Ethical Obligations and Decision Making in Accounting

Text and Cases

Fifth Edition

Steven M. Mintz, DBA, CPA
Professor Emeritus of Accounting
California Polytechnic State University,
San Luis Obispo

Roselyn E. Morris, Ph.D., CPA
Professor Emerita of Accounting
Texas State University–San Marcos

Mc
Graw
Hill
Education

ETHICAL OBLIGATIONS AND DECISION MAKING IN ACCOUNTING

Published by McGraw-Hill Education, 2 Penn Plaza, New York, NY 10121. Copyright © 2020 by McGraw-Hill Education. All rights reserved. Printed in the United States of America. No part of this publication may be reproduced or distributed in any form or by any means, or stored in a database or retrieval system, without the prior written consent of McGraw-Hill Education, including, but not limited to, in any network or other electronic storage or transmission, or broadcast for distance learning.

Some ancillaries, including electronic and print components, may not be available to customers outside the United States.

This book is printed on acid-free paper.

1 2 3 4 5 6 QVS 23 22 21 20 19

ISBN 978-1-260-56545-4
MHID 1-260-56545-9

Cover Image: ©Frank Peters/Shutterstock

All credits appearing on page or at the end of the book are considered to be an extension of the copyright page.

The Internet addresses listed in the text were accurate at the time of publication. The inclusion of a website does not indicate an endorsement by the authors or McGraw-Hill Education, and McGraw-Hill Education does not guarantee the accuracy of the information presented at these sites.

mheducation.com/highered

Dedication

We dedicate this book to all the students we have taught over the years, without whom our burning desire to teach ethics would lay dormant. In this book, we strive to awaken students' interest in ethics and ethical behavior. Our goals are to educate accounting students to be future leaders in the accounting profession, stimulate your ethical perception so that you not only know what the right thing to do is but have the courage to do it, and sensitize you to your duty to serve the public interest above all else.

"Educating the mind without educating the heart is no education at all."

Aristotle

About the Authors

Courtesy of Steven Mintz

Steven M. Mintz, DBA, CPA, is a Professor Emeritus of Accounting from the Orfalea College of Business at the California Polytechnic State University–San Luis Obsipo. Dr. Mintz received his DBA from George Washington University. His first book, titled *Cases in Accounting Ethics and Professionalism,* was also published by McGraw-Hill. Dr. Mintz has been acknowledged by accounting researchers as one of the top publishers of research papers on accounting ethics and accounting education. He was selected for the 2014 Max Block Distinguished Article Award in the "Technical Analysis" category by The CPA Journal. Dr. Mintz received the 2015 Accounting Exemplar Award of the Public Interest Section of the American Accounting Association. He also has received the Faculty Excellence Award of the California Society of CPAs. Dr. Mintz writes three award-winning blogs under the names "ethicssage," "workplaceethicsadvice," and "higheredethicswatch."

Courtesy of Roselyn E. Morris

Roselyn E. Morris, Ph.D., CPA, is a professor emerita of accounting of the Accounting Department of McCoy College of Business, Texas State University. Dr. Morris received her Ph.D. in business administration from the University of Houston. She is a past president of the Accounting Education Foundation. She is currently appointed for a six year term as chair of the Qualifications Committee of the Texas State Board of Public Accountancy (TSBPA) and is a board member of the National Association of State Boards of Accountancy (NASBA).

Both Professors Mintz and Morris have developed accounting ethics courses at their respective universities.

Preface

Ethical Obligations and Decision Making in Accounting was written to guide students through the mine-fields of ethical conflict in meeting their responsibilities under the accounting professions' codes of conduct. Our book is devoted to helping students cultivate the ethical commitment needed to ensure that their work meets the highest standards of integrity, independence, and objectivity. We hope that this book and classroom instruction will work together to provide the tools to help students to instill the ethical values of the accounting profession and professionalism in everything they do. Here is a brief overview of enhancements to the fifth edition. Additional details follow.

Overview of 5th Edition

An expanded discussion of professional judgment highlights the challenges to ethical decision-making for internal accountants and auditors, and external auditors. New material on behavioral ethics addresses cognitive challenges in the performance of an audit. We examine emerging issues in organizations related to equity, diversity, and inclusion, as well as sexual harassment. We build on traditional philosophical reasoning methods by taking the process one step further, that is, to convert ethical intent into ethical action by applying the "Giving Voice to Values" methodology. GVV coverage has been expanded to include new cases in order to provide instructors with more choices when and how to use GVV in class discussions. Whistleblowing obligations of CPAs are covered in full including the 2018 U.S. Supreme Court decision in *Digital Realty Trust, Inc. v. Somers* that clarifies when an accountant must report financial wrongdoing to the SEC under the Dodd-Frank Financial Reform Act. We also examine whether protections against retaliation under the Sarbanes-Oxley Act are working as intended. A 2018 court decision in *Erhart v. Bofl Holdings* held that whistleblowers can use confidential company documents to expose fraud may be a game changer. In this book, we are committed to thoroughly exploring ethical obligations of accountants and auditors. In that regard, we have expanded discussion of some of the rules of conduct including independence, objectivity and integrity, and professional skepticism. We also devote more coverage to acts discreditable to the profession, a growing problem of professional behavior. New rules to disclose critical audit matters and when to include a separate paragraph in the audit report are discussed. Expanded coverage of non-GAAP metrics raises questions about the usefulness of such data, its conformity with GAAP, and SEC guidelines. Ethical leadership is discussed in the context of professional role, professional obligations as a CPA, and dealing with organizational influences.

Several states now require their accounting students to complete an ethics course prior to being licensed as a CPA. This book has been designed to meet the guidelines for accounting ethics education including:

- encouraging students to make decisions in accordance with prescribed values, attitudes, and behaviors.

- providing a framework for ethical reasoning, knowledge of professional values, and ethical standards.

- prescribing attributes for exercising professional skepticism and behavior that is in the best interest of the investing and consuming public and the profession.

- instilling the desire to do the right thing and adhere to the standards set forth in the AICPA Code of Professional Conduct.

Accounting students should strive to be the best accounting professionals possible. To that end, we dedicate the book to instilling a sense of ethics and professionalism.

What's New in the 5th Edition?

In response to feedback and guidance from numerous accounting ethics faculty, the authors have made many important changes to the fifth edition of *Ethical Obligations and Decision Making in Accounting: Text and Cases,* including the following:

Connect

- **Connect is available** with assignable cases, test bank assessment material, and SmartBook. **SmartBook** is an excellent way to ensure that students are reading and understanding the basic concepts in the book and it prepares them to learn from classroom discussions. Several of the **Chapter Cases** are available in an auto-graded format to facilitate grading by instructors. The purpose of using the digital format is to better prepare students ahead of class to free up instructors to discuss a broader range of topics in their lectures and in the give-and-take between teacher and student. **Connect Insight Reports** will also give the instructor a better view into the overall class's understanding of core topics prior to class to appropriately focus lectures and discussion. The **Connect Library** also offers materials to support the efforts of first-time and seasoned instructors of accounting ethics, including a comprehensive Instructor's Manual, Test Bank, Additional Cases, and PowerPoint presentations.
- **Learning Objectives** have been added and linked to specific content material in each chapter.

End-of-Chapter Assignments

Each chapter includes 25 discussion questions (20 in chapter 8) that are designed to review important topics in the text with students and apply their knowledge to new situations. Ten cases (5 in chapter 8) cover a variety of topics deemed most important in each chapter. We have purposefully kept most of these cases short to provide ample time for discussion in class about the ethical issues and to not get too bogged down with financial analysis. However, we do provide many SEC cases that focus on the numbers and are more comprehensive. We hope the mixture will serve the interests of all instructors.

The major cases have been restructured in the fifth edition to provide a selection of short and long cases, all of which have one thing in common: through the questions at the end of each case students are given the opportunity to tie together important topics discussed in the text and apply their knowledge of ethical reasoning to more complex situations. We have included on the web some of the discussion questions, end-of-chapter cases, and major cases from the third and fourth editions not carried over to the fifth edition to make way for new cases and keep the book fresh and up to date. Instructors may find this material useful for assignment purposes. We have also revised and enhanced additional Instructor's Resource Materials and supplements.

Chapter-by-Chapter Enhancements

Chapter 1

- Expanded discussion of Egoism to include Ayn Rand's *Rational Egoism,* a method of ethical reasoning popular with today's young adults and millennials.
- **New** coverage of moral turpitude and other "Acts Discreditable to the Profession." Recent studies have indicated violations of this ethics rule by CPAs are on the rise because of DUI and other offenses. Additional concerns in this area may exist over time especially in those states that permit recreational use of cannabis.
- Expanded discussion of the Principles of the AICPA Code of Professional Conduct, the public interest obligation, and regulation in the accounting profession.

Chapter 2

- **New** discussion of cognitive biases that can influence audit decision-making.
- **New** discussion of *equity, diversity, and inclusion.*
- Enhanced discussion of the GVV technique. Chapter 2 discusses the foundation of the approach including examples on applying the methodology. There are twenty cases in the book that apply GVV. These cases are designated as "a GVV case."
- Discussion of Volkswagen "Dieselgate" scandal.

Chapter 3

- Updated results from the Association of Certified Fraud Examiners Global Survey of Fraud.
- **New** discussion of corporate social responsibility including *sexual harassment.*
- Expanded discussion of the Sarbanes-Oxley Act and whistleblower protections.
- Expanded discussion of the Dodd-Frank Financial Reform Act and when to report financial wrongdoing to the SEC.
- Implications of the U.S. Supreme Court decision in *Digital Realty Trust, Inc. v. Somers* and how it may influence when would-be-whistleblowers inform the SEC of financial wrongdoing.
- Analyze when whistleblowers can use confidential company documents to expose fraud.
- Examine Equifax Data Breach in the context of corporate governance.

Chapter 4

- Enhanced discussion of professional judgment in accounting.
- Expanded coverage of KPMG Professional Judgment Framework.
- **New** discussion of problems for auditors who uncritically accept management's representations in an audit.
- Comprehensive discussion of the Revised AICPA Code of Professional Conduct including the threats and safeguards approach to determine when violations exist of independence, integrity and objectivity, and the presence of ethical conflicts.
- **New** discussion of confidentiality and disclosing fraud.
- Expanded discussion of ethics in tax practice.
- Discussion of recent cases brought against CPA firms for violating the AICPA Code.

Chapter 5

- Expanded discussion of errors, illegal acts, and fraud.
- Expanded discussion of Private Securities Litigation Reform Act and reporting requirements to the SEC; fraud and confidentiality issues explored.
- **New** Discussion of Professional Skepticism Scale that measures traits conducive to developing a questioning mind and informed judgment.
- Discussion of findings of the Center for Audit Quality of audit deficiencies.

- Expanded discussion of PCAOB audit inspection process and high rate of deficiencies of audit firms.
- **New** requirements to disclose critical audit matters in the audit report.

Chapter 6

- **New** cases that explore in depth legal obligations of accountants and auditors.
- **New** discussion of audit malpractice.
- Expanded section on legal liabilities under Sarbanes-Oxley.
- Expanded discussion on regulatory issues and PCAOB inspections.
- **New** requirements under SSARS No. 21 for compilations and issuing non-compilation reports.
- Enhanced coverage of auditor liability for internal control over financial reporting.

Chapter 7

- **New** discussion of earnings guidance and forward-looking-statements.
- **New** discussion of SEC Regulation G and Item 10(e) of Regulation S-K that define a "non-GAAP financial measure" including Compliance and Disclosure guidelines.
- Expanded discussion of non-GAAP financial measures including EBITDA and other non-GAAP performance measures.
- **New** examples of GAAP to non-GAAP reconciliations.
- **New** examples of lack of professional judgment in critical areas of the audit and auditing estimates.
- Expanded discussion of the use of accruals and earnings management.
- **New** discussion of revenue recognition standard, *Revenue from Contracts with Customers*
- Detailed examples of financial statement restatements including Hertz Corporation.

Chapter 8

Chapter 8 links back to discussions in Chapters 1 through 7 by incorporating material on "Ethical Leadership." The purpose is to leave students with a positive message of the importance of being a leader and ethical leadership in building organizational ethics. Leadership in decision-making in accounting, auditing, tax, and advisory services engagements is addressed. If there is one theme that describes what this chapter is about it is: "Businesses don't fail; leaders do." The chapter includes the following major topics:

- **New** discussion of audit quality controls, audit leadership, and audit failures.
- Expanded discussion of professional role and leadership.
- Revisiting moral intensity in the context of ethical leadership.
- Expanded discussion of ethical leadership in the practice of public accounting.
- **New** case studies on ethical leadership.
- Implications of ethical leadership for whistleblowing activities.
- Ethical leadership and the GVV technique.
- Ethical leadership competence.

 McGraw-Hill Connect® is a highly reliable, easy-to-use homework and learning management solution that utilizes learning science and award-winning adaptive tools to improve student results.

Homework and Adaptive Learning

- Connect's assignments help students contextualize what they've learned through application, so they can better understand the material and think critically.

- Connect will create a personalized study path customized to individual student needs through SmartBook®.

- SmartBook helps students study more efficiently by delivering an interactive reading experience through adaptive highlighting and review.

Connect's Impact on Retention Rates, Pass Rates, and Average Exam Scores

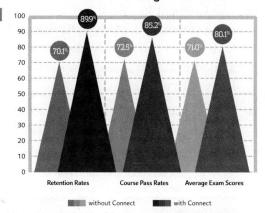

Using **Connect** improves retention rates by **19.8** percentage points, passing rates by **12.7** percentage points, and exam scores by **9.1** percentage points.

Over **7 billion questions** have been answered, making McGraw-Hill Education products more intelligent, reliable, and precise.

73% of instructors who use **Connect** require it; instructor satisfaction **increases** by 28% when **Connect** is required.

Quality Content and Learning Resources

- Connect content is authored by the world's best subject matter experts, and is available to your class through a simple and intuitive interface.

- The Connect eBook makes it easy for students to access their reading material on smartphones and tablets. They can study on the go and don't need internet access to use the eBook as a reference, with full functionality.

- Multimedia content such as videos, simulations, and games drive student engagement and critical thinking skills.

©McGraw-Hill Education

Robust Analytics and Reporting

©Hero Images/Getty Images

- Connect Insight® generates easy-to-read reports on individual students, the class as a whole, and on specific assignments.

- The Connect Insight dashboard delivers data on performance, study behavior, and effort. Instructors can quickly identify students who struggle and focus on material that the class has yet to master.

- Connect automatically grades assignments and quizzes, providing easy-to-read reports on individual and class performance.

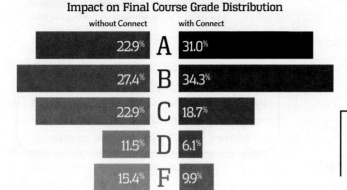

Impact on Final Course Grade Distribution

without Connect		with Connect
22.9%	A	31.0%
27.4%	B	34.3%
22.9%	C	18.7%
11.5%	D	6.1%
15.4%	F	9.9%

More students earn **As** and **Bs** when they use **Connect**.

Trusted Service and Support

- Connect integrates with your LMS to provide single sign-on and automatic syncing of grades. Integration with Blackboard®, D2L®, and Canvas also provides automatic syncing of the course calendar and assignment-level linking.

- Connect offers comprehensive service, support, and training throughout every phase of your implementation.

- If you're looking for some guidance on how to use Connect, or want to learn tips and tricks from super users, you can find tutorials as you work. Our Digital Faculty Consultants and Student Ambassadors offer insight into how to achieve the results you want with Connect.

www.mheducation.com/connect

Acknowledgments

The authors want to express their sincere gratitude to these reviewers for their comments and guidance. Their insights were invaluable in developing this edition of the book.

- Donald Ariail, *Southern Polytechnic State University*
- Stephanie Bacik, *Wake Tech Community College*
- Charles Bunn, Jr., *Wake Tech Community College*
- Kevin Cabe, *Indiana Wesleyan University*
- Rick Crosser, *Metropolitan State University of Denver*
- Denise Dickins, *East Carolina University*
- Dennis L. Elam, *Texas A&M University-San Antonio*
- Rafik Elias, *California State University-Los Angeles*
- Athena Jones, *University of Maryland University College*
- Patrick Kelly, *Providence College*
- Lorraine S. Lee, *University of North Carolina-Wilmington*
- Stephen McNett, *Texas A&M University-Central Texas*
- Kenneth Merchant, *University of Southern California*
- Michael Newman, *University of Houston*
- Robin Radtke, *Clemson University*
- John Sennetti, *NOVA Southeastern University*
- Edward Smith, *St. John's University*
- Dale Wallis, *University of California Los Angeles Extension*

We also appreciate the assistance and guidance given us on this project by the staff of McGraw-Hill Education, including Tim Vertovec, managing director; Rebecca Olson, portfolio manager; Zach Rudin, marketing manager; Caitlyn Johnston (Agate Publishing), product developer; Daryl Horrocks, program manager; Pat Frederickson, content project manager; Jacob Sullivan, content licensing specialist; and Sandy Ludovissy, buyer. We greatly appreciate the efforts of Justin Ross, copyeditor and proofreader of the book.

We are very grateful for the help provided by William F. Miller, University of Wisconsin - Eau Claire, in providing new content for the book, developing new cases, and his work on the Instructor Resources. We also wish to thank Tara Shawver for her work in developing digital materials to accompany the book.

Finally, we would like to acknowledge the contributions of our students, who have provided invaluable comments and suggestions on the content and use of these cases.

If you have any questions, comments, or suggestions concerning *Ethical Obligations and Decision Making in Accounting,* please send them to Steve Mintz at smintz@calpoly.edu.

Case Descriptions

Major Cases: See this section at the back of the book for details.

Brief Contents

Table of Contents

Chapter 3
Organizational Ethics and Corporate Governance   115

Chapter 4
Ethics and Professional Judgment in Accounting   209

Chapter 8
Ethical Leadership and Decision-Making in Accounting   485

Chapter 1

Ethical Reasoning: Implications for Accounting

Learning Objectives

After studying Chapter 1, you should be able to:

LO 1-1 Explain how integrity enables a CPA to withstand pressures and avoid subordination of judgment.

LO 1-2 Discuss the relationship between ethics, morals, values, and legal obligations.

LO 1-3 Describe how the pillars of character support ethical decision making.

LO 1-4 Differentiate between moral philosophies and their effect on ethical reasoning in accounting.

LO 1-5 Describe the regulatory system in accounting and how professional accountants serve the public interest.

LO 1-6 Discuss the Principles section of the AICPA Code of Professional Conduct.

LO 1-7 Explain what is meant by an act discreditable to the profession.

LO 1-8 Apply the IMA Statement of Ethical and Professional Practice and ethical reasoning methods to a case study.

Ethics Reflection

What is Your Ethics IQ?

Your Ethics IQ measures your level of ethics intelligence. This is not an exact science but does provide insight into your ability to reason through ethical dilemmas and make the right choice. The concept of an "Ethics IQ" has been discussed by Bruce Weinstein, The Ethics Guy.[1]

Answer these questions honestly. Otherwise, you will not know where you stand at the beginning of this course. Each question below has three possible answers. Each question is scored from 1 (least appropriate) to 3 (most appropriate). The scores are totaled and an Ethics IQ will be provided by your instructor.

Grab a pen and paper and let's get started!

Choose the "best" answer for each question.

Questions:

1. You are in line to check out at your favorite bagel store when the customer in front of you reaches for cream cheese in a container in a refrigerated area. You notice she drops a $20 bill. She just paid for her food and left the store. You're late for work already and your boss is a stickler for punctuality. What would you do assuming you can catch up with the customer?
   a. Pocket the $20.
   b. Tell the cashier and give him the $20 to return to the customer who is a regular.
   c. Chase down the customer and return the $20.

2. You are a student in Government 101 and are scheduled to take an essay final at 2:00 pm. While online, you notice a friend of yours in the 9:00 am section shared an Instagram photo of the essay questions. You are spending the time between 10:00 a.m. and 2:00 pm in your study group. You need to ace this class to graduate with honors. What would you do?
   a. Use the posting to prepare for the exam but don't tell the group members about it.
   b. Inform the group members and use the posted information to prepare for the exam.
   c. Ignore the posting.

3. You have discovered through a reliable third party that your best friend is cheating on his wife. Your wife asks whether you know anything about it after seeing your friend with another woman at a restaurant. What would you do?
   a. Confide in her that the cheating is going on.
   b. Deny you know anything about it.
   c. Tell her your friend hasn't said anything to you about it.

4. Your boss comes on to you at work. He constantly asks about your dating life and if you're seeing anyone regularly. He regularly stares at you. His behavior makes

you feel uncomfortable. But, you are up for a promotion and he has the final say. What would you do?

   a. Ignore it, at least until you get the promotion.
   b. Tell him his behavior is unwanted and you feel uncomfortable.
   c. Inform the Human Resources Department.

5. Your best friend was diagnosed with cancer a year ago. You have seen him deteriorate and deal with excruciating pain since then. His doctor can't prescribe marijuana, which might alleviate the pain, because it is illegal to do so in your state. You are thinking about crossing state lines and buying marijuana in a neighboring state where it is legal to buy marijuana for medical and recreational purposes, but it is illegal to cross back into your state under the federal Controlled Substances Act. What would you do?

   a. Cross state lines into a state where buying and using marijuana is permitted and give it to your friend.
   b. Don't cross state lines because it is illegal under the federal Controlled Substances Act.
   c. Tell your friend to move to a state that has medical marijuana laws.

6. You work for a small business and do a lot of travel and entertaining of potential clients. The company issues a credit card for all employees to simplify the accounting function. The card is to be used solely for business expenses. One day while on an out-of-town trip and after business hours, you use the business card to go to the spa to get a massage to alleviate painful arthritis, a problem you have been dealing with for years. What would you do when questioned about this charge by the Accounting Department?

   a. Explain that the out-of-town trip included a five-hour flight that created stress for your osteoarthritis condition. The massage is a legitimate business expense and should be reimbursed.
   b. Explain to the responsible person in the Accounting Department that you know it is a personal expense but ask that it be reimbursed this one time since you have a cash flow problem.
   c. Offer to reimburse the company for the massage.

7. You have just been fired from your job. On the way out, you contemplate downloading some proprietary information about a new R&D project of your employer. You worked on the project so figure you had a right to do so. What would you do?

   a. Don't download the information.
   b. Download the information about the project.
   c. Ask your employer for permission to download the information.

8. You are one of five workers on a team that performs financial calculations for your company. In advance of a meeting between the team and your supervisor, you discover a member of the team, who is your boyfriend, made a mistake in a calculation. The mistake made it look like the company was making more money than it was. What would you do assuming you are convinced the mistake was an honest one?

   a. Ignore it: You don't want to get your friend in trouble.
   b. Speak to your friend: Give him the opportunity to correct the mistake.
   c. Inform the supervisor since it's your job to report what you have observed.

9. You manage a group of six employees. One day one of those employees calls in sick. Later that day you notice the employee posted photos at a restaurant to Instagram. What would you do?

   a. Speak to the employee the next day when she comes to work.

   b. Let it go and say nothing.

   c. Fire the employee.

10. You are a manager at a fast food restaurant and monitor your employee's social media posts on company equipment. You just read a Facebook post by an employee who commented that the working conditions were oppressive. Other employees commented; some agreeing and others disagreeing. Assuming you work in an "at will" employment state (either the employer or the employee may terminate employment at any time). What would you do?

    a. Fire the employee who posted the critical comments.

    b. Ignore the comments.

    c. Meet with the employee(s) to discuss the comments.

Have the courage to say no. Have the courage to face the truth. Do the right thing because it is right. These are the magic keys to living your life with integrity.

Source: W. Clement Stone (1902–2002)

This quote by William Clement Stone, a businessman, philanthropist, and self-help book author, underscores the importance of integrity in decision making. Notice that the quote addresses integrity in one's personal life. That is because one has to act with integrity when making personal decisions in order to be best equipped to act with integrity on a professional level. Integrity, indeed all of ethics, is not a spigot that can be turned on or off depending on one's whims or whether the matter at hand is personal or professional. As the ancient Greeks knew, we learn how to be ethical by practicing and exercising those virtues that enable us to lead a life of excellence.

In accounting, internal accountants and auditors may be pressured by superiors to manipulate financial results. The external auditors may have to deal with pressures imposed on them by clients to put the best face on the financial statements regardless of whether they conform to generally accepted accounting principles (GAAP). It is the ethical value of integrity that provides the moral courage to resist the temptation to stand by silently while a company misstates its financial statement amounts.

Integrity: The Basis of Accounting

LO 1-1

Explain how integrity enables a CPA to withstand pressures and avoid subordination of judgment.

According to Mintz (1995), "Integrity is a fundamental trait of character that enables a CPA to withstand client and competitive pressures that might otherwise lead to the subordination of judgment."[2] A person of integrity will act out of moral principle and not expediency. That person will do what is right, even if it means the loss of a job or client. In accounting, the public interest (i.e., investors and creditors) always must be placed ahead of one's own self-interest or the interests of others, including a supervisor or client.

Integrity means that a person acts on principle—a conviction that there is a right way to act when faced with an ethical dilemma. For example, assume that your tax client fails to inform you about an amount of earned income for the year, and you confront the client on this issue. The client tells you not to record it and reminds you that there is no W-2 or 1099 form to document the earnings. The client adds that you will not get to audit the company's financial statements anymore if you do not adhere to the client's wishes. Would you decide to "go along to get along"? If you are a person of integrity, you should not allow the client to dictate how the tax rules will be applied in the client's situation. You are the professional and know the tax regulations best, and you have an ethical obligation to report taxes in accordance with the law. If you go along with the client and the Internal Revenue Service (IRS) investigates and sanctions you for failing to follow the IRS Tax Code, then you may suffer irreparable harm to your reputation. An important point is that a professional must never let loyalty to a client cloud good judgment and ethical decision making.

WorldCom: Cynthia Cooper: Hero and Role Model

Cynthia Cooper's experience at WorldCom illustrates how the internal audit function should work and how a person of integrity can put a stop to financial fraud. It all unraveled in April and May 2002 when Gene Morse, an auditor at WorldCom, couldn't find any documentation to support a claim of $500 million in computer expenses. Morse approached Cooper, the company's director of internal auditing and Morse's boss, who instructed Morse to "keep going." A series of obscure tips led Morse and Cooper to suspect that WorldCom was cooking the books. Cooper formed an investigation team to determine whether their hunch was right.

In its initial investigation, the team discovered $3.8 billion of misallocated expenses and phony accounting entries.[3] Cooper approached the chief financial officer (CFO) Scott Sullivan, but was dissatisfied with his explanations. The chief executive officer (CEO) of the company, Bernie Ebbers, had already resigned under pressure from WorldCom's board of directors, so Cooper went to the audit committee. The committee interviewed Sullivan about the accounting issues and did not get a satisfactory answer. Still, the committee was reluctant to take any action. Cooper persisted anyway. Eventually, one member of the audit committee told her to approach the outside auditors to get their take on the matter. Cooper gathered additional evidence of fraud, and ultimately KPMG, the firm that had replaced Arthur Andersen—the auditors during the fraud—supported Cooper. Sullivan was asked to resign, refused to do so, and was fired.[4]

One tragic result of the fraud and cover-up at WorldCom is the case of Betty Vinson. It is not unusual for someone who is genuinely a good person to get caught up in fraud. Vinson, a former WorldCom mid-level accounting manager, went along with the fraud because her superiors told her to do so. She was convinced that it would be a one-time action. It rarely works that way, however, because once a company starts to engage in accounting fraud, it feels compelled to continue the charade into the future to keep up the appearance that each period's results are as good as or better than prior periods. The key to maintaining one's integrity and ethical perspective is not to take the first step down the proverbial *ethical slippery slope.*

Vinson pleaded guilty in October 2002 to participating in the financial fraud at the company. She was sentenced to five months in prison and five months of house arrest. Vinson represents the typical "pawn" in a financial fraud: an accountant who had no interest or desire to commit fraud but got caught up in it when Sullivan, her boss, instructed her to make improper accounting entries. The rationalization by Sullivan that the company had to "make the numbers appear better than they really were" did nothing to ease her guilty conscience. Judge Barbara Jones, who sentenced Vinson, commented that "Ms. Vinson was among the least culpable members of the conspiracy at WorldCom. . . . Still, had Vinson refused to do what she was asked, it's possible this conspiracy might have been nipped in the bud."[5]

Accounting students should reflect on what they would do if they faced a situation similar to the one that led Vinson to do something that was out of character. Once she agreed to go along with making improper entries, it was difficult to turn back. The company could have threatened to disclose her role in the original fraud and cover-up if Vinson then acted on her beliefs. From an ethical (and practical) perspective it is much better to just do the right thing from the very beginning, so that you can't be blackmailed or intimidated later.

Vinson became involved in the fraud because she had feared losing her job, her benefits, and the means to provide for her family. She must live with the consequences of her actions for the rest of her life. On the other hand, Cynthia Cooper, on her own initiative, ordered the internal investigation that led to the discovery of the $11 billion fraud at WorldCom. Cooper did all the right things to bring the fraud out in the open. Cooper received the Accounting Exemplar Award in 2004 given by the Public Interest Section of the American Accounting Association and was inducted into the American Institute of Certified Public Accountants (AICPA) Hall of Fame in 2005.

Cooper truly is a positive role model. She discusses the foundation of her ethics that she developed as a youngster because of her mother's influence in her book *Extraordinary Circumstances: The Journey of a Corporate Whistleblower.* Cooper says: "Fight the good fight. Don't ever allow yourself to be intimidated. . . . Think about the consequences of your actions. I've seen too many people ruin their lives."[6]

Religious and Philosophical Foundations of Ethics

Virtually all the world's major religions contain in their religious texts some version of the Golden Rule: "Do unto others as you would wish them to do unto you." In other words, we should treat others the way we would want to be treated. This is the basic ethic that guides all religions. If we believe honesty is important, then we should be honest with others and expect the same in return. One result of this ethic is the concept that every person shares certain inherent human rights, which will be discussed later in this chapter.

We can think of the Golden Rule as a formal principle that serves as the general basis for other principles (duties) we have in an ethical system. Exhibit 1.1 provides some examples of the universality of the Golden Rule in world religions provided by the character education organization Teaching Values.[7]

Greek Ethics

The origins of Western philosophy trace back to the ancient Greeks, including Socrates, Plato, and Aristotle. The ancient Greek philosophy of virtue deals with questions such as: What is the best sort of life for human beings to live? Greek thinkers saw the attainment of a good life as the *telos,* the end or goal

EXHIBIT 1.1   The Universality of the Golden Rule in the World Religions

Religion	Expression of the Golden Rule	Citation
Christianity	All things whatsoever ye would that men should do to you, Do ye so to them; for this is the law and the prophets.	Matthew 7:12
Confucianism	Do not do to others what you would not like yourself. Then there will be no resentment against you, either in the family or in the state.	Analects 12:2
Buddhism	Hurt not others in ways that you yourself would find hurtful.	Uda–navarga 5,1
Hinduism	This is the sum of duty, do naught onto others what you would not have them do unto you.	Mahabharata 5, 1517
Islam	No one of you is a believer until he desires for his brother that which he desires for himself.	Sunnah
Judaism	What is hateful to you, do not do to your fellow man. This is the entire Law; all the rest is commentary.	Talmud, Shabbat 3id
Taoism	Regard your neighbor's gain as your gain, and your neighbor's loss as your own loss.	Tai Shang Kan Yin P'ien
Zoroastrianism	That nature alone is good which refrains from doing to another whatsoever is not good for itself.	Dadisten-I-dinik, 94, 5

of human existence. For most Greek philosophers, the end is *eudaimonia,* which is usually translated as "happiness." However, the Greeks thought that the end goal of happiness meant much more than just experiencing pleasure or satisfaction. The ultimate goal of happiness was to attain some objectively good status, the life of excellence. The Greek word for excellence is *arete,* the customary translation of which is "virtue." Thus for the Greeks, "excellences" or "virtues" were the qualities that made a life admirable or excellent. They did not restrict their thinking to characteristics we regard as moral virtues, such as courage, justice, and temperance that are learned primarily through habit and practice, but included others we think of as intellectual virtues, such as wisdom, which governs ethical behavior and understanding. The combination of these virtues are necessary to achieve moral excellence.[8]

The Language of Ethics

LO 1-2

Discuss the relationship between ethics, morals, values, and legal obligations.

The term *ethics* is derived from the Greek word *ethikos,* which itself is derived from the Greek word *ethos,* meaning "character." Morals is from the Latin word *moralis,* meaning "customs," with the Latin word *mores* being defined as "manners, morals, or ethics."

In philosophy, ethical behavior is that which is "good." The Western tradition of ethics is sometimes called "moral philosophy." The field of ethics or moral philosophy involves developing, defending, and recommending concepts of right and wrong behavior. These concepts do not change as one's desires and motivations change. They are not relative to the situation. They are immutable.

In a general sense, ethics (or moral philosophy) addresses fundamental questions such as: How should I live my life? That question leads to others, such as: What sort of person should I strive to be? What values are important? What standards or principles should I live by?[9] There are various ways to define the concept of ethics. The simplest may be to say that ethics deals with "right" and "wrong." However, it is difficult to judge what may be right or wrong in a particular situation without some frame of reference.

Gaa and Thorne define ethics as "the field of inquiry that concerns the actions of people in situations where these actions have effects on the welfare of both oneself and others."[10] We adopt that definition and emphasize that it relies on ethical reasoning to evaluate the effects of actions on others—*the stakeholders*.

Ethics deals with well-based standards of how people ought to act, does not describe the way people actually act, and is prescriptive, not descriptive. Ethical people always strive to make the right decision in all circumstances. They may not always succeed, but their intentions are good ones. They do not rationalize their actions based on their own perceived self-interests and take responsibility for those actions. The best way to understand ethics may be to differentiate it from other concepts.

Difference between Ethics and Morals

Ethics and morals relate to "right" and "wrong" conduct. While they are sometimes used interchangeably, they are different. Ethics is concerned with how we should live, generally, while morality is about a certain proper subset of how we ought to live. One way of understanding the difference is to think of it this way. Ethics leans towards decisions based upon individual character, and the more subjective understanding of right and wrong by individual, whereas morals emphasizes the widely-held communal or societal norms about right and wrong.[11]

Ethics also refers to rules provided by an external source, such as codes of conduct for a group of professionals (i.e., CPAs), or for those in a particular organization. Morals refers to an individual's own principles regarding right and wrong and may be influenced by a religion or societal mores. Ethics tends to be more practical than morals, conceived as shared principles promoting fairness in social and business interactions. For example, a CEO involved in a sex scandal may involve a moral lapse, while a CEO misappropriating money from a company she is supposed to lead according to prescribed standards of behavior is an ethical problem. These terms are close and often used interchangeably, and both influence ethical decision making. In this text we oftentimes use the terms synonymously while acknowledging differences do exist.

Values and Ethics

Values are basic and fundamental beliefs that guide or motivate attitudes or actions. We conceive of it as something that is important to an individual (personal values) and to a community (professional values). In accounting, the values of the profession are embedded in its codes of ethics that guide the actions of accountants and auditors in meeting their professional responsibilities.

In accounting, the values of the profession include independence, integrity, objectivity, professional skepticism, and due care. They define what it means to be a professional and provide a framework for the enforceable rules of professional conduct that are designed to serve the public interests above all else.

Values are concerned with how a person behaves in certain situations and is predicated on personal beliefs that may or may not be ethical, whereas ethics is concerned with how a moral person should behave to act in an ethical manner. A person who values prestige, power, and wealth is likely to act out of self-interest, whereas a person who values honesty, integrity, and trust will typically act in the best interests of others. It does not follow, however, that acting in the best interests of others always precludes acting in one's own self-interest. Indeed, the Golden Rule prescribes that we should treat others the way we want to be treated.

The Golden Rule is best seen as a consistency principle, in that we should not act one way toward others but have a desire to be treated differently in a similar situation. In other words, it would be wrong to think that separate standards of behavior exist to guide our personal lives but that a different standard (a lower one) exists in business.

Ethics and Laws

Laws are a collection of rules and regulations that come with penalties and punishments if not followed. Ethics, on the other hand, is a collection of societal or professional norms of behavior that are based on moral principles and values. Ethics is what should be done whereas laws deal with behavior that is compelled. Contrary to popular belief, we can and do legislate ethics. We have laws against stealing, kidnapping, etc., which are based on ethical standards. In accounting, we legislate ethics through a system of ethical duties established in state board of accountancy rules.

Being ethical is not the same as following the law. Although ethical people always try to be law-abiding, there may be instances where their sense of ethics tells them it is best not to follow the law. These situations are rare and should be based on sound ethical reasons.

Assume that you are driving at a speed of 45 miles per hour (mph) on a two-lane divided roadway (double yellow line) going east. All of a sudden, you see a young boy jump into the road to retrieve a ball. The boy is close enough to your vehicle so that you know you cannot continue straight down the roadway and stop in time to avoid hitting him. You quickly look to your right and notice about 10 other children off the road. You cannot avoid hitting 1 or more of them if you swerve to the right to avoid hitting the boy in the middle of the road. You glance to the left on the opposite side of the road and notice no traffic going west or any children off the road. What should you do?

Ethical Perspective

If you cross the double yellow line that divides the roadway, you have violated the motor vehicle laws. We are told never to cross a double yellow line and travel into oncoming traffic. But the ethical action would be to do just that, given that you have determined it appears to be safe. It is better to risk getting a ticket than hit the boy in the middle of your side of the road or those children off to the side of the road.

There is a concept known as "ethical legalism," which holds that if an intended action is legal, it is, therefore ethical. However, there are situations where doing the right thing may not be the legal thing, and vice versa.

During the pre-Civil War years in the U.S., the law did not prohibit slavery and slaves were considered personal property. Yet, few would say it was an ethical practice. Similarly, lying or betraying the confidence of a friend is not illegal, but most people would consider it unethical. The contrary is true as well. The law also prohibits acts that some groups would perceive as ethically neutral behavior—behavior that is ethically permissible but not itself ethical. For instance, speeding is illegal, but many people do not have an ethical conflict with exceeding the speed limit.

Laws and Ethical Obligations

Benjamin Disraeli (1804–1881), the noted English novelist, debater, and former prime minister, said, "When men are pure, laws are useless; when men are corrupt, laws are broken." A person of goodwill honors and respects the rules and laws and is willing to go beyond them when circumstances warrant. As indicated by the previous quote, such people do not need rules and laws to guide their actions. They always try to do the right thing. On the other hand, the existence of specific laws prohibiting certain behaviors will not stop a person who is unethical (e.g., does not care about others) from violating those laws. Just think about a Ponzi scheme, such as the $65 billion one engaged in by Bernie Madoff, whereby he duped others to invest with him by promising huge returns that, unbeknownst to each individual investor, would come from additional investments of scammed investors and not true returns.

Laws create a minimum set of standards. Ethical people often go beyond what the law requires because the law cannot cover every situation a person might encounter. When the facts are unclear and the legal issues uncertain, an ethical person should decide what to do on the basis of well-established standards of ethical behavior. This is where moral philosophies come in and, for accountants and auditors, the ethical standards of the profession.

Ethical people often do less than is permitted by the law and more than is required. A useful perspective is to ask these questions:

- What does the law require of me?
- What do ethical standards of behavior demand of me?
- How should I act to conform to both?

The Moral Point of View

When the rules are unclear, an ethical person looks beyond his/her own self-interest and evaluates the interests of the stakeholders potentially affected by the action or decision. Ethical decision making requires that a decision maker be willing, at least sometimes, to take an action that may not be in his/her best interest. This is known as the "moral point of view."

Sometimes people believe that the ends justify the means. In ethics it all depends on one's motives for acting. If one's goals are good and noble, and the means we use to achieve them are also good and noble, then the ends do justify the means. However, if one views the concept as an excuse to achieve one's goals through any means necessary, no matter how immoral, illegal, or offensive to others the means may be, then that person is attempting to justify the wrongdoing by pointing to a good outcome regardless of ethical considerations such as how one's actions affect others. The process you follow to decide on a course of action is just as important, if not more important, than achieving the end goal. If this were not true from a moral point of view, then we could rationalize all kinds of actions in the name of achieving a desired goal, even if that goal does harm to others while satisfying our personal needs and desires.

Imagine that you work for a CPA firm and are asked to evaluate three software packages for a client. Your boss tells you that the managing partners are pushing for one of these packages, which just happens to be the firm's internal software. Your initial numerical analysis of the packages based on functionality, availability of upgrades, and customer service indicates that a competitor's package is better than the firm's software. Your boss tells you, in no uncertain terms, to redo the analysis. You know what she wants. Even though you feel uncomfortable with the situation, you decide to "tweak" the numbers to show a preference for the firm's package. The end result desired in this case is to choose the firm's package. The means to that end was to alter the analysis, an unethical act because it is dishonest and unfair to the other competitors (not to mention the client) to change the objectively determined results. In this instance, ethical decision making requires that we place the client's interests (to get the best software package for his needs) above those of the firm (to get the new business and not upset the boss).

Moral Relativism

Moral relativism is the view that moral or ethical statements, which vary from person to person, are all equally valid and no one's opinion of right and wrong is actually better than any others.[12] In moral relativism, there is no ultimate standard of good or evil, so every judgment about right and wrong is purely a product of a person's preferences and environment.

Moral relativism moves away from the notion there are fixed standards of behavior based on moral principles and toward a subjective approach to decision making. In this view, morals depends on one's culture, religion, place, and time in which they occur. Three examples are ethical relativism, cultural relativism, and situation ethics.

Ethical Relativism

Moral relativism and *ethical relativism* are often thought of as the same concept. *Ethical relativism* is the philosophical view that what is right or wrong and good or bad is not absolute but variable and relative, depending on the person, circumstances, or social situation. Slavery is a good example of ethical relativism, an immoral act that some might feel is ethically acceptable.

Relativists point to certain beliefs in making their case.[13]

- What's right for you may not be what's right for me.
- What's right for my culture won't necessarily be what's right for your culture.
- No moral principles are true for all people at all times and in all places.

Cultural Relativism

Ethical relativism holds that morality is relative to the norms of one's culture. That is, whether an action is right or wrong depends on the moral norms of the society in which it is practiced. The same action may be morally right in one society but be morally wrong in another. If cultural relativism is correct, then there can be no common framework for resolving moral disputes or for reaching agreement on ethical matters among members of different societies.

A basic tenet of cultural relativism is that one cannot fully understand certain actions or customs without also understanding the culture from which those actions are derived. A good example is bull fighting, a traditional spectacle of Spain, Portugal, and some Latin American countries. Proponents claim it is a cultural art form. The highly-regarded American novelist, Ernest Hemingway, said about bull fighting that it is "a decadent art in every way. . .[and] if it were permanent it could be one of the major arts."[14] The opposite view shared by many cultures is bullfighting is an indecent form of torture. Is one view right and the other wrong? It depends on your perspective.

Most ethicists reject the theory of moral relativism. Some philosophers criticize it because if it is true then one must obey the norms of one's society and to diverge from them is to act immorally. This means if I am a member of a society that believes sexist practices are morally permissible, then I must accept those practices as morally right. Such a view promotes social conformity and leaves no room for moral reform or improvement in a society.[15]

Just imagine we are back in 1920 before the Congressional ratification of the 19th Amendment to the U.S. Constitution that gave women the right to vote. If I were a firm believer in women's suffrage then, under cultural relativism, I must accept the fact that before that time it was morally appropriate that women were denied the right to vote.

Situation Ethics

Situation ethics, a term first coined in 1966 by an Episcopalian priest, Joseph Fletcher, is a body of ethical thought that takes normative principles—like the virtues, natural law, and Kant's categorical imperative that relies on the universality of actions—and generalizes them so that an agent can "make sense" out of one's experience when confronting ethical dilemmas. Unlike ethical relativism that denies universal moral principles, claiming the moral codes are strictly subjective, situational ethicists recognize the existence of normative principles but question whether they should be applied as strict directives (i.e., imperatives) or, instead, as guidelines that agents should use when determining a course of ethical conduct. In other words, situationists ask: Should these norms, as generalizations about what is desired, be regarded as intrinsically valid and universally obliging of all human beings? For situationists, the circumstances surrounding an ethical dilemma can and should influence an agent's decision-making process and may alter an agent's decision when warranted. Thus, situation ethics holds that "what in some times and in some places is ethical can be in other times and in other places unethical."[16]

A classic case of situation ethics is that of Anne Frank and her Jewish family that was hiding in a sealed off area in the home of a Christian family in Amsterdam to escape Nazi terror back in World War II. They were able to live in secrecy for two years during which time the family lied to the Nazi soldiers about the family's whereabouts. The Frank's were ultimately captured along with several others and all but Otto Frank were put to death at the concentration camps. Following the war, Otto returned to Amsterdam where he retrieved the diary Anne had kept of their ordeal. He honored her wishes by getting the diary published for all the world to read. Just imagine what might have happened if the family had told the truth in this situation.

Student Cheating

Another danger of situational ethics is it can be used to rationalize cheating. Cheating in general is at epidemic proportions in society. The *2012 Report Card on the Ethics of American Youth,* conducted by the Josephson Institute of Ethics, found that of 23,000 high school students surveyed, 51% admitted to having cheated on a test during 2012, 55% admitted to lying, and 20% admitted to stealing. Of 23,000 students surveyed, 45% of males and 28% of females agreed that a person must lie and cheat "at least occasionally" to succeed. Twenty percent of males and 10% of females also believe "it is not cheating if everyone is doing it."[17]

Who is to Blame?

Cheating in college has been prevalent for some time. The rate of students who admit to cheating at least once in their college careers has held steadily around 75% since the first major survey on cheating in higher education in 1963.[18]

Students give many reasons for cheating including:[19]

- Increasingly competitive atmosphere
- Culture that is accepting of cheating
- Everyone does it
- Institutional indifference
- Lack of understanding what cheating is
- Pursuit of self-interest.

A survey of college students reported in Campus Technology on February 23, 2017, indicates there are a variety of ways students use to cheat including:[20]

- Plagiarism from internet sources (79%)
- Copied text from somebody else's assignment (76%)
- Used mobile devices to cheat during class (72%)
- Purchased custom term papers or essays online (42%)
- Had a "service" take their online classes for them (28%).

Interestingly, only 12% of students said they'd never cheat because of ethics.

There is a relativistic element to cheating, and students clearly invoke self-interest to rationalize their actions. Arizona State University conducted a survey of 2,000 students and found the following circumstances were most likely to lead to cheating:[21]

- A scholarship was at risk (38%)
- Facing disqualification from the university or program of study (35%)
- Ran out of time on an assignment (30%)
- To maintain a grade point average (28%).

Students were less inclined to cheat just because other students are doing it (15%) or the professor ignores it (20%).

The results of the study indicate that Arizona State faculty were not entirely blameless for the existence of cheating. The institution was concerned that 16% of instructors didn't discuss academic integrity even once in class. Another concern is the difficulty of reporting violations and determining penalties and many faculty's reluctance to formally document a breach because of the time investment it requires. These issues are being addressed by the university.

A disturbing trend is the availability of electronic access to a variety of online resources including the solutions manual and test bank questions. Instructors have historically relied on these resources to assess student learning. All that may be assessed now is whether an otherwise unproductive student has suddenly become productive as a result of acquiring instructor's resource materials or accessing previous exams. Here, students are to blame for irresponsible behavior and basically cheat themselves out of learning materials needed in the workplace and for the CPA Exam. Faculty are not blameless since many do not change exams from term to term and turn a blind eye to what they know goes on in virtually every college and university today.

There have been a number of well-publicized cheating scandals at colleges and universities these past few years including in 2012 at Harvard University where dozens of students were forced to withdraw from the university after a cheating scandal in a class that gave a take-home exam. Students collaborated with other students by sharing notes or sitting in on sessions with the same teaching assistants. The university called them out for violating its academic policy against discussing the exam with others. The students blamed the professor for a lack of clear directions while others lauded students for their collaboration.

Student Cheating at the University of North Carolina

If you're a college sports fan, by now you have probably heard about the paper-class scandal that we call "Tar Heel Gate" in which 3,100 student-athletes at the University of North Carolina in Chapel Hill (UNC) were essentially allowed to take classes without attending classes and given grades good enough to keep them eligible to play men's football and basketball during a 20-year period.

For five years, UNC had insisted the paper classes were the doing of one rogue professor: the department chair of the African-American studies program, Julius Nyang'oro. However, an independent report found that five counselors actively used paper classes, calling them "GPA boosters," and that at least two counselors suggested to a professor the grade an athlete needed to receive to be able to continue to play.

Many of the academic-athletic staff who were named and implicated were also named by university learning specialist Mary Willingham. Willingham said that she had worked with dozens of athletes who came to UNC and were unable to read at an acceptable level, with some of them reading on par with elementary schoolchildren. She also said there were many members of the athletic staff who knew about the paper classes, and her revelations contradicted what UNC had claimed for years–that Nyang'oro acted alone in providing the paper classes.

Willingham went public with detailed allegations about paper classes and, after an assault on her credibility by the university, filed a whistleblower lawsuit. In March 2015, UNC announced it would pay Willingham $335,000 to settle her suit.

In an unusual twist to the story, the director of UNC's Parr Center for Ethics, Jeanette M. Boxill, was accused of steering athletes into fake classes to help them maintain their eligibility with the NCAA. Moreover, she covered up her actions after the fact. Boxill violated the most basic standards of academic integrity.

The motivating factor at UNC was to keep student athletes eligible so that the sports programs would continue to excel and promote and publicize the school, not to mention earn millions of dollars in advertising. The investigation was completed in October 2017 and while the NCAA did not dispute that UNC was guilty of running one of the worst academic fraud schemes in college sports history, it did not impose any penalties because "no rules were broken." How could that be? Well, the panel that investigated the case determined that it could not punish the university or its athletic program because the paper classes were not available exclusively to athletes. Other students at UNC had access to the fraudulent classes, too.[22]

The NCAA's decision defies logic and sets the bar low for ethics in college sports. We believe the ruling was influenced by the fact that UNC is one of only four Division I Men's Basketball programs to have ever achieved 2,000 victories and UNC has won seven men's college basketball national championships including in 2017.

An ethical analysis of the paper class scandal shows that UNC suffered from ethical blindness. It failed to see the ethical violations of its actions in establishing a route for student-athletes to remain academically eligible. It acted in its own self-interest regardless of the impact of its behavior on the affected parties. The blind spots occurred because of a situational ethic whereby those who perpetrated the fraud and covered it up came to believe their actions were for the greater good of those involved in the athletic program and the UNC community. Honesty was ignored, integrity was not in the picture, and the athletes were not provided with the education they deserved.

Social Media Ethics

The Ethics Resource Center conducted a survey of social networkers in 2012 to determine the extent to which employees use social networking on the job. The survey points out that social networking is now the norm and that a growing number of employees spend some of their workday connected to a social network. More than 10% are "active social networkers," defined as those who spend at least 30% of their workday linked up to one or more networks.[23]

One concern is whether active social networkers engage in unethical practices through communications and postings on social media sites. Survey respondents say they think about risks before posting online and consider how their employers would react to what they post. But, they do admit to discussing company information online: 60% would comment on their personal sites about their company if it was in the news; 53% share information about work projects once a week or more; greater than one-third say they often comment, on their personal sites, about managers, coworkers, and even clients. The survey concludes that nothing is secret anymore and, unlike in Las Vegas, management must assume that what happens at work does not stay at work and may become publicly known.

An interesting result of the survey is active social networkers are unusually vulnerable to risks because they witness more misconduct and experience more retaliation as a result when they report it than their work colleagues. A majority (56%) of active social networkers who reported misdeeds experienced retaliation compared to fewer than one in five (18%) of other employee groups.

A 2013/14 survey by Proskauer, *Social Media in the Workplace Around the World 3.0,* found that as many as 36% of employers block social media at work—up from 29% in 2012. One in five companies block Facebook, while 15% shut out Twitter and nearly 14% have banned You Tube. Meanwhile, employers who allow free access to all social media sites have dwindled from 53 to 43%.[24]

The survey results indicate that employee misuse of social networking sites can have a potentially costly impact on business with the following concerns raised:

- Misuse of confidential information (80%)
- Misrepresenting the views of the business (71%)
- Inappropriate non-business use (67%)
- Disparaging remarks about the business or employees (64%)
- Harassment (64%)

Our conclusion about using social networking sites at work is that the burden falls both on the employees, who should know better than to discuss company business online where anyone can see it, and employers, who have the responsibility to establish a culture that discourages venting one's feelings about the employer online for all to see. Organizational codes of ethics need to be expanded to create policies for the use of social networking sites, training to reinforce those policies, and consequences for those who violate the policies.

The Six Pillars of Character

LO 1-3
Describe how the pillars of character support ethical decision making.

It has been said that ethics is all about how we act when no one is looking. In other words, ethical people do not do the right thing because someone observing their actions might judge them otherwise, or because they may be punished as a result of their actions. Instead, ethical people act as they do because their "inner voice" or conscience tells them that it is the right thing to do.

Assume that you are leaving a shopping mall, get into your car to drive away, and hit a parked car in the lot on the way out. Let's also assume that no one saw you hit the car. What are your options? You could simply drive away and forget about it, or you can leave a note for the owner of the parked car with your contact information. What would you do and why? Now just imagine your car was hit. Further, it's a brand new car. What would you want the motorist to do and why? The point is The Golden Rule asks us to think about ethics as if we are the recipient of possible unethical behavior.

Virtues or Character Traits

According to "virtue ethics," there are certain ideals, such as excellence or dedication to the common good, toward which we should strive and which allow the full development of our humanity. These ideals are discovered through thoughtful reflection on what we as human beings have the potential to become.

Virtues are attitudes, dispositions, or character traits that enable us to be and to act in ways that develop this potential. They enable us to pursue the ideals we have adopted. Honesty, courage, compassion, generosity, fidelity, integrity, fairness, self-control, and prudence are all examples of virtues in Aristotelian ethics. A quote attributed to Aristotle is, "We are what we repeatedly do. Therefore, excellence is not an act. It is a habit."[25]

The Josephson Institute of Ethics identifies Six Pillars of Character that provide a foundation to guide ethical decision making. These ethical values include trustworthiness, respect, responsibility, fairness, caring, and citizenship. Josephson believes that the Six Pillars act as a multilevel filter through which to process decisions. So, being trustworthy is not enough—we must also be caring. Adhering to the letter of the law is not enough; we must accept responsibility for our actions or inactions.[26]

Trustworthiness

The dimensions of trustworthiness include being honest, acting with integrity, being reliable, and exercising loyalty in dealing with others.

Honesty

Honesty is the most basic ethical value. It means that we should express the truth as we know it and without deception. In accounting, the full disclosure principle supports honesty through transparency and requires that the accounting professional disclose all the information that owners, investors, creditors, and the government need to know to make informed decisions. To withhold relevant information is dishonest.

Let's assume a company is involved in pending litigation where the possibility exists that the litigation will have a material effect on its financial results. Honesty dictates that the lawsuit should be disclosed. Generally accepted accounting principles (GAAP) requires disclosure. If a loss in the case is probable, has a material effect on the financial results, and the company can estimate the amount of the financial loss, then the company should set up a "reserve" for possible losses due to the pending lawsuit typically by setting up a contingent liability on the balance sheet.

Integrity

The integrity of a person is an essential element in trusting that person. MacIntyre, in his account of Aristotelian virtue, states, "There is at least one virtue recognized by tradition which cannot be specified except with reference to the wholeness of a human life—the virtue of integrity or constancy."[27] A person of integrity takes time for self-reflection, so that the events, crises, and challenges of everyday living do not determine the course of that person's moral life. Such a person is trusted by others because that person is true to her word.

Ultimately, integrity means to act on principle rather than expediency. If my superior tells me to do something wrong, I will not do it because it violates the ethical value of honesty. If my superior pressures me to compromise my values just this one time, I will not agree because one time can lead to another and a slide down the proverbial *ethical slippery slope*.

Returning to the lawsuit, let's assume the loss is probable and reasonably estimable and my boss tells me just to disclose it. I know GAAP requires recording in this case so, as a person of integrity, I insist on making the adjustment. I do not want to subordinate my judgment to that of my superior, a violation of integrity.

Reliability

The promises that we make to others are relied on by them, and we have a moral duty to follow through with action. Our ethical obligation for promise keeping includes avoiding bad-faith excuses and unwise commitments. Imagine that you are asked to attend a group meeting on Saturday and you agree to do so. That night, though, your best friend calls and says she has two tickets to the basketball game between the Dallas Mavericks and San Antonio Spurs. The Spurs are one of the best teams in basketball and you don't get this kind of opportunity very often, so you decide to go to the game instead of the meeting. You've broken your promise and acted out of self-interest without regard for the consequences of your actions: Might the group end up with a lower grade because of your decision? Let's assume you call the group leader and say that you can't attend the meeting because you are sick. Now, you've lied as well and have begun the slide down the ethical slippery slope where it will be difficult to climb back to the top.

Loyalty

Loyalty requires that friends not violate the confidence we place in them. In accounting, loyalty requires that we keep financial and other information confidential when it deals with our employer and client. For example, if you are the in-charge accountant on an audit of a client for your CPA firm-employer and you discover that the client is "cooking the books," you shouldn't telephone the local newspaper and tell the story to a reporter. Instead, you should go to your supervisor and discuss the matter and, if necessary, go to the partner in charge of the engagement and tell her. Your ethical obligation is to report what you have observed to your supervisor and let her take the appropriate action. However, the ethics of the accounting profession allow for instances whereby informing those above your supervisor is expected, an act of internal whistleblowing, and, in rare circumstances, going outside the organization to report the wrongdoing. Whistleblowing obligations will be discussed in Chapter 3.

There are limits to the confidentiality obligation. For example, let's assume that you are the accounting manager at a publicly owned company and your supervisor (the controller) pressures you to keep silent about the manipulation of financial information. You then go to the CFO, who tells you that both the CEO and board of directors support the controller. Out of a misplaced duty of loyalty in this situation, you might rationalize your silence as did Betty Vinson. Ethical values sometimes conflict, and loyalty is the one value that should never take precedence over other values such as honesty and integrity. Otherwise, we can imagine all kinds of cover-ups of information in the interest of loyalty or friendship.

Being loyal to one's supervisor even though doubts exist about proper accounting can lead down the ethical slippery slope. If I agree to footnote the lawsuit rather than record the adjustment, then I may feel obligated to do the same next time a similar situation arises. I was complicit the first time and don't want that getting out.

Respect

All people should be treated with dignity. We do not have an ethical duty to hold all people in high esteem, but we should treat everyone with respect, regardless of their circumstances in life. In today's slang, we might say that respect means giving a person "props." The Golden Rule encompasses respect for others through notions such as civility, courtesy, decency, dignity, autonomy, tolerance, and acceptance.[28]

By age 16, George Washington had copied by hand 110 *Rules of Civility & Decent Behavior in Company and Conversation.* They are based on a set of rules composed by French Jesuits in 1595. While many of the rules seem out of place in today's society, Washington's first rule is noteworthy: "Every Action done in Company, ought to be with Some Sign of Respect, to those that are Present."[29]

Why is respect so important to the way we treat individuals? Just think of the words to a 1967 song by the iconic Aretha Franklin: R-E-S-P-E-C-T. Find out what it means to me.

Washington's vernacular was consistent with the times as indicated by the last of his rules: "Labour to keep alive in your Breast that Little Spark of Celestial fire Called Conscience."[30] We have found many definitions of conscience, but the one we like best is posted on Moral Sense. The definition is: "Motivation deriving logically from ethical or moral principles that govern a person's thoughts and actions."[31]

Responsibility

Josephson points out that our capacity to reason and our freedom to choose make us morally responsible for our actions and decisions. We are accountable for what we do and who we are.[32]

The judgments we make in life reflect whether we have acted responsibly. Eleanor Roosevelt, the former first lady, puts it well: "One's philosophy is not best expressed in words; it is expressed in the choices one makes . . . and the choices we make are ultimately our responsibility."[33]

A responsible person carefully reflects on the choices before making a final decision. Imagine if you were given the task by your group to interview five CPAs in public practice about their most difficult ethical dilemma, and you decided to ask one person, who was a friend of the family, about five dilemmas that person faced in the practice of public accounting. Now, even if you made an "honest" mistake in interpreting the requirement, it is clear that you did not exercise the level of care that should be expected in this instance in carrying out the instructions to interview five different CPAs. Responsibility for accounting professionals means:

- To meet one's ethical and professional obligations when performing services for an employer or client but never forgetting that it is the public interest that trumps all other interests.
- To act with due care by gathering and evaluating relevant evidence in an audit and maintaining professional skepticism.
- To accept responsibility of one's actions and be accountable for them.

Fairness

Fairness is a subjective concept but typically involves issues of equality, impartiality, and due process. As Josephson points out, "Fairness implies adherence to a balanced standard of justice without relevance to one's own feelings or inclinations."[34] The problem sometimes is what seems fair to one person or group seems unfair to another.

Let's assume your instructor divides the class into groups for purposes of case studies. Further, your instructor told the case study groups at the beginning of the course that the group with the highest overall numerical average would receive an A, the group with second highest a B, and so on. At the end of the term, the instructor gave the group with the second-highest average—90.5—an A and the group with the highest average—91.2—a B. Perhaps the instructor took subjective factors into account in deciding on the final grading. If your group had the highest average, the members no doubt would find the instructor's decision unfair. However, if the group with the second highest average went well beyond the requirements of the course, that group might find the instructor's decision quite fair.

Fairness in accounting can be equated with objectivity. Objectivity means the financial and accounting information needs to be presented free from bias, that is, consistent with the evidence and not based solely on one's opinion about the proper accounting treatment. Objectivity helps to ensure that financial statements are reliable and verifiable. The purpose of objectivity is to make financial statements more useful to investors and end users.

Caring

The late Edmund L. Pincoffs, a philosopher who formerly taught at the University of Texas at Austin, believed that virtues such as caring, kindness, sensitivity, altruism, and benevolence enable a person who possesses these qualities to consider the interests of others.[35] Such people gain empathy for others. They are able to "walk a mile in someone else's shoes," meaning that before judging another person, you must first understand that person's experiences and thought processes. Josephson believes that caring is the "heart of ethics and ethical decision making."[36]

Let's assume that on the morning of an important group meeting, your child comes down with a temperature of 103 degrees. You call the group leader and say that you can't make it to the meeting. Instead, you suggest that the meeting be taped and you will listen to the discussions later that day and telephone the leader with any questions. The leader reacts angrily, stating that you are not living up to your responsibilities. Assuming that your behavior is not part of a pattern and you have been honest with the leader up to now, you would have a right to be upset with the leader, who seems uncaring. In the real world, emergencies do occur, and placing your child's health and welfare above all else should make sense in this situation to a person of rational thought. You also acted diligently by offering to listen to the discussions and, if necessary, follow up with the leader.

Citizenship

Josephson points out that "citizenship includes civic virtues and duties that prescribe how we ought to behave as part of a community."[37] An important part of good citizenship is to obey the laws, be informed about the issues, volunteer in your community, and vote in elections.

Accounting professionals are part of a community with specific ideals and ethical standards that govern behavior. These include responsibilities to one another to advance the profession and not bring discredit on oneself or others.

Reputation

It might be said that judgments made about one's character contribute toward how another party views that person's reputation. In other words, what is the estimation in which a person is commonly held, whether favorable or not?

Often when we cover up information in the present, it becomes public knowledge later. The consequences at that time are more serious because trust has been destroyed. A good example is Lance Armstrong, who for years denied taking performance-enhancing drugs while winning seven Tour de France titles. In 2012, he finally admitted to doing just that, and as a result, all those titles were stripped away by the U.S. Anti-Doping Agency. Armstrong's reputation took a hit and the admiration many in the public had for him fell by the wayside.

The reputation of a CPA is critical to a client's trusting that CPA to perform services competently and maintain the confidentiality of client information. One builds "reputational capital" through favorable actions informed by ethical behavior.

Accountants and auditors work years to build a reputation for trust so that clients come to value their services and the public believes in them. Accounting professionals know it takes a person a long time to build a reputation for trust but not very long to destroy it. Just think about the Lance Armstrong situation.

Modern Moral Philosophies

LO 1-4

Differentiate between moral philosophies and their effect on ethical reasoning in accounting.

The ancient Greeks believed that reason and thought precede the choice of action and that we deliberate about things we can influence with our decisions. The ability to reason through ethical conflicts and act on moral intent is a necessary but sometimes insufficient skill to make ethical decisions. This is because, while we believe that we should behave in accordance with certain moral principles, peer pressure, pressure from one's superior(s), and a culture that favors the client's interest above the public interest together create a barrier to acting in accordance with those principles. For example, accountants know inventory obsolescence should be recorded at year-end. But what if the client insists on holding off on the write-down due to concerns about a low level of earnings? Will we stand by our moral principles? Will we satisfy our obligation to honor the public trust? Or will we go along to get along and be a "team player"?

The noted philosopher James Rest points out that moral philosophies present guidelines for "determining how conflicts in human interests are to be settled for optimizing mutual benefit of people living together in groups." However, there is no single moral philosophy everyone accepts.[38]

Moral philosophies provide specific principles and rules that we can use to decide what is right or wrong in specific instances. There are many such philosophies and they are quite complex. We limit the discussion to what is necessary for students to learn in order to apply these methods to a variety of conflict situations that occur in accounting. Later in this chapter we will address the ethical standards embedded in the profession's ethics codes. It is the combination of the two that establish the ethical expectations of the public for the accounting profession. We do not favor any one of these philosophies because there is no one correct way to resolve ethical issues in accounting. Exhibit 1.2 presents the underlying framework for ethical decision-making for each of the moral philosophies.

EXHIBIT 1.2   Understanding Ethics as a Framework for Guiding Behavior

Philosophical Method	Proponents →	Basis for Moral Behavior →	Achieving Moral Excellence →	End Goal/ Humanity
Classic Greek <u>Virtue Ethics</u>	Aristotle, Plato, Socrates	**Virtues** Develop ethical character traits	Develop moral and intellectual virtues	Human excellence/ a life of virtue
Modern Philosophies <u>Deontology</u> (Rights Theory)	Kant	**Moral Principle** Categorical Imperative/ Universality	Satisfying duties to oneself and others	Treat humanity as an end in itself not a means to an end
<u>Teleology</u> (Act Utilitarianism)	Bentham, Mill	**Moral Action** Greatest good for the greatest number	Make decisions that produce the best consequences for oneself and others	Maximize well-being for all concerned
(Rule Utilitarianism)		Actions that conform to general rules		
<u>Egoism</u> (Rational Egoism)	Rand	**Moral Principle** The virtue of rationality	Make decisions that promote one's own interests in accordance with reason	Rational Selfishness
(Enlightened Egoism)	Alexis de Tocqueville	**Moral Concept** Self-interest rightly understood	Pursue self-interest to maximize general prosperity	Allow for the well-being of others in pursuing one's own interest
<u>Justice</u>	Rawls	**Moral Principles** Liberty Principle Difference Principle	Fair treatment: Treat equals, equally; unequals, unequally	Give each person what they deserve

Teleology

In *teleology,* an act is considered morally right or acceptable if it produces some desired result such as pleasure, the realization of self-interest, fame, utility, wealth, and so on. Teleologists assess the moral worth of behavior by looking at its consequences, and thus moral philosophers often refer to these theories as *consequentialism.* Consequentialism is a theory about outcomes, not motives or intentions. Two important teleological philosophies are egoism and utilitarianism.

Egoism

Egoism defines right or acceptable behavior in terms of its consequences for the individual. *Egoists* believe that they should make decisions that maximize their own self-interest, which is defined differently by each individual. In other words, the individual should "[d]o the act that promotes the greatest good for oneself."[39] Many believe that egoistic people and companies are inherently unethical because they ignore the moral point of view: they are short-term-oriented and will take advantage of others to achieve their goals. We discuss three forms of egoism below: ethical egoism, enlightened egoism, and rational egoism.

Ethical Egoism

As a brand of egoism, *ethical egoism* claims that the promotion of one's own good is in accordance with morality. In the strong version, it is held that it is always moral to promote one's own good, and it is never moral not to promote it. In the weak version, even though it is always moral to promote one's own good, it is not necessarily never moral to not. Thus, there are conditions in which the avoidance of personal interest may be a moral action.[40]

The ethical egoist ranks as most important duties that bring the highest payoff to oneself. Standard moral theories determine importance, at least in part, by considering the payoff to those helped. The conclusion is what brings the highest payoff to me will not, necessarily, bring the highest payoff to those helped.[41]

Ethical egoism as a moral theory creates conflicts of interest that are difficult to resolve. It is argued that pursuing my own interest can conflict with another's interest—my actions may bring about a cost to others. Specifically, a critic may contend that personal gain logically cannot be in one's best interest if it entails doing harm to another: doing harm to another would be to accept the principle that doing harm to another is ethical—i.e., one would equate doing harm with one's own best interest. The ethical egoist could logically pursue their interests at the cost of others.[42]

Egoism/ethical egoism is not an acceptable standard for decision making in accounting. How could we justify ignoring the public interest because it is in our own best interest not to go against the client's wishes?

Enlightened Egoism

Enlightened self-interest was discussed by Alexis de Tocqueville in his work *Democracy in America.* The notion he held was that Americans voluntarily join together in associations to further the interests of the group and, thereby, to serve their own interests.[43] This certainly accurately characterizes the role and purpose of the accounting profession.

Alexis de Tocqueville used "self-interest rightly understood" to describe this concept. He combined the right of association with the virtue to do what was right. The following passage from his book sums up the concept of enlightened self-interest:

> The Americans, on the contrary, are fond of explaining almost all of their lives by the principle of interest rightly understood; they show with complacency how an enlightened regard for themselves constantly prompts them to assist each other, and inclines them willingly to sacrifice a portion of their time and property to the welfare of the state.

Enlightened self-interest poses the question of whether or not it is to the advantage of a person to work for the good of all.

Enlightened egoism is one form of egoism that emphasizes more of a direct action to bring about the best interests of society. Enlightened egoists take a long-range perspective and allow for the well-being of others because they help achieve some ultimate goal for the decision maker, although their own self-interest remains paramount. For example, enlightened egoists may abide by professional codes of ethics, avoid cheating on taxes, and create safe working conditions. They do so not because their actions benefit others, but because they help achieve some ultimate goal for the egoist, such as advancement within the firm.[44] In other words, enlightened egoism is advocated as a means rather than an end, based on the belief that for everyone to pursue their own interests will maximize general prosperity.

An enlightened egoist might call management's attention to a coworker who is falsifying the financial reports, but only to protect the company's reputation and thus the egoist's own job security. In addition, an enlightened egoist could become a whistle-blower and report misconduct to the Securities and Exchange Commission (SEC) to receive an award for exposing misconduct.

Let's examine the following example from the perspectives of egoism and enlightened egoism. The date is Friday, January 17, 2019, and the time is 5:00 p.m. It is the last day of fieldwork on an audit, and you are the staff auditor in charge of receivables. You are wrapping up the test of subsequent collections of accounts receivable to determine whether certain receivables that were outstanding on December 31, 2018, and that were not confirmed by the customer as being outstanding, have now been collected. If these receivables have been collected and in amounts equal to the year-end outstanding balances, then you will be confident that the December 31 balance is correct and this aspect of the receivables audit can be relied on. One account receivable for $1 million has not been collected, even though it is 90 days past due. You go to your supervisor and discuss whether to establish an allowance for uncollectibles for part of or the entire amount. Your supervisor contacts the manager in charge of the audit who goes to the CFO to discuss the matter. The CFO says in no uncertain terms that you should not record an allowance of any amount. The CFO does not want to reduce earnings below the current level because that will cause the company to fail to meet financial analysts' estimates of earnings for the year. Your supervisor informs you that the firm will go along with the client on this matter, even though the $1 million amount is material. In fact, it is 10% of the overall accounts receivable balance on December 31, 2018.

The junior auditor faces a challenge to integrity in this instance. The client is attempting to circumvent GAAP. The ethical obligation of the staff auditor is not to subordinate judgment to others' judgment, including that of top management of the firm. Easier said than done, no doubt, but it is the standard of behavior in this situation.

If you are an egoist, you might conclude that it is in your best interests to go along with the firm's position, to support the client's presumed interests. After all, you do not want to lose your job. An enlightened egoist would consider the interests of others, including the investors and creditors, but still might reason that it is in her long-run interests to go along with the firm's position to support the client because she may not advance within the firm unless she is perceived to be a team player. Moreover, you don't want the firm to lose a client if it does not go along with the client's wishes. While the interests of others are seen as a means to an end—maximize one's own self-interests—enlightened egoism has value in accounting decision making because the public interest can (and should) be considered in evaluating the competing interests in the course of maximizing one's own interests.

Rational Egoism

Rational egoism is a particular brand of ethical egoism that claims the promotion of one's own interest is always in accordance with reason. Rational egoism, also called rational selfishness, is the principle that an action is rational if and only if it maximizes one's self-interest. One of the most well-known proponents of rational egoism is the contemporary philosopher Ayn Rand (1905–1982).

Rand's philosophy is an ethics of choice, guided by reason, with human survival as its goal. This is diametrically opposed to altruism. Altruism, according to Rand, is a morality of the past. It is irrational to expect people to be motivated to act in whole or in part for the sake of another's interest(s). According to Rand, humans must choose their own values, goals, and actions in order to maintain their lives. Without the ability to choose, there could be no morality because morality deals only with issues open to man's choice (i.e., to his free will).

In Rand's *The Virtue of Selfishness: A New Concept of Egoism,* rationality is conceived of as man's basic virtue, the source of all other virtues. The virtue of rationality means the recognition and acceptance of reason as one's only source of knowledge, one's only judge of values, and one's only guide to action. It means a commitment to the reality of one's existence, i.e., to the principles that all of one's goals, values, and actions take place in reality and, therefore, that one must never place any value or consideration whatsoever above one's "perception of reality."[45]

It is popular today to link Rand's philosophy with the basic tenets of capitalism. She describes the capitalist system as the essence of individualism with a laissez-faire attitude in which the function of government is solely to protect individual rights, including property rights. The idea is for the government to have a hands-off approach and let each individual act in their rational self-interest and somehow this will lead to the ultimate best interests of society. Thus, Rand had a vision of capitalism as a moral ideal. Of course, this is a controversial issue today as many critics talk about the evils of capitalism and the unequal distribution of resources and wealth born out of a pursuit of self-interest mentality of corporations and well-heeled individuals.

Writing a column for the Public Broadcasting System, Denise Cummins examines why Rand's popularity among young adults continues to grow. They seem to be drawn to Rand's philosophy of unfettered self-interest. When questioned about their beliefs, some have said it taught them to rely on no one but themselves. Others believe it to be an idealized version of core American ideals: freedom from tyranny, hard work, and individualism. On this view, "It promises a better world if people are simply allowed to pursue their own self-interest without regard to the impact of their actions on others. After all, others are simply pursuing their own self-interest as well."[46]

The problem we see with Rand in the accounting arena is it is a profession where one's individual values need to conform to the profession's ethical standards and, if they do not, the individual runs the risk of acting in her own best interests but not the public interest. Moreover, individual's may have a different perception of reality and those perceptions may change with each new situation. Actions become more relativistic and this makes it difficult to have a consistent set of ethical standards such as exists in the AICPA Code of Professional Conduct (AICPA Code). The reality for accounting students to consider in evaluating Rand's philosophy is the ethical standards of the accounting profession are not up for debate.

Utilitarianism

Like egoism, *Utilitarianism* is concerned with consequences, but unlike the egoist, the utilitarian seeks to make decisions which bring about the greatest good for the greatest number of people. Utilitarians believe they should make decisions that result in the greatest total *utility* or the greatest benefit for all those affected by a decision.[47]

Utilitarians follow a relatively straightforward method for deciding the morally correct course of action for any particular situation. First, they identify the various courses of action that they could perform. Second, they determine the utility of the consequences of all possible alternatives and then select the one that results in the greatest net benefit. In other words, they identify all the foreseeable benefits and harms (consequences) that could result from each course of action for those affected by the action, and then choose the course of action that provides the greatest benefits after the costs have been taken into account.[48] Given its emphasis on evaluating the benefits and harms of alternatives on stakeholders, utilitarianism requires that people look beyond self-interest to consider impartially the interest of all persons affected by their actions.

The utilitarian theory was first formulated in the eighteenth century by the English writer Jeremy Bentham (1748–1832) and later refined by John Stuart Mill (1806–1873). Bentham sought an objective basis that would provide a publicly acceptable norm for determining what kinds of laws England should enact. He believed that the most promising way to reach an agreement was to choose the policy that would bring about the greatest net benefits to society once the harms had been taken into account. His motto became "the greatest good for the greatest number." Over the years, the principle of utilitarianism has been expanded and refined so that today there are many different variations of the principle. Modern utilitarians often describe benefits and harms in terms of satisfaction of personal preferences or in purely economic terms of monetary benefits over monetary costs.[49]

Utilitarians differ in their views about the kind of question we ought to ask ourselves when making an ethical decision. Some believe the proper question is: What effect will my doing this action in this situation have on the general balance of good over evil? If lying would produce the best consequences in a particular situation, we ought to lie.[50] These *act-utilitarians* examine the specific action itself, rather than the general rules governing the action, to assess whether it will result in the greatest utility. For example, a rule in accounting such as "don't subordinate judgment to the client" would serve only as a general guide for an act-utilitarian. If the overall effect of giving in to the client's demands brings net utility to all the stakeholders, then the rule is set aside.

Rule-utilitarians, on the other hand, claim that we must choose the action that conforms to the general rule that would have the best consequences. For the rule-utilitarian, actions are justified by appealing to rules such as "never compromise audit independence." According to the rule-utilitarian, an action is selected because it is required by the correct moral rules that everyone should follow. The correct moral rules are those that maximize intrinsic value and minimize intrinsic disvalue. For example, a general rule such as "don't deceive" (an element of truthfulness) might be interpreted as requiring the full disclosure of the possibility that the client will not collect on a material, $1 million receivable. A rule-utilitarian might reason that the long-term effects of deceiving the users of financial statements are a breakdown of the trust that exists between the users and preparers and auditors of financial information.

In other words, we must ask ourselves: What effect would everyone's doing this kind of action (subordination of judgment) have on the general balance of good over evil? So, for example, the rule "to always tell the truth" in general promotes the good of everyone and therefore should always be followed, even if lying would produce the best consequences in certain situations. Notwithstanding differences between act- and rule-utilitarians, most hold to the general principle that morality must depend on balancing the beneficial and harmful consequences of conduct.[51]

While utilitarianism is a very popular ethical theory, there are some difficulties in relying on it as a sole method for moral decision making because the utilitarian calculation requires that we assign values to the benefits and harms resulting from our actions. But it is often difficult, if not impossible, to measure and compare the values of certain benefits and costs. Let's go back to our receivables example. It would be difficult to quantify the possible effects of going along with the client. How can a utilitarian measure the costs to the company of possibly having to write off a potential bad debt after the fact, including possible higher interest rates to borrow money in the future because of a decline in liquidity? What is the cost to one's reputation for failing to disclose an event at a point in time that might have affected the analysis of financial results? On the other hand, how can we measure the benefits to the company of *not* recording the allowance? Does it mean the stock price will rise and, if so, by how much?

Deontology

The term *deontology* is derived from the Greek word *deon,* meaning "duty." *Deontology* refers to moral philosophies that focus on the rights of individuals and on the intentions associated with a particular behavior, rather than on its consequences.

Deontologists believe that moral norms establish the basis for action. Deontology differs from rule-utilitarianism in that the moral norms (or rules) are based on reason, not outcomes. Fundamental to deontological theory is the idea that equal respect must be given to all persons.[52] In other words, individuals have certain inherent rights and I, as the decision maker, have a duty (obligation, commitment, or responsibility) to respect those rights.

Philosophers claim that rights and duties are correlative. That is, my rights establish your duties and my duties correspond to the rights of others. The deontological tradition focuses on duties, which can be thought of as establishing the ethical limits of my behavior. From my perspective, duties are what I owe to others. Other people have certain claims on my behavior; in other words, they have certain rights against me.[53]

As with utilitarians, deontologists may be divided into those who focus on moral rules and those who focus on the nature of the acts themselves. In *act deontology,* principles are or should be applied by individuals to each unique circumstance allowing for some space in deciding the right thing to do. *Rule deontologists* believe that general moral principles determine the relationship between the basic rights of the individual and a set of rules governing conduct. It is particularly appropriate to the accounting profession, where the Principles of the AICPA Code support the rights of investors and creditors to receive accurate and reliable financial information and the duty of CPAs to meet their obligations to these users, so we emphasize rule deontology in this book.

Unlike utilitarians, deontologists argue there are things we should not do, even to maximize utility. We should not deceive investors and creditors by going along with improper accounting even if it enables a client to gain needed financing, expand operations, add jobs to the payroll, and, ultimately, earn greater profit for the company. To do so would violate the rights of investors and creditors to full and fair financial information to assist in their decision-making needs (i.e. buy/sell stock, loan money/don't loan).

Rule deontologists believe that conformity to general moral principles based on logic determines ethicalness. Examples include Kant's categorical imperative, discussed next, and the Golden Rule.

Rights Principles

A *right* is a justified claim on others. For example, if I have a right to freedom, then I have a justified claim to be left alone by others. Turned around, I can say that others have a duty or responsibility to leave me alone.[54] In accounting, because investors and creditors have a right to accurate and complete financial information, I have the duty to ensure that the financial statements "present fairly" the financial position, results of operations, and changes in cash flows.

Formulations of *rights theories* first appeared in the seventeenth century in writings of Thomas Hobbes and John Locke. One of the most important and influential interpretations of moral rights is based on the work of Immanuel Kant (1724–1804), an eighteenth-century philosopher. Kant maintained that each of us has a worth or dignity that must be respected. This dignity makes it wrong for others to abuse us or to use us against our will. Kant expressed this idea as a moral principle: Humanity must always be treated as an end, not merely as a means. To treat a person as a mere means is to use her to advance one's own interest. But to treat a person as an end is to respect that person's dignity by allowing each the freedom to choose for himself.[55]

An important contribution of Kantian philosophy is the so-called categorical imperative: "Act only according to that maxim by which you can at the same time will that it should become universal law."[56] The "maxim" of our acts can be thought of as the intention behind our acts. The maxim answers the question: What am I doing, and why? In other words, moral intention is a driver of ethical action. The categorical imperative is a useful perspective: How would I want others to decide the issue in similar situations for similar reasons? If I can confidently answer that question, then my decision would meet the universality standard.

Kant believed that truth telling could be made a universal law, but lying could not. If we all lied whenever it suited us, rational communication would be impossible. Thus, lying is unethical. Imagine if every company falsified its financial statements. It would be impossible to evaluate the financial results of one company accurately over time and in comparison to other companies. The financial markets might ultimately collapse because reported results were meaningless, or even misleading. This condition of universality, not unlike the Golden Rule, prohibits us from giving our own personal point of view special status over the point of view of others. It is a strong requirement of impartiality and equality for ethics.[57]

One problem with deontological theory is that it relies on moral absolutes—absolute principles and absolute conclusions. Kant believed that a moral rule must function without exception. The notions of rights and duties are completely separate from the consequences of one's actions. This could lead to making decisions that might adhere to one's moral rights and another's attendant duties to those rights, but which also produce disastrous consequences for other people. For example, imagine if you were the person hiding Anne Frank and her family in the attic of your home and the Nazis came banging at the door and demanded, "Do you know where the Franks are?" Now, a strict application of rights theory requires that you tell the truth to the Nazi soldiers. However, isn't this situation one in which an exception to the rule should come into play for humanitarian reasons?

Whenever we are confronted with a moral dilemma, we need to consider whether the action would respect the basic rights of each of the individuals involved. How would the action affect the well-being of those individuals? Would it involve manipulation or deception—either of which would undermine the right to truth that is a crucial personal right? Actions are wrong to the extent that they violate the rights of individuals.[58]

Sometimes the rights of individuals will come into conflict, and one has to decide which right has priority. There is no clear way to resolve conflicts between rights and the corresponding moral duties to respect those rights. One of the most widely discussed cases of this kind is taken from William Styron's novel *Sophie's Choice*. Sophie and her two children are at a Nazi concentration camp. A guard confronts Sophie and tells her that one of her children will be allowed to live and one will be killed. Sophie must decide which child will be killed. She can prevent the death of either of her children, but only by condemning the other to be killed. The guard makes the situation even more painful for Sophie by telling her that if she chooses neither, then both will be killed. With this added factor, Sophie has a morally compelling reason to choose one of her children. But for each child, Sophie has an equally strong reason to save him or her. Thus, the same moral precept gives rise to conflicting obligations.[59]

Now, we do not face such morally excruciating decisions in accounting (thank goodness). However, we may have to differentiate between the rights of one party versus another and should rely on our duties/obligations to each under the Principles in the AICPA Code that are discussed later.

Justice

Justice is usually associated with issues of rights, fairness, and equality. A just act respects your rights and treats you fairly. Justice means giving each person what she or he deserves. *Justice* and *fairness* are closely related terms that are often used interchangeably, although differences do exist. While *justice* usually has been used with reference to a standard of rightness, *fairness* often has been used with regard to an ability to judge without reference to one's feelings or interests.

Justice as Fairness

John Rawls (1921–2002) developed a conception of justice as fairness using elements of both Kantian and utilitarian philosophy. He described a method for the moral evaluation of social and political institutions this way.[60]

Imagine that you have set for yourself the task of developing a totally new social contract for today's society. How could you do so fairly? Although you could never actually eliminate all of your personal biases and prejudices, you would need to take steps at least to minimize them. Rawls suggests that you imagine yourself in an original position behind a veil of ignorance. Behind this veil, you know nothing of yourself and your natural abilities, or your position in society. You know nothing of your sex, race, nationality, or individual tastes. Behind such a veil of ignorance all individuals are simply specified as rational, free, and morally equal beings. You do know that in the "real world," however, there will be a wide variety in the natural distribution of natural assets and abilities, and that there will be differences of sex, race, and culture that will distinguish groups of people from each other.

Rawls says that behind the veil of ignorance the only safe principles will be fair principles, for you do not know whether you would suffer or benefit from the structure of any biased institutions. The safest principles will provide for the highest minimum standards of justice in the projected society.

Rawls argues that in a similar manner, the rational individual would only choose to establish a society that would at least conform to the following two rules:

1. *Each person is to have an equal right to the most extensive basic liberty compatible with similar liberty for others.*

2. *Social and economic inequalities are to be arranged so that they are both:*

   (a)   reasonably expected to be to everyone's advantage and

   (b)   attached to positions and offices open to all.

The first principle—often called the *Liberty Principle*—is very Kantian in that it provides for basic and universal respect for persons as a minimum standard for all just institutions. But while all persons may be morally equal, we also know that in the "real world" there are significant differences between individuals that under conditions of liberty will lead to social and economic inequalities.

The second principle—called the *Difference Principle*—permits such inequalities and even suggests that it will be to the advantage of all (similar to the utility principle), but only if they meet the two specific conditions. Thus the principles are not strictly egalitarian, but they are not laissez-faire either. Rawls is locating his vision of justice in between these two extremes.

When people differ over what they believe should be given, or when decisions have to be made about how benefits and burdens should be distributed among a group of people, questions of justice or fairness inevitably arise. These are questions of *distributive justice.*[61]

The most fundamental principle of justice, defined by Aristotle more than 2,000 years ago, is that "equals should be treated equally and unequals unequally." In other words, individuals should be treated the same unless they differ in ways that are relevant to the situation in which they are involved. The problem with this interpretation is in determining which criteria are morally relevant to distinguish between those who are equal and those who are not. It can be a difficult theory to apply in business if, for example, a CEO of a company decides to allocate a larger share of the resources than is warranted (justified), based on the results of operations, to one product line over another to promote that operation because it is judged to have more long-term expansion and income potential. If I am the manager in charge of the operation getting fewer resources but producing equal or better results, then I may believe that my operation has been (I have been) treated unfairly. On the other hand, it could be said that the other manager deserves to receive a larger share of the resources because of the long-term potential of that other product line. That is, the product lines are not equal; the former deserves more resources because of its greater upside potential.

Justice as fairness is the basis of the objectivity principle in the AICPA Code that establishes a standard of providing unbiased financial information. In our discussion of ethical behavior in this and the following chapters, questions of fairness will be tied to making objective judgments. Auditors should render objective judgments about the fair presentation of financial results. In this regard, auditors should act as impartial arbiters of the truth, just as judges who make decisions in court cases should.

For purposes of future discussions about ethical decision making, we elaborate on the concept of *procedural justice.* When there is strong employee support for decisions, decision makers, organizations, and outcomes, procedural justice is less important to the individual. In contrast, when employees' support for decisions, decision makers, organizations, or outcomes is not very strong, then procedural justice becomes more important.[62] Consider, for example, a potential whistleblower who feels confident about bringing her concerns to top management because specific procedures are in place to support that person. Unlike the Betty Vinson situation at WorldCom, an environment built on procedural justice supports the whistleblower, who perceives the fairness of procedures used to make decisions.

Virtue Ethics

Virtue considerations apply both to the decision maker and to the act under consideration by that party. This is one of the differences between virtue theory and the other moral philosophies that focus on the act. Virtue theory focuses on both the person engaging in the act and the act itself. This philosophy is called *virtue ethics,* and it posits that what is moral in a given situation is not only what conventional morality or moral rules require but also what a well-intentioned person with a "good" moral character would deem appropriate.

Virtue theorists place less emphasis on learning rules and instead stress the importance of developing *good habits of character,* such as kindness. Plato emphasized four virtues in particular, which were later called *cardinal virtues:* wisdom, courage, temperance, and justice. Other important virtues are fortitude, generosity, self-respect, good temper, and sincerity. In addition to advocating good habits of character, virtue theorists hold that we should avoid acquiring bad character traits, or vices, such as cowardice, insensibility, injustice, and vanity. Virtue theory emphasizes moral education because virtuous character traits are developed in one's youth. Adults, therefore, are responsible for instilling virtues in the young.

The philosopher Alasdair MacIntyre states that the exercise of virtue requires "a capacity to judge and to do the right thing in the right place at the right time in the right way." Judgment is exercised not through a routinizable application of the rules, but as a function of possessing those dispositions/tendencies (i.e. virtues) that enable choices to be made about what is good for people and by holding in check desires for something other than what will help achieve this goal.[63]

At the heart of the virtue approach to ethics is the idea of "community" and all who practice in it. MacIntyre relates virtues to the rewards of a practice. He differentiates between the external rewards of a practice (such as money, fame, and power) and the internal rewards, which relate to the intrinsic value of a particular practice. MacIntyre points out that every practice requires a certain kind of relationship between those who participate in it. The virtues are the standards of excellence that characterize relationships within the practice. To enter into a practice is to accept the authority of those standards, obedience to the rules, and commitment to achieve the internal rewards.[64] The accounting profession is a community with standards of excellence embodied in state board rules of conduct and the AICPA Code.

We have emphasized moral intent as an essential ingredient of ethical behavior. Moral intent is necessary to deal with the many conflicts in accounting among the interests of employers, clients, and the public interest. We realize that for students, it may be difficult to internalize the concept that, when forced into a corner by one's supervisor to go along with financial wrongdoing, you should stand up for what you know to be right, even if it means losing your job. However, ask yourself the following questions: Do I even want to work for an organization that does not value my professional opinion? If I go along with it this time, might the same demand be made at a later date? Will I begin to slide down that ethical slippery slope where there is no turning back? How much is my reputation for honesty and integrity worth? Would I be proud if others found out what I did (or didn't do)? To quote the noted Swiss psychologist and psychiatrist, Carl Jung: "You are what you do, not what you say you'll do."

By way of summarizing the material in this section, we present an analysis of ethical reasoning methods that form the basis for ethical judgments and related implementation issues in Exhibit 1.3. We elaborate on these judgments throughout the book.

EXHIBIT 1.3 Ethical Reasoning Method Bases for Making Ethical Judgments

	Teleology			Deontology	Justice	Virtue Ethics
	Egoism	**Enlightened Egoism**	**Utilitarianism**	**Rights Theory**		
Ethical Judgments	Defines "right" behavior by consequences for the decision maker.	Considers well-being of others within the scope of deciding on a course of action based on self-interest.	Evaluates consequences of actions (harms and benefits) on stakeholders. *Act* Evaluate whether the intended *action* provides the greatest net benefits. *Rule* Select the action that conforms to the correct *moral rule* that produces the greatest net benefits.	Considers "rights" of stakeholders and related duties to them. Treats people as an end and not merely as a means to an end. *Universality Perspective:* Would I want others to act in a similar manner for similar reasons in this situation?	Emphasizes rights, fairness, and equality. Those with equal claims to justice should be treated equally; those with unequal claims should be treated unequally.	Only method where ethical reasoning methods—"virtues" (internal traits of character)—apply both to the *decision maker* and the decision. Judgments are made not by applying rules, but by possessing those traits that enable the decision maker to act for the good of others. Similar to Principles of AICPA Code and IMA standards.
Problems with Implementation	Fails to consider interests of those affected by the decision.	Interests of others are subservient to self-interest.	Can be difficult to assign values to harms and benefits.	Relies on moral absolutes—no exceptions; need to resolve conflicting rights.	Can be difficult to determine the criteria to distinguish equal claims from unequal claims.	Virtues may conflict, requiring choices to be made.

Regulation and the Public Interest in Accounting

LO 1-5

Describe the regulatory system in accounting and how professional accountants serve the public interest.

Regulation of the Accounting Profession

Professions are defined by the knowledge, skills, attitudes, behaviors, and ethics of those in the (accounting) profession. Regulation of a profession is a specific response to the need for certain standards to be met by the members of the profession. The accounting profession provides an important public service through audits and other assurance services (together, attest services) and those who choose to join the community pledge to act in the public interest.

Regulations exist to address the knowledge imbalance between the client and the provider of services, who has professional expertise. Regulation also helps when there are significant benefits or costs from the provision of accountancy services that accrue to third parties, other than those acquiring and producing the services.

In the United States, the state boards of accountancy are charged with protecting the public interest in licensing candidates to become CPAs. The behavior of licensed CPAs and their ability to meet ethical and professional obligations is regulated by the state boards. Regulatory oversight is based on the statutorily defined scope of practice of public accountancy. There are 55 state boards (50 states, plus the District of Columbia, Guam, Commonwealth of Northern Mariana Islands, Puerto Rico, and the U.S. Virgin Islands).

The National Association of State Boards of Accountancy (NASBA) provides a forum for discussion of the different state board requirements to develop an ideal set of regulations in the Uniform Accountancy Act. The NASBA Center for the Public Trust advances ethical leadership in business, institutions and organizations. It does this, in part, through training and a certification program that teaches how to recognize ethical issues, resolve dilemmas and create an atmosphere that promotes positive ethical behavior.

The Public Interest in Accounting

Following the disclosure of numerous accounting scandals in the early 2000s at companies such as Enron and WorldCom, the accounting profession, professional bodies, and regulatory agencies turned their attention to examining how to rebuild the public trust and confidence in financial reporting. Stuebs and Wilkinson point out that restoring the accounting profession's public interest focus is a crucial first step in recapturing the public trust and securing the profession's future.[65] Copeland believes that in order to regain the trust and respect the profession enjoyed prior to the scandals, the profession must rebuild its reputation on its historical foundation of ethics and integrity.[66]

The CPA license has "public" in its title to remind all that the primary obligation of CPAs is to the public interest. Keeping the public interest in mind helps a CPA determine dilemmas such as: who is the primary client—the public, company, management, or shareholders; to whom ethical loyalty is owed; when services and clients present conflicts of interests; and when confidentiality must be upheld. The Principles in the AICPA Code state that "members should accept the obligation to act in a way that will serve the public interest, honor the public trust, and demonstrate commitment to professionalism" (AICPA 0.300.030.01, 2014). The responsibility to the public overrides the responsibilities to the clients or those who hire and pay them. The public interest includes those who rely on financial statements for lending, investing, and pension decisions.[67]

Ethics and Professionalism

The accounting profession is a community with values and standards of behavior. These are embodied in the various codes of conduct in the professional bodies, including the AICPA. The AICPA is a voluntary association of CPAs with more than 418,000 members in 143 countries, including CPAs in business and industry, public accounting, government, education, student affiliates, and international associates. CPA state societies also exist in the United States. Even though regulation of the profession and licensing is through state boards and state board rules of conduct, the AICPA Code of Professional Conduct is typically recognized as having accepted standards of behavior.

The Institute of Management Accountants (IMA) has a global network of accountants and financial professionals with more than 75,000 members in 140 countries. The IMA Statement of Ethical and Professional Practice provides guidelines for ethical conduct and is unique in that it provides guidelines to resolve ethical conflicts. The IMA standards appear in Exhibit 1.4.

EXHIBIT 1.4   Institute of Management Accountants Statement of Ethical Professional Practice

Members of IMA shall behave ethically. A commitment to ethical professional practice includes overarching principles that express our values, and standards that guide our conduct.

Principles

IMA's overarching ethical principles include: Honesty, Fairness, Objectivity, and Responsibility. Members shall act in accordance with these principles and shall encourage others within their organizations to adhere to them.

Standards

A member's failure to comply with the following standards may result in disciplinary action.

I. Competence

Each member has a responsibility to:

1. Maintain an appropriate level of professional expertise by continually developing knowledge and skills.
2. Perform professional duties in accordance with relevant laws, regulations, and technical standards.
3. Provide decision support information and recommendations that are accurate, clear, concise, and timely.
4. Recognize and communicate professional limitations or other constraints that would preclude responsible judgment or successful performance of an activity.

II. Confidentiality

Each member has a responsibility to:

1. Keep information confidential except when disclosure is authorized or legally required.
2. Inform all relevant parties regarding appropriate use of confidential information. Monitor subordinates' activities to ensure compliance.
3. Refrain from using confidential information for unethical or illegal advantage.

III. Integrity

Each member has a responsibility to:

1. Mitigate actual conflicts of interest, regularly communicate with business associates to avoid apparent conflicts of interest. Advise all parties of any potential conflicts.

(Continued)

2. Refrain from engaging in any conduct that would prejudice carrying out duties ethically.
3. Abstain from engaging in or supporting any activity that might discredit the profession.

IV. Credibility

Each member has a responsibility to:

1. Communicate information fairly and objectively.
2. Disclose all relevant information that could reasonably be expected to influence an intended user's understanding of the reports, analyses, or recommendations.
3. Disclose delays or deficiencies in information, timeliness, processing, or internal controls in conformance with organization policy and/or applicable law.

Resolution of Ethical Conduct

In applying the Standards of Ethical Professional Practice, you may encounter problems identifying unethical behavior or resolving an ethical conflict. When faced with ethical issues, you should follow your organization's established policies on the resolution of such conflict. If these policies do not resolve the ethical conflict, you should consider the following courses of action:

1. Discuss the issue with your immediate supervisor except when it appears that the supervisor is involved. In that case, present the issue to the next level. If you cannot achieve a satisfactory resolution, submit the issue to the next management level. If your immediate superior is the chief executive officer or equivalent, the acceptable reviewing authority may be a group such as the audit committee, executive committee, board of directors, board of trustees, or owners. Contact with levels above the immediate superior should be initiated only with your superior's knowledge, assuming he or she is not involved. Communication of such problems to authorities or individuals not employed or engaged by the organization is not considered appropriate, unless you believe there is a clear violation of the law.
2. Clarify relevant ethical issues by initiating a confidential discussion with an IMA Ethics Counselor or other impartial advisor to obtain a better understanding of possible courses of action.
3. Consult your own attorney as to legal obligations and rights concerning the ethical conflict.

The Institute of Internal Auditors (IIA) is an international professional association representing the internal audit profession with more than 185,000 members in 170 countries. Similar to the IMA code, internal auditors are held to standards that address their competence, integrity, and objectivity (credibility), as you can see by Exhibit 1.5. Both codes contain a provision for confidentiality because internal accountants and auditors gain access to sensitive financial and operating information that should not be disclosed because it might negatively affect the company's financial and operating positions. Note that the ethics guidelines of the IMA and IIA are virtually the same except for the resolution of conflicts in the IMA standards.

EXHIBIT 1.5   The Institute of Internal Auditors Code of Ethics

Principles

Internal auditors are expected to apply and uphold the following principles:

1. **Integrity**
   The integrity of internal auditors establishes trust and thus provides the basis for reliance on their judgment.

2. **Objectivity**
   Internal auditors exhibit the highest level of professional objectivity in gathering, evaluating, and communicating information about the activity or process being examined. Internal auditors make a balanced assessment of all the relevant circumstances and are not unduly influenced by their own interests or by others in forming judgments.

(Continued)

3. **Confidentiality**
Internal auditors respect the value and ownership of information they receive and do not disclose information without appropriate authority unless there is a legal or professional obligation to do so.

4. **Competency**
Internal auditors apply the knowledge, skills, and experience needed in the performance of internal audit services.

Rules of Conduct

1. Integrity

Internal auditors:

1.1. Shall perform their work with honesty, diligence, and responsibility.
1.2. Shall observe the law and make disclosures expected by the law and the profession.
1.3. Shall not knowingly be a party to any illegal activity, or engage in acts that are discreditable to the profession of internal auditing or to the organization.
1.4. Shall respect and contribute to the legitimate and ethical objectives of the organization.

2. Objectivity

Internal auditors:

2.1. Shall not participate in any activity or relationship that may impair or be presumed to impair their unbiased assessment. This participation includes those activities or relationships that may be in conflict with the interests of the organization.
2.2. Shall not accept anything that may impair or be presumed to impair their professional judgment.
2.3. Shall disclose all material facts known to them that, if not disclosed, may distort the reporting of activities under review.

3. Confidentiality

Internal auditors:

3.1. Shall be prudent in the use and protection of information acquired in the course of their duties.
3.2. Shall not use information for any personal gain or in any manner that would be contrary to the law or detrimental to the legitimate and ethical objectives of the organization.

4. Competency

Internal auditors:

4.1. Shall engage only in those services for which they have the necessary knowledge, skills, and experience.
4.2. Shall perform internal audit services in accordance with the *International Standards for the Professional Practice of Internal Auditing (Standards).*
4.3. Shall continually improve their proficiency and the effectiveness and quality of their services.

The fastest growing professional association is the Association of Certified Fraud Examiners (ACFE). The ACFE is the world's largest anti-fraud organization and provider of anti-fraud training and education. Together with more than 80,000 members, the ACFE aims to reduce business fraud worldwide and inspire public confidence in the integrity and objectivity within the profession.

On an international level, the International Federation of Accountants (IFAC) is a global professional body dedicated to serve the public interest with over 110-member organizations and 185 country profiles. IFAC supports the development of high-quality international standards and speaks out on public interest issues. IFAC issues a global code of ethics through the International Ethics Standards Board of Accountants (IESBA)—Handbook of Code of Ethics for Professional Accountants. The global environment in accounting has grown in importance since IFAC was formed in 1977. More will be said about the global ethics arena in accounting in Chapter 4.

Ethics Education

As a future accounting professional, it is important for you to understand the role of ethics in the practice of accounting. For many years there was no requirement for accounting students to satisfy an ethics course requirement to sit for the CPA Exam. That changed when Texas became the first state to require an ethics course as part of the education requirement for CPA candidates, thanks to the Enron scandal and Houston office of Arthur Andersen, LLP, both Texas embarrassments. Currently, six states require explicit ethics education for the CPA candidates. Those states are California, Colorado, Maryland, New York, Texas, and West Virginia.

Both California and Texas require an ethics course devoted to accounting ethics and professional regulation. For example, the Texas State Board of Public Accountancy (TSBPA) requirement is for a three-semester hour ethics course that provides students with a framework of ethical reasoning and core professional values and attitudes for exercising professional skepticism, including independence, objectivity, integrity, ethical reasoning, and other behavior that is in the best interest of the public and profession.[68] In California, the board of accountancy requires a standalone accounting ethics course devoted to accounting ethics or accounting professional responsibilities.[69]

Even if you do not live in one of the six states, you will have to meet the state ethics education requirement to practice public accountancy in these states. For example, Oklahoma State University offers a course in Ethical Issues in Accounting while the University of Southern California's course is Ethics for Professional Accountants. The TSBPA has approved these courses to meet Texas's requirement so students from these institutions that take the approved courses can move to Texas and practice public accounting without having to take an ethics course.[70]

All states require passage of a state ethics exam after completion of the CPA exam, normally with the state code of professional conduct. This is the final step in licensing. Some states use a Professional Ethics course developed by the AICPA.

As Continuing Professional Education (CPE) became a mandatory requirement for licensing by all state boards and membership in professional associations, ethics CPE began to be offered and many states saw a dip in ethics complaints. Some states experimented with requiring an ethics CPE course on a regular basis. After the bank and savings and loan crisis of the 1980s, dot.com and financial scandals crises in 1990s, and numerous business frauds in the early 2000s, all states now require ethics CPE on an on-going basis.

Regulation in the accounting profession is a necessary but insufficient condition to ensure ethical and professional behavior occurs; ethics education on an on-going basis is an essential ingredient, as is developing ethical cultures. Organizations should support ethical behavior by setting an ethical tone at the top. This will be further explored in Chapters 2 and 3.

AICPA Code of Conduct

LO 1-6

Discuss the Principles section of the AICPA Code of Professional Conduct.

Given that state boards of accountancy generally recognize the AICPA ethical standards in state board rules of conduct, we emphasize the AICPA Code in most of this book. The Principles section of the AICPA Code, which mirrors virtues-based principles, are discussed next. We discuss the rules of conduct that are the enforceable provisions of the AICPA Code in Chapter 4.

Principles in the Code

The Principles of the AICPA Code are aspirational statements that form the foundation for the Code's enforceable rules. The Principles guide members in the performance of their professional responsibilities and call for an unyielding commitment to honor the public trust, even at the sacrifice of personal benefits. While CPAs cannot be legally held to the Principles, they do represent the expectations for CPAs on the part of the public in the performance of professional services. In this regard, the Principles are based on values of the profession and traits of character (virtues) that enable CPAs to meet their obligations to the public.

The Principles include (1) Responsibilities, (2) The Public Interest, (3) Integrity, (4) Objectivity and Independence, (5) Due Care, and (6) Scope and Nature of Services.[71]

The umbrella statement in the Code is that the overriding responsibility of CPAs is to exercise sensitive professional and moral judgments in all activities. By linking professional conduct to moral judgment, the AICPA Code recognizes the importance of moral reasoning in meeting professional obligations.

The second principle defines the public interest to include "clients, credit grantors, governments, employers, investors, the business and financial community, and others who rely on the objectivity and integrity of CPAs to maintain the orderly functioning of commerce." This principle calls for resolving conflicts between these stakeholder groups by recognizing the primacy of a CPA's responsibility to the public as the way to best serve clients' and employers' interests. In discharging their professional responsibilities, CPAs may encounter conflicting pressures from each of these groups. According to the public interest principle, when conflicts arise, the actions taken to resolve them should be based on integrity, guided by the precept that when CPAs fulfill their responsibilities to the public, clients' and employers' interests are best served.

As a principle of CPA conduct, integrity recognizes that the public trust is served by (1) being honest and candid within the constraints of client confidentiality, (2) not subordinating the public trust to personal gain and advantage, (3) observing both the form and spirit of technical and ethical standards, and (4) observing the principles of objectivity and independence and of due care.

Objectivity requires that all CPAs maintain a mental attitude of impartiality and intellectual honesty and be free of conflicts of interest in meeting professional responsibilities. Objectivity pertains to all CPAs in their performance of all professional services. Independence applies only to CPAs who provide attestation services, not tax and advisory/consulting services. The audit opinion is relied on by external users—investors and creditors—thereby triggering the need to be independent of the client entity to enhance assurances. In tax and advisory engagements, the service is provided primarily for the client (internal user) so that the CPA might become involved in some relationships with the client that might otherwise impair audit independence but do not come into play when providing nonattest services; nonattest services do require objectivity in decision making and the exercise of due care.

The due care standard calls for continued improvement in the level of competency and quality of services by (1) performing professional services to the best of one's abilities, (2) carrying out professional responsibilities with concern for the best interests of those for whom the services are performed, (3) carrying out those responsibilities in accordance with the public interest, (4) following relevant technical and ethical standards, and (5) properly planning and supervising engagements. A key element of due care is professional skepticism, which means to have a questioning mind and critical assessment of audit evidence.

The importance of the due care standard is as follows. Imagine if a CPA were asked to perform an audit of a school district and the CPA never engaged in governmental auditing before and never completed a course of study in governmental auditing. While the CPA or CPA firm may still obtain the necessary skills to perform the audit—for example, by hiring someone with the required skills—the CPA/firm would have a hard time supervising such work without the proper background and knowledge.

Acts Discreditable

LO 1-7

Explain what is meant by an act discreditable to the profession.

The rules of conduct under the AICPA Code cover personal behavior as well as professional behavior. This occurs under the "Acts Discreditable Rule" (1.400.001). Acts Discreditable include behaviors that cause embarrassment to the accounting profession. An example is discrimination and harassment in employment practices. The rule goes on to say that an act discreditable occurs when "a final determination, no longer subject to appeal, is made by a court or an administrative agency (i.e. state board of accountancy) or competent jurisdiction that [the CPA] has violated any antidiscrimination laws of the U.S., state, or municipality, including those related to sexual and other forms of harassment."[72]

McGee writes, under this rule, "many kinds of personal behavior might subject a CPA to punishment for violations that do not involve fraud or the violation of rights." He summarizes the essence of the rule as proscribing certain kinds of behavior that does more to protect [the image] of the profession than the public.[73]

The purpose of an act discreditable rule is to encourage moral behavior both outside and within the accounting profession. Any act that brings disrepute on the actor or the profession presumably can tarnish the image of the profession in the minds of the public.

One argument for regulating such acts is one's behavior in their personal life may affect their decisions as a professional. Ethical behavior is based on the constancy of one's acts. A person who is ethical in one instance and not the other violates this standard. A professional builds character through the repetition of good acts over time and in all kinds of situations. How can we conclude that a CPA who fails to file her own income tax return possesses the necessary ethics to advise a client on filing its return?

LO 1-8

Apply the IMA Statement of Ethical and Professional Practice and ethical reasoning methods to a case study.

Application of Ethical Reasoning in Accounting

In this section, we discuss the application of ethical reasoning in its entirety to a common dilemma faced by internal accountants and auditors. The case deals with the classic example of prematurely recording revenue to inflate earnings and make it look as though the company is doing better than it really is.

3D Printing Case Study

3D Printing, a privately-held company, was formed in March 2017 after a successful Kickstarter funding campaign. The project to develop the first jet fusion printer brought in $1.1 million, 10% above its goal. The company has struggled through its first full year of operations and is now preparing its financial statements for fiscal year end September 30, 2018. Kyle Bloom is the chief executive officer (CEO) of the company. He reports to a twelve-member board of directors. Madison Rose is the chief financial officer (CFO). She holds the Certified Management Accountant designation from the Institute of Management Accountants.

Kyle is meeting with Madison on October 5, 2018, to review the financial statements. The key issue being discussed is recording revenue on a $200,000 order from A-1 Printers. It seems the product won't be shipped until October 15, 2018, yet Kyle wants Madison to include the $200,000 in the current year earnings since that amount was received on September 30, 2018.

The following is an overview of the October 5 meeting.

Kyle: Madison, you have to include the $200,000 from A-1 Printers in revenue for this year.

Madison: I can't. Generally Accepted Accounting Principles (GAAP) require at least shipment of the product to A-1 as of September 30.

Kyle: You know we will ship the product in ten days. What's the big deal? You know our Kickstarter funds have run out so I'm in negotiations with our bank to borrow $10 million for continued expansion of our product line. Omitting the $200,000 means our net income will be $50,000, 80-percent below the target we announced. There's no way we'll get the loan. Production will be halted and layoffs will begin.

Madison: I understand and don't want to be held responsible for missing our targets. Still, it's better to take the hit to earnings now and record the revenue next year when it can put us over the top with respect to targeted earnings.

Kyle: I'll worry about next year, next year. If you prefer, we can adjust out the $200,000 in the first quarter of fiscal year 2019 as a prior period adjustment to retained earnings.

Madison: Has the board of directors approved it?

Kyle: Don't worry about the board. I'll take care of them.

At this point the meeting broke up and Madison was told to make the adjustment and include the $200,000 revenue this year. The last thing Kyle said to Madison was that he is expected to be a team player.

What should Madison do?

IMA Statement of Ethical Professional Practice

Competence: Madison is expected to perform professional duties in accordance with relevant laws, regulations, and technical standards. Recording the revenue in 2018 violates GAAP and state board rules.

Integrity: Madison should not engage in any conduct that would prejudice carrying out duties ethically. Going along with improper financial reporting violates her ethical responsibilities to place the public interest above other interests, including Kyle's, the company, and even self-interest.

Resolution: The IMA standards call for Madison to discuss her concerns with the next level of management, which is the board of directors since her superior—the CEO—, Kyle, is involved. The key issue for Madison is whether to blow the whistle and inform the board of directors. She can also seek advice by calling the IMA's anonymous helpline and/or the company hotline if one exists. Consulting an attorney also makes sense so Madison is aware of any potential legal liabilities.

Ethical Reasoning Methods

Categorical Imperative: (Rights Theory): Madison knows that Kyle's proposed revenue recognition is not a universally-accepted method. It accelerates revenue into an earlier period than justified. She would not want (or expect) other accountants to record the revenue as proposed, so why should she? Kyle is promoting an "ends justify the means" approach to decision making in that the revenue needs to be recorded to obtain the needed financing regardless of the method used to do it. Current investors and creditors, and the bank financing the $10 million, have an ethical right to receive accurate and reliable financial statements and Madison has an ethical duty to see to it that the financial statements do just that.

Utilitarianism: Act Utilitarianism could be used to justify delaying the recording of revenue by reasoning the benefits to be derived from getting the loan now (continued financing, no production stoppage, avoid layoffs) exceeds the potential costs if the bank finds out about the improper reporting. A Rule Utilitarian approach would come to a different conclusion because, much like Rights Theory, certain rules should never be violated regardless of utilitarian benefits. The relevant rule is never to falsify financial statement information.

Madison should also consider whether the board of directors have a right to know what is going on and if she has an ethical obligation to tell them. The IMA standards seem to say so, although the board is not specifically mentioned. In any case, the board should know because it is ultimately responsible to ensure the financial statements are accurate and reliable.

Decision

Madison should do whatever it takes to delay the recording of revenue until fiscal year ended September 30, 2019. She needs to counteract Kyle's statement of being a team player by pointing out her ultimate loyalty is not to the team or the organization but to herself, as an ethical person, and the public (investors, creditors) as a responsible, professional accountant. Finally, her should go the board before considering going outside the company (i.e. external auditors, regulatory agencies). These external parties might rightly assume that has been done in advance of any contact.

Scope and Organization of the Text

Ethical decision making in accounting is predicated on moral reasoning. In this chapter, we have attempted to introduce the complex philosophical reasoning methods that help to fulfill the ethical obligations of accounting professionals. In Chapter 2, we address behavioral ethics issues and lay the groundwork for discussions of professional judgment. We introduce a model that provides a framework for ethical decision making and can be used to help analyze cases presented at the end of each chapter. We also explain the "Giving Voice to Values" methodology that has become an integral part of ethical behavior since a decision-maker who possesses the abilities to express personal and professional values in an effective manner may be able to positively influence superiors who advocate improper financial reporting. In Chapter 3, we transition to the culture of an organization and how processes and procedures can help to create and sustain an ethical organization environment, including effective corporate governance systems. We also address whistleblowing considerations for accounting professionals.

The remainder of this book focuses more directly on accounting ethics. Chapter 4 addresses the AICPA Code and provisions that establish standards of ethical behavior for accounting professionals. In Chapter 5, we address fraud in financial statements, including the Fraud Triangle, and the obligations of auditors to assess the risk of material misstatements in the financial statements.

Auditors can be the target of lawsuits because of business failures and deficient audit work. In Chapter 6, we look at legal liability and regulatory issues under the Sarbanes-Oxley Act, Sections 302 and 404, violation of which can lead to legal liability. The techniques used to manipulate earnings and obscure financial statement items are discussed in the context of earnings management in Chapter 7. These "financial shenanigans" threaten the reliability of the financial reports and can lead to legal liabilities for accountants and auditors. Finally, in Chapter 8, we look at ethical leadership, the heart and soul of an ethical organization. Leadership in the accounting profession is examined from the perspective of auditor and firm behavior. The discussion of leadership links back to several topics discussed earlier in the text.

Concluding Thoughts

Financial scandals, unreported sexual harassment cases in Hollywood, the media and Congress, government misuse of funds, and other improprieties litter the stage of life these days with unabated examples of bad behavior. When was the last time you picked up a newspaper and read a story about someone doing the right thing because it was the right thing to do? It is rare these days. We seem to read and hear more about pursuing one's own selfish interests, even to the detriment of others. It might be called the "What's in it for me?" approach to life. Nothing could be more contrary to leading a life of virtue.

The road is littered with CFOs/CEOs/CPAs who masterminded (or at least directed) financial frauds at public companies and had to pay the price: Andy Fastow (10 years) and Jeff Skilling (14 years) at Enron; Scott Sullivan (5 years) and Bernie Ebbers (25 years) at WorldCom; and Tyco's Mark Swartz and Dennis Kozlowski who were sentenced to 8 1/3 to 25 years and ordered to pay $134 million in restitution. These fraudsters lost their dignity, their livelihood, and the respect of their community.

We want to conclude on a positive note. Heroes in accounting do exist: brave people who have spoken out about irregularities in their organizations, such as Cynthia Cooper from WorldCom, whom we have already discussed. Another such hero is David Walker, who served as comptroller general of the United States and head of the Government Accountability Office from 1998 to 2008. Walker appeared before an appropriations committee of the U.S. Senate in 2008 and spoke out about billions of dollars in waste spent by the U.S. government, including on the Iraqi war effort. Then there was auditor Joseph St. Denis, who spoke out about improper accounting practices at his former company, AIG, which received a $150 billion bailout from the U.S. government during the financial crisis of 2008.

A final note for students. Keep in mind that you may be in a position during your career where you feel pressured to remain silent about financial wrongdoing. You might rationalize that you didn't commit the unethical act, so your hands are clean. That's not good enough, though, as your ethical obligation to the public and the profession is to do whatever it takes to prevent a fraud from occurring and, if it does, take the necessary steps to correct and, if necessary, report the matter to higher-ups and government agencies.

We hope that you will internalize the ethical standards of the accounting profession and look at the bigger picture when pressured by a superior to do something that you know in your gut is wrong. Trust your common sense. Trust your conscience. Don't make a decision that might haunt you the rest of your life.

Discussion Questions

1. A common ethical dilemma used to distinguish between philosophical reasoning methods is the following. Imagine that you are standing on a footbridge spanning some trolley tracks. You see that a runaway trolley is threatening to kill five people. Standing next to you, in between the oncoming trolley and the five people, is a railway worker wearing a large backpack. You quickly realize that the only way to save the people is to push the man off the bridge and onto the tracks below. The man will die, but the bulk of his body and the pack will stop the trolley from reaching the others. (You quickly understand that you can't jump yourself because you aren't large enough to stop the trolley, and there's no time to put on the man's backpack.) Legal concerns aside, would it be ethical for you to save the five people by pushing this stranger to his death? Use the deontological and teleological methods to reason out what you would do and why.

2. Another ethical dilemma deals with a runaway trolley heading for five railway workers who will be killed if it proceeds on its present course. The only way to save these people is to hit a switch that will turn the trolley onto a side track, where it will run over and kill one worker instead of five. Ignoring legal concerns, would it be ethically acceptable for you to turn the trolley by hitting the switch in order to save five people at the expense of one person? Use the deontological and teleological methods to reason out what you would do and why.

3. MacIntyre, in his account of Aristotelian virtue, states that integrity is the one trait of character that encompasses all the others. How does integrity relate to, as MacIntrye said, "the wholeness of a human life"?

4. David Starr Jordan (1851–1931), an educator and writer, said, "Wisdom is knowing what to do next; virtue is doing it." Explain the meaning of this phrase as you see it.

5. a. Do you think it is the same to act in your own self-interest as it is to act in a selfish way? Why or why not?

   b. Do you think "enlightened self-interest" is a contradiction in terms, or is it a valid basis for all actions? Evaluate whether our laissez-faire, capitalistic, free-market economic system does (or should) operate under this philosophy.

6. Is it ever appropriate to lie to someone? Explain why or why not using ethical reasoning. Give one example of when you believe lying might be justified.

7. Is there a difference between cheating on a math test, pocketing an extra $10 from the change given to you at a restaurant, and using someone else's ID to get a drink at a bar?

8. Sir Walter Scott (1771–1832), the Scottish novelist and poet, wrote: "Oh what a tangled web we weave, when first we practice to deceive." Comment on what you think Scott meant by this phrase.

9. One explanation about rights is that there is a difference between what we have the right to do and what the right thing to do is. Explain what you think is meant by this statement. Do you believe that if someone attacks your credibility on social media that gives you the right to attack them?

10. Do you think it is ethical for a prospective employer to investigate your social media footprint in making a hiring decision? What about monitoring social networking activities of employees while on the job? Use ethical reasoning in answering these questions.

11. According to the 2011 National Business Ethics Survey conducted by the Ethics Resource Center, *Generational Differences in Workplace Ethics,*[74] a relatively high percentage of Millennials consider certain behaviors in the workplace ethical when compared with their earlier counterparts. These include:

    - Use social networking to find out about the company's competitors (37%),
    - "Friend" a client or customer on a social network (36%),
    - Upload personal photos on a company network (26%),
    - Keep copies of confidential documents (22%),
    - Work less to compensate for cuts in benefits or pay (18%),
    - Buy personal items using a company credit card (15%),
    - Blog or tweet negatively about a company (14%), and
    - Take a copy of work software home for personal use (13%).

    a. Choose one or more behaviors and explain why Millennials might view the behavior as ethical.

    b. Choose one or more behaviors and explain why you think it is unethical.

12. The 2016 Deloitte Millennial Survey of 7,500 college educated, full-time employees from 29 countries found that the most significant factor influencing respondents' decision-making at work was their personal values and morals. Seventy-percent believe their personal values are shared by the organization they work for, and they rank a solid ethical foundation built on trust, integrity, and honesty as one of the three most important values to the long-term success of a business.[75] Given the numerous examples of fraud so far in the 2000s, including Enron et al. and the financial recession, how can we reconcile the survey results with reality?

13. For years, the Baseball Hall of Fame has officially steered clear of the question as to how voters should handle the candidacies of players connected to performance-enhancing drugs. On November 21, 2017, Hall of Famer Joe Morgan pleaded with voters to reject players who failed drug tests, admitted using steroids, or were identified as users in Major League Baseball's investigation (Mitchell Report). Initially, two of the game's best players—Roger Clemens and Barry Bonds—could only muster about one-half of the 75% approval needed to be voted in. However, in 2017 both players received more than 50%, a significant threshold that has historically indicated future election, although their support only increased to 57.3% and 56.4%, respectively, in 2018. Do you believe Clemens and Bonds should be voted into the Hall of Fame?

14. Your best friend is from another country. One day after a particularly stimulating lecture on the meaning of ethics by your instructor, you and your friend disagree about whether culture plays a role in ethical behavior. You state that good ethics are good ethics, and it doesn't matter where you live and work. Your friend tells you that in her country it is common to pay bribes to gain favor with important people. Comment on both positions from a relativistic ethics point of view. What do you believe and why?

15. Socrates said that the best way to solve a problem is by thinking. Do you agree? Is thinking enough to solve most problems that arise in accounting?

16. Do you agree with our decision to omit Rand's Rational Egoism as a basis for making ethical judgments in accounting? Explain.

17. How should an accounting professional go about determining whether a proposed action is in the public interest?

18. Distinguish between ethical rights and obligations from the perspective of accountants and auditors.

19. Using the concept of justice that holds equals should be treated equally, unequals unequally, discuss how an auditor would assess the equality of interests in the financial reporting process.

20. CPAs who make false statements in advertisements violate the AICPA rules of conduct. Do you think it would be ethical for a CPA to hire a person to advertise in this manner for them? Why or why not?

21. Do you think a CPA can justify allowing the unethical behavior of a supervisor by claiming, "It's not my job to police the behavior of others?"

22. In the discussion of loyalty in this chapter, a statement is made that "your ethical obligation is to report what you have observed to your supervisor and let her take the appropriate action." We point out that you may want to take your concerns to others. The IMA Statement of Ethical Professional Practice includes a confidentiality standard that requires members to "keep information confidential except when disclosure is authorized or legally required." How do you believe this confidentiality standard might affect the next step taken by a CFO who failed to gain the support of the board of directors to force a change in improper financial reporting?

23. Assume that a corporate officer or other executive asks you, as the accountant for the company, to omit certain financial figures from the balance sheet that may paint the business in a bad light to

the public and investors. Because the request does not involve a direct manipulation of numbers or records, would you agree to go along with the request? What ethical considerations exist for you in deciding on a course of action?

24. Assume you are preparing for an interview with the director of personnel. Given the following possible questions, craft a response that you would feel comfortable giving for each one.

    • Describe an experience in the workplace when your attitudes and beliefs were ethically challenged. Use a personal example if you have not experienced a workplace dilemma.

    • What are the most important values that would drive your behavior as a new staff accountant in a CPA firm?

    • What would you do if your position on an accounting issue differs from that of firm management?

25. Mark Twain once said, "If you tell the truth, you don't have to remember anything." Explain what you think Twain meant by this statement and how it addresses one's character.

Endnotes

1. Bruce Weinstein Ph.D., The Ethics Guy, Available at: http://theethicsguy.com/whats-your-ethics-iq/.

2. Steven M. Mintz, "Virtue Ethics and Accounting Education," *Issues in Accounting Education* 10, no. 2 (Fall 1995), p. 257.

3. Susan Pulliam and Deborah Solomon, "Ms. Cooper Says No to Her Boss," *The Wall Street Journal,* October 30, 2002, p. A1.

4. Lynne W. Jeter, *Disconnected: Deceit and Betrayal at WorldCom* (Hoboken, NJ: Wiley, 2003).

5. Jeff Clabaugh, Washington Business Journal, WorldCom's Betty Vinson gets 5 months prison, August 5, 2005, https://www.bizjournals.com/washington/stories/2005/08/01/daily51.html.

6. Cynthia Cooper, *Extraordinary Circumstances* (Hoboken, NJ: Wiley, 2008).

7. Teaching Values, *The Golden Rule in World Religions,* Available at: www.teachingvalues.com/golden-rule.html.

8. William J. Prior, *Virtue and Knowledge: An Introduction to Ancient Greek Ethics* (London: Routledge, 1991).

9. William H. Shaw and Vincent Barry, *Moral Issues in Business* (Belmont, CA: Wadsworth Cengage Learning, 2010), p. 5.

10. James C. Gaa and Linda Thorne, "An Introduction to the Special Issue on Professionalism and Ethics in Accounting Education," *Issues in Accounting Education* 1, no. 1 (February 2004), p. 1.

11. Paul Walker and Terry Lovat, You say morals, I say ethics—what's the difference, September 17, 2014, Available at: https://theconversation.com/you-say-morals-i-say-ethics-whats-the-difference-30913.

12. Moral Relativism, Available at: https://www.allaboutphilosophy.org/moral-relativism.htm.

13. Ethical Relativism, Available at: https://www.allaboutphilosophy.org/ethical-relativism-faq.htm.

14. Ernest Hemingway, *Death in the Afternoon,* (Scribner; Reprint edition, April 6, 1996: New York, N.Y.).

15. Manuel Velasquez, Claire Andre, Thomas Shanks, S.J., and Michael J. Meyer, Ethical Relativism. Markkula Center for Applied Ethics, Available at: https://www.scu.edu/ethics/ethics-resources/ethical-decision-making/ethical-relativism/.

16. Joseph Fletcher, *Situation Ethics: The New Morality* (Louisville: KY: Westminster John Knox Press), 1966.

17. Josephson Institute of Ethics, 2012 Report Card on the Ethics of American Youth, https://b3vj2d40qhgsjw53vra221dq-wpengine.netdna-ssl.com/wp-content/uploads/2014/02/ReportCard-2012-DataTables.pdf.

18. James M. Lang, How College Classes Encourage Cheating, *The Boston Globe,* August 4, 2013, Available at: http://www.bostonglobe.com/ideas/2013/08/03/how-college-classes-encourage-cheating/3Q34x5ysYcplWNA3yO2eLK/story.html.

19. Ralph Heibutzki, Statistics on Why College Students Decide to Cheat, Available at: https://classroom.synonym.com/statistics-college-students-decide-cheat-5940.html.

20. Dian Schaffhauser, 9 in 10 Students Admit to Cheating in College, Suspect Faculty Do the Same, Campus Technology, February 23, 2017, Available at: https://campustechnology.com/articles/2017/02/23/9-in-10-students-admit-to-cheating-in-college-suspect-faculty-do-the-same.aspx.

21. Allie Grasgreen, Who Cheats, and How, Insider Higher Ed, March 16, 2012, Available at: https://www.insidehighered.com/news/2012/03/16/arizona-survey-examines-student-cheating-faculty-responses.

22. Marc Tracy, N.C.A.A.: North Carolina Will Not Be Punished for Academic Scandal, October 13, 2017, New York Times, Available at: https://www.nytimes.com/2017/10/13/sports/unc-north-carolina-ncaa.html.

23. Proskauer, Change note 24 to: 2013/14 Survey Social media in the Workplace Around the World 3.0, http://www.proskauer.com/files/uploads/social-media-in-the-workplace-2014.pdf.

24. Proskauer, 2013/14 Survey Social Media in the Workplace Around the World 3.0, Available at: http://www.proskauer.com/files/uploads/social-media-in-the-workplace-2014.pdf.

25. Aristotle, *Nicomachean Ethics,* trans. W. D. Ross (Oxford, UK: Oxford University Press, 1925).

26. Michael Josephson, *Making Ethical Decisions,* rev. ed. (Los Angeles: Josephson Institute of Ethics, 2002).

27. Alasdair MacIntyre, *After Virtue,* 2nd ed. (Notre Dame, IN: University of Notre Dame Press, 1984).

28. Josephson et al.

29. George Washington, *George Washington's Rules of Civility and Decent Behavior in Company and Conversation* (Bedford, ME: Applewood Books, 1994), p. 9.

30. Washington et al.

31. Vocabulary.com, Moral Sense, https://www.vocabulary.com/dictionary/moral%20sense.

32. Josephson et al.

33. Amy Anderson, "Profiles in Greatness - Eleanor Roosevelt," Success, December 1, 2008, http://www.success.com/article/profiles-in-greatness-eleanor-roosevelt.

34. Josephson et al.

35. Edmund L. Pincoffs, *Quandaries and Virtues against Reductivism in Ethics* (Lawrence: University Press of Kansas, 1986).

36. Josephson et al.

37. Josephson et al.

38. James R. Rest, *Moral Development: Advances in Research and Theory* (New York: Praeger,1986).

39. O. C. Ferrell, John Fraedrich, and Linda Ferrell, *Business Ethics: Ethical Decision Making and Cases,* 11th ed. (Mason, OH: South-Western, Cengage Learning, 2011), p. 159.

40. Internet Encyclopedia of Philosophy, Egoism, Available at: http://www.iep.utm.edu/egoism/.

41. Stanford Encyclopedia of Philosophy, Egoism, Available at: https://plato.stanford.edu/entries/egoism/.

42. Internet Encyclopedia of Philosophy.

43. Alexis de Tocqueville, *Democracy in America,* (Originally published 1835), (Chicago, ILL: University of Chicago Press, 2000).

44. Ferrell et al., p. 159.

45. Ayn Rand, *The Virtue of Selfishness: A New Concept of Egoism,* NY: New American Library, 1964.

46. Denise Cummins, Column: This is what happens when you take Ayn Rand seriously, PBS Newshour, February 16, 2016, http://www.pbs.org/newshour/making-sense/column-this-is-what-happens-when-you-take-ayn-rand-seriously/.

47. Ferrell et al. p. 159.

48. Manuel Velasquez, Claire Andre, Thomas Shanks, and Michael J. Meyer, "Calculating Consequences: The Utilitarian Approach to Ethics," *Issues in Ethics* 2, no. 1 (Winter 1989), Available at: www.scu.edu/ethics.

49. Velasquez et al.

50. Velasquez et al.

51. Velasquez et al.

52. Velasquez et al.

53. Velasquez et al.

54. Claire Andre and Manuel Velasquez, "Rights Stuff," Markkula Center for Applied Ethics' *Issues in Ethics* 3, no. 1 (Winter 1990), Available at: www.scu.edu/ethics/publications/iie/v3n1/.

55. Velasquez et al.

56. Immanuel Kant, *Foundations of Metaphysics of Morals,* trans. Lewis White Beck (New York: Liberal Arts Press, 1959), p. 39.

57. Velasquez et al.

58. Velasquez et al.

59. William Styron, *Sophie's Choice* (London: Chelsea House, 2001).

60. Spencer J. Maxcy, *Ethical School Leadership,* (Plymouth, United Kingdom: Rowman & Littlefield Education, 2002).

61. Manuel Velasquez, Claire Andre, Thomas Shanks, and Michael J. Meyer, "Justice and Fairness," *Issues in Ethics* 3, no. 2 (Spring 1990).

62. Ferrell et al., p. 165.

63. MacIntyre, pp. 187–190.

64. MacIntyre, pp. 190–192.

65. Martin Stuebs and Brett Wilkinson, "Restoring the Profession's Public Interest Role," *The CPA Journal* 79, no. 11, (2009) pp. 62–66.

66. James E. Copeland, Jr., "Ethics as an Imperative," *Accounting Horizons* 19, no. 1 (2005), pp. 35–43.

67. American Institute of CPAs (AICPA), AICPA Code of Professional Conduct, Effective December 15, 2014, Available at: https://www.aicpa.org/content/dam/aicpa/research/standards/codeofconduct/downloadabledocuments/2014december15contentasof2016august31codeofconduct.pdf.

68. Texas State Board of Public Accountancy (TSBPA), Texas Administrative Code, Title 22, Part 22, Chapter 511 (C), Rule Section 511.58, http://www.tsbpa.state.tx.us/education/education-requirements.html.

69. California Board of Accountancy, Business and Professions Code, Chapter 1, Section 5094.3, http://leginfo.legislature.ca.gov/faces/codes_displaySection.xhtml?sectionNum=5093.&lawCode=BPC.

70. TSBPA, Board Approved Ethics Courses Meeting Education Requirements for the Uniform CPA Examination, November 10, 2017, http://www.tsbpa.state.tx.us/pdffiles/approved-ethics-courses.pdf.

71. American Institute of Certified Public Accountants, *Code of Professional Conduct* at June 1, 2012 (New York: AICPA, 2012); Available at: www.aicpa.org/Research/Standards/CodeofConduct/Pages/default.aspx.

72. AICPA Code.

73. Robert W. McGee, "Can Sexual Acts Between (or Among) Consulting Adults Be Considered an Act Discreditable to the Profession under AICPA Code of Professional Conduct Rule 501? A Philosophical Look at the Practical Ethical Question", *Journal of Accounting & Public Policy,* 2, no. 1, (December 2000).

74. Ethics Resource Center, Generational Differences in Workplace Ethics: A Supplemental Report of the 2011 National Business Ethics Survey, Available at: https://rsp.uni.edu/sites/default/files/ERC%20Generational%20Differences.pdf http://www.ethics.org/files/u5/2011GenDiffFinal_0.pdf.

75. Deloitte, 2016 Deloitte Millennial Survey, Available at: https://www2.deloitte.com/content/dam/Deloitte/global/Documents/About-Deloitte/gx-millenial-survey-2016-exec-summary.pdf.

Chapter 1 Cases

Case 1-1 Harvard Cheating Scandal

Yes. Cheating occurs at the prestigious Harvard University. In 2012, Harvard forced dozens of students to leave in its largest cheating scandal in memory, but the institution would not address assertions that the blame rested partly with a professor and his teaching assistants. The issue is whether cheating is truly cheating when students collaborate with each other to find the right answer—in a take-home final exam.

Harvard released the results of its investigation into the controversy, in which 125 undergraduates were alleged to have cheated on an exam in May 2012.[1] The university said that more than half of the students were forced to withdraw, a penalty that typically lasts from two to four semesters. Many returned by 2015. Of the remaining cases, about half were put on disciplinary probation—a strong warning that becomes part of a student's official record. The rest of the students avoided punishment.

In previous years, students thought of Government 1310 as an easy class with optional attendance and frequent collaboration. But students who took it in spring 2012 said that it had suddenly become quite difficult, with tests that were hard to comprehend, so they sought help from the graduate teaching assistants who ran the class discussion groups, graded assignments, and advised them on interpreting exam questions.

Administrators said that on final-exam questions, some students supplied identical answers (right down to typographical errors in some cases), indicating that they had written them together or plagiarized them. But some students claimed that the similarities in their answers were due to sharing notes or sitting in on sessions with the same teaching assistants. The instructions on the take-home exam explicitly prohibited collaboration, but many students said they did not think that included talking with teaching assistants.

The first page of the exam contained these instructions: "The exam is completely open book, open note, open Internet, etc. However, in all other regards, this should fall under similar guidelines that apply to in-class exams. More specifically, students may not discuss the exam with others—this includes resident tutors, writing centers, etc."

Students complained about confusing questions on the final exam. Due to "some good questions" from students, the instructor clarified three exam questions by e-mail before the due date of the exams.

Students claim to have believed that collaboration was allowed in the course. The course's instructor and the teaching assistants sometimes encouraged collaboration, in fact. The teaching assistants—graduate students who graded the exams and ran weekly discussion sessions—varied widely in how they prepared students for the exams, so it was common for students in different sections to share lecture notes and reading materials. During the final exam, some teaching assistants even worked with students to define unfamiliar terms and help them figure out exactly what certain test questions were asking.

Some have questioned whether it is the test's design, rather than the students' conduct, that should be criticized. Others place the blame on the teaching assistants who opened the door to collaboration outside of class by their own behavior in helping students to understand the questions better.

Harvard adopted an honor code on May 6, 2014. In May 2017, Harvard announced that more than 60 students enrolled in Computer Science 50 (CS50): Introduction to Computer Science I appeared before the College's Honor Council investigating cases of academic dishonesty. While the facts have been kept confidential so far, a statement

---

[1] The facts of this case are taken from Richard Perez-Peña, "Students Disciplined in Harvard Scandal," February 1, 2013, Available at www.nytimes.com/2013/02/02/education/harvard-forced-dozens-to-leave-in-cheating-scandal.html?_r=0.

on the course website establishes standards for behavior: "The course recognizes that interactions with classmates and others can facilitate mastery of the course's material, [but] there remains a line between enlisting the help of another and submitting the work of another." The site provides some guidance: Acts of collaboration that are reasonable include sharing a few lines of code. Acts not reasonable include soliciting solutions to homework problems online. CS50 introduced a "regret clause," allowing students who commit "unreasonable" acts to face only course-specific penalties [not institutional] if they report the violation within 72 hours.[2]

Questions

1. Using Josephson's Six Pillars of Character, which of the character traits (virtues) apply to the May 2012 Harvard cheating scandal and how do they apply with respect to the actions of each of the stakeholders in this case?

2. Who is at fault for the cheating scandal? Is it the students, the teaching assistants, the professor, or the institution? Use ethical reasoning to support your answer.

3. Evaluate the ethics of the "regret clause" established for CS50 from deontological and teleological points of view.

Case 1-2 Giles and Regas

Ed Giles and Susan Regas have never been happier than during the past four months since they have been seeing each other. Giles is a 35-year-old CPA and a partner in the medium-sized accounting firm of Saduga & Mihca. Regas is a 25-year-old senior accountant in the same firm. Although it is acceptable for peers to date, the firm does not permit two members of different ranks within the firm to do so. A partner should not date a senior in the firm any more than a senior should date a junior staff accountant. If such dating eventually leads to marriage, then one of the two must resign because of the conflicts of interest. Both Giles and Regas know the firm's policy on dating, and they have tried to be discreet about their relationship because they don't want to raise any suspicions.

While most of the staff seem to know about Giles and Regas, it is not common knowledge among the partners that the two of them are dating. Perhaps that is why Regas was assigned to work on the audit of CAA Industries for a second year, even though Giles is the supervising partner on the engagement.

As the audit progresses, it becomes clear to the junior staff members that Giles and Regas are spending personal time together during the workday. On one occasion, they were observed leaving for lunch together. Regas did not return to the client's office until three hours later. On another occasion, Regas seemed distracted from her work, and later that day, she received a dozen roses from Giles. A friend of Regas's who knew about the relationship, Ruth Revilo, became concerned when she happened to see the flowers and a card that accompanied them. The card was signed, "Love, Poochie." Regas had once told Revilo that it was the nickname that Regas gave to Giles.

> Revilo pulls Regas aside at the end of the day and says, "We have to talk."
>
> "What is it?" Regas asks.
>
> "I know the flowers are from Giles," Revilo says. "Are you crazy?"
>
> "It's none of your business," Regas responds.

Revilo goes on to explain that others on the audit engagement team are aware of the relationship between the two. Revilo cautions Regas about jeopardizing her future with the firm by getting involved in a serious dating relationship with someone of a higher rank. Regas does not respond to this comment. Instead, she admits to being distracted

---

[2] Hannah Natanson, More than 60 Fall CS50 Enrollees Faced Academic Dishonesty Charges, *The Harvard Crimson,* May 3, 2017, Available at: http://www.thecrimson.com/article/2017/5/3/cs50-cheating-cases-2017/.

lately because of an argument that she had with Giles. It all started when Regas had suggested to Giles that it might be best if they did not go out during the workweek because she was having a hard time getting to work on time. Giles was upset at the suggestion and called her ungrateful. He said, "I've put everything on the line for you. There's no turning back for me." She points out to Revilo that the flowers are Giles's way of saying he is sorry for some of the comments he had made about her.

Regas promises to talk to Giles and thanks Revilo for her concern. That same day, Regas telephones Giles and tells him she wants to put aside her personal relationship with him until the CAA audit is complete in two weeks. She suggests that, at the end of the two-week period, they get together and thoroughly examine the possible implications of their continued relationship. Giles reluctantly agrees, but he conditions his acceptance on having a "farewell" dinner at their favorite restaurant. Regas agrees to the dinner.

Giles and Regas have dinner that Saturday night. As luck would have it, the controller of CAA Industries, Mark Sax, is at the restaurant with his wife. Sax is startled when he sees Giles and Regas together. He wonders about the possible seriousness of their relationship, while reflecting on the recent progress billings of the accounting firm. Sax believes that the number of hours billed is out of line with work of a similar nature and the fee estimate. He had planned to discuss the matter with Herb Morris, the managing partner of the firm. He decides to call Morris on Monday morning.

"Herb, you son of a gun, it's Mark Sax."

"Mark. How goes the audit?"

"That's why I'm calling," Sax responds. "Can we meet to discuss a few items?"

"Sure," Morris replies. "Just name the time and place."

"How about first thing tomorrow morning?" asks Sax.

"I'll be in your office at 8:00 a.m.," says Morris.

"Better make it at 7:00 a.m., Herb, before your auditors arrive."

Sax and Morris meet to discuss Sax's concerns about seeing Giles and Regas at the restaurant and the possibility that their relationship is negatively affecting audit efficiency. Morris asks whether any other incidents have occurred to make him suspicious about the billings. Sax says that he is only aware of this one instance, although he sensed some apprehension on the part of Regas last week when they discussed why it was taking so long to get the audit recommendations for adjusting entries. Morris listens attentively until Sax finishes and then asks him to be patient while he sets up a meeting to discuss the situation with Giles. Morris promises to get back to Sax by the end of the week.

Questions

1. Analyze the behavior of each party from the perspective of the Six Pillars of Character. Assess the personal responsibility of Ed Giles and Susan Regas for the relationship that developed between them. Who do you think is mostly to blame?

2. If Giles were a person of integrity but just happened to have a "weak moment" in starting a relationship with Regas, what do you think he will say when he meets with Herb Morris? Why?

3. Assume that Ed Giles is the biggest "rainmaker" in the firm. What would you do if you were in Herb Morris's position when you meet with Giles? In your response, consider how you would resolve the situation in regard to both the completion of the CAA Industries audit and the longer-term issue of the continued employment of Giles and Regas in the accounting firm.

Case 1-3 Unintended Consequences

Veronica Betterman, a fifth-year accounting major at Anywhere University, wakes up in a cold sweat. Like many accounting majors, Veronica did an internship in public accounting the previous spring resulting in a full-time job offer with Anywhere CPAs to start after she graduates this spring which she readily accepted.

Now in her fifth and final year, Veronica decided she wanted to see what other job opportunities might be out there. So, she went through her university's career fair just two weeks before and was invited to participate in six on-campus interviews. Five of those potential employers then invited her to their offices for another round of interviews. She received full time job offers from four of the five and has yet to hear from the last. Her deadline for deciding on the first of those offers is two days away and she does not know what to do.

While everyone tells her that she should be excited, she is not. She is scared. Worried she may make the wrong decision, she seeks advice from her academic advisor. Her advisor listens to Veronica's dilemma and to Veronica's surprise the advisor tells her that she should never have gone through the career fair, done any of those recent interviews or be contemplating anything other than starting at the firm she interned with.

The advisor stated that she has made a commitment with that company that she has to honor. To do otherwise would be a breach of ethics and is not only an indication of a lack of integrity on Veronica's part, but could cause irreparable harm to the university. He requests that Veronica meet with him again the next day after she prepares a list of all the potential consequences that could happen (to her, the internship program, the other employers, the university, other students) should she take a job with one of the other potential employers.

Veronica gets out of bed, opens up her laptop, and starts working on the list of consequences.

Questions

1. What potential consequences are there for Veronica, the internship program, the other employers, the university, and other students should Veronica not honor her commitment?

2. Analyze Veronica's actions using the Six Pillars of Character. What do Veronica's actions tell you about her character? Do you think her advisor handled the situation appropriately?

3. Assume Anywhere CPAs is in an "employment-at-will" state, which allow employers to fire an employee under most circumstances and this law is generally applied to employer rescinded job offers as well. Should that affect Veronica's decision to take a job with one of the other potential employers? Why or why not?

4. If Veronica decided to accept one of those other job offers, and that employer subsequently learned about her backing out of her previous commitment, how might they react?

Case 1-4 Lone Star School District

Jose and Emily work as auditors for the state of Texas. They have been assigned to the audit of the Lone Star School District. There have been some problems with audit documentation for the travel and entertainment reimbursement claims of the manager of the school district. The manager knows about the concerns of Jose and Emily, and he approaches them about the matter. The following conversation takes place:

Manager: Listen, I've requested the documentation you asked for, but the hotel says it's no longer in its system.

Jose: Don't you have the credit card receipt or credit card statement?

Manager:	I paid cash.
Jose:	What about a copy of the hotel bill?
Manager:	I threw it out.
Emily:	That's a problem. We have to document all your travel and entertainment expenses for the city manager's office.
Manager:	Well, I can't produce documents that the hotel can't find. What do you want me to do?

Questions

1. Assume that Jose and Emily are CPAs and members of the AICPA. What ethical standards in the Code of Professional Conduct should guide them in dealing with the manager's inability to support travel and entertainment expenses?

2. Using Josephson's Six Pillars of Character as a guide, evaluate the statements and behavior of the manager.

3. a. Assume that Jose and Emily report to Sharon, the manager of the school district audit. Should they inform Sharon of their concerns? Why or why not?

   b. Assume that they don't inform Sharon, but she finds out from another source. What would you do if you were in Sharon's position?

Case 1-5 Moral Turpitude

Ed has a growing CPA practice. He worked in New York after graduation, but has since returned home to Orlando to be closer to his family. Ed has been married to Kristina, the girl of his dreams, for five years and they have two children.

Ed is catching up on work after the family vacation to Walt Disney World. Just a quick call to his wife and then off to see his client Ella at Spa Day. Ella is his wife's long-time friend and has become a big client of Ed's firm for both consulting and tax services. Ella has expanded to three locations in Orlando and is considering a new location in Tampa.

Ed arrives early for the meeting. Ella comes out and greets him.

Ella:	Ed, you look rested. I hope your family enjoyed the Disney vacation. [Ed nodded his head]. I am expecting a call from the leasing agent for the Tampa location. I need to delay our meeting about 30 minutes. While you wait, you can enjoy a shoulder massage by Carrie, courtesy of the spa.
Ed:	That sounds nice. Kristina will be jealous that that I am getting a massage. I could use some relaxation after three days on rides and trekking through the park. But, if today's inconvenient for you I can come back another day.
Ella:	No, no. I must move quickly on the new location and need to consult with you on some tax questions.
Ed:	Okay, but I need to make the soccer game at 4:30. This is the first time the girls are facing each other in a game. Frankly, I don't know who to root for. Kristina said she'll root for one and I'll root for the other.
Ella:	Very diplomatic. I like it. Anyway, I'll be done in 30 minutes and we'll have plenty of time to talk before you go to the game.

Carrie came out and led Ed to the massage room. As Ed is enjoying the massage, a commotion is heard in the hallway. All of a sudden, another masseuse comes in and screams, "Police!" Next thing Ed knows, the door is slammed open and a policeman and police woman shout: "You're all under arrest!" Ed is startled. He begins to talk with trepidation.

> **Ed:** What for? I am a CPA here for a meeting with my client, Ella.

> **Police:** This location is a front for prostitution and money laundering. All customers will be taken to the station and charged with criminal mischief.

At the station, there was total chaos. The customers and the employees were milling around, not knowing what to do. Ella was nowhere to be seen. After a phone call to his wife and attorney, Ed is told that he will be booked, arraigned, and then released on his own recognizance.

By the time the dust settled, Ed missed the game. His wife came to pick him up. The girls were in tears.

Ed felt confident that no charges would be brought against him and the whole matter was one big misunderstanding. It was a case of being in the wrong place at the wrong time. Unfortunately, Ella could not be found to vouch for him that he was only at the spa for a business meeting.

In the end and after a six month wait, Ed was convinced by his attorney to plead out and put the matter behind him. The district attorney agreed to a sentence of one-year probation and community service.

Just as Ed was starting to breathe more easily, a letter comes from the Florida Board of Accountancy telling him there will be a hearing to decide whether to suspend his license to practice public accounting. The hearing will be in front of the Disciplinary Committee of the board in two weeks. Ed contacts his attorney and they prepare for the hearing.

The hearing does not go well. The committee questions how Ed did not know that Spa Day was a front for a prostitution ring and money laundering. Ed is told that even if he had not pled out, he has violated the acts discreditable and moral turpitude clauses of the code of professional conduct.

Questions

1. Did Ed commit an act discreditable to the profession? Explain.

2. Does the case have any bearing on Ed's ability to provide competent services to his client and serve the public interest? Why or why not?

3. What should Ed's attorney say in defense of his client?

4. Should state board of accountancy rules regulate personal behavior not related to one's professional services?

Case 1-6 Capitalization versus Expensing

Gloria Hernandez is the controller of a public company. She just completed a meeting with her superior, John Harrison, who is the CFO of the company. Harrison tried to convince Hernandez to go along with his proposal to combine 12 expenditures for repair and maintenance of a plant asset into one amount ($1 million). Each of the expenditures is less than $100,000, the cutoff point for capitalizing expenditures as an asset and depreciating it over the useful life. Hernandez asked for time to think about the matter. As the controller and chief accounting officer of the company, Hernandez knows it's her responsibility to decide how to record the expenditures. She knows that the $1 million amount is material to earnings and the rules in accounting require expensing of each individual item, not capitalization. However, she is under a great deal of pressure to go along with capitalization to boost earnings and meet financial analysts' earnings expectations, and provide for a bonus to top management including herself. Her job may be at stake, and she doesn't want to disappoint her boss.

Questions

Assume both Hernandez and Harrison hold the CPA and CMA designations.

1. What are the loyalty obligations of both parties in this case?

2. Assume that you were in Gloria Hernandez's position. What would motivate you to speak up and act or to stay silent? Would it make a difference if Harrison promised this was a one-time request?

3. What would you do and why?

Case 1-7 Eating Time

Kevin Lowe is depressed. He has been with the CPA firm Stooges LLP for only three months. Yet the partners in charge of the firm—Bo Chambers and his brother, Moe—have asked for a "sit-down." Here's how it goes:

"Kevin, we asked to see you because your time reports indicate that it takes you 50% longer to complete audit work than your predecessor," Moe said.

"Well, I am new and still learning on the job," replied Lowe.

"That's true," Bo responded, "but you have to appreciate that we have fixed budgets for these audits. Every hour over the budgeted time costs us money. While we can handle it in the short run, we will have to bill the clients whose audit you work on a larger fee in the future. We don't want to lose clients as a result."

"Are you asking me to cut down on the work I do?" Lowe asked.

"We would never compromise the quality of our audit work," Moe said. "We're trying to figure out why it takes you so much longer than other staff members."

At this point, Lowe started to perspire. He wiped his forehead, took a glass of water, and asked, "Would it be better if I took some of the work home at night and on weekends, completed it, but didn't charge the firm or the client for my time?"

Bo and Moe were surprised by Kevin's openness. On one hand, they valued that trait in their employees. On the other hand, they couldn't answer with a yes. Moe looked at Bo, and then turned to Kevin and said, "It's up to you to decide how to increase your productivity on audits. As you know, this is an important element of performance evaluation."

Kevin cringed. Was the handwriting on the wall in terms of his future with the firm?

"I understand what you're saying," Kevin said. "I will do better in the future—I promise."

"Good," responded Bo and Moe. "Let's meet 30 days from now and we'll discuss your progress on the matters we've discussed today and your future with the firm."

In an effort to deal with the problem, Kevin contacts Joyce, a friend and fellow employee, and asks if she has faced similar problems. Joyce answers "yes" and goes on to explain she handles it by "ghost-ticking." Kevin asks her to explain. "Ghost-ticking is when we document audit procedures that have not been completed." Kevin, dumbfounded, wonders, what kind of a firm am I working for?

Questions

1. Kevin is not a CPA yet. What are his ethical obligations in this case?

2. Given the facts in the case, evaluate using deontological and teleological reasoning whether Kevin should take work home and not charge it to the job. What about engaging in ghost-ticking?

3. What would you do if you were Kevin and why? How would you explain your position to Bo and Moe when you meet in 30 days?

Case 1-8 Shifty Industries

Shifty Industries is a small business that sells home beauty products in the San Luis Obispo, California, area. The company has experienced a cash crunch and is unable to pay its bills on a timely basis. A great deal of pressure exists to minimize cash outflows such as income tax payments to the Internal Revenue Service (IRS) by interpreting income tax regulations as liberally as possible.

You are the tax accountant and a CPA working at the company and you report to the tax manager. He reports to the controller. You are concerned about the fact that your supervisor has asked you to go along with an improper treatment of section 179 depreciation on the 2018 tax return so you can deduct the $100,000 full cost of eligible equipment against taxable income. The problem as you see it is the 2017 limitation of $500,000, which would have been fine for 2018 had Congress extended it, was rolled back to a maximum of $25,000. Therefore, your supervisor is planning to allow Shifty to deduct $75,000 more than allowed by law. Using a 35% tax rate it means the company is "increasing" its cash flow by $26,250.

Answer the following questions to prepare for a meeting you will have tomorrow morning with the tax manager.

Questions

1. What values are most important to you in deciding on a course of action? Why?

2. Who are the stakeholders in this case and how might they be affected by your course of action?

3. What would you do and why, assuming your approach will be based on the application of the ethical reasoning methods discussed in the chapter?

Case 1-9 Cleveland Custom Cabinets

Cleveland Custom Cabinets is a specialty cabinet manufacturer for high-end homes in the Cleveland Heights and Shaker Heights areas. The company manufactures cabinets built to the specifications of homeowners and employs 125 custom cabinetmakers and installers. There are 30 administrative and sales staff members working for the company.

James Leroy owns Cleveland Custom Cabinets. His accounting manager is Marcus Sims, who reports to the director of finance. Sims manages 15 accountants. The staff is responsible for keeping track of manufacturing costs by job and preparing internal and external financial reports. The internal reports are used by management for decision making. The external reports are used to support bank loan applications.

The company applies overhead to jobs based on direct labor hours. For 2019, it estimated total overhead to be $4.8 million and 80,000 direct labor hours. The cost of direct materials used during the first quarter of the year is $600,000, and direct labor cost is $400,000 (based on 20,000 hours worked). The company's accounting system is old and does not provide actual overhead information until about four weeks after the close of a quarter. As a result, the applied overhead amount is used for quarterly reports.

On April 10, 2019, Leroy came into Sims's office to pick up the quarterly report. He looked at it aghast. Leroy had planned to take the statements to the bank the next day and meet with the vice president to discuss a $1 million working capital loan. He knew the bank would be reluctant to grant the loan based on the income numbers in Exhibit 1. Without the money, Cleveland could have problems financing everyday operations.

EXHIBIT 1 Cleveland Custom Cabinets

Net Income for the Quarter Ended March 31, 2019	
Sales	$6,400,000
Cost of goods sold	4,800,000
Gross margin	$1,600,000
Selling and administrative expenses	1,510,000
Net income	$ 90,000

Leroy asked Sims to explain how net income could have gone from 14.2% of sales for the year ended December 31, 2018, to 1.4% for March 31, 2019. Sims pointed out that the estimated overhead cost had doubled for 2019 compared to the actual cost for 2018. He explained to Leroy that rent had doubled and the cost of utilities skyrocketed. In addition, the custom-making machinery was wearing out more rapidly, so the company's repair and maintenance costs also doubled from 2018.

Leroy wouldn't accept Sims's explanation. Instead, he told Sims that the quarterly income had to be at least the same percentage of sales as at December 31, 2018. Sims looked confused and reminded Leroy that the external auditors would wrap up their audit on April 30. Leroy told Sims not to worry about the auditors. He would take care of them. Furthermore, "as the sole owner of the company, there is no reason not to 'tweak' the numbers on a one-time basis. I own the board of directors, so no worries there." He went on to say, "Do it this one time and I won't ask you to do it again." He then reminded Sims of his obligation to remain loyal to the company and its interests. Sims started to soften and asked Leroy just how he expected the tweaking to happen. Leroy flinched, held up his hands, and said, "I'll leave the creative accounting to you."

Questions

1. Do you agree with Leroy's statement that it doesn't matter what the numbers look like because he is the sole owner? Even if it is true that Sims "owns" the board of directors, what should be their role in this matter? What about the external auditors? Should Sims simply accept Leroy's statement that he would handle them?

2. a. Assume that Sims is a CPA and holds the CMA. Put yourself in Sims's position. What are your ethical considerations in deciding whether to tweak the numbers?

    b. Assume you do a utilitarian analysis to help decide what to do. Evaluate the harms and benefits of alternative courses of action. What would you do? Would your analysis change if you use a rights theory approach?

3. Think about how you would actually implement your chosen action. What barriers could you face? How would you overcome them? Is it worth jeopardizing your job in this case? Why or why not?

Case 1-10 Better Boston Beans

Better Boston Beans is a coffee shop located in the Faneuil Hall Marketplace near the waterfront and Government Center in Boston. It specializes in exotic blends of coffee, including Sumatra Dark Roast Black, India Mysore "Gold Nuggets," and Guatemala Antigua. It also serves a number of blended coffees, including Reggae Blend, Jamaican Blue Mountain Blend, and Marrakesh Blend. For those with more pedestrian tastes, the shop serves French Vanilla, Hazelnut, and Hawaiian Macadamia Nut varieties. The coffee of the day varies, but the most popular is Colombia Supremo. The coffee shop also serves a variety of cold-blended coffees.

Cyndie Rosen has worked for Better Boston Beans for six months. She took the job right out of college because she wasn't sure whether she wanted to go to graduate school before beginning a career in financial services. Cyndie hoped that by taking a year off before starting her career or going on to graduate school, she would experience "the real world" and find out firsthand what it is like to work a 40-hour week. (She did not have a full-time job during her college years because her parents paid for the tuition and books.)

Because Cyndie is the "new kid on the block," she is often asked to work the late shift, from 4 p.m. to midnight. She works with one other person, Jeffrey Levy, who is the assistant shift supervisor. Jeffrey has been with Boston Beans for three years but recently was demoted from shift supervisor. Jeffrey reports to Sarah Hoffman, the new shift supervisor. Sarah reports to David Cohen, the owner of the store.

For the past two weeks, Jeffrey has been leaving before 11 p.m., after most of the stores in the Marketplace close, and he has asked Cyndie to close up by herself. Cyndie feels that this is wrong and it is starting to concern her, but she hasn't spoken to Jeffrey or anyone else. Basically, she is afraid to lose her job. Her parents have told her that financially she is on her own. They were disappointed that Cyndie did not go to graduate school or interview for a professional position after graduating from college.

Something happened that is stressing Cyndie out and she doesn't know what to do about it. At 11 p.m. one night, 10 Japanese tourists came into the store for coffee. Cyndie was alone and had to rush around and make five different cold-blended drinks and five different hot-blended coffees. While she was working, one of the Japanese tourists, who spoke English very well, approached her and said that he was shocked that such a famous American coffee shop would only have one worker in the store at any time during the workday. Cyndie didn't want to ignore the man's comments, so she answered that her coworker had to go home early because he was sick. That seemed to satisfy the tourist.

It took Cyndie almost 20 minutes to make all the drinks and also field two phone calls that came in during that time. After she closed for the night, she reflected on the experience. Cyndie realized that it could get worse before it gets better because Jeffrey was now making it a habit to leave work early.

At this point, Cyndie realizes that she either has to approach Jeffrey about her concerns or speak to Sarah. She feels much more comfortable talking to Sarah because, in Cyndie's own words, "Levy gives me the creeps."

Questions

1. Do you think it was right for Cyndie to tell the Japanese tourist that "her coworker had to go home early because he was sick"?

2. Cyndie decided to speak with Jeffrey. From an ethical perspective, do you think Cyndie made the right decision as opposed to speaking directly with either Sarah Hoffman or David Cohen? Would you have done the same thing? Why or why not?

3. During their discussion, Jeffrey tells Cyndie that he has an alcohol problem. Lately, it's gotten to him really bad. That's why he's left early—to get a drink and calm his nerves. Jeffrey also explains that this is the real reason he was demoted. He had been warned that if one more incident occurred, David would fire him. He pleaded with Cyndie to work with him through these hard times. How would you react to Jeffrey's request if you were Cyndie? Would your answer change if Jeffrey was a close personal friend instead of someone who gave you the creeps? Why or why not?

4. Assume that Cyndie keeps quiet. The following week, another incident occurs. Cyndie gets into a shouting match with a customer who became tired of waiting for his coffee after 10 minutes. Cyndie felt terrible about it, apologized to the customer after serving his coffee, and left work that night wondering if it was time to apply to graduate school. The customer was so irate that he contacted David and expressed his displeasure about both the service and Cyndie's attitude. David asks to meet with Jeffrey, Sarah, and Cyndie the next day. What are Cyndie's ethical responsibilities at this point?

Chapter

2

Cognitive Processes and Ethical Decision Making in Accounting

---

Learning Objectives

After studying Chapter 2, you should be able to:

LO 2-1   Analyze the thought process involved in making decisions and taking ethical action.

LO 2-2   Explain how our thoughts might bias our decision-making process.

LO 2-3   Distinguish between equity, diversity, and inclusion.

LO 2-4   Describe Kohlberg's stages of moral development.

LO 2-5   Explain how cognitive processes influence ethical decision making in accounting.

LO 2-6   Explain Rest's model and how its components influence ethical decision making.

LO 2-7   Describe the link between moral intensity and ethical decision making.

LO 2-8   Explain how moral reasoning and virtue influence ethical decision making.

LO 2-9   Apply the steps in the Integrated Ethical Decision-Making Model to a case study.

LO 2-10 Describe the "Giving Voice to Values" technique and apply it to a case study.

Ethics Reflection

Enron's Fall From Grace

During the courtroom testimony of Kenneth Lay, former CEO and chairman of the board of directors of Enron, and Jeff Skilling, former CEO of Enron, some observers were shocked that both seemed to believe Enron was a healthy company up to the bitter end. Instead, the company became the poster-child for failed companies during to financial frauds of the early 2000s because of the arrogance of its top leaders and failure to accept responsibility for their actions. Enron's use of a sophisticated tool to hide debt, "special-purpose entities," pushed the envelope on what is proper accounting. The financial institutions that got burned blamed Enron for their losses and wanted to teach the company a lesson.

Enron used special purpose entities to mask debt by borrowing money from financial institutions and transferring the debt to off-balance-sheet entities that were set up precisely for this reason. The goal was to make the company look like it was more financially sound than it really was. At the time, the accounting rules were unclear as to the treatment of such transfers and Enron took advantage of the 'gap' in GAAP.

Enron used this device to hide debt over and over again. By all accounts there were some 3,000 such entities. Ultimately, the banks grew weary of helping to set up these entities and the questionable collateral for the debt. By the time Enron declared bankruptcy in January 2002, the company had $13.1 billion in debt on its books; $18.1 billion on its nonconsolidated subsidiaries' books; and an estimated $20 billion more off the balance sheets. Its stock price had gone from $90.75 per share on December 2, 2001, before it declared bankruptcy, to $0.67 by January 2002.

Enron was "creative" with its accounting for long-term investments. Mark-to-market is a technique used to value investments and was designed under GAAP to cover investments in marketable securities (e.g. stocks and bonds). Andy Fastow, the former CFO and mastermind of the fraud, used mark-to-market to value long-term contracts to provide power out of a new power plant still under construction. The company would immediately record all profits estimated to be made under the contract. The problem was that Enron created the market used to value its assets. Moreover, if the revenue from the power plant was less than the projected amount, instead of taking the loss the company would then transfer these assets to its off-balance-sheet entities, where the loss would go unreported.

According to the exposé of the Enron fraud by Bethany McLean and Peter Elkind, *The Smartest Guys in the Room,*[1] Lay and Skilling truly believed they had done nothing wrong. They were the victim of circumstances. In reality, they suffered from what has been called "moral blindness," or the state of unawareness or insensibility to moral issues both in oneself and to one's relations with others.

Another way to explain the behavior of Lay and Skilling is they had what Bazerman and Tenbrunsel calls "ethical blind spots"[2] where decision making was concerned. Ethical blind spots often obscure important aspects of a decision. Lay and Skilling didn't realize their decisions had ethical implications and made unethical choices without knowing it.

They didn't know or didn't care that their actions would have consequences for themselves, the company, employees, and shareholders. Their decisions were based on an end justifies the means approach. The company's end goal was to become the largest natural gas and utility company in the world. It didn't matter how it got there; just that it did.

We can also look at decision making at Enron through the lens of cognitive biases. A cognitive bias refers to a systematic pattern of deviation from norms or rationality in judgment that manifests itself as a mistake in reasoning, evaluating, reflecting, and other cognitive processes. Individuals create their own social reality from their perception of the input rather than an objective analysis of it.[3] Cognitive biases can fool an individual into thinking, depending on how an issue is framed, that one is not even facing a moral or ethical dilemma.[4]

Andy Fastow made a presentation about the fraud on April 6, 2016, and he explained the rationalizations Enron used for its improper actions.[5]

- Helping the company and its shareholders by increasing profits and stock price.
- Timing problem or "We'll grow out of it."
- Immaterial amounts.
- Rewarded and recognized behavior by the company.
- Systemic problem.
- It has been approved. I'm following the rules.

Fastow was correct in that the accounting was approved by Andersen, the now defunct auditors of Enron, and the company's board of directors. How could this be? Well, the board was under the control of Lay and Skilling, who benefited the most from the fraud. Others weren't about to say anything: the top five executives at Enron received payments of $282.7 million in the year 2000 alone. Of this amount, Lay received $67.4 million and Skilling, $41.8 million.

Think about the following as you read the chapter: (1) How can cognitive biases influence your decision making? (2) What would you do if your attitudes and beliefs about right and wrong are being tested by pressures within an organization? (3) How can you counteract the reasons and rationalizations given to you to go along with manipulated financial statements?

As we practice resolving dilemmas we find ethics to be less a goal than a pathway, less a destination than a trip, less an inoculation than a process.

Source: Ethicist Rushworth Kidder (1944–2012)

Kidder believed that self-reflection was the key to resolving ethical dilemmas, and a conscious sense of vision and deep core of ethical values provide the courage to stand up to the tough choices. The pathway one takes can be influenced by biases we have about ourselves and others that need to be understood and acted upon to successfully continue the journey to ethical decision making.

Behavioral Ethics

LO 2-1

Analyze the thought process involved in making decisions and taking ethical action.

The field of behavioral ethics emphasizes the need to consider how individuals actually make decisions, rather than how they would make decisions in an ideal world. Knowledge of behavioral ethics is important to understand the way individuals think and process information, and how they deal with biases that can influence ethical decision making.

System 1 versus System 2 Thinking

Research in behavioral ethics reveals that our minds have two distinct modes of decision making– "System 1" and "System 2" thinking.[6] Daniel Kahneman, the Nobel Prize–winning behavioral economist, points out that System 1 thinking is our intuitive system of processing information: fast, automatic, effortless, and emotional decision processes; on the other hand, System 2 thinking is slower, conscious, effortful, explicit, and a more reasoned decision process. Walter points out that the dominant role of System 1 in ethical decision making is evidenced by the fact that children, even babies, have a basic moral sense that is ingrained into their brains before they are taught morality by their parents and society.[7] For example, infants at the earliest levels of moral development in Kohlberg's model, discussed later, are aware of the importance of rules and the need to yield to authority figures.

Kahneman's fundamental proposition is that we identify with System 2, *"the conscious, reasoning self that has beliefs, makes choices and decides what to think about and what to do."* But the one that is really in charge is System 1 as it *"effortlessly originates impressions and feelings that are the main sources of the explicit beliefs and deliberate choices of System 2."*[8]

What follows is an example of using System 1 thinking instead of the more deliberate approach of System 2, and drawing the wrong conclusion as a result. To illustrate, answer the following question: A baseball bat and ball together cost $110. If the bat costs $100 more than the ball, how much does the ball cost? Most people say $10. They decide quickly, without doing the math or thinking through the question. However, it is the wrong answer. The ball actually cost $5, and the bat cost $105.

The broader point of this exercise is to explain how System 1 thinking can lead to snap decisions that make it more difficult to resolve an ethical dilemma in a morally appropriate way. It may occur because you lack important information regarding a decision, fail to notice available information, or face time and cost constraints. You don't have the time or inclination and fail to see the dangers of deciding too quickly.

Many decisions in business and accounting have ethical challenges. This is because of the impacts of those decisions and the fact that outcomes are likely to affect stakeholders in different ways and will express different ethical values. A decision-making model built on System 2 thinking can provide a more systematic analysis that enables comprehensible judgment, clearer reasons, and a more justifiable and defensible action than otherwise would have been the case.

Cognitive Errors

Some people do not make decisions as we might expect of a rational actor because rules of thumb and biases shape people's ethical decision making in ways they often do not understand or notice. Kahneman and Tversky point out that incrementalism (the slippery slope) may influence the behavior of even well-intentioned people who find themselves in situations in which ethical corners are being cut. It can be difficult to notice gradual changes in one's environment so that cutting corners grow until violations of the law occur.[9]

A good example of a cognitive error brought on by incrementalism is the case of Aaron Beam, the first CFO at HealthSouth Corporation, a company that had a $2.7 million accounting fraud in the 1990s. One day in 1996 the time came when the company couldn't make its projected earnings and CEO Richard Scrushy refused to report a bad quarter. Instead, he instructed the chief accountant to scatter false assets and revenues throughout the company's 1,500 ledgers to hit their targets. Beam watched this go on for a year before he decided to quit.[10] He was sentenced to three months in prison after pleading guilty to going along with the fraud out of fear of what the CEO, Richard Scrushy, might do if he did not agree.

Beam didn't notice the gradual changes in the health care environment brought on by increased competition and a slowing economy. He never considered that Scrushy would continue to pressure him to manipulate the numbers. Beam suddenly realized he had begun the slide down the slippery slope of reporting false numbers and the need to cover them up, and there was no turning back.

Some people fall victim to self-serving biases in their decision making whereby they tend to gather, process, and even remember information in a way that advances their perceived self-interest and to support preexisting views. People can readily notice how the self-serving bias might affect others' decisions on ethical matters, but they are often nearly blind in perceiving how they themselves might be affected. This kind of ethical blindness occurs because we fail to perceive or think about the ethical issues and contextual factors blinds us to right and wrong, such as occurred for Aaron Beam.

Drumwright et al. identify four additional cognitive shortcomings:[11]

- *The Tangible & the Abstract.* When people make ethically tinged decisions, they tend to consider immediate and tangible factors at the expense of more removed and abstract factors[12] (i.e., System 1 thinking).

- *Loss Aversion.* People have a tendency to detest losses even more than they enjoy gains so that they make more immoral decisions to avoid what they perceive to be a potential loss.[13]

- *Framing.* People have a tendency to make different decisions based upon how a question is framed so that other factors are framed as more important than ethical standards[14] (i.e., meet or beat financial statement earnings goals).

- *Overconfidence.* People have a tendency to believe that they are more ethical than they actually are, which can cause them to make decisions with serious ethical implications without proper reflection.[15]

Framing was an important factor in the Enron case. Top executives were fixated on share price, which caused them to focus on earnings projections. Knowing that missing earnings targets would lead to a steep reduction in share price, they engaged in accounting maneuvers to keep the stock price up. Ethical considerations were completely disregarded, despite Enron's code of ethics. Had the company's officers managed to keep ethics in their decision analysis, they might have acted differently.[16]

Social and Organizational Pressures

Matousek identifies two of the most common social and organizational pressures that can cause well-intentioned people to make poor ethical choices: the tendencies to be overly obedient to authority and to conform excessively to the ethical judgments and actions of peers. In accounting, it is important to follow superiors' instructions, especially if they are seen as being ethical.[17] However, the desire to please authority can bias one's outlook on a financial reporting issue, suspend one's own ethical judgment about right versus wrong, and bend to the wishes of a superior. Despite sensing she was being asked to do something wrong by WorldCom's CFO, Scott Sullivan, Betty Vinson rationalized that since he was the CFO, Sullivan must know better than herself what was the proper accounting.

Situational Factors

Situational factors can influence ethical decision making and the actor may not even be aware of the effect. Studies show that when people are under time pressure, they will often act less ethically than in situations when they are not. They will not realize the impact that time pressure has on their decision making and actions, but the impact is still there.[18] For example, a lead engagement auditor might be hustling to complete an audit on time and under budget and not realize certain steps in the audit process have not been properly completed.

Transparency is another important factor. Novelist C. S. Lewis famously said: "Integrity is doing the right thing, even when no one is watching." Research shows that if people feel that they are not being watched, they will tend to act less ethically.[19] A greater number of people will try to get away with wrongdoing if they feel they won't get caught. It's logical to conclude that the accounting frauds that took place in the late 1990s and early 2000s were masterminded by people who never thought they would be caught doing the deed. Bernie Madoff most likely would not have conned his investors out of $65 billion using a Ponzi scheme if he thought he was being watched by the authorities.

Cognitive Dissonance

One limitation of the philosophical reasoning approaches incorporated into decision-making models is that how we think we should behave is different from how we decide to behave. This creates a problem of *cognitive dissonance,* a term first coined by Leon Festinger in 1956. The inconsistency between our thoughts, beliefs, or attitudes and our behavior creates the need to resolve contradictory or conflicting beliefs, values, and perceptions.[20] Tompkins and Lawley point out that:

> This dissonance only occurs when we are "attached" to our attitudes or beliefs, i.e., they have emotional significance or consequences for our self-concept or sense of coherence about how the world works. The psychological opposition of irreconcilable ideas (cognitions) held simultaneously by one individual, create[s] a motivated force that [c]ould lead, under proper conditions, to the adjustment of one's beliefs to fit one's behavior instead of changing one's behavior to fit one's beliefs (the sequence conventionally assumed).[21]

Cognitive dissonance suggests that we have an inner drive to hold all our attitudes and beliefs in harmony and avoid disharmony. When there is inconsistency between attitudes or behaviors (dissonance), something must change to eliminate the dissonance. Festinger posits that dissonance can be reduced in one of three ways: (1) change one or more of the attitudes, behavior, or beliefs so as to make the relationship between the two elements a consonant one; (2) acquire new information that outweighs the dissonant beliefs; or (3) reduce the importance of the cognitions (beliefs, attitudes).[22]

The Betty Vinson situation illustrates the dangers of reducing dissonance by changing one's attitudes and behaviors. It also illustrates how situational factors and social and organizational pressures can create biased behavior. Vinson knew it was wrong to "cook the books." She felt it in her inner being, but she did not act on those beliefs. Instead, she followed the orders from superiors and later justified her behavior by rationalizing it as a one-time act and demanded by people who knew accounting better than herself. In a sense, she reduced the importance of her own intuitions about the appropriateness of what she was asked to do.

Bazerman and Gino ask: What makes even good people cross ethical boundaries?[23] Wittmer asks: Do individuals in organizations always act and behave consistently with what they know or believe to be the right thing to do?[24] The behavioral approach to ethics leads to understanding and explaining moral and immoral behavior in systematic ways. In reality, whether behaviors are viewed legally or ethically, we hold individuals accountable for their behaviors and choices, at least in part because they *should have* known better. Even if we agree on what someone should ethically do in a given situation, our judgment is often clouded by other factors that cause us to act against our intuition of what good sense dictates.

Why did CEO Richard Scrushy certify HealthSouth Corporation's financial statements when he knew or was reckless in not knowing they were materially false and misleading? What influenced him to behave unethically? Once we start asking these questions, we shift our attention from inquiring about what the right thing to do is, or what a good person should do. Rather, we are attempting to understand why such an individual acted the way he did, trying to identify the factors that influenced or caused the behaviors. We have moved from a prescriptive framework, such as with the philosophical reasoning methods, to a more descriptive mode of analysis. Such a perspective is important in leading organizations toward more ethical behavior.[25] It requires identifying levers at both the individual and the institutional level to change ethically questionable behaviors when individuals are acting in unethical ways that they would not endorse with greater reflection.[26]

Cognitive Biases

LO 2-2

Explain how our thoughts might bias our decision-making process.

Understanding the unconscious biases that people may have is an important first step to preventing unethical behavior. Messick and Bazerman believe that we have cognitive biases about the world, other people, and ourselves which can negatively influence our decision-making process. Understanding our own biases, and those of others, can help us avoid them and improve our ethical decision making.[27]

The biases identified above are often compounded by the false belief that the world is more deterministic (controllable) than it is. This illusion of control causes us to underestimate the risks involved with our decisions. Memories of past-experiences change to support this erroneous belief. A hindsight bias might develop where people tend to believe that they expected a past outcome before it occurred (even when they did not).

Theories about the world also suggest that we tend to blame individuals for events, rather than their work environment, policies and procedures, or incentive programs. This often leads to problems being framed inaccurately and can result in decisions which do not correct and may exacerbate the problem. Therefore, it is important to take time determining how a problem is framed in order to maximize the probability of finding a solution for it.

Theories About the World

According to Messick and Bazerman people have a tendency to simplify complex issues to make decision making easier. This can lead to underestimating risk and making poor decisions by ignoring low-probability events; failing to identify all stakeholders impacted; ignoring the possibility the public will find out; not thinking about long-term consequences; and undervaluing the magnitude of the consequences in total.[28]

A good example of the damage underestimating risk can have is the "Dieselgate" scandal at Volkswagen (VW). The scandal broke in July 2015 when the California Air Resources Board (CARB) shared its findings about carbon dioxide emissions from diesel vehicles produced by VW. CARB and the Environmental Protection Agency (EPA) refused to certify VW's 2016 diesel vehicles. VW at first blamed software irregularities. An increasing number of negative reports about VW's diesel vehicles and VW's culpability led to the auto company's admission in September 2015 that the cars were "designed and manufactured with a defeat device to bypass, defeat or render inoperative elements of the vehicles emission control system." The system was set to report levels of emission that would pass lab tests, even though they emitted as much as 40 times the legal limit of pollutants on the road.[29] Exhibit 2.1 elaborates on the facts of the case and legal liabilities.

As the criminal case against VW closed on April 4, 2017, many wondered who blew the whistle and first admitted to regulators that VW was lying about its dirty diesels? It was first reported in the book *Faster, Higher, Farther: The Volkswagen Scandal* by Jack Ewing, that an American engineer, Stuart Johnson, the head of VW's Engineering and Environmental Office which has responsibility for VW's interaction with U.S. regulators, was the first person to reveal to CARB the existence of VW's defeat device software.[30]

In March 2016, it was announced that Daniel Donovan, a former worker in VW's information technology group, alleged VW illegally destroyed electronic data in the days after the EPA publicly accused the company of cheating emissions tests by manipulating its vehicles' software. Donovan claimed he was fired for refusing to participate in destroying evidence and obstructing justice. He said the company violated its obligation to preserve evidence while under investigation and also kept documents from an outside accounting firm conducting an investigation.

VW's violation of just about every ethical standard portrays a company that ignored its own research and testing findings, covered-up the problem, lied to authorities, and failed to consider how its deceptive tactics would affect the driving public.

An interesting aspect of the case is VW's thought process in determining whether to fix the problem or hide it from the government. The company's cognitive shortcomings include miscalculating the consequences of not fixing the software problem. It began when the executives evaluated the costs to the company if they were caught. Reviewing previous cases of violations of environmental regulations by auto manufacturers in the U.S., they predicted that the likely fines posed "only a moderate cost risk." They cited the highest fine, imposed against Hyundai/Kia as amounting to "barely $91 per vehicle" and added, "fines in this amount are not even remotely capable of influencing the share price of a globally operative company such as Volkswagen."[31]

An independent analysis of VW's risk assessment shows that the company underestimated the risk of deliberately misleading regulators and the public. The company's error in reasoning was due to a belief that its chances of getting caught were slim, and even if it were caught, the size of the penalty would be manageable. Using numbers provided by the EPA and U.S. Justice Department, historically, the financial penalties imposed for Clean Air Act violations were in the range of about $96 to $292 per vehicle. These amounts were well below the maximum allowable of $37,500 per vehicle. The VW settlement called for a penalty of $29,000 per vehicle, well above previous settlements.[32]

VW significantly underestimated the risk of getting caught and resulting financial penalty if it did, which is why a cost-benefit analysis is risky. The company did not account for added costs because of the government's desire to teach the company a lesson. In imposing such a harsh penalty, the government indicated that not only was the magnitude of the excess emissions 40 times the legal limit, VW was also guilty of false advertising about their diesel engines. This was not an innocent mistake. It was a calculated attempt by VW management to get away with a wrongdoing, knowing that the wrongdoing existed, because it did not want to tarnish its image and figured it would be less expensive just to deal with any fines that might come its way.

Top management seemed indifferent to what was going on. Martin Winterkorn, the former CEO of VW, reacted to the scandal by blaming others. His reasoning process was influenced by a self-serving bias. He claimed he would have stopped the scandal had he known about it. In testimony before the *Bundestag,* Germany's Parliament, Winterkorn said he was "no software engineer and that the rogue acts didn't rise to his level." There were, however, indications that he may have missed the signs before the crisis erupted in public. VW said Winterkorn had received two memos informing him of discrepancies in U.S. diesel emissions in 2014 and that he participated in a meeting in July 2015 that touched on the matter. Winterkorn seems to have turned a blind eye to the warnings signs and may have fallen victim to how the issue was framed; those most responsible for the software problem focused more on the compliance issues and not enough on the ethical issues.[33]

VW was guilty of having a blind spot where ethics was concerned. Its management was overconfident about the company's ability to absorb losses. Its destruction of documents reflected a systemic problem fuelled by a lack of accountability and an organization that operated under an ends justifies the means approach to decision making. At the end of the day, VW's behavior tarnished the trust of the driving public and the company paid dearly for its lapse in judgment.

EXHIBIT 2.1   Volkswagen "Dieselgate" Scandal

The VW scandal began well-before the California Air Resources Board shared its results about software irregularities in VW diesel vehicles. In May 2014, researchers at West Virginia University and the International Council on Clean Transportation published findings that the 2012 VW Jetta TDI and 2013 Passat TDI had "significantly higher in-use emissions" in testing.[34] The Board tested updated emissions one year later and found some improvement, but not enough. That led to VW's admission and the beginning of a legal nightmare for the company that will probably end with close to a $25 billion payout for providing false information to the U.S. government about emissions and reimbursements to owners of the affected vehicles, far above the initial $14.7 billion estimate by VW.

Up to $10 billion of the projected $25 billion settlement were scheduled to be paid out to owners of the 487,000 affected diesel cars in the U.S., sold under the VW or luxury Audi brands. The owners had a choice to make: have VW fix the car or buy it back. 97.5% of Volkswagen diesel owners chose buyback, not repair.

Repurchasing the cars cost VW between $12,500 to $44,000 per car. The $14.7 billion estimated settlement assumed that all the cars would be repurchased. Owners who got their vehicles fixed will also receive a cash payment of between $5,100 and $10,000 to compensate them for the lost value of the cars, as well as for Volkswagen's deceptive promise of "clean diesel." Most of the buyers paid extra for a car with a diesel engine.

Two VW employees were given prison terms for their involvement in the VW scandal. Oliver Schmidt, the man who was in charge of VW's U.S. environmental and engineering office before the Dieselgate scandal, was sentenced to seven years in prison on December 6, 2017. Schmidt also pleaded guilty to violating the Clean Air Act and conspiracy to defraud the U.S. government for his role in VW's developing software to hide the fact that many of its cars were not meeting emission standards.

James Liang, a former VW engineer, was sentenced on August 25, 2017, to 40 months in prison and a $200,000 fine for his role in not reporting VW's use of software to cheat U.S. emission rules on nearly 600,000 diesel vehicles. Daniel Nixon, Liang's lawyer, said his client was not "greedy or immoral," but followed orders to keep his job and support his family. "What occurred here was wrong," Nixon said. "But he wasn't the mastermind. He was not motivated by greed."[35] It is interesting to note Nixon's "just following orders" defense, which is nothing more than a rationalization for unethical actions.

Theories About Other People

Business today operates in a global environment rich in diversity with people who speak different languages, have different customs, mores, cultural beliefs, religious beliefs, laws, and accepted ways of behavior. Unfortunately, people have a tendency to think of themselves and the groups they belong to or share their beliefs with as better than those they don't belong to whether based on factors of race, religion, nationality, political affiliation, and so on.

This perception that "our way" is normal and preferred and that other ways are somehow inferior has been called ethnocentrism. In the ethnocentric view, the world revolves around our group, and our values and beliefs become the standard against which to judge the rest of the world.

Ethnocentrism is best described an 'us versus them' mentality that is pervasive in most societies. Having national pride or being affiliated with a religious group is natural and there is nothing wrong with that. The problem lies in our tendency to inaccurately believe that our group is better than any other without taking the time to thoroughly analyze whether these beliefs are valid.

In business, these unconscious beliefs can manifest themselves through discriminatory hiring and promotion practices and favoritism for white employees over employees of color and men over women. Understanding the role that stereotypes can play in our decision-making process is critical if we hope to avoid their negative manifestations. It is essential, in an increasingly diverse workforce, to mold individuals with these differences into a coherent whole. This is the essence of ethical leadership.

Theories About Ourselves

Some people develop a hindsight bias, believing they are more capable than they actually are. We have a tendency to overestimate our positive attributes and to underestimate our weaknesses. A hindsight bias may creep up where people have the tendency to view events as more predictable than they really are. This can create a superiority bias whereby executives become overconfident in their abilities and make decisions based on incomplete or inaccurate information. The best decisions surrounding complex matters are made through consultation and inclusion of other points of view.

Overconfidence bias is important in accounting because auditors overconfident in their (conservative) risk assessments about certain areas of the audit (i.e., the risk of failure of internal controls) may fail to seek additional information to update their knowledge. One cost of overconfidence is a reluctance to learn more about how the internal controls work before determining whether they are working as intended.[36]

Asch found that people have a tendency to yield to group pressure, even when they know the majority view is incorrect. The greater the number of people in the majority, the more likely those in the minority change their view to conform with the majority. "Group Think" speaks to an unconscious need for approval and avoidance of conflict within the groups we belong. This bias can result in individual group members not sharing concerns they may have about potential consequences a decision may have, leading to poor decisions being made.[37]

Stanley Milgram's classic 1963 study involving a persons' willingness to administer increasingly more severe electrical shocks to others as punishment demonstrates our tendency to subjugate our will to authoritative figures. The experiment shows that people have a tendency to follow the instructions of those they perceive to be in authority, even when those instructions conflict with their own values.[38] This bias can result in a person unconsciously giving more weight to their loyalty to their employer than their own integrity when making a decision as to whether to go along with an unethical request made by that employer.

Obedience to authority played a role in the Enron case. Andy Fastow and David Duncan, the Andersen auditor who went along with Enron's improper accounting, explicitly raised the defense that they were just following orders. In fact, this was the rallying cry for many in the era of financial frauds at companies such as WorldCom (Betty Vinson) and other leading figures in the Enron-era scandals.[39]

Our awareness of situations that create bias is important in the audit function. Auditors need to understand how they might utilize their understanding of biases to improve their ethical decision making. We build on our discussion of biases in this chapter in Chapter 4 where we discuss the link between KPMG's Professional Judgment Framework and our cognitive processes.

Bystander Effect

People also have a tendency to not report incidents of wrong doing they may witness if they believe (or hope) others will report it. Each individual may think that others will come to the aid of the threatened person. This bias is known as the bystander effect. Studies have shown that the greater the number of people present, the fewer the incidents of assistance; we take our cues from the behavior of others, and that is, after all, less stress and hassle to ourselves to assume others will intervene.[40]

One example of the bystander effect at work is an incident that occurred on a subway platform in New York City on December 3, 2012. During a disagreement between two passengers waiting for the train, Ki-Suck Han was pushed off the platform by Naeem Davis. Han was killed by an oncoming train while observers did nothing to help him off the tracks. One such observer, R. Umar Abbasi, a freelance photographer, took pictures of the incident. When questioned, Abbasi said he was shocked that people nearer to Han didn't try to help in the 22 seconds before the train struck. He figured others were closer and could have grabbed him and pulled him to safety.

Another example of the bystander effect is the rash of sexual harassment charges during 2017, first against Hollywood moguls such as Harvey Weinstein, then media personalities like Matt Lauer, and finally, a large number of Congressmen, many of whom resigned, including Minnesota Senator Al Franken. In each of these cases, the women alleging sexual harassment did not come forward initially because they feared for their career. Moreover, consciously or unconsciously, they assumed others similarly affected would report the wrongdoing.

The bystander effect could manifest itself in accounting if a fraud occurs and those in the know don't report it believing others, such as higher-ups, would do so. Failing to report fraud violates the integrity principle in the AICPA Code. An accountant or auditor cannot turn a blind eye to wrongdoing that affects the accuracy and reliability of the financial statements.

Equity, Diversity, and Inclusion

> ### LO 2-3
> Distinguish between equity, diversity, and inclusion.

We hear a lot about equity these days. It tends to be thought of as one of three key values necessary in the 21st century workplace. Equity, Diversity, and Inclusion (EDI) loosely means to give each person the same opportunity, accepting people from different races, genders, religions, and nationalities, and inviting those who have been historically locked-out of society to come in. EDI policies should promote ethical behavior and tear down biases that might influence the fair treatment of all people.

Diversity versus Inclusion

Diversity and inclusion are often viewed the same way. However, there are important differences. The U.S. government's Office of Personnel Management indicates that diversity is hiring and retaining employees that "reflect America's diversity," while inclusion is making them feel motivated, and a true part of the organization.[41]

The concept of diversity encompasses acceptance and respect. It means to treat each person as unique and to recognize our individual differences. It means understanding each other and moving beyond simple tolerance to embracing and to celebrating the rich dimensions of individuality. A diverse workforce is one where similarities and differences among employees in terms of different dimensions are molded together to produce the best outcome.

Inclusion has often been defined in the context of a society that leaves no one behind. It is one in which the cultural, economic, political, and social life of all individuals and groups can take part. The United Nations report, *Creating an Inclusive Society: Practical Strategies to Promote Social Integration,* points out: An inclusive society is one that overrides differences of race, gender, class, generation, and geography, and ensures inclusion and equality of opportunity, as well as capability of all members of the society to determine an agreed set of social institutions that govern social interaction.[42]

Equality vs. Equity

People tend to think about equality of opportunity and fairness in treatment as one and the same. It means having the same rights, social status, etc. Equality aims to ensure that everyone gets the same things in order to enjoy full, healthy lives. Like equity, equality aims to promote fairness and justice, but it can only work if everyone starts from the same place and needs the same things. But when we place it next to equity, that's when the lines get blurred. Equity can be thought of in terms of equal opportunity that fit a person's circumstances and abilities. It may mean giving a group of people different access to resources, as with disabled individuals who deserve special access for entry or different testing procedures in the classroom. In the workplace, it means to provide accommodations as needed.

A good analogy is to think of runners sprinting around an oval track during a competition. The concept of equality would mean treating runners the same way; having them start at the same place on the track. While this may seem fair at first, we quickly realize that those starting from an inside position have an advantage over runners in the outside lanes because the distance they have to travel is shorter. As a result, equality – starting at the same place – doesn't result in fairness. The concept of equity would mean the starting positions should be staggered so runners in the outer lanes have an equal chance to win the competition. In this case, different or tailored treatment leads to fairness and justice, not the same treatment.[43]

Deloitte Surveys

EDI policies are an integral part of ethics because the way we treat people with different demographic characteristics says a lot about the culture of an organization. The underlying principles of fairness and justice provide the foundation for EDI policies. The virtues of caring, kindness, and empathy should drive behavior in an ethical organization that wants to be known as a welcoming and supportive place to work.

According to the Deloitte survey, *Global Human Capital Trends,* 69% of executives rate diversity and inclusion an important issue, up from 59% in 2014.[44] Why has diversity and inclusion become so important? One answer is, in today's global business environment, it is common to have a diverse workforce that needs to be managed in ways that recognize equity and fairness in treatment. A diverse workforce poses challenges in the way people of different religions, genders, generations, and other types of diversity blend together to create an ethical corporate culture that values individuals from many walks of life.

The Deloitte survey indicates that 78% of respondents believe diversity and inclusion is a competitive advantage. Yet, despite this increased level of interest, only six percent of companies actually tie compensation to diversity outcomes. Solving diversity challenges is very difficult. Also, trending upward is a focus on eliminating measurable bias from talent processes, including hiring, promotion, performance management, leadership development, succession, and compensation.

In another survey by Deloitte – the *Inclusion Pulse Survey* – it was found that 72% of working Americans surveyed would or may consider leaving an organization for one they think is more inclusive. Thirty percent of millennials surveyed say they have already left a job for one with a more inclusive culture.[45]

The Deloitte Pulse survey gathered online responses during April 13-20, 2017, from more than 1,300 full-time employees from different sized companies across the U.S. The survey reported that inclusivity was perceived differently by different groups, but when it comes to workplace culture, most respondents relate more to the way inclusion "feels" over how it may "look." Nearly half of all respondents (47%) chose "an environment that makes me feel comfortable being myself" as one of the top three attributes of an inclusive workplace.

Why the differences? One reason is different definitions of inclusion create different perceptions of what it is and could be. Here are four definitions cited in the survey.

Inclusion: Respect for and appreciation of differences in demographic characteristics such as race, ethnicity, gender, age, national origin, disability, sexual orientation, and/or non-demographic characteristics such as religion, experiences, communication style, or work habits.

Stereotype-biased bias: Attitudes or generalized beliefs about people that affect understanding, actions, and decisions, such as assuming one group of people are more intelligent or hard working than other groups.

Inclusive: Embracing all people; making all people feel valued and they belong in their organization.

Inclusion initiatives: Efforts to help all people feel that they are valued and belong in their organization.

EDI policies are significantly more important in the 21st century than ever before. One reason is young adults and millennials have grown up in a culture that talks about these issues even though they may be lacking in reality. The expectations are high for an inclusive environment and the failure to do so can have negative consequences as the survey results indicate.

Deloitte's 2017 *Global Human Capital Trends* survey reports that diversity and inclusion at the workplace are now CEO-level issues, but they continue to be frustrating for many companies.

Sexual Harassment

Issues of equality, equity, and fairness are front and center when men (or women) with power and influence use their positions to extract favors from subordinates of the same or other sex. The allegations of sexual harassment and its relation to the bystander effect illustrates an environment where treating women (or men) equally might be dependent on whether they are willing to accept sexual overtones and other forms of threatening behavior.

Sexual harassment oftentimes implies a "quid pro quo"—something for something. A harassed woman may come to believe that her boss could stifle her career advancement unless she tolerates such behavior . . . and maybe more.

Sexual harassment is unwelcome behavior of a sexual nature that is severe, pervasive, or persistent enough to create a hostile or intimidating work environment. It can include physical touching, verbal comments, non-verbal conduct such as leering or emails, or a combination of these things.

As far as biases go, harassing behavior can create the belief that the recipient will not be treated equally and have the same opportunities unless they give in to sexual advances.

Uber Sexual Harassment Case

Charges of sexual harassment lodged against Uber by Susan Fowler in 2017 led to an investigation of the company's practices and corporate culture. Fowler's blog post, "Reflecting on one very, very strange year at Uber," detailed allegations of harassment, discrimination, and retaliation during her employment at Uber, and the ineffectiveness of the then-existing policies and procedures. Exhibit 2.2 provides details of

Fowler's experiences and the role and responsibilities of the Covington law firm that investigated these practices and their recommendations in general.

Covington was instructed to evaluate three issues: (1) Uber's workplace environment as it related to the allegations of discrimination, harassment, and retaliation in Fowler's post; (2) whether the company's policies and practices were sufficient to prevent and properly address discrimination, harassment, and retaliation in the workplace; and (3) what steps Uber could take to ensure that its commitment to a diverse and inclusive workplace was reflected not only in the company's policies but made real in the experiences of each of Uber's employees.

The recommendations for Uber were numerous and covered areas such as changing senior leadership and board oversight to develop and oversee diversity and inclusion policies, strengthening internal controls, reformulating Uber's cultural values, mandatory training for managerial personnel and the human resources department, diversity and inclusion enhancements in recruiting women and other underrepresented minority groups, providing an effective complaint process, recognizing and supporting efforts of employees to improve the workplace environment, and eliminating bias and misuse of the performance evaluation system.

The following specific recommendations illustrate the extensive steps Uber pledged to take in accepting the recommendations of the Covington report.

- Empowering senior leadership through the Head of Diversity who is responsible for diversity and inclusion.
- Creating a Board oversight committee, such as an Ethics and Culture Committee, to oversee Uber's efforts and enhance a culture of ethical business practices, diversity, and inclusion within the organization.
- Enhancing the role and responsibilities of the audit committee and internal controls with respect to diversity and inclusion compliance.
- Training key personnel in inclusive leadership and to combat implicit bias.
- Providing an effective complaint process for employees to address harassment, discrimination, and retaliation in the workplace.
- Establishing an employee diversity advisory board to funnel input and ideas to the Head of Diversity.
- Targeting diverse sources of talent, including alternative and non-traditional sources of recruiting, and developing deeper partnerships with Historically Black Colleges and Universities and Hispanic-Serving Institutions.
- Adopting a version of the "Rooney Rule" originally established by the National Football League (NFL) that requires each NFL franchise to interview at least one woman and one member of an underrepresented minority group for key managerial positions.
- Supporting employee efforts to enhance a diverse workplace environment through the performance review process.
- Eliminating bias and misuse of the performance review process.
- Reviewing compensation practices to ensure compensation policies and practices comply with state and federal equal pay laws.

Ferrell et al. point out that people can act unethically by failing to identify the ethical dimensions of a situation. Ethical blindness results from individuals who fail to sense the nature and complexity of their decisions.[46] Decision-making at Uber with respect to how female employees were treated illustrates what can happen when a company has a blind spot with respect to equity, diversity, and inclusion. The Covington report identifies the areas of risk for Uber and concludes that if the company commits to following the recommendations, Uber should be better positioned to create a corporate culture that values EDI and commits to incorporating it into their strategic policies.

EXHIBIT 2.2   Sexual Harassment Charges at Uber

Sexual harassment charges at Uber came to light on February 19, 2017, when former Uber engineer, Susan Fowler, published a blog post about behavior towards women at Uber.[47] Fowler detailed how, after joining Uber, she became part of a team. Her manager quickly sent her a string of messages about the open relationship he had with his girlfriend, and how he wasn't having as much luck as she was in finding sexual partners. Fowler took this as a blatant attempt by her superior to get her to sleep with him. She took a screen shot of his come-on and reported him. Human Resources told her even though this was harassment, nothing would be done. The manager was highly regarded and it was his first offense. Fowler was told her choice was to forget about it, be reassigned, or stay put even though the manager, who knew he had been reported, might give her a poor performance review.

Reassigned, Fowler wrote she later found out that the manager was openly propositioning female team members. She also discovered and wrote about a sexist corporate culture where women saw their performance evaluations retroactively downgraded when it suited male managers.

Ultimately, in response to Fowler's claim of sexual harassment and similar accusations, Uber fired 20 employees, including senior executives, and reprimanded 40 more employees. Uber commissioned an investigation of its workplace practices by Covington & Burling LLP ("Covington"), which was headed by Eric Holder, former Attorney General of the U.S. Specifically, Covington was asked to conduct a thorough and objective review regarding "the specific issues relating to work place environment raise by Fowler, as well as diversity and inclusion at Uber more broadly."

The Covington report was issued on June 13, 2017. Uber founder and CEO Travis Kalanick accepted responsibility for the company's state and told employees that he'd be taking an indefinite leave of absence. Following that, the company announced that Emil Michael, vice president for business, was also leaving. Then Uber board member and hedge fund partner David Bonderman resigned after making what he called an inappropriate remark about women at a company meeting.[48]

The sexual harassment case took a strange turn on November 30, 2017, when one of Uber's early investors and Hyperloop co-founder, Shervin Pishevar, was accused by at least five women of sexual harassment or assault. Pishevar allegedly made unwanted sexual advances or harassed them. The women accused Pishevar of exploiting a professional connection or offering the prospect of a job or investment to commit sexual assaults.[49]

The Covington report lays out a strong case for a company that lacked guidelines on issues of diversity and inclusion and an indifference to what was going on in the company. Holder suggested that Uber change its written cultural values to promote positive behavior, inclusion, and collaboration. That means doing away with values that justified poor behavior, such as "Let Builders Build," "Always Be Hustlin'," Meritocracy and Toe-Stepping" and "Principled Confrontation."

The recommendations in the report are designed to improve Uber's culture, promote fairness and accountability, and establish processes and systems to ensure the mistakes of the past would not repeated. The goal is to rebuild trust with Uber employees, riders, and drivers. Specifically, the new plan calls for Uber to forbid "any type of romantic or intimate relationship between individuals in a reporting relationship."[50]

Kohlberg and the Cognitive Development Approach

LO 2-4

Describe Kohlberg's stages of moral development.

Cognitive development refers to the thought process followed in one's moral development. An individual's ability to make reasoned judgments about moral matters develops in stages. The psychologist Lawrence Kohlberg concluded, on the basis of 20 years of research, that people develop from childhood to adulthood through a sequential and hierarchical series of cognitive stages that characterize the way they think about ethical dilemmas. Moral reasoning processes become more complex and sophisticated with development. Higher stages rely upon cognitive operations that are not available to individuals at lower stages, and higher stages are thought to be "morally better" because they are consistent with philosophical theories of justice and rights.[51] Kohlberg's views on ethical development are helpful in understanding how individuals may internalize moral standards and, as they become more sophisticated in their use, apply them more critically to resolve ethical conflicts.

Kohlberg developed his theory by using data from studies on how decisions are made by individuals. The example of Heinz and the Drug, given here, illustrates a moral dilemma used by Kohlberg to develop his stage-sequence model.

Heinz and the Drug

In Europe, a woman was near death from a rare type of cancer. There was one drug that the doctors thought might save her. It was a form of radium that a druggist in the same town had recently discovered. The drug was expensive to make, but the druggist was charging 10 times what the drug cost him to make: It cost $200 for the radium, and he charged $2,000 for a small dose of the drug. The sick woman's husband, Heinz, went to everyone he knew to borrow the money, but he could get together only about $1,000—half the cost. He told the druggist that his wife was dying and asked him to sell it cheaper or let him pay later. But the druggist said, "No, I discovered the drug and I'm going to make money from it." Heinz got desperate and broke into the man's store to steal the drug for his wife.

Should the husband have done that? Was it right or wrong? Most people say that Heinz's theft was morally justified, but Kohlberg was less concerned about whether they approved or disapproved than with the reasons they gave for their answers. Kohlberg monitored the reasons for judgments given by a group of 75 boys ranging in age from 10 to 16 years and isolated the six stages of moral thought. The boys progressed in reasoning sequentially, with most never reaching the highest stages. He concluded that the universal principle of justice is the highest claim of morality.

The dilemma of Heinz illustrates the challenge of evaluating the ethics of a decision. Table 2.1 displays three types of responses.[52]

TABLE 2.1	Three Sample Responses to the Heinz Dilemma
A:	It really depends on how much Heinz likes his wife and how much risk there is in taking the drug. If he can get the drug in no other way and if he really likes his wife, he'll have to steal it.
B:	I think that a husband would care so much for his wife that he couldn't just sit around and let her die. He wouldn't be stealing for his own profit; he'd be doing it to help someone he loves.
C:	Regardless of his personal feelings, Heinz has to realize that the druggist is protected by the law. Since no one is above the law, Heinz shouldn't steal it. If we allowed Heinz to steal, then all society would be in danger of anarchy.

Kohlberg considered how the responses were different and what problem-solving strategies underlie the three responses. Response A (Preconventional) presents a rather uncomplicated approach to moral problems. Choices are made based on the wants of the individual decision maker (egoism). Response B (Conventional) also considers the wife's needs. Here, Heinz is concerned that his actions should be motivated by good intentions (i.e., the end justifies the means). In Response C (Postconventional), a societywide perspective is used in decision making. Law is the key in making moral decisions[53] (for example, rule utilitarianism; justice orientation).

The examples in Table 2.2 demonstrate the application of Kohlberg's model of cognitive development to possible decision making in business.

Relating Kohlberg's stages to cognitive biases, individual's reasoning at stage 3 could be affected by "groupthink." Groupthink manifests itself in group decision making that discourages individuality and

TABLE 2.2	Kohlberg's Stages of Moral Development

Level 1—Preconventional
At the preconventional level, the individual is very self-centered. Rules are seen as something external imposed on the self.

Stage 1: Obedience to Rules; Avoidance of Punishment
At this stage, what is right is judged by one's obedience to rules and authority.
Example: A company forbids making payoffs to government or other officials to gain business. Susan, the company's contract negotiator, might justify refusing the request of a foreign government official to make a payment to gain a contract as being contrary to company rules, or Susan might make the payment if she believes there is little chance of being caught and punished.

Stage 2: Satisfying One's Own Needs
In Stage 2, rules and authority are important only if acting in accordance with them satisfies one's own needs (egoism).
Example: Here, Susan might make the payment even though it is against company rules if she perceives that such payments are a necessary part of doing business. She views the payment as essential to gain the contract. Susan may believe that competitors are willing to make payments, and that making such payments are part of the culture of the host country. She concludes that if she does not make the payment, it might jeopardize her ability to move up the ladder within the organization and possibly forgo personal rewards of salary increases, bonuses, or both. Because everything is *relative,* each person is free to pursue her individual interests.

Level 2—Conventional
At the conventional level, the individual becomes aware of the interests of others and one's duty to society. Personal responsibility becomes an important consideration in decision making.

Stage 3: Fairness to Others
In Stage 3, an individual is not only motivated by rules but seeks to do what is in the perceived best interests of others, especially those in a family, peer group, or work organization. There is a commitment to loyalty in the relationship.
Example: Susan wants to be liked by others. She might be reluctant to make the payment but agrees to do so, not because it benefits her interests, but in response to the pressure imposed by her supervisor, who claims that the company will lose a major contract and employees will be fired if she refuses to go along.

(Continued)

Stage 4: Law and Order

Stage 4 behavior emphasizes the morality of law and duty to the social order. One's duty to society, respect for authority, and maintaining the social order become the focus of decision making.

Example: Susan might refuse to make the illegal payment, even though it leads to a loss of jobs in her company (or maybe even the closing of the company itself), because she views it as her duty to do so in the best interests of society. She does not want to violate the law.

Level 3—Postconventional

Principled morality underlies decision making at this level. The individual recognizes that there must be a societywide basis for cooperation. There is an orientation to principles that shape whatever laws and role systems a society may have.

Stage 5: Social Contract

In Stage 5, an individual is motivated by upholding the basic rights, values, and legal contracts of society. That person recognizes in some cases that legal and moral points of view may conflict. To reduce such conflict, individuals at this stage base their decisions on a rational calculation of benefits and harms to society.

Example: Susan might weigh the alternative courses of action by evaluating how each of the groups is affected by her decision to make the payment. For instance, the company might benefit by gaining the contract. Susan might even be rewarded for her action. The employees are more secure in their jobs. The customer in the other country gets what it wants. On the other hand, the company will be in violation of the Foreign Corrupt Practices Act (FCPA), which prohibits (bribery) payments to foreign government officials. Susan then weighs the consequences of making an illegal payment, including any resulting penalties, against the ability to gain additional business. Susan might conclude that the harms of prosecution, fines, other sanctions, and the loss of one's reputational capital are greater than the benefits.

Stage 6: Universal Ethical Principles

Kohlberg was still working on Stage 6 at the time of his death in 1987. He believed that this stage rarely occurred. Still, a person at this stage believes that right and wrong are determined by universal ethical principles that everyone should follow. Stage 6 individuals believe that there are inalienable rights, which are universal in nature and consequence. These rights, laws, and social agreements are valid not because of a particular society's laws or customs, but because they rest on the premise of universality. Justice and equality are examples of principles that are deemed universal. If a law conflicts with an ethical principle, then an individual should act in accordance with the principle.

An example of such a principle is Immanuel Kant's categorical imperative, the first formulation of which can be stated as: "Act only according to that maxim [reason for acting] by which you can at the same time will that it would become a universal law."[54] Kant's categorical imperative creates an absolute, unconditional requirement that exerts its authority in all circumstances, and is both required and justified as an end in itself.

Example: Susan would go beyond the norms, laws, and authority of groups or individuals. She would disregard pressure from her supervisor or the perceived best interests of the company when deciding what to do. Her action would be guided only by universal ethical principles that would apply to others in a similar situation.

personal responsibility. In this stage, peer pressure influences decision making. A good example is the case of Cynthia Cooper at WorldCom. Cooper was pressured not only by the CFO, Scott Sullivan, but also the audit committee that initially backed away from any support for her position. Still, she persisted and eventually uncovered and reported the fraud at the company. Cooper's reasoning was at the postconventional level.

Let's return to the receivables example in Chapter 1 that applies ethical reasoning to the methods discussed in Exhibit 1.3 (Ethical Reasoning Method Bases for Making Ethical Judgments). In the receivables example, an auditor who reasons at Stage 3 might go along with the demands of a client out of loyalty or because she thinks the company will benefit by such inaction. At Stage 4, the auditor places the needs of society and abiding by the law (GAAP, in this instance) above all else, so the auditor will insist on recording an allowance for uncollectibles.

An auditor who reasons at Stage 5 would not want to violate the public interest principle embedded in the profession's ethical standards, which values the public trust above all else. Investors and creditors have a right to know about the uncertainty surrounding collectibility of the receivables. At Stage 6, the auditor would ask whether she would want other auditors to insist on providing an allowance for the uncollectibles if they were involved in a similar situation. This creates an objective standard for determining the right decision. The auditor reasons that the orderly functioning of markets and a level playing field require that financial information should be accurate and reliable, so another auditor should also decide that the allowance needs to be recorded. The application of the ethical principles of objectivity and integrity in the AICPA Code enables her to carry out the ethical action and act in a responsible manner.

Kohlberg's model suggests that people continue to change their decision priorities over time and with additional education and experience. They may experience a change in values and ethical behavior.[55] In the context of business, an individual's moral development can be influenced by corporate culture, especially ethics training.[56] Ethics training and education have been shown to improve managers' moral development. More will be said about corporate culture in Chapter 3.

Kohlberg maintains that his stage sequence is universal; it is the same in all cultures. William Crain addresses whether different cultures socialize their children differently, thereby teaching them different moral beliefs.[57] He points out that Kohlberg's response has been that different cultures do teach different beliefs, but that his stages refer not to specific beliefs, but to underlying modes of reasoning. We might assume, then, in a collectivist society, which exists in many Asian cultures, blowing the whistle on a member of a work group would be considered improper because of the "family" orientation or team player mentality (Stage 3), while in a more individualistic one, such as exists in the U.S., it is considered acceptable because it is in the best interests of society (Stage 4). Thus, individuals in different cultures at the same stage-sequence might hold different beliefs about the appropriateness of whistleblowing but still reason the same because, from a fairness perspective, it is the right way to behave.

The Ethical Domain in Accounting and Auditing

LO 2-5

Explain how cognitive processes influence ethical decision making in accounting.

A commitment to serve the public interest is the bedrock of the accounting profession. Snoeyenbos, Almeder, and Humber have described this as a "social contract" in which the professional discharges his obligation by operating with high standards of expertise and integrity. When the profession does not maintain these standards, the social contract is broken, and society may decide to limit the role or the autonomy of the profession. This occurred in the aftermath of the accounting scandals when Congress passed the Sarbanes-Oxley Act (SOX) and established the Public Company Accounting Oversight Board (PCAOB) to oversee the auditing, ethics, and independence practices of CPA firms that audit companies with stock listed on the New York Stock Exchange (NYSE) and NASDAQ. For nonpublicly-owned companies, the standards of the AICPA still apply.[58]

The ethical domain for accountants and auditors usually involves four key constituent groups, including (1) the client organization that hires and pays for accounting services; (2) the accounting firm that employs the practitioner, typically represented by the collective interests of the firm's management; (3) the accounting profession, including various regulatory bodies such as the Securities and Exchange Commission (SEC) and the PCAOB; and (4) the general public, who rely on the attestations and representations of the practitioner and the firm.[59] Responsibilities to each of these groups may conflict. For example, fees are paid by the client organization rather than by the general public, including investors and creditors who are the direct beneficiary of the independent auditing services, so the public interest may conflict with client interests. These conflicts might influence the cognitive development of auditors, thereby influencing their ethical reasoning.

The accounting profession's codes of conduct that were discussed in Chapter 1 encourage the individual practitioner's ethical behavior in a way that is consistent with the stated rules and guidelines of the profession. These positive factors work in conjunction with an individual's attitudes and beliefs and ethical reasoning capacity to influence professional judgment and ethical decision making. Biases can creep into decision making, leading the auditor to be overconfident about his ability to properly assess risk on the audit.

One type of bias that fits into the discussion of moral development is conformity bias. In every aspect of their lives, people take cues from those around them about the proper way to act. By observing others in the workplace new hires learn the culture of the organization and expected behavior. The conformity bias strongly pushes people to conform their judgments to those of their reference group. A good example is at Enron where freshly minted MBAs were acculturated into Enron's fast-and-loose corporate style without fully recognizing the ethical implications of company practices. At Enron, the "everybody else is doing it" explanation was used to justify the earnings manipulations.[60]

Kohlberg's theory of ethical development provides a framework that can be used to consider the effects of conflict areas on ethical reasoning in accounting. For example, if an individual accountant is influenced by the firm's desire to "make the client happy," then the result may be reasoning at Stage 3. The results of published studies during the 1990s by accounting researchers indicate that CPAs reason primarily at Stages 3 and 4. One possible implication of these results is that a larger percentage of CPAs may be overly influenced by their relationship with peers, superiors, and clients (Stage 3) or by rules (Stage 4). A CPA who is unable to apply the technical accounting standards and rules of conduct critically when these requirements are unclear is likely to be influenced by others in the decision-making process.[61] If an auditor reasons at the postconventional level, then that person may refuse to give in to the pressure applied by the supervisor to overlook the client's failure to follow GAAP. This is the ethical position to take, although it may go against the culture of the firm to "go along to get along."

Empirical studies have explored the underlying ethical reasoning processes of accountants and auditors in practice. Findings show that ethical reasoning may be an important determinant of professional judgment, such as the disclosure of sensitive information[62] and auditor independence.[63] Results also show that unethical and dysfunctional audit behavior, such as the underreporting of time on an audit budget, may be systematically related to the auditor's level of ethical reasoning.[64] In reviewing these and other works, Ponemon and Gabhart conclude that the results imply that ethical reasoning may be an important cognitive characteristic that affects individual judgment and behavior under a wide array of conditions and events in extant professional practice.[65]

The role of an accountant is to tell a story—to make an account—of a series of business activities. This story can be told from a variety of perspectives (i.e., employer or client) and can therefore result in many accounts. It is the role of the accountant to determine the perspective that will fairly present the information in accordance with laws and accounting standards, but they contain options and ambiguities. A higher level of understanding is required to deal with these different perspectives, the options and ambiguities that exist within the standards, and the uncertainties of business life. This higher level of understanding is encapsulated in the postconventional level of reasoning.[66]

Moral Reasoning and Moral Behavior

Within the cognitive-developmental paradigm the most distinguishing characteristic of morality is the human capacity to reason. Moral judgment has long been regarded as the single most influential factor—and the only truly moral determinant—of a person's moral behavior.[67] By definition, morality requires that a person's actions be rational, motivated by purpose or intent, and carried out with autonomous free will. Kohlberg maintained that it is as a result of development in moral reasoning that one becomes truly a moral person in both mind and deed.[68]

Kohlberg's work is not without its critics. Some philosophers complain it draws too heavily from Rawls's Theory of Justice and makes deontological ethics superior to other ethical perspectives. They note that the theory applies more to societal issues than to individual ethical decisions. A number of psychologists have challenged the notion that people go through "rigid" stages of moral reasoning, arguing instead that they can engage in many ways of thinking about a problem, regardless of their age.[69]

Although he later admitted to having underestimated the complexity of the relation between moral stage and action and revised his thinking to include two intervening cognitive functions to explain it—a prescriptive judgment of the moral right and a personal judgment of responsibility to act accordingly—Kohlberg still contended that it is the logic of a person's reasoning that most strongly influences his moral behavior. Thus, reason constitutes the essential core and strength of character of a person's moral maturity in Kohlberg's theory.[70]

Kohlberg's commitment to reason has been challenged by some who claim he disregarded other factors also associated with moral functioning, such as emotion[71] and traits of character.[72] Others have criticized Kohlberg's emphasis on reason without considering its interaction with other components of morality and its link to moral behavior in particular.[73] Still others claim the over-reliance on dilemmas, such as Heinz and the Drug, to evaluate moral reasoning shortchanges the role of virtue ethics and its focus on the character of individuals and their overall approach to life.[74]

Noted moral psychologist James Rest attempted to address some of the problems that are recognized in Kohlberg's work, and in doing so has moved from the six-stage model to one with three levels of understanding: personal interest, maintaining norms, and postconventional. Rest focuses on the maintaining norms (similar to the conventional level) and postconventional schemas. By maintaining norms, Rest means recognizing the need for societywide norms; a duty orientation; the need for cooperation; uniform and categorical application of norms, laws, and rules; and that individuals will obey the norms and laws and expect others to do the same even though it may not benefit all affected parties equally.[75]

Rest's conception has particular appeal for accountants who, at this level of moral development, recognize the importance of various laws and standards, comply with them, understand that sometimes compliance would benefit them and sometimes not, but recognize that obeying these norms is important for society. Rest recognized that, while operating at this level would be ideal for an accountant, it does not ensure that the accountant can make good decisions when there are options and ambiguities within accounting and auditing standards, nor does it ensure that he will have the ability to make good decisions when business circumstances arise that are outside the current laws, norms, or standards.[76]

A higher level of understanding is needed to deal with these different perspectives. The postconventional schema integrates such issues by recognizing that accountants do not have to follow the norms but should seek the moral criteria behind the norms for guidance in action. In accounting this means the fair presentation of financial information in a way that benefits society—that is, the public interest.

Rest's Four-Component Model of Ethical Decision Making

LO 2-6
Explain Rest's model and how its components influence ethical decision making.

Cognitive-developmental researchers have attempted to understand the process of ethical decision making. In particular, Rest asserts that ethical actions are not the outcome of a single, unitary decision process, but result from a combination of various cognitive structures and psychological processes. Rest's model of ethical action is based on the presumption that an individual's behavior is related to his level of moral development. Rest built on Kohlberg's work by developing a four-component model of the ethical decision-making process. The four-component model describes the cognitive processes that individuals use in ethical decision making; that is, it depicts how an individual first identifies an ethical dilemma and then continues through to his moral motivation and finally finds courage to behave ethically. Each component of the model must be present before the moral action will be undertaken.[77]

Rest built his four-component model by working backward. He started with the end product—to take ethical action—and then determined the steps that produce such behavior. He concluded that ethical action is the result of four psychological processes: (1) moral sensitivity (recognition), (2) moral judgment (reasoning), (3) moral focus (motivation), and (4) moral character (action).

Moral Sensitivity

The first step in moral behavior requires that the individual interpret the situation as moral. Absent the ability to recognize that one's actions affect the welfare of others, it would be virtually impossible to make the most ethical decision when faced with a moral dilemma.

Aaron Beam was unable to spot the ethical issues. He felt uncomfortable with what Richard Scrushy had asked him to do and that it was wrong to manipulate the numbers, yet he went along anyway; perhaps because he figured it was a one-time maneuver. He failed to see how his silence would affect others but found out the hard way on March 26, 2003 when HealthSouth's shares lost 97% of their value as news of the accounting fraud surfaced.

Moral Judgment

An individual's ethical cognition of what "ideally" ought to be done to resolve an ethical dilemma is called *prescriptive reasoning*.[78] The outcome of one's prescriptive reasoning is his ethical judgment of the ideal solution to an ethical dilemma. Generally, an individual's prescriptive reasoning reflects his cognitive understanding of an ethical situation as measured by his level of moral development.[79] Once a person is aware of possible lines of action and how people would be affected by the alternatives, a process aided by the philosophical reasoning methods, a judgment must be made about which course of action is more morally justifiable (which alternative is just or right).

Moral judgment relates to developing moral reasoning abilities over time. Kohlberg believed that people engage in more complex reasoning as they progress up the stages and become less self-centered and develop broader definitions of morality. Rest added that developing moral judgment is a social and cognitive construct that progressed from a self-focused view of moral issues through a group-based moral perspective to a reliance on postconventional moral principles and a primary factor in the understanding of moral actions and emotions.

Moral Focus

After concluding what course of action is best, decision makers must be focused on taking the moral action and follow through with ethical decision making. Moral values may conflict with other values. Moral motivation reflects an individual's willingness to place ethical values (e.g., honesty, integrity, trustworthiness, caring, and empathy) ahead of nonethical values (e.g., wealth, power, and fame) that relate to self-interest. An individual's ethical motivation influences his intention to comply or not comply with his ethical judgment in the resolution of an ethical dilemma.

Sometimes individuals want to do the right thing but are overwhelmed by countervailing pressures that may overpower their ethical intentions because of perceived personal costs. The loss of a job or a client can be motivating factors that compromise integrity and block ethical action. With Betty Vinson, fear for her job and ability to support her family tainted her motivation to do the right thing and refuse to record improper accounting.

Emotions also play a part in moral motivation. Organizations should create ethically rewarding environments to increase moral motivation. To reduce the costs of behaving morally, policies and procedures should be instituted that make it easier to report unethical behavior, prevent retaliation, and create an ethical culture in the organization. Leaders have to inspire employees and build confidence that their ethical intentions are supported by organizational systems.

Moral Character

As we learned in the discussion of cognitive dissonance, individuals do not always behave in accordance with their ethical intention. An individual's intention to act ethically and his ethical actions may not be aligned because of pressures or biases that influence decision making. Individuals with strong ethical character will be more likely to carry out their ethical intentions with ethical action than individuals with a weak ethical character because they are better able to withstand any pressures (i.e., have courage and maintain integrity to do otherwise).

Executing a plan of action takes character. Moral agents have to overcome indifference and opposition, resist distractions, cope with fatigue, and develop tactics and strategies for reaching their goals. Johnson points out that this helps to explain why there is only a moderate correlation between moral judgment and moral behavior. Many times deciding does not lead to doing.[80]

The four components of Rest's model are processes that must take place for moral behavior to occur. Rest does not offer the framework as a linear decision-making model, suggesting instead that the components interact through a complicated sequence of "feed-back" and "feed-forward" loops. An individual who demonstrates adequacy in one component may not necessarily be adequate in another, and moral failure can occur when there is a deficiency in any one component.[81] For example, an individual who has good moral reasoning capacity, a skill that can be developed (Component 2), may fail to perceive an ethical problem because he does not clearly understand how others might feel or react—a lack of empathy (Component 1).

Moral Intensity

LO 2-7

Describe the link between moral intensity and ethical decision making.

The lack of research on the characteristics of a moral issue prompted Thomas Jones to develop the moral intensity model. He argued that the characteristics of the moral issue—what he collectively termed moral intensity—influence ethical decision making. Jones's model links moral intensity to Rest's Four-Component Model. For example, social consensus and magnitude of consequences are strong predictors of moral judgment. Social consensus, magnitude of consequences, and probability of effect are strong predictors of moral intention. The six dimensions of Jones's model are briefly explained below.[82]

Magnitude of Consequences refers to the degree to which an individual may be harmed or benefited by the decision maker's action. A greater degree of harm or benefit results in an increase in moral intensity.

Temporal Immediacy refers to the length of time between the action and its consequences. An action with immediate negative consequences will cause a greater increase in moral intensity than an action for which the consequences are delayed.

Social Consensus refers to the degree of agreement among a social group that an action is good or bad. This social group could be society as a whole (e.g., a fraudulent financial statement is not morally accepted by society because accounting rules and SEC laws prohibit it). A strong Social Consensus that an act is morally wrong increases moral intensity.

Proximity refers to the nearness of the decision maker to the individuals potentially affected by the consequences. An increase in proximity results in an increase of moral intensity. An auditor who becomes too close to a client and is dealing with fraudulent financial statements is likely to feel more pressure from the client because of their close relationship.

Probability of Effect refers to the likelihood that the predicted consequences and the expected level of harm/benefit will occur. Moral intensity increases with an action that has a high probability of occurrence and high likelihood of causing predicted harm. Pressures increase on auditors when harm to the public interest intensifies with the likelihood of fraudulent financial statements.

Concentration of Effect refers to the relationship between the number of people affected and the magnitude of harm. Moral intensity increases if the Concentration of Effect is great. Fraudulent financial statements issued by a publicly owned company that is also using the statements for a significant loan creates additional pressures on auditors to make the most ethical decision possible.[83]

Morally intense situations raise the stakes with respect to ethical decision making. In accounting, possible harms to investors and creditors, the likelihood of occurring, and deviation from GAAP increase the intensity of decisions and can create obstacles to ethical decision making.

Aligning Ethical Behavior and Ethical Intent

LO 2-8

Explain how moral reasoning and virtue influence ethical decision making.

One question that arises from Rest's model is how to align ethical behavior with ethical intent. The answer is through the exercise of virtue, according to a study conducted by Libby and Thorne.[84] The authors point out that audit failures at companies such as Enron and WorldCom demonstrate that the rules in accounting cannot replace auditors' professional judgment. Transactions such as the special-purpose entities at Enron can be structured around rules, and rules cannot be made to fit every situation. The rules may be unclear or nonexistent, in which case professional judgment is necessary for decisions to be made in accordance with the values of the profession as embodied in its codes of conduct. Professional judgment requires not only technical competence, but also depends on auditors' ethics and virtues that inform ethical decision making.

Libby and Thorne surveyed members of the Canadian accounting community with the help of the Canadian Institute of Chartered Accountants (CICA), the equivalent of the AICPA in the United States, to develop a set of virtues important in the practice of auditing.[85] The authors divided the virtues into two categories: intellectual virtues which indirectly influence an individual's intentions to exercise professional judgment and instrumental virtues which directly influence an individual's actions. The most important intellectual virtues were found to be integrity, truthfulness, independence, objectivity, dependability, being principled, and healthy skepticism. The most important instrumental virtues were diligence (i.e., due care) and being alert, careful, resourceful, consultative, persistent, and courageous. The authors concluded from their study that virtue plays an integral role in the intention to exercise professional judgment, the exercise of professional judgment, and the necessity of possessing both intellectual and instrumental virtues for auditors.

Intellectual virtues aim at cognitive goods through the pursuit of truth, knowledge, and understanding. They can be thought of as qualities of mind and character that enable an auditor to act with good purpose. Intellectual virtues are developed over time by gaining knowledge and skills through experiences that develop one's ability to reason through difficult situations, develop good judgment, and ultimately gain practical wisdom.

Returning now to Rest's model, Thorne contends that the model fails to provide a theoretical description of the role of personal characteristics, except for level of moral development, in auditors' ethical decision processes. Thorne develops a model of individuals' ethical decision processes that integrates Rest's components with virtue-based characteristics, which, taken together, tend to increase the decision maker's propensity to exercise sound ethical judgment. Thorne believes that virtue theory is similar to the approach advocated by the cognitive-developmental perspective in three ways. First, both perspectives suggest that ethical action is the result of a rational decision-making process. Second, both perspectives are concerned with an individual's ethical decision-making process. Third, both perspectives acknowledge the critical role of cognition in individuals' ethical decision making. Exhibit 2.3 presents Thorne's integrated model of the ethical decision-making process.[86]

EXHIBIT 2.3   Thorne's Integrated Model of Ethical Decision Making[87]

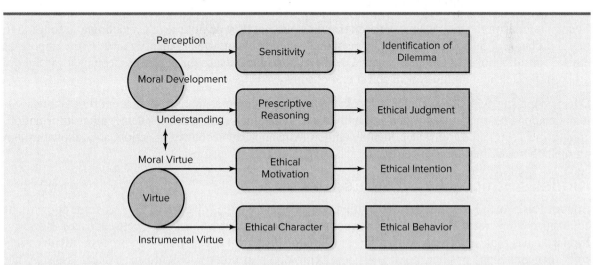

Exhibit 2.3 indicates that moral development and virtue are both required for ethical behavior. In her examination of the model, Armstrong suggests that moral development comprises sensitivity to the moral content of a situation or dilemma and prescriptive reasoning, or the ability to understand the issues, think them through, and arrive at an ethical judgment. Similarly, virtue comprises ethical motivation which

describes an individual's willingness to place the interests of others ahead of his own interest and ethical character which leads to ethical behavior.[88]

Even though virtue is a critical component of ethical behavior, other factors may get in the way of taking ethical action, including situational pressures, business norms, and the moral intensity of the issue itself that influences ethical decision making. Also, one's strength of character deepens with experience, and reflection on ethical dilemmas can bolster one's resolve.

Ethical Decision-Making Models

LO 2-9

Apply the steps in the Integrated Ethical Decision-Making Model to a case study.

Dealing with moral issues can be perplexing. How, exactly, should we think through an ethical issue? What questions should we ask? What factors should we consider? The philosophical methods of moral reasoning suggest that once we have ascertained the facts, we should ask ourselves five questions when trying to resolve a moral issue:

- What benefits and what harms will each course of action produce, and which alternative will lead to the best overall consequences?

- What moral rights do the affected parties have, and which course of action best respects those rights?

- Which course of action treats everyone the same, except where there is a morally justifiable reason not to, and does not show favoritism, discrimination, or other biased behaviors?

- Which course of action advances the common good?

- Which course of action develops moral virtues?

In commenting on these questions, Velasquez points out that they do not provide an automatic solution to moral problems. It is not meant to. The reasoning is merely meant to help identify most of the important ethical considerations. In the end, we must deliberate on moral issues for ourselves, keeping a careful eye on both the facts and on the ethical considerations involved.[89]

Decision-making guidelines can help us make better ethical choices. Johnson points out that taking a systematic approach encourages teams and individuals to carefully define the problem, gather information, apply ethical standards and values, identify and evaluate alternative courses of action, and follow through on their choices. They are also better equipped to defend their decisions.

Kidder's Ethical Checkpoints

Ethicist Rushworth Kidder acknowledges that ethical issues can be "disorderly and sometimes downright confusing." They can arise suddenly, create complex issues, and have unexpected consequences. However, Kidder argues that there is an underlying structure to the ethical decision-making process.[90] Kidder suggests that nine steps or checkpoints can help bring order to otherwise confusing ethical issues. What follows is a brief summary of the major points.

1. *Recognize that there is a moral issue.* Similar to Rest's notion of ethical sensitivity, we must acknowledge that an issue deserves our attention and moral questions exist.

2. *Determine the actor.* Kidder distinguishes between involvement and responsibility. Because we are members of larger communities, we are involved in any ethical issue that arises in the group. Yet we are only responsible for dealing with problems that we can do something about. For example, I may be concerned that clients threaten to fire their auditors if they plan to give a negative opinion on the financial statements. However, there is little I can do about it unless it happens in my firm.

3. *Gather the relevant facts.* Adequate, accurate, and current information is important for making effective decisions of all kinds, including ethical ones. Consider the motives of affected parties, patterns of behavior, likely consequences if the problem persists, and likely outcome of one course of action or another.

4. *Test for right-versus-wrong issues.* Kidder suggests using four determinations including a *legal test.* If lawbreaking is involved (i.e., fraudulent financial statements), then the problem becomes a legal matter, not a moral one. The *smell test* relies on intuition. If you have an uneasy feeling about the decision or course of action, chances are it involves right-versus-wrong issues. The *front-page test* asks how you would feel if your decision made it to the front page of the local newspaper. If you feel uncomfortable about it, then you should consider choosing another alternative. The *mom test* asks how you would feel if your mother or some other important role model became aware of your choice. If you have a queasy feeling, then it is best to reconsider your choice.

5. *Test for right-versus-right paradigms.* If an issue does not involve wrong behavior, then it likely pits two important positive values against each other. Kidder identified four such models: truth-telling versus loyalty to others and institutions; personal needs versus needs of the community; short-term benefits versus long-term negative consequences; and justice versus mercy. When an ethical dilemma pits two core values against each other, a determination should be made whether they are in conflict with one another in this situation. For example, it is important to be loyal to one's supervisor, but not at the risk of presenting biased financial information.

6. *Apply the ethical standards and perspectives.* Consider which ethical principle is most relevant and useful to this specific issue. Is it utilitarianism? Kant's categorical imperative? Justice as fairness? What is the role of virtue? Or, is it a combination of perspectives?

7. *Look for a third way.* Compromise is one way to reveal a new alternative that will resolve the problem or to develop a creative solution. A third way can also be the product of moral imagination. One's conception of the moral and ethical issues can change when considering different perspectives from a moral point of view. We may discover a better, economically viable, and morally justifiable solution.

8. *Make the decision.* At some point we have to make the decision. However, we may be mentally exhausted from wrestling with the problem, get caught up in analysis paralysis, or lack the necessary courage to come to a decision.

9. *Revisit and reflect on the decision.* Return to the decision later, after the issue has been resolved, to debrief. Reflect on the lessons to be learned. How can you apply them to future decisions? What ethical issues did it raise?

Johnson points out that it is not easy to determine who has responsibility for solving a problem, the facts may not be available, or a time constraint prevents gathering all the relevant information, and decisions do not always lead to action. The model seems to equate deciding with doing and, as we saw in our earlier discussion of moral action, we can decide on a course of action but not follow through. Johnson concludes that Kidder is right to say that making ethical choices takes courage. However, it takes even more courage to put the choice into effect.[91]

We believe that a decision-making process in accounting helps to organize one's thoughts about the ethical issues that accounting professionals face and can serve as a basis for analysis in many of the cases in this book. The integrated model explained below draws on Rest's Model and Kidder's Checkpoints to provide a basis for ethical decision making when accounting issues create ethical dilemmas. Consideration is given to moral intensity and how intellectual and instrumental virtues enable ethical action to occur.

The integrated model links to Rest's framework as follows:

Integrated Ethical Decision-Making Process

1. **Identify the ethical and professional issues (ethical sensitivity).**
   - *What are the ethical and professional issues in this case (i.e., GAAP and GAAS)?*
   - *Who are the stakeholders (i.e., investors, creditors, employees, management, the organization)?*
   - *Which ethical/professional standards apply (i.e., AICPA Code Principles, IMA Ethical Standards, and IIA code of ethics)?*

2. **Identify and evaluate alternative courses of action (ethical judgment).**
   - *What legal issues exist?*
   - *What can and cannot be done in resolving the conflict under professional standards?*
   - *Which ethical reasoning methods apply to help reason through alternatives (i.e., rights theory, utilitarianism, justice, and virtue)?*

3. **Reflect on the moral intensity of the situation and virtues that enable ethical action to occur (ethical intent).**
   - *Evaluate the magnitude of the consequences if specific actions are taken; likelihood of those consequences; ability to effect ethical responses by one's actions; consensus view within the profession about the appropriateness of the intended actions.*
   - *Consider whether anyone's rights are at stake and how they manifest in the decision-making process.*
   - *Consider how virtue (i.e., intellectual virtues) motivates ethical actions.*
   - *Evaluate social and organizational pressures and its effect on decision making.*

4. **Take action (ethical behavior).**
   - *Decide on a course of action consistent with one's professional obligations.*
   - *How can virtue (i.e., instrumental virtue) support turning ethical intent into ethical action?*
   - *What steps can I take to strengthen my position and argument?*
   - *How can I counter reasons and rationalizations that mitigate against taking ethical action? Who can I go to for support?*

Reflection would follow after the decision has been made. What was the outcome? How should it affect my approach to ethical decision making? How can I do better in the future?

Application of the Integrated Ethical Decision-Making Model: Ace Manufacturing

In order to illustrate the use of the model, a short case appears in Exhibit 2.4. The facts of the case and ethical issues are analyzed below using the Integrated Model. It is not our intention to cover all points; instead, it is to illustrate the application of the model and consideration of Rest's framework, moral intensity, and the virtues previously discussed and identified in Thorne's study.

EXHIBIT 2.4   Ace Manufacturing

Ace Manufacturing is a privately held company in Anytown, USA. There are three stockholders of the company—Joe Smith, Sue Williams, and Jack Jones. Jones manages the business, including the responsibility for the financial statements. Smith and Williams are in charge of sales and marketing. Each owner has a one-third stake in the business.

Jones recently hired his son, Paul, to manage the office. Paul has limited managerial experience, but his father hopes Paul will take over in a few years when he retires, and this is a good opportunity for Paul to learn the business.

Paul is given complete control over payroll, and he approves disbursements, signs checks, and reconciles the general ledger cash account to the bank statement balance. Previously, the bookkeeper was the only employee with such authority. However, the bookkeeper recently left the company and Jack Jones needed someone he could trust to be in charge of these sensitive operations. He did ask his son to hire someone as soon as possible to help with these and other accounting functions. Paul hired Larry Davis shortly thereafter based on a friend's recommendation. While Davis is relatively inexperienced, he did graduate with honors in Accounting from Anytown University and recently passed all parts of the CPA Exam.

On March 21, one year after hiring Davis, Paul discovered that he needed surgery. Even though the procedure was fairly common and the risks were minimal, Paul planned to take three weeks off after the surgery because of other medical conditions that might complicate the recovery. He told Davis to approve vouchers for payment and present them to his father during the three-week period for payment. Paul had previously discussed this plan with his father, and they both agreed that Davis was ready to assume the additional responsibilities. They did not, however, discuss the matter with either Smith or Williams.

The bank statement for March arrived on April 4. Paul did not tell Davis to reconcile the bank statement. In fact, he specifically told Davis to just put it aside until he returned. But Davis looked at the March statement while trying to trace a payment to a vendor who had billed the company for an invoice that Davis thought had already been paid, which was true. In the course of examining the bank statement, Davis noticed five separate payments to Paul, each for $2,000, during March. He became suspicious because Paul's salary was $3,950 per month. What's more, a check for that amount appeared on the statement.

Curiosity got the better of Davis and he decided to trace the checks paid to Paul to the cash disbursements journal. He looked for supporting documentation but couldn't find any. He noticed that the five checks were coded to different accounts including supplies, travel and entertainment, office expense, and two miscellaneous expenses. He then reviewed the banks statements for January and February and found five separate check payments each month to Paul each for $2,000.

Davis didn't know what to do at this point. He was quite certain there was no business justification for the $30,000 payments to Paul for the first three months of the year and he was concerned that if the same pattern continued unabated for the next three months, the total of $60,000 payments to Paul might threaten the ability of the company to secure a $100,000 loan for working capital.

What would you do if you were in the position of Larry Davis? Use the Integrated Ethical Decision-Making Model to craft your responses.

Ace Manufacturing: Integrated Ethical Decision-Making Process

1. **Identify the ethical and professional issues (ethical sensitivity).**

GAAP

- Appears there may be fraud in the financial statements. Expense accounts were charged for personal withdrawals.

- Financial statements do not fairly present financial position and results of operations due to improper expensing of personal expenditures.
- Taxable income may be similarly misstated.

Stakeholders/Interests

- Owners including Jack Jones
- Paul Jones (son)
- Larry Davis (new accountant/CPA)
- IRS
- Banks that may be approached about the loan
- Smith and Williams were not informed of Davis's increased responsibilities during Paul's recovery.

Ethical/professional standards

- Objectivity: Davis should not permit bias or influence, because of Paul's authority position, to interfere with making the right choice.
- Integrity: Don't subordinate judgment to Paul even though he is your boss.
- Due care: Professional skepticism has been exercised; carry through diligently and insist on supporting evidence for the recorded expenditures.

2. Identify and evaluate alternative courses of action (ethical judgment).

Legal issues

- Lacking evidence to the contrary, GAAP appears to have been violated and the financial statements are fraudulent. Legal liabilities may exist.
- Tax payments will be understated assuming the improper accounting carries over to taxable income.
- Jack Jones (through his son's actions) may have some liability to the other owners.

Alternatives/ethical analysis

- Do nothing: Davis knows about the highly questionable personal withdrawals by Paul. He can't stand idly by and do nothing. That would violate the integrity standard in the AICPA Code.
- Confront Paul and insist on an explanation: (a) allow him to repay the amount if he agrees to do so, (b) insist on adjusting entries, and/or (c) bring the matter to the attention of the owners and let them deal with it.
- Report the matter to Jack Jones—let Paul's dad deal with it: He may pay back the amounts for his son, which sweeps the ethical problem under the rug; he may read the riot act to his son.
- Report the matter to all of the owners without confronting Paul. Possible outcomes: (a) Jack Jones may insist Davis should be fired; (b) The other owners may insist Paul must be fired; (c) Paul's dad makes good on the amount owed to the company by his son's wrongdoing.

Prevailing ethical theories: Rule utilitarianism dictates that certain rules should never be violated (i.e. GAAP) regardless of any utilitarian benefits. Owners have a right to know about Paul's ethical lapse. Davis has an ethical obligation to the owners to make them aware of the situation. Davis has a professional, ethical obligation to avoid subordinating his judgment to Paul and/or his father. Justice requires Paul suffer the consequences of his action. If a different employee submitted improper expenses for reimbursement, that employee would (should be) reported to top management—the owners.

3. **Reflect on the moral intensity of the situation and virtues that enable ethical action to occur (ethical intent).**

- Do I want to be responsible for getting Paul in trouble with his dad, possibly fired? Paul may be prosecuted for his actions. The consequences for Ace are severe so I need to be sure of my decision.

- I want to do the right thing but will my actions do irreparable harm to others? What organizational pressures exist that may influence my decision?

- Can I ever trust Paul again? What he did is wrong and I shouldn't become a party to a cover-up. I need to avoid the slippery slope.

- I am accountable for my actions; I need to maintain my integrity.

- I need to avoid the effects of cognitive dissonance and not act in a manner that is inconsistent with the way I think I should act as an ethical person.

- What are my responsibilities given the company's pending bank loan?

4. **Take action (ethical behavior).**

- I should give Paul an opportunity to explain why he did what he did, out of fairness, but be prepared to approach the owners if his explanation and intended actions are not satisfactory.

- I should insist that steps be taken to correct the accounting and have the courage to stand up for my beliefs.

Giving Voice to Values

LO 2-10

Describe the "Giving Voice to Values" technique and apply it to a case study.

Once I decide what to do and why, I need to assess how best to express myself and be true to my values. I should expect Paul to come up with reasons and rationalizations for what he did. I need to be prepared to counter them using sound judgment. This is where a "Giving Voice to Values" framework comes in handy.

"Giving Voice to Values" (GVV) is a behavioral ethics approach that builds on the traditional philosophical reasoning methods and emphasizes developing the capacity to effectively express one's values to ensure ethical action is taken. There is a need to develop an approach to express one's values in a way that positively influences others by finding the levers to effectively voice and enact one's values.[92] GVV asks the protagonist to think about the arguments others might make that create barriers to expressing one's values and how best to counteract these "reasons and rationalizations."[93]

GVV links to ethical intent and ethical action in Rest's Model. An ethical decision maker should start by committing to expressing his values. The intent is there, but it may fall short of the mark of taking ethical action unless a pathway can be found to effectively express what one believes is the proper course of action in workplace dilemma situations. It is the pathway to that action that GVV addresses.

GVV is used post–decision making; that is, you have already decided what to do and have chosen to voice your values. According to Mary Gentile who developed the GVV methodology, "It shifts the focus away from awareness and analysis to action by addressing a series of questions for protagonists after identifying the right thing to do," including: How can you get it done effectively and efficiently? What do you need to say, to whom, and in what sequence? What will the objections or pushback be and, then, what will you say next? What data and examples do you need to support your point of view?[94]

The underlying theme of GVV is that we can effectively voice values in the workplace if we have the proper tools to do so. GVV relies on developing arguments and action plans and rehearsing how to voice/enact not just any values, but moral values specifically. For our purposes, the six pillars of character and intellectual and instrumental virtues discussed in this and the previous chapter are our target behaviors.

Reasons and Rationalizations

An important part of the GVV methodology is to develop ways to confront barriers we may encounter when value conflicts exist in the workplace. These barriers often appear in the form of "reasons and rationalizations" that can confound our best attempts to fulfill our sense of organizational and personal purpose. These are the objections one might hear from colleagues when attempting to point out an ethical problem in the way things are being done, as Cynthia Cooper experienced in the WorldCom case. Or sometimes you do not hear them because they are the unspoken assumptions of the organization.[95]

GVV provides a framework to deal with the opposing points of view based on the following series of questions.[96]

- What are the main arguments you are trying to counter? That is, what are the *reasons and rationalizations* you need to address?
- What is at *stake* for the key parties, including those who disagree with you?
- What *levers* can you use to influence those who disagree with you?
- What is your most *powerful and persuasive response* to the reasons and rationalizations you need to address? To whom should the argument be made? When and in what context?

Gentile identifies the most frequent categories of argument or rationalization that we face when we speak out against unethical practice.

Expected or Standard Practice: "Everyone does this, so it's really standard practice. It's even expected."

Materiality: "The impact of this action is not material. It doesn't really hurt anyone."

Locus of Responsibility: "This is not my responsibility; I'm just following orders here."

Locus of Loyalty: "I know this isn't quite fair to the customer, but I don't want to hurt my reports/team/boss/company."

An additional argument we include is:

Isolated Incident: "This is a one-time request; you won't be asked to do it again."

Think back to Andy Fastow's "explanation" for why the financial statement amounts were manipulated by Enron and you'll see a good example of a company that readily rationalized its unethical behavior.

Ace Manufacturing: GVV Analysis

We assume that Davis has decided to give Paul a chance to explain why he is receiving $10,000 a month with coding the expenditures to different accounts and no further substantiation. Giving Paul the opportunity to explain enhances the GVV methodology because Davis needs to be prepared to counter the arguments provided by Paul.

Davis needs to find a way to communicate his values powerfully and persuasively in the face of strong countervailing organizational or individuals norms, reasons, and rationalizations. In other words, how can Davis find a way to effectively articulate his point of view so that others can be convinced of its rightness? He may need to find a way not only to counteract Paul's position but that of his dad as well if he provides reasons to go along with what he and Paul decide is best in this situation.

Kohlberg argues that higher moral development requires role-taking ability. Role-taking ability involves understanding the cognitive and affective (i.e., relating to moods, emotions, and attitudes) aspects of another person's point of view. Davis needs to consider how Paul might react, what he might say, and how Davis might counter those statements when he meets with Paul.

We assume Paul and Davis will meet to discuss the matter. Using the GVV framework, what follows is a brief explanation of how such a meeting might go.

What are the main arguments you are trying to counter? That is, what are the reasons and rationalizations you need to address?

These could be addressed from the perspective of Paul trying to convince Davis to remain silent about the apparent misappropriation of company cash. Developing a script, such as the one below, can help Davis get to the next step, which is to understand the full scope of his dilemma, and then develop responses to Paul and other detractors with an opposing view (i.e., his dad) followed by involving other parties that can serve as enablers for his position.

- Davis was told to put bank statements aside and not to do reconciliations.
- The company is privately owned, no one gets hurt by what he did.
- The use of company cash for personal purposes is a common practice in the company because it's not publicly owned. (*Expected or Standard Practice*)
- He needed the money to pay for hospitalization costs.
- The amount of money involved is not significant. (*Materiality*)
- His monthly salary is low for someone in his position; he's not being compensated adequately.
- It was a one-time event and won't happen again. (*Isolated Incident*)
- His dad knows about it and has approved the withdrawals.
- He promises to pay the money back as soon as he gets out of the hospital (no harm, no foul).

What is at stake for the key parties, including those who disagree with you? (Moral intensity issues exist here.)

- Paul's reputation is on the line because he committed a fraud on the company.
- Jack Jones will feel embarrassed for himself and his son if Davis discloses what Paul has done to the other owners.
- The other owners have a right to know what has happened and may feel betrayed if no one discloses the problem.
- Davis may lose his job if he confronts Paul even if he drops the matter later on.
- The ability of the company to secure the $100,000 loan is at stake.
- Davis' reputation for integrity is at stake.

What levers can you use to influence those who disagree with you?

- Davis can ask Paul for supporting documentation to back up the coding of expenses to different accounts; he can share with Paul his analysis of the bank statements. When faced with the evidence, Paul may agree to repay the amount and not do it again.

- Davis can try to convince Paul that his actions are harmful to the company and potentially very embarrassing for his dad; he needs to come forward sooner rather than later and correct the "mistake."
- Davis can try to convince Paul that he needs to look at the long-term effects of taking money from the company that has not been properly authorized, rather than focus on short-term gain such as covering hospital bills. He certainly could have asked his dad to pay for these amounts.
- Davis should try and convince Paul of the dangers of producing financial statements with fraudulent expenses both in terms of the bank loan and taxes.
- Davis can use the leverage of threatening to go to all the owners if Paul doesn't admit the mistake and take corrective action; his loyalty obligation is to the three owners, not just Paul. They are the ones with the most at stake.
- Davis can enlist the help of Smith and Williams to serve as supporters to help counteract the reasons and rationalizations provided by Paul for his actions.
- Davis' reputation is at stake: he cannot violate the ethics of the profession; the accounting is wrong and needs to be corrected; he needs to explain about his ethical obligations as a CPA.

What is your most powerful and persuasive response to the reasons and rationalizations you need to address? To whom should the argument be made? When and in what context?

- Davis should explain to Paul that he was acting diligently when he looked at the bank statements because he didn't want to pay the same vendor twice and needed to see whether the first check had cleared the bank statement. In fact, Davis saved the company money by examining the bank statements and identifying the duplicate request for payment by a vendor.
- He should explain that using company cash for personal purposes is never acceptable unless Paul can demonstrate that the other owners knew about it and approved it.
- He should stress to Paul that taking company funds without offsetting business expenditures is a personal withdrawal, not an operating expense.
- Davis should challenge Paul's statement that his dad knows about it and approved it by suggesting they both go to Jack Jones and discuss the matter; he is calling Paul's bluff. Paul may back off at this point, which confirms the asset misappropriation.
- He should explain to Paul that it is not enough to simply pay the money back. Davis doesn't want to get caught up in a cover-up. He should ask himself: What if Paul persists in his actions even after repaying the $30,000? If he doesn't inform the owners now, Davis could be accused of being part of the problem and dismissed from his job. While this may seem remote at the time, Davis needs to ask himself: How would I feel if the state board of accountancy is contacted?

Role-playing Exercise

The script is developed and now it's time to turn it into a role-playing exercise where key participants can practice voicing their beliefs in a contentious situation.

Assume that Larry Davis calls Paul Jones and they set a 2:00 p.m. meeting on Friday at Paul's home where he is convalescing. The meeting goes like this:

"Paul, how are you feeling?"

"OK, Larry. What's happening at work?"

"That's why I wanted to see you."

"Yeah, why's that?"

"I noticed $10,000 payments to you each month for the first three months of the year. I can't find any supporting documentation for these amounts."

Paul immediately becomes indignant. "I told you not to look at the bank statements. You ignored my orders and disrespected my position. Your job is on the line here."

Davis is taken aback. He hesitates at first but explains about the vendor billing and tells Paul he saved the company $40,000 by detecting the duplicate billing. Paul abruptly says: "Don't you think I would have found this discrepancy?" Davis can tell Paul's anger is growing so he tries to defuse the situation.

"Paul, I may have overstepped my bounds here, and I apologize, but I believe, on balance, that I did the right thing."

Paul starts to get tired and Davis can tell he's stressed out so they agree to meet in Paul's office on Monday when he returns to work.

Paul's final comment is, "Tell no one about this meeting!" Davis returns to the office and starts to reflect on the meeting. He is not sure what to do at this point. He is thinking about his options, including not waiting for the meeting with Paul before acting.

What would you do if you were in Davis's position? You might seek out some advice at this point. Perhaps you have a trusted friend or adviser who can bring a fresh perspective to the situation? *The role-playing exercise might be extended for such a discussion.*

Cognitive issues play a role in what Davis decides to do. He needs to follow a Systems 2 approach, which he has already begun to do, by carefully evaluating the possible consequences of his actions for himself and others. He knows what is the right thing to do and must be certain his actions reflect his beliefs.

Concluding Thoughts

Good intentions are a necessary but insufficient condition to ensure that ethical action occurs. You have learned in the first two chapters that an ethical person knows what the right thing to do is but can struggle doing it. Sometimes biases influence our actions and decisions. At other times, organizational pressures dissuade us from the rightful course. In the end it is a matter of conforming our beliefs with our actions.

Ethical decisions are not made in a vacuum. Pressures exist in the real world of business and accounting; cultures may support or work against ethical behavior; and individuals react differently to the reasons and rationalizations given for not taking the ethical path. Therefore, it is important to understand how best to make your case when faced with an ethical dilemma. You need to learn how to overcome obstacles and effectively deal with those who would distract you from the goal of making the ethical choice and following through with ethical action. This is where the GVV framework is most valuable.

You will face dilemmas in the workplace; all of us do. You may make some mistakes, but in truth the only mistake is not trying to correct wrongdoing. In this chapter we have tried to provide you with the tools to deal with ethical conflicts in the workplace. We've given you a pathway to serve as part of a process for making ethical decisions. Perhaps the least likely person to choose for our final inspirational quote is Kristi Loucks, a sports writer, author, and freelance pastry chef who also covers the National Hockey League team Chicago Blackhawks. Loucks has said, "The road to success is littered with failures, but the lessons learned are crucial in plotting your course to success!"

Discussion Questions

1. Why do you think good people sometimes do bad things? Explain.

2. How do theories about the world, other people, and ourselves influence ethical decision making?

3. On November 21, 2017, a story broke that *New Yorker* reporter Ronan Farrow had alleged that Harvey Weinstein used lengthy nondisclosure agreements attached to hefty monetary settlements to prevent accusers from coming forward with reports of his alleged sexual activities. Do you think it would be right or wrong for someone who alleges Weinstein sexually harassed them to violate the nondisclosure agreement in order to get their story out in the press and potentially help other victims? Explain using ethical reasoning.

4. Back in August 2017, a leaked memo by Google employee James Damore alleged that the company was discriminating in its hiring practices based on race or gender. He claimed that Google was "pressing individual managers to increase diversity" and is "using race or gender" to decide which workers are promoted and with which teams job candidates are placed. Damore made controversial statements like: "Women, on average, have more openness directed towards their feelings and aesthetics rather than ideas. Women generally also have a stronger interest in people rather than things, relative to men . . . These two differences in part explain why women relatively prefer jobs in social or artistic areas. More men like coding because it requires systemizing and even within software engineers, comparatively more women work on the front end, which deals with both people and aesthetics." Google's CEO, Sundar Pichai, criticized the memo that claimed women had biological issues that prevented them from being as successful as men in technology. He said Damore's statements had "crossed the line by advancing harmful gender stereotypes in our workplace."[97] Damore was fired by Google after 3 1/2 years for writing the memo critical of the company's diversity efforts. Evaluate Damore's statements with respect to the discussion in this chapter of equity, diversity, and inclusion.

5. In 2016, an incident of price gouging raised issues similar to those in the Heinz and the Drug discussion in this chapter. Turing Pharmaceuticals purchased the right to the prescription drug Diaprim, a life-saving drug that treats toxoplasmosis, an infection that affects people with compromised immune systems, particularly those with HIV/AIDS and some forms of cancer. Lacking competition for their drug, Turing raised the price from $13.50 per tablet to $750 per tablet, or an increase of 5,000%. The reason given for the increase was to help the company fund its research work on toxoplasmosis, along with new education programs for the disease. Turing's CEO, Martin Shkreli, explained that it was a great business decision that benefited the company's stakeholders. From an ethical perspective, what's wrong with a pharmaceutical company charging whatever price the market will bear?

6. Do you believe all sexual relationships should be forbidden in the workplace? Use ethical reasoning to support your view.

7. How do you assess at what stage of moral development in Kohlberg's model you reason at in making decisions? Do you believe your level of reasoning is consistent with what is expected of an accounting professional? How does the stage you indicate relate to the findings of research studies discussed in this chapter about moral reasoning in accounting?

8. In his research into the components of ethical decision making, Rest raised the following issue: Assuming someone possesses sound moral reasoning skills, "Why would they ever choose the moral alternative, especially if it involves sacrificing some personal value or suffering some hardship? What motivates the selection of moral values over other values?" How does Rest's model deal with such a question? How would you answer it from the point of view of an accounting professional?

9. In the text, we point out that Rest's model is not linear in nature. An individual who demonstrates adequacy in one component may not necessarily be adequate in another, and moral failure can occur when there is a deficiency in any one component. Give an example in accounting when ethical intent may not be sufficient to produce ethical behavior and explain why that is the case.

10. In teaching about moral development, instructors often point out the threefold nature of morality: It depends on emotional development (in the form of the ability to feel guilt or shame), social development (manifested by the recognition of the group and the importance of moral behavior for the group's existence), and cognitive development (especially the ability to adopt another's perspective). How does this perspective of morality relate to ethical reasoning by accountants and auditors?

11. Do you believe that our beliefs trigger our actions, or do we act and then justify our actions by changing our beliefs? Explain.

12. Explain why moral problems may be of greater intensity than nonmoral problems.

13. Michael just graduated with a degree in Accounting from State University. He worked hard in school but could only achieve a 2.95 GPA because he worked 40 hours a week to pay his own way through college. Unfortunately, Michael was unable to get a job because the recruiters all had a 3.0 GPA cut-off point. Michael stayed with his college job for another year but is anxious to start his public accounting career. One day he reads about a job opening with a local CPA firm. The entry-level position pays little but it's a way for Michael to get his foot in the door. However, he knows there will be candidates for the position with a higher GPA than his so he is thinking about using his overall GPA, which was 3.25 including two years of community college studies, rather than his major GPA and the GPA at State, even though the advertisement asks for these two GPAs. Michael asks for your opinion before sending in the résumé. What would you say to Michael and why?

14. In this chapter, we discuss the study by Libby and Thorne of the association between auditors' virtue and professional judgment. The most important virtues identified were truthful, independent, objective, and having integrity. The authors note that the inclusion of these virtues in professional codes of conduct (such as the Principles of the AICPA Code) may account for their perceived importance. Explain how these virtues relate to an auditor's intention to make ethical decisions.

15. You are in charge of the checking account for a small business. One morning, your accounting supervisor enters your office and asks you for a check for $150 for expenses that he tells you he incurred entertaining a client last night. He submits receipts from a restaurant and lounge. Later, your supervisor's girlfriend stops by to pick him up for lunch, and you overhear her telling the receptionist what a great time she had at dinner and dancing with your supervisor the night before. What would you do and why?

16. According to a survey reported by the *Daily Mail* in the United Kingdom, one in eight women has bought expensive clothes, worn them on a night out, and then returned them the next day. Nearly half of those who did confess said they were motivated by money because they couldn't afford to keep the clothes given their current economic condition. But 18% said they did it because they enjoyed the "buzz." Those most likely to do it were 18- to 24-year-olds, 16% of whom admitted to returning worn clothes.[98]

    Assume you are best friends with one such woman. She asks you to go shopping with her for a dress for the Senior Prom. She says the dress will be returned after the prom. What would you do or say to your friend and why? How might you counter the likely reasons and rationalizations she will give for her actions?

17. Sharon is an intern with a local CPA firm. Prior to returning to school, her supervisor goes on sick leave and asks her to do some complicated reconciliation work for him. She is given what seems to her to be an unrealistic deadline. Sharon looks at the workpapers and supporting documentation

and realizes she doesn't have the skills to complete the work without help. She contacts her supervisor who tells her to talk to Holly, a good friend of Sharon and former intern at the firm, for help. Holly returned to school one semester ago. What ethical considerations do you have in this matter? What would you do and why?

18. Identify the ethical issues in each of the following situations and what your ethical obligations are, assuming you are faced with the dilemma.

    a. A consultant for a CPA firm is ordered by her superior to downgrade the ratings of one company's software package being considered for a client and increase the ratings for another company, which is run by the superior's wife. What would you do and why?

    b. A tax accountant is told by his superior to take a position on a tax matter that is not supportable by the facts in order to make the client happy. This is a common practice in the firm and the likelihood of the IRS questioning it is remote. Would you go along with your supervisor?

    c. An auditor for a governmental agency concluded a contractor's accounting system was inadequate; her supervisor changed the opinion to adequate in order to minimize the audit hours on the job and make the process seem more efficient. Would you go above your supervisor in this matter and bring your concerns to high-ups in the agency?

19. One expression in particular seems to sum up why the accounting frauds at companies such as Enron, WorldCom, and HealthSouth were allowed to persist for so long: "If I Do It, I Must Do It Again." Explain what is meant by this statement in the context of ethical decision making.

20. Explain why the process of ethical decision making depends on a number of moral, social, psychological, and organizational factors.

21. Select one of the rationalizations for Enron's actions identified by Andy Fastow in the chapter opening and explain how you would counteract that statement by emphasizing its ethical deficiencies.

22. Windsor and Kavanagh propose in a research study that client management economic pressure is a situation of high moral intensity that sensitizes auditors' emotions and thus motivates their moral reasoning to make deliberative decisions either to resist or accede to client management wishes. Explain how you think such a process might work.

23. Explain how an overconfidence bias might influence an auditor's judgment about the proper balance sheet value of inventory?

24. Explain what you think each of the following statements means in the context of moral development.

    a. How far are you willing to go to do the right thing?

    b. How much are you willing to give up to do what you believe is right?

    c. We may think we would blow the whistle on client wrongdoing but what should we do if firm management tells us to drop the matter?

25. A major theme of this chapter is that our cognitive processes influence ethical decision making. Use the theme to comment on the following statement, which various religions claim as their own and has been attributed to Lao Tzu and, some say, the Dalai Lama:

    "Watch your thoughts; they become your words.

    Watch your words; they become your actions.

    Watch your actions; they become your habits.

    Watch your habits; they become your character.

    Watch your character; it becomes your destiny."

Endnotes

1. Bethany McLean and Peter Elkind, *The Smartest Buys in the Room: The Amazing Rise and Scandalous Fall of Enron* (New York: Penguin Group, 2003).

2. Max Bazerman and Ann E. Tenbrunsel, *Blind Spots: Why We Fail to Do What's Right and What to Do about it* (Princeton, NJ: Princeton University Press, 2011).

3. Martie G. Haselton, Daniel Nettle, and Paul W. Andrews, The Evolution of Cognitive Bias. In. D. M. Buss (Ed.), *The Handbook of Evolutionary Psychology* (Hoboken, NJ: John Wiley & Sons Inc., 2005), pp. 724–746.

4. The Psychology of Enron, https://peopletriggers.wordpress.com/2014/06/29/the-psychology-of-enron/.

5. Julia La Roche, The former CFO of Enron warned a group of execs that large US companies are doing the same things he did, *Business Insider,* April 6, 2016, http://www.businessinsider.com/andy-fastow-talk-2016-4.

6. Richard F. West and Keith Stanovich, "Individual Differences in Reasoning: Implications for the Rationality Debate," *Behavioral & Brain Sciences* (2000), 23, pp. 645–665.

7. Chip Walter, *Last ape standing,* (NY: Bloomsbury, 2013).

8. Leon Festinger, *A Theory of Cognitive Dissonance* (Evanston, IL: Row & Peterson, 1957).

9. Daniel Kahneman and Amos Tversky, "Choices, values and frames,"*American Psychologist,* Volume 39, 1984, pp. 341–350.

10. Amber Walkowiak, "The Wagon to Disaster: Aaron Beam on Fraud in HealthSouth and the Price He Paid," *McCombs TODAY,* April 21, 2010, http://www.today.mccombs.utexas.edu/2010/04/the-wagon-to-disaster-aaron-beam-on-fraud-in-healthsouth-and-the-price-he-paid.

11. Minette Drumwright, Robert Prentice, and Cara Biasucci, "Behavioral Ethics and Teaching Ethical Decision Making," *Decision Sciences,* Vol. 13, No. 3, 2015, pp. 431–458.

12. Jonathan Glover, *Humanity: a moral history of the 20th century,* 2nd ed. (New Haven, CT: Yale University Press, 2012).

13. Cass Sunstein, *Simpler: The future of government.* (NY: Simon & Schuster, 2013).

14. Max H. Bazerman and Ann E. Trebunsel, *Blind Spots.* (Princeton, NJ: Princeton University Press, 2011).

15. Cordelia Fine, *A Mind of Its Own.* (NY: W.W. Norton & Co, 2006).

16. Robert A. Prentice, "Ethical Decision Making: More Needed Than Good Intentions," *Financial Analysts Journal* Vol. 63 No. 6, https://www.cfapubs.org/doi/pdf/10.2469/faj.v63.n6.4923.

17. Mark Matousek, *Ethical Wisdom.* (NY: Anchor Books, 2011).

18. John M. Darley and Daniel Bateson, "From Jerusalem to Jericho": A Study of situational and dispositional variables in helping behavior," *Journal of Personality and Social Psychology,* Vol. 27. No. 1, pp. 100–108.

19. Adam Alter, *Drunk Tank Pink.* (NY: Oxford University Press, 2013.

20. Leon Festinger, *A Theory of Cognitive Dissonance* (Evanston, IL: Row & Peterson, 1957).

21. Penny Tompkins and James Lawley, "Cognitive Dissonance and Creative Tension—The Same or Different?" from presentation at The Developing Group, October 3, 2009, Available at: http://www.cleanlanguage.co.uk/articles/articles/262/0/Cognitive-Dissonance-and-Creative-Tension/Page0.html.

22. Leon Festinger, *A Theory of Cognitive Dissonance* (Evanston, IL: Row & Peterson, 1957).

23. Max H. Bazerman and Francesca Gino, "Behavioral Ethics: Toward a Deeper Understanding of Moral Judgment and Dishonesty," *Annual Review of Law and Social Science* 8 (December 2012), pp. 85–104.

24. Dennis P. Wittmer, "Behavioral Ethics in Business Organizations: What the Research Teaches Us," in *Encyclopedia of Business Ethics and Society,* ed. Robert W. Kolb (NY: Sage Publications, 2008).

25. Wittmer et al.

26. Bazerman et al.

27. David M. Messick and Max H. Bazerman, "Ethical Leadership in the Psychology of Decision Making," *Sloan Management Review, Vol. 37,* 1996, pp. 9–22.

28. Messick et al.

29. Volkswagen emissions scandal – Timeline, December 15, 2015, https://www.theguardian.com/business/2015/dec/10/volkswagen-emissions-scandal-timeline-events.

30. Jack Ewing, Faster, *Higher, Farther: The Volkswagen Scandal,* NY: (W. W. Norton & Co., Inc., 2017.)

31. Ewing et al.

32. Drew Kodjak, "Taking stock of the VW settlement agreement," *The International Council on Clean Transportation,* July 15, 2016, https://www.theicct.org/blogs/staff/taking-stock-vw-settlement-agreement.

33. Karin Matussek, Ex-VW CEO Winterkorn Deflects Blame for Emissions Cheating, *Bloomberg Technology,* January 19, 2017, https://www.bloomberg.com/news/articles/2017-01-19/ex-vw-ceo-winterkorn-defends-tenure-in-first-speech-since-exit.

34. VW Diesel Crisis: Timeline of Events, December 7, 2017, https://www.cars.com/articles/vw-diesel-crisis-timeline-of-events-1420681251993/.

35. VW executive given the maximum prison sentence for his role in Dieselgate, December 6, 2017, https://www.theverge.com/2017/12/6/16743308/volkswagen-oliver-schmidt-sentence-emissions-scandal-prison.

36. Messick and Bazerman.

37. Solomon Asch, Effects of Group Pressure Upon The Modification and Distortion of Judgement. Chapter 5 in Eleanor Maccoby, *Readings in Social Psychology.* (NY: Holt, 1958). A summary and video of the experiment can be found here: http://www.psychologyconcepts.com/solomon-aschs-conformity-study/.

38. Stanley Milgram, "Behavioral Study of Obedience," *Journal of Abnormal and Social Psychology,* 1963, Vol. 67 No.4, pp. 371–378.

39. Robert A. Prentice.

40. Kristy Mathewson, "Whistleblowing and Bystander Apathy: Connecting Ethics with Social Responsibility", The Corporate Social Responsibility Newswire, Posted August 7, 2012, http://www.csrwire.com/blog/posts/494-whistleblowing-and-bystander-apathy-connecting-ethics-with-social-responsibility.

41. U.S. Government Office of Personnel Management, Diversity and Inclusion, https://www.opm.gov/policy-data-oversight/diversity-and-inclusion/.

42. United Nations Department of Economic and Social Affairs, Creating an Inclusive Society: Practical Strategies to Promote Social Integration, 2009, http://www.un.org/esa/socdev/egms/docs/2009/Ghana/inclusive-society.pdf.

43. SGBA e-Learning Resource: Rising to the Challenge, "Distinguish Between Equity and Equality," http://sgba-resource.ca/en/concepts/equity/distinguish-between-equity-and-equality/.

44. 2017 Deloitte Global Human Capital Trends, https://www2.deloitte.com/content/dam/Deloitte/global/Documents/About-Deloitte/central-europe/ce-global-human-capital-trends.pdf.

45. Deloitte, Seventy-Two Percent of Working Americans Surveyed Would or May Consider Leaving an Organization for One They Think is More Inclusive, Deloitte Poll Finds, https://www.prnewswire.com/news-releases/seventy-two-percent-of-working-americans-surveyed-would-or-may-consider-leaving-an-organization-for-one-they-think-is-more-inclusive-deloitte-poll-finds-300469961.html. The well-being pulse survey is available at: https://www2.deloitte.com/us/en/pages/about-deloitte/articles/well-being-survey.html.

46. O.C. Ferrell, John Fraedrich, and Linda Ferrell, *Business Ethics: Decision Making for Personal Integrity & Social Responsibility,* (Boston, MS: Cengage Learning, 2018), p. 3).

47. Susan Fowler, "Reflecting on one very, very strange year at Uber," https://www.susanjfowler.com/blog/2017/2/19/reflecting-on-one-very-strange-year-at-uber.

48. Tom Krisher and Barbara Ortutay, Uber CEO to Take Leave as Board Adopts Sweeping Reforms, https://www.nbcbayarea.com/news/local/Uber-Sexual-Harassment-Review-Released-425727804.html.

49. Seung Lee, Uber investor Shervin Pishevar accused of sexual misconduct, report says, *The Mercury News,* http://www.mercurynews.com/2017/11/30/uber-investor-shervin-pishevar-accused-of-sexual-misconduct-report-says/.

50. Krisher and Ortutay.

51. Lawrence Kohlberg, "Stage and Sequence: The Cognitive Developmental Approach to Socialization," in *Handbook of Socialization Theory and Research,* ed. D. A. Goslin (Chicago: Rand McNally, 1969), pp. 347–480.

52. Rest and Narvaez.

53. Rest et al.

54. Muriel J. Bebeau and S. J. Thoma, "Intermediate Concepts and the Connection to Moral Education," *Educational Psychology Review* 11, no. 4 (1999), p. 345.

55. O. C. Ferrell, John Fraedrich, and Linda Ferrell, *Business Ethics: Ethical Decision Making and Cases* (Mason, OH: South-Western, Cengage Learning, 2009 Update), pp. 162–163.

56. Clare M. Pennino, "Is Decision Style Related to Moral Development Among Managers in the U.S.?" *Journal of Business Ethics* 41 (December 2002), pp. 337–347.

57. William Crain, *Theories of Development: Concepts and Applications,* 6th ed. (Upper Saddle River, NJ, 2010).

58. Milton Snoeyenbos, Robert F. Almeder, and James M. Humber, *Business Ethics, Corporate Values and Society* (Buffalo, NY: Prometheus Books, 1983). pp. 239–264.

59. Lawrence A. Ponemon and David R. L. Gabhart, "Ethical Reasoning Research in the Accounting and Auditing Professions," in *Moral Development in the Professions: Psychology and Applied Ethics,* eds. James R. Rest and Darcia Narvaez, (New York: Psychology Press, 1994), pp. 101–120.

60. Robert A. Prentice.

61. See Michael K. Shaub, "An Analysis of the Association of Traditional Demographic Variables with the Moral Reasoning of Auditing Students and Auditors," *Journal of Accounting Education* (Winter 1994), pp. 1–26; and Lawrence A. Ponemon, "Ethical Reasoning and Selection Socialization in Accounting," *Accounting, Organizations, and Society* 17 (1992), pp. 239–258.

62. David Arnold and Larry Ponemon, "Internal Auditors' Perceptions of Whistle-blowing and the Influence of Moral Reasoning: An Experiment," *Auditing: A Journal of Practice and Theory* (Fall 1991), pp. 1–15.

63. Larry Ponemon and David Gabhart, "Auditor Independence Judgments: A Cognitive Developmental Model and Experimental Evidence," *Contemporary Accounting Research* (1990), pp. 227–251.

64. Larry Ponemon, "Auditor Underreporting of Time and Moral Reasoning: An Experimental-Lab Study," *Contemporary Accounting Research* (1993), pp. 1–29.

65. Ponemon and Gabhart, 1994, p. 108.

66. Plummer, p. 244.

67. Lawrence Kohlberg, *Essays on Moral Development: Vol. II: The Psychology of Moral Development: The Nature and Validity of Moral Stages* (San Francisco: Harper & Row, 1984).

68. Mary Louise Arnold, "Stage, Sequence, and Sequels: Changing Conceptions of Morality, Post-Kohlberg," *Educational Psychology Review,* Vol. 12, No. 4, 2000, p. 365–383.

69. James R. Rest, Darcia Narvaez, Muriel J. Bebeau, and Stephen J. Thoma, *Postconventional Moral Thinking: A Neo-Kohlbergian Approach,* (Mahwah, NJ: Lawrence Erlbaum, 1999).

70. M. L. Arnold, pp. 367–368.

71. John C. Gibbs, "Toward an Integration of Kohlberg's and Hoffman's Moral Development Theories," *Human Development* 34, 1991, pp. 88–104.

72. Richard S. Peters, *Moral Development and Moral Education* (London: George Allen & Unwin, 1982).

73. Augusto Blasi, "Bridging Moral Cognition and Moral Action: A Critical Review of the Literature," *Psychological Bulletin* Vol. 88, No. 1, 1980, pp. 1–45.

74. William Damon and Anne Colby, "Education and Moral Commitment," *Journal of Moral Education,* Vol. 25, No. 1, 1996, pp. 31–37.

75. Craig E. Johnson, *Organizational Ethics: A Practical Approach,* 3rd ed. (NY: Sage Publications, Inc., 2015).

76. Plummer, pp. 242–244.

77. James R. Rest, "Morality," in *Handbook of Child Psychology: Cognitive Development,* Vol. 3, series ed. P. H. Mussen and vol. ed. J. Flavell (New York: Wiley, 1983), pp. 556–629.

78. Lawrence Kohlberg, *The Meaning and Measurement of Moral Development* (Worcester, MA: Clark University Press, 1979).

79. Rest and Narvaez, p. 24.

80. Craig E. Johnson, *Meeting the Ethical Challenges of Leadership* (New York: Sage Publications, 2011).

81. Steven Dellaportas, Beverly Jackling, Philomena Leung, Barry J. Cooper, "Developing an Ethics Education Framework for Accounting," *Journal of Business Ethics Education,* 8, no.1 (2011), pp. 63–82.

82. Thomas Jones, "Ethical Decision Making by Individuals in Organizations: An Issue-Contingent Model," *Academy of Management Review* 16, pp. 366–395.

83. Jones, p. 379.

84. Libby, Theresa, and Linda Thorne. "The Development of a Measure of Auditors' Virtue." *Journal of Business Ethics,* 2007, pp. 89–99., doi:10.1007/s10551-006-9127-0.

85. Libby and Thorne.

86. Libby et al.

87. Libby et al.

88. Mary Beth Armstrong, J. Edward Ketz, and Dwight Owsen, "Ethics Education in Accounting: Moving Toward Ethical Motivation and Ethical Behavior," *Journal of Accounting Education* 21 (2003), pp. 1–16.

89. Manuel Velasquez, Claire Andre, Thomas Shanks, and Michael J. Meyer, "Thinking Ethically: A Framework for Moral Decision Making," Available at: http://www.scu.edu/ethics/practicing/decision/thinking.html#sthash.zMGI3C7i.dpuf.

90. Rushworth M. Kidder, *How Good People Make Tough Choices* (NY: Simon & Schuster, 1995).

91. Johnson, 2011, pp. 249–250.

92. The University of Texas uses a program, "Ethics Unwrapped," to teach GVV to its students. Videos are available on the following Web site: http://ethicsunwrapped.utexas.edu/

93. Materials to teach GVV and cases are available on the GVV Web site: http://www.babson.edu/Academics/teaching-research/gvv/Pages/curriculum.aspx

94. M.C. Gentile, *Giving Voice to Values: How to Speak Your Mind When You Know What's Right.* (New Haven, CT: Yale University Press, 2010).

95. M.C. Gentile et al.

96. M.C. Gentile et al.

97. John Shinal, Fired Google engineer Damore says the company is hiring and promoting workers based on race or gender, *CNBC,* August 14, 2017, https://www.cnbc.com/2017/08/14/fired-google-engineer-james-damore-says-this-.html.

98. Larisa Brown, The women who wear an expensive new dress for a night out - then take it back to the shop the next day, Daily Mail, June 10, 2012, http://www.dailymail.co.uk/femail/article-2157430/How-women-wear-expensive-new-frock-shop.html#ixzz3ea5m2mo.

Chapter 2 Cases

Case 2-1 A Team Player? (a GVV case)

Barbara is working on the audit of a client with a group of five other staff-level employees. After the inventory audit was completed, Diane, a member of the group, asks to meet with the other employees. She points out that she now realizes a deficiency exists in the client's inventory system whereby a small number of items were double counted. The amounts are relatively minor and the rest of the inventory observation went smoothly. Barbara suggests to Diane that they bring the matter to Jessica, the senior in charge of the engagement. Diane does not want to do it because she is the one responsible for the oversight. Three of the other four staff members agree with Diane. Haley is the only one, along with Barbara, who wants to inform Jessica.

After an extended discussion of the matter, the group votes and decides not to inform Jessica. Still, Barbara does not feel right about it. She wonders: What if Jessica finds out another way? What if the deficiency is more serious than Diane has said? What if it portends other problems with the client? She decides to raise all these issues but is rebuked by the others who remind her that the team is already behind on its work and any additional audit procedures would increase the time spent on the audit and make them all look incompetent. They remind Barbara that Jessica is a stickler for keeping to the budget and any overages cannot be billed to the client.

Questions

1. Explain how cognitive shortcomings play a role in Diane's position.

2. Explain what Barbara should do if she reasons at each of the six stages of Kohlberg's model.

3. Assume you are in Barbara's position. What would you do and why? Consider the following in answering the question:

- How can you best express your point of view effectively?

- What do you need to say, to whom, and in what sequence?

- What do you expect the objections or pushback will be and, then, what would you say next?

Case 2-2 FDA Liability Concerns (a GVV case)

Gregory and Alex started a small business based on a secret-recipe salad dressing that got rave reviews. Gregory runs the business end and makes all final operational decisions. Alex runs the creative side of the business.

Alex's salad dressing was a jalapeno vinaigrette that went great with barbeque or burgers. He got many requests for the recipe and a local restaurant asked to use it as the house special, so Alex decided to bottle and market the dressing to the big box stores. Whole Foods and Trader Joe's carried the dressing; sales were increasing every month. As the business grew, Gregory and Alex hired Michael, a college friend and CPA, to be the CFO of the company.

Michael's first suggestion was to do a five-year strategic plan with expanding product lines and taking the company public or selling it within five to seven years. Gregory and Alex weren't sure about wanting to go public and losing control, but expanding the product lines was appealing. Michael also wanted to contain costs and increase profit margins.

At Alex's insistence, they called a meeting with Michael to discuss his plans.

"Michael, we hired you to take care of the accounting and the financial details," Alex said. "We don't understand profit margins. On containing costs, the best ingredients must be used to ensure the quality of the dressing. We must meet all FDA requirements for food safety and containment of food borne bacteria, such as listeria or e. coli, as you develop cost systems."

"Of course," Michael responded. "I will put processes in place to meet the FDA requirements."

At the next quarterly meeting of the officers, Alex wanted an update on the FDA processes and the latest inspection. He was concerned whether Michael understood the importance of full compliance.

"Michael," Alex said, "the FDA inspector and I had a discussion while he was here. He wanted to make sure I understood the processes and the liabilities of the company if foodborne bacteria are traced to our products. Are we doing everything by the book and reserving some liabilities for any future recalls?"

Michael assured Alex and Gregory that everything was being done by the book and the accounting was following standard practices. Over the next 18 months, the FDA inspectors came and Michael reported everything was fine.

After the next inspection, there was some listeria found in the product. The FDA insisted on a recall of batch 57839. Alex wanted to recall all the product to make sure that all batches were safe.

"A total recall is too expensive and would mean that the product could be off the shelves for three to four weeks. It would be hard to regain our shelf advantage and we would lose market share," Michael explained.

Alex seemed irritated and turned to Gregory for support, but he was silent. He then walked over to where Michael was sitting and said, "Michael, nothing is more important than our reputation. Our promise and mission is to provide great-tasting dressing made with the freshest, best, organic products. A total recall will show that we stand by our mission and promise. I know we would have some losses, but don't we have a liability reserve for recall, like a warranty reserve?"

"The reserve will not cover the entire expense of a recall," Michael said. "It will be too expensive to do a total recall and will cause a huge loss for the quarter. In the next six months, we will need to renew a bank loan; a loss will hurt our renewal loan rate and terms. You know I have been working to get the company primed to go public as well."

Alex offered that he didn't care about going public. He didn't start the business to be profitable. Gregory, on the other hand, indicated he thought going public was a great idea and would provide needed funds on a continuous basis.

Alex told Michael that he needed to see all the FDA inspection reports. He asked, "What is the FDA requiring to be done to address the issue of listeria?"

"I'm handling it, Alex," Michael said. "Don't worry about it. Just keep making new salad dressings so that we can stay competitive."

"Well, Michael, just answer what the FDA is asking for."

"Just to sterilize some of our equipment, but it shouldn't be too bad."

"Michael, it's more than that," Alex responded. "The FDA contacted me directly and asked me to meet with them in three days to discuss our plans to meet the FDA requirements and standards. We will be fined for not addressing issues found in prior inspections. I want to see the past inspection reports so I can better understand the scope of the problem."

"Listen, Alex," Michael said. "I just completed a cost–benefit analysis of fixing all the problems identified by the FDA and found the costs outweighed the benefits. We're better off paying whatever fines they impose and move on."

"Michael, I don't care about cost–benefit analysis. I care about my reputation and that of the company. Bring me all the inspection reports tomorrow."

The three of them met the following day. As Alex reviewed the past inspection reports, he realized that he had relied on Michael too much and his assurances that all was well with the FDA. In fact, the FDA had repeatedly noted that more sterilization of the equipment was needed and that storage of the products and ingredients needed additional care. Alex began to wonder whether Michael should stay on with the company. He also was concerned about the fact that Gregory had been largely silent during the discussions. He wondered whether Gregory was putting profits ahead of safety and the reputation of the company.

Questions

Alex knows what the right thing to do is. As Alex prepares for a meeting on the inspection reports the next day, he focuses on influencing the positions of Michael and Gregory, both of whom will be involved in the meeting. Put yourself in Alex's position and answer the following questions.

1. What are the main arguments you are trying to counter? That is, what are the reasons and rationalizations you need to address?
2. What is at stake for the key parties, including those who disagree with you?
3. What levers can you use to influence those who disagree with you?
4. What is your most powerful and persuasive response to the reasons and rationalizations you need to address? To whom should the argument be made? When and in what context?

Case 2-3 Taxes and the Cannabis Business (a GVV case)

Hailey Declaire, a CPA, just sent the tax return that she prepared for a client in the marijuana growing and distribution business, Weeds 'R' Us, to Harry Smokes the manager of the tax department. Harry had just fielded a phone call from the president of Weeds 'R' Us who gave him an ear full because Hailey insisted on reporting all of the cash sales from the marijuana business on the 2019 tax return. Hailey arrives at Harry's office and the following conversation ensues.

"Hailey, come in," Harry said.

"Thank you, Harry," Hailey responded.

"Do you know why I asked to see you?"

"I'm not sure. Does it have something to do with the tax return for Weeds 'R' Us?" asked Hailey.

"That's right," answered Harry.

"Is there a problem?" Hailey asked.

Harry answered: "I just spoke with the company's president. He said you insisted on reporting 100% of the cash sales from the marijuana business. He's upset. He wants to hold back 25% of that amount and figures no one will be the wiser because marijuana is a cash business. The company can't get a bank account in the state because, even though the cannabis business is legal in the state, it still is prohibited under federal law under the Controlled Substances Act."

"Why would we risk our reputation by going along with the client's position?" Hailey asked.

"It's not that simple," Harry responded. "The client needs an audit report under state regulations. We have been pushing hard to get that business. It's lucrative and may open the door to even more services including personal financial planning."

Harry knew he could simply change the tax return and submit it for the client. However, he wanted Hailey to get onboard because the firm intended to go after other clients in the marijuana business. So, Harry asked Hailey to meet with him and the partner in charge of the tax practice first thing on Monday morning. Hailey says she'll be there and returns to her office.

Questions

Assume you are in Hailey's position and answer the following questions.

1. Explain how social and organizational pressures might influence your position at Monday's meeting.

2. What role might cognitive dissonance play in developing your position?

3. Think of your response in the context of developing a script and consider the following:

   • What are the main arguments you are trying to counter? That is, what are the reasons and rationalizations you need to address?

   • What is at stake for the key parties?

   • What levers can you use to influence those who disagree with you?

   • What is your most powerful and persuasive response to the reasons and rationalizations you need to address? To whom should the argument be made? When and in what context?

Case 2-4 A Faulty Budget (a GVV Case)

Jackson Daniels graduated from Lynchberg State College two years ago. Since graduating from college, he has worked in the accounting department of Lynchberg Manufacturing. Lynchberg is publicly-owned with an eleven-member board of directors.

Daniels was recently asked to prepare a sales budget for the year 2019. He conducted a thorough analysis and came out with projected sales of 250,000 units of product. That represents a 25% increase over 2018.

Daniels went to lunch with his best friend, Jonathan Walker, to celebrate the completion of his first solo job. Walker noticed Daniels seemed very distant. He asked what the matter was. Daniels stroked his chin, ran his hand through his bushy, black hair, took another drink of scotch, and looked straight into the eyes of his friend of 20 years. "Jon, I think I made a mistake with the budget."

"What do you mean?" Walker answered.

"You know how we developed a new process to manufacture soaking tanks to keep the ingredients fresh?"

"Yes," Walker answered.

"Well, I projected twice the level of sales for that product than will likely occur."

"Are you sure?" Walker asked.

"I checked my numbers. I'm sure. It was just a mistake on my part."

Walker asked Daniels what he planned to do about it.

"I think I should report it to Pete. He's the one who acted on the numbers to hire additional workers to produce the soaking tanks," Daniels said.

"Wait a second, Jack. How do you know there won't be extra demand for the product? You and I both know demand is a tricky number to project, especially when a new product comes on the market. Why don't you sit back and wait to see what happens?"

"Jon, I owe it to Pete to be honest. He was responsible for my hire."

"You know Pete is always pressuring us to 'make the numbers.' Also, Pete has a zero tolerance for employees who make mistakes. That's why it's standard practice around here to sweep things under the rug. Besides, it's a one-time event—right?"

"But what happens if I'm right and the sales numbers were wrong? What happens if the demand does not increase beyond what I now know to be the correct projected level?"

"Well, you can tell Pete about it at that time. Why raise a red flag now when there may be no need?"

As the lunch comes to a conclusion, Walker pulls Daniels aside and says, "Jack, this could mean your job. If I were in your position, I'd protect my own interests first."

Jimmy (Pete) Beam is the vice president of production. Jackson Daniels had referred to him in his conversation with Jonathan Walker. After several days of reflection on his friend's comments, Daniels decided to approach Pete and tell him about the mistake. He knew there might be consequences, but his sense of right and wrong ruled the day. What transpired next surprised Daniels.

"Come in, Jack" Pete said.

"Thanks, Pete. I asked to see you on a sensitive matter."

"I'm listening."

"There is no easy way to say this so I'll just tell you the truth. I made a mistake in my sales budget. The projected increase of 25% was wrong. I checked my numbers and it should have been 12.5%. I'm deeply sorry, want to correct the error, and promise never to do it again."

Pete's face became beet red. He said, "Jack, you know I hired 20 new people based on your budget."

"Yes, I know."

"That means ten have to be laid off or fired. They won't be happy and once word filters through the company, other employees may wonder if they are next."

"I hadn't thought about it that way."

"Well, you should have." Here's what we are going to do . . . and this is between you and me. Don't tell anyone about this conversation."

"You mean not even tell my boss?"

"No," Pete said. "JB can't know about it because he's all about correcting errors and moving on. Look, Jack, it's my reputation at stake here as well."

Daniels hesitated but reluctantly agreed not to tell the controller, JB, his boss. The meeting ended with Daniels feeling sick to his stomach and guilty for not taking any action.

Questions

1. What are Daniels's options in this situation? Use ethical reasoning to identify the best alternative. What would you do if you were in Daniels' position?

   Assume that you have decided to take some action, based on the ethical analysis, even though you had agreed not to do so. Consider the following in deciding what your next step should be.

2. What is at stake for the key parties?

3. Based on your chosen action, develop a list of the main arguments you are likely to encounter in making the strongest case possible to the relevant stakeholders?

4. What is your most powerful and persuasive response to the reasons and rationalizations you may need to address? To whom should the argument be made? When and in what context?

Case 2-5 Gateway Hospital

Troy just returned from a business trip for health-care administrators in Orlando. Kristen, a relatively new employee who reports to him, also attended the conference. They both work for Gateway Hospital, a for-profit hospital in the St. Louis area. The Orlando conference included training in the newest reporting requirements in the health-care industry, networking with other hospital administrators, reports on upcoming legislation in health care, and the current status of regulations related to the Affordable Care Act. The conference was in late March and coincided with Troy's kids' spring break, so the entire family traveled to Orlando to check out Walt Disney World and SeaWorld.

The hospital's expense reimbursement policy is very clear on the need for receipts for all reimbursements. Meals are covered for those not provided as part of the conference registration fee, but only within a preset range. Troy has never had a problem following those guidelines. However, the trip to Orlando was more expensive than Troy expected. He did not attend all sessions of the conference in order to enjoy time with his family. Upon their return to St. Louis, Troy's wife suggested that Troy submit three meals and one extra night at the hotel as business expenses, even though they were personal expenses. Her rationale was that the hospital policies would not totally cover the business costs of the trip. Troy often has to travel and misses family time that cannot be recovered or replaced. Troy also knows that his boss has a reputation of signing forms without reading or careful examination. He realizes the amount involved is not material and probably won't be detected.

Kristen is approached by Joyce, the head of the accounting department, about Troy's expenses, which seem high and not quite right. Kristen is asked about the extra night because she did not ask for reimbursement for that time. Kristen knows it can be easily explained by saying Troy had to stay an extra day for additional meetings, a common occurrence for administrators, although that was not the case. She also knows that the hospital has poor controls and a culture of "not rocking the boat," and that other employees have routinely inflated expense reports in the past.

Assume you, as Kristen, have decided the best approach, at least in the short run, is to put off responding to Joyce so that you can consider the matter further.

Questions

1. Should you discuss the matter first with Troy before responding to Joyce? Explain.

2. Assume Kristen is a Certified Management Accountant and member of the Institute of Management Accountants. As such, she falls under The IMA Statement of Ethical and Professional Practice. Discuss how these ethical provisions should affect what Kristen decides to do in the context of the Integrated Ethical Decision-Making Process.

3. Apply each of the four steps of the Integrated Ethical Decision-Making Process to help you decide what your course of action should be.

Case 2-6 The Normalization of Unethical Behavior: The Harvey Weinstein Case

On October 5, 2017, New York Times investigative reporters Jodi Kantor and Megan Twohey broke the story 'Harvey Weinstein Paid Off Sexual Harassment Accusers for Decades.'[1] Harvey Weinstein was one of the most powerful and influential movie executives in Hollywood. Weinstein co-founded both the Weinstein Company and

---

[1] Jodi Kantor and Megan Twohey, Harvey Weinstein Paid Off Sexual Harassment Accusers for Decades. *New York Times* October 5, 2017: https://www.nytimes.com/2017/10/05/us/harvey-weinstein-harassment-allegations.html.

Miramax Films. His movies have garnered over 300 Oscar nominations. Ronan Farrow suggests in his article, 'From Aggressive Overtures To Sexual Assault: Harvey Weintein's Accusers Tell Their Stories,' that Weinstein has been publicly thanked at award ceremonies more than anyone else in movie history (with the exception of Steven Spielberg and God).[2] The allegations against Weinstein span three decades and range from sexual harassment to sexual assault and rape.

Kantor's and Twohey's report found at least eight women in which Weinstein entered into settlement agreements with to presumably keep from pursuing any further legal action against him. The release of this article resulted in a flood of women coming forward and telling their stories regarding similar encounters with Weinstein. It also led to the resignation of four of the Weinstein Companies Board members and the firing of Weinstein himself. NPR interviewed Kantor and Twohey about their investigation of Weinstein and is available via podcast.[3]

On October 10, 2017, The New Yorker published Farrow's article, which corroborates what is in the report of Kantor and Twohey with three of the thirteen women he interviewed accusing Weinstein of rape. As with the Kantor and Twohey article, Farrow suggests that Weinstein's exploits were common knowledge throughout the entertainment industry. They point toward a systemic problem in the industry where people turned a blind eye to what was happening and even normalized this behavior in their responses to it. In fact, Seth MacFarlane while announcing the Best Supporting Actress Nomination's at the 2013 Oscars joked "Congratulations, you five ladies no longer have to pretend to be attracted to Harvey Weinstein."[4]

One of the first women to be interviewed was Ashley Judd. The actress was interviewed by ABC News' Diane Sawyer about her experiences. She expressed regret that she didn't come forward sooner about her allegations of sexual harassment in a hotel room years ago from Weinstein. In the segment that first aired on ABC's "Good Morning America," Judd said she wished she had a "magic wand" that would allow her to change the past, for her and others. "I wish I could prevent it for anyone, always." Judd did tell her parents and other people in Hollywood, including agents and actors, but didn't think she would be believed by going public. "Who was I to tell," she said. "I knew it was disgusting. Was I going to tell the concierge who sent me up to the room?"[5]

Emboldened by what had become a scandal of epic proportions in the entertainment industry, dozens of women started to speak out and tell their story. It motivated actress Alyssa Milano to tweet a call-out to victims "so we might give people a sense of the magnitude of the problem." The hashtag #MeToo caught fire and became the rallying cry for all women similarly abused.

The bravery exhibited by these women empowered other women throughout the entertainment industry, media, and politics to step forward and finally tell their stories about gender sexual harassment, bullying, and rape. Time magazine named these brave women the 2017 Person(s) of the Year "Silence Breakers – the voices that launched a movement." Over the rest of 2017, we witnessed an unprecedented number of men being accused of and fired or being forced to resign because of sexual harassment allegations. These include the firing of CBS Good Morning America's host Charlie Rose, NBC's News Anchor Matt Lauer, PBS's Tavis Smiley, and a host of other high-profile media figures. Congress had its own problems with the resignation of Rep. John Conyers Jr. (D-MI.) and Senator Al Franken (D-MN).

---

[2]Ronan Farow, From Aggressive Overtures To Sexual Assault: Harvey Weinstein's Accusers Tell Their Stories. *The New Yorker,* October 10, 2017: https://www.newyorker.com/news/news-desk/from-aggressive-overtures-to-sexual-assault-harvey-weinsteins-accusers-tell-their-stories.

[3]https://www.npr.org/2017/11/15/564310240/times-reporters-describe-how-a-paper-trail-helped-break-the-weinstein-story.

[4]Ashley Lee, Seth MacFarlane Explains 2013 Oscars Jab at "Abhorrent, Indefensible" Harvey Weinstein, *The Hollywood Reporter,* October 11, 2017, https://www.hollywoodreporter.com/news/seth-macfarlane-explains-harvey-weinstein-at-2013-oscars-jab-1047829.

[5]Cynthia Littleton, Ashley Judd Gives First TV Interview on Harvey Weinstein: 'I Had No Warning.', October 26, 2017, http://variety.com/2017/biz/news/ashley-judd-harvey-weinstein-good-morning-america-diane-sawyer-1202599726/.

Questions

1. Why do you think this type of behavior was allowed to go on for nearly thirty years?

2. What biases do you think may have played a role in the decisions made by both victims and others who were aware of Weinstein's crimes but did nothing?

3. What responsibility did the Weinstein board of directors have to the victims? What about agents who continued to send their clients to meetings with him? What about the Screen Actors Guild-American Federation of Television and Radio Artists (SAG-AFTRA) that claims to have a zero-tolerance policy on sexual harassment?

4 Is it fair to judge a person on his/her worst act after a lifetime of seemingly doing good things?

Case 2-7 Milton Manufacturing Company

Milton Manufacturing Company produces a variety of textiles for distribution to wholesale manufacturers of clothing products. The company's primary operations are located in Long Island City, New York, with branch factories and warehouses in several surrounding cities. Milton Manufacturing is a closely held company, and Irv Milton is the president. He started the business in 2008, and it grew in revenue from $500,000 to $5 million in 10 years. However, the revenues declined to $4.5 million in 2018. Net cash flows from all activities also were declining. The company was concerned because it planned to borrow $20 million from the credit markets in the fourth quarter of 2019.

Irv Milton met with Ann Plotkin, the chief accounting officer (and also a CPA), on January 15, 2019, to discuss a proposal by Plotkin to control cash outflows. He was not overly concerned about the recent decline in net cash flows from operating activities because these amounts were expected to increase in 2019 as a result of projected higher levels of revenue and cash collections. However, that was not Plotkin's view.

Plotkin knew that if overall negative capital expenditures continued to increase at the rate of 40% per year, Milton Manufacturing probably would not be able to borrow the $20 million. Therefore, she suggested establishing a new policy to be instituted on a temporary basis. Each plant's capital expenditures for 2019 for investing activities would be limited to the level of those capital expenditures in 2017, the last year of an overall positive cash flow. Operating activity cash flows had no such restrictions. Irv Milton pointedly asked Plotkin about the possible negative effects of such a policy, but in the end, he was convinced that it was necessary to initiate the policy immediately to stem the tide of increases in capital expenditures. A summary of cash flows appears in Exhibit 1.

Sammie Markowicz is the plant manager at the headquarters in Long Island City. He was informed of the new capital expenditure policy by Ira Sugofsky, the vice president for operations. Markowicz told Sugofsky that the new policy could negatively affect plant operations because certain machinery and equipment, essential to the production process, had been breaking down more frequently during the past two years. The problem was primarily with the motors. New and better models with more efficient motors had been developed by an overseas supplier. These were expected to be available by April 2019. Markowicz planned to order 1,000 of these new motors for the Long Island City operation, and he expected that other plant managers would do the same. Sugofsky told Markowicz to delay the acquisition of new motors for one year, after which time the restrictive capital expenditure policy would be lifted. Markowicz reluctantly agreed.

Milton Manufacturing operated profitably during the first six months of 2019. Net cash inflows from operating activities exceeded outflows by $1,250,000 during this time period. It was the first time in two years that there was a positive cash flow from operating activities. Production operations accelerated during the third quarter as a result of increased demand for Milton's textiles. An aggressive advertising campaign initiated in late 2018 seemed to bear fruit for the company. Unfortunately, the increased level of production put pressure on the machines, and the degree of breakdown was increasing. A big problem was that the motors wore out prematurely.

EXHIBIT 1   Milton Manufacturing Company

	Summary of Cash Flows **For the Years Ended December 31, 2018 and 2017 (000 omitted)**	
	December 31, 2018	**December 31, 2017**
Cash Flows from Operating Activities		
Net income	$ 372	$ 542
Adjustments to reconcile net income to net cash provided by operating activities	(2,350)	(2,383)
Net cash provided by operating activities	$(1,978)	$ (1,841)
Cash Flows from Investing Activities		
Capital expenditures	$(1,420)	$ (1,918)
Other investing inflows (outflows)	176	84
Net cash used in investing activities	$(1,244)	$ (1,834)
Cash Flows from Financing Activities		
Net cash provided (used in) financing activities	$ 168	$ 1,476
Increase (decrease) in cash and cash equivalents	$(3,054)	$ (2,199)
Cash and cash equivalents—beginning of the year	$ 3,191	$ 5,390
Cash and cash equivalents—end of the year	$ 147	$ 3,191

Markowicz was concerned about the machine breakdown and increasing delays in meeting customer demands for the shipment of the textile products. He met with the other branch plant managers, who complained bitterly to him about not being able to spend the money to acquire new motors. Markowicz was very sensitive to their needs. He informed them that the company's regular supplier had recently announced a 25% price increase for the motors. Other suppliers followed suit, and Markowicz saw no choice but to buy the motors from the overseas supplier. That supplier's price was lower, and the quality of the motors would significantly enhance the machines' operating efficiency. However, the company's restrictions on capital expenditures stood in the way of making the purchase.

Markowicz approached Sugofsky and told him about the machine breakdowns and the concerns of other plant managers. Sugofsky seemed indifferent but reminded Markowicz of the capital expenditure restrictions in place and that the Long Island City plant was committed to keeping expenditures at the same level as it had in 2017. Markowicz argued that he was faced with an unusual situation and he had to act now. Sugofsky hurriedly left, but not before he said to Markowicz, "You and I may not agree with it, but a policy is a policy."

Markowicz reflected on his obligations to Milton Manufacturing. He was conflicted because he viewed his primary responsibility and that of the other plant managers to ensure that the production process operated smoothly. The last thing the workers needed right now was a stoppage of production because of machine failure.

At this time, Markowicz learned of a 30-day promotional price offered by the overseas supplier to gain new customers by lowering the price for all motors by 25%. Coupled with the 25% increase in price by the company's supplier, Markowicz knew he could save the company $1,500, or 50% of cost, on each motor purchased from the overseas supplier.

After carefully considering the implications of his intended action, Markowicz contacted the other plant managers and informed them that, while they were not obligated to follow his lead because of the capital expenditure policy, he planned to purchase 1,000 motors from the overseas supplier for the headquarters plant in Long Island City.

Markowicz made the purchase at the beginning of the fourth quarter of 2019 without informing Sugofsky. He convinced the plant accountant to record the $1.5 million expenditure as an operating (not capital) expenditure because he knew that the higher level of operating cash inflows resulting from increased revenues would mask the effect of his expenditure. In fact, Markowicz was proud that he had "saved" the company $1.5 million, and he did what was necessary to ensure that the Long Island City plant continued to operate.

The acquisitions by Markowicz and the other plant managers enabled the company to keep up with the growing demand for textiles, and the company finished the year with record high levels of profit and net cash inflows from all activities. Markowicz was lauded by his team for his leadership. The company successfully executed a loan agreement with Second Bankers Hours & Trust Co. The $20 million borrowed was received on October 3, 2019.

During the course of an internal audit of the 2019 financial statements, Beverly Wald, the chief internal auditor (and also a CPA), discovered that there was an unusually high number of motors in inventory. A complete check of the inventory determined that $1 million worth of motors remained on hand.

Wald reported her findings to Ann Plotkin, and together they went to see Irv Milton. After being informed of the situation, Milton called in Sugofsky. When Wald told him about her findings, Sugofsky's face turned beet red. He told Wald that he had instructed Markowicz *not* to make the purchase. He also inquired about the accounting since Wald had said it was wrong.

Wald explained to Sugofsky that the $1 million should be accounted for as inventory, not as an operating cash outflow: "What we do in this case is transfer the motors out of inventory and into the machinery account once they are placed into operation because, according to the documentation, the motors added significant value to the asset."

Sugofsky had a perplexed look on his face. Finally, Irv Milton took control of the accounting lesson by asking, "What's the difference? Isn't the main issue that Markowicz did not follow company policy?" The three officers in the room nodded their heads simultaneously, perhaps in gratitude for being saved the additional lecturing. Milton then said he wanted Wald and Plotkin to discuss the alternatives on how best to deal with the Markowicz situation and present the choices to him in one week.

Questions

Use the Integrated Ethical Decision-Making Process to guide you in answering the following:

1. Identify the ethical and professional issues of concern to Beverly Wald and Ann Plotkin.
2. Identify and evaluate alternative courses of action using ethical reasoning.
3. Explain how the moral intensity of the situation might influence ethical action.
4. Decide on a course of action to present to Milton. Why did you select that alternative?

Case 2-8 Juggyfroot (a GVV case)

"I'm sorry, Lucy. That's the client's position," Ricardo said.

"I just don't know if I can go along with it, Ricardo," Lucy replied.

"I know. I agree with you. But, Juggyfroot is our biggest client, Lucy. They've warned us that they will put the engagement up for bid if we refuse to go along with the reclassification of marketable securities," Ricardo explained.

"Have you spoken to Fred and Ethel about this?" Lucy asked.

"They recommended giving in to the client on this matter," Ricardo responded.

"Listen," Lucy said. "I understand the pressures of being an engagement partner and the need to keep the client happy, but this goes too far."

The previous scene took place in the office of Deziloo LLP, a large CPA firm in Beverly Hills, California. Lucy is the manager of the engagement of Juggyfroot, a publicly owned global manufacturer of pots and pans and other household items. Ricardo is the managing partner of the office. Fred and Ethel are the engagement review partners that make final judgments on difficult accounting issues, especially when there is a difference of opinion with the client. All four are CPAs.

Ricardo is preparing for a meeting with Norman Baitz, the CEO of Juggyfroot. Ricardo knows that the company expects to borrow $5 million next quarter and it wants to put the best possible face on its financial statements to impress the banks. That would explain why the company reclassified a $2 million market loss on a trading investment to the available-for-sale category so that the "loss" would now show up in stockholder's equity, not as a charge against current income. The result was to increase earnings in 2018 by 8%. Ricardo knows that without the change, the earnings would have declined by 2% and the company's stock price would have taken a hit.

In the meeting, Ricardo decides to overlook the recommendation by Fred and Ethel. He felt Lucy made valid points. Ricardo points out to Baitz that the investment in question was marketable, and in the past, the company had sold similar investments in less than one year. Ricardo adds there is no justification under GAAP to change the classification from trading to available-for-sale.

What happened next shocked Ricardo back to reality. The conversation between Baitz and Ricardo went this way.

"I hate to bring it up, Ricardo, but do you recall what happened last year at about the same time?"

"What do you mean?"

"You agreed that we could record $1 million as revenue for 2017 based on a sale of our product that we held at an off-site distribution warehouse until the client asked for delivery, which occurred in 2018."

Ricardo remembered all too well. It almost cost the firm the Juggyfroot account. "Are you going to throw that in my face?"

"No, Ricardo. Just a gentle reminder that you had agreed to go along with what we had asked at that time. We believe there is enough gray area to do the same here. Who knows. We may hold on to the investment for more than one year."

The meeting broke up when Baitz received a confidential phone call. They agreed to continue it first thing in the morning. Baitz's parting words were "we value loyalty in our accountants."

Questions

1. Explain how incrementalism might influence Ricardo's position with respect to the not so subtle statement by Norman Baitz.

2. Assume you are in Ricardo's position and preparing for the meeting with Baitz in the morning. Consider the following in crafting a response to Baitz.

   • What are the main arguments you are trying to counter?

   • What is at stake for the key parties?

   • What levers can you use to influence Baitz?

   • What is your most powerful response to the reasons and rationalizations you need to address? To whom should the argument be made? When and in what context?

Case 2-9 Racially Charged Language Inhibits Inclusive Cultures

Leaving home for the first time and going off to college is an exciting and stressful time for tens of thousands of students across the U.S. each year. Leaving the familiarity of family, friends, and community behind and entering an often much more diverse community filled with people with different social, political, religious, racial, national, and sexual orientation backgrounds can create challenges. Luckily, there is currently an effort across the United States to reduce the impact of potential biases by educating people on and promoting the benefits of having diversity in communities, businesses, schools, and social groups people belong to. These efforts are more commonly known as Equity, Diversity, and Inclusion (EDI) Initiatives. One example of a college that seems to have it right with respect to EDI policies is the University of Wisconsin, Eau Claire. A brief review of those policies and programs appear in Exhibit 1.

EXHIBIT 1   Equity, Diversity, and Inclusion Policies and Programs at UWEC

Faculty and staff at the University of Wisconsin, Eau Claire (UWEC) have incorporated EDI initiatives into their core mission. The core mission is to create an inclusive community where all students thrive and find the programs and support needed to reach their full potential. Too often, members of underrepresented groups feel alienated and/or are unconsciously or consciously discriminated against resulting in them transferring schools or dropping out completely.

To operationalize this mission, the faculty, staff, and administration came together setting goals surrounding student enrollment and retainment specifically for underrepresented groups. The faculty have common language surrounding EDI within all course syllabi and encourage all their students to help make the classroom environment more welcoming and inclusive to all. They have all agreed to participate in EDI initiatives in some way and to have that participation be a part of their annual performance review. In 2017, they created the first office of EDI and hired an Assistant Chancellor of Equity, Diversity, and Inclusion to lead the effort.

UWEC has also developed a 12-week training program called Circles of Change to start an open in-person dialogue about race throughout the region the university is located within. Launched as a pilot in the Spring of 2017, the fall of 2017 had more than 120 people participating in Circles of Change action groups, gathering weekly to discuss race relations on campus and in the community. "The goal is to help make the Chippewa Valley a more welcoming place for everyone."

As discussed in Chapter 2, some people have unconscious biases and stereotypical beliefs that can lead to making poor decisions. This can be magnified by instances of bias on college campuses. Many colleges and universities across the country have implemented freshman orientation programs to help students transition into college life and to make them feel welcome.

There is a need for diversity and inclusivity training. During 2017, there were many reported instances of racial bias through the use of racial slurs on college and university campuses. Many were reported during the September to December 2017 period, magnifying the growing need for EDI programs on campus. The following examples were chosen not only to illustrate the hateful speech but to describe admirable responses by the universities affected.

1. At Eastern Michigan University, racial fliers promoting a white supremacist organization were found posted on several buildings. Officials removed them because they ran counter to the school's values. According to a spokesperson, "The fliers and the hateful, racist causes they promote run completely counter to Eastern's core values of diversity, inclusiveness and respect."[1]

2. At Cabrini University in Radnor, PA, a number of instances were reported of the words "N-word go away" written on the dormitory room door of a female black student and a second occurrence stating "go away too" just a

---

[1]https://www.freep.com/story/news/2017/09/07/racist-fliers-found-removed-eastern-michigan-university/644473001/.

few days later. The reaction of the university was: "As we ensure a thorough investigation into the incident, we want to remind everyone that hate has no home on our campus — hate speech of any kind goes against who we are as an institution and as a diverse community of learners."[2]

3. A few racial incidents occurred between October and December 2017 at Framingham State University in Framingham, MA. In one such incident, a flyer defaced with racially offensive writing was found under an African-American student's door. The President of the University responded: "Framingham State University draws strength from its diversity. We are an institution where individuals of differing cultures, perspectives, and experiences are welcomed, respected, valued and supported. In response to recent events, we must not allow those with hate in their hearts to divide us. The best way to stand up to this type of vile behavior is by uniting as a community against it."[3]

4. Flyers containing a racist slogan and anti-African-American imagery were found at the University of Texas at Austin. The flyers depict a racist caricature of a black man holding a knife and bear the words "Around blacks . . . never relax." The University was quick to condemn such hatred and pointed to their new Hate and Bias Policy that addresses such issues.[4]

A good illustration of a proactive response to incidents of hatred occurred at the University of Hartford in West Hartford, CT. In response to an incident of racial harassment and bullying, Gregory Woodward, president of the University, stated that "the harsh reality is that racism in America is part of our reality. It is here on our campus and on campuses across the country. We are a reflection of the society at large. It is disturbing and inexcusable, and needs our constant attention and vigilance. We must all speak up, speak out, and be relentless in our pursuit of a more inclusive environment for our students. Acts of racism, bias, or other abusive behaviors will not be tolerated in any way, shape, or form on this campus."[5]

Questions

1. Identify which biases and/or stereotypes might exacerbate the type of behavior described in this case.

2. What responsibility does a college or university have in ensuring all students feel safe and welcome at their institutions? Answer this question using Rights Theory and theories of Justice.

3. Why is it important for EDI policies to be implemented in the workplace? Refer to the Deloitte surveys in answering this question.

Case 2-10 WorldCom

The WorldCom fraud was the largest in U.S. history, surpassing even that of Enron. Beginning modestly during mid-year 1999 and continuing at an accelerated pace through May 2002, the company—under the direction of Bernie Ebbers, the CEO; Scott Sullivan, the CFO; David Myers, the controller; and Buford Yates, the director of accounting—"cooked the books" to the tune of about $11 billion of misstated earnings. Investors collectively lost $30 billion as a result of the fraud.

[2]http://www.phillytrib.com/news/racial-epithets-reported-at-cabrini-university/article_6e46de74-2f6c-5813-bae5-cfe0553955ad.html.

[3]https://www.framingham.edu/the-fsu-difference/inclusive-excellence/bias-education-response-team/racism-response.

[4]http://www.statesman.com/news/local/updated-racist-flyers-found-say-around-blacks-never-relax/J0sDeYiBgauXj7oS3pWyUP/.

[5]http://wtnh.com/2017/11/01/pd-university-of-hartford-student-arrested-for-bullying-roommate/.

The fraud was accomplished primarily in two ways:

1. Booking "line costs" for interconnectivity with other telecommunications companies as capital expenditures rather than operating expenses.

2. Inflating revenues with bogus accounting entries from "corporate unallocated revenue accounts."

During 2002, Cynthia Cooper, the vice president of internal auditing, responded to a tip about improper accounting by having her team do an exhaustive hunt for the improperly recorded line costs that were also known as "prepaid capacity." That name was designed to mask the true nature of the costs and treat them as capitalizable costs rather than as operating expenses. The team worked tirelessly, often at night and secretly, to investigate and reveal $3.8 billion worth of fraud.

Soon thereafter, Cooper notified the company's audit committee and board of directors of the fraud. The initial response was not to take action, but to look for explanations from Sullivan. Over time, Cooper realized that she needed to be persistent and not give in to pressure that Sullivan was putting on her to back off. Cooper even approached KPMG, the auditors that had replaced Arthur Andersen, to support her in the matter. Ultimately, Sullivan was dismissed, Myers resigned, Andersen withdrew its audit opinion for 2001, and the Securities and Exchange Commission (SEC) began an investigation into the fraud on June 26, 2002.

In an interview with David Katz and Julia Homer for *CFO Magazine* on February 1, 2008, Cynthia Cooper was asked about her whistleblower role in the WorldCom fraud. When asked when she first suspected something was amiss, Cooper said: "It was a process. My feelings changed from curiosity to discomfort to suspicion based on some of the accounting entries my team and I had identified, and also on the odd reactions I was getting from some of the finance executives."[1]

Cooper did exactly what is expected of a good auditor. She approached the investigation of line-cost accounting with a healthy dose of skepticism and maintained her integrity throughout, even as Sullivan was trying to bully her into dropping the investigation.

When asked whether there was anything about the culture of WorldCom that contributed to the scandal, Cooper laid blame on Bernie Ebbers for his risk-taking approach that led to loading up the company with $40 billion in debt to fund one acquisition after another. He followed the same reckless strategy with his own investments, taking out loans and using his WorldCom stock as collateral. Cooper believed that Ebbers's personal decisions then affected his business decisions; he ultimately saw his net worth disappear, and he was left owing WorldCom some $400 million for loans approved by the board.

Betty Vinson, the company's former director of corporate reporting, was one of five former WorldCom executives who pleaded guilty to fraud. At the trial of Ebbers, Vinson said she was told to make improper accounting entries because Ebbers did not want to disappoint Wall Street. "I felt like if I didn't make the entries, I wouldn't be working there," Vinson testified. She said that she even drafted a resignation letter in 2000, but ultimately she stayed with the company. It was clear she felt uneasy with the accounting at WorldCom.

Vinson said that she took her concerns to Sullivan, who told her that Ebbers did not want to lower Wall Street expectations. Asked how she chose which accounts to alter, Vinson testified, "I just really pulled some out of the air. I used some spreadsheets."[2]

Her lawyer urged the judge to sentence Vinson to probation, citing the pressure placed on her by Ebbers and Sullivan. "She expressed her concern about what she was being directed to do to upper management, and to Sullivan and Ebbers, who assured her and lulled her into believing that all was well," he said.

[1] David K. Katz and Julia Homer, "WorldCom Whistle-blower Cynthia Cooper," *CFO Magazine,* February 1, 2008. Available at: www.cfo.com/article.cfm/10590507.

[2] Susan Pulliam, "Ordered to Commit Fraud, a Staffer Balked, Then Caved: Accountant Betty Vinson Helped Cook the Books at WorldCom," *The Wall Street Journal,* June 23, 2003. Available at: www.people.tamu.edu/~jstrawser/acct229h/Current%20 Readings/E.%20WSJ.com%20-%20A%20Staffer%20Ordered%20to%20Commit%20Fraud,%20Balked.pdf.

On December 6, 2002 the SEC reached an agreement with Betty Vinson about her role in the WorldCom fraud and suspended her from appearing or practicing before the Commission as an accountant. In its Administrative Proceeding, the SEC alleged that: "At the direction of WorldCom senior management, Vinson and other WorldCom employees caused WorldCom to overstate materially its earnings in contravention of GAAP for at least seven successive fiscal quarters, from as early as October 2000 through April 2002." The overstatement included improperly capitalized line costs to overstate pre-tax earnings by approximately $3.8 billion. The agreement went on to say: "Vinson knew, or was reckless in not knowing, that these entries were made without supporting documentation, were not in conformity with GAAP, were not disclosed to the investing public, and were designed to allow WorldCom to appear to meet Wall Street analysts' quarterly earnings estimates."

Questions

1. Explain the role of cognitive shortcomings in the WorldCom fraud and how social and organizational pressures influenced Betty Vinson's actions.

2. The SEC action against Vinson was deemed "appropriate and in the public interest." How was the public interest affected by what Vinson did and WorldCom's actions broadly?

3. In a presentation at James Madison University in November 2013, Cynthia Cooper said, "You don't have to be a bad person to make bad decisions." Discuss what you think Cooper meant and how it relates to our discussion of ethical and moral development in the chapter.

Chapter

3

Organizational Ethics and Corporate Governance

Learning Objectives

After studying Chapter 3, you should be able to:

LO 3-1 Describe the link between organizational culture, climate, ethical leadership, and ethical decision making.

LO 3-2 Explain the link between organizational ethics, individual ethics, and corporate culture.

LO 3-3 Describe the signs that an organization has collapsed ethically.

LO 3-4 Explain the models of corporate social responsibility.

LO 3-5 Discuss the scope and role of corporate governance systems in the ethical decision-making process.

LO 3-6 Discuss compliance, integrity, and employee views about ethics in the workplace.

LO 3-7 Describe the causes of fraud, detection methods, and preventative controls.

LO 3-8 Explain how the provisions of the Sarbanes-Oxley Act relate to corporate governance, including relationships with key parties.

LO 3-9 Analyze the moral basis for whistleblowing and accountants' obligations to whistle blow.

Ethics Reflection

Wells Fargo: The Lessons of an Ethics Failure

On September 8, 2016, Wells Fargo announced it was paying $185 million in fines to Los Angeles city and federal regulators to settle allegations that its employees created millions of fake bank accounts for customers. Top management had set unrealistic sales goals that promoted aggressive sales tactics without regard for the ethics of these policies and what it meant for the public trust.

Wells Fargo engaged in fraud when its employees set up fake accounts for customers, charged them for services not requested, and sold products not wanted because of aggressive cross-selling goals set by the bank. The impact of the Wells Fargo scandal continued well into 2018 as legal settlements with the government were drawn out, class-action lawsuits worked its way through the courts, and whistleblower retaliation lawsuits became resolved. Many questions can be raised as a result of the incident, including why the ethics and compliance machinery at Wells Fargo failed so miserably.[1]

The facts of the case illustrate a company that put 'profits-over-people.'

- 3.5 million of fake bank and credit card accounts opened in customer names. Wells Fargo paid $185 million in fines for the fraud under a national class action lawsuit.
- Improperly charged mortgage fees known as rate-lock extensions when loan approvals exceeded the 30 to 45-day period. These fees were charged even though the delay in approvals were due to the bank, not the customer.
- Set up about 528,000 unauthorized online bill paying services. Wells agreed to pay $910,000 in refunds to customers.
- Forced up to 570,000 borrowers into unneeded auto insurance. The cost of unneeded insurance pushed about 274,000 Wells Fargo customers into delinquency and caused nearly 25,000 wrongful vehicle repossessions. It is estimated the bank will pay $80 million to reimburse customers.
- Additional $5.4 million for illegal vehicle seizures by repossessing more than 860 vehicles of U.S. service members in violation of the Servicemembers Civil Relief Act.

How did Wells Fargo, a bank that once had a strong reputation for customer service, get to this point? It was a failure at all levels of management, but blame was laid at the doorstep of the former CEO, John Stumpf, who was forced to resign. Under his watch, Wells violated just about every standard of ethical behavior, most of which will be addressed in this chapter. For now, here is a list of the systemic failures.

- A failure of leadership.
- Creating a toxic culture.
- Ignoring employee reports of fraudulent accounts.
- Not living up to the standards in its ethics code.
- Retaliating against whistleblowers, including violations of the Sarbanes-Oxley Act.

The retaliation against Wells Fargo whistleblowers illustrates how a company's own ethics and compliance procedures are no better than the paper they are written on unless top management 'walks the talk' of ethics. Wells had an ethics hotline expressly for the purpose of reporting behavior they suspected as suspicious or fraudulent; then they retaliated against those employees who did just that.[2]

Bill Bado, a former Wells Fargo banker, was one of six former Wells employees who spoke to CNN about their experiences. Bado, who refused orders to open phony bank and credit accounts, called the hotline and sent an email to human resources, flagging unethical sales activities as he had been instructed to do. Eight days after reporting it, Bado was terminated. The reason given was "excessive tardiness."[3]

One unnamed whistleblower, who was a former branch manager in Ponoma, California, received $577,500 in back wages and damages after being fired for reporting co-workers who engaged in allegedly fraudulent activities related to the fake-account scandal by opening accounts and enrolling customers in bank products without their knowledge, consent, or disclosures.

A number of Wells Fargo employees reportedly lodged whistleblower complaints with the Occupational Safety and Health Administration (OSHA) of the U.S. Department of Labor after being fired for reporting ethics violations to the company. The Sarbanes-Oxley Act contains a provision that protects whistleblowers who have been unlawfully retaliated against. One such employee, Claudia Ponce de Leon, was reinstated by OSHA, but the bank is fighting the order, claiming de Leon was fired for inappropriate behavior, not reporting that colleagues were opening fake accounts in order to meet sales goals.[4]

An important device in setting an ethical tone in an organization is to establish a code of ethics and a hotline to report alleged improper activity. Wells Fargo had both but that didn't seem to matter. It's Ethics Policy states:

"Our ethics are the sum of all the decisions each of us makes every day. We have a responsibility to always act with honesty and integrity. When we do so, we earn the trust of our customers. We have to earn that trust every day by behaving ethically, rewarding open, honest communications, and holding ourselves accountable for our decisions and actions."[5]

The saga of Wells Fargo is a company that suffered from ethical blind spots, gave in to situational pressures to meet sales goals at all costs, and functioned in a social and organizational environment that that led employees to do things they otherwise would not have done, i.e., set up fake accounts and charge customers for unwanted services.

Think about the following as you read the chapter: (1) What steps should an organization take to establish an ethical culture? (2) How can corporate governance mechanisms influence ethical decision making? (3) What are the whistleblowing obligations of accounting professionals and their ethical and legal obligations to report financial wrongdoing?

The thing I have learned at IBM is that culture is everything. Underneath all the sophisticated processes, there is always the company's sense of values and identity.

Source: Louis V. Gerstner, Jr., former CEO, IBM

This statement by former IBM chief executive officer (CEO) Louis Gerstner highlights one of the themes of this chapter: The culture of an organization establishes the boundaries within which ethical decisions must be made. As we learned from previous chapters, it is one thing to know that you should behave in a certain way, but it is quite another to do it (or even want to do it) given the pressures that may exist from within the organization.

What Makes for an Ethical Organization?

LO 3-1
Describe the link between organizational culture, climate, ethical leadership, and ethical decision making.

Organizational ethics can be thought of as the generally accepted principles and standards that guide behavior in business and other organizational contexts. High ethical standards require both organizations and individuals to conform to sound moral principles. In organizations, a critical component of creating an ethical organization environment is the culture that includes shared values, beliefs, goals, norms, and problem solving mechanisms.

Ethical Culture

Corporate culture starts with an explicit statement of values, beliefs, and customs from top management. The statement provides the framework for top management on how to manage themselves and other employees, and how they should conduct their business(es). A code of ethics builds on those values and serves as a guide to support ethical decision making. It clarifies an organization's mission, values, and principles, linking them with standards of professional conduct.

Microsoft is recognized as an ethical company and is a recipient of the designation for 2017 of The World's Most Ethical Companies. Microsoft is one of 124 companies to receive such recognition by *Ethisphere,* an organization that makes the designation based on an Ethics Quotient rating system that includes the following factors: Ethics and Compliance Program; Corporate Citizenship and Responsibility; Culture of Ethics; and Leadership, Innovation, and Reputation. Microsoft has been included in the list for the last seven years.[6]

Microsoft's Standards of Business Conduct define what it stands for: "We are more likely to make ethical choices when integrity, honesty, and compliance guide our decisionmaking." It links building trust with applying the company's culture and values to build lasting relationships inside and outside the company: "Our values are the enduring principles that we use to do business with integrity and win trust every day. Our culture is our operating framework—who we are and how we behave."[7]

An important element of ethical culture is the tone at the top. Tone at the top refers to the ethical environment that is created in the workplace by the organization's leadership. An ethical tone creates the basis for standards of behavior that become part of the code of ethics. Microsoft has established a tone that reflects a commitment to ethical practices.

The tone set by managers influences how employees respond to ethical challenges and is enhanced by ethical leadership. When leaders are perceived as trustworthy, employee trust increases; leaders are seen as ethical and as honoring a higher level of duties. Employees identify with the organization's values and the likely outcome is high individual ethics, high organization ethics, and a lack of dissonance.[8]

If the tone set by management upholds ethics and integrity, employees will be more inclined to uphold those same values. However, if top management appears unconcerned about ethics and focuses solely on the bottom line, employees will be more prone to commit fraud, whether occupational (i.e., Wells Fargo's manipulation of customer accounts and services) or participation in fraudulent financial reporting as occurred with Aaron Beam and Betty Vinson.

Ethical Climate

The ethical climate of an organization plays an important role in organizational culture. Whereas an organization's overall culture establishes ideals that guide a wide variety of member behaviors, the ethical climate focuses specifically on issues of right and wrong. We have seen how a toxic climate, such as the one at Wells Fargo, can corrupt virtually all the systems and negate checks and balances designed to ensure ethical standards are followed.

As we discussed in Chapter 2, theories about the world suggest that top management tends to blame individuals for events, rather than their work climate, operational policies and procedures or incentive programs. This often leads to problems being framed inaccurately and can result in unethical decisions, much as occurred at Wells Fargo.

Organizational ethical climate refers to the moral atmosphere of the work environment and the level of ethics practiced within a company. Leaders determine organizational climate, establish character, and define norms. Character plays an important role in leadership. Leaders of good character have integrity, courage, and compassion. They are careful and prudent. Their decisions and actions inspire employees to think and act in a way that enhances the well-being of the organization, its people, and society in general. Ralph Waldo Emerson, the American essayist, poet, and philosopher, said, "Our chief want is someone who will inspire us to be what we know we could be."

Johnson points out that virtues are woven into the inner lives of leaders, shape the way they see and behave, operate independent of the situation, and help leaders to live more fulfilling lives. He identifies courage, temperance, wisdom, justice, optimism, integrity, humility, reverence, and compassion as underlying traits of character of effective leaders. Ethical leaders recognize that moral action is risky but continue to model ethical behavior despite the danger. They refuse to set their values aside to go along with the group, to keep silent when customers may be hurt, or to lie to investors. They strive to create ethical environments even when faced with opposition from their superiors and subordinates. Ethical leaders serve as role models for those within the organization and stakeholders that rely on it.[9]

There is no one size fits all for ethical climates. Johnson believes that an organization must first identify principles and practices that characterize positive ethical climates and then adapt them to a particular organization setting. He identifies key markers of highly ethical organizations including humility, zero tolerance for individual and collective destructive behaviors, justice, integrity, trust, a focus on process, structural reinforcement, and social responsibility. An ethical climate is enhanced through a values-driven organization that encourages openness and transparency and provides a supportive environment to voice matters of concern without fear of retribution or retaliation.[10] An ethical climate should also support policies related to equity, diversity, and inclusion.

Is there a difference between ethical decision making in general, as we discussed in Chapter 2, and ethical decision making in an organizational setting? We believe there are important differences that incorporate both individual and organizational factors into the process. Ferrell et al. describe a process that is depicted in Exhibit 3.1.[11] What follows is a brief explanation of the components of the framework.

Ethical Issue Intensity

Ethical issue intensity reflects the relevance or importance of an event or decision as viewed by the individual, work group, and/or organization. The relative importance of the issue is based on the values, beliefs, and norms involved, as well as situational pressures in the workplace. Ferrell et al. point out that

EXHIBIT 3.1   Framework for Understanding Ethical Decision Making in Business

```
┌──────────────────┐
│  Ethical Issue   │────┐
│    Intensity     │    │
└──────────────────┘    │
                        │
┌──────────────────┐    │    ┌──────────────────┐      ┌──────────────────┐
│ Individual       │────┤    │ Business Ethics  │      │                  │
│ Factors          │    ├──▶ │ Evaluations and  │ ──▶  │ Ethical or       │
└──────────────────┘    │    │ Intentions       │      │ Unethical Behavior│
                        │    └──────────────────┘      └──────────────────┘
┌──────────────────┐    │
│ Organizational   │────┤
│ Factors          │    │
└──────────────────┘    │
                        │
┌──────────────────┐    │
│   Opportunity    │────┘
└──────────────────┘
```

Source: O.C. Ferrell, John Fraedrich, and Linda Ferrell, *Business Ethics: Ethical Decision Making and Cases*, 11th ed. (Stamford, CT: Cengage Learning, 2017, p. 130).

senior employees and those with administrative authority contribute significantly to ethical issue intensity because they typically dictate an organization's position on ethical issues.[12]

Individuals' moral intensity increases their awareness of potential ethical problems for the organization, which in turn reduces their intention to act unethically. However, obedience to authority and pressures of peers can create social and organizational pressures that can lead to cognitive dissonance. At Wells Fargo, many employees adjusted their beliefs to match their behaviors in order to alleviate the dissonance.

Individual Factors

When people need to resolve issues in their daily lives, they often make their decisions based on their own values and principles of right or wrong. Values of individuals can be derived from moral philosophies, such as those discussed in Chapter 1. These provide principles or rules people use to decide what is right or wrong from a moral and personal perspective. Although an individual's intention to engage in ethical behavior relates to individual values, organizational and social forces also play an important role by shaping behavioral intentions and decision making.[13]

Values applied to business can also be used in negative rationalizations, such as "Everyone does it" or "We have to do what it takes to get the business."[14] We learned how Wells Fargo set unrealistic sales goals and pressured employees to go along by rationalizing their behavior as "I'm just following orders."

Organizational Factors

Research has established that in the workplace, the organization's values often have a greater influence on decisions than a person's own values. Ethical decisions in the workplace are made jointly in work groups or other organizational settings. The strength of personal values, the opportunities to behave unethically, and the exposure to others who behave ethically or unethically influence decision making. An alignment between an individual's own values and the values of the organization help create positive work environments and organizational outcomes.[15]

An important component of organizational culture is the company's ethical culture. Ethical culture reflects the integrity of decisions made and results from corporate policies, top management's leadership on ethical issues, the influence of coworkers, and the opportunity for unethical behavior. Research indicates that ethical values integrated into the organization's culture are positively correlated to employees' commitment to the firm and their sense that they fit into the company.[16] The more employees perceive an organization's culture to be ethical, the less likely they are to make unethical decisions.

Opportunity

Ferrell et al. point out that opportunity describes the conditions in an organization that limit or permit ethical or unethical behavior.[17] Opportunity results from conditions that either provide internal or external rewards or fail to erect barriers against unethical behavior. The opportunities that employees have for unethical behavior in an organization can be reduced or eliminated with aggressive enforcement of rules and codes of ethics.

Opportunity existed at Wells Fargo because of the incentive pay program in effect for tellers and other bank workers. On January 10, 2017, the bank announced its incentive compensation system that was at the root of its fake-accounts scandal would be changed. No longer would sales goals to push workers to open more accounts be the basis for incentive compensation. Instead, the new system would judge employees on how often customers use their accounts and whether customers are satisfied with the bank's services.[18]

Business Ethics Intentions, Behavior, and Evaluations

Ethical dilemmas involve problem-solving situations when the rules governing decisions are often vague or in conflict. The results of an ethical decision are often uncertain; it is not always immediately clear whether or not we made the right decision. Moreover, the decision we make may not always comport with the one we intended to make because of pressures within the organization.

One's intentions influence the final decision but our actions may not match our intentions because of reasons and rationalizations given by superiors to act in a different way. We need a mechanism to evaluate pressures and effectively respond to claims such as everyone does it. Here is where we rely on GVV, which asks the decision maker to identify levers to counteract the pressures and find enablers to support our point of view.

Organizational Influences on Ethical Decision Making

LO 3-2

Explain the link between organizational ethics, individuals ethics, and corporate culture.

Smith and Carroll presented a detailed argument that organizational factors such as socialization processes, environmental influences, and hierarchical relationships collectively constitute a "stacked deck," which impedes moral behavior.[19] Organizational factors are likely to play a role in moral decision making and behavior at two points: establishing moral intent and engaging in moral behavior. Explicit organizational behaviors may cause unethical (or ethical) behavior to result despite good (or bad) intention.

Thomas Jones developed an explanatory model[20] that merged Rest's four-component ethical decision-making model with Fiske and Taylor's work on social cognition to illustrate the ethical decision-making process of an individual who encounters an ethical dilemma within the context of work.[21] Of particular importance is the role that moral intensity plays in recognizing moral issues. Moral issues of high intensity will be more salient because the magnitude of consequences is greater, their effects stand out, and their effects involve significant others (greater social, cultural, psychological, or physical proximity).

While Jones's model illustrates the impact that moral intensity has on ethical choices and behavior and acknowledges that organizational factors influence the establishment of moral intent and behavior—the last two steps in Rest's model—the model fails to address what Burchard calls the cyclical, ongoing dynamic exchange between the individual and organization, which affects the development and sustaining of one's code of conduct in the organizational context.[22] It was left to Jones and Hiltebeitel to fill the gap when they conducted a study of organizational influence on moral decisions and proposed a model that demonstrated organizational influence on the moral decision-making process.[23] As Jones had done with his previous model, Jones and Hiltebeitel based their model on Rest's moral reasoning and Kohlberg's moral development theory.

The Jones-Hiltebeitel model looks at the role of one's personal code of conduct in ethical behavior within an organization. When an employee was called upon to perform routine tasks—those with no internal conflict or cognitive dissonance—the actions taken were almost automatic. However, when those tasks diverged from the routine, the employee would refer to her personal code of conduct for ethical cues. The implications for ethical behavior within the organization are significant because an unethical individual might act dishonestly in one case, while a virtuous person would act in a truthful, trustworthy manner.

According to the model, when one's personal code is insufficient to make the necessary moral decision, the individual will look at the factors that influenced the formation of the code, including professional and organizational influences to resolve the conflict. The influences that are strongest are the ones that determine the reformation of the individual's code of conduct. The implications for the culture of an organization are significant because an organization that values profits above all else might elicit one kind of response, such as to go along with improper accounting, while an organization that values integrity above all else might lead to questioning improper accounting and doing what one can to reverse false and misleading financial results.[24]

Ethical Dissonance Model

Burchard points out that the Jones-Hiltebeitel model and others like it pay too little attention to the examination of ethical person-organization fit upon the person-organization exchange, within each of the four potential fit options. Burchard presents what she calls the Ethical Dissonance Cycle Model to illustrate the interaction between the individual and the organization, based on the person-organization ethical fit at various stages of the contractual relationship in each potential ethical fit scenario.[25] The model is complex, so we restrict our coverage to the basics of the person-organization interchange and its implications for ethical behavior within organizations. This is an important consideration because the ethics of an individual influences the values that one brings to the workplace and decision making, while the ethics (through its culture) of an organization influences that behavior. To keep it simple, we adopt the idea that there can be a dissonance between what is considered ethical and what may actually be "best" for the subject inviting ethical consideration.

Of the four potential fit options, two possess high person-organization fit: (1) high organizational ethics, high individual ethics (High-High), and (2) low organizational ethics, low individual ethics (Low-Low); and two possess low person-organization fit: (1) high organizational ethics, low individual ethics (High-Low) and (2) low organizational ethics, high individual ethics (Low-High).[26]

Let's pause for a moment and consider the practical implications of this model. Imagine that you are interviewing for a position with a mid-sized company in your town. You can easily find out information about the company on the Internet to prepare for the interview, such as the scope of its operations, products and services, customer base, and geographical locations. However, it is less easy to find out about its reputation for ethics, although reports in the media about specific events might be of some use. Now, let's assume that you knew (and understood) what is meant by organizational fit and in this case the fit is

Low-High. Would that affect whether you interview with the company? Might you ask questions to better understand why that fit exists? Would it affect your final decision whether to work for the company? The information you might gather during the process could be invaluable when you face ethical dilemmas in the workplace.

In two of the fit options (High-High and Low-Low), no ethical dissonance exists. Person-organization fit is optimal, and the organization is highly effective, either to constructive or destructive ends. The other two (High-Low and Low-High) demonstrate a lack of person-organization fit in the realm of ethics and values.[27]

High Organizational Ethics, High Individual Ethics (High-High)

Assume that you know your values and beliefs are an ethical match for the company you work for. You are likely to continue to stay employed in the organization. The issue for us is how you might assess organizational ethics. Koh and Boo identified three distinct measures of organizational ethics: support for ethical behavior from top management, the ethical climate of the organization, and the connection between career success and ethical behavior.[28] These three factors relate to the culture of the organization and may have implications for actions such as whistleblowing, as discussed later on. Koh and Boo found that positive ethical culture and climate produces favorable organizational outcomes by setting down the ethical philosophy and rules of conduct and practices (i.e., code of ethics).

Low Organizational Ethics, Low Individual Ethics (Low-Low)

When both the individual and organization possess low moral and ethical development, the fit is there, but it is turns in a negative direction. A culture of corruption is difficult to change, and, for the employee, it takes more conscious effort to stop the corruption than to participate in it. You might say that the employee adopts the attitude of going along to get along. Padilla et al. contends that "dysfunctional leader behaviors and susceptible followers interacting in the context of a contributing environment produce negative organizational outcomes in which 'followers must consent to, or be unable to resist, a destructive leader.'"[29]

High Organizational Ethics, Low Individual Ethics (High-Low)

According to Hamilton and Kelman, if the individual possesses lower ethics than that which is held by the organization, the discovery of an individual's lack of person-organization fit is often pointed out by socialized members within the ethical organization.[30] Those assimilated members of the organization may attempt to socialize the individual to the ways of the organization to alleviate the ethical dissonance. Once this dissonance is discovered, the likelihood that the mismatched employee will leave the company rises. The more the individual's personal decisions are seen to be in conflict with the ethical decisions that are perceived to be encouraged by the organization, the greater the discomfort of the individual. Imagine, for example, a newly hired employee thought there was nothing wrong with accepting free gifts from contractors doing business with one's employer, but the employer has a code of ethics forbidding such practices. The culture of the organization conflicts with the individual's low ethical standards in this instance, and others in the organization that identify with organizational values may attempt to resolve the dissonance and alter the employee's behavior. If the employee's behavior does not change, the employee may be let go for cause or insubordination.

Low Organizational Ethics, High Individual Ethics (Low-High)

A reduction in job satisfaction is likely if an employee striving to be ethical perceives little top management support for ethical behavior, an unfavorable ethical climate in the organization, and/or little association between ethical behavior and job success.[31] Once this ethical dissonance is discovered, the likelihood of employee turnover rises. Sims and Keon found a significant relationship between the ethical rift between one's personal decisions and the perceived unwritten/informal policies of the organization, and the individual's level of comfort within the organization. The greater the difference between the decisions that the individual made and the decisions perceived as expected and reinforced by the organization, the greater levels of discomfort the individual would feel, and the more likely the individual would be to report these feelings of discomfort.[32] The case of Cynthia Cooper, discussed in Chapter 1, illustrates the low organizational, high individual ethics environment. Cooper reported her concerns to top management, and once she was convinced that nothing would be done to address the improper accounting for capitalized costs, she blew the whistle by going to the audit committee and external auditors.

Seven Signs of Ethical Collapse

LO 3-3
Describe the signs that an organization has collapsed ethically.

We can think of the ethical culture of an organization as a piece of the overall organizational culture. So, if the organizational culture represents "how we do things around here," the ethical culture represents "how we do things around here in relation to ethics and ethical behavior in the organization." The ethical culture represents the organizations "ethics personality." A strong ethical culture is essential in creating an organization that supports people making good ethical decisions and behaving ethically at all times and in all decisions. When all relevant organizational systems are pushing people in the same ethical direction, ethical failure is much less likely.[33]

In her book *The Seven Signs of Ethical Collapse,* Marianne Jennings analyzes the indicators of possible ethical collapse in companies and provides advice how to avoid impending disaster. She starts with a description of ethical collapse, saying that it "occurs when any organization has drifted from the basic principles of right and wrong," and she uses financial reporting standards and accounting rules as one area where this might occur. She points out that "not all companies that have drifted ethically have violated any laws."[34] Enron did not necessarily violate GAAP in treating the effects of *some* of its transactions with special-purpose entities off-balance-sheet. However, the company ignored conflicts of interest of Andy Fastow who managed some of the entities while wearing a second hat as CFO of Enron during the time the two entities had mutual dealings.

According to Jennings, "When an organization collapses ethically, it means that those in the organization have drifted into rationalizations and legalisms, and all for the purpose of getting the results they want and need at almost any cost." A good example is Dennis Kozlowski at Tyco International who misappropriated company resources for personal purposes without the approval of the board of directors and rationalized that he was just doing what those before him had done. Thus, he invoked one of the reasons and rationalizations that we discussed in GVV—Expected or Standard Practice. Jennings links the rationalizations and legalisms to a culture that leads to behavior based on the notion "It's not a question of should we do it." It is a culture of "Can we do it legally?" This mentality occurs because of the combination of the seven factors working together to cloud judgment.[35]

Jennings identifies seven common ethical signs of moral meltdowns in companies that have experienced ethical collapse. The common threads she found that make good people at companies do really dumb things include (1) pressure to maintain numbers; (2) fear and silence; (3) young 'uns and a bigger-than-life CEO (i.e., loyalty to the boss); (4) weak board of directors; (5) conflicts of interest overlooked or unaddressed; (6) innovation like no other company; and (7) goodness in some areas atones for evil in others.[36] We briefly review them next.

Pressure to Maintain the Numbers

Jennings points out that the tension between ethics and the bottom line will always be present. The first sign of a culture at risk for ethical collapse occurs when there is not just a focus on numbers and results, but an unreasonable and unrealistic obsession with meeting quantitative goals. This "financial results at all costs" approach was a common ethical problem at both Enron and WorldCom. At WorldCom, the mantra was that financial results had to improve in every quarter, and the shifting of operating expenses to capitalized costs was used to accomplish the goal regardless of the propriety of the accounting treatment. It was an "end justifies means" culture that sanctioned wrongdoing in the name of earnings. Accountants like Betty Vinson got caught up in the culture and did not know how to extricate themselves from the situation.

Fear of Reprisals

A culture of fear and silence can easily mask ethical problems. Employees may be reluctant to raise issues of ethical concern because they may be ignored, treated badly, transferred, or worse. Others might rationalize leaving it up to the next employee to report it, or the bystander effect. The whistleblowing process in many organizations does not work as intended because while ethical employees want to blow the whistle, they are reluctant to do so because they fear reprisals, so they stay silent. One aspect of such a culture is a "kill the messenger syndrome," whereby an employee brings bad news to higher-ups with the best intentions of having the organization correct the matter, but instead the messenger is treated as an outcast. The employee finds herself in a situation where her ethics are high but the organization's is low.

Loyalty to the Boss

Dennis Kozlowski, the dominant, larger-then-life CEO of Tyco, had an appetite for a lavish style of living. He surrounded himself with young people who were taken by his stature and would not question his actions. Kozlowski, who once spent $6,000 on shower curtains for an apartment paid for by the company, made sure these "young 'uns" received all the trappings of success so they would be reluctant to speak up when ethical and legal issues existed for fear of losing their expensive homes, boats, and cars and the prestige that comes along with financial success at a young age. Jennings quoted Kozlowski as saying, "I hire them just like me: smart, poor, and want to be rich." Kozlowski selected them for their positions based on their inexperience, possible conflicts of interest, and unlikelihood to question the boss's decisions. Of course, not all bigger-than-life CEOs are unethical (e.g., Warren Buffett).

Weak Board of Directors

A weak board of directors characterizes virtually all the companies with major accounting frauds in the early part of the 2000s. One example is HealthSouth. Richard Scrushy surrounded himself with a weak board so that when he made decisions as CEO that contributed to an accounting scandal where the company's earnings were falsely inflated by $1.4 billion, the board would go along, in part because of their interrelationships with Scrushy and HealthSouth that created conflicts of interest. Jennings identifies the following conflicts of interest:[37]

- One director earned $250,000 per year from a consulting contract with HealthSouth over a seven-year period.
- Another director had a joint investment venture with Scrushy on a $395,000 investment property.
- Another director's company was awarded a $5.6 million contract to install glass at a hospital being built by HealthSouth.
- MedCenter District, a hospital-supply company that was run online, did business with HealthSouth and was owned by Scrushy, six directors, and the wife of one of those directors.

- The same three directors had served on both the audit committee and the compensation committee for several years.
- Two of the directors had served on the board for 18 years.
- One director received a $425,000 donation to his favorite charity from HealthSouth just prior to his going on the board.

Weak boards can often indicate an organization's ethical collapse, simply because they lack the experience or cohesiveness to challenge an unethical CEO or senior management team.

Culture of Conflicts

A conflict of interest occurs when a person holds a position of trust that requires her to exercise judgment on behalf of others, but where her personal interests and/or obligations conflict with those of others. Andy Fastow was making a lot of money as the general partner of the off-balance-sheet entities that did many deals with Enron. Some at Enron felt the deals were not in its best interests. Still, Fastow was able to convince the Enron board that the entities couldn't exist without his working both sides of the table. Consequently, the board repeatedly gave Fastow a limited waiver of the company's conflict of interest rules in its code of ethics so he could run the off-balance-sheet entities and, simultaneously, serve as Enron's CFO.

Conflicts of interest were pronounced before the passage of the Sarbanes-Oxley Act (SOX) and revision of the New York Stock Exchange corporate governance rules that call for the splitting of the roles of CEO and chair of the board of directors. The problem with having a single person perform dual roles is the CEO is also setting the agenda for the board, thereby creating an inherent conflict because the board is supposed to supervise the CEO. Moreover, it is the board's responsibility to vote on executive compensation packages, so when the CEO is also the chair, she is voting on her own compensation package. Publicly held corporations in the U.S. are required to have a board of directors to oversee top management and ensure top management decisions reflect shareholder interest. In 2010, the SEC under the Dodd-Frank Financial Reform Act adopted rules that required companies to disclose in their proxy statements why the board chair and CEO positions are unified or separated.

Innovations

Too many companies that dissolve in fraud and other wrongdoings felt they were above fray because they were so innovative. In entering a guilty plea to fraud, Sanjay Kumar, former CEO of Computer Associates, remarked: ". . . standard accounting rules [were] not the best way to measure [CA's] results because it had changed to a new business model offering its clients more flexibility."[38] The innovators may come to believe they are immune from the business cycle and almost untouchable. In a sense, they become blind to the ethical issues that arise during and after the innovation process.

Goodness in Some Areas Atones for Evil in Others

Does it make sense that a company steeped in good works for a community and socially responsible behavior should be given a pass if it gets involved in wrongful acts? Many companies rely on their culture of diversity, safety, volunteerism, or environmentally-conscious operations as evidence of their overall ethical goodness, despite improprieties elsewhere as if two "rights" undo a "wrong." Jennings quotes John Rigas, the founder of Adelphia Communications that had a multi-billion dollar fraud in 2002 that included $2.3 billion of co-borrowing between Adelphia subsidiaries and some Rigas family-owned entities: "It's more than money. You've got to give back to the community that supported you." Jennings points out that while he was CEO of Adelphia, John Rigas "gave back" to his daughter and others in business with him.[39]

Corporate Social Responsibilities

LO 3-4

Explain the models of corporate social responsibility.

It's clear that business has a social responsibility to obey the law. Relationships with employees, customers, suppliers, creditors, etc. create contractual obligations. Legal obligations also exist to avoid negligence, fraud, and other liabilities under tort law. Economists point out that business has a social responsibility to produce the goods and services required for society to function. The philosopher and ethicist, Chris MacDonald, believes the primary question of corporate social responsibilities (CSR) is the extent to which business organizations and their managers have ethical responsibilities that go beyond producing needed goods and services within the law.[40]

For our purposes, when we address issues of CSR, we are referring to the ethical expectations that society has for business. Ethical responsibilities are those things that we ought to, or should, do, even if we prefer not to.[41] A business may not want to develop the systems to remove toxic waste because of cost concerns, but it chooses to do so to garner goodwill through environmentally friendly policies and act in society's interests.

We also address the more obligatory sense of ethical responsibility to prevent harm. A good example is developing (and enforcing) policies against sexual harassment in the workplace. Sexual harassment cases are often fueled by a toxic culture such as the one at the Fox News Channel where it was revealed that Roger Ailes, the former chairman and CEO, had repeatedly harassed one of its hosts, Gretchen Carlson, who turned down Ailes's sexual advances during her eleven-year career at Fox. Her sexual harassment lawsuit was settled for a reported $20 million in 2016. Bill O'Reilly, Fox's top draw, settled a $32 million lawsuit in 2017 just before he signed a new contract. The station knew of the charges by Lis Wiehl, a former Fox News analyst, prior to extending his contract.

The fallout from these high-profile cases led Twenty-First Century Fox, Inc. to issue a statement that it was committed to zero tolerance for sexual harassment, race discrimination, and all other forms of discrimination prohibited by law, and a corporate policy that creates a safe, productive, and welcoming workplace for everyone. Fox claims to have taken steps to address concerns regarding workplace civility and governance. It established the Fox News Workplace Professionalism and Inclusion Council, a committee comprising experts in workplace and inclusion matters, with a majority serving from outside the company.[42]

A few points here. First, there is no doubt that sexual harassment and other forms of discrimination, and we would add cyberbullying in the workplace, do harm to the recipients of these offensive behaviors. Second, the Fox News case illustrates a new corporate commitment to policies of equity, diversity, and inclusion, issues we addressed in Chapter 2. Lastly, in the case of Fox News there seems to have been a climate where top executives turned a blind eye to the toxic culture that pervaded the environment at Fox.

The final way we address CSR issues is whether business has a social responsibility to do good things and make society a better place. Michael Stroik, Manager, Research and Analytics, for the Committee Encouraging Corporate Philanthropy (CECP), spoke about a report issued by CECP that indicates a changing global environment whereby markets are mandating social investments as a price of doing business. The top trends in CSR were found to be: 1) linking a corporation's performance and corporate societal investments, 2) aligning philanthropic efforts with their goals for impact, 3) increasing employee engagement, and 4) increasing non-cash methods of giving.[43]

Socially responsible workplace policies and socially-responsible investments can help with millennial engagement. Millennials are passionate about social causes. According to a 2015 Cone Communications

Millennial CSR Study, more than 9-in-10 millennials would switch brands to one associated with a cause, and millennials are "prepared to make personal sacrifices to make an impact on issues they care about, whether that's paying more for a product, sharing products rather than buying, or taking a pay cut to work for a responsible company."[44] Socially responsible companies should leverage this commitment to engage in practices that, we might say, illustrate 'Doing Good by Being Good.'

Models of CSR

Economic Model

A business exists to serve the interests of society. This may mean to produce goods and services needed, create jobs, and providing wealth for investors. The economic model of CSR holds that businesses' sole social responsibility is to fulfill the economic functions they were designed to serve. As R. Edward Freemen points out, managers are employees, or agents, of those owners and must work to further the owners' interests. He identifies this perspective as the dominant model of CSR and refers to it as "managerial capitalism."[45]

The economic model of CSR places the shareholders at the center of the corporation and the ethical responsibility of management is to serve those shareholders. Specifically, managers have a primary responsibility to pursue profit within the law. Nobel Prize-winning economist Milton Friedman's classic 1970 *New York Times* article, "The Social Responsibility of Business is to Increase Profits," argues for the economic model.

Some critics contend that Friedman ignored the ethical dimension of business in his statement: "There is one and only one social responsibility of business—to use its resources and engage in activities to increase profits so long as it stays within the rules of the game, which is to say, engages in open and free competition without deception or fraud."[46] Friedman certainly recognized the importance of staying within the law. Beyond that, it may seem Friedman's statement implies that decisions that are not driven by fraud or deception are likely to be ethical decisions. Perhaps, but there's more to it than that interpretation. Specifically, we should question whether it's ethical to cut wages in order to maximize profits. There's no deception or fraud, but is it right to harm another to accomplish one's self-interest goals? Is this end justifies the means approach ethical when employees work hard, haven't had a pay raise for five years, and must contend with rising consumer prices?

Did Friedman intend to recognize the moral responsibilities of business and somehow link them to profit-making activities? Hartmann et al. believe so. They state that contrary to popular belief, Friedman does not ignore ethical responsibilities in his analysis but suggested that managers fulfill their ethical responsibility by increasing shareholder wealth and pursuing profit.[47] In other words, so long as shareholder wealth and profitability increase or are benefited by managers' actions, the corporation has met its ethical responsibilities to society. But what happens when laws are passed that impose costs on business and do not increase profits, yet they have an ethical basis to them? Does that mean the company can't meet its ethical responsibilities to shareholders?

A good example is the Sarbanes-Oxley Act (SOX) that was enacted into law on July 30, 2002. Section 404 of the Law imposes significant costs on business to develop internal controls to help prevent and detect wrongful behavior, including fraud, and to minimize the risk that CEOs and CFOs will sign off on financial statements that contain material misstatements. A study by Charles River Associates in 2004 shows that on average, companies in the sample were estimated to have spent $7.8 million each to implement Section 404, including $1.9 million of audit and compliance fees. Some business leaders observed that the costs of compliance exceed the benefits in terms of improved internal control systems over financial reporting and they have urged regulators to modify the implementation rules to reduce the costs associated with Section 404.[48] Of course, determining the benefits is no easy task because how can we know the "savings" by having in place strong controls that cut down on instances of fraud?

Stakeholder Model

A second perspective on CSR is known as the stakeholder model. The stakeholder model takes a broader view than the shareholder model and recognizes that business exists to create value for a range of parties, including employees, customers, suppliers, and communities as well as investors and stockholders. Business managers have responsibilities to all those who have a stake in the success or failure of the company, not only those who have invested financially.[49]

Freeman's version of stakeholder theory is widely recognized as the most influential. Stakeholder theory begins by recognizing that every business decision affects a wide variety of people, benefiting some and imposing costs on others. Think about the Volkswagen case. The decision makers probably thought the company would benefit by not having to redesign the diesel engines to meet pollution requirements. Most likely they thought profits would be higher as a result. Beyond that, the costs were more significant since customers were cheated, communities were harmed, and, ultimately, shareholder value was lost.[50]

Stakeholder theory recognizes that every business decision imposes costs on someone that must be recognized. A manager who seeks to maximize profits is imposing costs on employees, consumers, and suppliers because the maximization is, typically, driven by price increases or cost reductions. The dominant economic model argues that these costs are justified because management owes an ethical duty to shareholders. The stakeholder model acknowledges this but argues that other ethical duties have an equal claim on managerial decision making.[51]

Examples of CSR

The Case of the Ford Pinto

The case of the Ford Pinto illustrates a classic example of how a company can make a fatal mistake in its decision making by failing to consider the interests of the stakeholders adequately. The failure was due to total reliance on utilitarian thinking instead of the universality perspective of rights theory, to the detriment of the driving public and society in general.

The Pinto was Ford Motor Company's first domestic North American subcompact automobile, marketed beginning on September 11, 1970. It competed with the AMC Gremlin and Chevrolet Vega, along with imports from makes such as Volkswagen, Datsun, and Toyota. The Pinto was popular in sales, with 100,000 units delivered by January 1971, and was also offered as a wagon and Runabout hatchback. Its reputation suffered over time, however, especially from a controversy surrounding the safety of its gas tank.

The public was shocked to find out that if the Pinto cars experienced an impact at speeds of only 30 miles per hour or less, they might become engulfed in flames, and passengers could be burned or even die. Ford faced an ethical dilemma: what to do about the apparently unsafe gas tanks that seemed to be the cause of these incidents. At the time, the gas tanks were routinely placed behind the license plate, so a rear-end collision was more likely to cause an explosion (whereas today's gas tanks are placed on the side of the vehicle). However, the federal safety standards at the time did not address this issue, so Ford was in compliance with the law. Ford's initial response was based on ethical legalism—the company complied with all the laws and safety problems, so it was under no obligation to take any action.

Eventually, Ford did use ethical analysis to develop a response. It used a risk–benefit analysis to aid decision making. This was done because the National Highway Traffic Safety Administration (NHTSA) excused a defendant from being penalized if the monetary costs of making a production change were greater than the "societal benefit" of that change. The analysis followed the same approach modeled after Judge Learned Hand's ruling in *United States v. Carroll Towing* in 1947 that boiled the theory of negligence down to the following: If the expected harm exceeded the cost to prevent it, the defendant was obligated to take the precaution, and if he (or it, in the case of a company) did not, liability would result. But if the cost was larger than the expected harm, the defendant was not expected to take the precaution. If there was an accident, the defendant would not be found guilty.[52] A summary of the Ford analysis follows.

Ford's Risk-Benefit Analysis[53]

Benefits of Fixing the Pintos

Savings: 180 burn deaths, 180 serious burn injuries, 2,100 burned vehicles

Unit cost: $200,000 per death (figure provided by the government); $67,000 per burn injury and $700 to repair a burned vehicle (company estimates)

Total benefits: 180 × ($200,000) + 180 × ($67,000) + 2,100 × ($700) = **$49.5 million**

Costs of Fixing the Pintos

Sales: 11 million cars, 1.5 million light trucks

Unit cost: $11 per car, $11 per light truck

Total cost: 11,000,000 × ($11) + 1,500,000 × ($11) = **$137 million**

Based on this analysis and other considerations, including not being required by law to change its product design, Ford decided not to change the placement of the fuel tank.

Ford's risk–benefit analysis relied only on act-utilitarian reasoning, an approach that ignores the rights of various stakeholders. A rule-utilitarian approach might have led Ford to follow the rule "Never sacrifice public safety." A rights theory approach would have led to the same conclusion, based on the reasoning that the driving public has an ethical right to expect that their cars will not blow up if there is a crash at low speeds.

Ethical decision making is more difficult when an important factor is omitted from the analysis, which can happen if a cognitive error occurs. The framing of the problem may be inadequate to the task and make it more difficult to properly define the scope of the problem. For example, Ford did not include as a potential cost the lawsuit judgments that might be awarded to the plaintiffs and against the company. For example, in May 1972, Lily Gray was traveling with 13-year-old Richard Grimshaw when their Pinto was struck by another car traveling approximately 30 miles per hour. The impact ignited a fire in the Pinto, which killed Gray and left Grimshaw with devastating injuries. A judgment was rendered against Ford, and the jury awarded the Gray family $560,000 and Matthew Grimshaw, the father of Richard Grimshaw, $2.5 million in compensatory damages. The surprise came when the jury also awarded $125 million in punitive damages. This was subsequently reduced to $3.5 million.[54]

In the aftermath of the scandal, it is interesting to consider whether any of the Ford executives who were involved in the decision-making process would have predicted in advance that they would have made such an unethical choice. Dennis Gioia, who was in charge of recalling defective automobiles at Ford, did not advocate ordering a recall. Gioia eventually came to view his decision not to recall the Pinto as a moral failure—what De Cremer and Tenbrunsel call a failure to think outside his prevailing background narrative or script at the point of decision. "My own schematized (scripted) knowledge influenced me to perceive recall issues in terms of the prevailing decision environment and to unconsciously overlook key features of the Pinto case . . . mainly because they did not fit an existing script." While personal morality was very important to Gioia, he admits that the framing narrative of his workplace "did not include ethical dimension."[55] The moral mistake was that there were other, better choices that he could have made—albeit ones outside the purview of Gioia's framing narrative.

Lessons Learned?

Has the automobile industry learned a lesson from Ford's experience with the Pinto? The answer is an unequivocal no. We've learned about the VW defeat device case, and here is another example of moral blindness by a supplier of parts to an automobile company.

On September 1, 2017, Honda agreed to a $605 million so-called economic loss settlement covering up to 16.5 million U.S. vehicles with potentially faulty Takata air bag inflators. The settlement covers damages linked to inflators, including claims that vehicles were inaccurately represented to be safe, and that buyers had overpaid for cars with defective or substandard air bags. At least 18 deaths and 180 injuries worldwide have been tied to the defect that led to Takata filing for bankruptcy protection. At the time of this writing, 19 automakers had recalled more than 42 million vehicles in the largest auto safety callback in history. Takata expects 125 million vehicles worldwide will eventually be recalled due to its defect-prone inflators.[56] Various reports indicate that Honda and Takata knew about the faulty inflators since 2004 but failed to notify the National Highway Traffic Safety Administration in previous recalls (which began in 2008) that the affected airbags actually ruptured or were linked to injuries or deaths.

Johnson & Johnson

It's not easy finding a company that did the right thing when faced with an ethical dilemma about the safety of a product sold to the public. Even though it occurred more than thirty-five years ago, Johnson & Johnson's experience with poisoned Tylenol capsules stands as an example of how at least one company properly framed the ethical issues and made decisions to protect the public rather than take advantage of it.

Johnson & Johnson faced a crisis in the fall of 1982, when seven people in the Chicago area collapsed suddenly and died after taking Tylenol capsules that had been laced with cyanide. These five women and two men became the first victims ever to die from what came to be known as "product tampering." The news of this incident traveled quickly and was the cause of a massive, nationwide panic.

Johnson & Johnson reacted swiftly to the news and by all accounts the company took the steps necessary to gain the public trust. Many wondered why Johnson & Johnson was able to do what other companies like Ford could not. The company pointed to their corporate credo that detailed the ethical values of the company. The credo appears in Exhibit 3.2.

EXHIBIT 3.2   Johnson & Johnson Credo

We believe our first responsibility is to the doctors, nurses, and patients, to mothers and fathers and all others who use our products and services. In meeting their needs, everything we do must be of high quality. We must constantly strive to reduce our costs in order to maintain reasonable prices. Customers' orders must be serviced promptly and accurately. Our suppliers and distributors must have an opportunity to make a fair profit.

We are responsible to our employees, the men and women who work with us throughout the world. Everyone must be considered as an individual. We must respect their dignity and recognize their merit. They must have a sense of security in their jobs. Compensation must be fair and adequate, and working conditions clean, orderly, and safe. We must be mindful of ways to help our employees fulfill their family responsibilities. Employees must feel free to make suggestions and complaints. There must be equal opportunity for employment, development, and advancement for those qualified. We must provide competent management, and their actions must be just and ethical.

We are responsible to the communities in which we live and work, and to the world community as well. We must be good citizens—support good works and charities and bear our fair share of taxes. We must encourage civic improvements and better health and education. We must maintain in good order the property we are privileged to use, protecting the environment and natural resources.

Our final responsibility is to our stockholders. Business must make a sound profit. We must experiment with new ideas. Research must be carried on, innovative programs developed, and mistakes paid for. New equipment must be purchased, new facilities provided, and new products launched. Reserves must be created to provide for adverse times. When we operate according to these principles, the stockholders should realize a fair return.

Source: Johnson & Johnson Credo, http://www.jnj.com/sites/default/files/pdf/jnj_ourcredo_english_us_8.5x11_cmyk.pdf.

Unlike a code of ethics that details expectations for behavior and consequences for failure, a credo is an aspirational statement of what the company values. The Johnson & Johnson credo clearly sets a positive tone. Notice how it emphasizes the company's primary obligations to those who use and rely on the safety of its products. The credo focuses on rights and obligations—to the health care community, patients and employees—and it implies that shareholders will earn a fair return if the company operates in accordance with its ethical values. Johnson & Johnson was credited with being an ethical organization in part because of the way it handled the Tylenol poisoning incidents in 1982 and its experience is discussed in most business ethics textbooks.

Tamara Kaplan, a professor at Penn State University, contends that Johnson & Johnson used the Tylenol poisonings to launch a public relations program immediately to preserve the integrity of both their product and their corporation as a whole. We find this to be a vacuous position, however. By Kaplan's own admission, "Johnson & Johnson's top management put customer safety first, before they worried about their company's profit and other financial concerns."[57] This hardly sounds like a company that used a catastrophic event to boost its image in the eyes of the public.

Johnson & Johnson's stock price dropped precipitously after the initial incident was made public. In the end, the stock price recovered because the company's actions gained the support and confidence of the public. Johnson & Johnson acted swiftly to remove all the product from the shelves of supermarkets, provide free replacements of Tylenol capsules with the tablet form of the product, and make public statements of assurance that the company would not sell an unsafe product. To claim that the company was motivated by a public relations agenda (even though in the end, its actions did provide a public relations boon for the company) is to ignore a basic point that Johnson & Johnson's management may have known all along: that is, good ethics is good business. We wish this story had a happier ending. Unfortunately, Johnson & Johnson has been involved in several incidents of unsafe products and has absorbed billions in lawsuits from the public during the past ten years.

The Wharton School looks at some of the product recalls and concludes the company had quality control problems with several of its brands. For example, the painkiller Motrin was found to be dissolving improperly and two hip replacement devices that were recalled in 2010 after the shredding of metal fragments led to post-surgical complications in some patients. The company also agreed to pay the state of Texas $158 million to settle claims it improperly marketed the anti-psychotic drug Risperdal to patients on Medicaid. Ironically, the article questions whether Johnson & Johnson was putting profits over patient safety. A marketing professor offered that it was a failure in the quality of management at all levels and says the company has to be more responsive than ever to potential problems.[58] No doubt, letting problems fester makes them worse and invites the slippery slope into ethical decision making.

Trust in Business

"Responsibility creates trust" is the credo of Bosch, the German multinational engineering and electronics company. Trust in business is the cornerstone of relationships with customers, suppliers, employees, and others who have dealings with an organization. Trust means to be reliable and carry through words with deeds. Trust becomes pervasive only if the organization's values are followed and supported by top management. By modeling the organization's values, senior leaders provide a benchmark for all employees.

A good example of building trust in an organization is from Paul O'Neill, former CEO at Alcoa Inc., the world's third-largest producer of aluminum. O'Neill created a reputation for trust among his employees by setting strict ethical standards and carrying through with them. In an interview with "PBS Newshour" on July 9, 2002, O'Neill was asked by reporter Jim Lehrer why Alcoa was able to avoid the accounting scandals that infected so many companies in the late 1990s and early 2000s. He responded with the following statement: "When I went there [to Alcoa], I called the chief financial officer and the controller and I said to them, 'I don't want to ever be accused of or guilty of managing earnings,' that is to say making earnings that really aren't as a consequence of operations." O'Neill went on to express in the interview his dismay at the number of cases where employees of a company were told that here are our company's values, and then senior management totally ignored those same values.

Trust can be lost, even if once gained in the eyes of the public, if an organization no longer follows the guiding principles that helped to create its reputation for trust. The long list of product defects at Johnson & Johnson proves that point.

Foundations of Corporate Governance Systems

LO 3-5

Discuss the scope and role of corporate governance systems in the ethical decision-making process.

In his book *Corporate Governance and Ethics,* Zabihollah Rezaee points out that corporate governance is shaped by internal and external mechanisms, as well as policy interventions through regulations. Internal mechanisms help manage, direct, and monitor corporate governance activities to create sustainable stakeholder value. Examples include the board of directors, particularly independent directors; the audit committee; management; internal controls; and the internal audit function. External mechanisms are intended to monitor the company's activities, affairs, and performance to ensure that the interests of insiders (management, directors, and officers) are aligned with the interests of outsiders (shareholders and other stakeholders). Examples of external mechanisms include the financial markets, state and federal statutes, SEC regulations, court decisions, and shareholder proposals.[59] Three noteworthy points are: (1) independent directors enhance governance accountability; (2) separation of the duties of the CEO and board chair minimizes conflicts of interest; and (3) separate meetings between the audit committee and external auditors strengthen control mechanisms.

Ethical and Legal Responsibilities of Officers and Directors

Duty of Care—Managers and Directors

Directors and officers are deemed fiduciaries of the corporation because their relationship with the corporation and its shareholders is one of trust and confidence. As fiduciaries, directors and officers owe ethical—and legal—duties to the corporation and to the shareholders. These fiduciary duties include the duty of care and the duty of loyalty.

The standard of *due care* provides that a director or officer act in good faith, exercise the care that an ordinarily prudent person would exercise in similar circumstances, and act in the way that she considers to be in the best interests of the corporation. Directors and officers who have not exercised the required duty of care can be held liable for the harms suffered by the corporation as a result of their negligence. Notice how this standard ties into Kant's Categorical Imperative: Act only according to that maxim whereby you can, at the same time, will that it should become a *universal law.* The universal standard is one of due care.

The duty of care also involves the exercise of reasonable care by a board member to ensure that the corporate executives with whom she works carry out their management responsibilities and comply with the law in the best interests of the corporation.[60]

Duty of Loyalty

The *duty of loyalty* requires faithfulness; a director must place the interests of the corporation ahead of personal interests. For example, directors must not use corporate funds or confidential corporate information for personal advantage. A conflict occurs when a board member hears of a potential deal that might affect the selling price of company stock (up or down). The board member's attempt to profit from this knowledge is called insider trading; it's illegal as well as being a conflict of interest.[61] Another conflict would be if a board member is involved in a personal relationship with an employee of the company. The employee's position with the company might be affected by the relationship and allegations of sexual harassment could harm corporate interests.

Duty of Good Faith

The obligation of *good faith* requires an honesty of purpose that leads to caring for the well-being of the constituents of the fiduciary. Vice Chancellor Leo Strine of the Delaware Chancery Court linked good faith to fiduciary analysis in the Enron fraud by suggesting that the Enron case might influence courts to look more carefully at whether directors have made a good faith effort to accomplish their duties. He connected good faith with directors' "state of mind." Strine identified certain kinds of director conduct that may call good faith into question. These include "a failure to monitor if [the directors'] laxity in oversight was so persistent and substantial that it evidences bad faith." It can also arise in situations where "committee members knew that their inadequate knowledge disabled them from discharging their responsibilities with fidelity."[62]

Business Judgment Rule

A corporate director or officer may be able to avoid liability to the corporation or to its shareholders for poor business judgments under the *business judgment rule.* Directors and officers are expected to exercise due care and to use their best judgment in guiding corporate management, but they are not insurers of business success. Honest mistakes of judgment and poor business decisions on their part do not make them liable to the corporation for resulting damages.

To obtain the business judgment rule's protection, directors must be independent and disinterested as to the matter acted upon. Directors must act with due care and good faith. The due care inquiry is process-oriented, and due care is measured by a standard of gross negligence (i.e., reckless behavior), not simple negligence. The burden of proof is on the party challenging the board's decision, to establish facts rebutting the presumption in favor of upholding the decision. Unless a plaintiff succeeds in rebutting the rule, the court will not substitute its views for those of the board's if the latter's decision can be "attributed to any rational business purpose."

The business judgment rule generally immunizes directors and officers from liability for the consequences of a decision that is within managerial authority, as long as the decision complies with management's fiduciary duties and as long as acting on the decision is within the powers of the corporation. Therefore, if there is a reasonable basis for a business decision, it is unlikely that a court will interfere with that decision, even if the corporation suffers as a result.

Chancery Court

The Chancery Court located in Delaware is the preeminent forum for the resolution of commercial business litigation matters including the duties of officers and directors. The Court's fundamental purpose is to be an equity court—to provide relief suited to the circumstances when no adequate remedy is available at law.

The broad interpretation of the business judgment rule was on display on August 9, 2005, when Chancellor William B. Chandler III of the Delaware Court ruled that the directors of the Walt Disney Company acted in good faith when Michael Ovitz was hired in 1995 to be the CEO of Disney and then allowed to walk away 15 months later with a severance package valued at $130 million after being fired by Michael Eisner, the chair of the board of directors. In a lawsuit challenging the board's action, the shareholder plaintiffs alleged that the Disney's directors had breached their fiduciary duties both in approving Ovitz's employment agreement and in later allowing the payment of the non-fault termination benefits. The Delaware Supreme Court affirmed the Court of Chancery's conclusion that the shareholder plaintiffs had failed to prove that the defendants had breached any fiduciary duty of care. As to the ensuing no-fault termination of Ovitz and the resulting termination payment pursuant to his employment agreement, the Supreme Court affirmed the trial court's holdings that the full board did not (and was not required to) approve Ovitz's termination, that Michael Eisner had authorized the termination, and that neither Eisner, nor Sanford Litvack, Disney's General Counsel, had breached his duty of care or acted in bad faith in connection with the termination.[63]

Components of Corporate Governance Systems

An essential part of creating an ethical organization environment is to put in place effective corporate governance systems that establish control mechanisms to ensure that organizational values guide decision making and that ethical standards are being followed. Corporate governance entails developing formal systems of accountability, oversight, and control. Strong corporate governance mechanisms lessen the opportunity for employees to make unethical decisions. Research has shown that corporate governance has a positive relationship with social responsibility. Moreover, firms with strong corporate governance mechanisms that call for the disclosure of social responsibility initiatives can establish legitimacy and trust among their stakeholders.[64]

There are many ways to define corporate governance. We prefer the definition by Ferrell et al.[65] described below.

> Accountability refers to how closely workplace decisions align with a firm's strategic direction and its compliance with ethical and legal considerations. Oversight provides a system of checks and balances that limit employees' and managers' opportunities to deviate from policies and strategies aimed at preventing unethical and illegal activities. Control is the process of auditing and improving organizational decisions and actions.

Models of Corporate Governance

Differences exist about the role of corporate governance in business. Some organizations take the view that as long as they are maximizing shareholder wealth and profitability, they are fulfilling their core responsibilities. Other firms take a broader view based on the stakeholder perspective.

The shareholder model of corporate governance is founded on classic economic precepts, including maximizing wealth for investors and creditors. In a public corporation, firm decisions should be oriented toward serving the best interests of investors. Underlying these decisions is a classic agency problem, in which ownership (investors) and control (managers) are separate. Managers act as the agents of the investors (principals), who expect those decisions to increase the value of the stock they own.[66] However, managers may have motivations beyond stockholder value such as increasing market share or more personal ones including maximizing executive compensation. In these instances, decisions may be based on an egoist approach to ethical decision making that ignores the interests of others. An enlightened egoist approach is more in keeping with capitalistic theory whereby other interests are considered by managers prior to deciding how best to serve their own interests. For example, it could be that managers believe an increase in the corporate dividend serves their interest because it may convince shareholders that managers are acting like responsible agents.

Albrecht et al. point out that the principal-agent relationship involves a transfer of trust and duty to the agent, while also assuming that the agent is opportunistic and will pursue interests that are in conflict with those of the principal, thereby creating an "agency problem."[67] Because of these potential differences, corporate governance mechanisms are needed to align investor and management interests. A fundamental challenge underlying all corporate governance affairs dates back to the days of Adam Smith. In *The Wealth of Nations,* Smith said that "the directors of companies, being managers of other people's money, cannot be expected to watch over it with the same vigilance with which they watch over their own."

One traditional approach is for shareholders to give the CEO shares or options of stock that vest over time, thus inducing long-term behavior and deterring short-term actions that can harm future company value. When the interests of top management are brought in line with interests of shareholders, agency theory argues that management will fulfill its duty to shareholders, not so much out of any sense of moral duty to shareholders, but because doing what shareholders have provided incentives for maximizes their own utility.[68]

Jensen and Meckling demonstrate how investors in publicly traded corporations incur (agency) costs in monitoring managerial performance. In general, agency costs arise whenever there is an "information asymmetry" between the corporation and outsiders because insiders (the corporation) know more about a company and its future prospects than do outsiders (investors).[69]

Agency costs can occur if the board of directors fails to exercise due care in its oversight role of management. Enron's board of directors did not monitor the company's incentive compensation plans properly, thereby allowing top executives to "hype" the company's stock so that employees would add it to their 401(k) retirement plans. While the hyping occurred, often through positive statements about the company made by CEO Ken Lay, Lay himself sold about 2.3 million shares for $123.4 million.

The agency problem can never be perfectly solved, and shareholders may experience a loss of wealth due to divergent behavior of managers. Investigations by the SEC and U.S. Department of Justice of 20 corporate frauds during the Enron-WorldCom era indicate that $236 billion in shareholder value was lost between the time the public first learned of the first fraud and September 3, 2002, the measurement date.

An alternative to agency theory is stewardship theory. In this theory, managers and directors are viewed as stewards of their companies and have a fiduciary duty to act in the best interests of the shareholders. The theory holds that as stewards, managers and directors will choose the interests of shareholders, perhaps psychologically identified as the best interests of "the company," over self-interests, regardless of personal motivations or incentives.[70] Contrary to agency theory, stewardship theory believes that directors do not inevitably act in a way that maximizes their own personal interests: They can and do act responsibly with independence and integrity. Even though some will fail, it does not invalidate the theory.[71]

Stewardship advocates recognize that directors need to consider a broader range of interests, including employees, customers, suppliers, and other legitimate stakeholders, but under the law their first responsibility is to the shareholders. They argue that conflicts of interest between stakeholder groups and the company should be met by competitive pressures in free markets, backed by legislation and legal controls to protect various stakeholder interests (i.e., environmental law; health and safety law; employment discrimination law).

Executive Compensation

One of the most common approaches to the agency problem is to link managerial compensation to the financial performance of the corporation in general and the performance of the company's shares. Typically, this occurs by creating long-term compensation packages and stock option plans that tie executive wealth to an increase in the corporation's stock price. These incentives aim to encourage managers to maximize the market value of shares. One of the biggest issues that corporate boards of directors face is executive compensation. It has been found that most boards spend more time deciding how much to compensate top executives than they do ensuring the integrity of the company's financial reporting systems.[72]

Executive Pay Packages

A problem arises when top management purposefully manipulates earnings amounts to drive up the price of stock so they can cash in more lucrative stock options. During the financial crisis of 2008–2009, Congress charged executives at some of the nation's largest companies with gaining pay packages in the millions while their companies suffered losses, and they may have even accepted funds from the government to keep them liquid. The Obama administration named a "compensation czar," Kenneth Feinberg, to set salaries and bonuses at some of the biggest firms at the heart of the economic crisis, as part of a broader government campaign to reshape pay practices across corporate America. The initiative reflected public uproar over executive compensation at companies such as American International Group (AIG), which received a $180 billion bailout from the government and decided to pay $165 million in bonuses to executives.

A 2016 study by the Economic Policy Institute in the U.S. indicates that the CEOs at one of the largest 350 companies made an average of $15.6 million in compensation, or 271 times the annual average pay of the typical worker. The ratio was 20-to-1 in 1965.[73] On a global basis, based on 2014 figures, this compares with a ratio of 148:1 in Switzerland, the nearest country, 84:1 in the United Kingdom, and 67:1 in Japan.[74]

Similar to the Disney example, a troubling situation occurred when the former CEO of CVS received a severance package worth $185 million when he left in early 2011, even though the company's net earnings had declined in the prior year. In 2014, the former chief operating officer of Yahoo, who was fired earlier in the year, received about $96 million in compensation for his 15 months on the job, including about $58 million in severance packages.

The disparity between average worker and CEO pay raises issues of equity. Thomas Dunfee, a Wharton professor of legal studies and business ethics, puts it this way: Do executive compensation figures reflect an efficient market, or a failed one? Are pay levels adequately disclosed? Should shareholders have more say? Are there issues of fairness and justice?[75]

Backdating Stock Options

An executive compensation scandal erupted in 2006 when it was discovered that some companies had changed the grant dates of their options to coincide with a dip in the stock price, making the options worth more because less money would be needed to exercise them and buy stock. Although backdating was legal, it must be expensed and disclosed properly in the financial statements. Legalities aside, it is difficult to justify such a practice from an ethical perspective because it purposefully manipulates the option criteria that determine their value.

In the wake of this scandal, hundreds of companies conducted internal probes and the SEC launched investigations into more than 140 firms. The agency filed charges against 24 companies and 66 individuals for backdating-related offenses, and at least 15 people have been convicted of criminal conduct. An interesting case is that of Nancy Heinen, Apple Computer's general counsel until she left in 2006. She was investigated by the SEC for receiving backdated options and wound up agreeing to pay $2.2 million in disgorgement (return of ill-gotten gains), interest, and penalties. Steve Jobs, the former CEO of Apple, apologized on behalf of the company, stating that he did not understand the relevant accounting laws. Of course, ignorance of the law is no excuse for violating it, especially by someone like Jobs, who presumably had dozens of accountants on staff to advise on these matters. Notably, the Sarbanes-Oxley Act includes stricter reporting requirements that are supposed to cut down on such practices.

Clawbacks

The Dodd-Frank Wall Street Reform and Consumer Protection Act (H.R. 4173)[76] was signed into federal law by President Barack Obama on July 21, 2010. Passed as a response to the late-2000s recession, it brought the most significant changes to financial regulation in the U.S. since the regulatory reform that followed the Great Depression. Two areas where Dodd-Frank relates to corporate governance are in executive compensation and in whistleblowing procedures, which will be discussed later on.

Clawbacks have been on the regulatory radar screen in a big way since 2002, when SOX gave the SEC power to recover compensation and stock profits from CEOs and CFOs of public companies in the event of financial restatements caused by misconduct. Clawback policies among Fortune 100 companies were already on the rise before the financial crisis, jumping from 17.6% in 2006 to 42.1% in 2007. In 2010, the year Dodd-Frank was passed, 82.1% of the Fortune 100 had them. In 2012, 86.5% of the Fortune 100 firms had adopted publicly disclosed policies. Now, about 90% have such policies. The ethical justification for clawbacks is the breach of fiduciary duty owed by top management to shareholders and inequities when they benefit from their own wrongful acts.

On July 1, 2015, the SEC proposed rules directing U.S. stock exchanges to create listing standards requiring listed companies to implement policies to recover or "claw back" incentive-based compensation received by executive officers as a result of materially incorrect financial statements. These proposed rules are mandated by Section 954 of Dodd-Frank. Because the SEC has not finalized its Clawback Policy Rules, it is unlikely that companies will be required to adopt the proposed clawback policies in 2017 or even soon thereafter.

According to a PwC study, many companies have modified their clawback policies since enactment of SOX and Dodd-Frank, and others have indicated that their policies will likely change once the SEC issues its clawback rules. Of the 100 companies in the study, 90% have policies to recover compensation if there is a restatement of financial results. However, of those that claw back upon restatement, 73% require evidence that the employee caused or contributed to false or incorrect financial reporting, while 27% require repayment in the event of a restatement even without any personal accountability. Another prevalent reason for clawbacks was misconduct (83%), which includes breaking a companies code of conduct or ethics policies.[77]

The scandal at Wells Fargo led to millions in clawbacks of executive compensation. Carrie Tolstedt, former head of the bank's retail division, had a $67 million clawback; John Stumpf, $69 million; and an additional $44 million from three other executives, for a total of $180 million. This is the largest clawback ever for a financial services firm.

Say on Pay

Dodd-Frank includes "say-on-pay" provisions (Section 951) that require SEC-registered issuers to provide shareholders at least once every three calendar years a separate nonbinding say-on-pay vote regarding the compensation of the company's named executive officers (i.e., CEO and CFO) and the company's three other most highly compensated officers. Although the vote on compensation is nonbinding, the company must include a statement in the "Compensation Discussion and Analysis" of the proxy statement whether its compensation policies and decisions have taken into account the results of the shareholder-say-on-pay vote and, if so, how. The idea is for the vote of the shareholders to be taken seriously not only by the company, but also by other companies in the same marketplace.

In perhaps the most widely followed shareholder action, in April 2012, 55% of Citigroup's shareholders voted against CEO Vikram Pandit's $15 million compensation package for 2011, a year when the bank's stock tumbled. At the time of the vote, Pandit had received nearly $7 million in cash for 2011, with the remainder to be paid in restricted stock and cash over the next few years (and thus subject to possible restructuring by the board). Citigroup's shareholders expressed concerns that the compensation package lacked significant and important goals to provide incentives for improvement in the shareholder value of the institution. Soon after the vote, a shareholder filed a derivative lawsuit against the CEO, the board of directors, and other directors and executives for allegedly awarding excessive pay to its senior officers.

On April 29, 2015, the SEC proposed new rules requiring public companies to make it easier for investors to judge whether top executives' compensation is in step with the company's financial performance. The proposal aims to give investors greater clarity about the link between what corporate executives are paid each year and total shareholder return–the annual change in stock price plus reinvested dividends. If finalized, companies would have to include a new table in their annual proxy filings disclosing top executives' "actual pay." The new figure is based on the total compensation public companies already calculate for their five highest-paid executives, though it would exclude certain components of pay that officers do not actually take home, such as share grants that have yet to vest.

Questions raised by shareholders and others about the size of executive compensation packages and say-on-pay votes are designed to build equity into the compensation system. Issues with respect to whether CEOs are overpaid, as many have said, do bring up questions of fairness and justice. Without transparency, it is difficult to have accountability. Over the long haul, the question is whether these nonbinding referendums are likely to have any impact on the potential civil liability of directors for approving allegedly excessive executive compensation that the shareholders reject. According to Robert Scully, who analyzed the law in the January 2011 *The Federal Lawyer,* the answer is probably not. Scully maintains that Dodd-Frank does not preempt state fiduciary law or entirely occupy the field of director liability for excessive compensation. Instead, the act focuses on the process by which public company executive compensation is set, thereby enforcing the primacy of the business judgment rule in determining executive compensation.[78]

Corporate Governance Oversight and Regulation

Following the large number of frauds and business failures in the later 1990s and early 2000s, regulators turned to the systems in place to monitor corporate behavior. This led to developing policies and procedures to strengthen the oversight and regulation of corporate governance mechanisms, in particular the board of directors and audit committee. Prior to the passage of SOX in the U.S., the United Kingdom had dealt with this problem and established the Cadbury Committee.

The Committee on the Financial Aspects of Corporate Governance, (Cadbury Committee), was established in May 1991 by the Financial Reporting Council, the London Stock Exchange, and the accountancy profession. The motivation for the Committee's creation was an increasing lack of investor confidence in the honesty and accountability of listed companies, following a large number of bank failures in the early 1990s including the collapse of the Bank of Credit and Commerce International and exposure of its widespread criminal practices.

The essence of Cadbury recommendations was to develop an approach 'based on compliance with a voluntary code coupled with disclosure, that would prove more effective than a statutory code'. The central components of this voluntary code, the Cadbury Code, are:[79]

- that there be a clear division of responsibilities at the top, primarily that the position of Chairman of the Board be separated from that of Chief Executive, or that there be a strong independent element on the board;
- that the majority of the Board be comprised of outside directors;
- that remuneration committees for Board members be made up in the majority of non-executive directors;
- that the Board should appoint an Audit Committee including at least three non-executive directors.

An outside or non-executive director is a member of a company's board of directors who is not part of the executive team. Non-executive directors, also known as external directors, independent directors, or outside directors, do not hold executive level or managerial positions. These directors are thought to hold the interests of the company in higher regard than executive directors, who may have an agency problem or conflict of interest between management and stockholders. A non-executive director typically does not engage in the day-to-day management of the organization, but is involved in policy making and planning exercises. In addition, non-executive directors' responsibilities include the monitoring of the executive directors and acting in the interest of the company stakeholders.

Requirements for Public Company Boards in the U.S.

Public companies in the U.S. that list their equity securities on the New York Stock Exchange (NYSE) or the Nasdaq Stock Market (Nasdaq) are required to have in place a board of directors with the following features:[80]

Independent Directors

Independent directors must comprise a majority of the board. An "independent director" is one who has no material relationship with the company either directly or as a partner, shareholder, or officer of an organization that has a relationship with the company. The company must have a minimum three-member audit committee composed of entirely independent directors.

Audit Committee

In addition to the independence requirements above, the audit committee must meet the independence requirements enumerated in Section 301 of SOX and the Securities Exchange Act Rule 10A-3(b)(1). This prohibits a director from accepting any direct or indirect consulting, advisory, or other compensatory fee from the listed company other than compensation for director service and not being affiliated with the company or its subsidiaries.

Not addressed by the NYSE, SEC Regulation S-K requires disclosure in annual reports whether or not the audit committee includes at least one "financial expert." An audit committee financial expert has an understanding of the financial statements and GAAP; experience in preparing, auditing, analyzing, or evaluating financial statements of companies comparable to the company or experience in actively supervising one or more persons engaged in such activities; experience in applying GAAP to accounting for estimates, accruals, and reserves; and an understanding of internal accounting controls, procedures for financial reporting, and audit committee functions.

Audit committee duties and responsibilities include, among others:

- To meet at least annually with the independent auditor and review the audit report describing independent auditor's internal quality control procedures.
- Discuss any material issues raised by the auditor's most recent internal quality control review or peer review of the firm, or by any inquiry or investigation by governmental or professional authorities within the preceding five years with regard to one or more independent audits carried out by the firm and steps taken to deal with any such issues.
- Discuss all relationships between the independent auditor and the company to enable assessment of the auditor's independence.
- Meet and discuss with the independent auditor and management the annual audited financial statements and quarterly financial statements, including review of Management's Discussion and Analysis of Financial Condition and Results of Operations.

- Discuss earnings press releases and financial information and earnings guidance given to analysts and rating agencies.

- Discuss policies with respect to risk assessment and risk management.

- Meet separately, from time to time, with management, with internal auditors, and with independent auditors.

- Review with the independent auditor any audit problems or difficulties and management's response to such issues.

- Set clear hiring policies for employees or former employees of the independent auditor.

- Report regularly to the board of directors.

- Evaluate work of the audit committee annually.

Public companies also should have a compensation committee composed only of independent directors. It's best not to have the same members serve on the audit and compensation committees to reduce the likelihood of any conflict of interest.

Corporate Governance Failures at Lehman Brothers

The Great Recession that officially lasted from December 2007 to June 2009, ushered in a period of bank failures and fraud that shook the economy of the U.S. Many people blamed excessive risk taking and failed corporate governance systems. Some point out that "moral hazard" was a major contributing factor. *Moral hazard* occurs where one party is responsible for the interests of another, but has an incentive to put its own interests first. The banks used collateral debt obligations (CDOs) to repackage individual mortgage loans into a product sold to investors on the secondary market. By so doing, Lehman transferred the risk of nonpayment on these financial instruments to other parties. Given the transfer of risk, Lehman initially issued loans to uncreditworthy borrowers, knowing the bank would not be responsible if the homeowners defaulted. Unfortunately, the extra liquidity created an asset bubble in housing, credit cards, and auto debt. Housing prices skyrocketed beyond their actual value. People bought homes so they could sell them. The easy availability of debt meant people used their credit cards too much. That drove credit card debt to almost $1 trillion in 2008.

For two and a half years, the U.S. Senate focused on the role of financial institutions in the financial crisis that started with the failure of Lehman Brothers. A bankruptcy examiner's report issued on April 12, 2011, shed light on the role of auditing firms in the financial meltdown. The report was written by Jenner & Block Chairman Anton Valukas. The details of Lehman's financial activities that vaulted the company into bankruptcy are too complicated to discuss in detail, but we do provide a brief summary in Exhibit 3.3 because of its significance to the great financial recession.

At the Senate Banking Committee hearings on the Lehman failure and subsequent financial crisis, Valukas spoke about the general principle that auditors play a critical role in the proper functioning of public companies and financial markets. He said:

> Boards of directors and audit committees are entitled to rely on external auditors to serve as watchdogs—to be important gatekeepers who provide an independent check on management. And the investing public is entitled to believe that a 'clean' report from an independent auditor stands for something. The public has every right to conclude that auditors who hold themselves out as independent will stand up to management and not succumb to pressure to avoid rocking the boat. I found that [valid] claims exist against Lehman's external auditor in connection with Lehman's issuance of materially misleading financial reports.

The Lehman failure illustrates how things can go so wrong when sound corporate governance mechanisms are not in place or not working as intended. The following is a brief description of those failures, many of which were in the area of corporate risk management.

- Failed risk management procedures brought on by excessive use of CDOs with exposure that far exceeded Lehman's understanding of the inherent risks.
- Ignoring warnings signs of liquidity risk.
- Failure to disclose material information on foreseeable risk factors.
- The Valukas report indicated that Lehman repeatedly exceeded its own internal risk limits and controls.
- Richard S. Fuld, Jr. served as chairperson and CEO.
- Make up of the board was inadequate given the complex nature of Lehman's financial transactions: only two of ten members had direct experience in the financial services industry.
- Significant payments were made to members of the board, which did not result from remuneration granted to them. These were payments from investment activity of limited partnerships set up by the company and that directors could engage.
- Top executive managers at Lehman received about $1 billion from cash bonuses and equity sales between 2000 and 2008; chairperson Fuld received close to $500 million just four days before the collapse.
- The staff owned four percent of the bank in 1994 when it went public and about 30% by 2006, mostly due to stock and options, the equivalent of $11 billion on paper.
- Ernst & Young know of potential accounting irregularities and failed to raise the issue with Lehman's board.

The relationships and activities described above illustrate a breakdown in ethics and failure of the board to exercise objective independent judgment on bank affairs. The board did not effectively monitor activities and did not meet the corporate governance standard of accountability to shareholders. It failed to meet its fiduciary responsibilities and duty of care to the shareholders. During the court process the Lehman officers stated that "Ernst & Young did not approve the Accounting Policy," instead the firm "became comfortable with the Policy for purposes of auditing financial statements."

EXHIBIT 3.3 Lehman's Financial Transactions and Accounting Irregularities

The financial recession started when Lehman Brothers failed because it was unable to retain the confidence of its lenders and counterparts and because it did not have sufficient liquidity to meet its current obligations. Lehman engaged in a series of business decisions and transactions that had left it with heavy concentrations of illiquid assets with deteriorating values such as residential and commercial real estate. Confidence eroded when Lehman reportedly had two consecutive quarters of huge reported losses, $2.8 billion in the second quarter of 2008 and $3.9 billion in the third quarter of that year.

The business decisions that had brought Lehman to its crisis of confidence may have been in error but were deemed by the bankruptcy examiner to be largely within the business judgment rule. But the decision not to disclose the effects of those judgments created a valid claim against the senior officers who oversaw and certified misleading financial statements. Legal claims of failing to meet professional responsibilities were charged against Lehman's CEO, Richard Fuld, and its CFOs, Christopher O'Meara, Erin M. Callan, and Ian Lowitt. A valid claim also existed against its external auditor, Ernst & Young, for its failure to question and challenge improper or inadequate disclosures in those financial statements, among other things.

(Continued)

Lehman had used an accounting device (known within Lehman as "Repo 105") to manage its balance sheet by temporarily removing approximately $50 billion of assets from the balance sheet at the end of the first and second quarters of 2008.

In an ordinary "repo," Lehman raised cash by selling assets with a simultaneous obligation to repurchase them the next day or several days later; such transactions were accounted for as financings, and the assets remained on Lehman's balance sheet. In a Repo 105 transaction, Lehman did exactly the same thing, but because the assets were 105% or more of the cash received, accounting rules permitted the transactions to be treated as sales rather than financings, so that the assets could be removed from the balance sheet. With Repo 105 transactions, Lehman's reported net leverage was 12.1 at the end of the second quarter of 2008, but if Lehman had used ordinary repos, net leverage would have been reported at 13.9.

Lehman did not disclose its use—or the significant magnitude of its use—of Repo 105 to the federal government, to the rating agencies, to its investors, or to its own board of directors. Ernst & Young was aware of its use but did not question it or the nondisclosure of the Repo 105 accounting transactions. It took Lehman until September 2008, several months into the financial meltdown, to publicly disclose the liquidity issues. On September 10, 2008, the company announced that it was projecting a $3.9 billion loss for the third quarter of 2008. By the close of trading on September 12, its stock price had declined to $3.65 a share, a 94% drop from the $62.19 price on January 2, 2008.

Over the weekend of September 12–14, 2008, a series of meetings were held by U.S. Treasury Secretary Henry Paulson, president of the Federal Reserve Bank of New York Timothy Geithner, SEC chairman Christopher Cox, and the chief executives of leading financial institutions. The government made a decision that many believe ushered in the financial crisis. It refused to fund a solution to the Lehman problem, stating that it did not have the legal authority to make a direct capital investment in Lehman, and Lehman's assets were insufficient to support a loan large enough to avoid its collapse. The bank collapsed on September 15, when it filed for bankruptcy protection. The filing remains the largest bankruptcy filing in U.S. history, with Lehman holding over $600 billion in assets.

Ethics in the Workplace

LO 3-6

Discuss compliance, integrity, and employee views about ethics in the workplace.

When we think about workplace ethics, the first thing that comes to mind is a code of conduct that influences the development of an ethical culture and provides direction to steer the ethical climate toward right behavior. A code goes beyond what is legal for an organization and provides normative guidelines for ethical conduct. Support for ethical behavior from top management is a critical component of fostering an ethical climate. Employees who sense that top managers act unethically quickly lose trust in those managers. The result can be to become disillusioned with the goals of the organization and question whether the corporate culture is one that is consistent with individual, personal values and beliefs.

Here is a list of measures that should be taken to establish an ethical culture:

1. Establish clear policies on ethical conduct including a code of ethics.
2. Develop an ethics training program that instills a commitment to act ethically and explains code provisions.
3. Assign a top-level officer, such as the Chief Ethics and Compliance Officer (CECO) to oversee compliance with ethics policies.

4. Use the internal auditors to investigate whether ethics policies have been followed in practice.

5. Establish strong internal controls to prevent and detect unethical behaviors, such as fraud.

6. Establish whistleblowing policies, including reporting outlets.

7. Establish an ethics hotline where employees can discuss questionable behavior on an anonymous basis.

8. Have employees sign a statement that they have complied with ethics policies.

9. Enforce ethics policies fairly and take immediate action against those who violate the policies.

10. Reward ethical behavior by including it in the performance evaluation system.

Compliance Function

On August 4, 2015, it was announced that the Ethics Resource Center (ERC), the oldest nonprofit advancing high ethical standards and practices in public and private institutions, and the Ethics Compliance and Officer Association (ECOA), a member-driven association for practitioners responsible for their organization's ethics and compliance programs, joined together to form a strategic alliance to become the go-to organization for ethics and compliance resources in the workplace. The resulting Ethics Compliance Initiative (ECI) provides leading ethics and compliance research and best practices, networking opportunities, and certification to its membership, which represents more than 450 organizations across all industries.

The 2016 State of Compliance study conducted by PricewaterhouseCoopers (PwC) reports on the views of 800 executives globally in three important categories: tone at the top, risk assessment, and oversight and responsibility.[81]

Tone at the Top

The results indicate a high level of senior executive support for compliance and ethics programs, but less visible engagement in leading their companies' programs.

98% have senior leadership that is committed to compliance and ethics.

55% indicate senior leadership provides only ad hoc program oversight or delegates most compliance and ethics oversight activities.

48% report their organization assesses its "tone at the top."

Tone at the top includes: (1) communicating compliance and ethics messaging to employees; (2) regularly reminding employees of the importance of ethical and compliant behavior, raising concerns, and the Company's non-retaliation policy; and (3) modeling the Company's values and demonstrating ethical and compliant behavior in everyday decision making and when enforcing disciplinary measures.

Risk Assessment

54% conduct compliance and ethics-specific risk assessment activities beyond enterprise risk management efforts.

21% use employee surveys to gather information for their risk assessments.

67% have a process to identify owners of specific compliance and ethics-related risk.

Even though 67% of respondents indicated there is a process in place in their organizations to identify owners, the study concludes organizations may be relying too heavily on the legal and/or compliance and ethics functions to manage these risk areas on a day-to-day basis. One reason for not relying on the in-house or external counsel is the lawyer's job is to defend the organization. The CECO's job is to bring the bad news to the boss and keep the company out of regulatory or other trouble and help to restore its reputation when ethics or compliance problems arise.

Oversight and Responsibility

20% have Boards of Directors that formed a separate, stand-alone compliance/ethics committee.

72% have dedicated business unit or business area compliance officers.

89% select compliance monitoring as a primary area of responsibility.

The study found that compliance and ethics functions have become more visible with their Boards of Directors and senior leaders. Sixty-three percent of respondents indicated their Boards receive reports on their organizations' compliance and ethics performance on at least a quarterly basis, and 67% indicated their senior leadership receives similar reports on at least a quarterly basis.

The accounting function in ethics and compliance is important. Specifically, 65% of respondents indicated that the audit committee in their organizations oversees most compliance and ethics programs. This makes sense because audit committees are responsible for oversight of internal controls over financial reporting including corporate culture and the tone at the top. The audit committee is responsible for compliance with laws such as SOX and Dodd-Frank. The committee must ensure that the audited financial statements do not contain any material misstatements due to non-compliance with SEC regulations and GAAP. The audit committee also communicates with both the external and internal auditors on matters related to compliance and ethics.

Integrity: The Basis for Trust in the Workplace

Albert Camus, the French Nobel Prize winning author, journalist, and philosopher, said, "Integrity has no need of rules." People of integrity are self-driven to do the right thing. Leaders of integrity act on the knowledge that their actions are ethical and provide the basis for others in the workplace to follow their lead.

KPMG's *Integrity Survey 2013* provides an inside look at organizational misconduct based upon responses from more than 3,500 U.S. working adults. Key findings from the report include:[82]

- Nearly three out of four employees reported that they had observed misconduct within their organizations in the previous 12 months.

- More than half of employees reported that what they observed could potentially cause a significant loss of public trust if discovered.

- Some of the driving forces behind fraud and misconduct in the corporate environment include pressure to do "whatever it takes" to meet targets, not taking the code of conduct seriously, believing employees will be rewarded based upon results and not the means used to achieve them, and fear of losing one's job for not meeting performance targets.

- Nearly half of employees were uncertain that they would be protected from retaliation if they reported concerns to management. And more than half suggested a lack of confidence that they would be satisfied with the outcome.

- Ethics and compliance programs continue to have a favorable impact on employee perceptions and behaviors.

Employees were asked what they would do if they observed a violation of their organization's standards of conduct. The results were: 78% would notify their supervisor or another manager; 54% would try resolving the matter directly; 53% would call the ethics or compliance hotline; 26% would notify someone outside the organization; and 23% would look the other way or do nothing.

It's encouraging to learn that over three-fourths would inform their supervisor, in part because it is the generally recognized initial step in considering whether to blow the whistle. It is somewhat troubling that almost one-quarter of the workers would look the other way or do nothing. Perhaps they do not believe they would be taken seriously or a "kill the messenger" culture exists in the organization. There is also the possibility that dissonance exists if the individual has a high ethics orientation while the organization's is low.

The tone at the top set by top management is a determining factor in creating organizational commitment to high ethics and integrity. Employees were asked whether the chief executive officer and other senior executives exhibited characteristics attributable to personal integrity and ethical leadership. Approximately two-thirds of the employees agreed that their leaders set the right tone regarding the importance of ethics and integrity and served as positive role models for their organization, leaving one-third unsure or in disagreement.

Perhaps not surprisingly, a large percentage (64%) indicated that the root cause of misconduct was pressure to do "whatever it takes" to meet business objectives, while 59% said they believed they would be rewarded for results, not the means used to achieve them. In such instances, the corporate culture does not foster integrity or ethical behavior; instead, expedience and self-interest drive workplace behavior. Moreover, the findings seem to indicate a majority of respondents believe their organizations follow an end justifies the means approach to decision making: what is most important is results, not the way they were achieved.

Employees Perceptions of Ethics in the Workplace

Going beyond the Integrity Survey, it is important to understand how employees view the ethics of the organizations they work for, in part to better understand corporate governance systems and whistleblowing. The *2013 National Business Ethics Survey* (NBES) conducted by the Ethics Resource Center provides interesting data about ethics in the workplace. The report is the eighth in a series. The 2013 survey provides information on the views of 6,579 respondents that represent a broad array of employees in the for-profit sector.[83] Exhibit 3.4 summarizes observed misconduct. It is encouraging that all such instances have declined between 2011 and 2013.

EXHIBIT 3.4   2013 NBES Survey of Reporting of Observed Misconduct

Type of Misconduct	2013	2011
Stealing or theft	64%	69%
Falsifying time reports or hours worked	49%	61%
Falsifying expense reports	48%	66%
Falsifying and/or manipulating financial reporting information	45%	62%
Falsifying invoices, books, and/or records	40%	N/A
Accepting inappropriate gifts or kickbacks from suppliers or vendors	36%	52%

The results of the NBES survey depicted in Exhibit 3.5 indicate a lessening of observed misconduct, virtually no change in reporting it, and a decline in pressure to compromise ethical standards from 2011 to 2013, which may reflect an improving corporate culture. This seems to be the case since the "weak-leaning" culture response went down by 6 points in the same time period. Other results include an increase in ethics training programs and the use of ethical conduct as a performance measure in employee evaluations.

EXHIBIT 3.5   Views of Employees on Ethics in the Workplace from the 2013 National Business Ethics Survey

Item	2013	2011	2009
Pressure to compromise ethical standards	9%	13%	8%
Weak/weak-leaning ethical culture	34%	40%	35%
Observed misconduct	41%	45%	55%
Reported observed misconduct	63%	65%	63%
Experienced retaliation after reporting (i.e., whistleblowing)	21%	22%	15%

The percentage of employees experiencing retaliation since 2009 is up, indicating it still remains a problem in corporate America. Perhaps the new protections under SOX and Dodd-Frank will help to stem the rising tide.

One concern is that, while misconduct is down overall, a relatively high percentage of misconduct is committed by managers—the very people who should be establishing an ethical culture and providing ethical leadership. Workers reported that 60% of misconduct involved someone with managerial authority from the supervisory level up to top management. Nearly a quarter (24%) of observed misdeeds involved senior managers. Also, workers said that 26% of misconduct is ongoing within their organizations and about 12% of wrongdoing was reported to take place company-wide.

Perhaps not surprising, the results indicate that occupational fraud and financial statement fraud are of greatest concern because of their effects on the accuracy and reliability of the financial statements.

Using Social Media to Criticize the Employer[84]

The National Labor Relations Act protects the rights of employees to act together in a concerted manner to address conditions at work, with or without a union. This protection extends to certain work-related conversations conducted on social media, such as Facebook and Twitter. Employees who act together on workplace issues—by, for example, meeting with a manager to lobby for better benefits or having a group discussion about the company's safety record—are protected from employer retaliation.

An activity is concerted only if it involves more than one employee's concerns. For example, employees discussing working conditions is protected. An employee who complains, after consulting with or on behalf of coworkers, that the company's performance evaluation system unfairly penalizes employees who speak up in safety meetings is engaged in concerted activity. However, an employee who complains about her own performance evaluation is not taking concerted action. As the National Labor Relations Board (NLRB) puts it, "personal gripes" are not protected. Even if employees are clearly acting in a concerted way, they won't be protected if they cross the line from constructive behavior to malicious or reckless actions.

As an example of what not to do: The former employee handbook of fast-food chain Wendy's included a rule requiring authorization before workers could make comments on social media about Wendy's business, policies, or employees. As part of an agreement with the NLRB, Wendy's social media policy now prohibits comments on "trade secrets and proprietary company information."

In 2010, the NLRB began receiving charges related to employer social media policies and to specific instances of discipline for Facebook postings. Following investigations, the agency found reasonable cause to believe that some policies and disciplinary actions violated federal labor law, and the NLRB

Office of General Counsel issued complaints against employers alleging unlawful conduct. In other cases, investigations found that the communications were not protected and so disciplinary actions did not violate the Act.

On September 28, 2012, the NLRB found that the firing of a BMW salesman for photos and comments posted to his Facebook page did not violate federal labor law. The question came down to whether the salesman was fired exclusively for posting photos of an embarrassing accident at an adjacent Land Rover dealership, which did not involve fellow employees, or for posting mocking comments and photos with co-workers about serving hot dogs at a luxury BMW car event. Both sets of photos were posted to Facebook on the same day; a week later, the salesman was fired. The Board ruled that the salesman was fired solely for the photos he posted of a Land Rover incident, which was not concerted activity and so was not protected.

The best advice for any employee when it comes to what they post on social media is to take a step back and think about the ramifications. You might be engaging in protected speech, and you might not.

Oftentimes an employer will claim that an employee who was fired ostensibly for comments on social media was fired instead for legitimate performance reasons. In these cases, the employer must prove it would have fired them even if they had not engaged in protected concerted activity.

Human Resource mangers can't infringe on employee rights or individual rights to freedom of speech, but they can help educate employees about how to properly conduct themselves in the workplace. In this digital age, employers must develop a social media policy so employees know just what is the expected standard of behavior.

Fraud in Organizations

LO 3-7

Describe the causes of fraud, detection methods, and preventative controls.

Fraud can be defined as a deliberate misrepresentation to gain an advantage over another party. Fraud comes in many different forms, including fraud in financial statements, the misappropriation of assets (theft) and subsequent cover-up, and disclosure fraud. We introduce the concept of fraudulent financial statements in this chapter and discuss it more fully in Chapter 5. We begin by examining the results of the *2018 Global Study on Occupational Fraud and Abuse: Report to the Nations,* conducted by the Association of Certified Fraud Examiners (ACFE).

Occupational Fraud

The 2018 ACFE survey is a follow-up to three prior biennial surveys. The 2018 survey reports on 2,690 cases of occupational fraud in 125 different countries that were reported by Certified Fraud Examiners. The total cost of occupational fraud exceeded $7.1 billion.[85]

Corruption represents one of the most significant fraud risks for organizations (38%), causing a median loss of $250,000. This includes conflicts of interest, bribery, illegal gratuities, and economic extortion.

Asset misappropriation was the most common type of occupational fraud. Examples of cost and relative frequency of such schemes include: check and payment tampering (150,000; 12%); billing ($100,000; 20%); noncash ($98,000; 21%); cash larceny ($75,000; 11%); payroll ($63,000; 7%); skimming ($50,000; 11%); expense reimbursements ($31,000; 14%); register disbursements ($29,000; 3%); and cash on hand ($20,000; 15%).

The ACFE report focuses on *occupational fraud* schemes in which an employee abuses the trust placed in him by an employer for personal gain. The ACFE defines occupational fraud as "the use of one's occupation for personal enrichment through the deliberate misuse or misapplication of the employing organization's resources or assets."[86] A summary of key findings follows:

- Survey participants estimated that the typical organization loses 5% of its revenues to fraud each year.

- The mean, or average, loss due to the frauds was $2.75 million.

- The frauds reported lasted a median of 16 months before being detected.

- Asset misappropriation schemes were the most common type of occupational fraud, comprising 89 percent of the reported cases, but causing the smallest median loss of $114,000.

- Financial statement fraud schemes made up less than 10% of the cases, but causing a median loss of $800,000.

- Occupational fraud is more likely to be detected by a tip (40%).

- Only 12% of organizations provided rewards for whistleblowers.

- Whistleblowers were most likely to report fraud to their direct supervisors (32% of cases), company executives (15%), a fraud investigation team (13%), a coworker (12%), or internal audit (10%).

- 80% of organizations reporting had a code of conduct in place at the time the fraud occurred.

- External audits of financial statements were the most commonly implemented anti-fraud control with nearly 80 percent of the organizations undergoing independent audits.

- The most prominent organizational weaknesses that contributed to the frauds was a lack of internal controls (30% of cases), followed by an override of existing controls (19%), lack of management review (18%), and poor tone at the top (10%).

- The perpetrators level of authority was strongly correlated with the size of the fraud. The median loss in a scheme committed by an owner/executive was $1 million for executives with six years or more of service but only $672,000 for those with five years or less. This is compared to managers ($200,000 for six years or more and $125,000 for five years or less) and employees ($100,000 for six years or more and $35,000 for five years or less).

- Fraudsters who had been with their company longer stole twice as much: $200,000 (5 years' tenure) versus $100,000 (less than 5 years' tenure).

How Occupational Fraud Is Committed and Detected

Asset misappropriation schemes include when an employee steals or misuses resources, such as charging personal expenses to the company while traveling on business trips. Corruption schemes include misusing one's position or influence in an organization for personal gain, something that Dennis Kozlowski was known for doing. Kozlowski and CFO Mark Swartz were convicted on June 21, 2005, of taking bonuses worth more than $120 million without the approval of Tyco's directors, abusing an employee loan program, and misrepresenting the company's financial condition to investors to boost the stock price while selling $575 million in stock.

The most common method of detection was a "tip," with 40% reporting. Additionally, 14% of tips came from an anonymous source, demonstrating that a significant portion of those who reported fraud did not want their identities known. In organizations with hotlines, 46% come from a tip but declines to 30% in organizations with no hotline. Internal audit was next with 15% followed by management review with 13%. Taken together these results indicate the need for strong internal controls to help prevent and detect fraud. More effective internal audits serve to strengthen internal controls, a goal of Section 404 of SOX. Exhibit 3.6 shows the frequency of detection methods as reported by survey respondents.

EXHIBIT 3.6 Initial Detection of Occupational Frauds from the *ACFE 2018 Global Study on Occupational Fraud and Abuse*

Detection Method	Percentage Reported	Median Loss
Tip	40%	$126,000
Internal Audit	15%	$108,000
Management Review	13%	$110,000
By Accident	7%	$ 50,000
Other	6%	N/A
Account Reconciliation	5%	$ 52,000
Document Examination	4%	$130,000
External Audit	4%	$250,000
Surveillance/Monitoring	3%	$ 50,000
Notified by Law Enforcement	2%	$935,000
IT Controls	1%	$ 39,000
Confession	1%	$186,000

An important point is that controls such as management reviews and internal audits account for a significant percentage of detection methods (28%), while the external audit accounts for only 4%. The point is that companies should not rely on the external audit to detect fraud but should put in place internal mechanisms to prevent and detect it.

Survey respondents provided information about how perpetrators were internally punished or dealt with. Not surprisingly, termination was the most common disciplinary action taken in occupational fraud cases (65%).

Frequency of Anti-Fraud Controls

The survey points out that while the presence of internal controls does not guarantee protection against fraud, it can help to both mitigate losses and deter some potential fraudsters by enhancing the perception of detection. Consequently, enacting internal controls specifically designed to prevent and detect fraud is a necessary part of a fraud risk management program; proactive fraud prevention and detection controls are a vital part in managing the risk of fraud.

With 40% of frauds being detected by tips, hotlines should play an essential role in organizations' anti-fraud programs. However, only 63% had a hotline mechanism in place and 12% provided rewards for whistleblowers. Exhibit 3.7 summarizes the frequency of anti-fraud controls.

Red-Flag Warnings of Fraud

Individuals who are engaged in occupational fraud schemes often exhibit certain behavioral traits or warning signs associated with their illegal activities. These are presented in Exhibit 3.8. Of particular note is living beyond one's means (41%) and financial difficulties (29%). The question is how can the anti-fraud controls identify these issues? These behavioral red flags might show up through work absences and poor performance. There may be warnings signs such as erratic behavior in the workplace.

EXHIBIT 3.7   Frequency of Anti-Fraud Controls: 2018 ACFE Global Fraud Survey

Anti-Fraud Control	Percentage Reported
External Audit of Financial Statements	80%
Code of Conduct	80%
Internal Audit Department	73%
Management Certification of Financial Statements	72%
External Audit of Internal Controls over Financial Reporting	67%
Management Review	66%
Hotline	63%
Independent Audit Committee	61%
Employee Support Programs	54%
Anti-Fraud Policy	54%
Fraud Training for Employees	53%
Fraud Training for Managers/Executives	52%
Dedicated Fraud Department, Function, or Team	41%
Formal Fraud Risk Assessments	41%
Surprise Audits	37%
Proactive Data Monitoring/Analysis	37%
Job Rotation/Mandatory Vacations	19%
Rewards for Whistleblowers	12%

EXHIBIT 3.8   Behavioral Red Flags Displayed by Perpetrators: *2018 ACFE Global Fraud Survey*

Behavioral Indicators of Fraud	Percentage Reported
Living Beyond Means	41%
Financial Difficulties	29%
Unusually Close Association with Vendor/Customer	20%
Control Issues, Unwillingness to Share Duties	15%
No Behavioral Red Flags	15%
Divorce/Family Problems	14%
"Wheeler-Dealer" Attitude	13%
Irritability, Suspiciousness, or Defensiveness	12%
Addiction Problems	10%
Complained about Inadequate Pay	9%
Excessive Pressure From Within the Organization	7%

(*Continued*)

Behavioral Indicators of Fraud	Percentage Reported
Refusal to Take Vacations	6%
Past Employment Related Problems	6%
Complained about Lack of Authority	5%
Excessive Family/Peer Pressure for Success	4%
Other	4%
Instability in Life Circumstances	3%

The results of the survey clearly indicate that internal auditors should have their "eyes wide open" with respect to whether managers have close relationships with outsiders that create conflicts of interest, one of the signs of ethical collapse. The results indicate that tip, internal audit, and management review accounted for 68% of frauds. That's not bad but organizations should be able to do better by strengthening their audit committee and ensuring an independent board of directors. Similarly, the internal auditors need to be aware of financial and/or personal problems of employees that might create pressures to misappropriate cash and/or create fictitious entries to cover up occupational fraud.

Example of Occupational Fraud

What follows is a description of a payroll fraud scheme. According to the ACFE study, payroll schemes accounted for 8.5% of the asset misappropriations, had a median cost of $90,000, and lasted a median of two years before being detected.

> The head of a department distributed paychecks to her employees on a weekly basis. Typically, the department head received the payroll checks each week from a payroll processing company and then distributed them to employees. One day another employee noticed the department head had locked his door after the checks were received and wondered about it. She became suspicious and reported it to his manager. A payroll audit discovered that several former employees were still receiving paychecks. It was discovered that the department head had the ability to access and edit electronic time keeping records for hourly employees and knew the passwords to the payroll system for their supervisors. She used this access to falsify hours, and thus paychecks, for previous employees. She then took the paychecks to check cashing companies to redeem them. The department head ultimately confessed to over 100 instances of payroll fraud over a 10-month period totaling almost $100,000.

In this case a lack of proper internal controls contributed to the fraud. The company lacked a proper separation of duties, did not regularly monitor payroll records for "ghost employees," did not require that employees regularly change their passwords, and allowed the department head who distributed the checks to also accept them from the payroll service. Perhaps a fraud hotline for employees to report suspicious behavior would have led to earlier reporting of the fraud.

Financial Statement Fraud

A variety of factors discourage the reporting of fraud according to a report by the Anti-Fraud Collaboration including:

- Poor tone at the top.
- Dominating and intimidating personalities.
- Mistrust.

- Excessive team loyalty.
- Management does not want to hear about problems.
- A lack of sound policies and procedures.
- Perception that wrongdoing will not be addressed if misconduct is reported.

Participants in the study identified the following factors that potentially discourage employees from coming forward and reporting fraud:

- Fear of the unknown.
- Fear that the report will not be handled anonymously or confidentially.
- Fear that the reporter's identity will be revealed to others in the organization.
- Concern that the person perpetrating the misconduct will not be held responsible.

The potential consequences to reporting suspected fraudulent financial reporting include:

- Retaliation by co-workers.
- Termination.
- Future reputation.
- Impact on others.
- Results of investigation determine that the misconduct is unsubstantiated.
- Emotional cost of whistleblowing.

Looking at the overall results of the study, it becomes clear why employees may be reluctant to report suspected fraudulent financial reporting. Concerns whether their reports will do any good and the potential consequences for them both professionally and personally discourage reporters from coming forward. A perceived lack of support makes it more difficult to want to do the right thing and report the fraud. It all comes down to the culture of the organization and whether top management genuinely encourages the reporting of financial statement fraud or just gives lip service to it.

Financial statement fraud is discussed in greater detail in Chapter 5. Here, we introduce the term and give examples of fraud techniques to provide context for the types of transactions that raise concerns for those in the corporate governance system.

Financial statement fraud schemes occur because an employee—typically a member of top management—causes a misstatement or omission of material information in the organization's financial reports. Examples include recording fictitious revenues, understating reported expenses, artificially inflating reported assets, failing to accrue expenses at the end of the year, and accelerating the recording of revenue into an earlier period as occurred in the 3D Printing case in Chapter 1.

A report by Ernst & Young, *Detecting Financial Statement Fraud: What Every Manager Needs to Know,*[87] provides examples of common methods to overstate revenue, understate expenses, and make improper asset valuations. Revenue overstatements include the following:

- Recording gross, rather than net, revenue.
- Recording revenues of other companies when acting as a "middleman."
- Recording sales that never took place.
- Recording future sales in the current period.
- Recording sales of products that are out on consignment.

Another would be recording revenue from increases in asset values that are not in accordance with GAAP, as Enron did by using mark-to-market accounting for for a fixed asset—power plants.

Common methods of understating expenses include the following:

- Reporting cost of sales as a non-operating expense so that it does not negatively affect gross margin.
- Capitalizing operating costs, recording them as assets on the balance sheet instead of as expenses on the income statement (i.e., WorldCom).
- Not recording some expenses at all, or not recording expenses in the proper period.

Examples of improper asset valuations include the following:

- Manipulating reserves.
- Changing the useful lives of assets.
- Failing to take a write-down when needed.
- Manipulating estimates of fair market value.

Why Does Financial Statement Fraud Occur?

Why does financial statement fraud occur? This question has been examined since the 1980s when well-publicized financial statement frauds occurred at companies including ZZZZ Best, Miniscribe, Phar-Mor, Cendant, and Waste Management. Theoretically, there are three factors that appear to be present in every case of financial statement fraud that are addressed in auditing standards.[88]

Situational pressure. Situational pressures may prompt an otherwise honest person to commit fraud. It typically occurs as a result of immediate pressure within either her internal or external environment. For example, financial analysts project earnings and companies feel the pressure to meet or exceed these amounts. An accountant may come to believe she has no option other than to go along with the fraud. The Betty Vinson situation at WorldCom is a case in point. She did not know where to turn; she was unequipped to deal with the fraud.

Perceived opportunity. The opportunity to commit fraud and conceal it must exist. People do not normally commit fraud believing they will get caught. They do it because they believe they can get away with it (i.e., have access to the underlying financial information or override internal controls). The opportunity to commit fraud and conceal it often involves the absence of or improper oversight by the board of directors or audit committee, weak or nonexistent internal controls, unusual or complex transactions, accounting estimates that require sufficient subjective judgment by management, and ineffective internal audit staff.

Rationalization. People who commit financial statement fraud are able to rationalize the act. Being able to justify the act makes it possible. The individual must first convince herself that the behavior is temporary or is acceptable. She may believe it is in the best interest of the company to commit the fraud, perhaps because a needed loan will not be secured without financial statements to back it up. There is often the belief that everything will return to normal after the trigger event has passed.

Financial statement fraud does not occur in a vacuum. It is enabled by the absence of an ethical culture. Oftentimes, a culture is created and a tone at the top established that presents the image of a company willing to do whatever it takes to paint a rosy picture about financial results. Effective oversight and strong internal controls give way to greed, moral blindness, and inattentiveness to the important details that help to prevent and detect fraud. As with most situations in business, the desire to succeed crowds out ethical behavior. Those in the way are pressured to be team players; go along just this one time; and, in the end, compromise their values.

Corporate Governance Structures and Relationships

LO 3-8
Explain how the provisions of the Sarbanes-Oxley Act relate to corporate governance, including relationships with key parties.

In response to accounting scandals at Enron and WorldCom that caused huge losses to shareholders and led to a crisis of confidence in the financial markets, the U.S. Congress adopted the SOX in 2002.

The following is a summary of key requirements under SOX.[89]

Sarbanes-Oxley Act

Section 301

Section 301 requires publicly traded corporations to "establish procedures" for accepting employee complaints (both anonymously and non-anonymously) concerning "questionable accounting or auditing matters." Section 301 also requires independent audit committees to oversee the procedures for receiving and handling confidential whistleblower reports including (1) the receipt, retention, and treatment of reports received by the issuer regarding accounting, internal accounting controls, or auditing matters and (2) the confidential, anonymous submission by employees of the issuer of concerns regarding questionable accounting or auditing matters.

Section 302

Section 302 requires that principal executive and financial officers certify that they have reviewed the findings of annual or quarterly reports, and find the statements within to be accurate and free of any material errors. Those officers, normally the CEO and CFO, must also certify that they understand their responsibility for creating and monitoring internal controls within their organization, and have evaluated the effectiveness of those controls within 90 days prior to the report being issued.

Section 404

Section 404 requires public companies to include in their annual reports a report of management on the company's internal control over financial reporting. The internal control report must include a statement of management's responsibility for establishing and maintaining adequate internal control over financial reporting for the company and management's assessment of the effectiveness of those controls. The external auditor must evaluate management's conclusions and issue its own report on the assessment of internal controls.

Section 406

Section 406 outlines code of ethics requirements for senior financial officers. A code for financial officers comprises the standards necessary to promote honest and ethical conduct; full, fair, accurate, timely, and understandable disclosure in periodic reports; and compliance with applicable governmental rules and regulations.

Section 806

Section 806 links to section 12 of the Securities Exchange Act of 1934 and prohibits "any officer, employee, contractor, subcontractor, or agent of such company" to "discharge, demote, suspend, threaten, harass, or in any other manner discriminate against an employee in the terms and conditions of employment because of any lawful act done by the employee. This includes providing information concerning any conduct which the employee reasonably believes constitutes a violation of any rule or regulation of the SEC, or any provision of federal law relating to fraud against shareholders, when the information or assistance is provided to or the investigation is conducted by federal officials, members of Congress, and "a person with supervisory authority over the employee (or such other person working for the employer who has the authority to investigate, discover, or terminate misconduct.)"

SOX also establishes the Public Company Accounting Oversight Board (PCAOB) to: (1) oversee the audit of public companies that are subject to the securities laws; (2) establish audit report standards and rules; and (3) inspect, investigate, and enforce compliance on the part of registered public accounting firms, their associated persons, and certified public accountants. PCAOB also establishes (or modifies) the auditing and related attestation standards, quality control, and the ethics standards used by registered public accounting firms to prepare and issue audit reports.

False Certifications of Financial Statements

There have been very few cases of false certifications of financial statements under section 302 of SOX that have led to sanctions by the SEC. In fact, perhaps the best-known case is one of failure to impose sanctions when sanctions were warranted. Richard Scrushy, the former HealthSouth Corporation CEO, falsely certified the financial statements of the company that had a $2.8 billion accounting fraud but was not sent to jail for that crime. On the other hand, HealthSouth CFO Weston L. Smith was sentenced in 2005 to 27 months in prison for his role in the fraud. Smith had pleaded guilty to one count each of conspiracy to commit wire and securities fraud, falsely certifying a financial report, and falsifying a report to the SEC.

The SEC's disclosure on July 30, 2014, of an enforcement action against two corporate executives of a small Florida-based computer equipment company exemplifies the type of emerging theory of fraud it is now pursuing. The commission went after both the CEO and CFO of Quality Services Group Inc. (QSGI) solely for alleged misrepresentations in public disclosures about the company's internal controls environment, which are required by SOX.

The SEC alleged that QSGI's CEO (Marc Sherman) and former CFO (Edward Cummings) knew of significant internal controls issues in the company's inventory practices that they failed to disclose to auditors and investors. Central to the SEC's theory of fraud is that Sherman and Cummings (1) signed Form 10-Ks (annual financial statements filed with the SEC) with management reports on internal controls that falsely omitted issues and (2) signed certifications in which they falsely represented that they had evaluated the management report on internal controls and disclosed all significant deficiencies to auditors.[90]

The SEC found that Sherman falsely certified in the certifications attached to the Forms 10-K and 10-K/A for the fiscal year December 31, 2008, and 10-Q (quarterly statements) forms for the quarter ended March 31, 2009, respectively, that he had: (1) evaluated QSGI's internal controls over financial reporting and (2) disclosed all significant deficiencies to the external auditors which were reasonably likely to adversely affect QSGI's ability to record, process, summarize, and report financial information. As a result, Sherman violated Securities Exchange Act Rule 13a-14 by signing false Section 302 certifications. Sherman was sanctioned by the SEC and prohibited from committing or causing any future violations of specified Securities Exchange Act rules, prohibited for five years from acting as an officer or director of any issuer that has a class of securities registered under the Exchange Act, and ordered to pay a civil monetary penalty in the amount of $7,500.[91]

So, the question in the end is, why have there not been more prosecutions under Section 302? Allison Frankel believes that the answer may lie partly in how corporations have responded to SOX. Most major corporations have implemented internal compliance systems that make it very difficult to show that the CEO or CFO knowingly signed a false certification. And when prosecutors have enough evidence to show that those internal systems failed and top executives knowingly engaged in wrongdoing, they often prefer, for strategic reasons, to charge crimes other than false certification.[92]

After SOX was passed, most large corporations put in place multiple layers of subcertification, requiring lower-level officials to attest to the accuracy of financial reports all the way up the chain of command to the CEO and CFO. The subcertifications forces corporations to be more vigilant about financial reporting at all levels but it also insulates CEOs and CFOs from false certification charges.

The SEC seems to be going after CFOs now because they typically mastermind financial frauds. Emboldened by legislative expansions of liability for financial executives under SOX and Dodd-Frank, the SEC increasingly is pursuing claims against CFOs that do not allege actual wrongdoing. It does so by alleging that the CFO's subordinates violated securities laws and that the CFO either certified the resulting reports or failed to implement adequate internal safeguards.

Relationships between Audit Committee, Internal Auditors, and External Auditors

Following the passage of SOX, the audit committee was seen as the one body that was (or at least should be) capable of preventing identified fraudulent financial reporting. The audit committee has an oversight responsibility for the financial statements. The internal auditors should have direct and unrestricted access to the audit committee so that they can take any matters of concern directly to that group without having to go through top management. The external auditors rely on the support and actions of the audit committee to resolve differences with management over proper financial reporting. The goal of such relationships should be to establish an ethical corporate culture that supports good corporate governance. Exhibit 3.9 depicts the ideal relationship between the internal auditors and audit committee. The framework is identified in the Treadway Commission Report titled *Report of the National Commission on Fraudulent Financial Reporting.*[93]

EXHIBIT 3.9   Internal Control Environment—"Corporate Culture"

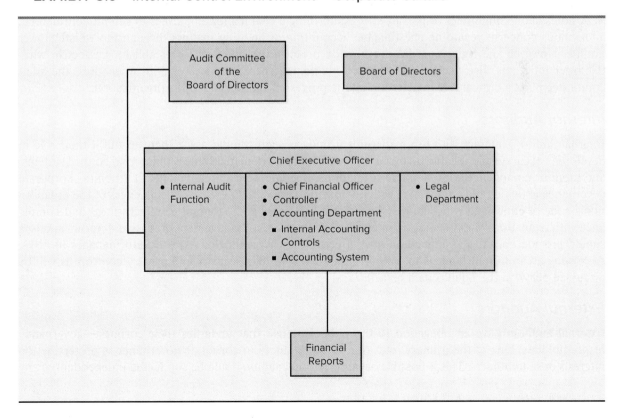

Audit Committee

In the accounting scandals of the early 2000s, the audit committee either didn't know about the fraud or chose to look the other way. A conscientious and diligent audit committee is an essential ingredient of an effective corporate governance system—one that takes its role in financial statement oversight to heart and follows basic principles of responsibility, accountability, and transparency.

An effective device to ensure audit committee independence is for the committee to meet separately with the senior executives, the internal auditors, and the external auditors. The perception of internal auditors as the "eyes and ears" of the audit committee suggests that the head of the internal audit department attend all audit committee meetings. Recall the role of Cynthia Cooper, the director of internal auditing at WorldCom. She informed the audit committee every step of the way as her department uncovered the fraud, and ultimately she gained the support of the external auditors.

The audit committee's duties include: (1) monitor the integrity of the financial statements; (2) review any formal announcements relating to the company's financial performance; (3) review significant financial reporting judgments contained in the statements and performance statements; (4) review the company's internal financial controls and risk management procedures; (5) monitor the effectiveness of the company's internal audit function; (6) review the company's whistleblower processes and compliance program; and (7) review and monitor the external auditor's independence and objectivity and the effectiveness of the audit process.

The audit committee should also seek assurances from the CEO and CFO, as part of the CEO/CFO financial statement certification process under Section 302 of SOX, that they have put in place effective disclosure controls and procedures to ensure that all reports have been prepared and filed properly with the appropriate authorities in accordance with applicable requirements.

SOX calls on audit committees to create formal procedures to collect, track, and process hotline claims received by the issuer company related to accounting, internal controls, or auditing matters. Additionally, SOX holds audit committees responsible for establishing a channel for employees to submit confidential, anonymous concerns regarding questionable accounting or auditing matters through the whistleblower hotline. However, the legislation did not provide prescriptive guidance for establishing effective whistleblower programs. Because the SEC has not mandated specific processes and procedures, the audit committee plays a critical role in determining the processes appropriate for its organization.

Internal Auditors

Internal auditors interact with top management and, as such, should assist them to fulfill their role in developing accurate and reliable financial statements, ensure the effectiveness of internal control systems, and monitor compliance with laws and regulations. Specific obligations include: (1) monitor corporate governance activities and compliance with organization policies; (2) review effectiveness of the organization's code of ethics and whistleblower provisions; (3) assess audit committee effectiveness and compliance with regulations; and (4) oversee internal controls and risk management processes. Internal auditors should provide objective assurance on how effectively the organization assesses and manages its risks. A growing area of importance is to provide assurance with data security and privacy controls as will be discussed below in the Equifax data breach.

External Auditors

External auditors have an obligation to the public interest that underlies their corporate governance responsibilities. One of the primary roles of external auditors in corporate governance is protecting the interests of shareholders. This is possible because external audits should be conducted independent of any influence of management or the board of directors of the company. External audits should be designed to introduce a measure of accountability into the financial reporting process.

The PCAOB has recognized the importance of two-way communication between audit committees and external auditors with the adoption of Auditing Standard No. 16, *Communications with Audit Committees* ("AS 16"). Required communications include:

- Matters relating to the company's accounting policies and practices, including why certain accounting policies and practices are considered critical.

- Estimates made by management and the process used to develop these estimates, including significant changes to the process used by management to develop estimates, reasons for the changes, and the effects on the financial statements.

- The auditor's judgment about the quality of the entity's financial reporting, including the auditor's evaluation of and conclusions about the qualitative aspects of the company's significant accounting policies and practices. Auditors should also discuss significant unusual transactions and their opinion on the business rationale thereof.

- Whether the audit committee is aware of matters relevant to the audit including, but not limited to, violations or potential violations of laws or regulations, including fraud risks.

A company's audit committee is the primary link between the board of directors, management, and the independent auditors. Improving communication among these parties will play a vital role in improving the overall value of the audit for all stakeholders.

Internal Controls as a Monitoring Device

The internal controls that are established by management should help prevent and detect fraud, including materially false and misleading financial reports, asset misappropriations, and inadequate disclosures in the financial statements. These controls are designed to ensure that management policies are followed, laws are strictly adhered to, and ethical systems are built into corporate governance.

The internal control report required by Section 404 of SOX must include a statement of management's responsibility for establishing and maintaining adequate internal control over financial reporting for the company, management's assessment of the effectiveness of the company's internal control over financial reporting as of the end of the company's most recent fiscal year, a statement identifying the framework used by management to evaluate the effectiveness of the company's internal control over financial reporting, and a statement that the registered public accounting firm that audited the company's financial statements included in the annual report has issued an attestation report on management's assessment of the company's internal control over financial reporting.

An internal control system, no matter how well conceived and operated, can provide only reasonable—not absolute—assurance to management and the board of directors regarding achievement of an entity's objectives. The likelihood of achievement is affected by a variety of factors including: judgments in decision making can be faulty; breakdowns can occur due to simple mistakes and errors in the application of controls; and controls can be circumvented by the collusion of two or more people. Management override of internal controls may be a problem as well, similar to what happened at Enron and WorldCom. Indeed, the ACFE Fraud Survey found that organizations that lacked internal controls were more susceptible to asset misappropriation schemes, while corruption schemes more often involved an override of existing controls. Further, a poor tone at the top was much more likely to contribute to a financial statement fraud scheme than either of the other two categories of occupational fraud.

COSO Framework

The system of internal controls and whether it operates as intended enables the auditor to either gain confidence about the internal processing of transactions or create doubt for the auditor that should be pursued. *Internal Control–Integrated Framework,* published by the Committee of Sponsoring Organizations (COSO) of the Treadway Commission in 1992, establishes a framework that defines internal control as a process, effected by an entity's board of directors, management, and other personnel, designed to provide reasonable assurance regarding the achievement of the following objectives: (a) effectiveness and efficiency of operations; (b) reliability of financial reporting; and (c) compliance with applicable laws and regulations.[94]

The COSO report states that management should enact five components related to these objectives as part of the framework: (1) the control environment; (2) risk assessment; (3) control activities; (4) monitoring; and (5) information and communication.

1. The *control environment* sets the tone of an organization, influencing the control consciousness of its people. It is the foundation for all aspects of internal control, providing discipline and structure.

2. *Risk assessment* is the entity's identification and evaluation of how risk might affect the achievement of objectives.

3. *Control activities* are the strategic actions established by management to ensure that its directives are carried out.

4. *Monitoring* is a process that assesses the efficiency and effectiveness of internal controls over time.

5. *Information and communication* systems provide the information in a form and at a time that enables people to carry out their responsibilities.

Enterprise Risk Management

In 2001, COSO initiated a project, and engaged PwC, to develop a framework that would be readily usable by managements to evaluate and improve their organizations' enterprise risk management. The need was there following a large number of business scandals born out of a failure of internal controls, corporate governance systems, and risk management.

According to the report, enterprise risk management enables management to effectively deal with uncertainty and associated risk and opportunity, enhancing the capacity to build value. Value is maximized when management sets strategy and objectives to strike an optimal balance between growth and return goals and related risks and efficiently and effectively deploys resources in pursuit of the entity's objectives. Of particular importance, enterprise risk management encompasses:[95]

- Aligning risk appetite and strategy—Management considers the entity's risk appetite in evaluating strategic alternatives, setting related objectives, and developing mechanisms to manage related risks.

- Enhancing risk response decisions—Enterprise risk management provides the rigor to identify and select among alternative risk responses—risk avoidance, reduction, sharing, and acceptance.

Deloitte discusses the value of risk management by pointing out that management and the Board must know beforehand the firm's capacity for risk-taking, the previously specified amount of different risks they want the firm to take, and the current and targeted risk profile relative to the desired level and capacity-to be able to evaluate and take action. This is the essence of what a risk appetite framework can do for an organization. Information needs to flow up to the Board and be presented in a timely way that drives decision making.[96]

The capabilities inherent in enterprise risk management help management achieve the entity's performance and profitability targets and prevent loss of resources. Enterprise risk management helps ensure effective reporting and compliance with laws and regulations and helps avoid damage to the entity's reputation and associated consequences. In sum, enterprise risk management helps an entity get to where it wants to go and avoid pitfalls and surprises along the way.

COSO updated its enterprise risk management positions in *ERM Framework, Enterprise Risk Management—Integrating with Strategy and Performance.* The September 2017 revisions to the ERM framework highlight the importance of enterprise risk management in strategic planning. According to COSO's Chair, Robert B. Hirth Jr., COSO's "overall goal is to encourage a risk-conscious culture." PwC developed the framework and according to Miles Everson, PwC's Global Advisory Leader and Engagement Leader: "The Framework addresses the evolution of ERM, the benefits that can be achieved, and the need for organizations to improve their approach to managing risk."[97]

Drilling down on the Framework with respect to corporate culture, ERM suggests that each entity should link its culture—shared behaviors, emotions, and mindsets in the organization—to its strategy and risk appetite. The problem here is the ERM framework does not place sufficient emphasis on the ethical dimension of making strategic decisions opting, instead, for a focus on the entity's "hunger" for risk in terms of its strategic objectives. This tail-wagging-the-dog approach to developing an ethical culture allows management to create a culture in each situation after first determining its willingness to accept risk in developing strategic activities. Our concern is this approach sounds too much like ethical relativism because it allows each entity to define its own risk appetite rather than creating a standard built on ethical values.

Equifax Data Breach

In September 2017, Equifax disclosed that a flaw in a tool designed to build web applications created a security breach that had occurred two months prior and hackers gained access to its data. Some of the information hackers had access to included names, social security numbers, birth dates, addresses, and some driver's license numbers. The tool is called Apache Struts, and it's used by many large businesses and government organizations. A cybersecurity arm of the U.S. Department of Homeland Security "identified and disclosed" the flaw in March 2017, according to an Equifax statement. The company's security department "was aware of this vulnerability at that time, and took efforts to identify and to patch any vulnerable systems." Yet, the company admitted that hackers exploited the flaws months later. Equifax was widely criticized for waiting almost two months to alert its customers and shareholders about the hack.[98]

Congress conducted hearings to discover why the breach occurred and why it took so long for the company to inform the public about the hack of the personal information of 143 million consumers. Equifax responded by announcing that its chief information officer and chief security officer were "retiring," and that was followed by the chief executive and two other senior managers.

Francine McKenna, who writes for MarketWatch.com, points out that a company's external auditor is supposed to be an objective independent watchdog, the first line of defense for shareholders and the public when company executives and the board fail to protect them. She explains that even before the external auditors, Ernst & Young (EY), audited the financial statements of Equifax, it should have made sure the company executives set the right "tone at the top" about controls, including of its information technology systems. This was necessary to ensure Equifax was protecting its biggest asset—the consumer information it sells to banks and other organizations, which generates most of its revenues.[99]

Rani Hoitash, a Bentley University professor of accounting who is also a certified information systems auditor, told Market Watch that the assessment of cybersecurity risks is outside the scope of a financial statement and internal control over financial reporting audit based on auditing standards. He added, however, auditor's "are required to look at policies and practices related to financial-reporting-related information technology systems and data early in the annual audit process. If poor practices related to access controls or patch management are detected, they may not be confined to one system because these general information technology controls are not typically managed or controlled separately."[100]

Was EY asleep at the wheel? It was aware that the SEC had scrutinized Equifax for inadequate disclosures of its cyberrisk and poor overall disclosure controls. That was based on correspondence between the SEC and Equifax CEO and CFO dating from 2011 to 2014. In January 2014, the SEC asked Equifax's CEO about inadequate disclosures regarding a material weakness in internal controls over financial reporting in 2013. In its response, Equifax provided the SEC with a detailed timeline of its evaluation of the control weaknesses and concluded that its interim quarter disclosure controls were also ineffective. McKenna points out that EY's audit partner for Equifax was copied on the response to the SEC from the company's controller, along with the rest of the company's top executives. So, it appears, EY knew about the data security problems but did nothing about it.

In yet another embarrassing event for Equifax management, the U.S. Department of Justice (DOJ) announced in September 2017 that it had opened a criminal investigation into Equifax officials' stock sales just before the public disclosure of the security breach. DOJ is considering whether officials dumped nearly $1.8 million in stock just after the company discovered the breach and one month before it was announced. The company maintains the officials didn't know about the breach when they sold the stock. The SEC also announced it is investigating the possibility of insider trading.

The Equifax scandal raises some important questions in light of our discussion about internal controls, risk assessment, and the role of the internal auditors and audit committee in the data breach fiasco. A few items to consider are:

- External auditors rely on the work of internal auditors. What steps did Equifax's internal auditors take to ensure the information technology systems were operating as intended? Did it communicate this matter with the audit committee? The external auditors?

- Did the EY auditors adequately consider whether problems with the information security systems also affected the internal control systems thereby raising doubts whether the financial statements did or did not contain any material misstatements. A problem in one area of the audit heightens the possibility of problems in other areas.

- Did the company (i.e., CEO and CFO) adequately consider the controls when they certified under Section 302 that the internal controls over financial reporting were operating as intended?

- Should the SEC go after top officials of Equifax to clawback some of its executive compensation during the period nothing was done about the data breach even though the company was well aware of it?

The Equifax case illustrates what can happen when management seeks to protect its own interests and that of the company without regard to its responsibilities to consumers and the public. The audit deficiencies seem to be a fallout of the fraud. One concern we have is whether the EY auditors made a good faith attempt to understand information technology controls and how they may have influenced the internal controls over financial reporting.

We also are concerned about the role that "risk tolerance" may have played in the company's evaluations. The ERM document says that each entity should link its culture to its strategy and risk appetite, focusing on its "hunger" for risk. Does this mean that Equifax might have, knowingly or unknowingly, decided the risk of a data breach was acceptable because its risk tolerance was very high?

Whistleblowing

There is a symbiotic relationship between whistleblowing and an organization's culture. Effective internal whistleblowing processes are an important part of a healthy corporate culture. Internal auditors have a critical role to play in monitoring whistleblowing procedures, given the nature of internal control. The audit committee should ensure that matters of concern are raised through appropriate channels and promptly dealt with. Whistleblowing should be part of the internal control environment and an effective corporate governance system.

There is no one set definition of whistleblowing, although most definitions characterize the practice as disclosing to others in an organization an action that violates organizational norms or the law. Near and Miceli take a broad view of whistleblowing as "the disclosure by organization members (former or current) of illegal, immoral, or illegitimate practices under the control of their employers, to persons or organizations that may be able to effect action." This definition includes whistleblowers who use internal channels (e.g., a hotline or ombudsperson) or external channels (e.g., the external auditors or the SEC) to blow the whistle. They identify four elements of the whistleblowing process: the whistleblower, the whistleblowing act or complaint, the party to whom the complaint is made, and the organization against which the complaint is lodged. In discussing the act itself, they label it as an act of "dissidence" somewhat analogous to civil disobedience.[101]

Morality of Whistleblowing

Given that the act of whistleblowing is a personal choice, the key to whether an individual will blow the whistle on wrongdoing is whether the whistleblower perceives organizational policies are designed to encourage moral autonomy, individual responsibility, and organizational support for whistleblowers.

Whistleblowing always involves an actual or at least declared intention to prevent something bad that would otherwise occur. It always involves information that would not ordinarily be revealed. Most ethicists agree whistleblowing is an ethical action. According to the "standard theory" on whistleblowing of Michael Davis, whistleblowing is morally required when it is required at all; people have a moral obligation to prevent serious harm to others if they can do so with little costs to themselves.[102]

DeGeorge analyzes when whistleblowing is a moral act. His starting position is based on the universal ethical principle that "corporations have a moral obligation not to harm." DeGeorge identifies five criteria when whistleblowing is morally permitted: (1) the firm's actions will do serious and considerable harm to others; (2) the whistleblowing act is justifiable once the employee reports it to her immediate supervisor and makes her moral concerns known; (3) absent any action by the supervisor, the employee should take the matter all the way up to the board, if necessary; (4) documented evidence must exist that would convince a reasonable and impartial observer that one's views of the situation is correct and that serious harm may occur; and (5) the employee must reasonably believe that going public will create the necessary change to protect the public and is worth the risk to oneself.[103]

DeGeorge's criteria establish the foundation for moral behavior to occur when contemplating whistleblowing. He rejects the position that external whistleblowing is *always* morally justifiable, and also rejects the position that external whistleblowing is *never* morally justifiable. Basically his position is that the whistleblower should have a moral motivation to engage in the act (i.e., to expose unnecessary harm and illegal or immoral actions).

Rights and Duties

Researchers have posed the question of whether workplace whistleblowing is a right, and thus allows for responsible behavior, or whether it is an imposed corporate duty, thus resulting in liability of workers. If an organization institutes an internal whistleblowing policy, it is because it perceives moral autonomy to be weak so that employees need direction when and how whistleblowing should occur. When businesses then implement the policy, it leads to the conclusion that moral autonomy is strong, and employees are expected to blow the whistle.[104] Therefore, if employees do not blow the whistle in accordance with corporate policy, they then become liable for not doing so, rendering the policy a tool that controls employee behavior. Responsibility for misdeeds then shifts from the organization to the individual, and employees are further stripped of the right to moral autonomy.[105]

Miceli and Near's research has shown that what whistleblowers hope and believe their speaking out will achieve is the correction of what they perceive as an organizational wrongdoing (e.g., fraudulent financial statements). This research also found that not everyone who perceives a wrongdoing acts upon that perception. In fact, only 42% stated they were ready to blow the whistle. Those who observe wrongdoing but would not do so identify a "retaliatory climate" in their organizations as the primary barrier to blowing the whistle on corporate wrongdoing, while those who say they would speak up about it were confident that they "would not experience managerial retaliation if they blew the whistle."[106]

Whistleblowing regulations attempt to protect individuals when they behave responsibly toward society in light of irresponsible behavior by their organizations. This certainly is the motivation for the anti-retaliation provisions of both SOX and Dodd-Frank. The acknowledgement of the need for such protection, however, implies that moral agency, autonomy, and responsibility are problematic in organizations, or at the very least, that they do not come naturally and are not welcomed when they arrive. When organizations establish an ethical culture and anonymous channels to report wrongdoing, they create an environment that supports whistleblowing and whistleblowers while controlling for possible retaliation.[107]

Anthony Menendez v. Halliburton, Inc.[108]

Doing the right thing and blowing the whistle does not always pay off and can be an arduous task. A case in point is what happened to Anthony Menendez in his whistleblowing ordeal with Halliburton. One day in February 2006, he received an e-mail from Halliburton's chief accounting officer, Mark McCollum, that was addressed to much of the accounting department. It read, "The SEC has opened an inquiry into the allegations of Mr. Menendez." Everyone was told to retain their documents until further notice. Menendez had been outed. Thus began a nine-year ordeal to clear his name.

The key accounting issue was how to recognize revenue when goods are held for the customer in the seller's warehouse and not shipped pending customer request. Halliburton was engaging in "bill-and-hold" transactions. To meet the GAAP requirements to recognize revenue on these transactions, the following four criteria must be met: (1) the risks of ownership must have passed to the buyer; (2) delivery must be for a fixed date; (3) the seller must not retain any significant performance obligations; and (4) the goods or equipment must be complete and ready for shipment. Menendez knew the first criteria couldn't be met and in most cases neither could the second. All efforts to convince the company it was prematurely recognizing revenue were met with resistance because the company was under pressure to meet financial analysts' earnings projections. The KPMG auditors went along despite Menendez's efforts to convince them of the GAAP violation. Once he had been retaliated against, Menendez decided to lodge a complaint with the SEC under SOX.

The facts of the case are summarized in Exhibit 3.10. (An expanded version of this case with multiple areas for discussion appears in Case 3-8).

EXHIBIT 3.10   Accountant Takes on Halliburton and Wins

Tony Menendez was the Director of Technical Accounting Research and Training at Halliburton. Halliburton contracts with energy companies like Royal Dutch Shell and BP to find and exploit huge oil and gas fields. It sells services of its geologists and engineers who work intricate machinery that Halliburton built and sold to its customers. The company's accountants had been allowing the company to count the full value of the equipment right away as revenue, sometimes even before it had assembled the equipment. But the customers could walk away in the middle of the contracts. Menendez knew that if the equipment were damaged, Halliburton, not the customer, absorbed the loss. Menendez recommended the company wait until the work was completed to record the equipment sales as revenue.

Even though top Halliburton accounting executives, including Halliburton's chief accounting officer, Mark McCollum, agreed with Menendez's analysis, they didn't act to correct the accounting because of concern about its impact in slowing revenue growth. McCollum tried to dissuade Menendez by reminding him of the need to be a team player and that his persistence was not well received by colleagues. He told Menendez that the Halliburton team, working with the external auditors from KPMG, had reached a different conclusion. He also offered that Menendez shouldn't put things in writing and had to be more "circumspect about the use of e-mail to communicate." He finished by telling Menendez that he wasn't asking him to compromise his ethics and compromise the position he felt so strongly about.

Menendez waited to see what would happen. Given that billions in equipment sales were involved, he knew this was no trivial matter. Finally, in the fall he realized nothing would happen. Menendez agonized and several days later filed a confidential complaint with the SEC in November 2005.

He spoke to the SEC about the matter and was told to go to the audit committee. Menendez assumed the SEC would take action, but nothing seemed to occur, until February 4, 2006, when he heard the SEC was poking around.

Unbeknownst to Menendez, his complaint went to the Halliburton legal department as well as the board committee, an apparent violation of company policy. The audit committee was supposed to keep such reports confidential. A few days later, the SEC notified the company that it had opened an investigation into the company's revenue recognition. Then, the e-mail from McCollum got distributed. Halliburton's general counsel said "the SEC is investigating Mr. Menendez's complaints" to the company's chief financial officer, KPMG, other top executives, and McCollum. McCollum had forwarded it to at least 15 of Menendez's colleagues in accounting. As far as Halliburton was concerned, they had a traitor in their ranks.

The ramifications were immediate. Menendez was stripped of his responsibilities and became a pariah at the firm. Halliburton contracted with an outside law firm to conduct an "investigation." Not surprisingly, it cleared the company. The SEC informed Halliburton it would not bring any enforcement action against it.

Menendez went back to the SEC to no avail. The commission wouldn't even accept the documents he had provided. Finally, he felt he had to leave Halliburton having been punished for blowing the whistle. He brought a claim under SOX in May 2006 based on retaliation, but the government would not take up his case. He brought separate lawsuits, but lost. He persisted even when others told him he had no chance of prevailing. No one would take his case. Finally, he decided to represent himself in the appeals process. It went on for more than five years. In September 2011, the administrative laws appeals panel had ruled. It overturned the original trial judge.

Halliburton appealed the reversal. Another two years went by and in April 2013, the appeals panel ruled that he had been retaliated against for blowing the whistle, just as he had argued all along.

Menendez acted on principle in his quest for the truth. He only wanted to be proven right so he had asked for a token sum. The panel, noting the importance of punishing retaliations against whistleblowers, awarded him $30,000.

Menendez's case was filed before Dodd-Frank became effective. It is interesting to contemplate what might have happened had he filed a whistleblower claim under the act. Would he have been rewarded for his efforts?

Dodd-Frank Provisions

The Dodd-Frank Wall Street Reform and Consumer Protection Act was adopted by Congress on January 5, 2010, and became effective on August 12, 2011.[109] It changes the regulatory landscape for internal accountants and auditors, and external auditors and auditing firms, by protecting whistleblowers that "voluntarily" provide the SEC with "original information" about a violation of federal securities laws that leads to a successful enforcement proceeding. Under the United States Code, the enforcement action must result in monetary sanctions of more than $1 million.[110]

Dodd-Frank defines a whistleblower as any individual who provides information to the SEC relating to a violation of the securities laws that has occurred, is ongoing, or is about to occur. *Voluntarily* means the whistleblower has provided information prior to the government, a self-regulatory organization, or the PCAOB asking for it directly from the whistleblower. Original information must be based upon the whistleblower's independent knowledge or independent analysis, not already known to the SEC and not derived exclusively from an allegation made in a judicial or administrative hearing or a governmental report, hearing, audit, or investigation.[111]

Section 922 of Dodd-Frank provides an award for whistleblowers (who meet certain criteria) of "not less than 10% and not more than 30%, in total, of what has been collected of the monetary sanctions imposed in the section." Kastiel believes the award incentivizes whistleblowing and provides a bounty hunter's payment for disclosing the relevant information to the SEC.[112] This raises the question: Is it ethical to provide financial incentives to motivate employees to come forward and report financial wrongdoing? This is not an easy question to answer.

One major concern with Dodd-Frank is that it may cause would-be whistleblowers to go external with the information rather than internally using the organization's prescribed reporting mechanisms. The disclosure of confidential information about clients raises questions about a possible violation of Section 1.320.001 of the AICPA Code and of state privilege laws.[113] The external disclosure of confidential information can, under certain circumstances, be treated as an exception to the rule if disclosure is linked to compliance with applicable laws and government regulations, which include Dodd-Frank. The act defines the circumstances under which the disclosure of confidential information by external auditors will not violate confidentiality and entails a good faith effort to get the company or client to alter the accounting that triggers the concern.

We believe that once the internal reporting process has played out and nothing has been done to correct for the wrongdoing, from an ethical perspective, external whistleblowing is the proper course of action, especially if it is the *only* way for the public to know. An employee should not fall victim to the bystander effect and assume others will report it. Along with knowledge comes the responsibility to correct wrongdoings, which is in the best long-term interests of the organization.

Internal Accountants' Eligibility

Under Dodd-Frank, internal accountants are excluded from receiving whistleblower awards because of their pre-existing legal duty to report securities violations.[114] This includes individuals with internal compliance or audit responsibilities at an entity who receive information about potential violations since it is part of their job responsibilities to report suspicion of illegal acts and fraud to management.

Internal accountants are eligible to become Dodd-Frank whistleblowers in three situations: (1) disclosure to the SEC is needed to prevent "substantial injury" to the financial interest of an entity or its investors; (2) the whistleblower "reasonably believes" the entity is impeding investigation of the misconduct (e.g., destroying documents or improperly influencing witnesses); or (3) the whistleblower has first reported the violation internally and at least 120 days have passed with no action.

The substantial injury provision does not require the whistleblower to reasonably believe that the entity might commit a "material violation"; rather, the whistleblower will generally only need to demonstrate that responsible management or governance personnel at the entity were aware of an "imminent violation" and were not taking steps to prevent it. The 120-day "look-back" period begins after the internal accountant or auditor either provided information of a possible violation to the relevant entity's management (i.e., audit committee, chief legal officer, or chief ethics and compliance officer), or at least 120 days have elapsed since the whistleblower received the information, if the whistleblower received it under circumstances indicating that these people were already aware of the information. The internal accountant cannot become eligible for a whistleblower award by learning of possible misconduct, realizing that those responsible for the entity's compliance are not aware of the possible misconduct, failing to provide the information to them, waiting for the 120-day period to run, and then reporting the information to the SEC (SEC 2010).[115]

External Auditor Eligibility

External auditors are generally prohibited from blowing the whistle on their clients because the information gained during a mandated audit would not be considered to derive from an individual's independent knowledge or analysis. The Dodd-Frank Act prohibits an external auditor who is already obligated to report information to the SEC from personally profiting from reporting that same information as a whistleblower. However, for auditors and their firms, the whistleblower rules allow the auditor or an employee associated with the auditor to make a whistleblower submission alleging that the firm failed to assess, investigate, or report wrongdoing in accordance with Section 10A or that the firm failed to follow other professional standards.

Section 10A of the Securities Exchange Act sets out prescribed steps to take before deciding whether to inform the SEC of fraud.

1. Determine whether the violations have a material effect, quantitatively or qualitatively, on the financial statements.
2. If yes, has management, or the board of directors, caused management to take remedial action, including reporting externally if necessary?
3. If no, then the auditor must make a formal report of its conclusions and provide the report to the board. The board then has one business day to inform the SEC and provide a copy of the communication to the external auditor. If the auditing firm does not receive a copy within one business day, then it has two choices:
   a. Provide a copy of its own report to the SEC within one business day, or
   b. Resign from the engagement and provide a copy of the report to the SEC within one business day of resigning.

If the whistleblower makes such a submission to the SEC based on the firm's failure to follow Section 10A, the whistleblower will be able to obtain an award not only from a successful enforcement action against the auditing firm, but also from any successful action against the firm's engagement client. In allowing such claims, the goal of the SEC is to "help insure that wrongdoing by the [accounting] firm (or its employees) is reported on a timely fashion." According to the SEC, this goal is paramount "because of the important gatekeeper role that auditors play in the securities markets."[116]

Rosenthal and Smith point out that several members of the public accounting profession, including KPMG, Ernst & Young, PricewaterhouseCoopers, and the Center for Audit Quality, believe that permitting CPAs to obtain monetary rewards for blowing the whistle on their own firms' performance of services for clients could create several significant problems including: (1) undermining the ethical obligations of CPAs not to divulge confidential client information by providing a financial reward for whistleblowing; (2) harming the quality of external audits because client management might restrict access to client information for fear the financial incentive for whistleblowing could lead to reporting client-specific information to the SEC; (3) overriding the firms' internal reporting mechanisms for audit-related disagreements; and (4) incentivizing an individual to bypass existing programs to report disagreements including hotlines.[117]

Integrity Considerations

The Integrity and Objectivity rule in the AICPA Code requires that "In the performance of any professional service, a member shall maintain objectivity and integrity, shall be free of conflicts of interest, and shall not knowingly misrepresent facts or subordinate his or her judgment to others [1.100.001]."[118] This rule includes subordination of judgment issues when differences of opinion exist either between an internal accountant and his or her supervisor within the client entity as well as differences between an external auditor and the audit firm. The process to follow is depicted in Exhibit 3.11.

The basic consideration is whether threats exist to compliance with integrity and objectivity that cannot be resolved through adequate safeguards. These threats exist when differences of opinion on accounting matters are present. Under Sections 1.100.001 and 1.130.020, when differences of opinion exist on how best to handle disagreements with one's superior within the entity, or the auditor and audit firm, and the required adjustments are not made, then the CPA should consider whether safeguards exist to ensure that threats to compliance with the rules are eliminated or reduced to an acceptable level. Assuming the difference is between the internal accountant and her supervisor (i.e., the CFO), the internal accountant should determine whether internal reporting requirements exist within the entity to report differences of opinion and any responsibilities that may exist to communicate with third parties, such as regulatory authorities. In that regard, the CPA is advised to seek legal advice on the matter.

If the internal accountant concludes that safeguards cannot eliminate or reduce the threats to integrity and objectivity to an acceptable level or other appropriate action was not taken, then the accountant should consider whether the relationship with the organization should be terminated including possibly resigning one's position. These steps are necessary to prevent subordination of judgment.

The ethical standards in the AICPA Code, SOX provisions, and Dodd-Frank reporting requirements are all part of a healthy corporate governance system. The rules provide the foundation for professional obligations and when to report differences within the corporate governance system. SOX provides steps to ensure the underlying features of a strong corporate governance system exist and are operating as intended. Dodd-Frank addresses whistleblowing considerations when the corporate governance system has not worked as intended to rectify deficiencies in the financial statements. An ethical company is one that embraces these requirements and instills them in the corporate culture.

Whistleblowing Experiences

Since 2012, the SEC's whistleblower program under Dodd-Frank has paid more than $175 million to whistleblowers who provided the SEC with unique and useful information that contributed to a successful enforcement action. In 2016 alone, the office issued more than $57 million to 13 whistleblowers, including six of the ten largest whistleblower awards in the program's history. The details of most awards are not publicly available because many whistleblowers file anonymously through attorneys. However, we can learn a lot from the awards with respect to the types of incidents that trigger awards, confidentiality considerations, and whistleblowing and retaliation by the offenders.[119] Here are a few examples.

- September 29, 2016. The SEC ordered International Game Technology to pay a $500,000 penalty for terminating the employment of a whistleblower because he reported to senior management and to the SEC that the company's financial statements might be distorted.

EXHIBIT 3.11   Ethical Responsibilities of CPAs to Avoid Subordination of Judgment*

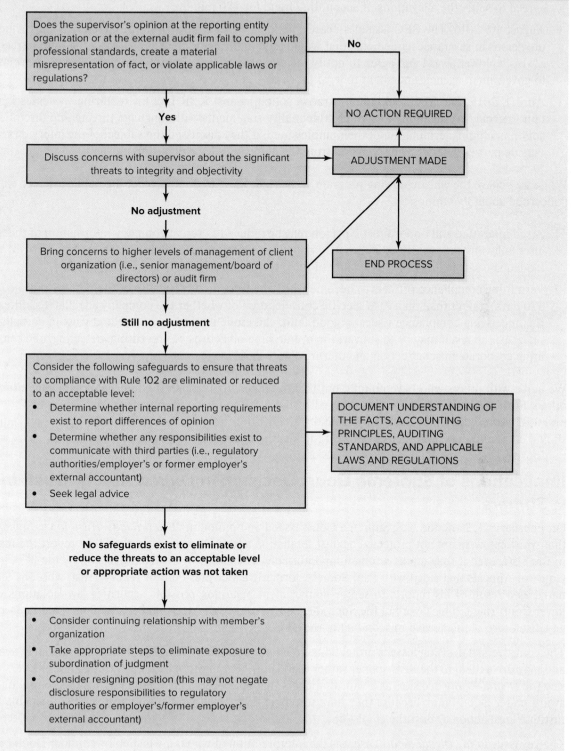

*Source: Exhibit 3.11 was developed by the author from AICPA Code Section 1.130.020

- August 30, 2016 ($22 million award). A former financial executive at Monsanto exposed weaknesses in the company's internal controls that failed to account for millions of dollars in rebates. Monsanto agreed to settle the allegations of accounting fraud for $80 million.

- August 10, 2016. The SEC issued a cease-and-desist order against BlueLinx Holdings for including provisions in severance agreements that would require former employees to waive the right to recover a whistleblower award and agree to notify the company's legal counsel before disclosing information to government agencies pursuant to legal process.

- April 1, 2015. The SEC took administrative action against KBR Inc. for requiring witnesses in certain internal investigations to sign confidentiality statements with language threatening disciplinary action, including termination of their employment, if they discussed the subject of the interviews with outside parties without prior approval from the company's legal department.

While we believe the whistleblowing program is the right thing to do to protect the public interest, we are concerned about two things:

1. A self-interested and opportunistic person may be induced to reveal company information to the SEC after following the prescribed internal compliance process, that led to no action by the company, with inadequate safeguards as to the quality of the information provided, and

2. Permitting compliance officers to become whistleblowers merely because of the passage of time (i.e., 120 days), rather than on a case-specific consideration of whether the company adequately addressed the underlying compliance issues in good faith, can erode corporate culture and trust in compliance officials; the result may be to subvert the overarching objectives of preventing, detecting, and remediating corporate misconduct on an enterprise-wide basis.[120]

We agree with others who have pointed out that, by reporting through the internal compliance process, others in the organization become informed of the facts and become potential whistleblowers.[121] As a practical matter, there may be no way around widening the circle of those in the know, but organizations should, at a minimum, take steps to protect the identity of the whistleblower.

Implications of Supreme Court Decision in *Digital Realty Trust, Inc. v. Somers*

On February 21, 2018, the U.S. Supreme Court issued an opinion in *Digital Realty Trust, Inc. v. Somers*[122] that whistleblowers are not protected against retaliation under Dodd-Frank unless they report the matter to the SEC, even if they report wrongdoing internally. The Court overruled a decision by the 9th Circuit Court of Appeals that sided with Paul Somers, formerly a vice-president of Realty Trust, who was terminated as a result of his reports to senior management regarding possible securities law violations. The lower Court ruled in his favor but the Supreme Court reversed the decision because Somers did not make any disclosure of the alleged misconduct to the SEC.

The controversial decision lessens protections for employees under Dodd-Frank who are retaliated against and may drive them to the SEC sooner rather than later. That may not be a good thing for employers who saw the *Digital Realty* decision as a win. It appears that employees can still qualify for the bounty hunter award under Dodd-Frank because they have to report the alleged wrongdoing to the SEC to enable it to institute legal action against the employer.

The key issue in the *Digital Realty* case was the interpretation of who is a whistleblower under Dodd-Frank and when does a would-be whistleblower qualify for protection against retaliation. The statute defines a whistleblower as a person who reports potential violations of the securities laws to the SEC. Under the anti-retaliation provisions, an employer is prohibited from discharging, harassing or otherwise discriminating against a whistleblower because of the whistleblower's having made protected disclosures in any of three situations: (1) providing information to the SEC, (2) testifying or assisting in the SEC's investigation, and (3) "making disclosures that are required or protected under" SOX, the Securities Exchange Act, specified criminal anti-retaliation prohibitions or "any other law, rule, or regulation subject to the jurisdiction of the Commission."[123]

The SEC had been interpreting the Act with respect to the retaliation provision broadly thereby allowing the protections to apply to internal company reporting even if the individual did not report to the SEC. The Supreme Court disagreed with that interpretation. Writing for the Court in its 9-0 unanimous decision, Justice Ruth Bader Ginsburg put it this way: "A whistleblower is any person who provides . . . information relating to a violation of the securities laws *to the Commission*" [emphasis added]. "That definition," she added, "describes who is eligible for anti-retaliation protection if the individual engages in any of the protected conduct enumerated in the three clauses." Moreover, she observed, "this interpretation is consistent with the 'core objective' of Dodd-Frank's robust whistleblower program," . . . [which] is 'to motivate people who know of securities law violations to *tell the SEC.*'" That's why, for example, the program provides for substantial monetary rewards for SEC reporting. By comparison, SOX had a broader mission to "disturb the 'corporate code of silence' that 'discourage[d] employees from reporting fraudulent behavior not only to the proper authorities, such as the FBI and the SEC, but even internally.'"[124]

As for auditors, attorneys and other employees who are subject to internal-reporting requirements, they are protected under the provision as soon as they also report to the SEC. This has significant implications for accountants and auditors who are CPAs. Rule 1.130.020 of the AICPA Code, that is depicted in Exhibit 3.11, calls for accounting professionals to first meet their internal reporting obligations and then and only then to determine whether any responsibilities exist to communicate with third parties (i.e., the SEC). Consider what might happen if a controller uses the internal reporting mechanisms and, during the process, is fired by the company. It would seem to be too late at that point to inform the SEC and qualify for whistleblower protection. Filing under the Sarbanes-Oxley Act may be an option but there is only a 180-day window of opportunity after the date on which the employee became aware of the violation. Dodd-Frank actions have a shelf life of three years in most cases.

The bottom line on the Supreme Court decision, at least for most employees, is whether they go to the SEC immediately even before they report the matter internally to ensure they qualify for Dodd-Frank protections. Accounting professionals have a tougher decision since they are professionally and ethically obligated to use the internal chain of command first before reporting to the SEC. The Supreme Court may have turned Dodd-Frank, and whistleblowing in general, on its head. Only time will tell whether employees rush off to the SEC to seek protection rather than try and resolve differences internally first. For now, a cynic might say you should go to the SEC and report wrongdoing then risk being fired and then go back to the SEC and claim retaliation.

Whistleblowers Can Use Confidential Company Documents to Expose Fraud

On January 26, 2018, Charles Matthew Erhart struck a blow for all would-be whistleblowers when he achieved a significant win on a critical challenge that nearly all corporate whistleblowers often face—whether they can use confidential company documents to expose fraud and other illegality. District Court Judge Cynthia Bashant's decision in *Erhart v. BofI Holdings*[125] clarifies that employer confidentiality agreements do not supersede federal whistleblower rights, and signals that retaliatory lawsuits against whistleblowers are unlikely to succeed. The decision also provides important guidance to corporate whistleblowers concerning precautions to take in using company documents to blow the whistle.

Erhart worked for BofI Federal Bank (BofI) as an internal auditor and sued BofI under the Sarbanes-Oxley Act and other whistleblower protection laws. Erhart alleged that BofI terminated his employment in retaliation for disclosing to the bank and federal regulators numerous violations of federal and state law. In particular, Erhart's whistleblower retaliation complaint alleged that he opposed the bank's decision to withhold information that was clearly responsive to an SEC subpoena and disclosed improprieties in the CEO's personal accounts and potential violations of bank rules.

Shortly after Erhart filed his retaliation claim, BofI further retaliated against him by suing him for alleged theft and dissemination of BofI's confidential information. In particular, BofI brought claims for (1) breach of contract; (2) conversion; (3) breach of the duty of loyalty; (4) negligence; (5) fraud; (6) violation of the Computer Fraud and Abuse Act; (8) unfair business practices; and (9) other violations of federal and state law.

The key aspects of the decision follow.

Confidentiality Agreements Do Not Trump Whistleblower Rights

The public policy protecting whistleblowers from retaliation, which is reflected in the Dodd-Frank Financial Reform Act and Sarbanes-Oxley, precludes companies from interfering with or preventing whistleblowing. In particular, an SEC rule implementing the Dodd-Frank whistleblower reward program bars companies from "enforcing, or threatening to enforce, a confidentiality agreement" to impede communicating with the SEC. Judge Bashant held that the "public policy in favor of whistleblower protection clearly outweighs the interest in the enforcement of [BofI's confidentiality] agreement, and the agreement is unenforceable."

Appropriating Company Documents is Protected Whistleblowing in Certain Circumstances

Judge Bashant held that whistleblowers are permitted to take company documents to disclose fraud to the government for two reasons. First, "whistleblowers often need documentary evidence to substantiate their allegations." Second, "[a]llowing a whistleblower to appropriate documents supporting believed wrongdoing also mitigates the possibility that evidence of the wrongdoing will be destroyed before an investigation can be conducted."

However, Judge Bashant also held that if a whistleblower engages in wholesale stripping of confidential documents or where the appropriation of confidential documents is "vast and indiscriminate," the public policy in favor of whistleblower might not immunize the whistleblower from potential liability. Here, Judge Bashant declined to reject Erhart's whistleblower defense to the appropriation claims because (1) Erhart testified in a declaration that he "was very careful in [selecting] the information [he] accessed and turned over. Each document was specifically related to one of the allegations of wrongdoing [he] had discussed with [his supervisor] and then reported to federal law enforcement"; and (2) Erhart states that "every document" he used was one he "had properly accessed in the course of performing [his] work as an internal auditor."

Disclosure of Confidential Information in a Retaliation Complaint Should Be Limited to What is Reasonably Necessary to Pursue the Claim

Judge Bashant rejected BofI's position that its confidentiality agreement barred Erhart from using any confidential information to pursue his retaliation claims. But she also noted that Erhart should be permitted to disclose BofI's information in his complaint if doing so was "reasonably necessary" to pursue his retaliation claim.

Taken together with the *Digital Realty Trust, Inc. v. Somers* ruling, these two court decisions seek to protect whistleblowers at the cost of harming employer interests. It remains to be seen whether these rulings result in more whistleblower activity against employers and increased involvement of the SEC at an earlier stage to shut down financial wrongdoing sooner rather than later.

Concluding Thoughts

It is essential for all organizations to take reasonable steps to ensure that they develop an ethical culture, enhance ethical climate by clearly defining right behavior through a code of ethics and ethics policies, and set an ethical tone at the top that encourages responsible behavior. Corporate governance is a key element of an ethical environment. Strong internal controls, an independent audit committee, periodic meetings between independent directors and the external auditors, and a clearly defined whistleblowing policy all contribute to an effective corporate governance system. Research supports the proposition that "strong ethical cultures" diminish organizational misconduct and thereby the need for employees to blow the whistle internally or externally.[126]

Creating an ethical culture is a necessary but insufficient condition to ensure that ethical behavior occurs. Individuals within the organization may attempt to subvert the systems and pressure others to look the other way or go along with wrongdoing under the guise of being a team player or accepting a one-time fix to a perceived problem. In these situations, outlets should exist for employees to voice their values when they believe unethical or fraudulent behavior has occurred. Just imagine how Anthony Menendez's experiences would have changed had Halliburton created such a supportive environment.

Employees who have made a good faith effort to report material misstatements in the financial statements or violations of applicable laws and regulations to top management and the board of directors to no avail now have the option of informing the SEC under SOX and be protected against retaliation. Dodd-Frank provides a whistleblower award to incentivize internal accountants and external auditors to report fraud after following the prescribed procedures so that management has an opportunity to adjust the financial statements. These are important parts of a healthy corporate governance system but may not solve the underlying problem, which is a tone at the top that says: This is the way things are done around here. It takes a strong commitment to ethics of those in the organization to change the culture and align ethical action with ethical beliefs.

Discussion Questions

1. What are the ethical lessons to be learned from the scandal at Wells Fargo?

2. In her book *The Seven Signs of Ethical Collapse,* Jennings explains: "When an organization collapses ethically, it means that those in the organization have drifted into rationalizations and legalisms, and all for the purpose of getting the results they want and need at almost any cost." Discuss what you think Jennings meant by this statement in the context of the "Giving Voice to Values" discussions in Chapter 2.

3. Explain the components of Burchard's Ethical Dissonance Model and how it describes the ethical person-organization fit at various stages of the contractual relationship in each potential fit scenario. Assume a *Low Organizational Ethics, High Individual Ethics (Low-High)* fit. How might this relationship influence your motivation to blow the whistle on corporate wrongdoing?

4. Explain the following statements: (1) It has been argued that an organization that does not support those that whistle blow because of violation of professional standards is indicative of a failure of organizational ethics; (2) It is a distinguishing mark of actions labeled whistleblowing that the agent intends to force attention to a serious moral problem. How does this statement relate to whistleblowers who come forward under provisions of the Dodd-Frank Financial Reform Act?

5. In an interview on Philosophy Talk, a national syndicated radio program, Edward Snowden, the National Security Agency whistleblower, was asked whether he sees himself as a hero or a traitor, considering the various depictions presented by the government and media. He answered by discussing the cost-benefit analysis that whistleblowers must consider before leaking information. Use the Snowden case and analyze his actions from a cost-benefit perspective. How might Rights Theory lead to a different analysis?

6. Explain the role of integrity in workplace ethics.

7. According to the 2013 *National Business Ethics Survey,* 60% of workplace misconduct involved someone with managerial authority. Roughly 25% of observed misconduct involved senior managers. Why are high-level employees more likely to behave unethically?

8. It has been said that recent graduates from a business school majoring in accounting and just entering the profession are especially vulnerable to ethical missteps because they are often naive and may not see the ethical aspects of situations they confront. Explain the various dimensions of such alleged ethical challenges in the workplace.

9. Organizational culture can influence moral behavior through the "stacked deck" phenomenon. Explain how this might work and lead to a defense of subordinates' behavior we might call "They made me do it".

10. Do you believe that employees who observe more occupational fraud in their organizations are more likely to engage in occupational fraud themselves?

11. The following questions are about corporate governance and executive compensation:

    (a) How does agency theory address the issue of executive compensation?

    (b) How might stakeholder theory argue against the current model of executive compensation in the United States?

    (c) What is meant by the statement, "Compensation systems always become in part *end* and not simply *means*"?

12. The issue of the size of executive compensation packages is explored in the text. The highest paid CEO in 2016 was Thomas Rutledge, CEO of Charter Communications, who received $98 million in executive compensation. As noted in the text, critics claim that CEOs receive excessive executive compensation packages when compared with the average worker (271:1). How would you evaluate the fairness of executive compensation pay packages?

13. Explain how internal auditors' sensitivity to ethical dilemmas might be influenced by corporate governance mechanisms.

14. What are the roles and responsibilities of independent members of the board of directors with respect to risk management and corporate governance?

15. How can a board of directors know whether the culture of the organization supports the right kind of risk taking?

16. Five months before the new 2002 Lexus ES hit showroom floors, the company's U.S. engineers sent a test report to Toyota City in Japan: The luxury sedan shifted gears so roughly that it was "not acceptable for production." Days later, another Japanese executive sent an e-mail to top managers saying that despite misgivings among U.S. officials, the 2002 Lexus was "marginally acceptable for production." The new ES went on sale across the nation on October 1, 2001.

In years to come, thousands of Lexus owners discovered that some of the vehicles had transmission problems, which caused it to hesitate when motorists hit the gas or lurch forward unintentionally. The 2002–2006 ES models would become the target of lawsuits, federal safety investigations, and hundreds of consumer complaints, including claims of 49 injuries.

In an August 15, 2005, memo explaining the company's position, a staff attorney wrote, "The objective will be to limit the number of vehicles to be serviced to those owners who complain and to limit the per-vehicle cost."

In 2010, Toyota was fined a record $16.4 million for delays in notifying U.S. federal safety officials about defects that could lead to sudden acceleration.

What are the common features in the automobile product defect cases discussed in the text and in this question? What role did corporate governance play in the way they were handled by management?

17. While on a lunch break following a dispute with a supervisor, an employee updated her Facebook status to an expletive and the name of the employer's company. Several coworkers "liked" her status. She later posted that the employer didn't appreciate its employees; no coworkers responded to this online. Do you believe the employee should be fired for her actions? Explain why or why not.

18. Brief and Motowidlo define prosocial behavior within the organizational setting as "behavior which is (a) performed by a member of an organization, (b) directed toward an individual, group, or organization with whom she interacts while carrying out her organizational role, and (c) performed with the intention of promoting the welfare of the individual, group, or organization toward which it is directed."[127]

The researchers on whistleblowing using this model have generally argued that stages 5 and 6 represent cognitive moral development consistent with prosocial behavior. Discuss why stages 5 and 6 of Kohlberg's model are more likely to be associated with prosocial behavior than lower stages of moral development.

19. How do the concepts of cognitive dissonance and organizational/ethical dissonance relate to whether an accountant might choose to blow the whistle on corporate wrongdoing?

20. Just because an accountant or auditor has a right to blow the whistle, does that mean she has a duty to blow the whistle? How might we make that determination?

21. Review the facts related to the reporting of financial statement fraud by Tony Menendez at Halliburton in the context of the factors identified in the Anti-Fraud Collaboration study. Discuss the similarities between the two with respect to Menendez's experiences and explain how an effective compliance function might have been used to mitigate the concerns of reporting suspected fraud.

22. When financial results aren't what they seemed to be—and a company is forced to issue material financial restatements –should it be required to develop policies to claw back incentive pay and bonuses that were awarded to senior managers on the basis of rosier outcomes? Use ethical reasoning to answer this question.

23. Is it a positive result that 40% of occupational fraud is initially detected by a "tip"? Explain why or why not.

24. Do you believe the U.S. Supreme Court decision in *Digital Realty Trust, Inc. v. Somers* and the decision in *Erhart v. Bofl* holdings were the "right" decisions? Explain the basis for your answer.

25. Is business ethics an oxymoron?

Endnotes

1. Tom Fox, Wells Fargo: The Lessons of an Ethics Failure, *National Defense Magazine,* November 30, 2016, http://www.nationaldefensemagazine.org/articles/2016/11/30/wells-fargo-the-lessons-of-an-ethics-failure.

2. Richard Bowen, Wells Fargo, Fried Again, August 17, 2017, http://www.richardmbowen.com/wells-fargo-fried-again/.

3. Matt Egan, I called the Wells Fargo ethics line and was fired, September 21, 2016, http://money.cnn.com/2016/09/21/investing/wells-fargo-fired-workers-retaliation-fake-accounts/index.html.

4. Matt Egan, More Wells Fargo workers allege retaliation for whistleblowing, November 7, 2017, http://money.cnn.com/2017/11/06/investing/wells-fargo-retaliation-whistleblower/index.html.

5. Wells Fargo, *Our Code of Ethics and Business Conduct: Living Our Vision, Values, and Goals,* https://www08.wellsfargomedia.com/assets/pdf/about/corporate/code-of-ethics.pdf.

6. Ethisphere Magazine, World's Most Ethical Companies, 2017, https://ethisphere.com/ethisphere-announces-2017-worlds-most-ethical-companies/.

7. Microsoft Standards of Business Conduct, https://www.microsoft.com/en-us/legal/compliance/sbc/download.

8. Cam Caldwell, Linda A. Hayes, and Do Tien Long, "Leadership, Trustworthiness, and Ethical Stewardship," *Journal of Business Ethics* 96 (2010), pp. 497–512.

9. Craig E. Johnson, *Meeting the Ethical Challenges of Leadership: Casting Light or Shadow* (New York: Sage Publications, 2015).

10. Johnson, pp. 321–323.

11. O.C. Ferrell, John Fraedrich, and Linda Ferrell, *Business Ethics: Ethical Decision Making and Cases,* 11th ed. (Stamford, CT: Cengage Learning, 2017, p. 130).

12. Ferrell et al., pp. 130–131.

13. Ferrell et al., pp. 131–132.

14. Ferrell et al., p. 132.

15. Ferrell et al., pp. 133–134.

16. Sean Valentine, Lynn Godkin, and Margaret Lucero, "Ethical Context, Organizational Commitment, and Person-Organization Fit," *Journal of Business Ethics* Vol. 41 No. 4 (December 2002), pp. 349–360.

17. Ferrell et al.

18. James Rufus Koren, Wells Fargo overhauls pay plan for branch employees following fake-accounts scandal, *L.A. Times,* January 10, 2017, http://beta.latimes.com/business/la-fi-wells-fargo-pay-20170110-story.html.

19. H. R. Smith and Archie B. Carroll, "Organizational Ethics: A Stacked Deck," *Journal of Business Ethics,* Vol. 3, No. 2 (May 1984), pp. 95–100.

20. Thomas M. Jones, "Ethical Decision Making by Individuals in Organizations: An Issue-Contingent Model," *Academy of Management Review,* Vol. 16, No. 2 (1991), pp. 366–395.

21. Susan E. Fiske and Shelley E. Taylor, *Social Cognition* (NY: McGraw-Hill, 1991).

22. MaryJo Burchard, "Ethical Dissonance and Response to Destructive Leadership: A Proposed Model," *Emerging Leadership Journeys,* 4, no. 1, pp. 154–176.

23. Scott K. Jones and Kenneth M. Hiltebeitel, "Organizational Influence in a Model of the Moral Decision Process of Accountants," *Journal of Business Ethics* 14, no. 6 (1995), pp. 417–431.

24. Jones.

25. Burchard.

26. Burchard, pp. 158–159.

27. Lawrence A. Pervin, "Performance and Satisfaction as a Function of Individual-Environment Fit," *Psychological Bulletin* 69, no. 1 (January 1968), pp. 56–68.

28. Hian Chye Koh and El'fred H. Y. Boo, "Organizational Ethics and Job Satisfaction and Commitment," *Management Decision* 4, nos. 5 and 6 (2004), pp. 677–693.

29. Art Padilla, Robert Hogan, and Robert B. Kaiser, "The Toxic Triangle: Destructive Leaders, Susceptible Followers, and Conducive Environments," *Leadership Quarterly* 18 (3), (2007), pp. 176–194.

30. V. Lee Hamilton and Herbert Kelman, *Crimes of Obedience: Toward a Social Psychology of Authority and Responsibility* (New Haven, CT: Yale University Press, 1989).

31. Koh and Boo.

32. Randi L. Sims and Thomas L. Keon, "The Influence of Ethical Fit on Employee Satisfaction, Commitment, and Turnover," *Journal of Business Ethics* 13, no. 12 (1994), pp. 939–948.

33. Corporate Culture, *Ethical Systems,* http://www.ethicalsystems.org/content/corporate-culture.

34. Marianne M. Jennings, *The Seven Signs of Ethical Collapse: How to Spot Moral Meltdowns in Companies Before It's Too Late* (New York: St. Martin's Press, 2006).

35. Jennings et al.

36. Jennings et al.

37. Jennings et al, pp.138-139.

38. Marianne Jennings, Seven Signs of Ethical Collapse, Markkula Center for Applied Ethics, April 4, 2007, https://www.scu.edu/ethics/focus-areas/business-ethics/resources/seven-signs-of-ethical-collapse/.

39. Jennings, Markkula Center for Applied Ethics.

40. Chris MacDonald, BP and Corporate Social Responsibility, *The Business Ethics Blog,* https://businessethicsblog.com/2010/09/01/bp-and-csr/.

41. Laura P. Hartman, Joseph DesJardins, and Chris MacDonald, *Business Ethics: Decision Making for Personal & Social Responsibility,* (New York: McGraw Hill Education, 2018), pp. 177–180.

42. Twenty-First Century Fox, Inc., Workplace Civility and Inclusion, https://www.21cf.com/corporate-governance/workplace-civility-and-inclusion.

43. Corporate Giving Data: Trends and Insights from CECP's Annual Benchmarking Report: A Conversation with Michael Stroik, Manager, Research an d Analytics, CECP, https://www.changingourworld.com/corporate-social-engagement/social-strategist/social-strategist-december-2014.

44. Kelsey Chong, Millennials and the Rising Demand for Corporate Social Responsibility, *Berkeley Haas,* https://cmr.berkeley.edu/blog/2017/1/millennials-and-csr/.

45. R. Edward Freeman, "Managing for Stakeholders," https://papers.ssrn.com/sol3/papers.cfm?abstract_id=1186402.

46. Milton Friedman, "The Social Responsibility of Business is to Increase its Profits, *NY Times,* September 13, 1970, http://www.nytimes.com/1970/09/13/archives/article-15-no-title.html.

47. Hartman et al., pp. 180–182.

48. Charles River Associates, Sarbanes-Oxley Section 404 Costs and Remediation of Deficiencies: Estimates from a Sample of Fortune 1000 Companies, April 2005, https://www.sec.gov/spotlight/soxcomp/soxcomp-all-attach.pdf.

49. Hartman et al., 185–187.

50. Freeman.

51. Hartman, p. 183–187.

52. *United States v. Carroll Towing,* 159 F.2d 169 (2d Cir. 1947).

53. Douglas Birsch and John H. Fiedler, *The Ford Pinto Case: A Study in Applied Ethics, Business, and Technology* (Albany: State University of New York, 1994).

54. *Grimshaw v. Ford Motor Co.,* 1 19 Cal.App.3d 757, 174 Cal. Rptr. 348 (1981).

55. David De Cremer and Ann E. Tenbrunsel, *Behavioral Business Ethics: Shaping an Emerging Field* (New York: Routledge, 2012).

56. Honda Settles Takata Air Bag Claims for $605 Million, *Reuters,* September 1, 2017, http://fortune.com/2017/09/01/honda-takata-air-bag-lawsuit-settlement/.

57. Tamara Kaplan, "The Tylenol Crisis: How Effective Public Relations Saved Johnson & Johnson," Pennsylvania State University. Available here: http://www.aerobiologicalengineering.com/wxk116/TylenolMurders/crisis.html.

58. Patients versus Profits at Johnson & Johnson: Has the Company Lost its Way,? Knowledge at Wharton, February 15, 2012, http://knowledge.wharton.upenn.edu/article/patients-versus-profits-at-johnson-johnson-has-the-company-lost-its-way/.

59. Zabihollah Rezaee, *Corporate Governance and Ethics* (New York: Wiley, 2009).

60. Hartman, pp. 508–509.

61. Jean Murray, Why a Conflict of Interest Policy is Needed for Corporate Boards. September 9, 2016, https://www.thebalance.com/conflict-of-interest-policy-for-your-corporate-board-397464.

62. Leo L. Strine, Jr., "Derivative Impact? Some Early Reflections on the Corporation Law Implications of the Enron Debacle," *57 Business Lawyer,* 1371, 1373 (2002).

63. Disney Affirmed: The Delaware Supreme Court Clarifies The Duty of Directors To Act In Good Faith, June 9, 2006, http://www.potteranderson.com/newsroom-news-90.html.

64. Arifur Khan, Mohammed Badrul Muttakin, and Javed Siddigui, "Corporate Governance and Corporate Social Responsibility Disclosures: Evidence from an Emerging Economy," *Journal of Business Ethics* Vol. 114 No. 2, 2013, pp. 207–223.

65. Ferrell, pp. 41–48.

66. O.C. Ferrell, John Fraedrich, and Linda Ferrell, *Business Ethics: Ethical Decision Making and Cases* (Stamford, CT: Cengage Learning, 2015, p. 44).

67. W. Steve Albrecht, Conan C. Albrecht, and Chad O. Albrecht, "Fraud and Corporate Executives: Agency, Stewardship, and Broken Trust," *Journal of Forensic Accounting* 5 (2004), pp. 109–130.

68. Lex Donaldson and James H. Davis, "Stewardship Theory," *Australian Journal of Management* 16, no. 1 (June 1991).

69. Michael Jensen and William H. Meckling, "Theory of the Firm: Managerial Behavior, Agency Costs, and Ownership Structure," *Journal of Financial Economics* (1976), pp. 305–360.

70. Chamu Sundaramurthy and Marianne Lewis, "Control and Collaboration: Paradoxes and Government," *Academy of Management Review* 28, Issue 3 (July 2003), pp. 397–416.

71. Tricker, pp. 65–71.

72. John A. Byrne with Louis Lavelle, Nanette Byrnes, Marcia Vickers, and Amy Borrus, "How to Fix Corporate Governance," *BusinessWeek,* May 6, 2002, pp. 69–78.

73. Economic Policy Institute, CEO pay remains high relative to the pay of typical workers and high-wage earners, July 20, 2017, http://www.epi.org/files/pdf/130354.pdf.

74. Ratio between CEOs and average workers in world in 2014, by country, https://www.statista.com/statistics/424159/pay-gap-between-ceos-and-average-workers-in-world-by-country/.

75. "Current Controversies in Executive Compensation: 'Issues of Justice and Fairness,'" Knowledge@Wharton, May 2, 2007, Available at: http://knowledge.wharton.upenn.edu/article/current-controversies-in-executive-compensation-issues-of-justice-and-fairness/.

76. Dodd-Frank Wall Street Reform and Consumer Protection Act (H.R. 4173), www.sec.gov/about/laws/wallstreetreform-cpa.pdf.

77. PwC, Executive Compensation Clawbacks: 2014 Proxy Disclosure Study, January 2015. https://www.pwc.com/us/en/hr-management/publications/assets/pwc-executive-compensation-clawbacks-2014.pdf.

78. Robert E. Scully, Jr. "Executive Compensation, the Business Judgment Rule, and the Dodd-Frank Act: Back to the Future for Private Litigation?" *The Federal Lawyer,* January 2011.

79. Institute of Chartered Accountants in England and Wales, Report of the Committee on The Financial Aspects of Corporate Governance, May 1991, https://www.icaew.com/-/media/corporate/files/library/subjects/corporate-governance/financial-aspects-of-corporate-governance.ashx?la=en.

80. New York Stock Exchange, NYSE Corporate Governance Guide, 2014, https://www.nyse.com/publicdocs/nyse/listing/NYSE_Corporate_Governance_Guide.pdf.

81. PricewaterhouseCoopers, PwC State of Compliance Study 2016, https://www.pwc.com/us/en/risk-assurance/state-of-compliance-study.html.

82. *KPMG Integrity Survey 2013,* https://assets.kpmg.com/content/dam/kpmg/pdf/2013/08/Integrity-Survey-2013-O-201307.pdf.

83. Ethics Resource Center (ERC), *2013 National Business Ethics Survey (NBES) of the U.S. Workforce.*

84. This section is taken from a blog posted by Steven Mintz: "Beware of Posting Critical Comments About Your Employer on Facebook," March 1, 2017, http://www.ethicssage.com/2017/03/beware-of-posting-critical-comments-about-your-employer-on-facebook.html.

85. Association of Certified Fraud Examiners, *2016 Global Fraud Study: Report to the Nations on Occupational Fraud and Abuse,* https://s3-us-west-2.amazonaws.com/acfepublic/2018-report-to-the-nations.pdf

86. ACFE, p. 6.

87. Ernst & Young, *Detecting Financial Statement Fraud: What Every Manager Needs to Know,* October 2010, Center for Audit Quality.

88. AICPA Professional Standards, *Consideration of Fraud in a Financial Statement Audit* (AU-C Section 240), (NY: AICPA, 2014).

89. House of Representative Financial Services Committee, HR 3763—Sarbanes-Oxley Act of 2002, July 24, 2002, https://www.congress.gov/bill/107th-congress/house-bill/3763.

90. Securities and Exchange Commission, "SEC Charges Company CEO and Former CFO With Hiding Internal Controls Deficiencies and Violating Sarbanes-Oxley Requirements," July 30, 2014.

91. *In the Matter of Marc Sherman, Respondent,* Securities Exchange Act of 1934, Release No. 74765, April 20, 2015, https://www.sec.gov/litigation/admin/2015/34-74765.pdf.

92. Alison Frankel, "Sarbanes-Oxley's Lost Promise: Why CEOs Haven't been Prosecuted," *Reuters.com On the Case* blog, July 27, 2012, Available at: http://blogs.reuters.com/alison-frankel/2012/07/27/sarbanes-oxleys-lost-promise-why-ceos-havent-been-prosecuted/.

93. Report of the National Commission on Fraudulent Financial Reporting (Treadway Commission), October 1987, https://www.coso.org/Documents/NCFFR.pdf.

94. Committee of Sponsoring Organizations of the Treadway Commission (COSO), 2013 *Internal Control–Integrated Framework,* Report Available at: http://www.coso.org/documents/Internal%20Control-Integrated%20Framework.pdf.

95. COSO, Enterprise Risk Management–Integrated Framework, September 2004, https://www.coso.org/Documents/COSO-ERM-Executive-Summary.pdf.

96. Deloitte, Risk appetite frameworks: How to spot the genuine article, https://www2.deloitte.com/content/dam/Deloitte/au/Documents/risk/deloitte-au-risk-appetite-frameworks-financial-services-0614.pdf.

97. COSO, Enterprise Risk Management Framework: Integrating with Strategy and Performance, https://www.coso.org/Documents/COSO-ERM-Presentation-September-2017.pdf.

98. Jackie Wattles and Selena Larson, How the Equifax data breach happened: What we know now, *CNNTech,* September 16, 2017, http://money.cnn.com/2017/09/16/technology/equifax-breach-security-hole/index.html.

99. Francine McKenna, Equifax auditors are on the hook for data security risk controls," *Market Watch,* October 3, 2017, http://money.cnn.com/2017/09/16/technology/equifax-breach-security-hole/index.html.

100. McKenna.

101. Janet P. Near and Marcia P. Miceli, "Organizational Dissidence: The Case of Whistle-blowing," *Journal of Business Ethics* 4 (1985), pp. 1–16.

102. Michael Davis, "Some Paradoxes of Whistleblowing," *Business and Professional Ethics Journal* Vol. 15 No. 1, 1996, https://philosophia.uncg.edu/media/phi361-metivier/readings/Davis-Paradoxes%20of%20Whistle-Blowing.pdf.

103. Richard T. De George, *Business Ethics,* 7th ed. (NY: Prentice-Hall, 2010).

104. Marion Mogielnicki, "Hunting for 'Bounty' and Finding 'Moral Autonomy': The Dodd-Frank Act Expansion of Whistle Blower Protections," *Academy of Business Research,* Vol. 2, (2011), pp. 74–84.

105. Tsahuridu et al.

106. Miceli and Near, pp. 698–699.

107. Tsahuridu et al.

108. Jesse Eisinger, "The Whistleblower's Tale: How an Accountant took on Halliburton and Won," *Pro Publica,* April 21, 2015.

109. Dodd-Frank et al.

110. SEC, "Implementation of the Whistleblower Provisions of Section 21F of the Securities Exchange Act of 1934," Available at: https://www.sec.gov/rules/final/2011/34-64545.pdf.

111. Dodd=Frank et al.

112. Kobi Kastiel, "Elements of an Effective Whistleblower Hotline," *Harvard Law School Forum on Corporate Governance and Financial Regulation,* October 25, 2014. Available at: http://corpgov.law. harvard.edu/2014/10/25/elements-of-an-effective-whistleblower-hotline/.

113. AICPA, *Code of Professional Conduct,* December 15, 2014, Available at: https://www.aicpa.org/content/dam/aicpa/research/standards/codeofconduct/downloadabledocuments/2014december15contentasof2016august31codeofconduct.pdf.

114. SEC et al.

115. SEC et al.

116. SEC et al.

117. Jason Rosenthal, Esq. and Lesley Smith, Esq, "Should CPAs be Financially Rewarded As Whistleblowers?" *CPA Insider,* 2011, Available at: https://www.cpa2biz.com/Content/media/PRODUCER_CONTENT/Newsletters/Articles_2011/CPA/Jul/Whistleblowers.jsp

118. AICPA Code.

119. Jason Zuckerman and Matthew Stock, SEC Whistleblower Program: What are the largest SEC whistleblower awards? November 30, 2017, https://www.zuckermanlaw.com/sp_faq/largest-sec-whistleblower-awards/.

120. Philip Stamatakos and Ted Chung, "Dodd-Frank's Whistleblower Provisions and the SEC's Rule: Compliance and Ethical Considerations," *Corporate Governance Advisor,* September/October 2011.

121. Daniel Hurson, "United States: Ten 'Rules' For Becoming A Successful SEC Whistleblower," September 11, 2013, Available at: http://www.mondaq.com/unitedstates/x/261844/Corporate+Commercial+Law/The+New+Rules+For+Becoming+A+Successful+SEC+Whistleblower.

122. Supreme Court of the United States, *Digital Realty Trust, Inc. v. Somers,*February 21, 2018, https://www.supremecourt.gov/opinions/17pdf/16-1276_b0nd.pdf.

123. Dodd-Frank Wall Street Reform and Consumer Protection Act (H.R. 4173).

124. Cydney Posner, SCOTUS says whistleblowers must whistle all the way to the SEC, *Cooley Pub Co,* February 21, 2018, https://cooleypubco.com/2018/02/21/scotus-says-whistleblowers-must-whistle-all-the-way-to-the-sec/.

125. *Charles Matthew Erhart v. BOFI Holding, Inc., Case No. 15-cv-02287-BAS(NLS),* February 14, 2017, https://cases.justia.com/federal/district-courts/california/casdce/3:2015cv02287/486757/22/0.pdf?ts=1474967833.

126. Mark S. Schwartz, "Developing and Sustaining an Ethical Corporate Culture: The Core Elements," *Business Horizons* 56 (2013), pp. 39–50.

127. Arthur P. Brief and Stephan J. Motowidlo, "Prosocial Organizational Behaviors," *The Academy of Management Review,* Vol. 11, No. 4 (Oct., 1986), pp. 710–725.

Chapter 3 Cases

Case 3-1 The Parable of the Sadhu

Bowen H. McCoy

Reprinted with permission from "The Parable of the Sadhu," by Bowen H. McCoy, *Harvard Business Review.* Copyright © Harvard Business Publishing.

Last year, as the first participant in the new six-month sabbatical program that Morgan Stanley has adopted, I enjoyed a rare opportunity to collect my thoughts as well as do some traveling. I spent the first three months in Nepal, walking 600 miles through 200 villages in the Himalayas and climbing some 120,000 vertical feet. My sole Western companion on the trip was an anthropologist who shed light on the cultural patterns of the villages that we passed through.

During the Nepal hike, something occurred that has had a powerful impact on my thinking about corporate ethics. Although some might argue that the experience has no relevance to business, it was a situation in which a basic ethical dilemma suddenly intruded into the lives of a group of individuals. How the group responded holds a lesson for all organizations, no matter how defined.

The Sadhu

The Nepal experience was more rugged than I had anticipated. Most commercial treks last two or three weeks and cover a quarter of the distance we traveled.

My friend Stephen, the anthropologist, and I were halfway through the 60-day Himalayan part of the trip when we reached the high point, an 18,000-foot pass over a crest that we'd have to traverse to reach the village of Muklinath, an ancient holy place for pilgrims.

Six years earlier, I had suffered pulmonary edema, an acute form of altitude sickness, at 16,500 feet in the vicinity of Everest base camp—so we were understandably concerned about what would happen at 18,000 feet. Moreover, the Himalayas were having their wettest spring in 20 years; hip-deep powder and ice had already driven us off one ridge. If we failed to cross the pass, I feared that the last half of our once-in-a-lifetime trip would be ruined.

The night before we would try the pass, we camped in a hut at 14,500 feet. In the photos taken at that camp, my face appears wan. The last village we'd passed through was a sturdy two-day walk below us, and I was tired.

During the late afternoon, four backpackers from New Zealand joined us, and we spent most of the night awake, anticipating the climb. Below, we could see the fires of two other parties, which turned out to be two Swiss couples and a Japanese hiking club.

To get over the steep part of the climb before the sun melted the steps cut in the ice, we departed at 3.30 a.m. The New Zealanders left first, followed by Stephen and myself, our porters and Sherpas, and then the Swiss. The Japanese lingered in their camp. The sky was clear, and we were confident that no spring storm would erupt that day to close the pass.

At 15,500 feet, it looked to me as if Stephen was shuffling and staggering a bit, which are symptoms of altitude sickness. (The initial stage of altitude sickness brings a headache and nausea. As the condition worsens, a climber may encounter difficult breathing, disorientation, aphasia, and paralysis.) I felt strong—my adrenaline was flowing—but

I was very concerned about my ultimate ability to get across. A couple of our porters were also suffering from the height, and Pasang, our Sherpa sirdar (leader), was worried.

Just after daybreak, while we rested at 15,500 feet, one of the New Zealanders, who had gone ahead, came staggering down toward us with a body slung across his shoulders. He dumped the almost naked, barefoot body of an Indian holy man—a sadhu—at my feet. He had found the pilgrim lying on the ice, shivering and suffering from hypothermia. I cradled the sadhu's head and laid him out on the rocks. The New Zealander was angry. He wanted to get across the pass before the bright sun melted the snow. He said, "Look, I've done what I can. You have porters and Sherpa guides. You care for him. We're going on!" He turned and went back up the mountain to join his friends.

I took a carotid pulse and found that the sadhu was still alive. We figured he had probably visited the holy shrines at Muklinath and was on his way home. It was fruitless to question why he had chosen this desperately high route instead of the safe, heavily traveled caravan route through the Kali Gandaki gorge. Or why he was shoeless and almost naked, or how long he had been lying in the pass. The answers weren't going to solve our problem.

Stephen and the four Swiss began stripping off their outer clothing and opening their packs. The sadhu was soon clothed from head to foot. He was not able to walk, but he was very much alive. I looked down the mountain and spotted the Japanese climbers, marching up with a horse.

Without a great deal of thought, I told Stephen and Pasang that I was concerned about withstanding the heights to come and wanted to get over the pass. I took off after several of our porters who had gone ahead.

On the steep part of the ascent where, if the ice steps had given way, I would have slid down about 3,000 feet, I felt vertigo. I stopped for a breather, allowing the Swiss to catch up with me. I inquired about the sadhu and Stephen. They said that the sadhu was fine and that Stephen was just behind them. I set off again for the summit.

Stephen arrived at the summit an hour after I did. Still exhilarated by victory, I ran down the slope to congratulate him. He was suffering from altitude sickness—walking 15 steps, then stopping, walking 15 steps, then stopping. Pasang accompanied him all the way up. When I reached them, Stephen glared at me and said, "How do you feel about contributing to the death of a fellow man?"

I did not completely comprehend what he meant. "Is the sadhu dead?" I inquired.

"No," replied Stephen, "but he surely will be!"

After I had gone, followed not long after by the Swiss, Stephen had remained with the sadhu. When the Japanese had arrived, Stephen had asked to use their horse to transport the sadhu down to the hut. They had refused. He had then asked Pasang to have a group of our porters carry the sadhu. Pasang had resisted the idea, saying that the porters would have to exert all their energy to get themselves over the pass. He believed they could not carry a man down 1,000 feet to the hut, reclimb the slope, and get across safely before the snow melted. Pasang had pressed Stephen not to delay any longer.

The Sherpas had carried the sadhu down to a rock in the sun at about 15,000 feet and pointed out the hut another 500 feet below. The Japanese had given him food and drink. When they had last seen him, he was listlessly throwing rocks at the Japanese party's dog, which had frightened him.

We do not know if the sadhu lived or died.

For many of the following days and evenings, Stephen and I discussed and debated our behavior toward the sadhu. Stephen is a committed Quaker with deep moral vision. He said, "I feel that what happened with the sadhu is a good example of the breakdown between the individual ethic and the corporate ethic. No one person was willing to assume ultimate responsibility for the sadhu. Each was willing to do his bit just so long as it was not too inconvenient. When it got to be a bother, everyone just passed the buck to someone else and took off. Jesus was relevant to a more individualistic stage of society, but how do we interpret his teaching today in a world filled with large, impersonal organizations and groups?"

I defended the larger group, saying, "Look, we all cared. We all gave aid and comfort. Everyone did his bit. The New Zealander carried him down below the snow line. I took his pulse and suggested we treat him for hypothermia. You and the Swiss gave him clothing and got him warmed up. The Japanese gave him food and water. The Sherpas carried him down to the sun and pointed out the easy trail toward the hut. He was well enough to throw rocks at a dog. What more could we do?"

"You have just described the typical affluent Westerner's response to a problem. Throwing money—in this case, food and sweaters—at it, but not solving the fundamentals!" Stephen retorted.

"What would satisfy you?" I said. "Here we are, a group of New Zealanders, Swiss, Americans, and Japanese who have never met before and who are at the apex of one of the most powerful experiences of our lives. Some years the pass is so bad no one gets over it. What right does an almost naked pilgrim who chooses the wrong trail have to disrupt our lives? Even the Sherpas had no interest in risking the trip to help him beyond a certain point."

Stephen calmly rebutted, "I wonder what the Sherpas would have done if the sadhu had been a well-dressed Nepali, or what the Japanese would have done if the sadhu had been a well-dressed Asian, or what you would have done, Buzz, if the sadhu had been a well-dressed Western woman?"

"Where, in your opinion," I asked, "is the limit of our responsibility in a situation like this? We had our own well-being to worry about. Our Sherpa guides were unwilling to jeopardize us or the porters for the sadhu. No one else on the mountain was willing to commit himself beyond certain self-imposed limits."

Stephen said, "As individual Christians or people with a Western ethical tradition, we can fulfill our obligations in such a situation only if one, the sadhu dies in our care; two, the sadhu demonstrates to us that he can undertake the two-day walk down to the village; or three, we carry the sadhu for two days down to the village and persuade someone there to care for him."

"Leaving the sadhu in the sun with food and clothing—where he demonstrated hand-eye coordination by throwing a rock at a dog—comes close to fulfilling items one and two," I answered. "And it wouldn't have made sense to take him to the village where the people appeared to be far less caring than the Sherpas, so the third condition is impractical. Are you really saying that, no matter what the implications, we should, at the drop of a hat, have changed our entire plan?"

The Individual versus the Group Ethic

Despite my arguments, I felt and continue to feel guilt about the sadhu. I had literally walked through a classic moral dilemma without fully thinking through the consequences. My excuses for my actions include a high adrenaline flow, a superordinate goal, and a once-in-a-lifetime opportunity—common factors in corporate situations, especially stressful ones.

Real moral dilemmas are ambiguous, and many of us hike right through them, unaware that they exist. When, usually after the fact, someone makes an issue of one, we tend to resent his or her bringing it up. Often, when the full import of what we have done (or not done) hits us, we dig into a defensive position from which it is very difficult to emerge. In rare circumstances, we may contemplate what we have done from inside a prison.

Had we mountaineers been free of stress caused by the effort and the high altitude, we might have treated the sadhu differently. Yet isn't stress the real test of personal and corporate values? The instant decisions that executives make under pressure reveal the most about personal and corporate character.

Among the many questions that occur to me when I ponder my experience with the sadhu are: What are the practical limits of moral imagination and vision? Is there a collective or institutional ethic that differs from the ethics of the individual? At what level of effort or commitment can one discharge one's ethical responsibilities?

Not every ethical dilemma has a right solution. Reasonable people often disagree; otherwise there would be no dilemma. In a business context, however, it is essential that managers agree on a process for dealing with dilemmas.

Our experience with the sadhu offers an interesting parallel to business situations. An immediate response was mandatory. Failure to act was a decision in itself. Up on the mountain, we could not resign and submit our résumés to a headhunter. In contrast to philosophy, business involves action and implementation—getting things done. Managers must come up with answers based on what they see and what they allow to influence their decision-making processes. On the mountain, none of us but Stephen realized the true dimensions of the situation we were facing.

One of our problems was that, as a group, we had no process for developing a consensus. We had no sense of purpose or plan. The difficulties of dealing with the sadhu were so complex that no one person could handle them. Because the group did not have a set of preconditions that could guide its action to an acceptable resolution, we reacted instinctively as individuals. The cross-cultural nature of the group added a further layer of complexity. We had no leader with whom we could all identify and in whose purpose we believed. Only Stephen was willing to take charge, but he could not gain adequate support from the group to care for the sadhu.

Some organizations do have values that transcend the personal values of their managers. Such values, which go beyond profitability, are usually revealed when the organization is under stress. People throughout the organization generally accept its values, which, because they are not presented as a rigid list of commandments, may be somewhat ambiguous. The stories people tell, rather than printed materials, transmit the organization's conceptions of what is proper behavior.

For 20 years, I have been exposed at senior levels to a variety of corporations and organizations. It is amazing how quickly an outsider can sense the tone and style of an organization and, with that, the degree of tolerated openness and freedom to challenge management.

Organizations that do not have a heritage of mutually accepted, shared values tend to become unhinged during stress, with each individual bailing out for himself or herself. In the great takeover battles we have witnessed during past years, companies that had strong cultures drew the wagons around them and fought it out, while other companies saw executives—supported by golden parachutes—bail out of the struggles.

Because corporations and their members are interdependent, for the corporation to be strong, the members need to share a preconceived notion of correct behavior, a "business ethic," and think of it as a positive force, not a constraint.

As an investment banker, I am continually warned by well-meaning lawyers, clients, and associates to be wary of conflicts of interest. Yet if I were to run away from every difficult situation, I wouldn't be an effective investment banker. I have to feel my way through conflicts. An effective manager can't run from risk either; he or she has to confront risk. To feel "safe" in doing that, managers need the guidelines of an agreed-upon process and set of values within the organization.

After my three months in Nepal, I spent three months as an executive-in-residence at both the Stanford Business School and the University of California at Berkeley's Center for Ethics and Social Policy of the Graduate Theological Union. Those six months away from my job gave me time to assimilate 20 years of business experience. My thoughts turned often to the meaning of the leadership role in any large organization. Students at the seminary thought of themselves as antibusiness. But when I questioned them, they agreed that they distrusted all large organizations, including the church. They perceived all large organizations as impersonal and opposed to individual values and needs. Yet we all know of organizations in which people's values and beliefs are respected and their expressions encouraged. What makes the difference? Can we identify the difference and, as a result, manage more effectively?

The word *ethics* turns off many and confuses more. Yet the notions of shared values and an agreed-upon process for dealing with adversity and change—what many people mean when they talk about corporate culture—seem to be at the heart of the ethical issue. People who are in touch with their own core beliefs and the beliefs of others and who are sustained by them can be more comfortable living on the cutting edge. At times, taking a tough line or a decisive stand in a muddle of ambiguity is the only ethical thing to do. If a manager is indecisive about a problem and spends time trying to figure out the "good" thing to do, the enterprise may be lost.

Business ethics, then, has to do with the authenticity and integrity of the enterprise. To be ethical is to follow the business as well as the cultural goals of the corporation, its owners, its employees, and its customers. Those who cannot serve the corporate vision are not authentic businesspeople and, therefore, are not ethical in the business sense.

At this stage of my own business experience, I have a strong interest in organizational behavior. Sociologists are keenly studying what they call corporate stories, legends, and heroes as a way organizations have of transmitting value systems. Corporations such as Arco have even hired consultants to perform an audit of their corporate culture. In a company, a leader is a person who understands, interprets, and manages the corporate value system. Effective managers, therefore, are action-oriented people who resolve conflict, are tolerant of ambiguity, stress, and change, and have a strong sense of purpose for themselves and their organizations.

If all this is true, I wonder about the role of the professional manager who moves from company to company. How can he or she quickly absorb the values and culture of different organizations? Or is there, indeed, an art of management that is totally transportable? Assuming that such fungible managers do exist, is it proper for them to manipulate the values of others?

What would have happened had Stephen and I carried the sadhu for two days back to the village and become involved with the villagers in his care? In four trips to Nepal, my most interesting experience occurred in 1975, when I lived in a Sherpa home in the Khumbu for five days while recovering from altitude sickness. The high point of Stephen's trip was an invitation to participate in a family funeral ceremony in Manang. Neither experience had to do with climbing the high passes of the Himalayas. Why were we so reluctant to try the lower path, the ambiguous trail? Perhaps because we did not have a leader who could reveal the greater purpose of the trip to us.

Why didn't Stephen, with his moral vision, opt to take the sadhu under his personal care? The answer is partly because Stephen was hard-stressed physically himself and partly because, without some support system that encompassed our involuntary and episodic community on the mountain, it was beyond his individual capacity to do so.

I see the current interest in corporate culture and corporate value systems as a positive response to pessimism such as Stephen's about the decline of the role of the individual in large organizations. Individuals who operate from a thoughtful set of personal values provide the foundation for a corporate culture. A corporate tradition that encourages freedom of inquiry, supports personal values, and reinforces a focused sense of direction can fulfill the need to combine individuality with the prosperity and success of the group. Without such corporate support, the individual is lost.

That is the lesson of the sadhu. In a complex corporate situation, the individual requires and deserves the support of the group. When people cannot find such support in their organizations, they don't know how to act. If such support is forthcoming, a person has a stake in the success of the group and can add much to the process of establishing and maintaining a corporate culture. Management's challenge is to be sensitive to individual needs, to shape them, and to direct and focus them for the benefit of the group as a whole.

For each of us, the sadhu lives. Should we stop what we are doing and comfort him, or should we keep trudging up toward the high pass? Should I pause to help the derelict I pass on the street each night as I walk by the Yale Club en route to Grand Central Station? Am I his brother? What is the nature of our responsibility if we consider ourselves to be ethical persons? Perhaps it is to change the values of the group so that it can, with all its resources, take the other road.

Questions

1. Throughout *The Parable of the Sadhu,* Bowen McCoy refers to the breakdown between the individual and corporate ethic. Explain what he meant by that and how, if we view the hikers on the trek up the mountain in Nepal as an organization, the ethical person-organization fit applied to the decisions made on the climb.

2. Using the various ethical discussions in the first three chapters as your guide, evaluate the actions of McCoy, Stephen, and the rest of the group from an ethical perspective.

3. What role did leadership and culture play in this case?

4. What is the moral of the story of the sadhu from your perspective?

Source: Reprinted with permission from "The Parable of the Sadhu," by Bowen H. McCoy, Harvard Business Review.

Case 3-2 Rite Aid Inventory Surplus Fraud

Occupational fraud comes in many shapes and sizes. The fraud at Rite Aid is one such case. In February 2015, VP Jay Findling pleaded guilty to fraud. VP Timothy Foster pleaded guilty to making false statements to authorities. On November 16, 2016, Foster was sentenced to five years in prison and Findling, four years. Findling and Foster were ordered to jointly pay $8,034,183 in restitution. Findling also forfeited and turned over an additional $11.6 million to the government at the time he entered his guilty plea. In sentencing Foster, U.S. Middle District Judge John E. Jones III expressed his astonishment that in one instance at Rite-Aid headquarters, Foster took a multimillion dollar cash pay-off from Findling, then stuffed the money into a bag and flew home on Rite Aid's corporate jet.[1]

The charges relate to a nine-year conspiracy to defraud Rite Aid by lying to the company about the sale of surplus inventory to a company owned by Findling when it was sold to third parties for greater amounts. Findling would then kick back a portion of his profits to Foster. Foster's lawyer told Justice Jones that, even though they conned the company, the efforts of Foster and Findling still earned Rite Aid over $100 million "instead of having warehouses filled with unwanted merchandise." Assistant U.S. Attorney Kim Daniel focused on the abuse of trust by Foster and persistent lies to the feds. "The con didn't affect some faceless corporation, Daniel said, "but harmed Rite Aid's 89,000 employees and its stockholders." Findling's attorney, Kevin Buchan, characterized his client as "a good man who made a bad decision." "He succumbed to the pressure. That's why he did what he did and that's why he's here," Buchan said during sentencing.

Findling admitted he established a bank account under the name "Rite Aid Salvage Liquidation" and used it to collect the payments from the real buyers of the surplus Rite Aid inventory. After the payments were received, Findling would send lesser amounts dictated by Foster to Rite Aid for the goods, thus inducing Rite Aid to believe the inventory had been purchased by J. Finn Industries, not the real buyers. The government alleged Findling received at least $127.7 million from the real buyers of the surplus inventory but, with Foster's help, only provided $98.6 million of that amount to Rite Aid, leaving Findling approximately $29.1 million in profits from the scheme. The government also alleged that Findling kicked back approximately $5.7 million of the $29.1 million to Foster.

Assume you are the director of internal auditing at Rite Aid and discover the surplus inventory scheme. You know that Rite Aid has a comprehensive corporate governance system that complies with the requirements of Sarbanes-Oxley, and the company has a strong ethics foundation. Moreover, the internal controls are consistent with the COSO framework. Explain the steps you would take to determine whether you would blow the whistle on the scheme applying the requirements of AICPA Interpretation 102-4 that are depicted in Exhibit 3.11. In that regard, answer the following questions.

Questions

1. Explain the following concepts in the context of the case and how it relates to individual and organizational factors that contribute to fraud:
   - Rationalizations for unethical actions.
   - Stakeholder effects.
   - Ethical dissonance.
   - Sometimes good people do bad things.

2. Assume you are the director of internal auditing and have uncovered the fraud. What would you do and why?

3. Assume, instead, that you are the audit engagement partner of KPMG and are the first to uncover the fraud. You approach management of the firm and discuss making the necessary adjustments. Top management tells you not to press the issue because the firm doesn't want to rock the boat with one of its biggest clients. What would you do and why?

---

[1] Matt Miller, Ex-Rite Aid VP, businessman, get years in federal prison for multimillion dollar scam, November 16, 2016, http://www.pennlive.com/news/2016/11/ex-rite_aid:vp_businessman_get.html.

Case 3-3 United Thermostatic Controls (a GVV case)

United Thermostatic Controls is a publicly owned company that engages in the manufacturing and marketing of residential and commercial thermostats. The thermostats are used to regulate temperature in furnaces and refrigerators. United sells its product primarily to retailers in the domestic market, with the company headquartered in Detroit. Its operations are decentralized according to geographic region. As a publicly owned company, United's common stock is listed and traded on the NYSE. The organization chart for United is presented in Exhibit 1.

EXHIBIT 1   United Thermostatic Controls Organization Chart

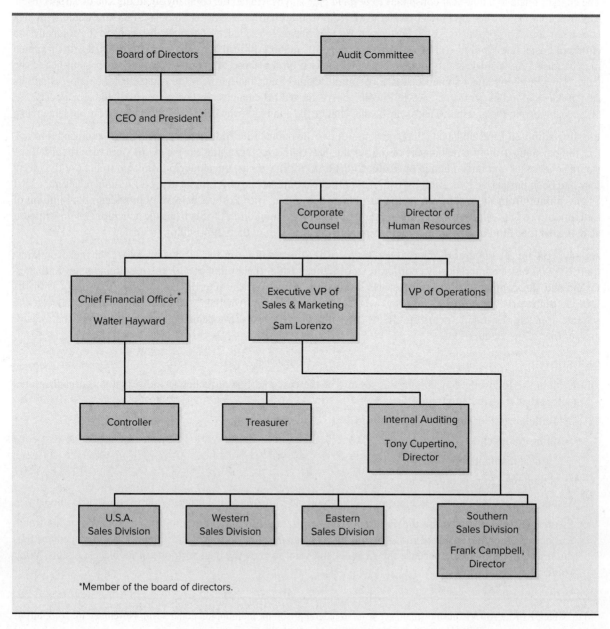

*Member of the board of directors.

Frank Campbell is the director of the Southern sales division. Worsening regional economic conditions and a reduced rate of demand for United's products have created pressures to achieve sales revenue targets set by United management nonetheless. Also, significant pressures exist within the organization for sales divisions to maximize their revenues and earnings for 2018 in anticipation of a public offering of stock early in 2019. Budgeted and actual sales revenue amounts, by division, for the first three quarters in 2018 are presented in Exhibit 2.

EXHIBIT 2   United Thermostatic Controls—Sales Revenue, 2018 (1st 3Qs)

	Budgeted and Actual Sales Revenue First Three Quarters in 2018					
	U.S.A. Sales Division			**Western Sales Division**		
Quarter Ended	**Budget**	**Actual**	**% Var.**	**Budget**	**Actual**	**% Var.**
March 31	$ 632,000	$ 638,000	.009%	$ 886,000	$ 898,000	.014%
June 30	640,000	642,000	.003	908,000	918,000	.011
September 30	648,000	656,000	.012	930,000	936,000	.006
Through September 30	$1,920,000	$1,936,000	.008%	$2,724,000	$2,752,000	.010%

	Eastern Sales Division			**Southern Sales Division**		
Quarter Ended	**Budget**	**Actual**	**% Var.**	**Budget**	**Actual**	**% Var.**
March 31	$ 743,000	$ 750,000	.009%	$ 688,000	$ 680,000	(.012)%
June 30	752,000	760,000	.011	696,000	674,000	(.032)
September 30	761,000	769,000	.011	704,000	668,000	(.051)
Through September 30	$2,256,000	$2,279,000	.010%	$2,088,000	$2,022,000	(.032)%

Campbell knows that actual sales lagged even further behind budgeted sales during the first two months of the fourth quarter. He also knows that each of the other three sales divisions exceeded their budgeted sales amounts during the first three quarters in 2018. He is very concerned that the Southern division has been unable to meet or exceed budgeted sales amounts. He is particularly worried about the effect this might have on his and the division managers' bonuses and share of corporate profits.

In an attempt to improve the sales revenue of the Southern division for the fourth quarter and for the year ended December 31, 2018, Campbell reviewed purchase orders received during the latter half of November and early December to determine whether shipments could be made to customers prior to December 31. Campbell knows that sometimes orders that are received before the end of the year can be filled by December 31, thereby enabling the division to record the sales revenue during the current fiscal year. It could simply be a matter of accelerating production and shipping to increase sales revenue for the year.

Reported sales revenue of the Southern division for the fourth quarter of 2018 was $792,000. This represented an 18.6% increase over the actual sales revenue for the third quarter of the year. As a result of this increase, reported sales revenue for the fourth quarter exceeded the budgeted amount by $80,000, or 11.2%. Actual sales revenue for the year exceeded the budgeted amount for the Southern division by $14,000, or 0.5%. Budgeted and actual sales revenue amounts, by division, for the year ended December 31, 2018, are presented in Exhibit 3.

EXHIBIT 3 United Thermostatic Controls—Sales Revenue, 2018 (4 Qs)

	Budgeted and Actual Sales Revenue in 2018					
	U.S.A. Sales Division			Western Sales Division		
Quarter Ended	Budget	Actual	% Var.	Budget	Actual	% Var.
March 31	$ 632,000	$ 638,000	.009%	$ 886,000	$ 898,000	.014%
June 30	640,000	642,000	.003	908,000	918,000	.011
September 30	648,000	656,000	.012	930,000	936,000	.006
December 31	656,000	662,000	.009	952,000	958,000	.006
2018 Totals	$2,576,000	$2,598,000	.009%	$3,676,000	$3,710,000	.009%

	Eastern Sales Division			Southern Sales Division		
Quarter Ended	Budget	Actual	% Var.	Budget	Actual	% Var.
March 31	$ 743,000	$ 750,000	.009%	$ 688,000	$ 680,000	(.012)%
June 30	752,000	760,000	.011	696,000	674,000	(.032)
September 30	761,000	769,000	.011	704,000	668,000	(.051)
December 31	770,000	778,000	.010	712,000	792,000	.112
2018 Totals	$3,026,000	$3,057,000	.010%	$2,800,000	$2,814,000	.005%

During the course of their test of controls, the internal audit staff questioned the appropriateness of recording revenue of $150,000 on two shipments made by the Southern division in the fourth quarter of the year. These shipments are described as follows:

1. United shipped thermostats to Allen Corporation on December 31, 2018, and billed Allen $85,000, even though Allen had specified a delivery date of no earlier than February 1, 2019, to take control of the product. Allen intended to use the thermostats in the heating system of a new building that would not be ready for occupancy until March 1, 2019.

2. United shipped thermostats to Bilco Corporation on December 30, 2018, in partial (one-half) fulfillment of an order. United recorded $65,000 revenue on that date. Bilco had previously specified that partial shipments would not be accepted. Delivery of the full shipment had been scheduled for February 1, 2019.

During their investigation, the internal auditors learned that Campbell had pressured United's accounting department to record these two shipments early to enable the Southern division to achieve its goals with respect to the company's revenue targets. The auditors were concerned about the appropriateness of recording the $150,000 revenue in 2018 in the absence of an expressed or implied agreement with the customers to accept and pay for the prematurely shipped merchandise. The auditors noted that, had the revenue from these two shipments not been recorded, the Southern division's actual sales for the fourth quarter would have been below the budgeted amount by $70,000, or 9.8%. Actual sales revenue for the year ended December 31, 2018, would have been below the budgeted amount by $136,000, or 4.9%. The revenue effect of the two shipments in question created a 5.4% shift in the variance between actual and budgeted sales for the year. The auditors felt that this effect was significant with respect to the division's revenue and earnings for the fourth quarter and for the year ended December 31, 2018. The auditors decided to take their concerns to Tony Cupertino, director of the internal auditing department. Cupertino is a licensed CPA.

Cupertino discussed the situation with Campbell. Campbell informed Cupertino that he had received assurances from Sam Lorenzo, executive vice president of sales and marketing, that top management would support the recording of the $150,000 revenue because of its strong desire to meet or exceed budgeted revenue and earnings amounts. Moreover, top management is very sensitive to the need to meet financial analysts' consensus earnings estimates. According to Campbell, the company is concerned that earnings must be high enough to meet analysts' expectations because any other effect might cause the stock price to go down. In fact, Lorenzo has already told Campbell that he did not see anything wrong with recording the revenue in 2018 because the merchandise had been shipped to the customers before the end of the year and the terms of shipment were FOB shipping point.

At this point, Cupertino is uncertain whether he should take his concerns to Walter Hayward, the CFO, who is also a member of the board of directors, or take them directly to the audit committee. Cupertino knows that the majority of the members of the board, including those on the audit committee, have ties to the company and members of top management. Cupertino is not even certain that he should pursue the matter any further because of the financial performance pressures that exist within the organization. However, he is very concerned about his responsibilities as a CPA and obligations to work with the external auditors who will begin their audit in a few weeks. It is at this point that Cupertino learns from Campbell that the CFO of Bilco agreed to accept full shipment when the goods arrive in return for a 20% discount on the total price that would be paid on February 1, 2019. Cupertino asked Campbell how he had found out. It seems Campbell took the initiative to help solve the revenue problem by going directly to the Bilco CFO.

Questions

1. Identify the stakeholders in this case and their interests.
2. Describe the ethical and professional responsibilities of Tony Cupertino.
3. Assume you are in Cupertino's position and know you have to do something about the improper accounting in the Southern sales division. Consider the following in crafting a plan how best to voice your values and take appropriate action:

   - How can you get it done effectively and efficiently?
   - What do you need to say, to whom, and in what sequence?
   - What will the objections or pushback be, and then,
   - What would you say next? What data and other information do you need to make your point and counteract the reasons and rationalizations you will likely have to address?

Case 3-4 Franklin Industries' Whistleblowing (a GVV Case)

Natalie got the call she had been waiting for over six long months. Her complaint to the human resources department of Franklin Industries had been dismissed. It was HR's conclusion that she was not retaliated against for reporting an alleged embezzlement by the Accounting Department manager. In fact, HR ruled there was no embezzlement at all. Natalie had been demoted from assistant manager of the department to staff supervisor seven months ago after informing Stuart Masters, the controller, earlier in 2018, about the embezzlement. Her blood started to boil as she thought about all the pain and agony she'd experienced these past six months without any level of satisfaction for her troubles.

Natalie Garson is a CPA who works for Franklin Industries, a publicly owned company and manufacturer of trusses and other structural components for home builders throughout the United States. Six months ago she filed a complaint with HR after discussing a sensitive matter with her best friend and coworker, Roger Harris. Natalie trusted Harris, who had six years of experience at Franklin. The essence of the discussion was that Natalie was informed by the accounting staff of what appeared to be unusual transactions between Denny King, the department manager, and an outside company no one had ever heard of before. The staff had uncovered over $5 million in payments, authorized by King, to Vic Construction. No one could find any documentation about Vic, so the staff dug deeper and discovered that the owner of Vic Construction was Victoria King. Further examination determined that Victoria King and Denny King were siblings.

Once Natalie was convinced there was more to the situation than meets the eye, she informed the internal auditors, who investigated and found that Vic Construction made a $5 million electronic transfer to a separate business owned by Denny King. One thing lead to another, and it was determined by the internal auditors that King had funneled $5 million to Vic Construction, which, at a later date, transferred the money back to King. It was a $5 million embezzlement from Franklin Industries.

Natalie met with Roger Harris that night and told him about the HR decision that went against her. She was concerned whether the internal auditors would act now in light of that decision She knew the culture at Franklin was "don't rock the boat." That didn't matter to her. She was always true to her values and not afraid to act when a wrongdoing had occurred. She felt particularly motivated in this case—it was personal. She felt the need to be vindicated. She hoped Roger would be supportive.

As it turned out, Roger cautioned Natalie about taking the matter any further. He had worked for Franklin a lot longer than Natalie and knew the board of directors consisted mostly of insider directors. The CEO of Franklin was also the chair of the board. It was well known in the company that whatever the CEO wanted to do, the board rubber-stamped it.

Natalie left the meeting with Roger wondering whether she was on her own. She knew she had to act but didn't know the best way to go about it. Even though Roger cautioned against going to the CEO or board, Natalie didn't dismiss that option.

Questions

Assume you are in Natalie's position. Answer the following questions.

1. What are the ethical values in this case? What about professional values?
2. Consider the following assuming you have decided to do something about the embezzlement:
   - What are the main arguments you are trying to counter? That is, what are the reasons and rationalizations you need to address?
   - What is at stake for the key parties, including those who disagree with you?
   - What levers can you use to influence those who disagree with you?
   - What is your most powerful and persuasive response to the reasons and rationalizations you need to address? To whom should the argument be made? When and in what context?
3. Assume you have exhausted all your options within Franklin Industries. Is this a situation where you would consider filing a complaint with the SEC under the Sarbanes-Oxley Act? What about Dodd-Frank? Explain.

Case 3-5 Walmart Inventory Shrinkage (a GVV Case)

The nation's retailers lost a staggering amount of money in 2016 due to shoplifting, organized crime, internal theft, and other types of inventory shrink.

Inventory shrink totaled $48.9 billion in 2016, up from $45.2 billion the year before, as budget constraints left retail security budgets flat or declining, according to the annual National Retail Security Survey by the National Retail Federation and the University of Florida. The thefts amounted to 1.44% of sales, up from 1.38%.

According to the study,[1] which was sponsored by The Retail Equation, 48.8% of retailers surveyed reported increases in inventory shrink, and 16.7% said it remained flat. Shoplifting and organized retail crime accounted for 36.5% of shrink, followed by employee theft/internal (30%), administrative paperwork error (21.3%), and vendor fraud or error (5.4%).

Shoplifting continued to account for the greatest losses of overall shrink. Shoplifting averaged $798.48 per incident, up from $377 in 2015. The rise was partially attributed to retailers allocating smaller budgets for loss prevention, leaving them with fewer security staff to fight theft, the report said.

The average loss due to employee theft per incident was put at $1,922.80, up from $1,233.77 in 2015. The average cost of retail robberies dropped to $5,309.72 from $8,170.17 in 2015, but remained at more than double the $2,464.50 seen in 2014.

For the first time in the survey, retailers were asked about return fraud, reporting an average loss of $1,766.27.

The facts of this case are from the Walmart shrinkage fraud discussed in an article in *The Nation* on June 11, 2014. "Literary license" has been exercised for the purpose of emphasizing important issues related to organizational ethics at Walmart. Any resemblance to actual people and events is coincidental.[2]

Shane O'Hara always tried to do the right thing. He was in touch with his values and always tried to act in accordance with them, even when the going got tough. But nothing prepared him for the ordeal he would face as a Walmart veteran and the new store manager in Atomic City, Idaho.

In 2013, Shane was contacted by Jeffrey Cook, the regional manager, and told he was being transferred to the Atomic City store in order to reduce the troubled store's high rate of "shrinkage" (i.e., theft including shoplifting and employees stealing) to levels deemed acceptable by the company's senior managers for the region. As a result of fierce competition, profit margins in retail can be razor thin, making shrinkage a potent—sometimes critical—factor in profitability. Historically, Walmart had a relatively low rate of about 0.8% of sales. The industry average was 1%.

Prior to his arrival at the Atomic City store, Shane had heard the store had shrinkage losses as high as $2 million or more—a sizable hit to its bottom line. There had even been talk of closing the store altogether. He knew the pressure was on to keep the store open, save the jobs of 40 people, and cut losses so that the regional manager could earn a bonus. It didn't hurt that he would qualify for a bonus as well, so long as the shrinkage rate was cut by more than two-thirds.

Shane did what he could to tighten systems and controls. He managed to convince Cook to hire an "asset-protection manager" for the store. The asset-protection program handles shrink, safety, and security at each of its stores. The program worked. Not only did shrinkage decline but other forms of loss, including changing price tags on items of clothing, were significantly reduced.

However, it didn't seem to be enough to satisfy Cook and top management. During the last days of August 2013, Shane's annual inventory audit showed a massive reduction in the store's shrinkage rate that surprised even him: down to less than $80,000 from roughly $800,000 the previous year. He had no explanation for it, but was sure the numbers had been doctored in some way.

During the remainder of 2013, a number of high-level managers departed from the company. Cindy Rondel, the head of Walmart's Idaho operations, retired; so did her superior, Larry Brooks. Walmart's regional asset-protection manager for Idaho, who was intimately involved with inventory tracking in the state, was fired as well. Shane wondered if he was next.

Shane decided to contact Cook to discuss his concerns. Cook explained why the shrinkage rate had shrunk so much by passing it off as improper accounting at the Atomic City store that had been corrected. He told Shane that an

---

[1] Marianne Wilson, Retailers losing billions to inventory, June 22, 2017, https://www.chainstoreage.com/article/retailers-losing-billions-inventory-shrink/.

[2] Spencer Woodman, "Former Managers Allege Pervasive Inventory Fraud at Walmart: How Deep Does the Rot Go?" *The Nation,* June 11, 2014.

investigation would begin immediately and he was suspended with pay until it was completed. Shane was in shock. He knew the allegations weren't true. He sensed he might become the fall guy for the fraud.

Shane managed to discretely talk about his situation with another store manager in the Atomic City area. That manager said she had been the target of a similar investigation the year before. In her case, she had discovered how the fraud was carried out and the numbers were doctored, but she had told no one—until now.

She explained to Shane that the fraud involved simply declaring that missing items were not, in fact, missing. She went on to say you could count clothing items in the store and if the on-hand count was off—as in, you were supposed to have 12 but you only had 10—you could explain that the other 2 were in a bin where clothing had been tried on by customers, not bought, and left in the dressing room, often with creases that had to be cleaned before re-tagging the clothing for sale. So, even though some items may have been stolen, they were still counted as part of inventory. There was little or no shrinkage to account for.

At this point Shane did not know what his next step should be. He needed to protect his good name and reputation. But what steps should he take? That was the question.

Questions

Assume you are in Shane O'Hara's position. Answer the following questions.

1. Put on "Your Thinking Cap" and explain how the provisions of the Sarbanes-Oxley Act might have helped to detect the fraud.

2. What anti-fraud controls might have helped detect the fraud. Why?

3. Assume you are in Shane O'Hara's position. What would you do next and why? Consider the following in crafting your response.

   - Who are the stakeholders in this case and what are the ethical issues?

   - What do you need to say, to whom, and in what sequence?

   - What are the reasons and rationalizations you are likely to hear in getting your point across?

   - What is your most powerful and persuasive response to these arguments? To whom should you make them? When and in what context?

4. Is this a situation where you would seriously consider blowing the whistle since you were suspended with pay? Under what conditions would you blow the whistle and what process might you follow?

Case 3-6 Full Disclosure: The Case of the Morally Challenged AP Clerk (a GVV case)

John Stanton, CPA, is a seasoned accountant who left his Big-4 CPA firm Senior Manager position to become the CFO of a highly successful hundred million-dollar privately held manufacturer of solar panels. The company wanted John's expertise in the renewable energy sector and his pedigree from working for one of the Big-4 firms. The company plans to go public later this year and wants John to lead the effort. Everything went well for the first two months until the controller, Diane Hopkins, who is also a CPA, came to John with a problem. She discovered that one of her accounts payable clerks has been embezzling money from the company by processing and approving fictitious invoices from shell companies for fictitious purchases that the AP clerk had created. Diane estimated that the clerk had been able to steal approximately $250,000 over the year and a half they worked at the company. Diane and John agreed to fire the clerk immediately and did so. They also agreed that John would report the matter to the police.

John picked up the phone and called the CEO, David Laskey, who was also the majority shareholder, to give him a heads up on what had transpired. Laskey asked John to come to his office the next day to discuss the need to report the matter to the police. Laskey shared with John that he did not think it was a good idea to report it to the police as he was fearful of the effect on taking the company public and the initial public offering share price.

After the call, John reflected on what it would mean to not report the matter to the police and whether there were others he needed to inform about the matter.

Questions

1. To whom do John Stanton and David Laskey owe their ultimate responsibility? Explain.

2. If Stanton were to agree not to report this embezzlement to the police or disclose it in the annual report and prospectus, would he be violating the integrity or due care rule in the AICPA Code of Professional Conduct? What about acts discreditable?

3. Assume Stanton is preparing for the meeting with Laskey. Consider the following in deciding what he should do.

   - What can he say to Laskey to counteract the reasons Laskey provided not to notify the police?
   - Who can Stanton rely on for support in this matter? What might he say to that person(s) to encourage their support?
   - What levers can Stanton use to convince Laskey as to the correct course of action given the company's impending IPO?
   - What should Stanton do next if Laskey orders him to drop the matter?

Case 3-7 Olympus

Summary of the Case[1]

On September 25, 2012, Japanese camera and medical equipment maker Olympus Corporation and three of its former executives pleaded guilty to charges related to an accounting scheme and cover-up in one of Japan's biggest corporate scandals. Olympus admitted that it tried to conceal investment losses by using improper accounting under a scheme that began in the 1990s.

The scandal was exposed in 2011 by Olympus's then-CEO, Michael C. Woodford. As the new president of Olympus, he felt obliged to investigate the matter and uncovered accounting irregularities and suspicious deals involving the acquisition of U.K. medical equipment manufacturer Gyrus. He called the company's auditors, PwC, to report it. The firm examined payments of $687 million related to financial advice on the acquisition paid to a non-existent Cayman Islands firm. A fraud of $1.7 billion emerged, including an accounting scandal to hide the losses. Along the way, the Japanese way of doing business came under attack by Woodford.

Olympus initially said that it fired Woodford, one of a handful of foreign executives at top Japanese companies, over what it called his aggressive Western management style. Woodford disclosed internal documents to show he was dismissed after he raised questions about irregular payouts related to mergers and acquisitions. Without any serious attempt by management to investigate, he went behind the board's back and commissioned a report by PwC into the Gyrus deal, including the unusually high advisory fee and apparent lack of due diligence. On October 11, 2011, he circulated the report to the board and called on the chair of the board, Tsuyoshi Kikukawa, and executive vice president Hisashi Mori to resign. Three days later, the board fired Woodford.

---

[1] The facts of this case are drawn from: Michael Woodford, *Exposure: Inside the Olympus Scandal: How I Went from CEO to Whistleblower* (NY: Penguin Books, 2012).

Ultimately, the accounting fraud was investigated by the Japanese authorities. "The full responsibility lies with me, and I feel deeply sorry for causing trouble to our business partners, shareholders, and the wider public," Kikukawa told the Tokyo district court. "I take full responsibility for what happened."

Prosecutors charged Kikukawa, Mori, and a former internal auditor, Hideo Yamada, with inflating the company's net worth in financial statements for five fiscal years up to March 2011 due to accounting for risky investments made in the late-1980s bubble economy. The three former executives had been identified by an investigative panel, commissioned by Olympus, as the main suspects in the fraud. In December 2011, Olympus filed five years' worth of corrected financial statements plus overdue first-half results, revealing a $1.1 billion hole in its balance sheet.

On April 28, 2017, following six years of scandal-ridden disclosures, a Tokyo court found Kikukawa and five others liable for $529 million. Kikukawa and two other executives who pleaded guilty never went to jail. Instead, they were given suspended sentences of up to three years.

Olympus Spent Huge Sums on Inflated Acquisitions, Advisory Fees to Conceal Investment Losses

Olympus's cover-up of massive losses has shed light on several murky methods that some companies employed to clean up the mess left after Japan's economic bubble burst. Many companies turned to speculative investments as they suffered sluggish sales and stagnant operating profits. The company used "loss-deferring practices" to make losses look smaller on the books by selling bad assets to related companies.

To take investment losses off its books, Olympus spent large sums of money to purchase British medical equipment maker Gyrus Group PLC and three Japanese companies and paid huge consulting fees. Olympus is suspected of having deliberately acquired Gyrus at an inflated price, and, in the year following the purchase, it booked impairment losses as a result of decreases in the company's value.

To avert a rapid deterioration of its financial standing, Olympus continued corporate acquisitions and other measures for many years, booking impairment losses to improve its balance sheet. Losses on the purchases of the three Japanese companies amounted to $34.5 billion. With money paid on the Gyrus deal included, Olympus may have used more than $62.5 billion in funds for past acquisitions to conceal losses on securities investments.

The previous method that recorded stocks and other financial products by book value—the price when they were purchased—was abolished. The new method listed them by market value (mark-to-market accounting). Under this change, Olympus had to report all the losses in its March 2001 report. However, Olympus anticipated this change a year in advance and posted only about $10.6 billion of the nearly $62.5 billion as an extraordinary loss for the March 2000 settlement term. The company did not post the remainder as a deficit; rather, it deferred it using questionable measures.

Olympus's Tobashi Scheme

At the heart of Olympus's action was a once-common technique to hide losses called *tobashi,* which Japanese financial regulators tolerated before clamping down on the practice in the late 1990s. *Tobashi,* translated loosely as "to blow away," enables companies to hide losses on bad assets by selling those assets to other companies, only to buy them back later through payments, often disguised as advisory fees or other transactions, when market conditions or earnings improve.

Tobashi allows a company with the bad assets to mask losses temporarily, a practice banned in the early 2000s. The idea is that you pay off the losses later, when company finances are better.

Olympus appears to have pushed to settle its *tobashi* amounts from 2006 to 2008, when the local economy was picking up and corporate profits were rebounding, in an effort to "clean up its act." Business was finally strong enough to be able to withstand a write-down. It was during those years that the company engineered the payouts that came under scrutiny: $687 million in fees to an obscure financial adviser over Olympus's acquisition of Gyrus in 2008, a fee that was roughly a third of the $2 billion acquisition price, more than 30 times the norm. Olympus also acquired three small Japanese companies from 2006 to 2008 with little in common with its core business for a total of $773 million, only to write down most of their value within the same fiscal year.

Olympus Scandal Raises Questions about the "Japan Way" of Doing Business

The scandal rocked corporate Japan, not least because of the company's succession of firings, denials, admissions, and whistleblowing. It also exposed weaknesses in Japan's financial regulatory system and corporate governance.

"This is a case where Japan's outmoded practice of corporate governance remained and reared its ugly head," according to Shuhei Abe, president of Tokyo-based Sparx Group Company. "With Olympus's case, it will no longer be justifiable for Japan Inc. to continue practicing under the excuse of the 'Japan way of doing things.'"

On the surface, Olympus seemed to have checks on its management. For example, it hired directors and auditors from outside the company, as well as a British president who was not tied to corporate insiders. In reality, however, the company's management was ruled by former chairman Kikukawa and a few other executives who came from its financial sections.

The company's management is believed to have been effectively controlled by several executives who had a background in financial affairs, including Kikukawa and Mori, both of whom were involved in the cover-up of past losses. Olympus's board of auditors, which is supposed to supervise the board of directors, included full-time auditor Hideo Yamada, who also had financial expertise.

After Woodford made his allegations, he was confronted by a hostile board of directors that acted based on the premise that whistleblowing offended their corporate culture. Subsequently, the board fired him saying that he had left because of "differences in management styles." Employees were warned not to speak to him or jeopardize their careers.

One problem with corporate governance in Japan is truly independent non-executive directors are unusual. Many Japanese do not see the need for such outside intervention. They question how outsiders can know enough about the company to make a valuable contribution. Moreover, how could they be sensitive to the corporate culture? They could even damage the credibility of the group.

Accounting Explanations

Olympus hid a $1.7 billion loss through an intricate array of transactions.

A one-paragraph summary of what it did appears in the investigation report:

> The lost disposition scheme is featured in that Olympus sold the assets that incurred loss to the funds set up by Olympus itself, and later provided the finance needed to settle the loss under the cover of the company acquisitions. More specifically, Olympus circulated money either by flowing money into the funds by acquiring the entrepreneurial ventures owned by the funds at the substantially higher price than the real values, or by paying a substantially high fee to the third party who acted as the intermediate in the acquisition, resulting in recognition of a large amount of goodwill, and subsequently amortized goodwill recognized impairment loss, which created substantial loss.

Here is a more understandable version of the event:

> Olympus indirectly loaned money to an off-the-books subsidiary and then sold the investments that had the huge losses to the subsidiary at historical cost, eventually paying a huge premium to buy some other small companies and writing off the underwater investments as if they were goodwill impairments.

A more detailed bookkeeping analysis of the complicated transactions appears in Exhibit 1.

EXHIBIT 1 Detailed Bookkeeping Analysis of Olympus's Accounting Fraud[2]

PHASE 1

Transaction 1:

This is a summary of a complex move—it involved purchasing a certificate of deposit (CD) at several banks that were asked to loan the money back to an unrelated entity, with the CD as collateral, so the subsidiary can buy investments from Olympus.

Note: According to the investigative committee's report, three banks were involved through the course of the whole project: Commerzbank, LGT, and Société Générale. The committee's report indicates that all three banks agreed to Olympus's request not to tell the auditors about the CDs being collateral for a loan.

(Olympus books)

DR Certificate of deposit
CR Cash
    (CD purchase at banks; banks loan it to unconsolidated subsidiary)

(Unconsolidated subsidiary books)

DR Cash
CR Note payable to banks
    (Cash from banks; collateralized by Olympus)

Transaction 2:

(Olympus books)

DR Cash
CR Financial assets (Investments)
    (Proceeds from selling underwater investments to unconsolidated subsidiary; may have triggered gain on sale)

(Unconsolidated subsidiary books)

DR Financial assets (Investments)
CR Cash
    (To buy underwater investments from Olympus)

PHASE 2

Eventually the CDs would have to be rolled over and brought back. In addition, the unrealized losses would have to be written down eventually, so the second phase was launched.

Transaction 3:

Olympus bought some tiny (startup) companies. It paid significantly more than they were worth and paid large amounts for consultants for their service as finders and intermediaries.

(Olympus books)

DR Investments (startup subsidiary)
DR Goodwill—(cash paid less fair market value of subsidiary net assets)
CR Cash
    (Investments in new subsidiaries)

(Continued)

[2] "Olympus Scandal: $1.5 billion in Losses Hidden in Dodgy Acquisitions," Available at http://factsanddetails.com/japan/cat24/sub157/item2305.html.

Note: The investment in the consolidated subsidiary shows a large amount of goodwill, which could then be written down.

(Entries by the newly formed consolidated subsidiary)

DR Cash
CR Common stock
   (Cash investment from Olympus)

Transaction 4:

The effect of these transactions was to transfer money into the newest consolidated subsidiary, which used the money to buy the bad investments from the older, unconsolidated subsidiary. The unconsolidated subsidiary then repaid the note payable to the bank and Olympus liquidated its CD.

(Entries by the newly formed consolidated subsidiary)

DR Financial assets (Investments)
CR Cash
   (Buy underwater investments from unconsolidated subsidiary at book value)

(Unconsolidated subsidiary books)

DR Cash (from consolidated subsidiary)
CR Financial assets (Investments)
   (Proceeds received from consolidated subsidiary from sale of underwater investments)
DR Note payable to banks
CR Cash
   (Repay loan to banks)

Entries by Olympus

DR Cash
CR Certificate of deposit
   (CD liquidated)

*Olympus Scandal: $1.5 billion in Losses Hidden in Dodgy Acquisitions.

Auditor Responsibilities

Arthur Andersen was the external auditor through March 31, 2002, after which Andersen closed its doors for good in the post-Enron era. Then KPMG AZSA LLC was the auditor through March 31, 2009. The 2010 and 2011 fiscal years were audited by Ernst & Young ShinNihon LLC.

The investigative report noted that the fraud was hidden quite well. Three banks were involved in hiding information from the auditors. The summary report said that all three of them agreed not to tell auditors the information that would normally be provided on an audit confirmation.

KPMG did come across one of the *tobashi* schemes carried out through one of the three different routes that had been set up. According to the investigative report:

Not everything was going smoothly. The report said that in 1999, Olympus's then-auditor, KPMG AZSA LLC, came across information that indicated the company was engaged in *tobashi,* which recently had become illegal in Japan. Mori and Yamada initially denied KPMG's assertion, but the auditor pushed them that same year to admit to the presence of one fund and unwind it, booking a loss of $10.5 billion. The executives assured KPMG that that was the only such deal, the report said. However, the schemes expanded, without detection, for another six years or so and was in place, without detection, until the last component was unwound at the end of fiscal year 2010. The last part of the bad investments was finally written off in March 2011.

Olympus Finally Had Enough of the Deception

Olympus removed KPMG AZSA as its group auditor in 2009 after a dispute over how to account for some controversial acquisitions. The camera-maker decided not to disclose this to the stock market. Instead, Olympus told investors at the time that KPMG's audit contract had expired and it was hiring Ernst & Young. Mori and Yamada had finally decided to unwind and write off the underwater financial assets and repay the loans that Olympus had made through its unconsolidated subsidiary. Of course, by then, the financial press had gotten wind of what was going on at Olympus.

Questions

1. What role did cultural relativism and situational ethics play in the Olympus fraud? Explain.
2. Describe the shortcomings in corporate culture at Olympus?
3. Did Michael Woodford violate his ethical and/or legal responsibilities as CEO of Olympus? Use the U.S. model of corporate governance to answer this question.
4. Compare the accounting techniques used by Olympus with those used by Enron. What was each designed to do? How did each affect financial reporting? Does it seem the auditors of Olympus should have done more to fully disclose these transactions?

Case 3-8 Accountant Takes on Halliburton and Wins!

The whistleblowing aspects of this case were first discussed in the text. What follows is a more comprehensive discussion of accounting and auditing issues.

In 2005, Tony Menendez, a former Ernst & Young LLP auditor and director of technical accounting and research training for Halliburton, blew the whistle on Halliburton's accounting practices. The fight cost him nine years of his life. Just a few months later in 2005, Menendez received an e-mail from Mark McCollum, Halliburton's chief accounting officer, and a top-ranking executive at Halliburton, that also went to much of the accounting department. "The SEC has opened an inquiry into the allegations of Mr. Menendez," it read. Everyone was to retain their documents until further notice.

What happened next changed the life of Menendez and brought into question how such a large and influential company could have such a failed corporate governance system. Further, the role of the auditors, KPMG, with respect to its handling of accounting and auditing matters seemed off, and independence was an issue. Exhibit 1 summarizes some of the relevant accounting and auditing issues in the case.

Nature of Halliburton's Revenue Transactions in Question

During the months following the "leaked" e-mail, Menendez waited and watched to see if Halliburton would act on his claims that the company was cooking the books. The issue was revenue recognition as discussed following.

Halliburton enters into long-term contracts with energy giants like Royal Dutch Shell or BP to find and exploit huge oil and gas fields. It sells services—the expertise of its geologists and engineers. Halliburton also builds massive and expensive machinery that its professionals use to provide those services. Then, the company charges its

EXHIBIT 1 Issues Related to the Sarbanes-Oxley Act, SEC, and KPMG

Tony Menendez contacted Halliburton's audit committee because he believed it was in the best interest of the employees and shareholders if he made himself available to the committee in its efforts to investigate the questionable accounting and auditing practices and properly respond to the SEC. It was discovered that Halliburton did not have in place, as required by Section 301 of the Sarbanes-Oxley Act (SOX), a process for "(1) the receipt and treatment of complaints received by the issuer regarding accounting, internal controls, or auditing matters; and (2) the confidential, anonymous submission of employees of the issuer of concerns regarding questionable accounting or auditing matters."

After waiting for the company to take action to no avail, Menendez felt there was no alternative to blowing the whistle, and on November 4, 2005, he contacted the SEC and PCAOB stating in part:

"As a CPA and the Director of Technical Accounting Research and Training for Halliburton, I feel it is my duty and obligation to report information that I believe constitutes both a potential failure by a registered public accounting firm, KPMG, to properly perform an audit and the potential filing of materially misleading financial information with the SEC by Halliburton."

Two weeks later, at the agencies' request, he met with SEC enforcement staff at their Fort Worth office. On November 30, 2005, he approached members of top management of Halliburton. On February 4, 2006, Menendez provided what he believed would be a confidential report to Halliburton's audit committee, giving the company yet another opportunity for self-examination. However, on the morning of February 6, 2006, Menendez's identity was disclosed to Mark McCollum, Halliburton's chief accounting officer, and less than an hour after finding out that Menendez had reported the questionable accounting and auditing practices to the SEC, McCollum distributed information about Menendez's investigation and identity.

The disclosure was followed by a series of retaliatory actions. Halliburton management stripped Menendez of teaching and researching responsibilities, ordered subordinates to monitor and report on his activity, excluded him from meetings and accounting decisions, and ordered financial and accounting personnel to pre-clear any conversations about accounting issues before discussing them with Menendez.

In May 2005, Menendez filed a civil whistleblower complaint under SOX. In July 2006, Halliburton told the Department of Labor committee handling the case that KPMG had insisted that Menendez be excluded from a meeting concerning accounting for a potential joint venture arrangement called "RTA." Halliburton indicated it acceded to KPMG's demand and excluded Menendez from the meeting. SOX prohibits an employer from discriminating against an employee, contractor, or agent and from prohibiting such party from engaging in activity protected under the Act, and the SEC stated that the assertion by the company that KPMG's presence was mandatory was misleading. In fact, the SEC opined that KPMG's presence was not even advisable since KPMG was supposed to be an independent auditor in both appearance and in fact.

The RTA meeting was scheduled to determine whether or not Halliburton would be required to consolidate the proposed joint venture. Senior management explicitly stated that the division management would not receive approval to proceed unless Halliburton could both avoid consolidation and maintain control over the joint venture activities. Earlier in the development of the accounting position regarding this joint venture, KPMG told management that it would allow the company to avoid consolidation and FIN 46R's Anti-Abuse criteria on the basis that the determination required professional judgment, and indicated that KPMG would be willing to support a conclusion that Halliburton was not significantly involved in the joint venture activities, when clearly the facts and circumstances did not support such a conclusion. Menendez had vehemently objected to KPMG and management's proposed conclusion on the basis that such a position was absurd.

According to the SEC, given KPMG's previous guidance to the company regarding RTA, and its willingness to accommodate unsupportable conclusions, continued input by KPMG on RTA was inappropriate and, once again, put KPMG in the position of auditing its own recommendations and advice. In the end, the concerted failures of management and the external auditor underscored the lack of independence between company and KPMG, which was a root cause of the accounting violations Menendez fought to correct and, at last, had to report.

customers for that equipment, which has particularly high profit margins. At the crux of the matter, the company's accountants had been allowing the company to count the full value of the equipment right away as revenue, sometimes even before it had assembled the equipment. But the customers could walk away in the middle of the contracts. Menendez realized that if the equipment were damaged, Halliburton, not the customer, was on the hook.

Menendez accused Halliburton of using so-called bill-and-hold techniques that distort the timing of billions of dollars in revenue and allowed Halliburton to book product sales before they occurred.

Menendez explained Halliburton's accounting this way:

> For example, the company recognizes revenue when the goods are parked in company warehouses, rather than delivered to the customer. Typically, these goods are not even assembled and ready for the customer. Furthermore, it is unknown as to when the goods will be ultimately assembled, tested, delivered to the customer, and, finally, used by the company to perform the required oilfield services for the customer.

Based on Menendez's claims, Halliburton's accounting procedures violated generally accepted accounting principles. For companies to recognize revenue before delivery, "the risks of ownership must have passed to the buyer," the SEC's staff wrote in a 2003 accounting bulletin. There also "must be a fixed schedule for delivery of the goods" and the product "must be complete and ready for shipment" among other things.

Shortly after joining Halliburton in March 2005, Menendez said he discovered a "terribly flawed" flow chart on the company's in-house Web site, called the Bill and Hold Decision Tree. The flow chart, a copy of which Menendez included in his complaint, walks through what to do in a situation where a "customer has been billed for completed inventory which is being stored at a Halliburton facility."

First, it asks: Based on the contract terms, "has title passed to customer?" If the answer is no—and here's where it gets strange—the employee is asked: "Does the transaction meet all of the 'bill-and-hold' criteria for revenue recognition?" If the answer to that question is yes, the decision tree says to do this: "Recognize revenue." The decision tree didn't specify what the other criteria were.

In other words, Halliburton told employees to recognize revenue even though the company still owned the product. Ironically, the accelerated revenue for financial statement purposes led to higher income taxes paid to the IRS.

"The policy in the chart is clearly at odds with generally accepted accounting principles," said Charles Mulford, a Georgia Institute of Technology accounting professor, who reviewed the court records. "It's very clear cut. It's not gray."

According to the accounting rules, it is possible to use bill-and-hold and comply with the rules. But it's hard. The customer, not the seller, must request such treatment. The customer also must have a compelling reason for doing so. Customers rarely do.

Top Halliburton accounting executives had agreed with Menendez's analysis, including McCollum, the company's chief accounting officer. But according to Menendez, they dragged their feet on implementing a change that was certain to slow revenue growth. In an e-mail response to detailed questions, a Halliburton spokeswoman wrote, "The accounting allegations were made by Mr. Menendez almost nine years ago and were promptly reviewed by the company and the Securities and Exchange Commission. The company's accounting was appropriate and the SEC closed its investigation." This seems curious when we examine the SEC's own rules for recognition.

Hocus Pocus Accounting: Bill-and-Hold Schemes

The proper accounting for Halliburton's bill-and-hold transactions was not lost on its external auditors, KPMG. In fact, in early 2005, KPMG published an article entitled: *Bill and Hold Transactions in the Oilfield Services Industry,* which made it clear that oilfield services companies had to comply with all four criteria of SEC Staff Accounting Bulletin (SAB 101) to recognize revenue early. These include:

- Persuasive evidence of an arrangement exists.

- Delivery has occurred or services have been rendered.

- The seller's price to the buyer is fixed or determinable.

- Collectibility is reasonably assured.

KPMG went on to recognize that it would be rare for an oilfield services company to actually meet the necessary criteria. The impact to Halliburton was highlighted by KPMG's recognition that bill-and-hold transactions for oilfield services companies were "common" and "involve very large and complex products and equipment that carry significant amounts of economic value." KPMG went on to state that "perhaps no area of revenue recognition has received as much scrutiny as bill-and-hold."

Menendez's Complaint to the DOL

Menendez's allegations are part of a 54-page complaint he filed against Halliburton with a Department of Labor (DOL) administrative-law judge in Covington, Louisiana, who released the records to Menendez in response to a Freedom of Information Act request. Menendez claimed Halliburton retaliated against him in violation of the Sarbanes-Oxley Act's whistleblower provisions after he reported his concerns to the SEC and the company's audit committee.

According to a company spokesperson, Halliburton's audit committee "directed an independent investigation" and "concluded that the allegations were without merit." She declined to comment on bill-and-hold issues, and Halliburton's court filings in the case don't provide any details about its accounting practices.

Menendez filed his complaint shortly after a DOL investigator in Dallas rejected his retaliation claim. His initial claim was rejected by the court and subsequently appealed after many years, and the decision was ultimately overturned, but not until after he and his family had endured a nine year ordeal during which time he was an outcast at Halliburton.

The Final Verdict Is In: Accountant Takes on Halliburton and Wins!

The appeals process went on for three years. In September 2011, the administrative-law appeals panel ruled. It overturned the original trial judge. After five years, Menendez had his first victory.

But it wasn't over. Halliburton appealed to the Fifth Circuit Court of Appeals. There were more legal filings, more hours of work, more money spent.

Finally, in November 2014, almost nine years after Menendez received "The E-mail," he prevailed. The appeals panel ruled that he indeed had been retaliated against for blowing the whistle, just as he had argued all along.

Because he had wanted only to be proven right, he'd asked for a token sum. The administrative-law panel, noting the importance of punishing retaliations against whistleblowers, pushed for an increase and Menendez was awarded $30,000.

To say that the outcome stunned experts is something of an understatement. "Accountant beats Halliburton!" said Thomas, the attorney and expert on whistleblower law. "The government tries to beat Halliburton and loses."

Post-Decision Interview about Whistleblowing

In an interview with a reporter, Menendez offered that Halliburton had a whistleblower policy prior to this incident as required under Sarbanes-Oxley. It was required to be confidential, and although Halliburton's policy promised confidentiality, at the same time it discouraged anonymous complaints on the basis that if you didn't provide your identity, the company might not be able to properly investigate your concern. Menendez added that confidentiality was absolutely central to his case and he relied on this policy, but it was Halliburton that blatantly ignored its own policy and betrayed his trust.

He was asked how the whistleblowing policy of the SEC might be improved. He said that all too often it is almost impossible for a whistleblower to prevail and that there needs to be more protections and a more balanced playing field. "It shouldn't take nine years and hundreds of thousands of dollars to even have a remote chance of prevailing," he said.

· *The Human Aspect of the Case*

Menendez felt he had to leave Halliburton because of the retaliation and how everyone treated him differently after the e-mail. During the appeals process, as Menendez and his wife waited for vindication and money got tight, he finally caught a break. Through the accounting experts he had met during his legal odyssey, he heard that General Motors was looking for a senior executive.

He agonized over whether to tell interviewers about his showdown with Halliburton. Ultimately, he figured they would probably find out anyway. When he flew up to Detroit and met with Nick Cypress, GM's chief accounting officer and comptroller, he came clean. Cypress had heard good things about Menendez from Doug Carmichael, the accounting expert who had been Menendez's expert witness at trial.

After telling him, Menendez asked Cypress, "Does this bother you?"

"Hell no!" the GM executive replied.

This was not the typical reaction top corporate officers have to whistleblowers. The interviewer asked Cypress about it: "I was moved by it," he explained. "It takes a lot of courage to stand tall like that, and I needed that in the work we were doing. I needed people with high integrity who would work hard who I could trust" to bring problems directly to senior management.

Today, Tony Menendez, is a litigation consultant, speaker and writer at Financial Fraud Examiner LLC. In the meantime, Halliburton has thrived. The SEC never levied any penalty for the accounting issue raised by Menendez. In 2014, the company generated $3.5 billion in profit on $33 billion in revenue. It's not possible to tell if the company maintains the same revenue recognition policy from its public filings, says GT professor Mulford. But since the SEC passed on an enforcement action on the issue, the company likely feels it is in accordance with accounting rules. (Mulford believes that Menendez was right back then and that the SEC should have looked harder at the issue initially.)

Many of the Halliburton and KPMG officials involved in the accounting issue or the retaliation have continued to prosper in the corporate ranks. One is now Halliburton's chief accounting officer. McCollum is now the company's executive vice president overseeing the integration of a major merger. The KPMG executive who disagreed with Menendez is now a partner at the accounting firm.

Menendez did not tell his friends and family of his legal victory. He's more cautious than he used to be. "I changed a lot. It was almost 10 years where everything was in question. Wondering what would people think of you."

He and his wife still worry that disaster could arrive in the next e-mail. "It can really weaken a soul and tear apart a family or a marriage, if you aren't careful. Because of the enormous powers of a company," said his wife. If people asked her advice, she said, "I'd probably say don't do it."

Recently, Menendez finally explained the story to his son, Cameron, who is now 13 and old enough to understand. Cameron's response: "You should have asked for more money, Dad," the teenager said. "We could use it."

Years ago, Menendez and his wife bought a bottle of champagne to celebrate his eventual victory. They still haven't opened it.

Questions

1. Describe the inadequacies in the corporate governance system at Halliburton.

2. Consider the role of KPMG in the case with respect to the accounting and auditing issues. How did the firm's actions relate to the ethical and professional expectations for CPAs by the accounting profession?

3. The Halliburton case took place before the Dodd-Frank Financial Reform Act was adopted by Congress. Assume Dodd-Frank had been in effect and Menendez decided to inform the SEC under Dodd-Frank rather than SOX because it had been more than 180 days since the accounting violation had occurred. Given the facts of the case would Menendez have qualified for whistleblower protection? Explain.

4. Some critics claim that while Menendez's actions may have been courageous, he harmed others along the way. His family was in limbo for many years and had to deal with the agony of being labeled a whistleblower and disloyal to Halliburton. The company's overall revenue did not change; a small amount was merely shifted to an earlier period. Halliburton didn't steal any money, cheat the IRS, or cheat their customers or their employees. In fact, it lessened its cash flows by paying out taxes earlier than it should have under the rules.

    How do you respond to these criticisms?

Case 3-9   Loyalty to the Boss, Company, and/or the Profession: Whistleblowing as a Lever (a GVV Case)

Jerry Maloney, CPA has been working at Mason Pharmaceuticals for fifteen years. Mason is a Fortune 1000 company whose stock trades on the New York Stock Exchange. He came to Mason after starting his career in the Audit practice of PwC working on clients in the Pharmaceuticals and Medical Device manufacturing industries. Jerry loves and is very loyal to both the industry he works in and the company he works for. He believes that the drugs they manufacture save lives and he is committed to the continued success of the company. He started out as an Assistant Manager of Internal Audit at Mason, later led the internal audit division, and then moved into the Financial Reporting Department. His hard work has paid off and he was recently promoted to Senior Manager of Financial Reporting, reporting directly to the CFO. His department is responsible for preparing and ensuring the accuracy of all the required filings to the SEC and the NYSE. While his boss must certify the accuracy of the financials, the CFO relies on Jerry to ensure compliance with GAAP and that all the reporting requirements of the SEC and the NYSE are followed.

Jerry is sitting in his office reviewing a preliminary draft of the 10Q for the third quarter ended September 30, 2018. He is smiling as he reads the report as their Earnings Per Share (EPS) figures have exceeded their projected numbers for the third quarter in a row and he knows upper management will be thrilled. As he sits and contemplates what this might mean in terms of bonuses, raises, and stock valuation, Sharon Diggins, the Manager of Financial Reporting, knocks on his door. He invites her in and she explains that their staff have just found a material understatement of expenses in the draft 10Q. She explains that Research and Development Costs had been inadvertently capitalized as direct materials inventory and they needed to reverse that entry before issuing a final 10Q with the SEC. The reversal will cause them to fall just short of their expected EPS figures.

Mason had a big win in gaining regulatory approval for an impressive new treatment for Colorectal Cancer. The company expects this new drug to produce more revenue than any drug they have manufactured to date. Sharon explains that some manager in purchasing had inadvertently purchased a six months supply of the primary compound needed to produce the drug a month before regulatory approval was received. Unfortunately, the compound was received just a week before regulatory approval was granted. The accounts payable clerk recorded the invoice for the compound as Direct Materials Inventory as the intent was to use the materials for the manufacture of the new drug. Under GAAP all such costs need to be expensed as Research and Development Costs up until regulatory approval is received.

Jerry is distraught over the fact that the internal audit department did not catch this error sooner. He discusses with Sharon that they will need to investigate the oversight later but right now their larger issue is getting the reports revised. He explains that convincing John Bender, the CFO, that they need to correct this error now will be difficult. Bender is also reviewing the same draft of the 10Q that Jerry has and must be delighted by the apparent results. Jerry is sure he will argue against expensing the cost of the compound. He can just imagine that at a minimum Bender will argue that following GAAP to the letter does not make sense. The intent of the purchase was to produce the drug, which they will do starting in the current quarter. He is sure Bender will state following GAAP will actually reduce the true cost of goods sold next quarter and, therefore, they should leave the cost in inventory. Sharon reminds Jerry that a violation of GAAP of this magnitude would be considered fraudulent financial reporting by the SEC and cannot be allowed to happen. She suggests that they put their GVV training to work and try to identify all the arguments that Bender will use to try and convince them to ignore this error and then prepare counter arguments. Jerry agrees and they get to work formulating their plan for discussing this matter with Bender.

Questions

1. What are the main arguments that Jerry and Sharon will need to counter? That is, what are the reasons and rationalizations they will need to address?

2. What is at stake should they not convince Bender to issue a revised 10Q?

3. What levers do Jerry and Sharon have available to them? Include in your answer a discussion of the provisions under SOX and how they might be used as a lever.

4. If they cannot convince Bender to issue the revised report, what is their next step? To whom should they report this matter to? Include other parties they might be able to involve who will support their position.

5. If they are unable to stop the draft report from being issued, what are their options?

Case 3-10 Accountability of Ex-HP CEO in Conflict of Interest Charges

How could a CEO and chairperson of the board of directors of a major company resign in disgrace over a personal relationship with a contractor that led to a sexual harassment charge and involved a conflict of interest, a violation of the code of ethics? It happened to Mark Hurd on August 10, 2010. Hurd was the former CEO for Hewlett-Packard (HP) for five years and also served as the chair of the board of directors for four years. On departure from HP, Hurd said he had not lived up to his own standards regarding trust, respect, and integrity.

HP hired Playboy model Jodie Fisher to be a hostess at several HP events in California. Fisher was paid $30,000 to appear at six events, plus she received other benefits like first-class travel. The purpose of these events was for Mark Hurd to sell HP to chief information officers of other companies. On one occasion, Hurd invited Fisher up to his room, fondled her breasts, and asked her to stay the night. On another, he went to her room and forcibly kissed her. To gain her favor, over the next two years he passed her inside information, showed her his ATM balance of one million dollars, and suggested he'd take care of her if she'd go away with him. At an event in Boise, Idaho, Hurd tried one last time to force her into having sex, but Fisher ran away to her room and never worked again for HP.

The board of directors of HP began an investigation of Hurd in response to a sexual harassment complaint by Fisher, who retained lawyer Gloria Allred to represent her.

While HP did not find that the facts supported the complaint, they did reveal behavior that the board would not tolerate. Subsequent to Hurd's resignation, a severance package was negotiated granting Hurd $12.2 million, COBRA benefits, and stock options, for a total package of somewhere between $40 and $50 million.

In a letter to employees of HP on August 6, interim CEO Cathie Lesjak outlined where Hurd violated the "Standards of Business Conduct (SBC)" and the reasons for his departure.[1] Lesjak wrote that Hurd "failed to maintain accurate expense reports, and misused company assets." She indicated that each was a violation of the standards and "together they demonstrated a profound lack of judgment that significantly undermined Mark's credibility and his ability to effectively lead HP." The letter reminded employees that everyone was expected to adhere strictly to the standards in all business dealings and relationships and senior executives should set the highest standards for professional and personal conduct.

As for the complaint by Fisher, it was pointed out she was a "marketing consultant" who was hired by HP for certain projects, but she was never an employee of HP. Still, during the investigation, inaccurately documented expenses were found that were claimed to have been paid to Fisher for her services. Falsifying the use of company funds violated the HP's Standards of Business Conduct (SBE).

As for the sexual harassment claim, Allred alleged in the letter that Hurd harassed Fisher at meetings and dinners over a several year period during which time Fisher experienced a number of unwelcome sexual advances from Hurd, including kissing and grabbing. Fisher said that this continual sexual harassment made her uncertain about her employment status.

In August 2013, HP and former CEO, Mark Hurd, won dismissal of a lawsuit that challenged the computer maker's public commitment to ethics at a time when Hurd was allegedly engaging in sexual harassment.

HP did not violate securities laws despite making statements such as a commitment to be "open, honest, and direct in all our dealings" because such statements were too vague and general, U.S. District Judge Jon Tigar in San Francisco wrote.

As a result, shareholders led by a New York City union pension fund could not pursue fraud claims over Hurd's alleged violations of HP's SBC, the judge ruled.

"Adoption of the plaintiff's argument [would] render every code of ethics materially misleading whenever an executive commits an ethical violation following a scandal," Tigar wrote.

Shareholders led by the Cement & Concrete Workers District Council Pension Fund of Flushing, New York, claimed in their lawsuit that the share price had been fraudulently inflated because of Hurd's alleged activities.

They also claimed that HP's statements about its rules of conduct implied that Hurd was in compliance, and that Hurd ignored his duty to disclose violations.

At most, Judge Tigar said, such statements "constitute puffery—if the market was even aware of them."

Tigar also said Hurd's alleged desire to keep his dealings with Fisher secret did not by itself give rise to a fraud claim.

"Nothing suggests that Hurd thought that he could mislead investors with the statements the court finds were immaterial," the judge wrote.

Shareholders filed multiple derivative claims in the wake of the scandal, all of which were settled. HP made some promises regarding compliance and ethics, improving ethics and compliance training programs, and strengthening HP's SBC. HP also promised to appoint a "Lead Independent Director" tasked with implementing and enforcing the ethics standards and appointing a chief ethics and compliance officer to report violations of the code. It also promised to appoint and Ethics and Compliance Committee to oversee HP's ethics activities, including in regard to whistleblowing.[2]

---

[1] Craig E. Johnson, *Meeting the Ethical Challenges of Leadership: Casting Light or Shadow* (New York: Sage Publications, 2015).

[2] Ex-HP CEO Mark Hurd Wins Fraud Suit Arising Out of Sexual Harassment, February 3, 2107, http://mimesislaw.com/fault-lines/ex-hp-ceo-mark-hurd-wins-fraud-suit-arising-out-of-his-sexual-harassment-scandal/15878.

Questions

1. How can companies best protect themselves from claims of sexual harassment in the workplace?

2. How did the expenditures mentioned in the case affect the financial results at HP? Did financial fraud occur during the time Fisher was involved with Mark Hurd? Should their relationship have been disclosed to the shareholders? Explain.

3. Mark Hurd left HP with a compensation package between $40 million and $50 million. Do you think executives who resign from their positions or are fired because of unethical actions should be forced to give back some of those amounts to the shareholders to make them whole? Why or why not?

4. Despite hundreds of pages of policies, codes of ethics, organizational values, and carefully defined work environments and company culture, lapses in workplace ethics occur every day. Explain why you think these lapses occur and what steps might be taken by an organization to ensure that its top executives live up to values it espouses.

Chapter

4

Ethics and Professional Judgment in Accounting

Learning Objectives

After studying Chapter 4, you should be able to:

LO 4-1	Explain the KPMG professional judgment framework.
LO 4-2	Describe how the public trust was regained following the failures at Enron, WorldCom, and other companies.
LO 4-3	Explain the threats and safeguards approach to independence.
LO 4-4	Describe SEC actions taken against auditors for a lack of independence.
LO 4-5	Describe the process to resolve ethical conflicts that may cause violations of the rules.
LO 4-6	Explain what is meant by subordination of judgment in the context of the integrity and objectivity rules.
LO 4-7	Describe the rules of conduct that pertain to CPAs in business.
LO 4-8	Explain the rules of conduct in the AICPA Code that pertain to the performance of professional services.
LO 4-9	Describe the ethics rules for tax practice.
LO 4-10	Describe the PCAOB independence and ethics rules.

Ethics Reflection

CPAs are expected to act in accordance with the ethical standards embodied in the AICPA Code of Professional Conduct in the performance of a variety of services, including audit, tax, and consulting. The AICPA Code is not legally enforceable although many state boards of accountancy point to its relevance in the practice of public accounting.

CPAs in public practice, in business, and other CPAs are expected to adhere to the provisions in the AICPA Code and, if they do not, they can be subject to enforcement action by the state board of accountancy. Enforcement actions generally include mandatory training and/or continuing professional education above the normal requirements, probation, suspension, or revocation of one's professional license.

The public interest requires that CPAs make sound professional judgments in the performance of professional services and to ensure that the financial statements do not contain any material misstatements, including fraud. These judgments can be influenced by cognitive biases and other factors, as was discussed in Chapter 2. Common problems include framing issues in a way that fails to adequately consider the ethical dimension of a problem, social and organizational pressures that create cognitive dissonance, and an ethical culture that emphasizes conformity to organizational standards rather than independent thought and ethical decision making.

An interesting study of why CPAs run into ethical problems with state boards of accountancy was done by Cynthia L. Krom from Franklin & Marshall College. She poses an important question first raised by Stephen Loeb back in 1972: "How effective is the profession's machinery in enforcing the code of ethics and protecting the public interest?"[1]

The Krom study examined the frequency and nature of state board disciplinary actions in four states that comprise nearly 41% of all regulated CPAs: California, Illinois, New York, and Texas. The study identified a relatively small number of enforcement actions against CPAs when compared to other licensed professionals such as attorneys and physicians.

The results show disciplinary penalties for wrongdoings related to attest engagements were less severe than the author expected. She points out this may be due to the inability of clients, peers, or financial statements users to detect problems that arise. The audit committee has a role to play here to protect the public interest.

Disciplinary actions for behaviors outside the scope of practice were comparatively harsh. These wrongdoings relate to one's personal behavior and generally are labeled as acts discreditable to the profession, as we discussed in Chapter 1. They include failing to maintain a good moral character and any crime or offense involving moral turpitude.

Enforcement actions were sorted into ten different causes for discipline, clustered into four categories, based on the description given in the formal discipline disclosure. We provide just a few examples.

1. Primary CPA Professional Activities: failure to follow generally accepted auditing standards (GAAS), including a lack of independence, tax fraud, filing false returns, and not filing one's own taxes.

2. Federal or State Convictions: felonies related to securities fraud, asset misappropriation, and obstruction of justice*; assault; sexual harassment; and driving under the influence (DUI).[2]

3. Disciplinary action for unprofessional behavior or technical incompetence brought by agencies external to the specific state's board of accountancy; another state board's enforcement action; enforcement actions by the SEC, PCAOB, and IRS.

4. State Licensing Requirement Issues: violation of state board ethics rules practicing with an expired license, failing to meet continuing education requirements, failure to undergo a peer or quality review of one's attest practice.

The results of the study are somewhat surprising in that federal or state convictions were the most frequent enforcement action followed by violating one's primary CPA professional activities, state licensing requirement issues, and disciplinary action by other agencies. Here are those results.

Reason for Enforcement Action	Frequency
Federal or State Convictions	37.3%
(about 60% financial felonies)	
Primary CPA Professional Activities	31.3%
(54% audit; 46% tax)	
State Licensing Requirement Issues	19.1%
(about 70% registration issues)	
Discipline/Sanction by Other Agencies	12.3%
Total	100.0%

It is important for you, as a future CPA, to be aware of the profession's enforcement mechanisms and how your license to practice may be in jeopardy if you fail to follow the prescribed ethical standards discussed in this chapter. These standards exist to protect the public interest by ensuring licensed CPAs are knowledgeable about professional standards, committed to ethical behavior, and adhere to the administrative requirements imposed by a state board of accountancy in its role to assist state government in the licensing and regulation of the accounting profession.

Think about the following as you read the chapter: (1) What are effective measures to deal with cognitive biases that can influence ethical behavior? (2) What is the risk-based approach to deal with situations where independence, integrity and objectivity, and adherence to other professional standards is threatened by external relationships? (3) What is the role of professional skepticism in gathering evidence, evaluating its usefulness, and assessing risk in an audit?

*These are often called "white collar crimes," or frauds committed by business and government professionals. These crimes are characterized by deceit, concealment, or violation of trust and are not dependent on the application or threat of physical force or violence.

By certifying the public reports that collectively depict a corporation's financial status, the independent auditor assumes a public responsibility transcending any employment responsibility with the client. The independent public accountant performing this special function owes ultimate allegiance to the corporation's creditors and stockholders, as well as to the investing public. This "public watchdog" function demands that the accountant maintain total independence from the client at all times and requires complete fidelity to the public trust.

Source: Chief Justice Warren Burger, writing the unanimous opinion of the Supreme Court in United States v. Arthur Young & Co.

This important ruling of the U.S. Supreme Court reminds us that the independent audit provides the foundation for the existence of the accounting profession in the United States. Even though independent audits were common before the passage of the landmark legislation of the Securities Act of 1933 and the Securities Exchange Act of 1934, there is no doubt that CPAs derive their franchise as a profession from these two pieces of legislation, which require independent audits of publicly owned companies.

The Burger Court opinion emphasizes the trust that the public places in the independent auditor. The accounting profession is the only profession where one's public obligation supersedes that to a client. The medical profession recognizes the primacy of the physician's responsibility to a patient. The legal profession emphasizes the lawyer's responsibility to the client. The Public Interest Principle in the AICPA Code of Professional Conduct states, "In discharging their professional responsibilities, members (of the AICPA) may encounter conflicting pressures from each of these groups [clients, employers . . .]. In resolving those conflicts, members should act with integrity, guided by the precept that when members fulfill their responsibility to the public, clients' and employers' interests are best served." Professional judgment and ethical reasoning enable CPAs to meet their professional obligations to resolve conflicts in a morally appropriate way when the public interest is at stake.

What is Professional Judgment in Accounting?

LO 4-1
Explain the KPMG professional judgment framework.

How are ethical judgments made in accounting? The AICPA Code is the foundation for such judgments. The Code links exercising sensitive and moral judgments to professional conduct. Personal values or virtues link to ethical sensitivity and judgment. Ethical reasoning enables professional accountants to sort out consequences, evaluate rights of stakeholders, and ensure that decisions are just and fair to those who rely on the accounting profession to maintain the accuracy and reliability of financial reports.

KPMG Professional Judgment Framework

KPMG developed a framework of the elements of professional judgment in its monograph, *Elevating Professional Judgment in Auditing and Accounting: The KPMG Professional Judgment Framework.* It starts with a common definition of judgment: Judgment is the process of reaching a decision or drawing a conclusion where there are a number of possible alternative solutions.[3]

Judgment occurs in a setting of uncertainty, risk, and often conflicts of interest. We can see the link between judgment and decision making not only in Rest's model but also in the Integrated Model of Ethical Decision Making described in Chapter 2. The evaluation of alternatives links to ethical intent, which leads to ethical action. Professional judgment follows a similar path with pressures along the way imposed by one's supervisor, top management, or CPA firm management that might lead to compromising judgment.

The KPMG framework identifies five components of professional judgment that revolve around one's mind-set. The components are: (1) clarify issues and objectives; (2) consider alternatives; (3) gather and evaluate information; (4) reach conclusion; and (5) articulate and document rationale. The framework recognizes that influences and biases might affect the process as could one's knowledge of professional standards.

The framework is prescriptive. In the real world we may deviate from the process because of pressures, time constraints, and limited capacity. These constraints, influences, and biases threaten good judgment. For example, let's assume on the last day of an audit you determine that copies of documents for equipment purchases were provided by the client rather than original ones. You realize that fraudulent alteration of documents can occur more readily with copies than if the documents are original. However, to ask the client to provide originals at the eleventh hour means extra time and budget pressures for the firm. Indeed, your supervisor wants to wrap up the audit at the end of the day. Since the firm has never had a problem with this client, you decide to let it go. The process then becomes altered at step three because of our biases and influences.

At the very center of the KPMG framework is *mindset.* Auditors should approach matters objectively and independently, with inquiring and incisive minds. Professional skepticism is required by auditing standards. It requires an objective attitude that includes a questioning mind and critical assessment of audit evidence. In the previous example, professional skepticism was sacrificed for expedience.

Professional skepticism is not the same as professional judgment, but it is an important component of professional judgment. It is a frame of reference to guide audit decisions and enhances ethical decision making.

As decision makers navigate through the professional judgment framework, judgment traps and tendencies can lead to bias. One common judgment trap is the tendency to want to immediately solve a problem by making a quick judgment. The auditor in the previous example may choose to shortcut the process by accepting copies of original documents rather than spending the time to convince the client of why originals are needed. This System 1 approach ignores the more deliberative System 2 side of the process that critically analyzes the reasons for and against examining additional documents to gather reliable evidence about the supportability of the expenditures.

Link between KPMG Framework and Cognitive Processes

Each of us have our own biases that may cloud decision making and alter our final choices. We may be easy going and avoid conflicts at all costs, which would not make for a very good auditor, who needs to have a questioning mind and be willing to critically assess audit data. We also need to be deliberative about our thought processes and consider both the why and the how we make decisions.

Our intuitive judgments can fall prey to cognitive traps and biases that negatively influence our judgments. Three common judgment traps are groupthink, a rush to solve a problems, and "judgment triggers." Groupthink finds a home in stage 3 of Kohlberg's model. We become influenced by the expectations of the group and, consequently, we subjugate our own beliefs and thought process. We may do so to avoid conflicts or save time. In an audit, this means the team might accept copies of documents if the majority of members convince the others that the client can be trusted and the group doesn't want to bust the budget.

Judgment triggers can lead to accepting a solution to the problem before it is properly identified and evaluated. Biased judgments might be made because of judgment tendencies. KPMG identifies four common judgment tendencies that are most applicable and important for audit professionals: the availability tendency, the confirmation tendency, the overconfidence tendency, and the anchoring tendency.

The *availability tendency* may lead to judgments based on the accessibility of information rather than a deliberative analysis of how the facts of the current situation differ from prior ones. Also, an auditor may rely on past procedures in the current audit even though that approach may not be relevant to the current situation. Information that is most available to an auditor's memory may unduly influence estimates, probability assessments, and other professional judgments. The auditor in our previous example may take the easy way out and just accept the copies of documents since he already has them, rather than try to verify the existence of new equipment and match it to original documents for equipment purchases.

The tendency for decision makers to put more weight on information that is consistent with their initial beliefs or preferences is the *confirmation tendency.* The danger is an auditor may not adequately consider potentially contradictory information that could result in a valid alternative to a preliminary conclusion. The auditor trusts the client based on past experiences and is more willing to accept the copies. However, in many instances, we cannot know something to be true unless we explicitly consider how and why it may be false. Confirmation bias in auditing may occur when auditors over-rely on management's explanations for a significant difference between the auditor's expectation and management's recorded value, even when the client's explanation is inadequate.

The *overconfidence tendency* is when decision makers overestimate their own abilities to perform tasks or to make accurate diagnoses or other judgments and decisions, as may be the case when estimating outcomes or likelihoods. This may occur because of one's personal motivation or self-interest. It can lead to an inability to recognize alternative points of view or contradictory evidence. It can also affect an auditor's willingness to involve others who could provide a meaningful perspective to the analysis.

The *anchoring tendency* relates to starting from an initial numerical value and then adjusting insufficiently away from it in forming a final judgment as when the auditor becomes anchored to management's estimate. The auditor may place too much reliance on one piece of information or set of circumstances and not enough on other perspectives or data that may confirm or disconfirm a particular position or issue. The danger is the auditor uses evidence-gathering techniques from prior engagements, rather than considering objectively a fuller set of techniques.

The audit of financial statements has always required auditors to exercise their professional judgment, but the use and importance of these judgments continues to grow as the overall complexity and estimation uncertainty inherent in financial statements increases. In an effort to facilitate auditors' use of sound professional judgment, audit firms have turned to developing professional judgment frameworks, such as the one provided by KPMG, to promote a rigorous, thoughtful, and deliberate judgment process to guide making reasonable accounting judgments.[4]

Link between Professional Judgment and AICPA Code of Professional Conduct

The way in which professional judgments are made is an integral part of whether CPAs meet their ethical obligation to make objective judgments. A professional accountant should not allow bias, conflict of interest, or undue influence of others to override professional or business judgments.

The decisions auditors make to deal with judgment triggers say a lot about whether they can meet the due care standard. Competent professional service requires the exercise of sound, independent, and objective judgment in applying professional knowledge and skill in the performance of professional services.

Professional skepticism links to professional judgment through the ethical standards of independent thought, objectivity, and due care. Professional skepticism is part of the skill set auditors should have and is closely interrelated to the fundamental concepts of auditor independence and professional judgment, which contribute to audit quality.[5]

To promote the application of professional skepticism, CPA-firm management should set an appropriate tone that emphasizes a questioning mind throughout the audit and the exercise of professional skepticism in gathering and evaluating evidence.

Accountability can be thought of as the requirement to justify one's judgments to others. Absent a healthy dose of professional skepticism, it would be difficult for the auditor to justify having made judgments in accordance with the ethical standards of the accounting profession. These standards exist to protect the public interest and honor the public trust.

Reclaiming the Public Trust

LO 4-2

Describe how the public trust was regained following the failures at Enron, WorldCom, and other companies.

Following the disclosure of numerous accounting scandals during the dark days of Enron, the accounting profession and professional bodies turned their attention to examining how to rebuild the public trust and confidence in financial reporting. The International Federation of Accountants (IFAC) addresses the public interest dimension in its Policy Position Paper #4, entitled *A Public Interest Framework for the Accountancy Profession*. The framework is designed to enable IFAC and other professional bodies to better evaluate whether the public interest is being served through actions of the profession and its institutions. IFAC considers the "public interest" to represent the common benefits derived by stakeholders of the accounting profession through sound financial reporting. It links these benefits to responsibilities of professional accountants, including the application of high standards of ethical behavior and professional judgment.

The spectacular financial failures at Enron and WorldCom raised questions about auditors' commitment to ethics. Former SEC Chief Accountant Lynn Turner reminded the profession in a speech in 2001 that "the accounting profession should be mindful of its obligation to serve the public interest in order to protect its franchise under the Securities Exchange Acts of 1933 and 1934 which forms the core of its professional status."[6]

Former SEC Chairman Arthur Levitt was deeply concerned about a loss of independence and financial failures and reminded the profession that "Independence means the auditor should not be in bed with the corporate managers whose numbers they audit."[7]

The failures at Enron and WorldCom led to the demise of professional regulation and the birth of government regulation. The Sarbanes-Oxley Act was adopted by Congress in 2002 to enhance auditor independence by restricting the performance of certain consulting services for audit clients and regain the public trust. At the same time, the SEC was modernizing its independence rules to reflect changed relationships between auditors and management and the likelihood that independence could be compromised.

The formation of the Public Company Accounting Oversight Board ended seventy years of professional regulation. PCAOB Chair James Doty addressed these issues at the AICPA's 41st Annual National Conference on Current SEC and PCAOB Developments: "As sophisticated as our markets and economy are, they are dependent on trust. We cannot take trust for granted. Independent audits provide that trust, and thus bridge the gap between entrepreneurs who need capital and lenders who can provide capital."[8]

Where Were the Auditors?

George Santayana, a Spanish philosopher, essayist, poet, and novelist, once said: "Those who cannot remember the past are condemned to repeat it." Winston Churchill later said in a speech to the British House of Commons: "Those who fail to learn from history are condemned to repeat it." Either way, the expression aptly captures what seemed to happen to the accounting profession between 1978 and 2002, when the Sarbanes-Oxley Act was passed.

The auditing profession in the United States has come under periodic scrutiny from Congress during the past 40 years as a result of a series of financial frauds. The question consistently asked was: Where were the auditors? Why didn't auditing firms detect and report the many frauds that occurred during this time period? Was it a matter of bending to the wishes of the client that hires (and can fire) the firm and pays its fee? Were these failures due to inadequate and sometimes sloppy audits by firms that may have been trying to cut corners because they lowballed their audit fees to lure clients with the hope of gaining lucrative tax advice and consulting fees down the road? Or was it a reaction to clients who threatened auditors with the loss of the engagement through opinion shopping (i.e., looking for another firm that would be more willing to accept the client's position on an accounting matter)?

Congressional investigations examined whether auditors were living up to their ethical and professional responsibilities (as stated in the Burger Court opinion). The major themes of these investigations were (1) whether nonauditing services impair auditor independence, (2) the need for management to report on internal controls, (3) the importance of developing techniques to prevent and detect fraud, and (4) the need to strengthen the role of the audit committee and communications between the auditor and audit committee.

Following a large number of financial frauds in the 1980s at companies such as ESM Government Securities and bank failures at Continental Illinois National Bank and Trust and Penn Square Bank, Congress turned its attention to the need for stronger internal controls to help prevent and detect financial fraud. In January and February 1988, Congress held two hearings concerning the failure of ZZZZ Best Company, a corporation that had "created" 80% or more of its total revenue in the form of fictitious revenue from the restoration of carpets, drapes, and other items in office buildings after fires and floods. John Dingell, House of Representatives Chair of the Subcommittee on Oversight and Investigations, characterized the fraud as follows:[9]

> The fact that auditors and attorneys repeatedly visited make-believe job sites and came away satisfied does not speak well for the present regulatory system. The fact that the auditing firm discovering the fraud resigned the engagement without telling enforcement authorities is even more disturbing. . . . Cases such as ZZZZ Best demonstrate vividly that we cannot afford to tolerate a system that fails to meet the public's legitimate expectations in this regard.

The proverbial straw that broke the camel's back occurred when it was determined that the cost to the public to clean up 1,043 failed savings and loan institutions with total assets of over $500 billion during the 1986–1995 period was reported to be $152.9 billion, including $123.8 billion of U.S. taxpayer losses. These failed institutions made questionable home mortgage loans and issued risky investments to the public. Sound familiar? Well, little did we know at the time that 20 years later banks and financial institutions would be embroiled in a scandal that involved risky investments emanating from subprime mortgages, including derivatives and worthless mortgage-backed securities, and some institutions would need federal bailout funds to stay in business, while others would be taken over by the government or other institutions. The banks clearly didn't learn their lesson and the great financial recession occurred.

Treadway Commission Report

The National Commission on Fraudulent Financial Reporting, referred to as the Treadway Committee after its chair James C. Treadway, was formed in 1985 to study and report on the factors that can lead to fraudulent financial reporting. The Committee identified three relevant factors in determining the size and scope of fraud: (1) the seriousness of the consequences of fraudulent financial reporting, (2) the risk of its occurring in any given company, and (3) the realistic potential for reducing that risk. It also laid blame at the doorstep of financial analysts who, through short-sighted views of profitability and other indicators of financial health, may pressure management to focus all their attention on achieving short-term gains.

The Committee of Sponsoring Organizations of the Treadway Commission (COSO) emphasized the need to change corporate culture and establish the systems necessary to prevent fraudulent financial reporting. It identified three components of a strong, ethical culture: (1) the tone set by top management that influences the corporate environment within which financial reporting occurs, (2) an effective and objective internal audit function with reporting responsibilities to the audit committee, and (3) an independent audit committee that ensures the integrity of the financial reports.

Treadway's lasting legacy is the development of the integrated framework for internal control that was discussed in Chapter 3, which serves as the foundation for companies to build effective internal control systems.

PCAOB Inspections

Historically, the SEC had allowed the accounting profession to police itself through a system of peer review that began in 1977 whereby one auditing firm would examine another firm and issue a report on its findings. The system seemed to work well until the failures at Enron and WorldCom when Congress, realizing that both companies received clean reviews, started to wonder whether the government needed to step in and regulate the profession. In 2004, the PCAOB was formed and it instituted a mandatory quality inspection program for CPA firms that audit public companies.

The average audit deficiency rate has ranged between 30-to-40% since the program started. The rate for Big-4 firms has gotten as low as 21% (Deloitte) and gone as high as 54% (KPMG). In the case of KPMG, it was determined that the firm too often failed to gather enough supporting evidence before signing off on a company's financial statements and internal controls.

A startling report on BDO USA, LLP came out in April 2016, when the PCAOB found problems in 17 of the 23 audits, a 74% deficiency rate and record high among big firms. The PCAOB concluded that BDO didn't do enough work to support its opinion in these 17 audits. In 15 of the 17 audits, problems were identified in both the audit of financial statements and the audit of internal control.

In an unprecedented event on January 22, 2018, it was announced that a former PCAOB staffer, Brian Sweet, who was hired by KPMG in 2015, leaked confidential information about PCAOB's plans to audit the company. Most of the leaked information concerned which audit engagements the PCAOB planned to inspect, the criteria it was using to select engagements for inspection, and on what these inspections would focus. The alleged conspiracy got its start when, while preparing to leave the PCAOB, Sweet copied confidential information showing which audits would be reviewed. He shared the information with his new colleagues at KPMG, according to court documents, and continued to acquire and share PCAOB information with KPMG executives through 2017 with the help of at least two other board employees. Three KPMG partners were charged with conspiracy—David Middendorf, KPMG's former national managing partner for audit quality and professional practice; Thomas Whittle, former national partner-in-charge of inspections; and David Britt, the banking and capital markets group co-leader. As the scheme unraveled, accountants at KPMG deleted messages and considered hiding their communications using prepaid "burner" phones and codes over Instagram, according to prosecutors. Steven Peikin, the SEC's co-director of enforcement was quoted in saying: "These accountants engaged in shocking misconduct—literally stealing the exam—in an effort to interfere with the PCAOB's ability to detect audit deficiencies at KPMG."[10]

According to the criminal indictment, during Sweet's first week at KPMG the three partners asked, knowing his background with the PCAOB, whether there were any plans to inspect a client of theirs. Reluctant at first to respond, Middendorf is said to have later told Sweet to "remember where [his] pay-check came from" and "to be loyal to KPMG." Sweet was asked about the plans again a few days later, this time by Whittle, who implied that his position within the firm was not secure. Sweet showed Whittle the inspection list later that day. The audit partners used this information to analyze and review audit workpapers relevant to the inspection and suggested revisions to avoid possible findings of deficiencies by the PCAOB.[11]

It seems that KPMG was motivated by a desire to improve its inspection results following a high rate of audit deficiency. The knowledge of PCAOB's audit plans for the firm gave it an unfair advantage over other firms and violates ethical principles of right and wrong.

Professionalism versus Commercialism

Boyce points out that whether or not it has been broadly recognized, the accounting profession has always been characterized, to differing degrees, both by the pursuit of professional self-interest and the public interest. Increasingly, professional firms, particularly the Big Four international firms, have turned their attention to deliver business and client-focused service that threatens the public's confidence in the profession.[12] The perception that auditors may not be and may not act independent of the client's interests has taken a hit in recent years as commercialism has once again bumped up against professionalism.

Alarm bells went off in October 2013, when PwC announced it was acquiring the consulting giant Booz & Company. Back in 2002, PwC had sold its previous consulting business to IBM for $3.5 billion, as a response to restrictions created by SOX on providing consulting services for audit clients. As a result of its acquisition of Booz, PwC added $9.2 billion in global consulting revenue and increased its consulting group's share of total global firm revenue of $32.1 billion to 28.5%, up from 21.7% in 2009. Lynn Turner raised an important question about the merger when he asked, "Are the auditors going to serve management, or are they going to serve the best interests of the investing public?"[13]

Not to be outdone, on April 13, 2015, KPMG announced that it had entered into an agreement to acquire substantially all of the assets of Beacon Partners, Inc., a provider of management consulting services to hospitals, physician groups, and other health-care providers. KPMG is trying to leverage its foothold in the health-care industry in light of the growth in services as a result of the Affordable Care Act (Obamacare). In June 2014, it bought Zanett Commercial Solutions, a consulting firm with a significant focus on health care.

The latest area for expansion in accounting firms is digital consulting. On November 4, 2013, PwC announced it had acquired digital consulting firm BGT. The acquisition added digital strategists, analysts, designers, and technologists to PwC's Advisory practice. PwC's acquisition enables it to leverage its broad range of global business and industry consultants.

Deloitte's digital practice is well established and the firm broadened its scope to include digital marketing when it announced on February 29, 2016, that it had acquired Heat. Heat will continue to operate within Deloitte Digital as a full-service advertising agency, working across traditional, digital, and social media. Heat has done work for companies such as videogame maker Electronic Arts Inc. and travel website Hotwire. With this acquisition, the big firms seem to be sending a message that they are in the market for traditional advertising firms that specialize in digital technology to compliment their growing digital consultancy practices.

The growth in consulting services raises questions about any conflict of interest that might arise between consulting and auditing. Unlike audits that are conducted primarily to satisfy the public interest, consulting services satisfy the client's interest and do not require independence from the client. However, independence might be impaired as a result of the relationship between the two services. Just imagine if the auditor determined that the consulting work done was deficient or led to financial problems for the client. Can the auditor still be independent when conducting the audit? The fact is it does not matter whether the auditor is independent because as long as the appearance of independence has been tainted by the consulting relationship, the independence standard would be compromised.

The big firms' appetite for digital and other advisory services has led to the reemergence of consulting practices. Consulting services grew by 10.2% in 2016 to $21.5 billion of the $58.7 total consulting market. In examining whether professionalism and commercialism can coexist in CPA firms, Love points out that the profession will lose its *raison d'etre* if the public believes that CPAs are not independent due to the type of, or amount of fees received for, advisory services performed for clients upon which they render any assurance opinion.[14] We would like to think that the profession learned its lesson from Enron where Andersen received $27 million for tax and consulting services and $25 million for auditing. Unfortunately, this may be an instance of going "back to the future" as the profession has been investigated over and over again since 1977 for certain practices that threaten the public interest, including providing consulting services for audit clients.

AICPA Code: Independence Considerations for Members in Public Practice

LO 4-3

Explain the threats and safeguards approach to independence.

Introduction to Revised Code

On June 1, 2014, the AICPA issued a codification of the principles, rules, and interpretations and rulings in the revised AICPA Code of Professional Conduct that simplifies the identification of topics that are now contained in designated areas, whereas a CPA used to have to wade through actual rules, interpretations, and rulings to be knowledgeable about all aspects of an ethical situation. A major improvement of the AICPA Code is the creation of three sections, one each for members in public practice, members in business, and other members. This simplifies identifying how the rules apply to practitioners in the performance of their professional services.[15]

The most significant change is the incorporation of two broad conceptual frameworks, one for members in public practice and another for CPAs in business.[16] These conceptual frameworks incorporate a "threats and safeguards" approach and are designed to assist users in analyzing relationships and circumstances that the code does not specifically address.

A significant improvement is the new section on "Ethical Conflicts" that arise from obstacles to following the appropriate course of action due to internal or external pressures and/or conflicts in applying relevant professional standards or legal standards. The ethical conflicts provision is used in combination with the conceptual framework to determine whether specific rules of conduct have been violated. The revised AICPA Code was transitioned in and became fully effective on December 15, 2015.

The numbering in the revised Code can be confusing and we have kept it at a minimum in order to focus on the important material that students should know. The Principles in the Code (Section 0.300) were discussed in Chapter 1. They are now categorized as follows:

- Responsibilities (0.300.020)
- The Public Interest (0.300.030)
- Integrity (0.300.040)
- Objectivity and Independence (0.300.050)
- Due Care (0.300.060)
- Scope and Nature of Services (0.300.070)

In the discussions below, we refer to the Revised Code as the "AICPA Code" to simplify matters.

Three important points about the applicability of the AICPA Code are as follows: (1) It applies to CPAs in the performance of all professional services except when the wording of the rule indicates otherwise; (2) it is a violation of the rules for a CPA to permit others acting on their behalf from engaging in behavior that, had the CPA done so, it would have violated the rules; and (3) when differences exist between AICPA rules and those of the licensing state board of accountancy, the CPA should follow the state board's rules.

Members in Public Practice

Section 1.000.010 describes a conceptual framework that applies to members in public practice and provides a foundation to evaluate whether threats to the CPA's compliance with the rules of conduct are at an acceptable level or whether safeguards should be developed to prevent a violation of the rules. Under the AICPA Code, in the absence of an interpretation of a specific rule of conduct that addresses a particular relationship or circumstance, a CPA should evaluate whether that relationship or circumstance would lead a reasonable and informed third party who is aware of the relevant information to conclude a threat exists to the CPA's compliance with the rules that is not at an acceptable level. In some circumstances no safeguards can reduce a threat to an acceptable level. For example, a CPA cannot subordinate professional judgment to others without violating the "Integrity and Objectivity" Rule.

Conceptual Framework for AICPA Independence Standards

The conceptual framework approach is used to evaluate independence matters in Section 1.210. The Code uses a risk-based approach to assess whether a CPA's relationship with a client would pose an unacceptable risk. Risk is unacceptable if the relationship would compromise (or would be perceived as compromising by an informed third party knowing all the relevant information) the CPA's professional judgment when rendering an attest service to the client (i.e., audit, review, or attestation engagement). Key to that evaluation is identifying and assessing the extent to which a threat to the CPA's independence exists, and, if it does, whether it would be reasonable to expect that the threat would compromise the CPA's professional judgment and, if so, whether it can be effectively mitigated or eliminated. Under the risk-based approach, steps are taken to prevent circumstances that threaten independence from compromising the professional judgments required in the performance of an attest engagement.

The risk-based approach involves the following steps:

1. Identifying and evaluating threats to independence.
2. Determining whether safeguards already eliminate or sufficiently mitigate identified threats and whether threats that have not yet been mitigated can be eliminated or sufficiently mitigated by safeguards.

3. If no safeguards are available to eliminate an unacceptable threat or reduce it to an acceptable level, independence would be considered impaired.

Threats to Independence

Independence in fact is defined as the state of mind that permits the performance of an attest service without being affected by influences that compromise professional judgment, thereby allowing an individual to act with integrity and professional skepticism. To *appear to be independent,* the CPA should avoid circumstances that might cause an informed third party to reasonably conclude that the integrity, objectivity, or professional skepticism of a firm or member of the audit (attest) engagement team has been compromised.

Threats to independence include a self-review threat, advocacy threat, adverse interest threat, familiarity threat, undue influence threat, financial self-interest threat, and management participation threat. A brief description of each threat follows, and Exhibit 4.1 provides examples of each threat.

Self-Review Threat

A self-review threat occurs when a CPA reviews evidence during an attest engagement that is based on his own or his firm's nonattest work. An example would be preparing source documents used to generate the client's financial statements.

Advocacy Threat

An advocacy threat occurs when a CPA promotes an attest client's interests or position in such a way that objectivity may be, or may be perceived to be, compromised. These are of particular concern when performing tax services.

Adverse Interest Threat

An adverse interest threat occurs when a CPA takes actions that are in opposition to an attest client's interests or positions.

EXHIBIT 4.1   Examples of Threats to Independence

Threat	Example
Self-Review Threat	Preparing source documents used to generate the client's financial statements.
Advocacy Threat	Promoting the client's securities as part of an initial public offering or representing a client in U.S. tax court.
Adverse Interest Threat	Commencing, or the expressed intention to commence, litigation by either the client or the CPA against the other.
Familiarity Threat	A CPA on the attest engagement team whose spouse is the client's CEO.
Undue Influence Threat	A threat to replace the CPA or CPA firm because of a disagreement with the client over the application of an accounting principle.
Financial Self-Interest Threat	Having a loan from the client, from an officer or director of the client, or from an individual who owns 10% or more of the client's outstanding equity securities.
Management Participation Threat	Establishing and maintaining internal controls for the client.

Familiarity Threat

A familiarity threat occurs when a close relationship is formed between the CPA and an attest client or its employees, members of top management, or directors of the client entity, including individuals or entities that performed nonattest work for the client (i.e., tax or consulting services).

Undue Influence Threat

An undue influence threat results from an attempt by the management of an attest client or other interested parties to coerce the CPA or exercise excessive influence over the CPA.

Financial Self-Interest Threat

A financial self-interest threat occurs when there is a potential benefit to a CPA from a financial interest in, or from some other financial relationship with, an attest client. It goes beyond simple situations where independence would be impaired, such as directly owning shares of stock of the client or having material indirect financial interest. Financial self-interest threats can also arise from business relationships with a client or a member of management that creates a mutual self-interest.

Management Participation Threat

A management participation threat occurs when a CPA takes on the role of client management or otherwise performs management functions on behalf of an attest client.

Safeguards to Counteract Threats

Safeguards are controls that eliminate or reduce threats to independence. These range from partial to complete prohibitions of the threatening circumstance to procedures that counteract the potential influence of a threat. The nature and extent of the safeguards to be applied depend on many factors, including the size of the firm and whether the client is a public interest entity. To be effective, safeguards should eliminate the threat or reduce to an acceptable level the threat's potential to impair independence.

There are three broad categories of safeguards. The relative importance of a safeguard depends on its appropriateness in light of the facts and circumstances.

1. *Safeguards created by the profession, legislation, or regulation.* For example, continuing education requirements on independence and ethics and external review of a firm's quality control system.

2. *Safeguards implemented by the client,* such as a tone at the top that emphasizes the attest client's commitment to fair financial reporting and a governance structure, such as an active audit committee, that is designed to ensure appropriate decision making, oversight, and communications regarding a firm's services.

3. *Safeguards implemented by the firm,* including policies and procedures to implement professional and regulatory requirements.

Exhibit 4.2 categorizes examples by source of the safeguard. It applies to the conceptual framework for independence and the Integrity and Objectivity Rule.

Sarbanes-Oxley Act (SOX): Nonaudit Services

Similar to AICPA and SEC rules, SOX prohibits CPAs and CPA firms from providing certain nonattest services for public company attest clients. The potential for a conflict of interest exists because of a self-review threat to independence that occurs when a CPA reviews, as part of an attest engagement, evidence that results from the CPA's own nonattest services.

EXHIBIT 4.2   Examples of Safeguards in Applying the Conceptual Framework

Source of the Safeguard	Examples of Safeguards
Created by the profession, legislation, or regulation	Professional resources, such as hotlines, for consultation on ethical issues.
Implemented by the client	The client has personnel with suitable skill, knowledge, or experience who make managerial decisions about the delivery of professional services and makes use of third-party resources for consultation as needed.
	The tone at the top emphasizes the client's commitment to fair financial reporting and compliance with the applicable laws, rules, regulations, and corporate governance policies.
	Policies and procedures are in place to achieve fair financial reporting and compliance with the applicable laws, rules, regulations, and corporate governance policies.
	Policies and procedures are in place to address ethical conduct.
	Policies are in place that bar the entity from hiring a firm to provide services that do not serve the public interest or that would cause the firm's independence or objectivity to be considered impaired.
Implemented by the firm	Policies and procedures addressing ethical conduct and compliance with laws and regulations.

Section 201 of SOX provides that the following nonattest services may not be performed for attest clients in addition to bookkeeping or other services related to the accounting records or financial statements of the audit client:

1. Financial information systems design and implementation.
2. Appraisal or valuation services, fairness opinions, or contribution-in-kind reports.
3. Actuarial services.
4. Internal audit outsourcing services.
5. Management functions or human resources.
6. Broker or dealer, investment adviser, or investment banking services.
7. Legal services and expert services unrelated to the audit.
8. Any other service that the board of directors determines, by regulation, is impermissible.

SOX allows an accounting firm to "engage in any nonaudit service, including tax services," that is not listed above, only if the activity is preapproved by the audit committee of the issuer company. The preapproval requirement is waived if the aggregate amount of all such nonaudit services provided to the issuer constitutes less than 5% of the total amount of revenues paid by the issuer to its auditor.

The rules do not give CPAs definitive guidance on how audit committees should determine whether a tax service is an allowable activity requiring preapproval or is a prohibited service that even preapproval cannot save other than saying that tax compliance, planning, and advice are acceptable once approved. It is generally understood that the SEC allows the provision of tax-minimization services to audit clients, except for transactions that have no business purpose other than tax avoidance (i.e., tax shelters).

The issue of whether a CPA firm should be allowed to do permitted tax services for audit clients can be evaluated ethically from a utilitarian perspective. The question is whether the benefits of auditor-provided tax services outweigh the risks that the audit will not be performed with the level of objectivity necessary to ensure the independence standard is met. An argument to allow permitted tax services is that the insight learned from providing tax services can enhance audit effectiveness and, in turn, the client's financial reporting quality. The argument against it would be that it creates a self-review threat and could lead to an advocacy relationship between the tax accountants and audit client, which creates a threat to independence that cannot be reduced or eliminated by any safeguards.

Relationships That May Impair Independence

A variety of relationships have the potential to impair audit independence because of conflicts of interest that may arise. Some of these potential conflicts arise from financial and other relationships with an audit client or members of top management of the client, providing nonattest services for an attest client, or being employed by a former attest client.

Financial Relationships

The ownership of stock in a client creates a financial self-interest threat to independence. The problem with owning direct and material indirect financial interests is that these arrangements might create the impression in the mind of an outside observer that the CPA cannot make decisions without being influenced by the stock ownership, even if that is not the case for any specific CPA. Appearances matter and the perception in the mind of the public that independent, objective judgment may be compromised by the financial relationship is enough for independence to be violated.

Another example of a financial self-interest threat is when a CPA becomes involved in a loan transaction to or from a client, including home mortgage loans from financial institution clients. This type of loan is prohibited under AICPA Code. It provides that independence is considered to be impaired if, during the period of the professional engagement, a covered member, such as a CPA on the attest engagement team or an individual in a position to influence the attest engagement team, has any loan to or from a client, any officer or director of the client, or any individual owning 10% or more of the client's outstanding equity securities or other ownership interests.

Examples of permitted loans include automobile loans and leases collateralized by the automobile, loans fully collateralized by cash deposits at the same financial institution (e.g., "passbook loans"), and aggregate credit card balances from credit cards and overdraft reserve accounts that are reduced to $10,000 or less on a current basis, taking into consideration the payment due and any available grace period.

One of the cases that led the SEC to require that the accounting profession tighten its independence rules was when Jose Gomez, the lead partner of Alexander Grant (now Grant Thornton) accepted loans from an audit client during its audit of ESM Government Securities from 1977 to 1984. Over the eight-year period, ESM committed fraud and, in the process, used its leverage against Gomez from $200,000 in loans to him so he would keep silent about the fact that ESM's financial statements did not fairly present financial position and the results of operations. Top management of ESM also threatened to pull the audit from Gomez's firm if he spoke out about the fraud. Gomez compromised his integrity, and the event ruined his reputation. Ultimately, Gomez was sentenced to a 12-year prison term and served 4½ years, and the firm paid approximately $175 million in civil payments.

The Independence Rule also extends to certain family members of the CPA. The detailed provisions are beyond the scope of this book, but we do want to emphasize two points to provide examples of familiarity threats to independence. First, when a CPA is part of the attest engagement team, which includes employees and contractors directly involved in an audit and those who perform concurring and second partner reviews, the rules extend to that CPA's immediate family members and close relatives. Immediate family members include the CPA's spouse, spousal equivalent, and dependents (whether or not they are related). The rules also extend to the CPA's close relatives, including parents, siblings, or nondependent children, if they hold a key position with the client (that is, one that involves direct participation in the preparation of the financial statements or a position that gives the CPA the ability to exercise influence over the contents of the financial statements). Close relatives are also subject to the Independence Rule if they own a financial interest in the client that is material to that person's net worth and of which the CPA has knowledge. The potential danger in these family relationships is that the family member's financial or employment relationship with the client might influence the perception that the CPA can be independent in fact or appearance.

There are other relationships that will bring a CPA under the Independence rules, including when a partner or manager provides 10 hours or more of nonattest services to the attest client. The problem is it may appear to an outside observer that the partner or manager may be able to influence the attest work because of the significant number of hours devoted to the nonattest services.

Let's stop at this point and consider that the Independence Rule is a challenging standard for the CPA and family members to meet, and it might present some interesting dilemmas. For example, imagine that a CPA knows that his father owns a financial interest in a client entity but does not know if that interest is material to the father's net worth. Should the CPA contact the father to find out? Or, might the CPA reason that it is better not to know because the Independence Rule applies only if the CPA has knowledge of the extent of the father's financial interest in the client? From an ethical perspective, the CPA should make a good-faith effort to determine the extent of his father's financial interest in the client entity.

Business Relationships

Another case that prompted the SEC to apply pressure on the AICPA to tighten its independence rules occurred after the SEC sanctioned EY because it was not independent in fact or appearance when it audited the financial statements of PeopleSoft for fiscal years 1994–1999. The SEC found independence violations arising from EY's business relationships with PeopleSoft while auditing the company's financial statements. These relationships created a mutuality of interests between the firm and PeopleSoft, resulting in a financial self-interest threat.

The basic facts are EY's Tax Group created a Global Expatriate Management System (EY/GEMS) as an in-house software program for assisting clients with the tax consequences of managing employees with international assignments. The EY/GEMS system was enhanced with the use of PeopleTools, a software product created by EY's audit client, PeopleSoft. A business relationship was created whereby a license to use PeopleTools was granted to EY in return for a payment to PeopleSoft of 15% of each licensee fee that EY received from outside customers purchasing the new software, 30% of each license renewal fee, and a minimum royalty of $300,000, payable in 12 quarterly payments of $25,000 each.

The licensing agreement provided that EY would make PeopleSoft a third-party beneficiary of each sublicense. PeopleSoft agreed to assist EY's efforts by providing technical assistance for a $15,000 quarterly fee. The agreement provided that EY could not distribute the derivative software to PeopleSoft's direct competitors. The agreement permitted EY to use PeopleSoft trademarks and trade names in marketing materials. PeopleSoft maintained a degree of control over the product by restricting EY's distribution rights and requiring the firm to work closely with PeopleSoft to ensure the quality of the product.

The SEC found that EY and PeopleSoft had a "symbiotic relationship," engaging in joint sales and marketing efforts and sharing considerable proprietary and confidential business information, and that EY partnered with PeopleSoft to accomplish increased sales and boost consulting revenues for EY. The findings of the SEC indicate that EY and PeopleSoft acted together to promote the product so that a reasonable investor with knowledge of all the facts would conclude that EY was closely identified in fact and appearance with its audit client.

Employment or Association with Attest Clients

It is not unusual for a CPA who has worked on an engagement for a client to be offered a position with that client. If the client has confidence in the abilities of the CPA and trusts that party, then the client may seek to hire the professional, for example, as the controller or CFO. The rules establish that independence may be impaired when a partner or professional employee leaves the firm and is subsequently employed by or associated with the client in a key position unless the following conditions are met:

- Amounts due to the former partner/professional are not material to the firm.
- The former partner/professional is not in a position to influence the accounting firm's operations or financial policies.
- The former partner/professional employee does not participate in or appear to participate in or is not associated with the firm once the relationship with the client begins.

An example of participating in the firm is continuing to consult for it or have one's name included in firm literature, which implies a relationship still exists.

Providing Nonattest Services to an Attest Client

An example of a prohibited activity under the AICPA Code is that a CPA should not perform management functions or make management decisions for an attest client. The relationship creates a management participation threat that places the CPA in the compromising position of making decisions for the client and then auditing those decisions. On the other hand, the CPA may provide advice, research materials, and recommendations to assist the client's management in performing its functions and making decisions.

Under Code Section 1.295, individual nonattest services may be permitted if adequate safeguards exist to mitigate potential threats to independence. However, when performing multiple services there may be unacceptable threats (i.e, management participation, self-review) to independence.

To protect against an impairment of independence, general requirements exist for the attest client when a CPA performs nonattest services, including:

- Assume all management responsibilities.
- Oversee the service, by designating an individual, preferably within senior management, who possesses suitable skill, knowledge, and/or experience.
- Evaluate the adequacy and results of the services performed.
- Accept responsibility for the results of the service.

Other requirements exist, including to clearly establish the objectives of the engagement, services to be performed, client's acceptance of its responsibilities, the CPA's responsibilities, and any limitations of the engagement.

Hosting Services

It's important for the rules of conduct to keep up with changing technology. The AICPA has recognized this by developing a new interpretation, *Hosting Services* (1.295.143), which appears in the Code's Independence Rule under "Nonattest Services," and applies to practitioners who provide nonattest services to attest clients. Under the new rule, hosting services can impair independence when a CPA assumes responsibility for maintaining internal control over an attest client's data or records. For example, the CPA assumes responsibility for safeguarding the information by:

- Acting as the sole host of a financial or nonfinancial information system of an attest client.
- Taking custody of or storing an attest client's data and records such that the client's data are incomplete and accessible only through the CPA.
- Providing electronic security and back-up services for an attest client's data or records.

Cathy Allen, a member of the AICPA's Professional Ethics Executive Committee, points out that, in recent years, it has become common for businesses and their CPAs to employ various software solutions, including cloud-based tools, to store, move, and manipulate data. A threat to independence exists because CPAs should not perform activities that are management's responsibility. The hosting of services creates a management participation threat because the CPA takes on the role of the attest client's management or otherwise assumes management responsibilities for the attest client, such as accepting responsibility for designing, implementing, or maintaining internal controls for the attest client (e.g., safeguarding information the company uses to run its business), whether financial or nonfinancial in nature. Accepting responsibility to perform a management function creates the threat to independence as stated in the interpretation.[17]

The following activities described by Allen are considered hosting services, and as such will impair independence if performed for an attest client, including responsibility for the following:

- Housing the attest client's website or other non-financial information on server(s) the firm leases.
- Keeping the attest client's data or records on behalf of the client, including the storage and safekeeping of the client's general and subsidiary ledgers, legal documents, and amortization and depreciation schedules, which are maintained on the CPA firm's server.
- Maintaining the original hard copies of the client's lease agreements in the CPA firm's facility.

The new interpretation applies to hard copy and electronic files, as both result in assumption of a management responsibility, which threatens independence.

Not all custody or control of a client's records results in hosting services, as a CPA may have to access, use, and/or take possession of a client's information when providing professional services. The key question is whether the CPA has accepted responsibility for maintaining custody or control of the information. For example, let's assume a CPA requests client records (e.g., time records and other employee payroll data), which he retains while preparing the client's payroll and related quarterly tax return. Once the engagement is completed, the CPA returns all original client records. He retains a copy of the tax return and any of the data he collected during the engagement that support his completed work product. Retaining copies of original documents does not impair independence.

Nontraditional Forms of Ownership

A variety of forms of organization exist today for providing professional accounting services to clients. For example, a traditional CPA firm may be acquired by a public company that will provide nonattest services to clients, while, at the same time, a spin-off of the original firm provides the attest services. The arrangement is necessary because only firms that are majority owned by CPAs can perform attest services. The problem with these so-called "alternative practice structures" is that the managers of the public company may attempt to exert pressure over those in the CPA firm because of their ownership leverage and because their ethical requirements are not likely to be as high as the ones for the CPAs. In these cases the CPAs remain responsible, financially and otherwise, for all the attest work performed.

Other forms of organization also provide ethical challenges for CPAs, including network firms where CPA firms join larger groups, which typically are membership associations that are legal separate entities otherwise unrelated to their members. Another is when the affiliate of a financial statement attest client is subject to the Independence Rule in the Code.

We expect new forms of organization will come into being as CPAs/CPA firms attempt to quench their seemingly never-ending thirst for more business and a broadened scope of professional services. This would not necessarily be a bad thing, in part because clients come to trust their auditors/audit firms. However, with the hiring of non-CPAs to service these clients, a legitimate question to raise is whether the CPA side of the practice can exercise restraint on the behavior of the non-CPAs when warranted.

Global Code of Ethics

We discussed the International Federation of Accountants (IFAC) and the International Ethics Standards Board for Accountants (IESBA) global code of ethics in Chapter 1. The global code is incorporated into *The Handbook of the Code of Ethics for Professional Accountants* and relies on the conceptual framework to evaluate all issues that may arise when specific rules do not address a matter. It also follows the threats and safeguards approach we discussed above.[18]

IFAC's "Fundamental Principles" of professional behavior differ slightly from the AICPA Code. The principles also describe the basic standards somewhat differently. The principles include:

Integrity. To be straightforward and honest in all professional and business relationships.

Objectivity. To not allow bias, conflict of interest, or undue influence of others to override professional or business judgment.

Professional Competence and Due Care. To maintain professional knowledge and skill at the level required to ensure that a client or employer receives competent professional service based on current developments in practice, legislation, and techniques and act diligently and in accordance with applicable technical and professional standards.

Confidentiality. To respect the confidentiality of information acquired as a result of professional and business relationships and therefore not disclose any such information to third parties without proper and specific authority, unless there is a legal or professional right or duty to disclose, nor use the information for the personal advantage of the professional accountant or third parties.

Professional Behavior. To comply with relevant laws and regulations and avoid any actions that discredits the profession.

The IFAC Code differs from the AICPA Code in that the former includes a separate principle for Confidentiality and one for Professional Behavior. The Confidentiality principle highlights growing concern with financial wrongdoing and laws such as SOX that protects whistleblowers from retaliation when reporting fraud against shareholders under Section 806. Reports to regulatory agencies such as the SEC would not violate confidentiality if it meets the required conditions as discussed in Chapter 3. The Professional Behavior principle recognizes the growing extent to which violations of ethics are due to non-practice issues that we discussed in the Introduction including federal and state convictions of crimes such as social crimes, discipline or sanctions by other agencies, and violations of state licensing requirements. We believe the AICPA Code would benefit from increasing the visibility of these principles as well.

SEC Actions on Auditor Independence

LO 4-4

Describe SEC actions taken against auditors for a lack of independence.

Publicly owned companies have been obligated to follow SEC rules since the passage of the Securities Act of 1933 and the Securities and Exchange Act of 1934. The PCAOB has taken some of that responsibility away from the SEC by establishing independence rules that are then approved by the SEC.

The SEC approach to independence emphasizes independence in fact and appearance in three ways: (1) proscribing certain financial interests and business relationships with the audit client, (2) restricting the provision of certain nonauditing services to audit clients, and (3) subjecting all auditor conduct to a general standard of independence. The general standard of independence is stated as follows: "The Commission will not recognize an accountant as independent, with respect to an audit client, if the accountant is not, or a reasonable investor with knowledge of all relevant facts and circumstances would conclude that the accountant is not, capable of exercising objective and impartial judgment on all issues encompassed within the accountant's engagement."

The general standard of independence is evaluated by applying four principles that are similar to the AICPA's conceptual framework and that indicate when auditor independence may be impaired by a relationship with the audit client. If a situation results in any of the following, the auditor's independence may be impaired: (1) creates a mutual or conflicting interest between an accountant and his audit client, (2) places an accountant in the position of auditing his own work, (3) results in an accountant acting as management or an employee of the audit client, or (4) places an accountant in a position of being an advocate for the audit client.

The SEC believes that these principles are "general guidance and their application may depend on particular facts and circumstances . . . [but they do] provide an appropriate framework for analyzing auditor independence issues." To provide further guidance on implementing the principles, the SEC identified three basic overarching principles that underlie auditor independence: (1) an auditor cannot function in the role of management, (2) an auditor cannot audit his own work, and (3) an auditor cannot serve in an advocacy role for his client.[19]

SEC Actions Against Audit Firms

The following describes actions taken by the SEC against audit firms during the past several years to provide examples of when threats to independence compromise professional judgment.

PwC and Logitech: Doing Governance, Risk, and Compliance Work for an Audit Client

On November 6, 2014, Logitech International S.A. filed a Form 8-K with the SEC informing it that its auditors, PwC, would not stand for re-election as Logitech's independent auditor because the firm had concluded it was not independent when it provided prohibited non-audit services to the audit client during the second quarter of Fiscal Year 2015. PwC took on a Governance, Risk, and Compliance (GRC) consulting engagement for Logitech, which PwC determined violated independence because its implementation of GRC software was designed to fix several material weaknesses in internal controls over financial reporting. PwC discussed the matter with Logitech's Audit Committee and they jointly agreed that PwC would give up the audit because the GRC engagement created a self-review threat to independence. Francine McKenna suggested that the firm gave up the audit engagement because "PwC decided it was more fun, less risky and more lucrative to consult with than audit" Logitech.[20] Perhaps PwC concluded that discretion was the better part of valor.

KPMG and Audit Clients: Performing Prohibited Nonaudit Services for an Audit Client

KPMG LLP agreed to pay $8.2 million on January 24, 2014, to settle charges by the SEC that the firm violated auditor independence rules by providing certain nonaudit services to affiliates of companies whose books KPMG was auditing. In audit reports, KPMG repeatedly represented that it was independent despite providing services at various times from 2007 to 2011 to three audit clients.[21]

"The prohibited services included restructuring, corporate finance, and expert services—to an affiliate of one company that was an audit client," the SEC stated. KPMG provided such prohibited nonaudit services as bookkeeping and payroll to affiliates of another audit client. These relationships created a self-review threat to independence.

In a separate instance, KPMG hired an individual who had recently retired from a senior position at an affiliate of an audit client. KPMG then loaned him back to that affiliate to do the same work he had done as an employee of that affiliate, which resulted in the professional acting as a manager, employee, and advocate for the audit client. An SEC investigation also revealed some KPMG personnel owned stock in companies or affiliates of companies that were KPMG audit clients, further violating auditor independence rules.

The SEC settlement reported that—without admitting or denying the findings—KPMG agreed to pay $5,266,347 in disgorgement of fees received from the three clients plus prejudgment interest of $1,185,002 and an additional penalty of $1,775,000. In addition, KPMG agreed to implement internal changes to educate firm personnel and monitor the firm's compliance with auditor independence requirements for nonaudit services and that an independent consultant would evaluate these changes.

Deloitte Consulting's Business Relationship with Audit Client Management

On July 1, 2015, the SEC charged Deloitte & Touche LLP with violating auditor independence rules when its consulting affiliate kept a business relationship with a trustee serving on the boards and audit committees of three funds Deloitte audited. Deloitte agreed to pay more than $1 million to settle the charges. Deloitte also disgorged to the SEC audit fees of nearly $500,000 plus prejudgment interest of about $116,000, and it paid a penalty of $500,000.[22]

Deloitte violated its own policies by failing to conduct an independence consultation before starting a new business relationship with trustee Andrew C. Boynton. Deloitte failed to discover that the required initial independence consultation was not performed until nearly five years after the independence-impairing relationship had been established between Deloitte Consulting and Boynton, who was paid consulting fees for his external client work.

Deloitte compromised its independence because the relationship made it appear that the firm may not be objective and impartial in conducting its audit of the three funds. Deloitte represented in audit reports that it was independent of the three funds while Boynton simultaneously served on their boards and audit committees.

Ernst & Young Lobbies on Behalf of Audit Clients

On July 14, 2014, Ernst & Young was sanctioned by the SEC for lobbying on behalf of two of its audit clients, thereby serving as an advocate for an audit client. In the case of one audit client, identified by the SEC only as Client A, the commission cited three lobbying efforts. It said EY had informed the client that a bill was scheduled to be voted on in the House of Representatives and arranged for a letter supporting the legislation to be delivered to legislative staff members before the vote was taken. In the second effort, the firm sent a letter to legislative leaders recommending legislation the client wanted, and in the third case it sought an amendment to pending legislation. There was no indication that any of those efforts had any practical effect.

These cases against the Big Four raise the red flag about consulting services and possible impairments of audit independence. CPA firms have to be more attentive to possible impairments of audit independence as they increase the nature and scope of nonaudit services provided to audit clients. Biases can creep into the decision making in a subtle way and compromise independent judgment.

EY Audit Partners Engage in Relationships With Client Personnel

On September 20, 2016, the SEC announced that EY had agreed to pay $9.3 million in total to settle charges against three of the firm's audit partners that engaged in relationships that created familiarity threats to independence. In one case, Gregory Bednar, a former senior partner on the engagement team of a public company client, "maintained an improperly close friendship" with the company's CFO, thus violating rules that ensure objectivity and impartiality during audits. Bednar reportedly spent close to $100,000 in travel and entertainment expenses between 2012-2015 while socializing with the CFO and his family. The firm was aware of the expenses but did nothing. Without admitting or denying the findings, Bednar and EY consented to the SEC order. The firm agreed to pay $4.975 million in monetary sanctions for the violations. Bednar agreed to a $45,000 penalty and was suspended from appearing and practicing before the SEC as an accountant for three years, but was allowed to apply for reinstatement after that time.[23]

Non–Big Four Firms Not Immune to Independence Violations

In what appears to be a common problem, at least for non–Big Four firms, on December 8, 2014, the SEC sanctioned eight firms and the PCAOB separately sanctioned seven others for violating auditor independence rules when they prepared the financial statements of brokerage firms that were their audit clients. The PCAOB said its enforcement actions grew out of information gathered by the board's inspection program. "The bedrock of audit quality is independence," said PCAOB chairman James Doty in a statement. "When an auditor's independence is impaired, the auditor's responsibility to exercise professional skepticism, and to serve the public trust, is also put at risk. Adhering to independence requirements is critically important."[24]

In the SEC action, the agency found that during audits the eight firms relied on data from financial statements and notes that the audit firms themselves had prepared for the clients. That meant the audit firms were auditing their own work, thereby creating a self-review threat to independence, and they inappropriately aligned themselves more closely with the interests of clients' management teams in helping prepare the books rather than strictly auditing them.

Insider Trading Cases

What possesses an accounting professional to trade on inside information or give tips about it to others and violate the accounting profession's most sacred ethical standard of audit independence? Is it carelessness, greed, or ethical blindness? Perhaps a bit of all three.

SEC rules 10b5-1 and 10b5-2 address insider trading situations. Insider trading refers generally to buying or selling a security, in breach of a fiduciary duty or other relationship of trust and confidence, while in possession of material, nonpublic information about the security. Insider trading violations may also include "tipping" such information, securities trading by the person "tipped," and securities trading by those who misappropriate and take advantage of confidential information of one's employer. Tipping includes providing confidential information of a client to one's family, business associates, and friends. An insider is responsible for assuring that his or her family members comply with insider trading laws. An insider may make trades in the market or discuss material information only after the material information has been made public.[25]

Under AICPA rules, CPAs are prohibited from disclosing or using confidential client information for their benefit because it impairs the independence of the CPA or CPA firm. A CPA who acquires securities of a client violates independence with respect to the client both individually and for the CPA firm because of the financial self-interest threat. A CPA in public practice should not disclose any confidential client information without the specific consent of the client. (1.700.001).

Insider trading rules apply to CPAs because all partners and employees (including non-CPA staff) are fiduciaries for all clients of the firm regardless of whether they perform audit or nonaudit services. Insider trading, including providing tips to others, violates the relationship of trust and confidence with the client. CPAs are required to maintain confidentiality of any confidential information obtained from an employer as well.

An act discreditable occurs when, in the course of providing professional services for one's employer, a CPA violates the confidentiality of his or her employer's or firm's confidential information and discloses any confidential information obtained as a result of an employment relationship, such as discussions with the employer's vendors, customers, or lenders (1.400.070).

Mayank Gupta, PwC

On September 13, 2017, the SEC announced that Mayank Gupta, a former auditor with PwC, agreed to settle charges he tipped his relative with inside information about a client on the verge of a merger. Cavium, a San Jose, California client, was making imminent preparations to acquire QLogic, an Aliso Viejo, California-based Corporation. Before the deal was announced to the public, Gupta called his cousin-in-law and told him Cavium was going to acquire QLogic and that QLogic was a "sure thing." The cousin immediately purchased call options in QLogic. QLogic's stock rose by more than nine percent, and the cousin profited by more than $23,785 from the illegal trades.[26]

Unlicensed Audit Staff Member

On March 14, 2017, the SEC agreed to accept an Offer of Settlement by Nima Hedayati, a junior audit staff member of a PCAOB-registered independent auditor. Hedayati had passed the CPA exam but did not hold a CPA license. Hedayati learned, in the course of her employment, material nonpublic information regarding a planned acquisition by Lam Research Corporation, a client entity, of KLA-Tencor Corporation. Soon thereafter, Hedayati purchased a total of 40 contracts for out-of-the-money KLA call options, both in his account and in the account of his then-fiancee. Hedayati also advised his mother to trade KLA, and on the basis of this suggestion, his mother purchased 1,400 shares of KLA common stock. On October 21, 2015, Lam and KLA issued a joint press release announcing their entry into a merger agreement. Shares of KLA closed that day at $63.98, up 19% from the previous day's close of $53.86. Collectively, Hedayati and his mother profited from the illegal trades by approximately $43,000.[27]

Thomas W. Avent, a Tax Partner

Thomas W. Avent, Jr. was a tax partner at an unidentified international accounting firm who led a practice group that performed due diligence in connection with pending mergers and acquisitions. Through his work, Avent learned secret, proprietary, carefully guarded information about upcoming acquisitions, including tender offers for publicly-traded companies. In 2011 and 2012, Avent tipped his stock broker about three acquisitions and the broker, in turn, passed the tips on to his former colleague and a friend. The friend then arranged to buy stocks or call options of the three target companies before the acquisitions were announced to the public. As a result, the broker got an illegal jump on other investors, and he and his family made over $111,000 in illicit insider-trading profits.

Scott London, KPMG

In the case of Scott London, the former partner in charge of the KPMG's Southern California regional audit practice, it seems greed and stupidity were the underlying causes of insider trading. On April 11, 2013, the SEC charged London with leaking confidential information to his friend, Brian Shaw, about Skechers and Herbalife. Shaw, a jewelry store owner and country club friend of London, repaid London with $50,000 in cash and a Rolex watch, according to legal filings.

After federal regulators froze Shaw's investment account because of suspicious activity, the jeweler fully confessed, paid back nearly $2 million in illegally gained profits and fines to the SEC, and cooperated in the investigation against London.

London was sentenced to 14 months in a federal prison and forced to pay a $100,000 fine. He also was fired from his $900,000-a-year job as an auditor for KPMG in 2012, and the company was forced to redo several of London's prior audits. The audit opinions signed by London on Skechers and Herbalife had to be withdrawn by the firm.

Thomas Flannigan, Deloitte & Touche

In 2010, Deloitte and Touche found itself involved in an SEC investigation of repeated insider trading by Thomas P. Flanagan, a former management advisory partner and a vice chairman at Deloitte. Flanagan traded in the securities of multiple Deloitte clients on the basis of inside information that he learned through his duties as a Deloitte partner. The inside information concerned market-moving events such as earnings results, revisions to earnings guidance, sales figures and cost cutting, and an acquisition. Flanagan's illegal trading resulted in profits of more than $430,000.

Flanagan also tipped his son, Patrick, to certain of this material nonpublic information. Patrick then traded based on that information. Patrick's illegal trading resulted in profits of more than $57,000. The SEC charges included: (1) Between 2003 and 2008, Flanagan made 71 purchases of stock and options in the securities of Deloitte audit clients. Flanagan made 62 of these purchases in the securities of Deloitte audit clients while serving as the advisory partner on those audits; and (2) on at least nine occasions between 2005 and 2008, Flanagan traded on the basis of material nonpublic information of Deloitte clients, including Best Buy, Motorola, Sears, and Option Care.

These insider trading cases illustrate the risk to audit independence when audit engagement team members, including partners, trade on information that is not publicly available. Beyond that, the use of sensitive financial information about a client for personal reasons violates the independence requirement because it creates a financial self-interest relationship between the partner and the client.

The leaking of confidential financial information about a company to anyone prior to its public release affects the level playing field that should exist with respect to personal and business contacts of an auditor and the general public. It violates the fairness doctrine in treating equals equally, and it violates basic integrity standards. Such actions cut to the core values of integrity and trust—the foundation of the public interest obligation of CPAs.

The increase in insider trading cases is troubling. The extent of the disclosure and subsequent trades seem to have no bounds, with audit partners, tax partners, management personnel at firms and even an unlicensed staff member all becoming embroiled in independence violations. Insider trading by the accounting professional, tips to one's broker, family members, and friends together illustrate the scope of the problem. We believe the SEC and AICPA should include these kinds of transactions as acts discreditable to the profession, as well as independence violations, to emphasize the social crime nature of these rule violations.

"Operation Broken Gate"

In October 2013, the SEC announced the launch of "Operation Broken Gate"—an initiative to identify auditors who neglect their duties and the required auditing standards. Operation Broken Gate is the SEC's effort to hold gatekeepers accountable. Around the same time, the SEC announced its "focus on auditors" program to increase its efforts to identify independence violations. The trigger event was the filing of multiple auditor independence cases whereby the firms loaned staff to their audit clients, similar to the KPMG case above. Technically, an independent auditor may loan staff to its client and clearly the auditor may provide tax services to its client. But if the loaned staff looks like a client employee, regardless of the services provided, the SEC may conclude the arrangement violates the independence rules.

The SEC's concerns go beyond independence violations. The underlying conduct that motivated Operation Broken Gate centers on a failure to comply with the pertinent professional standards. Cases have been filed against CPAs/CPA firms for a lack of due care, failure to obtain sufficient competent evidential matter, failure to properly assess audit risk, insufficient documentation of audit procedures in work papers, failure to properly assess internal controls, failure to perform an engagement quality review, and failure to communicate certain information with the audit committee. The possibility that audit firms are doing sloppy work is concerning.

AICPA Code: Ethical Conflicts

LO 4-5

Describe the process to resolve ethical conflicts that may cause violations of the rules.

Under the AICPA Code, when evaluating whether a CPA in public practice is in compliance with the rules, a CPA should assess whether an ethical conflict exists. Ethical Conflicts (1.000.020) create challenges to ethical decision making because they present barriers to meeting the requirements of the rules of conduct. An ethical conflict may exist, for example, if a CPA in public practice suspects a fraud may have occurred, but reporting the suspected fraud would violate the confidentiality obligation.

Exhibit 4.3 identifies the major considerations for CPAs in assessing the risk that ethical conflicts may lead to a violation of the rules of conduct. Briefly, the CPA should consider whether any departures exist to the rules, laws, or regulations and how they will be justified in order to ensure that conflicts are resolved in a way that permits compliance with these requirements. Resolution of the conflict may call for consulting with others in the entity or others, including legal counsel. Any unresolved conflicts can lead to a violation of the rules of conduct, which, in turn, should focus the CPA's attention on any continuing relationship with the engagement team, specific assignment, client, firm, or employer.

EXHIBIT 4.3   **Ethical Conflicts and Compliance with the Rules of Conduct for Members in Public Practice and Business***

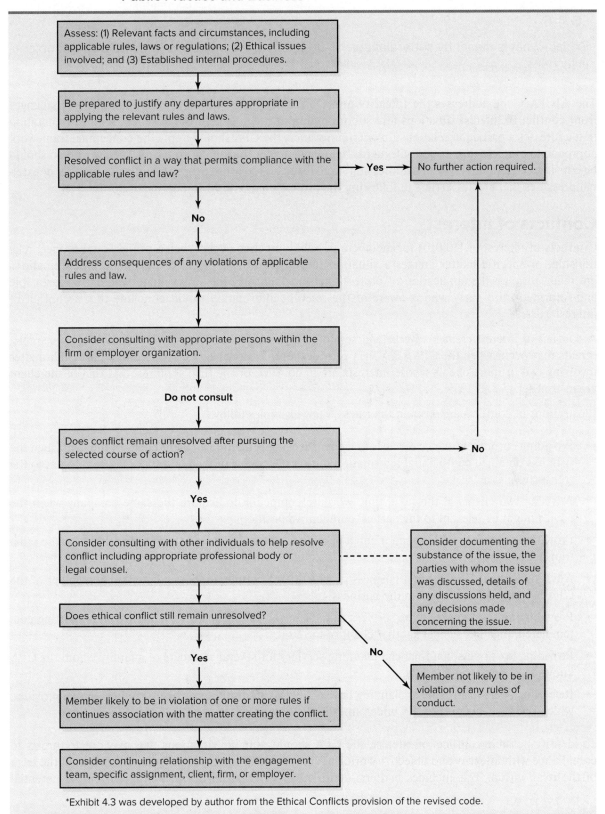

*Exhibit 4.3 was developed by author from the Ethical Conflicts provision of the revised code.

Integrity and Objectivity

LO 4-6

Explain what is meant by subordination of judgment in the context of the integrity and objectivity rules.

The AICPA Code addresses the Integrity and Objectivity Rule (1.100.001) by linking it to challenges from conflict of interest situations and subordination of judgment. In the absence of an interpretation that addresses a particular relationship or circumstance, the CPA should apply the conceptual framework approach to evaluate threats and safeguards. Guidance under the ethical conflicts framework also should be considered (Exhibit 4.3) when addressing such obstacles to ensure proper handling of internal or external pressures that create barriers to following the professional or legal standards, or both.

Conflicts of Interest

Conflicts of interest (1.110.010) for members in public practice occur when a professional service, relationship, or specific matter creates a situation that might impair objective judgment. Determinations are made through the application of professional judgment in order to evaluate whether a reasonable and informed third party who is aware of the relevant information would conclude that a conflict of interest exists.

A conflict of interest creates adverse and self-interest threats to integrity and objectivity. For example, threats may occur when the CPA/CPA firm provides a professional service related to a particular matter involving two or more clients whose interests are in conflict, or the firm's interest and that of the client are in conflict.

Illustrations of conflicts are given in the rules. A few examples follow.

- Providing corporate finance services to a client seeking to acquire an audit client of the firm when the firm has obtained confidential information during the course of the audit that may be relevant to the transaction.

- Advising two clients at the same time who are competing to acquire the same company when the advice might be relevant to the parties' competitive positions.

- Providing services to both a vendor and a purchaser who are clients of the firm in relation to the same transaction.

- Advising a client to invest in a business in which, for example, the immediate family member of the CPA has a financial interest in the business.

- Providing forensic investigation services to a client for the purpose of evaluating or supporting contemplated litigation against another client of the firm.

- Providing tax or personal financial planning services for several members of a family whom the CPA knows have opposing interests.

- Referring a personal financial planning or tax client to an insurance broker or other service provider, which refers clients to the CPA under an exclusive arrangement.

To identify possible conflicts of interest, the CPA should examine situations that may create threats to compliance with integrity and objectivity prior to acceptance of the engagement and throughout the term of the relationship. This includes matters identified by external parties including current or potential clients. The earlier a potential conflict is identified, the greater the likelihood of applying safeguards to eliminate or reduce significant threats to an acceptable level. If the threat has not been eliminated or reduced to an acceptable level, then appropriate safeguards should be applied to ensure acting with objectivity and integrity.

Examples of safeguards include: (1) implementing mechanisms to prevent unauthorized disclosure of confidential information of one or more clients when performing professional services for two or more clients whose interests conflict; (2) regularly reviewing the application of safeguards by a senior individual not involved in the engagements; (3) having a member of the firm not involved in providing the services or otherwise affected by the conflict review the work performed to assess whether key judgments and conclusions are appropriate; and (4) consulting with third parties, such as a professional body, legal counsel, or another professional accountant.

In cases where identified threats are so significant that no safeguards will eliminate them or reduce them to an acceptable level, or adequate safeguards cannot be implemented, the CPA should either decline to perform the service that would result in the conflict of interest, terminate the relevant relationship, or dispose of the relevant interests to eliminate the threat or reduce it to an acceptable level.

When a conflict of interest exists, the CPA should disclose the nature of the conflict to clients and other appropriate parties affected by the client and obtain their consent to perform professional services even if threats are at an acceptable level. If consent is not received, then the CPA should either cease performing the services or take action to eliminate or reduce the threat to an acceptable level.

An example of a potential conflict of interest is when a CPA offers gifts to clients or accepts gifts or entertainment from a client. Threats need to be evaluated as well as the significance of any such threats and safeguards that might mitigate their effects. Such situations may create self-interest, familiarity, or undue influence threats to compliance with the Integrity and Objectivity Rule.

Generally, gifts are differentiated from entertainment by whether the client participates in the activity with the firm. For example, giving tickets to a sporting event for the client to use would be considered a gift versus attending the event with the client, which would be considered entertainment. The determining factor as to whether the threats created by the gifts are at an acceptable or unacceptable level is the reasonableness of the circumstances, taking into consideration the nature of the gift or entertainment; occasion for which it is provided; cost or value; whether the entertainment was associated with the active conduct of business directly before, during, or after the entertainment; and the individuals from the client and the CPA's firm who participated in the entertainment.

Let's assume your client comes to your office one day. You are the partner in charge of the audit for the client. The client wants to show his appreciation for the audit engagement team's completion of the audit one week early and under budget. He gives you a dozen tickets for the baseball game between the Los Angeles Angels of Anaheim and L.A. Dodgers. It is just a regular, inter-league game and has no significance beyond that. Can you accept the gift?

If the audit is completed, the first question is whether the acceptance of the gift might make it appear to a reasonable observer that the gift is intended to influence the audit opinion. If so, that would create an undue influence threat and compromise integrity and objectivity. Also, it could be perceived as an advance payoff for future audit opinions. The influence does not have to be immediate. Beyond that, the key issue to consider is: Would acceptance violate any laws, regulations, or firm policies? If so, acceptance would create a threat that cannot be reduced or eliminated through any safeguards. If not, consider the following:

- What is the nature, value, and intent of the gift?
- Is it more than clearly inconsequential?

- Is it reasonable in the circumstances?
- Is it standard practice to accept or reject such gifts?
- Does the client expect a "quid pro quo"?

Ethically speaking, a good way to approach the issue is to, first, apply the "feel" test. If you have an uncomfortable feeling about the relationship and think it may influence others' opinions of you, don't get involved. Second, ask whether you would be comfortable explaining why you agreed to accept the gifts if you were questioned by a superior or a newspaper reporter? Third, you don't want to place yourself in a position where you have to "rationalize away" accepting a gift, which is increasingly challenged as being against the rules. Finally, remember to avoid taking the first step down the ethical slippery slope by having to justify your action even though you know it was wrong.

Subordination of Judgment

The Integrity Rule prohibits a CPA from knowingly misrepresenting facts or subordinating one's judgments when performing professional services for a client or employer. The Subordination of Judgment (1.130.020) interpretation addresses differences of opinion between a CPA and that person's supervisor or others within the organization. Originally, the interpretation was restricted to matters between internal accountants and supervisors but was extended in the revised code and now it also applies to external CPA auditors when differences of opinion exist between external auditors and senior management of the firm. The rule recognizes that pressures may be imposed by superiors in an accounting firm on an engagement team member because firm management is unaware of, unable to, or unwilling to reexamine its own conclusions regarding an accounting position that would result in a materially different financial statement presentation or footnote disclosure than that which the engagement team member believes accords with professional standards.

Differences of opinion on accounting matters can raise whistleblowing considerations, as was discussed in Chapter 3. Exhibit 3.11 describes the steps that should be taken by accounting professionals when faced with situations where differences of opinion exist in order to avoid subordinating judgment. A summary of the steps and related considerations follow.

- Consider any threats to integrity and objectivity including self-interest, familiarity, and undue influence threats and assess their significance.
- Evaluate the significance of threats to determine if they are at an acceptable level: Significance relates to whether the result of the position taken by the supervisor or other person fails to comply with applicable professional standards, creates a material misrepresentation of fact, or may violate applicable laws or regulations.
- If threats are at an acceptable level, discuss the conclusion with the person taking the position; if not at an acceptable level, bring concerns to supervisor.
- If differences of opinion are not resolved, discuss the matter with higher levels of management (i.e., supervisor's immediate superior, senior management, and those charged with governance).
- If appropriate action is not taken, consider the following safeguards to ensure that the threats are reduced to an acceptable level to avoid subordination of judgment:
  - Determine whether the organization's internal policies and procedures have any additional requirements for reporting differences of opinion.
  - Determine any reporting responsibilities to third parties, if applicable, and whether communication of confidentiality to the internal accountant/auditor employer or organization's external accountant are required.

- ■ Consult with legal counsel regarding responsibilities.
- ■ Document understanding of facts, accounting principles, auditing, other professional standards involved, applicable laws or regulations, and the conversations and parties with whom such matters were discussed.
- • If the CPA concludes that no safeguards can eliminate or reduce the threats to an acceptable level or that appropriate action was not taken, then consider whether to continue the relationship with the organization and take steps to eliminate exposure to any subordination of judgment.
- • Consider resigning from the organization, but that would not relieve the CPA from any reporting responsibilities to third parties, such as regulatory authorities or the employer's (former employer's) external accountant.

The threats and safeguards approach also applies to nonattest services performed for an attest client because they may cause an impairment of independence. These threats include self-review, management participation, and advocacy. When significant independence threats exist during the period of the professional engagement or the period covered by the financial statements, independence will be impaired unless the threats are reduced to an acceptable level and any other requirements are met as previously discussed. One final note, the rules recognize that, while one kind of nonattest service may not be significant enough individually to impair independence because adequate safeguards exist, the cumulative effect of multiple nonattest services can increase the significance of these threats as well as other threats to independence.

The broad scope of the threats and safeguards approach also reaches to tax services provided to an attest client. These services include preparation of a tax return and the transmittal of the return and any related payment to the taxing authority in paper or electronic form. Self-review and management participation threats to compliance with the Independence Rule may exist.

Threats would be at an acceptable level and independence would not be impaired provided the CPA does not have custody or control over the attest client's funds or assets and the individual designated by the client to oversee the tax services reviews and approves the return and related tax payment and, if required, signs the tax return prior to the CPA's transmitting it to the taxing authority.

Professional judgment is essential in applying the conceptual framework to independence, integrity and objectivity, and other professional requirements through evaluations of the significance of threats, whether they can be reduced to an acceptable level, and the steps to be taken to resolve differences of opinion on accounting issues with management of the employer or one's CPA firm. In making these determinations, the CPA must not only apply the "letter of the law" approach to the rules of conduct but also the spirit of the rules by asking: What is expected of me by the public as a CPA?

AICPA Code: Conceptual Framework for Members in Business

LO 4-7

Describe the rules of conduct that pertain to CPAs in business.

A major improvement in the revised AICPA Code is it now includes new material for CPAs in business to evaluate whether relationships may exist between the CPA and the employing organization that create threats to compliance with the Integrity and Objectivity Rule. The conceptual framework for members in business (2.000.010) applies to integrity and objectivity, as well as other rules of conduct, but not independence, because CPAs in business do not provide attest services to clients that require complete independence.

Similar to the guidance for CPAs in public practice, the threats and safeguards approach for CPAs in business identifies a variety of threats to compliance with the Integrity and Objectivity Rule, and other professional requirements, that create the need for safeguards to reduce the threat to an acceptable level or eliminate it. These threats and safeguards are different than those for CPAs in public practice. The examples below illustrate the differences.

Threats and Safeguards

Adverse interest threat. These threats to objectivity arise because the CPA's interests may be opposed to the interests of the employing organization. For instance, a CPA may have charged, or expressed an intention to charge, the employing organization with violations of law. The threat that arises is the result of the ethical conflict. An example would be if a CPA made a whistleblowing charge against the employer under SOX or Dodd-Frank. Other threats may exist because a CPA's or the CPA's immediate family or close relative has a financial or other relationship with a vendor, customer, competitor, or potential acquisition of the employing organization and when a CPA has sued or expressed an intention to sue the employing organization or its officers, directors, or employees.

Advocacy threat. Advocacy threats exist because a CPA may promote an employing organization's interests or position to the point that his objectivity is compromised. This would be the case if obtaining favorable financing or additional capital is dependent upon the accuracy of information included in or excluded from a prospectus, an offering, a business plan, a financing application, or a regulatory filing.

Familiarity threat. A familiarity threat arises from a long or close relationship with a person or an employing organization that causes a CPA to become too sympathetic to the latter's interests or too accepting of the person's or employing organization's product or service. Some examples include when a CPA uses an immediate family member's or a close relative's company as a supplier to the employing organization and when a CPA regularly accepts gifts or entertainment from a vendor or customer of the employing organization.

Self-interest threat. The existence of a self-interest threat means that a CPA could benefit, financially or otherwise, from an interest in or relationship with the employing organization or persons associated with the employing organization, such as when a CPA holds a financial interest in the employing organization and the value of that financial interest is directly affected by the CPA's decisions, as would be the case if the financial interest is in the form of shares or share options.

Self-review threat. A self-review threat may occur when a CPA is unable to appropriately evaluate the results of a previous judgment made or service performed or supervised by the CPA, or an individual in the employing organization, and the CPA relies on that service in forming a judgment as part of another service. An example is when performing an internal audit procedure, an internal auditor accepts work that he previously performed in a different position.

Undue influence threat. These threats occur because a CPA subordinates his judgment to that of an individual associated with the employing organization or any relevant third party due to that individual's position, reputation or expertise, aggressive or dominant personality, or attempts to coerce or exercise excessive influence over the CPA. An example is when a CPA is pressured to become associated with misleading information or to change a conclusion regarding an accounting or tax position.

The safeguards to reduce the threats to compliance with the rules for CPAs in business, or reduce them to an acceptable level, are different from those for CPAs in public practice. For CPAs in business, the safeguards are implemented by the employing organization not the firm, and client safeguards are not applicable.

Safeguards implemented by the employing organization include:

1. a tone at the top that emphasizes a commitment to fair financial reporting and compliance with applicable laws, rules, regulations, and corporate governance policies;

2. policies and procedures addressing ethical conduct and compliance with laws, rules, and regulations;

3. an audit committee charter, including independent audit committee members;

4. internal policies and procedures requiring disclosure of identified interests or relationships among the employing organization, its directors or officers, vendors, suppliers, or customers;

5. dissemination of corporate ethical compliance policies and procedures, including whistleblower hotlines, the reporting structure, dispute resolution, or similar policies to promote compliance with laws, rules, regulations, and other professional requirements;

6. policies and procedures for implementing and monitoring ethical practices;

7. a reporting structure whereby the internal auditor does not report to the financial reporting group;

8. policies and procedures that do not allow an internal auditor to monitor areas where the internal auditor has operational or functional responsibilities;

9. policies for promotion, rewards, and enforcement of a culture of high ethics and integrity; and

10. use of the third-party resources for consultation as needed on significant matters of professional judgment.

Ethical Conflicts

Similar to CPAs in public practice, ethical conflicts (2.000.020) for CPAs in business may arise that create threats to compliance with some or all of the rules of conduct. An ethical conflict occurs when obstacles to following an appropriate course of action exist due to internal or external pressures and/or conflicts exist in applying relevant professional and legal standards. Steps should be taken to best achieve compliance with the rules and laws by weighing the following factors: relevant facts and circumstances, ethical issues involved, and established internal procedures. CPAs in business must be prepared to justify any departures they believe may be appropriate in applying the relevant rules and laws. The failure to resolve the conflict in a way that permits compliance with the applicable rules and laws should lead the CPA to address the consequences of any violations. Beyond that, the process is similar to that for CPAs in public practice: consulting with appropriate persons within the organization; considering contacting an appropriate professional body or legal counsel for advice; documenting the findings and discussions; and, if necessary, considering whether to remain with the employer. Exhibit 4.3 describes the steps to be taken to deal with ethical conflicts and avoid violating the rules.

Integrity and Objectivity/Conflicts of Interest

The Integrity and Objectivity Rule (2.100.001) is similar to that for CPAs in public practice. It requires avoidance of conflicts of interest and not subordinating judgment to others as might be the case if a controller were pressured by a CFO to go along with misstated financial statements. The threats and safeguards framework is used when the rules or interpretations do not specifically address an issue.

A conflict of interest (2.000.020) for CPAs in business creates adverse interest and self-interest threats to compliance with the Integrity and Objectivity Rule. Examples include:

- Undertaking a professional service related to a particular matter involving two or more parties (i.e., vendors) whose interests with respect to that matter are in conflict; or

- Interests of the CPA with respect to the particular matter and the interests of a party for whom the services are undertaken related to that matter are in conflict (i.e., lender or shareholder).

An example of a situation in which conflicts of interest may arise is acquiring confidential information from one employing organization that could be used by the CPA to the advantage or disadvantage of the other employing organization.

When a conflict of interest has been identified, the CPA should apply the threats and safeguards approach. In general, the more direct the connection between the CPA and the matter causing the conflict, the more significant the threat to compliance with integrity and objectivity will be.

When a conflict of interest exists, the CPA should disclose the nature of the conflict to the relevant parties, including the appropriate levels within the employing organization and obtain their consent to undertake the professional service. This should be done even if the threat is at an acceptable level.

Threats to compliance with the Integrity and Objectivity Rule would not be at an acceptable level and could not be reduced to an acceptable level by the application of safeguards, and the CPA would be considered to have knowingly misrepresented facts in violation of the rule if the CPA:

- Makes, or permits or directs another party to make, materially false and misleading entries in an entity's financial statements or records;
- Fails to correct an entity's financial statements or records that are materially false and misleading when the CPA has the authority to record the entries; or
- Signs, or permits or directs another to sign, a document containing materially false and misleading information.

Subordination of Judgment

The Integrity and Objectivity Rule prohibits a CPA from knowingly misrepresenting facts or subordinating judgment when performing professional services for an employer. Self-interest, familiarity, and undue influence threats to compliance with the rule may exist when a CPA and the supervisor, or any other person within the organization, have a difference of opinion relating to the application of accounting principles; auditing standards; or other relevant standards, including standards applicable to tax and consulting services or applicable laws or regulations. The process to follow to resolve the difference is similar to that previously discussed for CPAs in public practice as depicted in Exhibit 3.11.

The Integrity and Objectivity Rule also requires the CPA in business (i.e., CFO) to be candid when dealing with the employer's external accountant and not knowingly misrepresent facts or knowingly fail to disclose material facts. This would include, for example, falsely certifying the financial statements under Section 302 of SOX.

Link between Conceptual Framework and Giving Voice to Values

The conceptual framework approach that underlies the ethical standards for CPAs in public practice and business is consistent with the thought process of the Giving Voice to Values methodology. For example, in bringing one's concerns to higher-ups in the organization, the goal should be to convince the appropriate party or parties that the position taken is the best one from both ethical and professional perspectives. In deciding what to say, how to say it, and to whom the discussion should be directed, the CPA should consider what the likely objections and pushbacks might be and how they can effectively be counteracted. Similarly, to meet one's professional responsibilities under the Integrity and Objectivity Rule, the CPA must convince others of the most ethical action.

Let's look at an example. Carl Kilgore is a CPA and the assistant controller of Linkage, Inc., a public company. He oversees the accounting for construction jobs for his company. One job has just been completed and the bill was prepared by the accounting department. Before Carl can even see it, the controller

(Jack Long), who is also a CPA, drops by and tells Carl to pad the bill by 50%. It seems this particular client never scrutinizes the bills from Linkage, Inc. because of a long-standing relationship of trust. In fact, this is the first time to your knowledge that any such padding has occurred. What would you do if you were Carl Kilgore and why?

Application of the conceptual framework calls for discussing the threat to integrity and objectivity with his supervisor, who is Jack Long, and trying to convince him to eliminate the padding. This may be a futile attempt, but, still, Carl should reason out his options because he can use it to bring the matter to those above Carl, if necessary. Carl reflects on the following:

- What are the main arguments by Jack you are trying to counter?
- What is at stake for the key parties, including those who disagree with you?
- What levers can you use to influence those who disagree with you?
- What is your most effective response to the reasons and rationalizations you need to address? To whom should the argument be made? When and in what context?

Carl's an ethical guy and he doesn't want to get caught up in a fraud or cover-up so he carefully develops a game plan to counteract Jack's request to pad the bill. Carl should drive home the point that the financials will be fraudulent if Jack's request is honored. Jack should be reminded that both he and Carl have ethical responsibilities to be objective in preparing the financial statements and Carl needs to maintain his integrity in light of Jack's request to falsify the statements. Carl should also point out the potential harm to the construction company of being billed for 150% of the correct amount and how it may react, and possible implications for trust and the reputation of Linkage, Inc. Carl may also have the option of using a hotline to report any unresolved differences. Carl's ultimate goal is to present the most convincing case in order to avoid the need to blow the whistle externally, either to the outside auditors or the regulatory authorities. Carl's most effective tool may be to emphasize the SOX Section 302 requirements for the CFO and CEO, and use them as leverage because, presumably, they would not want to commit fraud by falsely certifying the financial statements.

Rules for the Performance of Professional Services

LO 4-8

Explain the rules of conduct in the AICPA Code that pertain to the performance of professional services.

The remaining sections of the Code address ethics rules dealing with the performance of professional services for clients or one's employer. The standards for CPAs in public practice and those in business are similar with a few exceptions noted below. The rules are as follows:

- General Standards (1.300)
- Acts Discreditable (1.400)
- Fees and Other Types of Remuneration (1.500)
- Advertising and Other Forms of Solicitation (1.600)
- Confidential Information (1.700)
- Form of Organization and Name (1.800)

The conceptual framework applies to these rules in order to identify threats and safeguards when specific interpretations do not address a particular situation. If the CPA cannot demonstrate that safeguards were applied and eliminated or reduced threats to an acceptable level, then there would be a violation of the rules.

General Standards Rule (1.300.001)

The General Standards Rule establishes requirements for competence, compliance with professional standards, and adherence to accounting principles.

Competence (1.300.010)

Competence means having the appropriate technical qualifications to perform professional services and proper supervision and evaluation of the quality of work performed. While a reasonable care standard exists, CPAs are not expected to be infallible of knowledge or judgment.

To meet the competency standard, CPAs must be sensitive to situations when one's capabilities are limited and the conservative action may be to recommend another practitioner to perform the services. For example, a CPA or CPA firm should not undertake an audit of a school district without sufficient knowledge of generally accepted government accounting and auditing standards. Think of it this way: An accounting student who works on a group project with other students to develop a business plan might feel comfortable working on the financial plan, but presumably that student would not want to be responsible for developing the marketing plan. He would expect a marketing student to assume that responsibility.

The competence standard for CPAs in business includes a requirement that when a CPA who is a stockholder, partner, director, officer, or employee of an entity prepares or submits the entity's financial statements to third parties, the CPA should clearly communicate, preferably in writing, the CPA's relationship to the entity and should not imply that he is independent of the entity. In addition, if the communication states affirmatively that the financial statements are presented in conformity with the applicable financial reporting framework, the CPA should comply with the Accounting Principles Rule. It is important for CPAs in business to take note of these requirements because from time to time they may be asked to prepare and submit financial statements to support a loan request of the employer.

One interpretation of the competence standard establishes the requirements for the use of a third-party service provider (i.e., outsourcing). This occurs most often with bookkeeping services, tax preparation, or consulting services, including related clerical or data entry functions. The interpretation requires:

- Verifying that the third-party service provider has the required professional qualifications, technical skills, and other resources before engaging their services.
- Adequately planning and supervising the provider's services to ensure they are performed with competence and due care.
- Obtain sufficient relevant data to support the work product and comply with all technical standards applicable to professional services.
- Threats to compliance with the Integrity and Objectivity Rule should be considered.
- Confidentiality of client information must be secured.

Clients may not be aware of the use of a third-party service provider so before confidential information is provided to the service provider, the CPA should inform the client, preferably in writing, that a third-party service provider may be used and seek the client's approval. If the client objects, the CPA either should not use the service provider to perform professional services or should decline to perform the engagement.

A CPA is not required to inform the client when using a third-party service provider to provide administrative support services to the CPA (e.g., record storage, software application hosting, or authorized e-file tax transmittal services).

Compliance with Standards (1.310.001)

A variety of professional standards establish rules of conduct related to specific services including Statements on Auditing Standards (SAS), Statements on Standards for Accounting and Review Services (SSARS), Statements on Standards for Consulting Services (SSCS), and Statements on Standards for Tax Services (SSTS).

The Accounting Principles Rule obligates CPAs to ensure that the financial statements are prepared in accordance with GAAP and assess whether any material modifications to those statements are needed. If a CPA believes a departure from GAAP is justified to avoid misleading statements due to unusual circumstances, then the CPA can still comply with the rule by describing the departure; its approximate effects, if practicable; and the reasons why compliance with the principle would result in a misleading statement.

Of particular note is that the rule does not prohibit a CPA from preparing or reporting on financial statements based on other financial reporting frameworks such as International Financial Reporting Standards (IFRS)[28] promulgated by the International Accounting Standards Board (IASB) or statutory financial reporting requirements for an entity that are required by law or a U.S. or foreign governmental regulatory body to whose jurisdiction the entity is subject.

As is the case with most rules of conduct in the AICPA Code, in the absence of an interpretation that addresses a particular relationship or circumstance, the CPA should apply the conceptual framework approach to consider whether safeguards exist to mitigate any threats to compliance with the rule. Also, the CPA should consider guidance in ethical conflicts when addressing ethical conflicts that may arise when the CPA encounters obstacles to following an appropriate course of action.

Acts Discreditable (1.400.001)

The increase in disciplinary actions against licensed CPAs for acts discreditable was discussed in the Introduction to this chapter including fraudulent actions (i.e., tax fraud) and social crimes (i.e., DUI). Acts Discreditable covers a broad range of actions that may bring discredit to the profession. The list is long so we limit the discussion to confidential information obtained from employment, promoting or marketing professional services, returning client books and records, and removing client files or other proprietary information. As previously noted, the threats and safeguards approach is used and evaluation of ethical conflicts when interpretations do not address a particular relationship or circumstance.

Confidentiality of Information Gained through Employment

A confidentiality requirement exists for employees of firms that precludes disclosing confidential employer information obtained as a result of an employment relationship, such as discussions with the employer's vendors, customers, or lenders. An example where confidential information is generally protected is customer lists, target clients, costs, and marketing strategies that might afford competitive advantages. Perhaps the most dangerous situation is when an employee leaves the company, by choice or force, and decides to use confidential information for personal gain. Here, any covenants not to compete should be examined to determine restrictions and how they may affect downloading customer lists, taking client files, or using former client-related information to help start one's own practice.

Situations exist where a CPA is permitted or may be required to disclose confidential employer information under the law, such as occurs with whistleblowing disclosures when the conditions for doing so under Dodd-Frank have been met, as discussed in Chapter 3. Disclosure also may be required to comply with a validly issued and enforceable subpoena or summons. Other situations where disclosure is permissible include:

- Initiate a complaint to, or respond to any inquiry made by, the Professional Ethics Division, trial board of the AICPA, state CPA society, or state board of accountancy;
- Protect the CPA's professional interests in legal proceedings;
- Comply with professional standards and other ethics requirements; or
- Report potential concerns regarding questionable accounting, auditing, or other matters to the employer's confidential complaint hotline or those charged with governance.

Disclosure is also permitted on behalf of the employer to:

- Obtain financing with lenders;
- Communicate with vendors, clients, or customers; or
- Communicate with the employer's external accountant, attorneys, regulators, and other business professionals.

A CPA would be considered in violation of the Acts Discreditable Rule if he discloses or uses any confidential employer information acquired as a result of employment or volunteer relationships without the proper authority or specific consent of the employer or organization for whom he may work in a volunteer capacity, unless there is a legal or professional responsibility to use or disclose such information.

Promoting or Marketing Professional Services

CPA's violate the Acts Discreditable Rule if they promote or market their abilities to provide professional services or make claims about their experience or qualifications in a manner that is false, misleading, or deceptive. Promotional efforts would be false, misleading, or deceptive if they contain any claim or representation that would likely cause a reasonable person to be misled or deceived. This includes any representation about CPA licensure or any other professional certification or accreditation that is not in compliance with the requirements of the relevant licensing authority or designating body. False, misleading, or deceptive promotional efforts also violate the Advertising and Solicitation Rule (1.600.010).

Records Request

The records request rule is somewhat complicated and relies on basic definitions as explained below.

- *Client-provided records* are accounting or other records belonging to the client that were provided to the member [CPA] by or on behalf of the client, including hard-copy or electronic reproductions of such records.
- *Member-prepared records* are accounting or other records that the member was not specifically engaged to prepare and that are not in the client's books and records or are otherwise not available to the client, with the result that the client's financial information is incomplete. Examples include adjusting, closing, combining, or consolidating journal entries (including computations supporting such entries) and supporting schedules and documents that are proposed or prepared by the member as part of an engagement (e.g., an audit).

- *Member's work products* are deliverables as set forth in the terms of the engagement, such as tax returns.
- *Member's working papers* are all other items prepared solely for purposes of the engagement and include items prepared by the CPA, such as audit programs, analytical review schedules, and statistical sampling results and analyses.

The rules are summarized as follows.

1. Client-provided records in the custody or control of the member (CPA) should be returned to the client at the client's request.

2. Unless a member and the client have agreed to the contrary, when a client makes a request for member-prepared records, or a member's work products that are in the custody or control of the member or the member's firm and that have not previously been provided to the client, the member should respond to the client's request as follows:

    a. Member-prepared records relating to a completed and issued work product should be provided to the client, except that such records may be withheld if there are fees due to the member for the specific work product.

    b. Member's work products should be provided to the client, except that such work products may be withheld in any of the following circumstances:

        a. If there are fees due to the member for the specific work product.

        b. If the work product is incomplete.

        c. For purposes of complying with professional standards (for example, withholding an audit report due to outstanding audit issues).

        d. If threatened or outstanding litigation exists concerning the engagement or member's work.

State board rules on these matters can be confusing. The New York State Rules of the Board of Regents provide that certain information should be provided to a client upon request, including copies of tax returns and reports, or other documents that were previously issued to or for such client; copies of information that are contained in the accountant's working papers, if the information would ordinarily constitute part of the client's books and records and is not otherwise available to the client; and copies of client-owned records or records that the licensee receives from a client, and any records, tax returns, reports, or other documents and information that are contained in an accountant's working papers that were prepared for the client by the accountant and for which the accountant *has received payment from the client.* This implies that information can be withheld if payment has not been received. On the other hand, Texas State Board Rule 501.76 provides that a person's workpapers (to the extent that such workpapers include records that would ordinarily constitute part of the client's or former client's books and records and are not otherwise available to the client or former client) *should be furnished to the client within a reasonable time* (promptly, not to exceed 20 business days) after the client has made a request for those records. The person can charge a reasonable fee for providing such workpapers. The question is whether a "reasonable fee" precludes withholding working papers that constitute client books and records due to nonpayment of *client service fees.* As the saying goes, a word to the wise should be sufficient. Check with your state board rules on these matters once you become a licensed CPA.

The complexities of work-product privilege were brought to the forefront in a U.S. Supreme Court decision on May 24, 2010. In *United States v. Textron Inc.,* the Supreme Court declined to review a lower court opinion and let stand the decision by the First Circuit Court of Appeals that a corporation's tax accrual workpapers were not protected from an IRS summons by the work-product privilege. Exhibit 4.4 summarizes the facts of this case.

EXHIBIT 4.4 Supreme Court Declines to Hear *Textron* Work-Product Privilege Case

The case results from an IRS administrative summons for Textron's tax accrual workpapers with respect to the company's 1998–2001 tax returns. The workpapers were spreadsheets prepared by persons (some of whom were lawyers) in Textron's tax department to support Textron's calculation of its tax reserves for its audited financial statements. Textron refused to supply the workpapers to the IRS, and the dispute ended up in litigation.

In district court, Textron argued that its tax accrual workpapers were protected by either the attorney-client privilege, the tax practitioner privilege, or the work-product privilege. Textron acknowledged at trial that the documents' primary purpose was to support its reserve amounts for contingent tax liabilities, but it argued that they also analyzed the prospects for litigation over individual tax positions. The district court rejected Textron's attorney-client and tax practitioner privilege claims, saying that Textron waived those privileges by showing the documents to its outside accountants; however, it held that Textron's tax accrual workpapers were protected by the work-product privilege (*Textron Inc. v. United States,* 507 F. Supp. 2d 138 [D.R.I. 2007]).

A contentious issue in the case was whether Textron created the workpapers "in anticipation of litigation," because the work-product privilege does not protect documents prepared in the ordinary course of business. The district court concluded that although Textron undeniably created the workpapers to satisfy its financial audit requirements, but for the prospect of litigation, the documents would not have been created at all, and therefore they were protected by the work-product privilege.

On appeal, a three-judge panel of the First Circuit affirmed the district court. The court then granted an IRS petition to hear the case. The full court reversed the district court and held that the work-product privilege did not apply to Textron's tax accrual workpapers because the documents sought were prepared not for litigation, but for a statutorily required purpose of financial reporting, and so were prepared in the ordinary course of business; therefore, they were not protected by the privilege.

The Supreme Court decided not to review the case by denying a writ of certiorari.

Contingent Fees (1.510.001)

Years ago in the accounting profession, it was a violation of the rules of conduct for a CPA to accept a contingent fee for services performed for a client or for recommending a product or service to the client. These forms of payment were thought to be "unprofessional" and could potentially compromise the CPA's professional judgment. Over the years, however, professional accountants have become more involved in performing nonattest services that do not require independence and are largely provided to satisfy the client's interest, not the public interest. Thus, there is no third-party reliance on the work of the accountant. Moreover, CPAs who provide these nonattest services to clients are now competing with non-CPAs who perform similar services and are not bound by a professional code of conduct such as the AICPA Code. The result has been a loosening of the rules to permit the acceptance of contingent fees and commissions when performing advisory-type services for a nonattest client. Certain restrictions do apply, as discussed next.

Under the rule, a CPA is prohibited from performing for a contingent fee any professional services for, or to receive such a fee from, a client for whom the CPA or CPA firm performs any of the following services: (1) an audit or review of a financial statement; (2) a compilation of a financial statement when the CPA expects, or reasonably might expect, that a third party will use the financial statement, and the compilation report does not disclose a lack of independence; (3) an examination of prospective financial information; or (4) preparation of an original or amended tax return or claim for tax refund for a contingent fee for any client.

The danger of accepting a contingent fee for services provided to an attest client is it creates a financial self-interest threat to independence that may not be reduced or eliminated by any safeguards. Imagine if an accounting firm and audit client were to agree that the firm would receive 30% of any tax savings to the client resulting from tax advice provided by the firm. In this case, the fee is dependent on the outcome of the service. The fact that a government agency might challenge the amount of the client's tax savings, and thereby alter the final amount of the fee paid to the firm, heightens rather than lessens the mutuality of interest between the firm and client.

Exceptions do exist in tax practice where a contingent fee can be accepted, including: (1) if the fee is fixed by courts or other public authorities, (2) if the fee is determined based on the results of judicial proceedings or the findings of governmental agencies, (3) when filing an amended state or federal tax return claiming a tax refund based on a tax issue that is the subject of a tax case involving a different taxpayer or with respect to which the taxing authority is developing a position, or (4) when filing an amended federal or state income tax return (or refund claim) claiming a tax refund in an amount greater than the threshold for review by the Joint Committee on Internal Revenue Taxation ($1 million at March 1991) or state taxing authority.

Removing Client Files or Proprietary Information from a Firm

Once an employment relationship has been terminated, it would be an act discreditable for a CPA to take or retain (a) originals or copies (in any format) from the firm's client files or (b) proprietary information without the firm's permission, unless the CPA has a contractual arrangement with the firm allowing such action. A firm's ownership agreement would govern ownership of client files and proprietary information so that the employment relationship rules would not apply to owners of firms.

Commissions and Referral Fees (1.520.001)

The commission and referral fees rule is similar to that for contingent fees. Unlike a contingent fee, which is conditioned on the outcome of a service, a commission is typically paid to a CPA for recommending or referring to a client any product or service of another party, such as an investment product whereby the CPA receives a commission from the investment company if the client purchases the product. A similar arrangement exists when a CPA, for a commission, recommends or refers any product or service to be supplied by a client to another party. The restricted services identified under the contingent fees rule applies equally to the commissions rule. The same independence concerns exist because of the financial self-interest.

Imagine, for example, that a CPA is engaged to perform financial planning services for a client and to recommend a financial product or products based on the service. Now, if one of three products pays a commission to the CPA, assuming that the client purchases the product, while the other two do not, it may appear that the CPA can no longer be independent with respect to providing audit or other attest services for the client. The key point is that it doesn't matter if the CPA can, in fact, make independent decisions. The perception may be in the mind of a reasonable observer that such an independent mindset is no longer possible because of the commission arrangement. What if, for example, during the course of the audit and valuation of the investment product, the CPA discovers a flaw in the logic used to recommend the commission-based product to the client? Would the CPA disclose that fact to the client?

One requirement under the commission and referral fee rule that does not exist for contingent fees is to disclose permitted commissions and referral fees to any person or entity to whom the CPA recommends or refers a product or service to which the commission relates. In other words, the act of disclosing meets the CPA's ethical obligation under the AICPA Code. A protection beyond disclosure is that requirements for due care and adherence to the Objectivity and Integrity Rule applies in making product and service recommendations.

State board rules on these matters may differ from the AICPA rule, so it is important to understand and follow the state board rule that may have more restrictive guidelines. For example, the Texas State Board of Public Accountancy's commissions rule requires that a "person [licensed CPA] who receives, expects or agrees to receive, pays, expects, or agrees to pay other compensation in exchange for services or products recommended, referred, or sold by him shall, no later than the making of such recommendation, referral, or sale, disclose to the client in writing the nature, source, and amount, or an estimate of the amount when the amount is not known, of all such other compensation." In Washington State, the rule also includes a requirement to specify the CPA's role as the client's advisor.

In California, Section 5061 of the California Accountancy Act *prohibits* the acceptance or payment of a *referral fee* as follows: Except as expressly permitted by this section (applies only to commissions), a person engaged in the practice of public accountancy shall not (1) pay a fee or commission to obtain a client or (2) accept a fee or commission for referring a client to the products or services of a third party.

Advertising and Other Forms of Solicitation (1.600.001)

The advertising and solicitations rule establishes guidelines for when and how a CPA can promote professional services or solicit clients. While advertising and solicitation is permitted, these forms of communication cannot be done in a manner that is false, misleading, or deceptive. Solicitation by the use of coercion, overreaching, or harassing conduct is prohibited under the rule.

Advertising and solicitation practices of CPAs should never cross the line as might occur if they (1) create false or unjustified expectations of favorable results; (2) imply the ability to influence any court, tribunal, regulatory agency, or similar body or official; (3) contain a representation that specific professional services in current or future periods will be performed for a stated fee, estimated fee, or fee range when it was likely at the time of the representation that such fees would be substantially increased and the prospective client was not advised of that likelihood; and (4) contain any other representations that would be likely to cause a reasonable person to misunderstand or be deceived.

Given the new ways to engage current and future clients using social media outlets, it is fair to say the AICPA rules on advertising and solicitation lack specificity. Perhaps the AICPA believes its rules provide sufficient blanket coverage on all forms of practice. Still, some state boards provide clearer guidance such as Louisiana, which has issued a "Statement of Position" on Advertising and Communications that clarifies the advertising rule applies to licensees' Web sites, e-mails, and other electronic or Internet marketing, as well as all other forms of advertising, marketing, and public communications. In recent years, like so many professional service providers, CPAs have increasingly used the Internet and developed CPA firm Web sites. Prior to the advent of the Internet and universal access to marketing and advertising information, such information may have been in brochures or other printed material. Traditionally, such material was disseminated only by hand or mail and was not as available for general reference or scrutiny. Now, the information is available with one click, so the rules need to catch up with the technology.

Confidential Information (1.700.001)

The general requirement to maintain client confidentiality is that a CPA should not disclose confidential client information without the specific consent of the client. Confidentiality issues can be tricky from a legal perspective so CPAs are best served when they consult with legal counsel prior to disclosing, or determining whether to disclose, confidential client information.

Permitted Disclosure of Confidential Information

Client permission to discuss confidential issues generally is granted when there is a change of auditor and the successor auditor approaches the client for permission to discuss matters related to the audit with the predecessor. This step is required by GAAS. Of course, the client can always deny permission and cut off any such contact, in which case the successor auditor probably should run in the opposite direction of the client as quickly as possible. In other words, the proverbial "red flag" will have been raised. The CPA should be skeptical and wonder why the client may have refused permission.

The rule also permits the CPA to discuss confidential client information without violating the rule in the following situations: (1) in response to a validly issued subpoena or summons, or to adhere to applicable laws and government regulations (i.e, Dodd-Frank); (2) to provide the information necessary for a review of the CPA's professional practice (inspection/quality review) under PCAOB, AICPA, state CPA society, or board of accountancy authorization; and (3) to provide the information necessary for one's defense in an investigation of the CPA in a disciplinary matter.

Form of Organization and Name (1.800.001)

Ethics rules apply not only to individual CPAs who are licensed by state boards but also to accounting firms and certain members of alternative practice structures, networks, and affiliate firms. The forms of organization used by CPA firms over the years have changed to recognize the importance of nonattest services to the revenue flow of firms and competition with non-CPA firms in providing such services. Years ago, CPAs had to own 100% of a firm's equity interests. Today, most states simply require a majority ownership in the hands of licensed CPAs.

Clearly, the rules now accommodate non-CPA owners who perform a variety of advisory services and want a partial ownership interest in the firm. Toffler, in her book on the demise of Arthur Andersen,[29] laid blame on the proliferation of nonattest services at Andersen and non-CPA consultants, who operated under a less strict culture of ethical behavior than their CPA-attest colleagues. She claims that corners were cut and decisions were made that were in the interests of the client and firm, at the sacrifice of the public interest, as a result of compromises to independence and objectivity in audit services so as not to upset clients and possibly lose lucrative consulting services.

State boards need to have regulatory authority over practice units as well as CPAs because the members of a CPA firm might pressure an individual CPA within that firm to do something unethical. The firm should be sanctioned for the inappropriate behavior, and so should the CPA if he gives in to the pressure. Let's assume that you are working for a CPA firm in your hometown and your supervisor-CPA tells you to ignore a material sales return at year-end and wait to record it as a reduction of revenue until the first of next year. It seems that the client needs to maintain the level of revenue to meet targeted amounts and trigger bonuses to top management. If you go along with your supervisor, then you, the supervisor, and the firm itself can be cited for violating the ethics rules.

The rules provide that CPAs may practice public accounting only in a form of organization permitted by state law or regulation. The AICPA and virtually all state board rules prohibit the use of a firm name that is false, misleading, deceptive, and/or may imply the ability to provide services not justified. Imagine, for example, if the firm name is Maximum Tax Refunds, LLP.

Most states have rules far more extensive than the AICPA rules because of regulatory issues. For example, in North Carolina, the rules specify that non-CPA owners must be active participants in the business, the business must be the primary occupation of the non-CPA owners, and non-CPA owners must be of good moral character. Further, the name of a non-CPA owner may not be used in the name of the CPA firm.

An interesting question is whether the board of accountancy has any recourse against non-CPA owners even if they are registered with the board. In North Carolina, the board does not have any authority to discipline non-CPA owners of the CPA firm for violations of the state board rules on professional ethics and conduct. However, the rules do specify that the CPA partner who has been designated as the supervising partner of the CPA firm is held accountable for the non-CPA owners' compliance with the board's rules of conduct.

The Spirit of the Rules

The essence of professionalism is to follow the rules of conduct, act ethically at all times, and protect the public interest. The rules for the performance of professional services address these issues in a variety of ways. However, the rules can never cover every situation encountered, so the CPA needs to follow both the letter of the rule and the spirit of the rule. For example, the General Standards Rule calls for competence, due care, adequate planning and supervision, and gathering sufficient, relevant data. It does not directly address how to determine audit staffing and pricing. Murray points out that when charging fees, CPAs should ensure that their objectivity is not impaired by the hope of financial gain, and that such fees are proportional with the responsibilities they assume. Auditors need to be sure any threats to audit quality are met through adequate safeguards to ensure audit quality will not be adversely affected because the fee charged is insufficient to allow the necessary time and skill to be spent for this purpose.[30]

Ethics and Tax Services

LO 4-9

Describe the ethics rules for tax practice.

Students who graduate from college and take positions with accounting firms might end up providing tax services for a client at some time in their careers. Tax services include tax compliance, where much of the service is derived from audited financial records, tax consulting, tax planning, and tax shelters.

The AICPA explicitly recognizes the tax professional's dual obligations to the client to act as an advocate and to foster integrity in the tax system by honestly and fairly administering the tax laws. While client advocacy is an acceptable standard in tax practice, the tax accountant remains obligated to act objectively and with integrity, exercise due care, and follow the Statements on Standards for Tax Services issued by the AICPA.

In the performance of tax services for an audit client, the tax CPA is expected to consider whether any threats to independence exist that cannot be reduced or eliminated by safeguards and how such matters will be handled to avoid a violation of audit independence.

When a CPA prepares a tax return and transmits the tax return and related tax payment to a taxing authority in paper or electronic form, self-review and management participation threats to compliance with the Independence Rule may exist. In this case the CPA should apply the rules when providing non-attest services to an attest client to ensure all threats to independence have been adequately dealt with through safeguards.

Providing some tax services for audit clients can create a conflict of interests that threatens independence. Barrett points out that when auditors review the items for accrued taxes payable on the balance sheet and income tax expense on the income statement, they must reach conclusions about the validity of these amounts before they can express an opinion as to whether the financial statements fairly present the entity's financial condition and operating results in accordance with GAAP. As a result, auditors must examine the entity's tax returns and assess so-called "tax reserves" or "tax provisions" to evaluate tax expense for the current period and to determine whether any material unrecorded or undisclosed tax liabilities exist.[31] Here, a self-review threat may exist that cannot be reduced or eliminated by any safeguards.

An undue influence threat occurs if a CPA is pressured to change a conclusion regarding an accounting or a tax position. The client might seek to influence the tax position by linking it to additional attest work or consulting services.

Statements on Standards for Tax Services (SSTS)

The AICPA has issued seven Statements on Standards for Tax Services (SSTS) that explain CPAs' responsibilities to their clients and the tax systems in which they practice. The statements demonstrate a CPA's commitment to tax practice standards that balance advocacy and planning with compliance.

The statements establish required ethics rules for tax practitioners. Given the complexity of this area, we limit our discussion to the "realistic possibility" standard under *SSTS No. 1* and issues related to taking a tax position and tax planning.

SSTS No. 1—Tax Return Positions

This statement sets forth the applicable standards for CPAs when recommending tax return positions or preparing or signing tax returns (including amended returns, claims for refund, and information returns) filed with any taxing authority. The following definitions apply:

- A *tax return position* is a position reflected on a tax return on which a CPA has specifically advised a taxpayer or a position about which a CPA has knowledge of all material facts and, on the basis of those facts, has concluded whether the position is appropriate.

- A *taxpayer* is a client, a CPA's employer, or any other third-party recipient of tax services.

The statement addresses a CPA's obligation to advise a taxpayer of relevant tax return disclosure responsibilities and potential penalties. In addition to the AICPA and IRS tax regulations, various taxing authorities at the federal, state, and local levels may impose specific reporting and disclosure standards with regard to recommending tax return positions or preparing or signing a tax return. A CPA should determine and comply with the standards, if any, that are imposed by the applicable taxing authority with respect to recommending a tax return position or preparing or signing a tax return. If the applicable taxing authority has no written standards in this regard, then the following standards will apply.

A CPA should not recommend a tax return position or prepare or sign a tax return taking a position unless he has a good-faith belief that the position has at least a realistic possibility of being sustained administratively or judicially on its merits if challenged. This is known as the *realistic possibility of success* standard under *SSTS Interpretation No. 101-1.* It requires that the tax return position should not be recommended unless the position satisfies applicable reporting and disclosure standards.

Notwithstanding the previous statement, a CPA may recommend a tax return position if he concludes that there is a reasonable basis for the position and advises the taxpayer to disclose that position appropriately. An interesting aspect of the standard is the prohibition against recommending a tax return position or preparing or signing a tax return reflecting a position that the CPA knows exploits the "audit selection process of a taxing authority," or serves as a mere arguing position advanced solely to obtain leverage in a negotiation with a taxing authority. The former refers to the fact that a tax practitioner might recommend an overly aggressive position to a client hoping that the IRS does not choose to examine the client's tax return. Clearly, that would be a violation of basic ethical standards, including honesty (nondeceptiveness) and integrity.

SSTS Interpretation No. 1-1—Realistic Possibility Standard

SSTS No. 1-1 applies to CPAs when providing tax services that involve tax planning. A CPA can still recommend a nonfrivolous position provided appropriate disclosure is recommended. Tax planning includes recommending or expressing an opinion on a tax return position or a specific tax plan developed by the CPA, or a third party, that relates to prospective or completed transactions. The basic standards include:

- Establish the relevant background facts.
- Consider the reasonableness of the assumptions and representations.

- Apply the pertinent authorities to the relevant facts.
- Consider the business purpose and economic substance of the transaction, if relevant to the tax consequences of the transaction.
- Arrive at a conclusion supported by the authorities.

In conducting the required due diligence to establish a tax position, the CPA needs to decide whether to rely on the assumptions concerning facts rather than other procedures to support the advice or a representation from the taxpayer or another person. The CPA also should consider whether the tax advice provided will be communicated to third parties, particularly if those third parties may not be knowledgeable or may not be receiving independent tax advice with respect to a transaction.

When engaged in tax planning, the CPA should understand the business purpose and economic substance of the transaction when relevant to the tax consequences. The business purpose for the transaction should be described, and if the business reasons are relevant to the tax consequences, it is insufficient to merely assume that a transaction is entered into for valid business reasons without specifying what those reasons are.

Examples are provided in *SSTS No. 1-1* to assist in the application of the standards to fact situations. One such example is described in Exhibit 4.5.

EXHIBIT 4.5 Application of the Realistic Possibility Standard

Facts: The relevant tax regulation provides that the details (or certain information regarding) a specific transaction are required to be attached to the tax return, regardless of the support for the associated tax position (for example, if there is substantial authority or a higher level of comfort for the position). While preparing the taxpayer's return for the year, the CPA is aware that the attachment is required.

Conclusion: In general, if the taxpayer agrees to include the attachment required by the regulation, the CPA may sign the return if the CPA concludes that the associated tax return position satisfies the realistic possibility standard. However, if the taxpayer refuses to include the attachment, the CPA should not sign the return unless the CPA concludes the associated tax return position satisfies the realistic possibility standard and there are reasonable grounds for the taxpayer's position with respect to the attachment.

Tax Shelters

A listed transaction is defined by the IRS as a transaction that is the same as or substantially similar to one of the types of transactions that the IRS has determined to be a tax avoidance transaction. Such actions are identified by notice, regulation, or other form of published guidance as listed transactions. Tax avoidance transactions are sometimes labeled *tax shelters.* It is complicated, but basically the term *prohibited tax shelter transaction* means listed transactions, transactions with contractual protection, or confidential transactions.

The IRS guidelines for listed transactions identify participation in any of the following:

- A tax return reflects tax consequences or a tax strategy described in published guidance that lists the transaction.
- The CPA knows or has reason to know that tax benefits reflected on the tax return are derived directly or indirectly from such tax consequences or tax strategy.
- The client is in a type or class of individuals or entities that published guidance treats as participants in a listed transaction.

In other words, under IRS rules, any transaction that is the same or "substantially similar" to a transaction identified as a tax avoidance transaction by IRS notice, regulation, or other published guidance is a reportable transaction—it must be reported to the IRS.

KPMG Tax Shelter Case

One of the most controversial aspects of the Enron collapse was the alleged involvement of Andersen in marketing aggressive tax planning ideas that the IRS and the courts subsequently found to be abusive. After the Enron scandal, the accounting profession received a second serious blow in 2005, when KPMG settled a criminal tax case with the Department of the Treasury and the IRS for $456 million to prevent the firm's prosecution over tax shelters sold between 1996 and 2002. This is the largest criminal tax case ever filed.

The creation of tax shelter investments to help wealthy clients avoid paying taxes has been part of tax practice for many years. The difference in the KPMG case, according to the original indictment, is that tax professionals in the firm prepared false documents to deceive regulators about the true nature of the tax shelters. There appeared to be a clear intent to deceive the regulators, and that makes it fraud.

The indictment claimed that the tax shelter transactions broke the law because they involved no economic risk and were designed solely to minimize taxes. The firm had collected about $128 million in fees for generating at least $11 billion in fraudulent tax losses, and this resulted in at least $2.5 billion in tax evaded by wealthy individuals. On an annual basis, KPMG's tax department was bringing in for the firm nearly $1.2 billion of its $3.2 billion total U.S. revenue. Ultimately, the $128 million in fees were forfeited as part of the $456 million settlement.

Perhaps the most interesting aspect of the KPMG tax shelter situation is the culture that apparently existed in the firm's tax practice during the time the shelters were sold. In 1998, the firm had decided to accelerate its tax services business. The motivation probably was the hot stock market during the 1990s and the increase in the number of wealthy taxpayers. The head of the KPMG's tax department, Jeffrey M. Stein, and its CFO, Richard Rosenthal, created an environment that treated those who didn't support the "growth at all costs" effort as not being team players. From the late 1990s, KPMG established a telemarketing center in Fort Wayne, Indiana, that cold-called potential clients from public lists of firms and companies. KPMG built an aggressive marketing team to sell tax shelters that it created with names like Blips, Flip, Opis, and SC2.

In an unusual move, the Justice Department brought a lawsuit against two former KPMG managers on 12 counts of tax evasion using illegal tax shelters. On April 1, 2009, John Larson, a former senior tax manager, was sentenced to more than 10 years and ordered to pay a fine of $6 million. Robert Plaff, a former tax partner at KPMG, was sentenced to more than 8 years and fined $3 million. A third person convicted in the case, Raymond J. Ruble, a former partner at the law firm Sidley Austin, was sentenced to 6 years and 7 months. In handing down the ruling in the U.S. District Court in Manhattan, Judge Lewis A. Kaplan stated, "These defendants knew they were on the wrong side of the line," adding later that they had cooked up "this mass-produced scheme to cheat the government out of taxes for the purposes of enriching themselves." The losses through the scheme were estimated at more than $100 million.

Caterpillar Tax Fraud Case

Tax fraud cases occur from time to time that make us sit up, take notice, and ask where the tax accountants were. The Caterpillar case described in Exhibit 4.6 is one such case and the failure of PwC to detect and correct the fraud is troubling.

The IRS concluded in 2013 that Caterpillar had employed an "abusive" tax strategy and demanded $2 billion in back taxes and penalties. The strategy was designed to shift profits from the U.S. to a subsidiary in Switzerland to take advantage of that country's lower tax rate. Caterpillar's tax avoidance scheme had allegedly helped the company save more than $1 billion in taxes, according to Daniel Schlicksup, an accountant who had been with Caterpillar for 16 years.

Schlicksup tried to warn his bosses about the tax fraud as early as the spring of 2008. During that time, a company meeting was held at which the chair of the audit committee reminded attendees that they held Caterpillar's reputation in their hands. He stated that anyone aware of "financial malfeasance or trickery" was obliged to report it immediately. Later, the CEO, Jim Owens, pressed the point, saying he slept well because he couldn't imagine Caterpillar experiencing the sort of ethical lapses that had doomed Enron and other companies.

Following the meeting, Schlicksup had a crisis of conscience and sent an email to two of Owens's top underlings, with the subject line "Ethics issues important to you, the Board and Cat Shareholders." In a note, he shared his concerns about the tax strategy and described a systematic effort to shut him down. "I am now an example to my colleagues, peers, and others that they made the correct choice when they chose to not report ethical issues and ignore Company Policy." Attached to the email was a 15-page memorandum describing how his superiors had retaliated against him for speaking out. The next morning he sent 137 pages of documents purporting to show how, with the help of its auditor, PwC, Caterpillar had devised a way to shift billions in profit to Switzerland to avoid U.S. taxes.[32]

In his email that went to a group president Douglas Oberhelman, who would become CEO in 2010, Schlicksup said, "I do not believe you or the Board can manage risks if you are not aware" of them. The memo changed nothing except Schlicksup's career. Four months later he was told his position was being eliminated and he was being transferred to the information technology division. He resisted because he wasn't well-versed in IT and felt less valuable to the company. He was told this was his only option. Schlicksup took the new job, and then, later that year, filed an IRS whistleblower complaint accusing Caterpillar of tax fraud and filed a complaint with the Occupational Safety and Health Administration under SOX contending his employer had retaliated against him for raising concerns about "improper and illegal conduct."

Earlier, Schlicksup had gone public in June 2009 in a retaliation lawsuit against the company and a number of executives. Caterpillar asked a federal judge on two occasions to dismiss the lawsuit. The judge agreed that Schlicksup hadn't suffered financially but let the case proceed. On Valentine's Day in 2012, Schlicksup and the company settled. The terms were not disclosed.

At the time of writing, the IRS whistleblower case was still pending. The standard formula for whistleblower awards is 15% to 30% of what it collects. If Caterpillar pays the full $2 billion, Schlicksup stands to get $300 million to $600 million.

EXHIBIT 4.6   Caterpillar Tax Fraud Case

Tax fraud cases are not as common as financial statement fraud, but one case in particular, at Caterpillar, Inc., a client of PwC, illustrates the broad scope of tax fraud and length of time it takes to investigate tax fraud cases. An expose of the case appeared in a Bloomberg article by Bryan Gruley, David Vorecos, and Joe Deaux on June 1, 2017. What follows is a brief summary of the facts.[33]

In 2014, the U.S. Senate Permanent Subcommittee on Investigations headed by Michigan Senator Carl Levin detailed a program Caterpillar designed in 1999 with the advice of auditor PwC to use machinery part sales to shift its profits to low-tax Switzerland. The Senate investigation concluded these sales cut Caterpillar's U.S. bill by $2.4 billion between 2000 and 2012. The IRS, aided by documents provided by Caterpillar whistleblower Daniel Schlicksup, concluded in 2013 that Caterpillar had employed an "abusive" tax strategy. For years, Caterpillar accountants credited the Geneva, Switzerland office with 15% of the profits on parts sales,

(Continued)

while the other 85% was allocated as earnings in the United States. The company paid an effective tax rate of a little less than 30% on those U.S. profits. Shortly thereafter, Caterpillar reorganized the Geneva operation to cut the company's tax bill so it could compete better with Komatsu Ltd. and other foreign rivals that enjoyed lower tax rates. In planning documents, PwC said, "We are effectively more than doubling the profit on parts." Essentially, Caterpillar flipped the parts profit allocation so the new Swiss entity would be credited with 85% of the income on those sales. The company then paid taxes on those earnings at rates ranging from 4% to 6%, as negotiated with the Swiss tax authorities.

In effect, Caterpillar removed its U.S. operations from the outbound supply chain of parts sold in foreign countries. Before the accounting change, Caterpillar in the U.S. bought parts from third-party suppliers and resold them in Geneva for distribution overseas. After the change, CSARL, a parts subsidiary in Switzerland, bought parts directly from the suppliers. But that was merely on paper: U.S. facilities continued to handle and manage the bulk of inventory, supplies, and manufacturing. Of its 400 or so employees, the Geneva office had about 65 people working on parts, whereas the United States had about 5,000.

Caterpillar wound up effectively keeping two sets of books. The public one attributed the bulk of parts profits to Geneva, with its slight tax rate. An internal ledger known as "accountable profits" tracked the operating income of the divisions and calculated bonuses accordingly, according to a 2014 report by the Senate Subcommittee.

The IRS demanded $2 billion in back taxes and penalties. Additional investigations led to a final conclusion that Caterpillar had avoided taxes on more than $8 billion in revenue. On March 2, 2017, the federal government raided Caterpillar offices over possible tax fraud. Authorities seized documents and electronic information that could escalate a grand jury investigation into the company's tax avoidance strategies.

Resolving the tax fraud case is a complicated undertaking. Schlicksup worried that there seemed to be no reason for CSARL to exist other than to lower taxes. That creates a potential problem, because U.S. tax law requires a corporate structure to have clear "economic substance." In deciding tax shelter cases, the courts have mostly relied on the economic substance doctrine, which provides that transactions designed to yield tax benefits but which do not change the taxpayer's economic position independent of those benefits will not be respected. The common law doctrine normally requires the application of two separate tests—an objective test that focuses on the realistic potential of the transaction to generate a profit, and a subjective test focusing on the taxpayer's nontax business purpose in engaging in the transaction.

On March 30, 2010, the economic substance doctrine was codified in the Internal Revenue Code [IRC section 7701(o)]. It provides that, with respect to a transaction (or series of transactions) in which the common law economic substance doctrine is relevant, the transaction is treated as having economic substance only if the following tests are met:

- The transaction affects the taxpayer's economic position in a meaningful way, apart from any federal income tax effect; *and,*
- The taxpayer has a substantial purpose for engaging in the transaction, apart from any federal income tax effect.

The government's case against Caterpillar was still in process during 2018.

PCAOB Rules

LO 4-10

Describe the PCAOB independence and ethics rules.

The PCAOB now requires the lead engagement partner to file Form AP for identification purposes. Other standards follow.

Rule 3520—Auditor Independence

Rule 3520 establishes the requirement for the accounting firm to be independent of its audit client throughout the audit and professional engagement period as a fundamental obligation of the auditor. Under Rule 3520, a registered public accounting firm or an associated person's independence obligation with respect to an audit client that is an issuer encompasses not only an obligation to satisfy the independence criteria set out in the rules and standards of the PCAOB, but also an obligation to satisfy all other independence criteria applicable to the engagement, including the independence criteria set out in the rules and regulations of the commission under the federal securities laws.

Rule 3521—Contingent Fees

Rule 3521 treats registered public accounting firms as not independent of their audit clients if the firm, or any affiliate of the firm, during the audit and professional engagement period, provides any service or product to the audit client for a contingent fee or a commission or receives from the audit client, directly or indirectly, a contingent fee or commission. This rule mirrors Rules 1.520 and 1.510 of the AICPA Code that prohibit contingent fees, commissions, and referral fees for any service provided to an attest client.

Rule 3522—Tax Transactions

Under Rule 3522, a rule that was issued in the aftermath of the tax shelter transactions, a registered public accounting firm is not independent of its audit client if the firm, or any affiliate of the firm, during the audit and professional engagement period, provides any nonauditing service to the audit client related to marketing, planning, or opining in favor of the tax treatment of either a confidential transaction or an "aggressive tax position" transaction. An aggressive tax position transaction is one that was initially recommended, directly or indirectly, by the registered public accounting firm and a significant purpose of which is tax avoidance, unless the proposed tax treatment is at least more likely than not to be allowable under applicable tax laws.

Rule 3523—Tax Services for Persons in Financial Reporting Oversight Roles

Rule 3523 treats a registered public accounting firm as not independent if the firm provides tax services to certain members of management who serve in *financial reporting oversight roles* at an audit client or to immediate family members of such persons unless any of the following apply:

1. The person is in a financial reporting oversight role at the audit client only because she serves as a member of the board of directors or similar management or governing body of the audit client.

2. The person is in a financial reporting oversight role at the audit client only because of the person's relationship to an affiliate of the entity being audited:

   a. Whose financial statements are not material to the consolidated financial statements of the entity being audited.

   b. Whose financial statements are audited by an auditor other than the firm or an associated person of the firm.

3. The person was not in a financial reporting oversight role at the audit client before a hiring, promotion, or other change in employment and the tax services are provided pursuant to an engagement in process before the hiring, promotion, or other change in employment completed not after 180 days after the hiring or promotion event.

We are skeptical of ethics rules that build in exceptions, such as for members of the board of directors. From an ethical perspective, a practice is wrong if it violates certain standards of behavior, and it doesn't matter if the relationship with the other party is not deemed to be significant. After all, members of the board of directors at most companies today have ratcheted-up responsibilities under SOX and NYSE listing requirements. There does not appear to be a reasonable basis to exclude board members from the rule that prohibits providing tax services for persons in financial reporting oversight roles.

Rule 3524—Audit Committee Preapproval of Certain Tax Services

In connection with seeking audit committee preapproval to perform for an audit client any permissible tax service, a registered public accounting firm should do all of the following:

1. Describe, in writing, to the audit committee of the issuer:
   a. The scope of the service, the fee structure for the engagement, and any side letter or other amendment to the engagement letter, or any other agreement (whether oral, written, or otherwise) between the firm and the audit client relating to the service.
   b. Any compensation arrangement or other agreement, such as a referral agreement, a referral fee, or a fees-sharing arrangement, between the registered public accounting firm (or an affiliate of the firm) and any person (other than the audit client) with respect to the promoting, marketing, or recommending of a transaction covered by the service.
2. Discuss with the audit committee of the issuer the potential effects of the services on the independence of the firm.
3. Document the substance of its discussion with the audit committee of the issuer.

Rule 3525—Audit Committee Preapproval of Nonauditing Services Related to Internal Control over Financial Reporting

Rule 3525 provides that, when seeking audit committee preapproval to perform for an audit client any permissible nonauditing service related to internal control over financial reporting, a registered public accounting firm should describe, in writing, to the audit committee the scope of the service, discuss with the committee the potential effects of the service on the independence of the firm, and document the substance of its discussion with the audit committee of the issuer.

Rule 3526—Communication with Audit Committees Concerning Independence

Rule 3526 establishes guidelines when an accounting firm should discuss with the audit committee of the client information with respect to any relationships between the firm and the entity that might bear on auditor independence. Under the rule, a registered public accounting firm must do the following:

1. Prior to accepting an initial engagement, pursuant to the standards of the PCAOB, describe in writing, to the audit committee of the issuer, all relationships between the registered public accounting firm or any affiliates of the firm and the potential audit client or persons in financial reporting oversight roles at the potential audit client that, as of the date of the communication, may reasonably be thought to bear on independence.
2. Discuss with the audit committee the potential effects of the relationships on the independence of the firm, should it be appointed as the entity's auditor.
3. Document the substance of its discussion with the audit committee.

These requirements would also apply annually subsequent to being engaged as the auditor. An additional requirement annually is to affirm to the audit committee of the issuer of the communication that the registered public accounting firm is still independent in compliance with Rule 3520.

An important issue is whether the PCAOB has made a difference in reducing audit failures. Earlier in the chapter we discussed the significant audit deficiency rates so it would seem the PCAOB inspection process has not as yet made a notable difference in that regard, although detection may be greatly improved over the previous peer review process.

On June 1, 2017, the PCAOB adopted a new auditing standard to enhance the relevance and usefulness of the auditor's report by providing additional information to investors including a discussion of critical audit matters, which are matters that have been communicated to the audit committee, are related to accounts or disclosures that are material to the financial statements, and involve especially challenging, subjective, or complex auditor judgment.[34] More will be said about the new auditing standard in Chapter 5.

Concluding Thoughts

Professional judgment is more important today for auditors than ever before. Complex financial transactions and the broad application of fair value measurements require judgment. Judgment triggers can bias decision making by influencing the solution to problems without proper evaluation. Professional skepticism is important in judging decisions made by clients on accounting and financial reporting matters and keeping these biases in check.

Independent audits are the cornerstone of the profession. Accounting professionals are held to high ethical standards because of the public interest dimension of their work. In recent years, a renewed interest in providing nonattest services for attest clients has brought to the forefront the potential conflict between commercialism and professionalism. The AICPA Code's conceptual framework approach is important because it identifies safeguards to control threats that may occur as a result of the performance of nonattest services for attest clients and other relationships with the client and client management. CPA's are often pressured to compromise their judgment because of these relationships and it is through their commitment to serve the public interest that ethical standards are maintained.

CPAs in tax practice have their own challenges to objective judgment and in taking tax positions for clients. Tax positions should not be so aggressive that they push the envelope on the realistic possibility standard beyond the breaking point.

The PCAOB relies on inspections of registered accounting firms to identify deficiencies in audits. The deficiency rate is troubling, with some firms close to a 50% rate. CPAs and CPA firms should consistently monitor their own quality controls to ensure they are operating as intended.

CPA firms have been transitioning away from compliance-oriented services into more lucrative advisory services. On the one hand, we see this as a natural expansion in the scope of professional services and may very well benefit the client in more ways than one. Knowledge and expertise are important hallmarks of the profession. Clients benefit when trusted advisers provide services that otherwise might have been provided by professionals who have a lesser set of technical skills and lower ethical standards.

The problem is the expansion of nonattest services may threaten to alter the ethical culture of a firm. Consultants may have a different mindset than the objective judgment required of auditors. Moreover, increased opportunities to establish business relationships with clients and client management present a threat, and auditors must take care not to get too cozy with their clients.

Discussion Questions

1. In our discussion of the KPMG professional judgment framework, we pointed out that biased judgments can be made because of judgment tendencies. One such tendency that was not included in the framework is self-serving bias. Explain what you think this means and how it might influence audit judgment.

2. We all know people who say, "Don't bother me with the facts. I've already made up my mind." How might such an attitude influence judgment tendencies of auditors?

3. Explain the threats to professional skepticism that might influence audit judgment.

4. Explain the safeguards that can be used to reduce or eliminate threats to audit independence.

5. Do you believe the threats and safeguards approach establishes a situational or relativistic ethic? How might utilitarianism be used to evaluate the ethicality of permitting certain relationships when threats exist?

6. Can a CPA auditor be independent without being objective? Can a CPA auditor be objective without being independent? Explain.

7. Is independence impaired when an auditor is hired, paid, and fired by the same corporate managers whose activities are the subject of the audit? Does it matter that in most companies the audit committee hires, evaluates, fires (if appropriate), and determines the fees of the external auditor with minimal input from senior management?

8. When do ethical conflicts arise in the performance of professional accounting services? How should a CPA go about resolving ethical conflicts?

9. What are the specific threats to independence when a CPA accepts gifts or entertainment from an attest client? Does it matter whether the amount of the gift or entertainment was significant?

10. Do you believe that the SEC should prohibit auditors from providing *all* nonaudit services for audit clients? Use ethical reasoning to support your answer.

11. Assume that a CPA serves as an audit client's business consultant and performs each of the following services for the client. Identify the threats to independence. Do you believe any safeguards can be employed to reduce the threat to an acceptable level? Explain.

    a. Advising on how to structure its business transactions to obtain specific accounting treatment under GAAP.

    b. Advising and directing the client in the accounting treatment that the client employed for numerous complex accounting, apart from its audit of the client's financial statements.

    c. Selecting the audit client's most senior accounting personnel by directly interviewing applicants for those positions.

12. What is the problem with an auditor over-relying on management's representations on the financial statements?

13. Assume you disclosed information about a client. How would you determine if you violated the Confidential Client Information rule in the AICPA Code?

14. Andy Simmons is a CPA with his own accounting and tax practice. He occasionally does an audit for small business clients. One day an audit client shows Andy a letter from the local Property Tax Assessor's office. It seems the client inquired about the process to be followed to appeal the 20% increase in his property taxes. He already wrote an appeal and was denied. The letter said that most folks who appeal those decisions hire a CPA to represent them before the administrative board in

property tax assessment hearings. If your client asks you to represent him in the appeal process, can you do so under the AICPA Code? Explain.

15. You're struggling in your new accounting practice to tap into a potential client base. You have tried traditional advertising and marketing tools to no avail. Your friend tells you to use social media as a tool to reach potential customers. You're not sure about it. Your concern is one of ethics. The last thing you want to do is violate the ethical standards of the accounting profession. Identify the ethical issues that should be of concern to you in deciding whether and how to use social media for advertising and solicitation of new clients.

16. What are client hosting services? Would a CPA/CPA firm violate the Independence Rule if it provides hosting services for a client? Explain when it would or would not impair independence. Would independence be impaired in the following situations? Explain why or why not.

    (a) Electronically exchanging data or records with or on behalf of an attest client when the CPA has not been engaged to retain custody or control of the data or records on behalf of the client.

    (b) Maintaining the client's general ledger software and providing copies to the client.

17. You have decided to leave your CPA firm. Using the AICPA rules as a guide, answer the following questions: (1) Can you post some negative comments about your former employer on Twitter? (2) Can you call your former clients and tell them that you are leaving? (3) Can you take their files with you when you go?

18. You previously worked for the Department of Revenue, a governmental agency in your town. You cut all ties with the agency after you left two years ago to start your own tax accounting business. One day you receive a call from the agency asking you to conduct a tax audit of taxpayers in the town. You do not conduct a financial statement audit of any of these clients. Assume the proposed arrangement is to pay you 25% of additional amounts collected following your audits of property tax returns plus 50% of all first-year tax penalties. What ethical issues exist for you in deciding whether to accept the engagement? Would you accept it? Explain.

19. You were engaged to file the 2018 individual and corporate tax returns for a client. The client provided her records and other tax information on March 1, 2019, to help prepare the 2018 tax return. Your client paid you $12,000 in advance to prepare those returns. On April 1, after repeated requests to return her records, you informed the client that her tax returns for 2018 would be completed by April 15, and all of the records would be returned at that time. However, you failed to complete the return. The client paid another accountant $15,000 to complete the returns after the deadline and incurred tax penalties. Do you believe that you violated any of the rules of conduct in the AICPA Code? Did you violate any ethical standards beyond the Code? Explain.

20. You are the CFO of a privately owned business and prepare financial statements and tax returns (which are distributed to lenders, bonding/insurance providers, shareholders, and the IRS). What are the rules of conduct in the AICPA Code that you should follow?

21. In recent years the move by accounting firms to offshore tax and consulting work has grown and expanded into audit work. What are the ethical concerns that might be raised about the practice of electronically transmitting audit information to offshore centers like those in India that provide accounting professionals to audit U.S. corporations' financial statements?

22. In August 2008, EY agreed to pay more than $2.9 million to the SEC to settle charges that it violated ethics rules by co-producing a series of audio CDs with a man who was also a director at three of EY's audit clients. According to the SEC, EY collaborated with Mark C. Thompson between 2002 and 2004 to produce a series of audio CDs called *The Ernst & Young Thought Leaders Series.* Thompson served on the boards at several of EY's clients during the period when the CDs were produced. What threats to independence existed in the relationship between EY and Thompson? From

an ethical perspective, would it have mattered if it was not an audit client but one for whom advisory services only were performed?

23. Do you think the lead engagement partner in an audit should sign his or her name on the audit report itself or, instead, in the informational Form AP with the PCAOB? Use ethical reasoning to weigh the costs and benefits of such a requirement.

24. On August 31, 2017, the SEC charged Evan R. Kita, a CPA and former accountant at Celator Pharmaceuticals, Inc., and three others with insider trading on market-moving news about the New Jersey-based pharmaceutical company where the accountant formerly worked. Kita tipped two of his friends with confidential information about the clinical trial results for Celator's cancer drug and its acquisition by Dublin, Ireland-based Jazz Pharmaceuticals Plc almost three months later. Celator's stock rose 400% in March 2016 when it announced positive results for its drug to treat leukemia, and Jazz Pharmaceuticals offered to pay a hefty premium in May 2016 to acquire Celator.

According to the SEC's complaint, the two friends purchased Celator stock based on Kita's tips before the two announcements and agreed to share their trading profits with Kita. To avoid detection, Kita allegedly communicated with the two friends through an encrypted smartphone application.

Assuming the facts are correct, what ethical rules were violated by Evan Kita in this insider trading case? Do you think Kita committed an act discreditable to the profession? What do you think is the appropriate enforcement action the state board of accountancy should take against Kita?

25. Is accounting a trustworthy profession? How would you know whether it is or is not?

Endnotes

1. Cynthia L. Krom, "Disciplinary Action by State Board of Accountancy 2008-2014: Causes and Outcomes, *Accounting and the Public Interest* Vol. 16 No. 1, December 2016, pp. 1–27, https://doi.org/10.2308/apin-51609. The Loeb study is at: Stephen E. Loeb, "Enforcement of the code of ethics: A survey,"*The Accounting Review* Vol. 47 No. 1, 1972, pp. 1–10, http://www.jstor.org/stable/244561.

2. Krom labels DUI as a "social crime and includes other enforcement actions such as drug possession and nonpayment of child support."

3. Steven Glover and Douglas Prawitt, "Elevating Professional Judgment in Auditing and Accounting: The KPMG Professional Judgment Framework," Available at: https://www.researchgate.net/publication/258340692_Elevating_Professional_Judgment_in_Auditing_and_Accounting_The_KPMG_Professional_Judgment_Framework.

4. B. E. Christensen, S. M. Glover, and D. A. Wood, "Extreme Estimation Uncertainty in Fair Value Estimates: Implications for Audit Assurance," *Auditing: A Journal of Practice and Theory,* Vol. 31, No. 1 (2012), pp. 127–146.

5. Kathy Hurtt, "Development of a Scale to Measure Professional Skepticism," *Auditing: A Journal of Theory and Practice,* May 2012, Vol. 29, No. 1, pp. 149–171.

6. Lynn E. Turner, "We're Good but We Can Be Better," August 12, 2001, https://www.sec.gov/news/speech/spch511.htm.

7. Arthur Levitt, *Take on the Street* (NY: Penguin Random House, 2003).

8. James Doty, AICPA's 41st Annual National Conference on Current SEC and PCAOB Developments, December 2012, https://pcaobus.org/News/Speech/Pages/12032012_AICPA.aspx.

9. Mike Brewster, *Unaccountable: How the Accounting Profession Forfeited a Public Trust,* (Hoboken, NJ: John Wiley & Sons, Inc., 2003).

10. Aaron Elstein, Former KPMG executives charged with fraud and conspiracy, *CRAIN'S New York Business,* January 22, 2018, http://www.crainsnewyork.com/article/20180122/FINANCE/180129979/former-kpmg-executives-charged-with-fraud-and-conspiracy.

11. *United States of America v. David Middendorf. Thomas Whittle, David Britt, Cynthia Holder, and Jeffrey Wada,* U.S. District Court Southern District of NY, 18 CRIM 036 (Sealed Indictment).

12. Gordon Boyce, "Professionalism, the Public Interest, and Social Accounting," *Accounting for the Public Interest: Perspectives on Accountability, Professionalism and Role in Society,* ed. Steven Mintz (NY: Springer Dordrecht Heidelberg, 2014).

13. Ira Sager, "Arthur Levitt on PwC's Deal to Buy Booz: 'We Are Slipping Back,'" *Bloomberg Businessweek,* October 30, 2013, Available At: http://www.bloomberg.com/bw/articles/2013-10-30/arthur-levitt-on-pricewaterhousecoopers-deal-to-buy-booz-we-are-slipping-back.

14. Vincent J. Love, "Can Professionalism and Commercialism Coexist in CPA Firms?" *The CPA Journal,* February 2015, pp. 6–9.

15. Steven Mintz, "Revised AICPA Code of Professional Conduct: Analyzing the Ethical Responsibilities for Members in Public Practice and Members in Business," *The CPA Journal,* December 2014, pp. 62–71.

16. Ellen Goria, "Revised AICPA Code of Ethics . . . What's the Fuss?," *Journal of Accountancy,* February 2014, pp. 42–45.

17. Catherine R. Allen, "How data-hosting Services affect independence," *Journal of Accountancy,* September 27, 2017, https://www.journalofaccountancy.com/news/2017/sep/aicpa-ethics-interpretation-data-hosting-services.html.

18. IFAC, *Handbook of the Code of Ethics for Professional Accountants,* 2016 Edition, (NY: IFAC, 2016).

19. SEC, *Final Rule: Revision of the Commission's Auditor Independence Requirements,* February 5, 2001, Available at: www.sec.gov/rules/final/33-7919.htm.

20. Francine McKenna, "Piling Up For PwC," November 18, 2014, http://retheauditors.com/2014/11/18/piling-up-for-pwc/.

21. Sarah N. Lynch, "Deloitte to Pay $1mln to Resolve SEC Auditor Independence Rule Charges," *Reuters Business News,* July 1, 2015.

22. Michael Cohn, "SEC and PCAOB Discipline Firms for Violating Auditor Independence Rules," *Accounting Today,* December 8, 2014, Available at: http://www.accountingtoday.com/news/auditing/sec-pcaob-discipline-firms-violating-auditor-independence-rules-72953-1.html.

23. SEC, *In the Matter of Ernst & Young LLP and Gregory S. Bednar, CPA,* Accounting and Enforcement Release No. 3802, September 19, 2016, https://www.sec.gov/litigation/admin/2016/34-78872.pdf.

24. Michael Cohn, "SEC and PCAOB Discipline Firms for Violating Auditor Independence Rules," *Accounting Today,* December 8, 2014, Available at: http://www.accountingtoday.com/news/auditing/sec-pcaob-discipline-firms-violating-auditor-independence-rules-72953-1.html.

25. SEC, Insider Trading, https://www.sec.gov/fast-answers/answersinsiderhtm.html.

26. SEC, Litigation Release No. 23934, September 12, 2017, https://www.sec.gov/litigation/litreleases/2017/lr23934.htm.

27. SEC, Accounting and Auditing Enforcement Release No. 3863, March 14, 2017, *In the Matter of Nima Hedayati, Respondent,* https://www.sec.gov/litigation/admin/2017/34-80238.pdf.

28. IFRS has become widely adopted by countries for financial reporting, which includes the requirement for all companies operating in the European Union. Approximately 120 nations and reporting jurisdictions require IFRS to one extent or another.

29. Toffler, Barbara Ley. Final Accounting: Ambition, Greed, and the Fall of Arthur Andersen. New York :Broadway Books, 2003. Print.

30. Zowie Murray, The Politics of Audit Pricing, February 13, 2014, http://www.gaaaccounting.com/the-politics-of-audit-pricing/.

31. Barbara Ley Toffler with Jennifer Reingold, *Final Accounting: Ambition, Greed, and the Fall of Arthur Andersen* (New York: Broadway Books, 2003).

32. Bryan Gruley, David Voreacos, and Joe Deaux, "The Whistleblower Behind Caterpillar's Massive Tax Headache Could Make $600 Million," *Bloomberg News,* June 1, 2017, https://www.bloomberg.com/news/features/2017-06-01/the-whistleblower-behind-caterpillar-s-massive-tax-headache-could-make-600-million.

33. Bryan Gruley, David Voreacos, and Joe Deaux, "The Whistleblower Behind Caterpillar's Massive Tax Headache Could Make $600 Million," *Bloomberg News,* June 1, 2017, https://www.bloomberg.com/news/features/2017-06-01/the-whistleblower-behind-caterpillar-s-massive-tax-headache-could-make-600-million.

34. PCAOB, The Auditor's Report on an Audit of Financial Statements When the Auditor Expresses an Unuqlaified Opinion and Related Amendments to PCAOB Standards, PCAOB Release No. 2017-001, June 1, 2017, https://pcaobus.org/Rulemaking/Docket034/2017-001-auditors-report-final-rule.pdf.

Chapter 4 Cases

Case 4-1 KBC Solutions

The audit of KBC Solutions by Carlson and Smith, CPAs, was scheduled to end on February 28, 2019. However, Rick Carlson was uncertain whether it could happen. As the review partner, he had just completed going over the work paper files of the senior auditor in charge of the engagement, Grace Sloan, and had way too many questions to wrap things up by the end of the week. Rick called Grace into his office and asked her about some questionable judgments she had made. He hoped her explanations would be satisfactory and he could move on with completing the audit.

1. Why did you approve the accounting for new acquisitions of plant and equipment that were not supported by adequate underlying documentation?

2. Why did you accept the client's determinations of accrued expenses rather than make your own independent judgments?

3. How can you justify relying on last year's work papers to determine the proper allowance for uncollectibles one year later?

To say Grace was stressed out would be an understatement. This was her first engagement as a senior and she wondered whether it would be her last. Grace knew she had to make a convincing case for her judgments or suffer the consequences. She responded to each point as follows.

1. The client had problems with their systems and had to contact the vendor for a duplicate copy of the relevant invoices. She expects the copy within two days.

2. The client seemed to have a reasonable basis for those judgments so she saw no reason to delay completion of the audit over the accrued expenses.

3. Although the confirmation rate on the receivables was slightly below expected norms, there was no reason not to accept the client's explanation for those not confirmed as being correct in amount and due date.

Grace knew her answers would not completely satisfy Rick. She did, however, believe there were extenuating circumstances she felt compelled to explain even though it might reflect negatively on her leadership abilities. She explained that the audit team pressured her to let certain matters go because they were behind schedule in completion of the audit. She was convinced by the majority to trust the client on outstanding issues, which included the three raised by Rick.

Rick was not very happy with the explanation. He wondered about the professional judgments exercised by Grace and what her future with the firm should be.

Questions

1. Critically evaluate the judgments made by Grace as the senior by using the KPMG Professional Judgment Framework.

2. Did Grace violate any rules of conduct in the AICPA Code? Explain.

3. Does Rick have any ethical obligations in this matter? What should he do about signing off on the audit and why?

Case 4-2 Beauda Medical Center

Lance Popperson woke up in a sweat, with an anxiety attack coming on. Popperson popped two anti-anxiety pills, lay down to try to sleep for the third time that night, and thought once again about his dilemma. Popperson is an associate with the accounting firm of Hodgins and Gelman LLP. He recently discovered, through a "water cooler" conversation with Brad Snow, a friend of his on the audit staff, that one of the firm's clients managed by Snow recently received complaints that its heart monitoring equipment was malfunctioning. Cardio-Systems Monitoring, Inc. (CSM), called for a meeting of the lawyers, auditors, and top management to discuss what to do about the complaints from health-care facilities that had significantly increased between the first two months of 2018 and the last two months of that year. Doctors at these facilities claimed that the systems shut off for brief periods, and, in one case, the hospital was unable to save a patient who went into cardiac arrest.

Popperson tossed and turned and wondered what he should do about the fact that Beauda Medical Center, his current audit client, planned to buy 20 units of Cardio-Systems heart monitoring equipment for its brand-new medical facility in the outskirts of Beauda.

Question

Assume that both Popperson and Snow are CPAs. Do you think Snow violated his confidentiality obligation under the AICPA Code by informing Popperson about the faulty equipment at CSM? Explain.

Assume that Popperson informs the senior auditor in charge of the Beauda Medical audit, and the senior informs the manager, Kelly Kim. A meeting is held the next day with all parties in the office of Ben Smith, the managing partner of the firm. Here's how it goes:

Ben: If we tell Beauda about the problems at CSM, we will have violated our confidentiality obligation as a firm to CSM. Moreover, we may lose both clients.

Kelly: Lance, you are the closest to the situation. How do you think Beauda's top hospital administrators would react if we told them?

Lance: They wouldn't buy the equipment.

Ben: Once we tell them, we're subject to investigation by our state board of accountancy for violating confidentiality. We don't want to alert the board and have it investigate our actions. What's worse, we may be flagged for the confidentiality violation in our next peer review.

Kelly: Who would do that? I mean, CSM won't know about it, and the Beauda people are going to be happy we prevented them from buying what may be faulty equipment.

Senior: I agree with Kelly. They are not likely to say anything.

Ben: I don't like it. I think we should be silent and find another way to warn Beauda Medical without violating confidentiality.

Lance: What should we do? I need to be clear about my ethical responsibilities and the firm's as well.

Questions

1. Apply the steps in Exhibit 4.3, Ethical Conflicts and Compliance with the Rules of Conduct, and analyze whether the relationships described in this case create a conflict of interests and, if so, what safeguards should be implemented to mitigate the threat now and in the future?

2. What, if anything, should the accounting firm do about the malfunctioning equipment at Cardio-Systems Monitoring?

3. What should the firm do with respect to informing Beauda Medical about that equipment?

Case 4-3 Family Games, Inc. (a GVV case)

Family Games, Inc., is a privately-owned company with annual sales from a variety of wholesome electronic games that are designed for use by the entire family. The company sees itself as family-oriented and with a mission to serve the public. However, during the past two years, the company reported a net loss due to cost-cutting measures that were necessary to compete with overseas manufacturers and distributors.

"Yeah, I know all of the details weren't completed until January 2, 2019, but we agreed on the transaction on December 30, 2018. By my way of reasoning, it's a continuation transaction and the $12 million revenue belongs in the results for 2018. What's more, the goods were on the delivery truck on December 31, 2018, waiting to be shipped after the New Year."

This comment was made by Carl Land, the CFO of Family Games, to Helen Strom, the controller of Family Games, after Strom had expressed her concern that, because the lawyers did not sign off on the transaction until January 2, 2019, because of the holiday, the revenue should not be recorded in 2018. Land felt that Strom was being hyper-technical. He had seen it before from Helen and didn't like it. She needed to learn to be a team player.

"Listen, Helen, this comes from the top," Land said. "The big boss said we need to have the $12 million recorded in the results for 2018."

"I don't get it," Helen said to Land. "Why the pressure?"

"The boss wants to increase his performance bonus by increasing earnings in 2018. Apparently, he lost some money in Vegas over the Christmas weekend and left a sizable IOU at the casino," Land responded.

Helen shook her head in disbelief. She didn't like the idea of operating results being manipulated based on the personal needs of the CEO. She knew that the CEO had a gambling problem. This sort of thing had happened before. The difference this time was that it had the prospect of affecting the reported results, and she was being asked to do something that she knows is wrong.

"I can't change the facts," Helen said.

"All you have to do is backdate the sales invoice to December 30, when the final agreement was reached," Land responded. "As I said before, just think of it as a revenue-continuation transaction that started in 2018 and, but for one minor technicality, should have been recorded in that year. Besides, you know we push the envelope around here."

"You're asking me to 'cook the books,'" Helen said. "I won't do it."

"I hate to play hardball with you, Helen, but the boss authorized me to tell you he will stop reimbursing you in the future for child care costs so that your kid can have a live-in nanny 24-7 unless you go along on this issue. I promise, Helen, it will be a one-time request," Land said.

Helen was surprised by the threat and dubious "one-time-event" explanation. She sat down and reflected on the fact that the reimbursement payments for her child care were $35,000, 35% of her annual salary. As a single working mother, Helen knew there was no other way that she could afford to pay for the full-time care needed by her autistic son.

Questions

1. Assume that Carl Land and Helen Strom are CPAs. Explain the nature of the dilemma for Helen using the AICPA Code as a guide. What steps should she take to resolve the issue?

2. Apply the Giving Voice to Values methodology and answer the following questions from the perspective of Helen Strom.

What are the main arguments you are trying to counter? That is, what are the reasons and rationalizations you need to address?

What is at stake for the key parties, including those who disagree with you?

What levers can you use to influence those who disagree with you?

What is your most powerful and persuasive response to the reasons and rationalizations you need to address? To whom should the argument be made? When and in what context?

Case 4-4 A Potential Threat to Professional Judgment?

Katy Carmichael was just promoted to audit manager in the technology sector at PwC. She started at PwC six years ago and has worked on a number of the same client audits for multiple years. She prefers being placed on client audits year over year as she believes her knowledge about the client grows each year, resulting in a better audit. Public accounting firms, like PwC, do this as it provides continuity between the firm and the client and often results in a more efficient (less costly) audit as well.

Katy was thrilled to learn that she would be retaining three of her prior audit clients, including what she considers her favorite client (DGS- Drako Gaming Solutions) to audit. While she has not developed true friendships with the employees at those three clients, she does consider them good people. If she were not their auditor she would be very pleased to call them her friends. In fact, she greatly respects the senior management at DGS and likes the company enough that she has thought of going to work there on a number of occasions if she were ever to leave PwC. In describing the management of DGS to a friend, she stated they are as dedicated to their employees and minimizing their impact on the environment as they are to increasing shareholder value. She likes their culture, their people, and the games they produce and believes it would be a great place to work.

The audit planning for DGS's next audit is about to begin. As is common practice with all audits, each member of the PwC audit team is asked to fill out a questionnaire about any type of relationship (personal, business, or financial) they might have (or any other member of the engagement team might have) with the client company, any of their customers, suppliers, employees, or direct family members of their employees. There is no direct question which specifically addresses Katy's feelings toward the client and their management. As manager, Katy will be meeting with the PwC compliance partner assigned to DGS to go through the completed questionnaires to ensure there were no threats to independence and objectivity thereby hopefully ensuring no subordination of judgment would occur on the audit.

Questions

1. Identify any potential threats to judgment you think could exist based on the facts of the case?

2. Thinking back to the biases discussed in Chapter 2, what biases might the identified threat(s) make Katy more susceptible to and why?

3. This chapter discussed a link between the KPMG Professional Judgment Framework and Cognitive Processes specifically identifying four tendencies: availability, confirmation, overconfidence, and anchoring. How might Katy's feelings about the client exacerbate any or all of these tendencies? Provide specific examples of how these tendencies or biases might affect the audit?

4. Is Katy obligated to discuss her feelings about DGS with the compliance partner when they meet? If so, what should she say? Do you think the compliance partner should remove Katy from the audit? Explain.

5. What safeguards would you recommend to Katy and/or PwC to maintain integrity, professional skepticism, objectivity, and independence throughout this audit?

Case 4-5 Han, Kang & Lee, LLC (a GVV case)

Joe Kang is an owner and audit partner for Han, Kang & Lee, LLC. As the audit on Frost Systems was reaching its concluding stages on January 15, 2019, Kang met with Kate Boller, the CFO, to discuss the inventory measurement of one its highly valued products as of the balance-sheet date, December 31, 2018. Kang told Boller that a write-down of 20% had to be made because the net realizable value of the inventory on December 31 was 20% less than the original cost recorded on its books. That meant the earnings for the year would be reduced by $2 million and the client would show a loss for the year. In a heated exchange, Boller demanded Kang use the value at January 15, 2019, which reflects a full recovery of the "proposed" 20% writedown. Boller reminded Kang the financial statement issuance date would be January 31 so the recovery value is acceptable under GAAP. Besides, Boller said, the previous auditors had allowed her to do a similar thing. She went on to explain that the market value for this product was known to be volatile and a smoothing effect was justified in the accounting procedures.

Kang was under a great deal of pressure from the other two partners of the firm to keep Boller happy. It seems Frost Systems was about to provide hosting services for Boller and other management advisory services. The hosting services include providing electronic security and back-up services for the attest client's data and records. The revenue from these arrangements could turn out to be twice the audit fees. Kang called a meeting of the other partners. He was concerned that the final vote would be 2-1 to accept the client's interpretation of the accounting rules and record the inventory at the January 15 value.

The following are the rules for recognizing Subsequent Event values in accounting under the auditing standards, PCAOB AU 560.[1]

> An independent auditor's report ordinarily is issued in connection with historical financial statements that purport to present financial position at a stated date and results of operations and cash flows for a period ended on that date. However, events or transactions sometimes occur subsequent to the balance-sheet date, but prior to the issuance of the financial statements, that have a material effect on the financial statements and therefore require adjustment or disclosure in the statements. These occurrences hereinafter are referred to as "subsequent events."
>
> *Source: PCAOB AU 560 Subsequent Event.*

Questions

1. Did Boller apply the correct interpretation of GAAP rules for inventory valuation? What about PCAOB rules for subsequent events? What about the "smoothing effect" statement by Boller? Is this a valid basis for valuation? Explain.

2. Would independence be impaired if the firm were offered, and accepted, the hosting services? Consider whether any threats to independence would exist and, if so, how they might be reduced to an acceptable level.

3. Put yourself in Kang's position. You are preparing for the meeting with the other two partners. Consider the following in crafting an outline of points you may have to respond to.

What are the main arguments you are trying to counter? That is, what are the reasons and rationalizations you need to address?

What is at stake for the key parties, including those who disagree with you?

What levers can you use to influence those who disagree with you?

What is your most powerful and persuasive response to the reasons and rationalizations you may need to address? To whom should the argument be made? When and in what context?

---

[1] PCAOB, AU 560 Subsequent Event, https://pcaobus.org/Standards/Auditing/pages/au560.aspx.

Case 4-6 Tax Shelters

You are a tax manager and work for a CPA firm that performs audits, advisory services, and tax planning for wealthy clients in a large Midwestern city. You just joined the tax department after five years as a tax auditor for the county government. During the first six months in tax, you found out that the firm is aggressively promoting tax shelter products to top management officials of audit clients. Basically, the company developed a product and then looked for someone in management to sell it to, rather than the more conventional method whereby an officer might approach the firm asking it to identify ways to shelter income.

The way these products work is the firm would offer an opinion letter to the taxpayer to provide cover in case the IRS questioned the reasonableness of the transaction. The opinion would say that the firm "reasonably relied on a person who is qualified to know," and that would support the contention that the opinion was not motivated out of any intention to play the audit lottery. It also would protect the taxpayer against penalties in the event the firm is not correct and does not prevail in a tax case.

As time goes on, it becomes clear that the culture of the tax department is shifting from client service to maximization of tax revenues. You become concerned when you discover the firm did not register the tax shelter products, as required under the law.

One day you are approached by the tax partner you report to and asked to participate in one of the tax shelter transactions, with the end result being you would recommend to the tax partner whether he should sign off before presenting the product to the client. You feel uncomfortable with the request based on what you have learned about these products. You make an excuse about needing to complete three engagements that are winding down and buy some time.

The first thing you do is look for completed tax shelter arrangements with clients that had been reviewed and approved by the tax quality control engagement partner. What you find makes you more suspicious about the products. Several are marked "restricted" on the cover page without any further details. You then call a friend who is a manager in the audit department and set up a time to meet and discuss your concerns.

What you learn only heightens your concerns. Your friend confided that there is a culture in the tax department where business rationality sometimes displaces professional norms, a process accelerated by a conformist culture. Your friend also confided that the audit managers and partners are jealous of their tax peers because the tax managers and partners earn almost twice what the auditors earn because of the higher level of client revenues. It was clear your friend harbors ill feelings about the whole situation.

The following week the tax partner comes back and presents you with another tax shelter opportunity for the firm and all but demands that you oversee it. He implies in a roundabout way that your participation is a rite of passage to partnership in the firm. You manage to stall and put off the final decision a few days.

Questions

1. Evaluate the ethics of the tax shelter transactions, including your concerns about the practices.

2. Who are the stakeholders in this case, and what are your professional responsibilities to them?

3. What are the options available to you in this matter?

4. What would you do and why?

Case 4-7 Romance at EY Creates New Independence Policy

Per SEC release[1], from 2012 through 2014 then EY partner Pamela Hartford violated Independence Rules by having an affair with a client. Reports state she engaged in a personal relationship with Robert Brehl, the chief accounting officer of a public company that she serviced as a member of the audit engagement team. Another EY partner Michael Kamienski (the supervising partner on this engagement) became aware of facts suggesting an improper relationship between Hartford and Brehl. However, he failed to follow up on his suspicions. While Hartford and Brehl tried to keep their relationship a secret, they did attend client and EY social events. This suggests that others at both EY and the client could have been aware of the affair.

As part of the first SEC enforcement action of its kind, the SEC made charges of a breach of Independence against EY, Hartford, and Kaminski as well as Brehl. All parties agreed to settle the matter with the SEC without admitting guilt. EY agreed to pay $4.366 million, and both Hartford and Brehl each agreed to pay the SEC $25,000. While Kamienski did not have to pay a fine, Hartford, Brehl, and himself were suspended from appearing and practicing before the SEC as accountants, including not participating in either the financial reporting or auditing of publicly traded companies. The suspension allowed Brehl to apply for reinstatement after one year and both Hartford and Kamienski after 3 years.

The SEC release states that EY did not have specific policies in place to inquire about personal relations with clients and client personnel. EY subsequently added specific language to engagement team members' certifications on the firm's audit work asking about their own possible relationships with client personnel and whether they are aware of any personal relationships that any other member of the engagement team might have with client personnel.

The EY engagement team member certification added the following language subsequent to the settlement of this and another SEC investigation:

a. I am not aware of any other EY audit engagement team member who is or has been in such a relationship with any relevant individual of the audit client or a close or immediate family member of such a relevant individual.

b. I have not frequently entertained any relevant individual of the audit client and I am not aware of any other EY audit engagement team member who has frequently entertained any relevant individual of the audit client.

c. I have not frequently entertained immediate or close family members of a relevant individual of the audit client and I am not aware of any other EY audit engagement team member who has frequently entertained immediate or close family members of a relevant individual of the audit client.

d. I have not stayed at a residence of a relevant individual of the audit client and I am not aware of any other EY audit engagement team member who has stayed at a residence of a relevant individual of the audit client.

e. I am not aware of any other EY audit engagement team member that shares housing with a relevant individual of the audit client.

f. I have not vacationed with any relevant individuals (or in the case of Partners, Principals, Executive Directors and Directors who are covered persons, any employee) of **[Company]** or their close family members and I am not aware of any other EY audit engagement team member that has vacationed with any relevant individuals (or in the case of Partners, Principals, Executive Directors and Directors who are covered persons, any employee) of **[Company]** or their close family members.

g. I have not gone on a trip or attended an event with any relevant individual of **[Company]** where the trip or event required non-local travel or overnight accommodations and the predominant purpose of the trip or event was social, leisure or entertainment in nature, and I am not aware of any other EY audit engagement team member that has done so.

[1] *In the Matter of Ernst & Young LLP and Robert J. Brehl, CPA, Pamela J. Hartford, CPA, and Michael T. Kamienski, CPA*, SEC Release No. 34-78873 (Sept. 19, 2016).

Questions

1. What role does 'Auditor Independence' play in a CPA's responsibility to protect the public interest?

2. Explain the type of threat(s) to independence this case represents and explain why it is a threat to independence.

3. Do you think the questions added by EY are a sufficient safeguard to mitigate any such threats? Why or why not?

4. Explain how and why a sexual harassment situation might occur if the conflict of interests' matter is not properly addressed.

5. Do you think Pamela Hartford, Robert Brehl, and/or Michael Kamienski committed an act discreditable to the profession?

Case 4-8 Did the CPA Violate any Rules of Conduct?

Mark started his own practice ten years ago. He is a CPA and member of the AICPA. His firm grew quickly, helped along with the aid of his former employer Robert McAdams of Pure Water Company.

McAdams liked the way Mark performed all the payroll functions and filed tax returns and that Mark maintained all payroll and tax records for Pure Water Company. McAdams trusted Mark to make all necessary tax payments using e-filing for employee and employer taxes.

McAdams lauded Mark's services to all his acquaintances in social and professional organizations. The two discussed Mark paying a referral fee to McAdams for any future business, which they agreed to do. Fitzgerald Flooring was just referred to Mark by McAdams. Mark sent McAdams the agreed upon fee.

During the last two years McAdams' health began to fail, and Mark was often communicating with McAdams' wife Juanita. Juanita would send any correspondence from tax agencies directly to Mark with a blank check to cover the taxes and Mark's fees.

Recently, Juanita has also had some health issues and her son Lane is handling all financial matters for his parents. In the stack of bills, Lane finds three past due notices from the IRS. When discussing the correspondence with his mother, Juanita says to send all that to Mark as he handles all the tax records and filing. Lane shows his mother how the IRS claims that taxes have not been filed for the last six years.

Juanita says, "No, no, that cannot be right. Mark always handles that. He is such a nice young man. He files our taxes and maintains our records. He has done it for the last ten years. I sent him the correspondence with a check to cover the taxes and his fees. Mark takes good care of us and this can't be right."

In the meantime, Fitzgerald Flooring is being audited by the Workers' Compensation Insurance agency. The request for payroll records and filings is sent by Fitzgerald to Mark to make copies of all documents. Fitzgerald is quite dismayed to find that Mark tells them he has no payroll records or filings for Fitzgerald. Even though he promised Fitzgerald to maintain these records, he did not. He deleted them from the computer by mistake. Fitzgerald was miffed to learn of this and contacted the state board of accountancy, claiming an ethics violation by Mark.

Mark ignored three requests (emails, phone calls, and registered letters) from the state board to respond with documents and for an interview about Fitzgerald Flooring. In the meantime, the state board received notice from the IRS that Mark was banned from practicing before the IRS due to the six years of delinquent tax filings on behalf of McAdams and the Pure Water Company.

The state board reached out to the McAdams and Pure Water Company as a follow up on the IRS letter. They tried contacting Mark once again to no avail. Due to the failure of Mark to respond to the Board, the Board filed a cease and desist order with that state attorney general office for the suspension of Mark's license for failing to respond to the Board, accepting payments for services not rendered, failing to return client's records, delinquency in filing taxes for multiple years, and banned practicing before the IRS.

Questions

Evaluate Mark's conduct using the Six Pillars of Character. Did Mark violate any rules in the AICPA Code? Should he be permanently banned from practicing in the state? Explain.

Case 4-9 Eminent Domain: Whose Rights Should be Protected?

The leading New York court case concerning the enforcement of postemployment protective covenants concerned *BDO Seidman v. Hirschberg,* 93 N.Y.2d 382 (1999). The case demonstrates why accounting firms should include carefully drafted protective covenants in their employment, partnership, and shareholder agreements.

In *BDO Seidman,* the defendant Hirschberg was an accountant whose local Buffalo firm had been acquired by BDO. When Hirschberg was promoted to manager at BDO, he signed an agreement that prohibited him from servicing BDO's clients for 18 months after the termination of his employment. In addition, it required that if Hirschberg violated the agreement, he would have to pay BDO 150% of a particular client's fees from the fiscal year prior to his departure from BDO. When Hirschberg resigned four years after his promotion, he then provided accounting services to several BDO clients—the equivalent of $138,000 in revenues to BDO in the year prior to his departure.

The New York Court of Appeals examined BDO's agreement with Hirschberg to determine whether it was enforceable. The law is clear that, regardless of the actual language in the covenant, only reasonable restrictions will be enforced. A "restraint is reasonable only if it: (1) is no greater than is required for the protection of the legitimate interest of the employer, (2) does not impose undue hardship on the employee, and (3) is not injurious to the public."

The court scrutinized Hirschberg's covenant to determine whether BDO was indeed protecting a legitimate interest, and whether the covenant was tailored only as restrictively as necessary to protect that interest. The court ultimately held that the covenant was overly broad because it prohibited Hirschberg from servicing all BDO clients—even those Hirschberg himself recruited prior to joining BDO and those with whom Hirschberg had not developed any relationship as the result of his employment. Rather than simply discarding the overly broad covenant, however, the court next considered whether the covenant should have been enforced to the extent that it was reasonable. It found no evidence of BDO's deliberate overreaching, bad faith, or coercive abuse of superior bargaining power.

Because of this, the court rewrote—that is, "blue-penciled"— the covenant to effectively narrow it by precluding Hirschberg only from servicing those clients with whom he had developed a relationship as a result of his employment with BDO. The court then sent the case back to the trial judge to determine whether BDO was entitled to receive damages based on the formula of 150% of the client's prior year's revenue, as specified in the covenant.

This case demonstrates how valuable protective covenants can be in guarding an accounting firm's business interests. But *BDO Seidman* also highlights the importance of choosing appropriate covenants for given employees and carefully drafting such covenants so that they contain reasonable and clearly defined terms.

In addition to being clearly defined, a firm's protective covenants must be reasonable in scope. As *BDO Seidman* illustrated, courts will not enforce overly broad covenants. Thus, firms must be reasonable in defining their protected interests and their employees' prohibited conduct. Firms should not overreach; if a court sees overreaching, coercion, or bad faith by a firm, it may decline to partially enforce the agreement and may simply throw out the protective covenant in entirety.

Questions

1. Do you believe covenants not to compete, such as the one in *BDO Seidman,* are ethical? Do they violate any rules of conduct in the AICPA Code?

2. Who are the stakeholders in the BDO case and what are their interests? How might the various interests in a covenant be evaluated to determine whether these agreements are in the public interest?

3. Do you believe Hirschberg should have been allowed to service all of the clients he serviced while at BDO after leaving the firm?

4. Assume you are in Hirschberg's position and the NY Court of Appeals ruled you could not service any of the clients you serviced while at BDO—both the ones you brought in and those assigned to you by BDO. After the ruling, BDO approaches you and offers to rehire you at the same pay and give you the same client assignments. Would you accept the offer?

Case 4-10 Navistar International

In a bizarre twist to a bizarre story, on October 22, 2013, Deloitte agreed to pay a $2 million penalty to settle civil charges—brought by the PCAOB—that the firm violated federal audit rules by allowing its former partner to continue participating in the firm's public company audit practice, even though he had been suspended over other rule violations. The former partner, Christopher Anderson, settled with the PCAOB in 2008 by agreeing to a $25,000 fine and a one-year suspension for violating rules during a 2003 audit of the financial statements for a unit of Navistar International Corp. According to the charges, "Deloitte permitted the former partner to conduct work precluded by the Board's order and put investors at risk."[1]

After he settled the case and agreed to a one-year suspension, the PCAOB said Deloitte placed Anderson into another position that still allowed him to be involved in the preparation of audit opinions. Allowing a suspended auditor to continue working in that capacity is a violation of PCAOB rules, unless the SEC gives the firm permission. During the suspension, Anderson rendered advice on assignments involving three other Deloitte clients, according to the PCAOB. Deloitte said that it had taken "several significant actions to restrict the deployment" of Anderson. "However, we recognize more could have been done at that time to monitor compliance with the restrictions we put in place."[2]

In January 2013, Deloitte had settled a lawsuit alleging it committed fraud and negligence, forcing Navistar to restate earnings between fiscal year 2002 and the first nine months of 2005. Deloitte was dropped by Navistar in 2006, and the company was delisted by the New York Stock Exchange.

In response to charges by Navistar that sought to hold Deloitte liable for an incompetent audit, deceptive business practices, fraudulent concealment and basically everything that went wrong for Navistar, the Deloitte spokesman Jonathan Gandal, expressed the firm's position as follows:

> "A preliminary review shows it to be an utterly false and reckless attempt to try to shift responsibility for the wrongdoing of Navistar's own management. Several members of Navistar's past or present management team were sanctioned by the SEC for the very matters alleged in the complaint."[3]

---

[1] *Navistar Intern. Corp. v. Deloitte & Touche LLP,* 837 F.Supp.2d 926 (2011), Available at: No. 11 C 3507, http://www.leagle.com/decision/In%20FDCO%2020111028F31/NAVISTAR%20INTERN.%20CORP.%20v.%20DELOITTE%20&%20TOUCHE%20LLP.

[2] Steven R. Straher, "Deloitte fined $2 million for letting suspended exec work on audit," *October 23, 2013,* Available at: http://www.chicagobusiness.com/article/20131023/NEWS04/131029905/deloitte-fined-2-million-for-letting-suspended-exec-work-on-audit.

[3] "Navistar Sues Its Former Auditor Deloitte & Touche," April 26, 2011, Available at: http://www.bloomberg.com/news/articles/2011-04-26/navistar-sues-ex-auditor-deloitte-for-500-million-over-malpractice-claim.

Early in the fraud, Navistar denied wrongdoing and said the problem was with "complicated" rules under SOX. Cynics reacted by saying it is hard to see how the law can be blamed for Navistar's accounting shortcomings, including management having secret side agreements with its suppliers who received "rebates;" improperly booking income from tooling buyback agreements, while not booking expenses related to the tooling; not booking adequate warranty reserves; or failing to record certain project costs.

It is clear that Navistar employees committed fraud and actively took steps to avoid discovery by the auditors. The auditors did not discover the fraud, according to Navistar, and, in retrospect, the company wanted to hold the auditors responsible for that failure. Deloitte maintained that in each case, the fraudulent accounting scheme was nearly impossible to detect because the company failed to book items or provide information about them to the auditors.

Deloitte may have been guilty of failing to consider adequately the risks involved in the Navistar audit. After SOX was passed in mid-2002, all the large audit firms did some major cleanup of their audit clients and reassessed risk, an assessment that should have been done more carefully at the time of accepting the client. Big Four auditors, in particular, wanted to shed risky clients to protect themselves from new liability. Interestingly, to accomplish that goal with Navistar, Deloitte brought in a former Arthur Andersen partner to replace the engagement partner who might have become too close to Navistar and its management, thereby adjusting to the client's culture.

Whether because of his experience with Andersen's failure, fear of personal liability, a "not on my watch" attitude, or possibly a heads-up on interest by the SEC in some of Navistar's accounting, this new partner cleaned house. Many prior agreements between auditor and client and many assumptions about what could or could not be gotten away with were thrown out.

One problem for Navistar was that it was too dependent on Deloitte to hold its hand in all accounting matters, even after the SOX prohibited that reliance. According to Navistar's complaint, "Deloitte provided Navistar with much more than audit services. Deloitte also acted as Navistar's business consultant and accountant. For example, Navistar retained Deloitte to advise it on how to structure its business transactions to obtain specific accounting treatment under GAAP . . . Deloitte advised and directed Navistar in the accounting treatments Navistar employed for numerous complex accounting issues apart from its audits of Navistar's financial statements, functioning as a *de facto* adjunct to Navistar's accounting department. . . . Deloitte even had a role in selecting Navistar's most senior accounting personnel by directly interviewing applicants."[4]

The audit committee's role is detailed in the 2005 10-K filed in December 2007:

> "The audit committee's extensive investigation identified various accounting errors, instances of intentional misconduct, and certain weaknesses in our internal controls. The audit committee's investigation found that we did not have the organizational accounting expertise during 2003 through 2005 to effectively determine whether our financial statements were accurate. The investigation found that we did not have such expertise because we did not adequately support and invest in accounting functions, did not sufficiently develop our own expertise in technical accounting, and as a result, we relied more heavily than appropriate on our then outside auditor. The investigation also found that during the financial restatement period, this environment of weak financial controls and under-supported accounting functions allowed accounting errors to occur, some of which arose from certain instances of intentional misconduct to improve the financial results of specific business segments."

The complaint against Deloitte also references audit discrepancies cited in PCAOB inspections of Deloitte. Navistar believed the discrepancies related to Deloitte's audit of the company. However, the names of companies in PCAOB inspections are not made publicly available due to confidentiality and proprietary information concerns.

[4] *United States Securities Exchange Commission v. Navistar International Corp.,* In the United States District Court for the Northern District of Illinois, January 22, 2015, Available at: https://www.sec.gov/litigation/litreleases/2015/court-filing23183.pdf.

Questions

1. Would you characterize the Deloitte audit of Navistar a failed audit? Answer based on the ethics rules of conduct in the AICPA Code as they pertain to audit engagements and the facts of the Navistar case.

2. Evaluate the deficiencies in internal controls and corporate governance at Navistar. Do you believe external auditors should be expected to discover fraud when a company, such as Navistar, is so poorly run that its personnel did not have the necessary training and expertise, its internal controls were deficient, and it relied too heavily on Deloitte to determine GAAP compliance? Explain.

3. What is the purpose of the PCAOB audit firm inspection program with respect to ensuring that auditors meet their ethical and professional responsibilities and obligation to place the public interest above all else?

Chapter

5

Fraud in Financial Statements and Auditor Responsibilities

Learning Objectives

After studying Chapter 5, you should be able to:

LO 5-1   Distinguish between audit requirements for errors, fraud, and illegal acts.

LO 5-2   Explain the components of the Fraud Triangle.

LO 5-3   Describe fraud risk assessment procedures.

LO 5-4   Explain the standards for audit reports and auditor communications.

LO 5-5   Explain PCAOB standards to assess ICFR.

LO 5-6   Analyze a case study on auditor obligations when materially misstated financial statements exist.

Ethics Reflection

An audit of financial statements is intended to enhance the degree of confidence of intended users, such as lenders, creditors, and investors, and is achieved through an examination of the financial statements by an independent accountant the purpose of which is to provide reasonable assurance whether the financial statements are free of material misstatement, whether caused by error or fraud. The examination should be an objective evaluation of the statements in accordance with AICPA standards for private companies and PCAOB standards for public companies. A new requirement for PCAOB reports is for the auditor to determine and communicate "critical audit matters." More will be said about this later in this chapter.

The PCAOB is concerned about "audit quality." The term audit quality is not well defined. The PCAOB is in the process of identifying audit quality indicators (AQIs). The Center for Audit Quality (CAQ) believes that AQIs could be used to better inform audit committees about key matters that may affect the quality of an audit. The International Auditing and Assurance Standards Board (IAASB), which is an independent board under the umbrella of IFAC, defines audit quality by identifying the key elements that create an environment which maximizes the likelihood that quality audits are performed on a consistent basis. This includes inputs, processes, outputs, key interactions within the financial reporting supply chain, and contextual factors. The inputs include the values, ethics, and attitudes of auditors, which in turn are influenced by the culture prevailing within the audit firm.[1] The inputs are the link to ethics and ethical behavior that were addressed in Chapters 1-4.

The PCAOB Quality Control (QC) Section 20 standards for the *System of Quality Control for a CPA Firm's Accounting and Auditing Practice* emphasizes that the Scope and Nature of Services Principle in the AICPA Code calls for CPAs to practice in firms that have in place internal quality-control procedures to ensure that services are competently delivered and adequately supervised. A firm's system of quality control encompasses the firm's organizational structure and the policies adopted and procedures established to provide the firm with reasonable assurance of complying with professional standards. Quality control includes the maintenance of Integrity, Objectivity, and, where required, Independence, which requires a continuing assessment of client relationships, engagement performance, and monitoring.

Material misstatements discovered through the audit may require *Reissuance Restatements* or *Revision Restatements* of the financial statements. Reissuance Restatements, sometimes referred to as "Big R" restatements, address a material error that calls for the reissuance of past financial statements. Alternatively, Revision Restatements, or "little r" restatements, deal with immaterial misstatements, or adjustments made in the normal course of business. Because revision restatements are less severe, they are generally not looked at as a sign of poor reporting. According to Audit Analytics, SEC Form 8-K disclosures of Reissuance Restatements have been declining since 2007 through 2016; 2016 showed a record low of 130, a sharp decline from 2006's 941. The number of Revision Restatements has remained fairly steady, although as a percentage of overall restatements it increased to 78.3% in 2016.[2]

Digging deeper into financial restatements, Fatima Alali and Sophia I-Ling Wang reviewed the Audit Analytics data from 2000-2014 and found that Big R restatements are typically accompanied by filing amended financial restatements for the periods affected. The audit opinion is also revised to reflect the restatements. The users of financial statements are alerted not to rely on the originally issued financials because of the error or fraud. The authors point out that there is an increasing trend of filing restatements without first announcing them to the public, mainly because the determination of the exact day previously issued financial statements should no longer be relied upon is subject to the discretion of the companies and their auditors.[3] This seems to be a rationalization for failing to be transparent and can put the public at a disadvantage, especially investors.

Audit Analytics defines corporate financial restatements as "errors due to unintentional misapplication of U.S. GAAP" and corporate financial frauds as "intentional manipulation of financial data or misappropriation of assets." Financial reporting quality (i.e., the determination and detection of restatements or frauds) was examined using Audit Analytics data. The number of discovered financial restatements begins in 2000 at four percent of total public reporting companies, peaks in 2006 at 17%, then decreases to approximately eight percent of total reporting companies per year after 2007. The authors conclude that these statistics appear to support the view that the passage of SOX in 2002 and the implementation of SOX Section 404 later in 2004, that requires management issues a report on internal control over financial reporting, led to the initial spike in reporting restatements.[4] The good news is the rate has remained relatively steady for the last seven years.

As you read this chapter, reflect on the following: (1) What is the fraud triangle and how does it help to identify red flags that are indicators fraud may exist? (2) What are the auditor's responsibilities to assess the risks of material misstatement of the financial statements, whether due to error or fraud? (3) What are the most common causes of financial statement fraud and how can internal controls over financial reporting and the audit firms' quality controls keep them in check? (4) What information is communicated by the audit report?

The true standards of audit practice are found within the auditor's character: honesty, integrity, self control and high ethical values. The printed standards are merely guidelines for trying to make the art of auditing into a profession.

Source: Michael L.Piazza

This quote from Michael L. Piazza, director and producer of AuditWisdom.com, harkens back to our discussion of professional ethics in Chapter 4. The auditing standards discussed in this chapter can make a difference and help to prevent and detect material misstatements in the financial statements if the accounting professionals who are charged with following those standards adhere to the rules of conduct in the AICPA Code and, when appropriate, PCAOB ethics and independence standards.

Fraud in Financial Statements

LO 5-1

Distinguish between audit requirements for errors, fraud, and illegal acts.

Introduction

According to the AICPA audit standard on fraud, *Consideration of Fraud in a Financial Statement Audit* (AU-C Section 240), the primary responsibility for the prevention and detection of fraud rests with both those charged with governance of the entity and management. A strong emphasis should be placed on fraud prevention, which may reduce opportunities for fraud to take place, and fraud deterrence, which could persuade individuals not to commit fraud because of the likelihood of detection and punishment.[5] As we discussed in Chapter 3, this involves a commitment to creating a culture of ethical behavior, tone at the top, and reinforcement through governance structures.

Under AICPA standards, an auditor conducting an audit in accordance with generally accepted auditing standards (GAAS) is responsible for obtaining reasonable assurance that the financial statements as a whole are free from material misstatements, whether caused by fraud or error. Due to the inherent limitations of an audit, an unavoidable risk exists that some material misstatements of the financial statements may not be detected even though the audit was conducted in accordance with those standards.[6]

The auditing profession recognizes its obligation to look for fraud by being alert to certain red flags, assessing the control environment of the organization, passing judgment on internal controls, and considering audit risk and materiality when performing an audit. However, this is a far cry from guaranteeing that fraud will be detected, especially when top management goes to great lengths to hide it from the auditors.

A disconnect sometimes exists between a CPA's professional responsibility for detecting fraud and the public's perception of a CPA's duties in this regard. The "expectations gap" is one of understanding the actual role and responsibility of the external auditor with respect to detecting financial reporting fraud, and the public's perception with respect to the auditor's role therein.

The disconnect takes on a different character when members of the accounting profession and finance professionals are queried on their views. On April 24, 2013, the Center for Audit Quality (CAQ) held a roundtable on the subject of the expectation gap. The participants included representatives from CAQ, the Financial Executives International (FEI), the Institute of Internal Auditors (IIA), and the National Association of Corporate Directors (NACD). The following summarizes the results of these discussions.[7]

- The vast majority of survey respondents indicated that financial executives had primary responsibility for *deterring* financial reporting fraud.

- External auditors were more likely than any other financial reporting supply chain members to suggest that boards and audit committees bore primary responsibility.

- Respondents were more likely to identify financial management as having the primary role for *detecting* fraud, but these results were not as pronounced as they were for deterrence.

- Audit committee members and internal auditors were more likely than the other two groups to place primary responsibility for fraud detection on the external auditor.

These mixed results indicate the shared responsibility of many parties in the financial reporting chain for deterring, detecting, and reporting financial statement misstatements whether due to error or fraud.

Board members had confidence that management, internal audit, and external audit would be able to identify a material misstatement due to fraud. They also had a fairly high level of confidence in their own ability to identify a material misstatement, although this level of confidence was not shared by the other participants. This is somewhat surprising given management's role in designing processes and procedures (i.e., internal controls) and monitoring their effectiveness in developing accurate and reliable financial statement information. Moreover, the CEO and CFO are both required to certify financial statements under Section 302 of SOX. The question is whether management and the board take their responsibilities seriously enough to be responsive to auditors' need for cooperation and full disclosure of information that might bear on the fair presentation of financial results.

Nature and Causes of Misstatements

Fraudulent financial reporting involves either intentional misstatements or omissions of amounts or disclosures in financial statements that are intended to deceive financial statement users. Fraudulent financial reporting generally occurs in one of three ways: (1) Deception such as manipulation, falsification, or alteration of accounting records or supporting documents from which the financial statements are prepared; (2) misrepresentation in, or intentional omission from, the financial statements of events, transactions, or other significant information; and (3) intentional misapplication of accounting principles relating to measurement, recognition, classification, presentation, or disclosure. Because fraud involves an intentional act, the perpetrator of the falsehood knows, or should know, that what she proposes to do is wrong. Once financial statements have been falsified, the trust relationship between an auditor and the public breaks down.

A sensitive area that should receive heightened scrutiny by auditors is accounting estimates. The financial statements contain many estimates (i.e., depreciation, uncollectible accounts, estimated warranty obligations) that require professional judgment. Biases discussed in previous chapters can lead to estimating amounts that show management's side of the story rather than conform to GAAP. Auditors must be on the lookout to identify situations where management's interpretation of the data is at odds with their own determinations.

Errors, Fraud, and Illegal Acts

Material errors, fraud, and illegal acts represent situations where the financial statements should be restated. Exhibit 5.1 describes the auditors' obligations to detect and report each of these events. The following briefly describes the nature and effects of such acts.

EXHIBIT 5.1   Auditors' Responsibility to Detect Errors, Illegal Acts, and Fraud

	Responsible for Detection		Required to Communicate Findings	
	Material	**Immaterial**	**Material**	**Immaterial**
Errors	Yes	No	Yes (audit committee)	No
Illegal acts	Yes (direct effect)	No	Yes (audit committee)	Yes (one level above)
Fraud	Yes	No	Yes (audit committee)	Yes (by low-level employee, to one level above) (by management-level employee, to audit committee)

Errors

Errors are unintentional acts and may involve mistakes in gathering or processing data, unreasonable accounting estimates arising from oversight or misinterpretation of facts, or mistakes in the application of GAAP. Auditors are responsible for detecting errors that have a material effect on the financial statements and reporting their findings to the audit committee. An error correction is the correction of an error in previously issued financial statements. The amount is determined by calculating the cumulative effect of the error on periods prior to those presented in the financial statements. The effected asset and/or liability account(s) are adjusted with an offsetting adjustment to the opening balance of retained earnings for the current period. Financial statements should be restated for each period presented to reflect the error correction.

Fraud

Auditors should be sensitive to red flags that warn fraud is possible, if not likely. Fraud, whether fraudulent financial reporting or misappropriation of assets, involves incentive or pressure to commit fraud, a perceived opportunity to do so, and some rationalization of the act. The intentional act of fraud occurs when an individual(s) in management, those charged with governance, employees, or third parties use deception in a way that results in a material misstatement in the financial statements. In its most common form, management fraud involves top management's deceptive manipulation of financial statements.

In an "Analysis of Alleged Auditor Deficiencies in SEC Fraud Investigations: 1998–2010" conducted for the CAQ, it was determined that the failure to exercise due professional care and appropriate levels of professional skepticism resulted in auditors' inability to detect fraud. Being more attuned to the red flags that fraud may exist is an essential component of enhanced professional judgment.[8]

The intent of management determines whether the misapplication of GAAP is an error in judgment or a deliberate decision to manipulate earnings. In a court of law, it typically comes down to the credibility of the CFO and CEO who are charged with fraud. Absent a "smoking gun," the court might look for parallel actions by these top officers, such as selling their own shares of corporate stock after the fraudulent act but before it becomes public knowledge, as occurred at Enron and WorldCom.

Illegal Acts

Illegal acts are violations of laws or governmental regulations. For example, a violation of the Foreign Corrupt Practices Act (FCPA) that prohibits bribery constitutes an illegal act. Illegal acts include those attributable to the entity whose financial statements are under audit or as acts by management or employees acting on behalf of the entity. Such acts expose the company to both legal liability and public disgrace. The auditor's responsibility is to determine the proper accounting and financial reporting treatment of a violation once it has been determined that a violation has in fact occurred.

The auditor's responsibility is to detect and report misstatements resulting from illegal acts that have a direct and material effect on the determination of financial statement amounts (i.e., they require an accounting entry). The auditors' responsibility for detecting direct and material effect violations is greater than their responsibility to detect illegal acts arising from laws that only indirectly affect the client's financial statements. An example of the former would be violations of tax laws that affect accruals and the amount recognized as income tax liability for the period. Tax law would be violated, triggering an adjustment in the current period financial statements if, say, a company, for tax purposes, were to expense an item all in one year that should have been capitalized and written off over three years. Examples of items with an indirect effect on the statements include the potential violation of other laws such as the FCPA, occupational safety and health regulations, environmental protection laws, and equal employment regulations. The events are due to operational, not financial, matters and their financial statement effect is indirect, such as a possible contingent liability that should be disclosed in the notes to the financial statements.

The auditor's obligation when she concludes that an illegal act has or is likely to have occurred is first to assess the impact of the actions on the financial statements, including materiality considerations. This should be done regardless of any direct or indirect effect on the statements. The auditor should consult with legal counsel and any other specialists in this regard. Illegal acts should be reported to those charged with governance such as the audit committee. Consideration should be given to whether the client has taken appropriate remedial action concerning the act. Such remedial action may include taking disciplinary actions, establishing controls to safeguard against recurrence, and, if necessary, reporting the effects of the illegal acts in the financial statements. Ordinarily, if the client does not take the remedial action deemed necessary by the auditor, then the auditor should withdraw from the engagement. This action on the part of the auditor makes clear that she will not be associated in any way with illegal activities.

The Private Securities Litigation Reform Act (PSLRA) of 1995

The Private Securities Litigation Reform Act (PSLRA) of 1995 places additional requirements upon public companies registered with the SEC and their auditors when (1) the illegal act has a material effect on the financial statements, (2) senior management and the board of directors have not taken appropriate remedial action, and (3) the failure to take remedial action is reasonably expected to warrant departure from a standard (i.e., unmodified audit report) or to warrant resignation.

Once the auditor reports to the board that remedial action has not been taken to correct the detected illegal act, the client has one business day to inform the SEC under the requirements of Section 10A(b) of the Securities Exchange Act of 1934 ("Required Responses to Audit Discoveries"). The board should provide the auditor with a copy of the notice provided to the SEC. If, however, the client fails to report such conduct to the SEC, or the auditor fails to receive a copy of the board's notice to the SEC, then the reporting obligation falls to the auditor, who must then resign from the engagement or furnish the SEC with a copy of the audit report the following day. If the auditor resigns, she must still provide the SEC with a copy of the auditor's report within one day following the client's failure to do so.

A good example of the application of Section 10A is the litigation in the Xerox fraud. The accounting issues are discussed in Chapter 7; here, we look at the reporting requirements for fraud and illegal acts and whether KPMG met those standards with regard to its client Xerox.

In *SEC v. KPMG LLP, Joseph T. Boyle, Michael A. Conway, Anthony P. Dolanski, and Ronald A. Safran,* the SEC alleged, among other claims, violations of Section 10A by KPMG and four of its partners.[9] On January 29, 2003, the SEC filed an action against the firm and its partners, claiming as follows:

> "Defendants KPMG . . . and certain KPMG partners permitted Xerox Corporation to manipulate its accounting practices and fill a $3 billion "gap" between actual operating results and results reported to the investing public from 1997 through 2000. Instead of putting a stop to Xerox's fraudulent conduct, the KPMG defendants themselves engaged in fraud by falsely representing to the public that they had applied professional auditing standards to their review of Xerox's accounting, that Xerox's financial reporting was consistent with GAAP and that Xerox's reported results fairly represented the financial condition of the company . . . Section 10(A) of the Exchange Act requires a public accountant conducting an audit of a public company such as Xerox to: (1) determine whether it is likely that an illegal act occurred and, if so, (2) determine what the possible effect of the illegal act is on the financial statements of the issuer, and (3) if the illegal act is not clearly inconsequential, inform the appropriate level of management and assure that the Audit Committee of the client is adequately informed about the illegal act detected. If neither management nor the Audit Committee takes timely and appropriate remedial action in response to the auditor's report, the auditor is obliged to take further steps, including reporting the likely illegal act to the Commission."

In November 2004, KPMG reached a settlement with the SEC. KPMG consented to a finding that it violated Section 10(A) of the Securities Exchange Act of 1934; to pay disgorgement of $9,800,000, plus prejudgment interest; to pay a civil penalty of $10 million; and to implement a number of internal reforms. A final judgment against KPMG was issued on April 20, 2005.

Confidentiality Obligation

Recall that Section 1.700 of the AICPA Code of Professional Conduct prohibits CPAs from directly disclosing information to outside parties, including illegal acts, *unless the auditors have a legal duty to do so.* Compliance with the PSLRA would qualify as an exception to the bar on disclosing confidential client information, as would compliance with SOX and Dodd-Frank provisions.

A duty to notify parties outside the client may exist in each of the following circumstances:

- When the entity reports an auditor change under the appropriate securities law on Form 8-K.
- To a successor auditor when the successor makes inquiries in accordance with *Terms of Engagement* (AU-C Section 210).
- In response to a subpoena.
- To a funding agency or other specified agency in accordance with requirements for the audits of entities that receive financial assistance from a government agency.

Because potential conflicts with the auditor's ethical and legal obligations for confidentiality may be complex, the auditor should always consider consulting with legal counsel before discussing illegal acts with parties other than the client.

The Fraud Triangle

LO 5-2

Explain the components of the Fraud Triangle.

Donald R. Cressey, a noted criminologist, is mostly credited with coming up with the concept of a Fraud Triangle. Albrecht points out that Cressey developed a hypothesis of why people commit fraud. He found that trusted persons become trust violators when they conceive of themselves as having a financial problem that is nonsharable, are aware that this problem can be secretly resolved by violation of the position of financial trust, and are able to apply to their contacts in that situation verbalizations which enable them to adjust their conceptions of themselves as users of the entrusted funds or property.[10]

Edwin Sutherland, another criminologist, argued that persons who engage in criminal behavior have accumulated enough feelings and *rationalizations* in favor of law violation that outweigh their pro-social definitions. Criminal behavior is learned and will occur when perceived rewards for criminal behavior exceed the rewards for lawful behavior or *perceived opportunity.* So, while not directly introducing the Fraud Triangle, Sutherland did introduce the concepts of rationalizations and opportunities. It is interesting to think about how Sutherland's thesis relies on a utilitarian analysis of harms and benefits of criminal behavior.[11]

The Fraud Triangle in auditing is discussed in AU-C Section 240. The deception that encompasses fraudulent financial reporting is depicted in Exhibit 5.2.[12]

EXHIBIT 5.2   The Fraud Triangle

Some depict the fraud triangle with the opportunity at the base. We prefer to show pressure at the base because we believe, absent pressure to commit fraud, it is unlikely to occur simply because a fraudster needs access to do the deed.

Three conditions generally are present when fraud occurs. First, management or other employees have an incentive or are under pressure, which provides the motivation for the fraud. Second, circumstances exist that provide an opportunity for a fraud to be perpetrated. Examples include the absence of, or ineffective, internal controls and management's override of internal controls. Third, those involved are able to rationalize committing a fraudulent act much like the rationalizations we discussed in the GVV methodology.

As noted in the auditing standard, some individuals possess an attitude, character, or set of ethical values that allow them to commit a dishonest act knowingly and intentionally. For the most part, this is the exception rather than the rule. However, even honest individuals can commit fraud in an environment that imposes sufficient pressure on them. The greater the incentive or pressure, the more likely that an individual will be able to rationalize the acceptability of committing fraud.[13] Two good examples previously discussed are Betty Vinson and Aaron Beam.

It is important for students to understand the link between elements of the Fraud Triangle and our earlier discussions about cognitive development. The disconnect between one's values and actions may be attributable to motivations and incentives to act unethically, perhaps because of a perceived gain or as a result of pressures imposed by others who might try to convince us it is a one-time request or standard practice, or to be loyal to one's supervisor or the organization. These also become rationalizations for unethical actions invoked by the perpetrator of the fraud.

Incentives/Pressures to Commit Fraud

The incentive to commit fraud typically is a self-serving one. Egoism drives the fraud in the sense that the perpetrator perceives some benefit by committing the fraud, such as a higher bonus or promotion. The fraud may be caused by internal budget pressures or financial analysts' earnings expectations that are not being met. Personal pressures also might lead to fraud if, for example, a member of top management is deep in personal debt or has a gambling or drug problem. AU-C 240 identifies other factors that directly result from operations include:[14]

- Recurring negative cash flows from operations and an inability to generate cash flows from operations while reporting earnings and earnings growth.

- Need to obtain additional debt or equity financing to stay competitive—including financing of major research and development or capital expenditures.

- Rapid growth or unusual profitability, especially compared to that of other companies in the same industry.

Opportunity to Commit Fraud

The second side of the Fraud Triangle connects the pressure or incentive to commit fraud with the opportunity to carry out the act. Employees who have access to assets such as cash and inventory should be monitored closely through an effective system of internal controls that helps safeguard assets. Two common red flags that involve internal controls are domination of management by a single person or small group (in a nonowner-managed business) without compensating controls and when an organization has ineffective oversight over the financial reporting process and internal control by those charged with governance. Other factors that directly result from operations include:

- Significant related-party transactions not in the ordinary course of business or with related entities not audited or audited by another firm.

- Assets, liabilities, revenues, or expenses based on significant estimates that involve subjective judgments or uncertainties that are difficult to corroborate.

- Significant, unusual, or highly complex transactions, especially those close to period end that pose difficult "substance over form" questions.

Rationalization for the Fraud

Fraud perpetrators typically try to explain away their actions as acceptable. For corporate executives, rationalizations to commit fraud might include thoughts such as "We need to protect our shareholders and keep the stock price high," "All companies use aggressive accounting practices," "It's for the good of the company," or "The problem is temporary and will be offset by future positive results." Other rationalizations might include "My boss doesn't pay me enough" or "I'll pay the money back before anyone notices it's gone." The underlying motivation for the fraud in these instances may be dissatisfaction with the company and/or personal financial need. External factors may influence the attitude of management and lead to future rationalizations including:

- A practice by management of committing to analysts, creditors, and other third parties to achieve aggressive or unrealistic forecasts.

- Management failing to correct known significant deficiencies or material weaknesses in internal control on a timely basis.

Frisch's Restaurant: Trust but Verify

Michael Hudson, the former assistant treasurer at Frisch's Restaurant in Cincinnati that owns 95 Big Boy Restaurants in Ohio, embezzled at least $3.3 million between 2008-2014, during which time he gambled at the Horseshoe Casino. Hudson even occasionally sent coworkers pictures of jackpots he won.[15]

Hudson had the opportunity to commit fraud as assistant treasurer. He took advantage of his position by programming the company's payroll computer to pay himself hundreds of thousands extra annually. The company said he then hid the depleted cash by forging internal and vendor statements to show higher costs at store operations. The missing money wasn't noticed by Frisch's because they were recorded as expenses spread throughout the years and across almost all the stores. Hudson made unauthorized wire or automated transfers of funds from Frisch's bank accounts for his own benefit.

Hudson didn't seem to rationalize his actions. It appears he committed the fraud because he could do so by virtue of his position in the company, the trust placed in him by management, and, in all likelihood, the absence of effective internal controls meant he was able to get away with it for seven years.

Were there red flags that fraud was occurring at Frisch's? Company officials say no, yet the signs were there if the company looked hard enough. Consider the following:

- Hudson was helpful to others; somehow, he ended up doing some of the work for colleagues that might have exposed the theft. He built confidences to leverage the possible disclosure of the fraud by fellow employees.

- No one seemed to review the underlying documentation evidencing the fraud. A routine review of records following the fraud uncovered discrepancies when a new worker conducting an internal audit got credit card transaction records from the processing company that didn't coincide with Hudson's records.

- While Hudson didn't have a flashy car or expensive home that might have raised red flags, fellow employees knew he gambled a lot from the pictures he sent.

On September 22, 2016, Hudson pleaded guilty in federal district court in Ohio to charges of wire fraud and filing a false tax return and was sentenced to 60 months in prison, 3 years of supervised release and ordered, among other things, to pay restitution to Frisch's in the amount of approximately $3.1 million. On August 4, 2017, the SEC announced fraud charges against Hudson. Among other charges, it is alleged that Hudson falsely certified to Frisch's CFO that the company's internal control over financial reporting for which he was responsible was effective. To settle the SEC's charges, Hudson agreed to the entry of a judgment imposing permanent injunctions, an officer-and-director bar, and ordering him liable for disgorgement of approximately $3.9 million, payment of which is deemed satisfied by the restitution ordered in the parallel federal criminal case. As a result of Hudson's felony conviction, he was immediately suspended from appearing and practicing before the SEC as an accountant, which includes not participating in the financial reporting or audits of public companies.

Is There a Dark Triad Personality Risk?

One theory that has gained traction in the last few years is that there may be certain personality types that make it more likely fraud will occur and, if so, auditors should consider the risk that the existence of such personality types in top management may compromise the internal controls over financial reporting and lead to financial fraud.

Epstein and Ramamoorti discuss the existence of *the dark triad* deviant personalities, "whose behaviors may imply different risk profiles for audit—and financial reporting fraud—risk assessments, engagement planning, and audit execution." They suggest that "the existence and prevalence within the executive ranks of so-called dark triad personalities challenge the logic of applying the most commonly cited fraud risk models" including the Cressey Fraud Triangle. The authors identify three personality types: narcissism, Machiavellianism, and psychopathy.[16]

Kari Joseph Olsen conducted research into personality characteristics and accounting and found there is a growing prevalence today of individuals with narcissistic personality tendencies. Narcissistic personalities can bias cognitive processing to suit a person's self-view. These persons are obsessed with power, prestige, and vanity and are mentally unable to see the destructive damage they cause to themselves and others. Olsen asks: Do narcissistic personality tendencies of the CEO influence and motivate accounting decisions? His research suggests that earnings per share is a potential avenue through which narcissistic CEOs can receive needed praise and affirmation to support their inflated sense of self-importance.[17]

Journalist Jay Ronson interviewed Al Dunlap, former CEO of Sunbeam, who was responsible for a turn-around at the company best illustrated by an increase in earnings per share (EPS) from $12.50, on the day he was hired in 1997, to a peak of $52.50 in 1998 when the board doubled his salary to $2 million. Dunlap gained the nickname "Chainsaw Al" because of his "gleeful fondness for firing people and shutting down factories." That worked at first to improve the earnings outlook, but Dunlap hit a snag once those maneu-vers had all been played out. He turned to fraudulent techniques to inflate earnings including recording bogus revenue. Ronson observed that Dunlap "had a 'Grandiose sense of self worth'—which would have been a hard one for him to deny because he was standing underneath a giant oil painting of himself. When asked about it, Dunlap said: 'You've got to like yourself if you're going to be a success.'"[18]

Research conducted on opportunistic behavior (earnings management and fraud) in accounting choices suggests that internal motivations, specifically the emotions and the Machiavellianism personality traits, influence choices that are made.[19] Former HealthSouth CEO Richard Scrushy acted like a bully in pres-suring a series of CFOs to go along with a $2.7 billion fraud undertaken by recording fake revenues on the company's books over six years and correspondingly adjusting the balance sheets and paper trails.

Epstein and Ramamoorti point out that Machiavellians are calculating and cunning and they use charm, friendliness, self-disclosure, guilt, and pressure to get what they want. Former HealthSouth CFO Aaron Beam writes that Scrushy was a charismatic leader who could get employees to follow him either through charm, encouragement, or outright intimidation.[20]

Dr. Alejandro Adrian LeMon suggests that psychopaths are fascinating, impressive, and charming. They are articulate and exude confidence. Oftentimes thought of as sociopaths, they are controlling and manip-ulative. As a co-worker, they are unethical and willing to use you for their own personal gain, even it means ruining your reputation. They are also master liars, highly successful, and use sophisticated methods to achieve their high ambitions. According to LeMon, one example of a high-profile psychopath is Jeffrey Skilling, the former president of Enron. Skilling sold shares of his company's stock while already having inside information of Enron's impending bankruptcy. He knew many families would lose their lifetime savings, their jobs, and their homes. But that did not stop him from misleading investors and his employ-ees. In his view, he was far more important than the well-being of others. Not once did Skilling express genuine remorse or guilt for his crimes in court.[21]

Epstein and Ramamoorti state that the existence of psychopaths in corporate management suggests that auditors might find it useful to incorporate the "dark triad personality risk" factor into their risk assess-ments to better identify when fraud might be present. It is common for auditors to use checklists to watch out for the elements of the fraud triangle and use such indications when making decisions about audit scope.[22] We agree with the authors that auditors should consider the personality type when dealing with management. Being on the lookout for certain behavioral traits may raise red flags sooner and enable the auditors to better assess the risk of fraud. However, as the saying goes, the devil is in the details.

Tyco Fraud

In a "60 Minutes" interview, Dennis Kozlowski, the former CEO of Tyco, explained to Morley Safer that his motivation to steal from the company was to keep up with "the masters of the universe." This meant keeping up with other CEOs of large and successful companies that had pay packages in the hundreds of millions. He rationalized his actions by claiming that he wasn't doing anything different from what was done by his predecessor. In 2005, a jury found that Kozlowski and ex-CFO Marc Swartz stole about $137 million from Tyco in unauthorized compensation and made $410 million from the sale of inflated stock.

The corporate governance system at Tyco completely broke down, thereby creating the opportunity for fraud to occur and thrive. Most members of Tyco's board of directors benefited personally as a result of Tyco's practices. For example, one board member worked for a law firm that "just happened" to receive as much as $2 million in business from Tyco. This person's pay at the law firm was linked to the amount of work that he helped bring in from Tyco.

Obviously, when the fraud is perpetrated by the CEO or CFO, as was the case with Tyco, access is a given. Then it is just a matter of circumventing the controls or overriding them or, in the case of Kozlowski, enlisting the aid of others in the organization to hide what was going on.

We believe it's fair to characterize Kozlowski as having a narcissistic personality. He had an inflated view of himself and cultivated others in the company to view him the same way. Kozlowski was generous with his lieutenants because he thought they would be loyal to the boss. He was obsessed with his own self-worth, made decisions that infected the culture of the company, and failed to see how his actions were destructive, not only to himself but to Mark Swartz, board members, and the company.

Fraud Considerations and Risk Assessment

LO 5-3
Describe fraud risk assessment procedures.

Fraud Risk Assessment

Fraud considerations in an audit require that the auditor should evaluate the risk of fraud, including the effectiveness of internal controls, and communicate with those charged with governance responsibilities about fraud. Most of the requirements of AU-C 240 call for the auditor to engage in risk assessment during the audit. Actually, the assessment of risk starts with an evaluation of evidence about the potential client before agreeing to do the audit. One important step is to communicate with the predecessor auditor to find out the reasons for the firing or the reasons for no longer servicing the client. Of particular importance is assessing the integrity of the top management and key accounting personnel. The successor auditor also should clarify with the predecessor whether there were any differences of opinion with management over the application of accounting principles and how these were handled, including the role of the audit committee.

Fraud risk assessment depends in large part on maintaining professional skepticism when evaluating the reliability of audit evidence obtained and assessing whether a material misstatement due to fraud exists. In making the assessment, of course, the auditor should not approach the audit with an attitude toward management of "You are crooks. Prove me wrong." Instead, a healthy attitude is one that informs management in word and deed that the auditor's responsibility is to ask the tough questions, thoroughly examine relevant documentation, and probe to determine whether the organization culture promotes ethical decision making and whether there is support for financial statement amounts and disclosures.

AU-C 240 identifies the broad goals of fraud risk assessment as to (1) make inquiries of management and others within the organization to obtain their views about the risks of fraud and how they are addressed; (2) consider any unusual or unexpected relationships that have been identified in performing analytical procedures (i.e., financial statement comparisons over time and ratio analysis) in planning the audit; (3) consider whether one or more fraud risk factors exist; and (4) consider other information (i.e., interim financial results and factors associated with the acceptance of the client) that may be helpful in identifying risks of material misstatement due to fraud.

Internal Control Assessment

The risk that internal controls will not help prevent or detect a material misstatement in the financial statements is a critical evaluation to provide reasonable assurance that the statements are free of error or fraud.

The system of internal controls and whether it operates as intended enables the auditor to gain either confidence about the internal processing of transactions, which is fine, or doubt, which the auditor should pursue.

Building on the description of the control environment in the COSO internal control framework first discussed in Chapter 3, the auditor should assess:

- Whether management's philosophy and operating style promote effective internal control over financial reporting;
- Whether sound integrity and ethical values, particularly of top management, are developed and understood; and
- Whether the board or audit committee understands and exercises oversight responsibility over financial reporting and internal control.

A direct relationship exists between the degree of risk that a material weakness could exist in a particular area of the company's internal control over financial reporting (ICFR) and the amount of audit attention that should be devoted to that area. In addition, the risk that a company's internal control over financial reporting will fail to prevent or detect misstatement caused by fraud usually is higher than the risk of failure to prevent or detect error. The auditor should focus more of his or her attention on the areas of highest risk.

As discussed in Chapter 3, COSO's enterprise risk management framework (ERM) is designed to help an entity get where it wants to go and avoid pitfalls and surprises along the way. ERM is defined as a process, effected by an entity's board of directors, management, and other personnel and applied in strategy settings and across the enterprise, designed to identify potential events that may affect the entity and to manage risk within its risk appetite. ERM adds a number of strategic issues, including objective setting by management, identification of risks and opportunities affecting achievement of an entity's objectives, and risk responses selected by management to align risk tolerance and risk appetite.

Audit Committee Responsibilities for Fraud Risk Assessment

The audit committee should evaluate management's identification of fraud risks, implementation of anti-fraud measures, and creation of the appropriate tone at the top. Active oversight by the audit committee can help reinforce management's commitment to create a culture with "zero tolerance" for fraud. An entity's audit committee also should ensure that senior management (in particular, the CEO and CFO) implements appropriate fraud deterrence and prevention measures to better protect investors, employees, and other stakeholders. Evaluation and oversight not only helps ensure that senior management fulfills its responsibility, but also can serve as a deterrent to senior management engaging in fraudulent activity (that is, by ensuring an environment is created whereby any attempt by senior management to involve employees in committing or concealing fraud would lead promptly to reports from such employees to appropriate persons, including the audit committee).

The audit committee also plays an important role in helping those charged with governance fulfill their oversight responsibilities with respect to the entity's financial reporting process and the system of internal control. In exercising this oversight responsibility, the audit committee should consider the potential for management override of controls or other inappropriate influence over the financial reporting process. Some examples follow:

- Solicit the views of the internal auditors and independent auditors with respect to management's involvement in the financial reporting process and, in particular, the ability of management to override information processed by the entity's financial reporting system (for example, the ability of management or others to initiate or record nonstandard journal entries).

- Consider reviewing the entity's reported information for reasonableness compared with prior or forecasted results, as well as with peers or industry averages.

- Information received in communications from the independent auditors can assist the audit committee in assessing the strength of the entity's internal control and the potential for fraudulent financial reporting.

As part of its oversight responsibilities, the audit committee should encourage management to provide a mechanism for employees to report concerns about unethical behavior, actual or suspected fraud, or violations of the entity's code of conduct or ethics policy and receive periodic reports describing the nature, status, and eventual disposition of any fraud or unethical conduct. A summary of the activity, follow-up, and disposition also should be provided to all of those charged with governance.

Auditor's Communication with Those Charged with Governance

Whenever the auditor has determined that there is evidence that fraud may exist, the matter should be brought to the attention of the appropriate level of management. AU-C 240 requires such communication even if the matter might be considered inconsequential, such as a minor misappropriation by an employee. Fraud (whether caused by senior management or other employees) that causes a material misstatement of the financial statements should be reported directly to those charged with governance. In addition, the auditor should reach an understanding with those charged with governance regarding the nature and extent of communications with them about misappropriations perpetrated by lower-level employees.

The Auditor's Communication With Those Charged With Governance (AU-C Section 260) identifies the auditor's communication responsibilities to strengthen governance:

- The auditor has access to the audit committee as necessary.

- The chair of the audit committee meets with the auditor periodically.

- The audit committee meets with the auditor without management at least annually unless prohibited by law or regulation.

Given the importance of an independent audit in detecting fraud in financial statements, the auditor should discuss with the audit committee relationships that create threats to auditor independence and the related safeguards that have been applied to eliminate or reduce those threats to an acceptable level.

Another important area for communication is about accounting estimates. Certain accounting estimates are particularly sensitive because of their significance to the financial statements and because of the possibility that future events affecting them may differ significantly from management's current judgments. In communicating with those charged with governance about the process used by management in formulating sensitive estimates, including fair value estimates, and about the basis for the auditor's conclusions regarding the reasonableness of those estimates, the auditor should consider the following:

- The nature of significant assumptions;

- The degree of subjectivity involved in the development of the assumptions; and

- The relative materiality of the items being measured to the financial statements as a whole.

If the auditor, as a result of the assessment of the risks of material misstatement, has identified such risks due to fraud that have continuing control implications, the auditor should consider whether these risks represent significant deficiencies or material weaknesses in the entity's internal control that should be communicated to management and those charged with governance. Consideration should also be given to whether the absence of or deficiencies in controls to prevent, deter, and detect fraud represent significant deficiencies or material weaknesses that should be communicated to management and those charged with governance.

Management Representations and Financial Statement Certifications

Section 302 of SOX requires certification of the financial statements by the CFO and CEO for public companies. For many years, the AICPA has required written representations as part of audit evidence gathered. One way to deal with the problem that some significant errors may not be detected, although not foolproof, is to obtain written representations (also known as management representations or client representations) to confirm certain matters and support other evidence obtained during the audit. AU-C Section 580, *Written Representations,* requires representations by the CEO, the CFO, and other appropriate officers.[23] The purpose of the representation is for management to acknowledge its responsibility for the fair presentation of financial statements, the design and implementation of programs and controls to prevent and detect fraud, whether management has knowledge of any allegations of fraud or suspected fraud affecting the entity, and whether any fraud that exists could have a material effect on the financial statements.

The representations generally include:

- A statement that the client has provided access to all known information that bears on the fair presentation of the financial statements.

- Confirmation that management has performed an assessment of the effectiveness of internal control over financial reporting based on criteria established in the Internal Control–Integrated Framework issued by COSO.

- Conclusions as to whether the company has maintained an effective ICFR.

- Disclosure of any deficiencies in the design or operation of ICFR.

Qwest Communications International Inc.

False representations occurred in one of the largest frauds back in the late 1990s and early 2000s at Qwest Communications International Inc. that certainly contributed to the SEC's inclusion of Section 302 in SOX. From at least April 1, 1999, through March 31, 2002, senior executives and others at Qwest engaged in a massive financial fraud that hid from the investing public the true source of the company's revenue and earnings growth, caused the company to fraudulently report approximately $3 billion of revenue, and facilitated the company's June 2000 merger with U.S. West. Joseph P. Nacchio, Qwest's former CEO, and the company's two former CFOs, Robert S. Woodruff and Robin R. Szeliga, directed the fraudulent scheme to carry out Nacchio's aggressive and rigid targets for revenue and earnings growth. Extreme pressure was placed on subordinate Qwest executives to meet these aggressive targets at all costs and the pressure spread throughout the company, causing a "culture of fear." For example, at a January 2001 all-employee meeting, Nacchio stated, "[T]he most important thing we do is meet our numbers. It's more important than any individual product, it's more important than any individual philosophy, it's more important than any individual cultural change we're making. We stop everything else when we don't make the numbers."[24]

The pressure on employees to meet revenue and earnings targets was intense. The opportunity to manipulate the numbers was there and carried out by top management. Qwest fraudulently and repeatedly relied on immediate revenue recognition from one-time sales of assets known as "IRUs" and certain equipment while falsely claiming to the investing public that the revenue was recurring. By hiding non-recurring revenue and making false and misleading public statements, Nacchio, Woodruff, and Szeliga fraudulently and materially misrepresented Qwest's performance and growth to the investing public.

Nacchio had consistently said that he did nothing wrong and he did not instruct anyone else to do anything wrong during his tenure at Qwest. One has to wonder why, then, did he sell $52 million worth of Qwest shares in April and May 2001 after receiving private warnings that the company would miss revenue targets? Nacchio was found guilty by the U.S. Justice Department of insider trading and received a prison sentence of six years and a $19 million fine. Nacchio's sentence was reduced by about 1 ½ years for good behavior and participation in a residential drug-treatment program.

As for Robin Szeliga, she settled with the SEC for her role in the fraud. Her mistake was signing the relevant filings with the SEC as the CFO of Qwest. Szeliga signed all of Qwest's materially false 10-Q reports filed with the SEC, and its materially false 10-K annual reports for 2000 and 2001. She signed false management representation letters to Qwest's outside auditors. She drafted and reviewed all earnings releases and spoke at financial analyst calls.

Section 302 SOX certifications from the CEO and CFO is the SEC's way to regulate management representations in light of frauds at companies such as Qwest. It's interesting to consider whether Szeliga (and Nacchio) would have falsely certified the financial statements and the design and effectiveness of disclosure controls and procedures had the SOX requirement been in effect during the fraud period.

Audit Report and Auditing Standards

LO 5-4
Explain the standards for audit reports and auditor communications.

Background

The free market for stocks and bonds can only exist if there is sharing of reliable financial information, strengthened by information that is transparent and unbiased. The external audit is intended to enhance the confidence that users can place on the financial statements that have been prepared by management. Since 1926 the New York Stock Exchange (NYSE) has required an auditor's report with public companies' financial statements. Then the Securities Exchange Act of 1934, which is discussed further in Chapter 6, required all public companies to have an independent auditor's report on annual financial statements. For both public and nonpublic entities, the auditor's report on financial statements and related disclosures provides (or disclaims) an opinion on whether the entity's financial statements and related disclosures are presented in accordance with generally accepted accounting principles in the U.S. (AICPA report) or based on an evaluation of the accounting principles used (PCAOB report). The PCAOB report takes a broader view because public companies with global operations may be required to follow IFRS as well as the accounting principles in the home country.

Audit Report

The auditors' unmodified or standard report for nonpublic companies under the AICPA requirements is presented in Exhibit 5.3. The auditors' unqualified report for public companies under the PCAOB requirements is presented in Exhibit 5.4.

EXHIBIT 5.3 Unmodified Opinion for Nonpublic Companies

Independent Auditor's Report
To the Board of Directors and Stockholders, XYZ Company
Introductory Paragraph

We have audited the accompanying consolidated financial statements of XYZ Company and its subsidiaries, which comprise the consolidated balance sheets as of December 31, 2018, 2017, and 2016, and the related consolidated statements of income, changes in stockholders' equity, and cash flows for the years then ended, and the related notes to the financial statements.

Management's Responsibility for the Financial Statements

Management is responsible for the preparation and fair presentation of these consolidated financial statements in accordance with accounting principles generally accepted in the United States of America; this includes the design, implementation, and maintenance of internal control relevant to the preparation and fair presentation of consolidated financial statements that are free from material misstatement, whether due to fraud or error.

Auditor's Responsibility

Our responsibility is to express an opinion on these consolidated financial statements based on our audits. We conducted our audits in accordance with auditing standards generally accepted in the United States of America. Those standards require that we plan and perform the audit to obtain reasonable assurance about whether the consolidated financial statements are free of material misstatement.

An audit involves performing procedures to obtain audit evidence about the amounts and disclosures in the consolidated financial statements. The procedures selected depend on the auditor's judgment, including the assessment of the risks of material misstatement of the consolidated financial statements, whether due to fraud or error. In making those risk assessments, the auditor considers internal controls relevant to the entity's preparation and fair presentation of the consolidated financial statements in order to design audit procedures that are appropriate in the circumstances, but not for the purpose of expressing an opinion on the effectiveness of the entity's internal controls. Accordingly, we express no such opinion. An audit also includes evaluating the appropriateness of accounting policies used and the reasonableness of significant accounting estimates made by management, as well as evaluating the overall presentation of the consolidated financial statements.

We believe that the audit evidence we have obtained is sufficient and appropriate to provide a basis for our audit opinion.

Opinion

In our opinion, the consolidated financial statements referred to above present fairly, in all material respects, the financial position of XYZ Company and its subsidiaries as of December 31, 2018, 2017, and 2016, and the results of its operations and its cash flows for the years then ended in accordance with accounting principles generally accepted in the United States of America.

Optional Paragraph

Report on Other Legal and Regulatory Requirements *[This section usually won't apply unless the auditor has other reporting responsibilities. If so, then the opening paragraph after the salutation should be titled Report on the Financial Statements]*

[Auditor's signature]

[Auditor's city and state]

[Date of the auditor's report]

EXHIBIT 5.4   The Auditors' Unqualified Report Including Critical Audit Matters

---

Report of Independent Registered Public Accounting Firm

To the shareholders and the board of directors of ABC Company.

Opinion on the Financial Statements

We have audited the accompanying balance sheets of ABC Company (the "Company") as of December 31, 2018, and 2017, the related statements of [titles of the financial statements, e.g., income, comprehensive income, stockholders' equity, and cash flows] for each of the three years in the period ended December 31, 2018, and the related notes [and schedules] (collectively referred to as the "financial statements"). In our opinion, the financial statements present fairly, in all material respects, the financial position of the Company as of [at] December 31, 2018 and 2017, and the results of its operations and its cash flows for each of the three years in the period ended December 31, 2018, in conformity with [the applicable financial reporting framework].

Basis for Opinion

These financial statements are the responsibility of the Company's management. Our responsibility is to express an opinion on the Company's financial statements based on our audits. We are a public accounting firm registered with the Public Company Accounting Oversight Board (United States) ("PCAOB") and are required to be independent with respect to the Company in accordance with the U.S. federal securities laws and the applicable rules and regulations of the Securities Exchange Commission and the PCAOB.

We conducted our audits in accordance with the standards of the PCAOB. Those standards require that we plan and perform the audit to obtain reasonable assurance about whether the financial statements are free of material misstatement, whether due to error or fraud. Our audits included performing procedures to assess the risks of material misstatement of the financial statements, whether due to error or fraud, and performing procedures that respond to those risks. Such procedures included examining, on a test basis, evidence regarding the amounts and disclosures in the financial statements. Our audits also included evaluating the accounting principles used and significant estimates made by management, as well as evaluating the overall presentation of the financial statements. We believe that our audits provide a reasonable basis for our opinion.

Critical Audit Matters [if applicable]

The critical audit matters communicated below are matters arising from the current period audit of the financial statements that were communicated or required to be communicated to the audit committee and that: (1) relate to accounts or disclosures that are material to the financial statements and (2) involved our especially challenging, subjective, or complex judgments. The communication of critical audit matters does not alter in any way our opinion on the financial statements, taken as a whole, and we are not, by communicating the critical audit matters below, providing separate opinions on the critical audit matters or on the accounts or disclosures to which they relate.

[Include critical audit matters]

[Signature]

We have served as the Company's auditor since [year].

[City and State or Country]

[Date]

Differences exist between the unmodified report used for nonpublic companies' audits and the PCAOB unqualified audit report including:

- The PCAOB report is titled Report of Independent Registered Public Accounting Firm, and the AICPA report is titled Independent Auditor's Report.

- The audit opinion in the PCAOB report is included in the first section of the report whereas it appears in the last paragraph of the AICPA report.

- Reference to whether the financial statements are free of material misstatement, whether due to error or fraud, appears in the Basis for Opinion section of the PCAOB report, not the Auditor's Responsibility section as in the AICPA report.

- The PCAOB report language specifically references the independence requirement under relevant laws and rules of the SEC and PCAOB; the AICPA report is titled Independent Auditor's Report.

- The AICPA report specifically references considering the internal controls in order to design audit procedure but not to express an opinion; the PCAOB report doesn't specifically mention internal controls but addresses the role of audit procedures. The internal control report of management is required for public companies as a separate report by SOX Section 404.

- The PCAOB report that was revised on June 1, 2017, now includes a separate section on Critical Audit Matters (CAMs) that are not included in the AICPA report.

- The PCAOB report includes a statement disclosing the year in which the auditor began serving consecutively as the company's auditor; no such statement exists in the AICPA report.

PCAOB AS 1301: Communications with Audit Committees[25]

Previously we discussed auditor communications with those charged with governance as it pertains to AICPA standards. In this section we address exactly what should be communicated between the registered public accounting firm and the audit committee of a public entity under PCAOB standards. The following items should be communicated to ensure the audit committee is aware of situations that may affect the auditors' evaluation of accounting and financial reporting results and problems with management in carrying out the audit.

1. *Significant accounting policies and practices.* Significant accounting policies include management's initial selection of, or changes in, significant accounting policies or the application of such policies in the current period and the effect on financial statements or disclosures of significant accounting policies in controversial areas or areas for which there is a lack of authoritative guidance, consensus, or diversity in practice.

2. *Critical accounting policies and practices.* All critical accounting policies and practices to be used should be communicated to the audit committee, including the reasons certain policies and practices are considered critical and how current and future events might affect the determination of whether certain policies are considered critical.

3. *Critical accounting estimates.* A description of the process management used to develop critical accounting estimates should be communicated, along with management's significant assumptions used in critical accounting estimates that have a high degree of subjectivity. Additional communications include any significant changes that management made to the processes used to develop critical accounting estimates or significant assumptions, a description of management's reasons for the changes, and the effects of the changes on the financial statements.

4. *Significant unusual transactions.* Significant unusual transactions include those that are outside the normal course of business for the company or that otherwise appear to be unusual due to their timing, size, or nature and the policies and practices management used to account for significant unusual transactions.

The auditor should communicate to the audit committee a variety of matters dealing with the quality of the company's financial reporting including, for example, situations in which the auditor identified bias in management's judgments about the amounts and disclosures in the financial statements. Also, the results of the auditor's evaluation of the differences between estimates best supported by the audit evidence and estimates included in the financial statements, which are individually reasonable but that indicate a possible bias on the part of the company's management.

The auditor should communicate to the audit committee any disagreements with management about matters, whether or not satisfactorily resolved, that individually or in the aggregate could be significant to the company's financial statements or the auditor's report. Disagreements with management do not include differences of opinion based on incomplete facts or preliminary information that are later resolved by the auditor obtaining additional relevant facts or information prior to the issuance of the auditor's report.

The auditor should communicate to the audit committee any significant difficulties encountered during the audit. Significant difficulties encountered during the audit include, but are not limited to:

- Significant delays by management, the unavailability of company personnel, or an unwillingness by management to provide information needed for the auditor to perform her audit procedures.

- An unreasonably brief time within which to complete the audit.

- Unexpected extensive effort required by the auditor to obtain sufficient appropriate audit evidence.

- Unreasonable management restrictions encountered by the auditor on the conduct of the audit.

- Management's unwillingness to make or extend its assessment of the company's ability to continue as a going concern when requested by the auditor.

Audit committee communications are an essential part of an effective governance system and a key ingredient in creating an ethical organization environment. Open communications between the auditor and audit committee are essential to supporting the financial reporting oversight role assigned to the audit committee under SOX. The audit committee plays a critical role in resolving differences between the auditor and management and supporting the goal of a fair presentation of the financial statements and efficient and effective internal controls over financial reporting.

PCAOB AS 3101: The Auditor's Report on an Audit of Financial Statements When the Auditor Expresses an Unqualified Opinion[26]

The new PCAOB audit report went into effect for audits of fiscal years ending on or after December 15, 2017, except for the requirements related to critical audit matters (CAMs), which is effective for audits of fiscal years ending on or after June 30, 2019, for large accelerated filers and for fiscal years ending on or after December 15, 2020, for all other companies to which the requirements apply.

Critical Audit Matters

The PCAOB rule for disclosing CAMs is designed to improve audit quality. In determining whether a matter to be disclosed involved especially challenging, subjective, or complex auditor judgment, the auditor should take into account, alone or in combination, the following factors, as well as other factors specific to the audit:

- The auditor's assessment of the risks of material misstatement, including significant risks;
- The degree of auditor judgment related to areas in the financial statements that involved the application of significant judgment or estimation by management, including estimates with significant measurement uncertainty;
- The nature and timing of significant unusual transactions and the extent of audit effort and judgment related to these transactions;
- The degree of auditor subjectivity in applying audit procedures to address the matter or in evaluating the results of those procedures;
- The nature and extent of audit effort required to address the matter, including the extent of specialized skill or knowledge needed or the nature of consultations outside the engagement team regarding the matter; and
- The nature of audit evidence obtained regarding the matter.

The auditor must communicate in the auditor's report CAMs or state that none were determined to exist. For each CAM, the auditor should:

- Identify the CAM;
- Describe the principal considerations that led the auditor to determine that the matter is a CAM;
- Describe how the CAM was addressed in the audit; and
- Refer to the relevant financial statement accounts or disclosures that relate to the CAM.

Deloitte points out that management and audit committees should consider the implications of the new CAM requirements and discuss them with their auditors. Here are a few items to consider:[27]

- What matters might be included in CAMs?
- How will management and audit committees engage with the auditor as CAMs are identified and the auditor's descriptions of the CAMs are developed and finalized?
- How will the timing of auditor communications with management and the audit committee accommodate the discussion of CAMs?
- How do the auditor's statements regarding CAMs compare to management's disclosures regarding the same matters?

The reason to communicate with investors about CAMs is to inform them of key areas of the audit that might not otherwise be disclosed. As Jermakowicz et al. observe, "Reducing the level of information asymmetry between management and investors could result in more efficient capital allocation and lower the average cost of capital. ... The result should be to elevate the overall level of confidence in audited financial reports."[28]

Disclosure of Engagement Partner and Certain Other Participants in Audits

On December 15, 2015, the PCAOB adopted new rules and amendments to its auditing standards about involvement in audits. This information will be filed with the PCAOB on a new form, Auditor Reporting of Certain Audit Participants ("Form AP") and will be searchable on the PCAOB's website. The rules require disclosure of:[29]

- The name of the engagement partner;
- The names, locations, and extent of participation of other accounting firms that took part in the group audit (i.e., network firms) if their work constituted 5% or more of the total group audit hours; and
- The number and aggregate extent of participation of all other accounting firms that took part in the group audit whose individual participation was less than 5% of the total group audit hours.

This requirement brings U.S. audits into line with international standards and practices. However, one difference is the IAASB standards requires that engagement partners physically sign the audit report with their names instead of the name of the firms, as is done in the U.S. The final PCAOB standard was a compromise from the original proposal that called for having the engagement partner sign the audit report. Those who argued against it say because more than one partner is typically involved in an engagement, why single out the engagement partner to sign the report? The CAQ warned of adverse outcomes. The CAQ emphasized that engagement partners must answer to their employers, regulators, firms, audit committees, and investors already. CAQ opined that these multiple layers of accountability provide a significant incentive for engagement partners to conduct high quality audits in accordance with professional standards.

Audit Opinions

AICPA audit standards provide that auditors can express an unmodified/unqualified opinion, a qualified opinion, an adverse opinion, or a disclaimer. An auditor also can withdraw from the engagement under restricted circumstances. The qualified opinion, adverse opinion, or disclaimer of opinion is a "modified" opinion.

Opinion Paragraph—Unmodified or Unqualified

An auditor should give an unmodified or unqualified opinion when the financial statements "present fairly" financial position, results of operations, and cash flows. Certain situations may call for adding an additional paragraph: either an emphasis-of-matter or other-matter paragraph.

An emphasis-of-matter paragraph is a paragraph in the auditor's report that refers to a matter appropriately presented or disclosed in the financial statements (e.g., going concern, litigation uncertainty, subsequent events, etc.). It is added when, in the auditor's professional judgment, the item is of such importance that it is fundamental to users' understanding of the financial statements. Some emphasis-of-matter paragraphs are required by AICPA standards and others are added at the discretion of the auditor.

An other-matter paragraph is a paragraph included in the auditor's report that refers to a matter other than those presented or disclosed in the financial statements that, in the auditors' professional judgment, is relevant to users' understanding of the audit, the auditor's responsibilities, or the auditor's report (e.g., supplemental information).

An emphasis-of-matter or other-matter paragraph follows the opinion paragraph and has a section heading of "Emphasis-of-Matter" or "Other-Matter" for the AICPA report.

The PCAOB report also allows for an "emphasis paragraph" that might explain the following matters:

*   Significant transactions with related parties;
*   Unusually important subsequent events;
*   Accounting matters, other than those involving a change in accounting principles, affecting the comparability of the financial statements with those of the preceding period;
*   An uncertainty relating to the future outcome of significant litigation or regulatory actions; and
*   That the entity is a component of a larger business enterprise.

Opinion Paragraph—Modified

Recall that Rule 203 of the AICPA Code of Professional Conduct precludes rendering an opinion that states that the financial statements have been prepared in accordance with GAAP, or any statement that the auditor is not aware of any material modifications that should be made to such statements or data to make them conform with GAAP, if such statements or data contain any departure from an accounting principle that has a material effect on the statements or data taken as a whole. Instead, the auditor should modify the opinion and explain the GAAP deviation.

The auditor should modify the opinion in the auditor's report when (1) the auditor concludes, based on the audit evidence obtained, the financial statements as a whole are materially misstated; or (2) the auditor is unable to obtain sufficient appropriate audit evidence to conclude that the financial statements as a whole are free from material misstatement. The circumstances when each opinion is proper are discussed next.

A qualified opinion would be appropriate when (1) the auditor, having obtained sufficient appropriate audit evidence, concludes that misstatements, individually or in the aggregate, are material but not pervasive to the financial statements; or (2) the auditor is unable to obtain sufficient appropriate audit evidence on which to base the opinion, but the auditor concludes that the possible effects on the financial statements of undetected misstatements, if any, could be material but not pervasive.

An adverse opinion is proper when the auditor, having obtained sufficient appropriate audit evidence, concludes that misstatements, individually or in the aggregate, are both material and pervasive to the financial statements. Pervasive is a term used in the context of misstatements to describe the effects on the financial statements of misstatements, if any that are undetected due to an inability to obtain sufficient appropriate audit evidence. Pervasive effects on the financial statements require professional judgment by the auditor and are not generally confined to specific elements, accounts, or items of the financial statements, but if they are, they would represent or could represent a substantial proportion of the financial statements.

A disclaimer of opinion is warranted when the auditor is unable to obtain sufficient appropriate audit evidence on which to base the opinion, and the auditor concludes that the possible effects on the financial statements of undetected misstatements, if any, could be both material and pervasive.

For modifications, the audit report should include a separate paragraph that describes the matter giving rise to the modification. This paragraph should be placed immediately before the opinion paragraph in the auditor's report and include a heading such as "Basis for Qualified Opinion," "Basis for Adverse Opinion," or "Basis for Disclaimer of Opinion" as appropriate.

Exhibit 5.5 includes a summary of various paragraphs that can be included in the standard audit report and modified opinions.

EXHIBIT 5.5   Examples of Paragraphs in the Audit Report

Type of Report/Opinion	Management's Responsibility	Auditor's Responsibility	Opinion	Emphasis-of-Matter OR Other-Matter
Unmodified Opinion	Standard	Standard	Standard	
Emphasis-of-Matter				
Going Concern Issue	Standard	Standard	Standard	Description
Consistent GAAP Application	Standard	Standard	Standard	Description
Modified Opinions				
Qualified	Standard	Include departure from GAAP or scope limitation	"Except for the [GAAP departure or effects of scope limitation] . . . the financial statements present fairly . . ."	
Adverse	Standard	Include substantial reasons for adverse opinion	". . . the financial statements do not present fairly . . ."	
Disclaimer	Omitted	Omitted	Changed to indicate that an opinion cannot be expressed on the financial statements and why	

PCAOB standards require that, in certain circumstances, the auditor include explanatory language (or an explanatory paragraph) in the auditor's report that, while not affecting the auditor's opinion on the financial statements, it would shine light on certain matters that may be of concern to the users of the statements now and into the future. Here are a few examples:

- There has been a change between periods in accounting principles or in the method of their application that has a material effect on the financial statements;

- A material misstatement in previously issued financial statements has been corrected;

- Management is required to report on the company's internal controls over financial reporting, but such reporting is not required to be audited, and the auditor has not been engaged to perform an audit of management's assessment of the effectiveness of the company's internal control over financial reporting; and

- Other information in a document containing audited financial statements is materially inconsistent with information appearing in the financial statements.

Withdrawal from the Engagement

From time to time, an auditor might consider withdrawing from an engagement. Withdrawal generally is not appropriate because an auditor is hired by the client to do an audit and render an opinion, not walk away from one's obligations when the going gets tough. However, if a significant conflict exists with management or the auditor decides that management cannot be trusted, then a withdrawal may be justified. Factors that affect the auditor's conclusion include the implication of the involvement of a member of management or those charged with governance in any misconduct. Trust issues are a matter of ethics. Once pressure builds up in the auditor–client relationship and it boils over, the auditor must consider whether the breakdown in the relationship has advanced to the point that any and all information provided by the client is suspect. An auditor should not allow herself to be in the position of questioning the client's motives with every statement made and piece of evidence gathered. Withdrawal triggers the filing of the SEC's 8-K form by management.

Limitations of the Audit Report

Three phrases in the AICPA audit report are critical to understanding the limits of the report: (1) *reasonable assurance,* (2) *material,* and (3) *present fairly.* These expressions are used to signal the reader about specific limitations of the audit report.

Reasonable Assurance

The term *reasonable* is often used in law to define a standard of behavior to decide legal issues. For example, an auditor should exercise a *reasonable* level of care (due care) to avoid charges of negligence and possible liability to the client. Reasonable assurance is not an absolute guarantee that the financial statements are free of material misstatement. Auditors do not examine all of a company's transactions. The transactions selected for examination are determined based on materiality considerations and risk assessment. Even then, only a small percentage of transactions may be selected, often by statistical sampling techniques. Professional judgment is critical in making these determinations. Notably, increased use of data analytics could make it possible for external financial statement auditors to improve audits by testing complete sets of data.

Materiality

The concept of *materiality* recognizes that some matters are important to the fair presentation of financial statements, while others are not. The materiality concept is fundamental to the audit because the audit report states that an audit is performed to obtain reasonable assurance about whether the financial statements are free of material misstatement. Materiality judgments can be most challenging when determining whether audit adjustments are necessary.

Materiality judgments require the use of professional judgment and are based on management and auditor perceptions of the needs of a reasonable person who will rely on the financial statements. *Materiality* is defined in the glossary of Statement of Financial Accounting Concepts (SFAC) 2, Qualitative Characteristics of Accounting Information,[30] as: *The magnitude of an omission or misstatement of accounting information that, in the light of surrounding circumstances, makes it probable that the judgment of a reasonable person relying on the information would have been changed or influenced by the omission or misstatement.*

Materiality in the context of an audit reflects the auditor's judgment of the needs of users in relation to the information in the financial statements and the possible effect of misstatements on user decisions as a group. Materiality is judged by assessing whether the omissions or misstatements of items in the statements could, individually or collectively, influence the economic decisions of users taken on the basis of financial statements. Materiality depends on the size and nature of the omission or misstatement judged in the surrounding circumstances.

Typically, an auditor might use a percentage for the numerical threshold, such as 5%. Materiality is then judged by comparing an item in question to some amount such as total assets or net income. If the questionable item is equal to or greater than 5% of the comparison amount, then it is material and must be reported in the financial statements.

Assume that a company has one item in inventory that cost $400,000. The auditor believes the current market value is $381,000, or $19,000 (4.75%) below cost. Under the 5% rule, the item may be judged immaterial and the write-down ignored. However, what if the net income for the year is only $300,000? Then the $19,000 write-down becomes material because it equals 6.33% of net income.

One unintended consequence of the accounting profession's approach to materiality is that a controller—knowing the 5% rule is in effect—may attempt to decrease expenses or increase revenues by an amount less than 5% to increase earnings by an amount that will not be challenged by the auditor. It is somewhat ironic that the auditor can let the difference go unchallenged, even though it may be due to the misapplication of GAAP, simply because it is not "material" in amount. A good example is at North Face Inc. where the company engaged in barter transactions in the late 1990s. The CFO knew the materiality criteria used by the Deloitte auditors, and he structured a transaction to produce gross profit ($800,000) below the materiality amount. The auditors had recommended an adjustment for that amount, which was part of a $1.64 million revenue transaction. The auditors passed on the adjustment using materiality as the explanation.

Staff Accounting Bulletin (SAB) 99,[31] issued by the SEC, clarifies that the exclusive use of a percentage materiality criteria to assess material misstatements in the financial statements has no basis in law and is unacceptable. The commission did state that the use of a percentage as a numerical threshold, such as 5%, may provide the basis for a preliminary assumption that, without considering all relevant circumstances, a deviation of less than the specified percentage with respect to a particular item on the registrant's financial statements is unlikely to be material. However, the SEC ruled that both qualitative and quantitative factors must be considered when assessing materiality.

Materiality is judged both by the relative amount and by the nature of the item. For example, even a small theft by the president of a company is material because it raises doubts about the trustworthiness of the president, may indicate that other misappropriations have occurred, and brings into question the tone set from the top.

The SEC lists some of the qualitative factors that may cause quantitatively small misstatements to become material in SAB 99, including:

- It arises from an item capable of precise measurement.
- It arises from an estimate and, if so, the degree of imprecision inherent in the estimate.
- It masks a change in earnings or other trends.
- It hides a failure to meet analysts' consensus expectations for the enterprise.
- It changes a loss into income or vice versa.
- It concerns a segment or other portion of the registrant's business that has been identified as playing a significant role in the registrant's operations or profitability.
- It affects the registrant's compliance with regulatory requirements.
- It affects the registrant's compliance with loan covenants or other contractual requirements.
- It has the effect of increasing management's compensation—for example, by satisfying the requirements for the award of bonuses or other forms of incentive compensation.
- It involves concealment of an unlawful transaction.

Auditors should be on the alert for these red flags, which signal that qualitatively material items may not have been recorded and disclosed in accordance with GAAP.

What Is Meant by "Present Fairly"?

Without an understanding of the term *present fairly,* the users of a financial statement would be unable to assess its reliability. For the purposes of our discussion about fair presentation, we will proceed with the following guideline: that the auditor's assessment of fair presentation depends on whether (1) the accounting principles selected and applied have general acceptance; (2) the accounting principles are appropriate in the circumstances; (3) the financial statements, including the related notes, are informative of matters that may affect their use, understanding, and interpretation; (4) the information presented in the statements is classified and summarized in a reasonable manner—that is, neither too detailed nor too condensed; and (5) the financial statements reflect transactions and events within a range of reasonable limits.

Present fairly is a determination made in accordance with a financial reporting framework—i.e., U.S. GAAP or IFRS. Compliance with the framework includes (1) acknowledging explicitly or implicitly that, to achieve fair presentation of the financial statements, it may be necessary for management to provide disclosures beyond those specifically required by the framework; or (2) acknowledging explicitly that it may be necessary for management to depart from a requirement of the framework to achieve a fair presentation of the financial statements. Such departures are expected to be necessary only in extremely rare circumstances.

We wonder how the term *fair* in *fair presentation* relates to the traditional ethics notion of fairness as justice. Does this mean that financial statements that present fairly are just statements? We think not, because justice means, in part, to treat equals equally and unequals unequally. There is no such distinction in accounting to provide a different level of information for different user groups that might have different needs for information to assist decision making.

Outside the U.S., in European and other countries that have adopted IFRS, the term *true and fair view* replaces *fair presentation.* Historically, the former is associated with a higher degree of professional judgment, while the latter is more rules-based. However, determinations of fair presentation have moved more to the professional judgment arena as standards in the U.S. evolve to better accord with the International Standards on Auditing (ISA). Evidence of the movement toward increased professional judgment and professional skepticism can be seen in frameworks such as the KPMG Professional Judgment Framework discussed in Chapter 4.

Generally Accepted Auditing Standards (GAAS)

The whole of GAAS are comprehensive and more detailed than we need to focus on for our purposes. Instead, we address matters that pertain to professional judgment and professional skepticism in keeping with one of the themes in Chapter 4.

An independent auditor plans, conducts, and reports the results of an audit in accordance with GAAS. *Auditing standards* provide a measure of audit quality and the objectives to be achieved in an audit. Auditing standards differ from auditing procedures because the procedures are steps taken by the auditor during the course of the audit to comply with GAAS. The application of auditing standards entails making judgments with regard to the nature of audit evidence, sufficiency, competency, and reliability. Materiality considerations also are important to assess whether the audit opinion should be modified.

The GAAS have been seen as the bedrock foundation of the auditor's obligations to conduct a proper audit. These standards address the overall responsibilities of the independent auditor and the objectives of the conduct of an audit in accordance with AU-C Section 200. The PCAOB and the AICPA both adapted these standards that are applied to audits of historical financial information, compliance audits, and audits of internal control over financial reporting.

General Responsibilities of the Independent Auditor

The general responsibilities relate to the quality of the professionals who perform the audit. These include adequate technical training and proficiency, independence in mental attitude, and due care in the performance of the audit and preparation of the report. As discussed in Chapter 4, to be independent means to avoid all appearances that one's judgment may be clouded by events and relationships. Due care in performing an audit requires an objective outlook on audit evidence, diligence in meeting professional responsibilities, and competence in making professional judgments, including to exercise professional skepticism.

Objectives of Audit Procedures and Evidence

Objectives of audit procedures and evidence establish the criteria for judging whether the audit has met quality requirements. The standards include adequately planning the audit work and supervising assistants so that the audit is more likely to detect a material misstatement; obtaining a sufficient understanding of the entity and its internal control, to assess the risk of material misstatement of the financial statements, whether due to error or fraud; planning effectively the nature, timing, and extent of further audit procedures; and gathering sufficient competent evidential matter through audit procedures, including inspection, observation, inquiries, and confirmations to provide a reasonable basis (support) for an opinion regarding the financial statements under audit.

Objectives of Reporting

The objectives of reporting guide auditors in rendering an audit report and in determining the degree of responsibility that the auditor is taking with respect to the expression of an opinion of the financial statements. They include determination of whether the statements have been prepared in conformity with GAAP, identification of situations where the accounting principles have not been observed consistently in the current period in relation to the preceding period, and discussion in the report of any situation identified in the footnotes to the financial statements where informative disclosures are inadequate. In each case, professional judgments are necessary to meet the requirements of these standards.

Audit Evidence

Gathering and objectively evaluating audit evidence requires the auditor to consider the competency and sufficiency of the evidence. Representations from management, while part of the evidential matter the auditor obtains, are not a substitute for the application of those auditing procedures necessary to afford a reasonable basis for an opinion regarding the financial statements under audit.

Audit risk and materiality need to be considered together in determining the nature, timing, and extent of auditing procedures and in evaluating the results of those procedures. According to AU-C Section 315, the auditor should consider audit risk and materiality both in (a) planning the audit and designing auditing procedures and (b) evaluating whether the financial statements taken as a whole are presented fairly, in all material respects, in conformity with GAAP.[32]

The auditor's response to the risks of material misstatement due to fraud involves the application of professional skepticism when gathering and evaluating audit evidence. Examples of the application of professional skepticism in response to the risks of material misstatement due to fraud are obtaining additional corroboration of management's explanations or representations concerning material matters, such as through third-party confirmation, the use of a specialist, analytical procedures, examination of documentation from independent sources, or inquiries of others within or outside the entity. The independent auditor's direct personal knowledge, obtained through physical examination, observation, computation, and inspection, is more persuasive than information obtained indirectly.

Audit procedures are specific acts performed by the auditor to gather evidence about whether specific assertions are being met. For example, the client may state that the inventory value is $1 million. That is a specific assertion. The auditor then uses the procedure of observing the physical count of inventory to assess inventory quantity and traces certain year-end purchases and sales of inventory to invoices and other documentation as part of the cutoff process to determine whether year-end transactions should be part of the inventory. Typically, the auditor also tests the pricing of the inventory to assess the application of methods such as first-in, first-out (FIFO); last-in, first-out (LIFO); and the weighted average methods. The current market value of the inventory also has to be assessed.

Audit procedures help obtain an understanding of the entity and its environment, including its internal controls, to assess the risks of material misstatements. Audit procedures also test the operating effectiveness of controls in preventing or detecting material misstatements.

Professional skepticism plays an important role in gathering audit evidence and evaluating its usefulness. Recall that the term means to have a questioning mind and make a critical assessment of audit evidence. However, these requirements are somewhat ambiguous and leave open to interpretation what constitutes appropriate levels of questioning and critical assessment and how such behavior is demonstrated and can be documented.

The PCAOB in its inspection process looks for adequate judgments and skepticism when reviewing the audit reports of registered public companies. Shortcomings in these areas may reflect audit deficiencies. The PCAOB's Observations from 2016 Inspections of Auditors of Issuers (Staff Inspection Brief) describes the three key areas with the most frequent audit deficiencies observed in the 2016 inspection cycle: assessing and responding to risks of material misstatement, auditing ICFR, and auditing accounting estimates. Audit deficiencies include the failure to design and perform audit procedures to assess fraud risks and other significant risks. The Staff Inspection Brief specifically mentions that auditors should presume that there is a fraud risk involving improper revenue recognition and evaluate the types of revenue, revenue transactions, or assertions that may give risk to such risks.[33] The failure to adequately assess the fraud risk due to improper revenue can lead to materially misstated financial statements that require reissuance or restatement.

Internal Control Over Financial Reporting (ICFR)

LO 5-5

Explain PCAOB standards to assess ICFR.

As part of its oversight mission, the PCAOB aims to improve the quality of U.S. public company audits by evaluating auditors' assessment of companies' ICFR, as required by SOX. Recall that Section 404 requires registered accounting firms to report on management's assessment on the effectiveness of the internal control structure and procedures for financial reporting.

According to the PCAOB Staff Inspection Brief, audit deficiencies related to non-compliance with AS 2201, *An Audit of Internal Control Over Financial Reporting That is Integrated with An Audit of Financial Statements,* continue to be the most frequently identified deficiencies. The most frequent ICFR deficiencies identified related to insufficient testing of the design and operating effectiveness of selected controls, particularly with a review element. Specifically, some auditors did not evaluate the nature and/ or the appropriateness of the procedures performed by management during the review, including the criteria used to identify matters for investigation and the actions taken in investigating and resolving such matters.[34]

PCAOB Staff Audit Practice Alert No. 11 provides a Sample Inspection Finding–Review Control Deficiency.[35]

> An auditor selected for testing certain issuer controls related to the assessment of possible impairment of the issuer's long-lived assets. These controls consisted of the preparation and review of quarterly impairment memoranda and meetings to discuss various matters that could have an effect on accounting for these assets.
>
> The auditor limited the procedures to test these controls to obtaining evidence of management approval of the memoranda, attending certain issuer meetings, and reading the issuer's memoranda, which did not include detailed information such as the relevant indicators of possible asset impairment that management reviewed.
>
> The procedures performed by the auditor were not sufficient, as the auditor did not obtain an understanding of the actions performed by management during the review, which was necessary to evaluate whether the control was designed and operating to prevent or detect on a timely basis misstatements that could cause the financial statements to be materially misstated.

Calderon et al. examined PCAOB inspection reports published from August 2004 to November 2013 for inspection years 2002 through 2012. The authors used Audit Analytics data to categorize five types of ICFR-related audit deficiencies, and then collected detailed descriptions from the inspection reports. The authors reviewed 2,047 completed inspection reports during the period. Of the 1,025 inspection reports with audit deficiencies (about 50%), the authors identified 131 ICFR-related deficiencies: 89 U.S. inspection reports by U.S. auditors and 42 foreign inspection reports (31 foreign auditors). The following deficiencies were found:[36]

1. Testing the design of controls or operating effectiveness of controls (i.e., management review controls)	94
2. Application of the top-down risk-based approach to the audit of internal control (i.e., thought process auditors should employ in identifying risks)	53
3. Identifying information technology risks (i.e., obtaining an understanding of specific risks to the ICFR resulting from information technology)	40
4. Performing extensive testing of the work done by third parties in high-risk areas involving significant judgment and fraud risk	28
5. Evaluating identified control deficiencies	21

In a speech on the "PCAOB's Role in Improving Audit Quality," PCAOB Board member, Jeanette Franzel, addressed the importance of audit quality indicators to monitor on a regular basis audit quality. We discussed AQIs in the introduction and are mindful of their importance in identifying possible fraud risks and deficiencies in ICFR.

Franzel stated that the Board has seen significant improvements in audit quality as evidenced by the large firms dedicating significant resources toward remediating deficiencies and improving quality control systems. She also pointed to improvements in tone at the top, coaching and support to audit teams, and training and monitoring of audit quality.[37] These results are encouraging although we believe the accounting profession still has a long way to go to fully address why such a high deficiency rate exists in the inspections of audit reports.

Medicis Pharmaceutical Corporation Case

LO 5-6

Analyze a case study on auditor obligations when materially misstated financial statements exist.

Overview of the Case

The issuance of materially misstated financial statements by Medicis Pharmaceutical Corporation for the 2003 through 2007 fiscal years and the first two quarters of 2008 illustrates what can happen when audits fail to follow PCAOB standards and auditors do not conduct an audit with due care and exercise appropriate professional skepticism. Medicis used an accounting technique not acceptable under GAAP to reserve for its product returns. The company reserved for most of its estimated product returns at the cost of replacing the product rather than the correct method based on gross sales price. Since estimated costs were below sales value, the company overstated net revenues, net income, and EPS in some years with reversal effects in others thereby creating material misstatements in most of the years reported between 2003 and 2007. Exhibit 5.6 summarizes the facts of the case including accounting procedures followed, audit deficiencies, material misstatements, and improper unqualified opinions issued by EY. The information is taken from the PCAOB's findings as a result of its inspection of EY's audits of Medicis and other determinations.[38]

Ernst & Young

Ernst & Young and its auditors were cited by the PCAOB for deficient audits and disciplined pursuant to SOX. The auditors included: Jeffrey S. Anderson, lead engagement auditor; Robert H. Thibault, the independent review partner; Ronald Butler, Jr., a second partner supervised by Anderson; and Thomas A. Christie, also supervised by Anderson. The external auditors failed to obtain sufficient competent evidential matter to support the accounting, accepted management's representations, ignored its own internal audit quality review (AQR) of the client thereby violating PCAOB's quality control requirements (QC Section 20), and issued unqualified audit reports that the financial statements presented fairly, in all material respects, Medicis's financial position and results of operations in conformity with GAAP in each of the periods audited. The PCAOB inspected EY's audits of Medicis in some of those years, discovered mistakes in the application of GAAP, and highlighted the deficiencies in the audits in its inspection report.

The deficiencies in EY's audit can be summarized as follows:

- Failed to follow GAAS.
- Relied on management representations rather than independently gathered audit evidence.
- Developed alternative accounting methods for the reserve for sales returns in lieu of the client doing so and didn't inform the client of the alternative.
- Failed to act on its own AQR and correct deficiencies in its audit of Medicis.
- Issued unqualified opinions when it knew there were material misstatements in the financial statements.

PCAOB Actions

The PCAOB censured EY; barred Anderson and Thibault from being associated with a registered public accounting firm; censured Butler and Christie; and imposed civil monetary penalties in the amounts of $2 million, as to EY, $50,000, as to Anderson, $25,000 as to Thibault, and $25,000 as to Butler. All parties violated PCAOB rules and auditing standards related to EY's audits of the December 31, 2005, 2006, and 2007 financial statements of Medicis and in the consultation memorandum concerning Medicis' accounting for products returns stemming from EY's AQR of the December 31, 2005, Medicis audit in 2006.

Audit Committee

On September 24, 2008, Medicis announced that the Audit Committee of its Board of Directors determined that the quarterly periods in fiscal years 2003 through 2007 and the first two quarters of 2008, will need to be restated and should no longer be relied upon as well as EY's reports on the financial statements and effectiveness of ICFR for the related periods. The restatements relate to a modification in the Company's technical interpretation of GAAP relating to sales return reserve calculations.

Medicis restated its net revenues and diluted net income (loss) per share on Form 10/KA for the year ended December 31, 2007, as shown in Exhibit 5.6, including transition to calendar-year end reporting at 12/31/05" to the end of the sentence.

Exhibit 5.7 summarizes the facts of the case. Considering Medicis' accounting for sales returns over the five-year period, it's not unreasonable to say this was a company that was using accounting methods in search of appropriate transactions, rather than the reverse as is normally understood.

EXHIBIT 5.6   Medicis Form 10K/A (in millions) For the year ended December 31, 2007

Net revenues (in millions)	Fiscal Year Ended 12-31-2007	Fiscal Year Ended 12-31-2006	Transition Period Ended 12-31-2005	Fiscal Year Ended 06-30-2005	Fiscal Year Ended 06-30-2004	Fiscal Year Ended 06-30-2003
Reported	$464.7	$349.2	$164.0	$376.9	$303.7	$247.5
Adjustment	(7.3)	44.0	1.3	(11.2)	11.5	(37.2)
Restated	$457.4	$393.2	$165.3	$365.7	$315.2	$210.3
Diluted net income (loss) per share (in dollars)	Fiscal Year Ended 12-31-2007	Fiscal Year Ended 12-31-2006	Transition Period Ended 12-31-2005	Fiscal Year Ended 06-30-2005	Fiscal Year Ended 06-30-2004	Fiscal Year Ended 06-30-2003
Reported	$1.14	($1.39)	$0.76	$1.01	$0.52	$0.84
Adjustment	(0.06)	0.51	0.03	(0.09)	0.06	(0.34)
Restated	$1.08	($0.88)	$0.79	$0.92	$0.58	$0.50

EXHIBIT 5.7   Medicis Pharmaceutical Corporation Summary of the Case

Medicis sold pharmaceutical products to wholesale distributors and retail chain drug stores, which resold Medicis' products to others. Medicis' standard "Return Goods Policy" gave customers the right to return the product if the product was returned within four to six months before expiration or up to 12 months after expiration (collectively, "expired product"). When customers returned expired product, Medicis' Return Goods Policy provided that the company would give customers a full credit by issuing a credit memo in the amount of "the original purchase price or pricing one year prior to the date the warehouse receives the return." The

(Continued)

Policy did not require customers to purchase the same or similar product as a condition of receiving or using a credit for returning expired product. Customers routinely applied return credits to purchases of the same or similar products as the products that were returned due to expire. Most of the subsequent purchases occurred during the same quarter in which the return was issued.

Medicis' Revenue Recognition and Returns and Applicable GAAP

The proper accounting method for revenue recognition and the estimated returns reserve should have been based on *Statement of Financial Accounting Standards (SFAS) 48—Revenue Recognition When Right of Return Exists.*[39] Under SFAS 48, a company which sells a product subject to a right of return, may recognize revenue from those sales transactions at the time of sale only if certain conditions, including the ability to estimate future returns, are met. Medicis represented to EY that it recognized product revenue at the time of sale in accordance with SFAS 48. Because its customers had the right to return expired product, Medicis also recorded estimates of future product returns at the time of sale. Medicis used these estimates to establish a sales return reserve that reduced revenue reported in its financial statements. The audit evidence obtained by EY auditors indicated that SFAS 48 applied and that Medicis used the correct method. However, by reserving at replacement costs for most of its estimated returns, Medicis recorded its 85% gross margin as revenue at the time of sale even though it would issue as credit for gross sales price when the product was eventually returned months or years later. Audit evidence obtained by EY indicated that the reserving at replacement costs, and not at gross sales price, had a material impact on Medicis's return reserve estimate. The PCAOB pointed to information in EY's 2005 audit work papers that demonstrated had Medicis reserved for all estimated returns at gross sales price versus using both gross sales price and replacement cost, the company's reserve would have increased by over $54 million.

Compliance with PCAOB Rules and Audit Standards

Financial Statements for Six-Months-Ended December 31, 2005

Medicis adopted an interpretation of SFAS 48 by designating the transaction an "exchange," an exception to the gross sales reserve requirement. Exchanges by ultimate customers of one item for another of the same kind, quality, and price (i.e., one color or size for another) are not considered returns by exchanges. Medicis used this misinterpretation of the rules because exchanges are limited to transactions with "ultimate customer" and not the reseller as was the case for Medicis. The PCAOB determined that EY auditors were aware that the majority of Medicis product sales were to resellers. Further, the auditors know or should have known that the returns were not returns of products in exchange for products of a similar kind, quality, and price. Rather, they were of unsalable product for which a credit equal to the original gross sales price was issued.

Although the auditors knew about use of replacement cost, not gross sales price, they failed to adequately consider whether Medicis needed to disclose this practice in its financial statements. They also failed to consider disclosing the company's interpretation of SFAS 48. The auditors failed to obtain, or ensure the procedures to obtain, sufficient competent evidential matter supporting the conclusion that estimated returns replaced were eligible for the exchange exception. They were aware of the contradictory audit evidence indicating that returns replaced were not eligible for the exchange exception to SFAS 48, but failed to appropriately consider, or ensure performance of audit procedures to consider, such contradictory audit evidence.

2006 EY Audit Quality Review of the December 31, 2005 Audit

In May 2006, the December 31, 2005 Medicis audit was the subject of an EY AQR. The AQR program was part of EY's system of quality controls and procedures and designed to identify any deficiencies in selected EY audits and to require engagement teams to remediate such deficiencies. Rather than remediating the deficiency in using the exchange exception, the auditors concluded that a new equally deficient rationale supported Medicis' continued use of replacement cost. The new justification was to treat the transaction using warranty accounting. A consultation memorandum was prepared regarding the warranty accounting rationale. It was approved by Anderson and Thibault. The stated rationale was "by allowing customers to send back expired product the Company is essentially offering a 'warranty' on products sold. This means that the

(Continued)

economic cost to the Company of 'guaranteeing freshness' of the product is the cost basis of the product." This statement was contradicted by EY's internal accounting guidance which provided: "Warranty provisions differ from right-of-return provisions because the ultimate customer is returning a defective product."

During the December 31, 2005 audit and at the time of the 2006 AQR, Medicis had no documentation setting forth a warranty accounting rationale for reserving at replacement cost. EY did not inform Medicis of the warranty accounting rationale for reserving at replacement cost before EY concluded that the rationale was appropriate. It was not until the 2006 audit procedures (performed in the first quarter of 2007) that Medicis provided EY with any documentation setting forth a warranty rationale for reserving at replacement cost. The PCAOB charged that the auditors knew or should have known that the accounting did not conform to GAAP and a change to the gross sales price method would have a material effect on Medicis' financial statements and required it to restate December 31, 2005 financial statements.

December 31, 2006 Audit

During 2006, Medicis continued to rely on the warranty accounting to support its sales returns reserve but developed a new methodology at year-end to estimate the reserve for newer products. As a result of over $17 million of unexpected returns during the fourth quarter of 2006, Medicis broke its reserve into two categories: (1) products launched within the last four years ("non-legacy products") and (2) products launched more than four years earlier ("legacy products"). For legacy products, Medicis used historical return rates and lag times and reserved for returns at replacement costs ("historical method"). For non-legacy products, the returns reserve was based on estimating the total units of inventory in the distribution and retail channels and comparing that total estimate to an estimate of the units in the channels that would not be returned for expiration due to product demand. Medicis reserved for the difference between these two estimates at gross sales price.

As part of the 2006 year-end audit procedures, Medicis prepared a memorandum dated March 1, 2007, documenting its reliance on the SFAS 5 warranty accounting rationale, to support reserving for legacy product returns replaced at replacement cost under the historical method. The PCAOB determined that the auditors failed to obtain sufficient competent evidential matter supporting the conclusions and they knew or should have known that the application of warranty accounting to legacy product returns was not prescribed by GAAP.

December 31, 2007 Audit

Over the course of 2007, Medicis continued to change how it estimated its sales return reserve estimate. As shown in the audit work papers, Anderson and Christie knew that the December 31, 2006 returns reserve of $35.2 million—which was intended to cover approximately 18 months' worth of future returns—was insufficient to cover the 12 months of 2007 returns alone, which totaled $53.8 million at gross sales price. Management's December 31, 2007 return reserves of $9.6 million was less than the actual returns in the fourth quarter of 2007 alone. EY failed to adequately consider these facts and, to the extent management believed its historical return pattern would not continue, obtain sufficient competent evidential matter to support the reasonableness of the year-end reserve estimate.

Anderson and Christie failed to adequately test or ensure the performance of audit procedures to test management's estimate that 12 weeks of product inventory in the distribution channel was an appropriate estimate of the number of units of product not likely to be returned. Instead, the engagement team relied on management's representation that the 12-week assumption was appropriate and on the prior year's audit team's insufficiently supported acceptance of the 12-week assumption as the basis for the continued used of the assumption in 2007. The PCAOB charged that Anderson and Christie knew or should have known that the December 31, 2006 reserve estimate had proven not to be sufficient to cover anticipated returns.

The failure of EY, Anderson, and Christie to comply with PCAOB standards meant they improperly authorized the issuance of EY's audit report dated February 26, 2008, on Medicis' financial statements for the year-ended December 31, 2007, which incorrectly expressed an unqualified opinion that the financial statements presented fairly, in all material respects, Medicis' financial position and results of operations in conformity with GAAP.

Concluding Thoughts

Financial statement fraud threatens the foundation of the financial reporting process and jeopardizes the integrity of the auditing function. Signposts that fraud may exist need to be ingrained in the DNA of auditors. Influences that might bias their approach to an audit and their evaluation of audit evidence must be controlled through an ethical approach that emphasizes objectivity, due care, and the exercise of professional skepticism.

Auditors need to be more diligent in looking for the signs that fraud may exist. The Fraud Triangle provides a valuable framework to evaluate risks of fraud and better understand how to detect it and to prevent it from occurring. Beyond that, management and the audit committee must meet their obligations to monitor ICFR and make needed adjustments as warranted. Auditors must review management's assessments and make their own determination whether internal controls are operating as intended. Audit firms need to strengthen their own quality control systems to ensure they meet quality control standards and help to identify material misstatements in the financial statements, whether due to error or fraud.

Audit estimates are a problematic area. The aggressive judgments by management, such as the in the Medicis Pharmaceutical case, creates challenges for auditors in verifying the estimates and determining whether they contribute to improper financial reporting.

Financial statement restatements are also of concern. It's encouraging that the rate of restatements seems to be on the decline. Still, auditors must be mindful of the pressures placed on them by the management to cut corners in reporting revenues.

We are concerned about the quality of audits. The high deficiency rates found in PCAOB inspection reports indicates to us that auditors are not meeting their obligations to the public. Overreliance on management's representations seems to be the culprit, causing many of the audit deficiencies. As the saying goes, "trust but verify" should be the mantra of a sound audit.

Discussion Questions

1. What are the objectives of audit risk assessment, and why is it important to assess the likelihood that fraud may occur? How might the assessment influence the auditors' evaluation of ICFR?

2. Distinguish between an auditor's responsibilities to detect and report errors, illegal acts, and fraud. What role does materiality have in determining the proper reporting and disclosure of such events?

3. AU-C 240 points to three conditions that enable fraud to occur. Briefly describe each condition. How does one's propensity to act ethically, as described by Rest's model of morality, influence each of the three elements of the Fraud Triangle?

4. How might the existence of the dark triad personalities underlie undesirable behaviors by management and how might it influence the audit?

5. Describe the types of audit deficiencies that might arise because of problems with ICFR.

6. Explain the content of each section of the AICPA audit report. Evaluate the importance of each section with respect to the users of financial reports.

7. Give one example each of when an auditor might render an unmodified opinion and include either an emphasis-of-matter paragraph and/or an other-matter paragraph. What is the value of such paragraphs in the audit report?

8. Gary James works for Hill & Beans, a professional services firm. James was a onetime business partner of former Florida state Senator Howard Clark and a donor to his campaign. Clark was recently charged with conspiring to defraud the IRS out of hundreds of thousands of dollars during the time James prepared tax returns for Clark's business. The allegation is that Clark misclassified $2,268,520 as business expenses, when the money went to his children's tuition, a trip to Turks and Caicos Islands, home remodeling, and more. The amount of taxes Clark's business owed for these deductions was $850,748, but only $56,766 was paid. The IRS is preparing charges against James for his role in the matter.

   a. Discuss the ethics violations that may have been committed by James with respect to the AICPA Code discussed in Chapter 4.

   b. Assume you are the director of auditing for Hill & Beans and Clark approaches you requesting that your firm audit the financial statements of his business and prepare a report that would be submitted along with a loan request for $1 million for his business. How might the facts of this case influence whether you agree to provide the audit service?

9. Rationalization for fraud can fall under two categories: "no harm" and "no responsibility." Assume an employee is directed by management to reduce recorded expenses at year-end by insignificant amounts individually, but which are material in total. How might the employee justify her actions if questioned by the auditor with respect to no harm and no responsibility? What stage of moral development in Kohlberg's model is best illustrated by the employee's actions? Why?

10. The PCAOB believes there have been improvements in audit quality during the past few years. Discuss the indicators of audit quality and why they are important to protect the public interest.

11. Some criticize the accounting profession for using expressions in the audit report that seem to be building in deniability should the client commit a fraudulent act. What expressions enable the CPA to build a defense should the audit wind up in the courtroom? Do you see anything wrong with these expressions from an ethical point of view?

12. Do you think the concept of materiality is incompatible with ethical behavior? Consider in your answer how materiality judgments affect risk assessment in an audit of financial statements.

13. Data analysis, often in the form of continuous monitoring of transactions and controls, is increasingly used as a key component of risk management and audit processes overall. How might data analytics contribute to fraud detection? What are the potential drawbacks to the use of data analytics?

14. Mr. Arty works for Smile Accounting Firm as a senior accountant. Currently, he is doing a review of rental property compliance testing of rental receipts and expenses of the property owned by the client. He determines that the staff accountants tested only two tenants per property, instead of the three required by the audit program based on materiality considerations. However, to request more information from the client would cause massive delays, and the manager on the engagement is pressing hard for the information now. The manager did approach the client, who stated that she "needed the report yesterday." The manager reminds Arty that no problems were found from the testing of the two properties, in past years the workpapers called for just two properties to be reviewed, the firm has never had any accounting issues with respect to the client, and he is confident the testing is sufficient. Explain the relationship between the manager's explanations and the judgment tendencies discussed in Chapter 4.

15. Auditing standards require that a "brainstorming" session should be held at the beginning of each audit to help identify steps to assess the possibility that material misstatements/fraud in the financial statements exist. Discuss how brainstorming sessions might enhance audit judgments, professional skepticism, and decision making. Consider the groupthink dimension in your discussion.

16. Discuss the link between skeptical judgment and skeptical action and Rest's Four-Component Model of Ethical Decision Making.

17. What are the auditor's responsibilities to communicate information to the audit committee under PCAOB standards? If the auditor discovers that the audit committee routinely ignores such communications, especially when they are critical of management's use of GAAP in the financial statements, what step(s) might the auditor take at this point?

18. In 1995, Congress added Section 10A to the Securities Exchange Act of 1934 as part of the Private Securities Litigation Reform Act. Is it accurate to say that Congress enacted Section 10A with the intent to require auditors to blow the whistle on the fraudulent activities of their clients? Explain.

19. Explain how PCAOB inspections can lead to improvements in audit engagement quality.

20. What is the purpose of an audit firm developing a system of quality controls?

21. Answer the following questions about financial statement restatements.

    a. What are financial statement restatements?

    b. When should financial statements be restated?

    c. Assume the auditor has determined that prior financial statements need to be restated. What disclosures and other information should be communicated to shareholders, investors, and creditors about this matter?

22. Do you believe the end-user cares whether the lead audit engagement partner signs his or her name to the report or the firm simply files Form AP with the PCAOB? Explain.

23. Do you agree that a professional accountant providing professional services to a client *that is not an audit client* of the firm or a network firm, who is unable to escalate a matter pertaining to an illegal act within the client, should be required to disclose the suspected illegal act to the entity's external auditor? If not, why not and what action should be taken? What about informing the SEC? Under what circumstances, if any, should the auditor consider a whistleblowing action against the client and/or the firm under Dodd-Frank?

24. Assume you are inspecting EY's audit of Medicis Pharmaceutical Corporation for the PCAOB. Read through the information provided about the case in the chapter and identify the factors the auditors should have taken into account in determining critical audit matters.

25. You may know the difference between right and wrong behavior and never would consider committing fraud. But how do you maintain the highest level of professional conduct as it relates to fraudulent behaviors in others or when fraud is suspected?

Endnotes

1. International Auditing and Assurance Standards Board (IAASB), *A Framework for Audit Quality: Key Elements that Create an Environment for Audit Quality,* February 2014, https://www.ifac.org/system/files/publications/files/A-Framework-for-Audit-Quality-Key-Elements-that-Create-an-Environment-for-Audit-Quality-2.pdf.

2. Audit Analytics, *2016 Financial Restatements Review,* June 12, 2017, http://www.auditanalytics.com/blog/2016-financial-restatements-review/.

3. Fatima Alali and Sophia I-Ling Wang, "Characteristics of Financial Restatements and Frauds: An Analysis of Corporate Reporting Quality from 2000-2014," *The CPA Journal,* November 2017, https://www.cpajournal.com/2017/11/20/characteristics-financial-restatements-frauds/.

4. Alali and I-Ling Wang.

5. American Institute of Certified Public Accountants (AICPA), *Consideration of Fraud in a Financial Statement Audit* (AU-C Section 240).

6. AICPA, AU-C Section 240.

7. Center for Audit Quality (CAQ), Closing the Expectation Gap in Deterring and Detecting Financial Statement Fraud: A Roundtable Summary, October 21, 2013, http://www.thecaq.org/closing-expectation-gap-deterring-and-detecting-financial-statement-fraud-roundtable-summary.

8. *Securities and Exchange Commission v. KPMG LLP,* Joseph T. Boyle, Michael A. Conway, Anthony P. Dolanski, and Ronald A. Safaran, Civil Action No. 03-CV-0671 (DLC), Available at: www.sec.gov/litigation/complaints/comp17954.htm.

9. Mark S. Beasley, Joseph V. Carcello, Dana R. Hermanson, and Terry L. Neal, "An Analysis of Alleged Auditor Deficiencies in SEC Fraud Investigations: 1998–2010," Center for Audit Quality (2013).

10. W. Steve Albrecht, "Iconic Fraud Triangle Endures," *Fraud Magazine,* July–August 2014, Available at: http://www.fraud-magazine.com/article.aspx?id=4294983342.

11. Albrecht.

12. AICPA, AU-C Section 240.

13. AU-C Section 240.

14. AICPA, AU-C Section 240.

15. Alexander Coolidge, Frisch's: Top exec stole millions, January 20, 2015, https://www.cincinnati.com/story/money/2015/01/20/frischs-top-exec-stole-millions/22038045/.

16. Barry Jay Epstein and Sridhar Ramamoorti, "Today's Fraud Risk Models Lack Personality, *The CPA Journal,* March 2016, https://www.cpajournal.com/2016/03/16/todays-fraud-risk-models-lack-personality/.

17. Kari Joseph Olsen, Kelsey Kay Dworkis, and S. Mark Young (*2014*) CEO Narcissism and Accounting: A Picture of Profits. Journal of Management Accounting Research: Fall 2014, Vol. 26, No. 2, pp. 243-267, https://doi.org/10.2308/jmar-50638.

18. Jon Ronson, *The Psychopath Test: A journey Through the Madness Industry,* (NY: Riverview Publishing, 2011).

19. Juliana Moore and Elinor Jreige Weffort, Opportunistic Behavior in Accounting Choices: The Influence of Emotions and Personality, 2015, https://www.fea.usp.br/sites/default/files/arquivos/anexos/paper_oportunistic_behavior_in_accounting_choices_milan_et_al_2015_0.pdf.

20. Aaron Beam and Chris Warner, *HealthSouth: The Wagon to Disaster, (Fairhope, AL: Wagon Publishing, 2009).*

21. Alenjandro Adrian LeMon, Ph.D., Your Life Is This Dark Room and Only I Have the Key: A Closer Look into the Mind of the Psychopath, http://psychone.net/blogs/self-education/your-life-is-a-dark-room-and-i-have-the-key-a-closer-look-into-the-mind-of-the-psychopath.html.

22. Epstein and Ramamoorti.

23. AICPA, *Written Representations,* (AU-C Section 580).

24. *In the United States District Court for the District of Colorado, SEC v. Joseph Nacchio, Robert S. Woodruff, Robin R. Szeliga, Afshin Mohebbi, Gregory Casey, James T. Kozlowski, Frank T. Noyes,* Civil Action No. 05-MK-480.

25. PCAOB, AS 1301: Communications with Audit Committees, PCAOB release No. 2012-04, December 15, 2012, https://pcaobus.org/Standards/Auditing/Pages/AS1301.aspx.

26. PCAOB, AS 3101: The Auditor's Report on an Audit of Financial Statements When the Auditor Expresses an Unqualified Opinion, PCAOB Release No. 2017-001, June 1, 2017, https://pcaobus.org/Standards/Auditing/Pages/AS3101.aspx.

27. Deloitte, PCAOB adopts changes to the auditor's report, Heads Up, Volume 24, Issue 16 June 20, 2017. https://www2.deloitte.com/us/en/pages/audit/articles/hu-pcaob-adopts-changes-to-the-auditors-report-062017.html

28. Eva K. Jermakowicz, Barry J. Epstein, and Sridhar Ramamoorti, "CAM versus KAM—Making Judgments in Reporting Critical Audit Matters," *The CPA Journal,* February 2018, pp. 34-40.

29. PCAOB, Form AP—Auditor Reporting of Certain Audit Participants, https://pcaobus.org/Rules/Pages/Form-AP-Instructions.aspx.

30. Financial Accounting Standards Board (FASB), *Statement of Financial Accounting Standards* (Stamford, CT: FASB, November 1977).

31. SEC, Staff Accounting Bulletin 99: Materiality, Available at: https://www.sec.gov/interps/account/sab99.htm.

32. AICPA, *Understanding the Entity and its Environment and Assessing the Risks of Material Misstatement,* (AU-C Section 315).

33. PCAOB Staff Inspection Brief, Preview of Observations from 2016 Inspections of Auditors of Issuers, November 2017, https://pcaobus.org/Inspections/Documents/inspection-brief-2017-4-issuer-results.pdf.

34. PCAOB Staff Inspection Brief.

35. PCAOB, Staff Audit Practice Alert No. 11: Considerations for Audits of Internal Control Over Financial Reporting, October 24, 2013, https://pcaobus.org/Standards/QandA/10-24-2013_SAPA_11.pdf.

36. Thomas G. Calderon, Hakjoon Song, and Li Wang, "Audit Deficiencies Related to Internal Control, *The CPA Journal,* February 2016, https://www.cpajournal.com/2016/02/01/audit-deficiencies-related-internal-control/.

37. Jeanette Franzel, "The PCAOB's Role in Improving Audit Quality, *The CPA Journal,* August 2017, https://www.cpajournal.com/2017/08/21/pcaobs-role-improving-audit-quality/.

38. PCAOB, *Order Making Findings and Imposing Sanctions: In the Matter of Ernst & Young LLP, Jeffrey S. Anderson, CPA, Ronald Butler, Jr., CPA, Thomas A Christie, CPA, and Robert H. Thibault, CPA,* PCAOB Release No. 105-2012-01, February 8, 2012, https://pcaobus.org/Enforcement/Decisions/Documents/Ernst_Young.pdf.

39. Financial Accounting Standards Board (FASB), Statement of Financial Accounting Standards No. 48 – Revenue Recognition When Right of Return Exists, http://www.fasb.org/jsp/FASB/Document_C/DocumentPage?cid=1218220126701&;acceptedDisclaimer=true.

Chapter 5 Cases

Case 5-1 Loyalty and Fraud Reporting (a GVV case)

Assume Ethan Lester and Vick Jensen are CPAs. Ethan was seen as a "model employee" who deserved a promotion to director of accounting according to Kelly Fostermann, the CEO of Fostermann Corporation, a Maryland-based, largely privately held company that is a prominent global designer and marketer of stereophonic systems. The company has an eleven person board of directors.

Kelly considered Ethan to be an honest employee based on performance reviews and his unwillingness to accept the promotion, stating that he wasn't ready yet for the position. Kelly admired his willingness to learn and grow, not just expect a promotion. Little did she know that Ethan was committing a $50,000 fraud during 2018 by embezzling cash from the company. In fact, no one seemed to catch on because Ethan was able to override internal controls. However, the external auditors were coming in and to solidify the deception, he needed the help of Vick Jensen, a close friend who was the accounting manager and also reports to Ethan. Ethan could "order" Vick to cover up the fraud but hoped he would do so out of friendship and loyalty. Besides, Ethan knew Vick had committed his own fraud two years ago and covered it up by creating false journal entries for undocumented sales, returns, transactions, and operating expenses.

Ethan went to see Vick and explained his dilemma. He could see Vick's discomfort in hearing the news. Vick had thought he had turned the corner on being involved in fraud after he quietly paid back the $20,000 he had stolen two years ago. Here is how the conversation went.

"Vick, I need your help. I blew it. You know Mary and I split up 10 months ago."

"Yes," Vick said.

"Well, I got involved with another woman who I tried to impress by buying her things. I wound up taking $50,000 from company funds."

"Ethan, what were you thinking?"

"Don't get all moral with me. Don't you recall your own circumstances?"

Vick was quiet for a moment and then asked, "What do you want me to do?"

"I need you to make some entries in the ledger to cover up the $50,000. I promise to pay it back, just as you did. You know I'm good for it."

Vick reacted angrily, saying, "You told me to skip the bank reconciliations—that you would do them yourself. I trusted you."

"I know. Listen, do this one favor for me, and I'll never ask you again."

Vick grew increasingly uneasy. He told Ethan he needed to think about it . . . his relationship with the auditors was at stake.

Questions

1. Analyze the facts of the case using the Fraud Triangle. Would you characterize what Ethan Lester did as a failure of internal controls? Explain.

2. Assume Ethan sets a meeting with Vick in two days to follow-up on his request. Vick has decided not to be part of the cover-up. Use the GVV framework to help Vick prepare for the meeting. Consider the following:

   • What should Vick say to counteract Ethan's request?

   • How might Vick's intended action affect the company and the external auditors?

   • Who can Vick go to for support?

3. Assume Ethan gets upset after the meeting and decides to fire Vick. He tells Vick to leave quietly or Ethan will disclose the $20,000 fraud. What should Vick do next?

Case 5-2 ZZZZ Best[1]

The story of ZZZZ Best is one of greed and audaciousness. It is the story of a 15-year-old boy from Reseda, California, who was driven to be successful, regardless of the costs. His name is Barry Minkow. Although this case dates back over 30 years, it does serve as an example of what can happen when auditors do not look too hard to find fraud.

Minkow had high hopes to make it big—to be a millionaire very early in life. He started a carpet cleaning business in the garage of his home. Minkow realized early on that he was not going to become a millionaire cleaning other people's carpets, but that he could in the insurance restoration business. In other words, ZZZZ Best would contract to do carpet and drapery cleaning jobs after a fire or flood. Because the damage from the fire or flood probably would be covered by insurance, the customer would be eager to have the work done, and perhaps not be all that concerned with how much it would cost. The only problem with Minkow's insurance restoration idea was that it was all a fiction. Allegedly, over 80% of his revenue was from this work. In the process of creating the fraud, Minkow was able to dupe the auditors, Ernst & Whinney (now EY), into thinking the insurance restoration business was real. The auditors never caught on until it was too late.

How Barry Became a Fraudster

Minkow wrote a book, *Clean Sweep: A Story of Compromise, Corruption, Collapse, and Comeback,*[2] that provides some insights into the mind of a 15-year-old kid who was called a "wonder boy" on Wall Street until the bubble burst. He was trying to find a way to drum up customers for his fledgling carpet cleaning business. One day, while he was alone in his garage-office, Minkow called Channel 4 in Los Angeles. He disguised his voice so he wouldn't sound like a teenager and told a producer that he had just had his carpets cleaned by the 16-year-old owner of ZZZZ Best. He sold the producer on the idea that it would be good for society to hear the success story about a high school junior running his own business. The producer bought it lock, stock, and carpet cleaner. Minkow gave the producer the phone number of ZZZZ Best and waited. It took less than five minutes for the call to come in. Minkow answered the phone and when the producer asked to speak with Mr. Barry Minkow, Minkow said, "Who may I say is calling?" Within days, a film crew was in his garage shooting ZZZZ Best at work. The story aired that night, and it was followed by more calls from radio stations and other television shows wanting to do interviews. The calls flooded in with customers demanding that Barry Minkow personally clean their carpets.

As his income increased in the spring of 1983, Minkow found it increasingly difficult to run the company without a checking account. He managed to find a banker that was so moved by his story that the banker agreed to allow an

---

[1]The facts are derived from a video by the ACFE, *Cooking the Books: What Every Accountant Should Know about Fraud,* Available at: http://www.acfe.com/selfstudy.aspx?id=2590&terms=(video+cooking+the+books)+.

[2]Barry Minkow, *Clean Sweep: A Story of Compromise, Corruption, Collapse, and Comeback* (Nashville, TN: Thomas Nelson, 1995).

underage customer to open a checking account. Minkow used the money to buy cleaning supplies and other necessities. Even though his business was growing, Minkow ran into trouble paying back loans and interest when due.

Minkow developed a plan of action. He was tired of worrying about not having enough money. He went to his garage—where all his great ideas first began—and looked at his bank account statement, which showed that he had more money than he thought he had based on his own records. Minkow soon realized it was because some checks he had written had not been cashed by customers, so they didn't yet show up on the bank statement. Voilá! Minkow started to kite checks between two or more banks. He would write a check on one ZZZZ Best account on the last day of the reporting period and deposit it into another. The check wouldn't clear Bank #1 for at least one day so he could count the cash in both accounts (back then, checks weren't always processed in real time the way they are today).

It wasn't long thereafter that Minkow realized he could kite checks big time. Not only that, he could make the transfer of funds at the end of a month or a year and show a higher balance than really existed in Bank #1 and carry it onto the balance sheet. Because Minkow did not count the check written on his account in Bank #1 as an outstanding check, he was able to double-count.

Time to Expand the Fraud

Over time, Minkow moved on to bigger and bigger frauds, like having his trusted cohorts confirm to banks and other interested parties that ZZZZ Best was doing insurance restoration jobs. Minkow used the phony jobs and phony revenue to convince bankers to make loans to ZZZZ Best. He had cash remittance forms made up from nonexistent customers with whatever sales amount he wanted to appear on the document. He even had a co-conspirator write on the bogus remittance form, "Job well done." Minkow could then show a lot more revenue than he was really making.

Minkow's phony financial statements enabled him to borrow more and more money and expand the number of carpet cleaning outlets. However, Minkow's personal tastes had become increasingly more expensive, including purchasing a Ferrari with the borrowed funds and putting a down payment on a 5,000-square-foot home. So, the question was: How do you solve a perpetual cash flow problem? You go public! That's right, Minkow made a public offering of stock in ZZZZ Best. Of course, he owned a majority of the stock to maintain control of the company.

Minkow had made it to the big leagues. He was on Wall Street. He had investment bankers, CPAs, and attorneys all working for him—the now 19-year-old kid from Reseda, California, who had turned a mom-and-pop operation into a publicly owned corporation.

Barry Goes Public

Pressured to get a big-time CPA firm to do his audit by the underwriting firm selling his stock, Minkow hired Ernst & Whinney to perform the April 30, 1987, fiscal year-end audit. Minkow continued to be one step ahead of the auditors—that is, until the Ernst & Whinney auditors insisted on going to see an insurance restoration site. They wanted to confirm that all the business—all the revenue—that Minkow had said was coming in to ZZZZ Best was real.

The engagement partner drove to an area in Sacramento, California, where Minkow did a lot of work—supposedly. He looked for a building that seemed to be a restoration job. Why he did that isn't clear, but he identified a building that seemed to be the kind that would be a restoration job in progress.

Earlier in the week, Minkow had sent one of his cohorts to find a large building in Sacramento that appeared to be a restoration site. As luck would have it, Minkow's associate picked out the same site as had the partner later on. Minkow's cohorts found the leasing agent for the building. They convinced the agent to give them the keys so that they could show the building to some potential tenants over the weekend. Minkow's helpers went up to the site before the arrival of the partner and placed placards on the walls that indicated ZZZZ Best was the contractor for the building restoration. In fact, the building was not fully constructed at the time, but it looked as if some restoration work was going on at the site.

Minkow was able to pull it off in part due to luck and in part because the Ernst & Whinney auditors did not want to lose the ZZZZ Best account. It had become a large revenue producer for the firm, and Minkow seemed destined for greater and greater achievements. Minkow was smart and used the leverage of the auditors not wanting to lose the ZZZZ Best account as a way to complain whenever they became too curious about the insurance restoration jobs. He would even threaten to take his business from Ernst & Whinney and give it to other auditors. To get on their good side, he would wine and dine the auditors and even invite them to his house.

Minkow also took a precaution with the site visit. He had the auditors sign a confidentiality agreement that they would not make any follow-up calls to any contractors, insurance companies, the building owner, or other individuals involved in the restoration work. This prevented the auditors from corroborating the insurance restoration contracts with independent third parties.

The Fraud Starts to Unravel

It was a Los Angeles housewife who started the problems for ZZZZ Best that would eventually lead to the company's demise. Because Minkow was a well-known figure and flamboyant character, the *Los Angeles Times* did a story about the carpet cleaning business. The Los Angeles housewife read the story about Minkow and recalled that ZZZZ Best had overcharged her for services in the early years by increasing the amount of the credit card charge for its carpet cleaning services.

Minkow had gambled that most people don't check their monthly statements, so he could get away with the petty fraud. However, the housewife did notice the overcharge and complained to Minkow, and eventually he returned the overpayment. She couldn't understand why Minkow would have had to resort to such low levels back then if he was as successful as the *Times* article made him out to be. So she called the reporter to find out more, and that ultimately led to the investigation of ZZZZ Best and future stories that weren't so flattering.

Because Minkow continued to spend lavishly on himself and his possessions, he always seemed to need more and more money. It got so bad over time that he was close to defaulting on loans and had to make up stories to keep the creditors at bay, and he couldn't pay his suppliers. The complaints kept coming in, and eventually the house of cards that was ZZZZ Best came crashing down.

During the time that the fraud was unraveling, Ernst & Whinney decided to resign from the ZZZZ Best audit. It had started to doubt the veracity of Minkow and his business at ZZZZ Best. Of course, by then it mattered little because the firm had been a party to the cover-up for some time.

Legal Liability Issues

The ZZZZ Best fraud was one of the largest of its time. ZZZZ Best reportedly settled a shareholder class action lawsuit for $35 million. Ernst & Whinney was sued by a bank that had made a multimillion-dollar loan based on the financial statements for the three-month period ending July 31, 1986. The bank claimed that it had relied on the review report issued by Ernst & Whinney in granting the loan to ZZZZ Best. However, the firm had indicated in its review report that it was not issuing an opinion on the ZZZZ Best financial statements. The judge ruled that the bank was not justified in relying on the review report because Ernst & Whinney had expressly disclaimed issuing any opinion on the statements. The firm lucked out in that the judge understood that a review engagement only provides limited assurance rather than the reasonable assurance of the audit.

Barry Minkow was charged with engaging in a $100 million fraud scheme. He was sentenced to a term of 25 years.

Questions

1. Do you believe that auditors should be held liable for failing to discover fraud in situations such as ZZZZ Best, where top management goes to great lengths to fool the auditors? Explain.

2. Discuss the red flags that existed in the ZZZZ Best case and evaluate Ernst & Whinney's efforts with respect to fraud risk assessment.

3. These are selected numbers from the financial statements of ZZZZ Best for fiscal years 1985 and 1986. What calculations or analyses would you make with these numbers that might help you assess whether the financial relationships are "reasonable"?

	1985	**1986**
Sales	$1,240,524	$4,845,347
Cost of goods sold	576,694	2,050,779
Accounts receivable	0	693,773
Cash	30,321	87,014
Current liabilities	2,930	1,768,435
Notes payable—current	0	780,507

4. Analyze Minkow's behavior from the perspective of being a "Dark Triad Personality." Does he fit one or more of the personality types? Explain.

Case 5-3 Reauditing Financial Statements

Margaret Dairy is a CPA and the managing partner of Dairy and Cheese, a regional CPA firm located in northwest Wisconsin. She just left a meeting with a well-respected regional credit union headquartered in her hometown. Margaret was asked whether her firm would be willing to reaudit the previous years' financial statements and, subsequently, conduct an audit of the current years' financials. This is the first time Margaret has been asked to conduct a reaudit, although she realizes it has become more common as a result of problems like Enron and WorldCom experienced. Some companies switching auditors have elected to have the new audit firm re-examine prior-period financial statements because of concerns about the quality of the earlier audit.

On her way back to the office, Margaret calls her brother Mark, who is a Senior Audit Manager at a firm in Margaret's hometown, to share her good news. She tells him that doing the audit work for the two years will increase her firm's revenue by 10%. Mark is taken aback by the news. The new client was a client of Mark's firm. He did not know the firm had lost the client and it might be picked up by Dairy & Cheese.

Questions

1. What issues should be of concern to Margaret in deciding whether Dairy and Cheese should accept the reaudit engagement?

2. What are Mark's ethical obligations in this matter? Should he discuss the situation with Margaret? How about bringing it up at his firm?

3. Regardless of your answer to part 2, what inquiries should Margaret make of the predecessor auditor?

4. Assume Margaret's firm discovers undetected fraud in the previous years' financial statements, what should she do?

Case 5-4 GE Multibillion Insurance Charge

On January 30, 2018, General Electric (GE) announced that it was taking an after-tax charge of $6.2 billion in the December 31, 2017 financial statements and additional cash funding of $15 billion in statutory capital contributions to its insurance subsidiary. GE acknowledged a Securities and Exchange Commission investigation into the process leading to the sudden multibillion-dollar charge and an additional review of revenue recognition and controls over its long-term contracts. When GE first announced the charge on January 16, 2018, which related to the remnants of its long-term care reinsurance portfolio, CEO John Flannery told analysts he had "underappreciated the risk in this book." [A book of business, in the context of insurance, is a database or "book" that lists all of the insurance policies the insurance company has written.][1]

GE's North America Life & Health subsidiary is a reinsurance portfolio the company held on to after mostly exiting the business between 2004 and 2006. A reinsurer buys the right to receive premiums from the primary insurers that deal directly with consumers in exchange for eventually shouldering any potential losses. Those primary insurers underwrite and administer the policies and process claims when they come in.

The majority of GE Capital's remaining insurance business, 60%, is related to long-term care insurance. At the time, Flannery told analysts, GE believed that a gradual runoff of existing claims—no new business has been added since 2006—would be more profitable than selling the whole business. Unfortunately, Flannery said, GE didn't anticipate the low interest rate environment, low policy lapse rates, and higher claims cost that it is seeing now.

GE warned analysts as long ago as the second-quarter of 2017 that a review of its claims experience and reserves was under way, and any charge would happen in the fourth quarter. In its 2017 second quarter filing with the SEC, GE wrote: "We have recently experienced elevated claim experience for a portion of our long-term care insurance products, which may result in a deficiency in reserves plus future premiums compared to future benefit payments. Should such a deficiency exist, we would record a charge to earnings in the second half of 2017 upon completion of this review." And in its third quarter 2017 filing with the SEC, GE warned about the potential charge again but with more details.

"We have recently experienced elevated claim experience for a portion of our long-term care insurance contracts and are conducting a comprehensive review of premium deficiency assumptions across all insurance contracts, including a reassessment of future claim projections for long-term care contracts that will be incorporated within our annual test of future policy benefit reserves for premium deficiencies in the fourth quarter of 2017. We would record a charge to earnings for any premium deficiencies in the fourth quarter of 2017 upon completion of this review."

Accounting experts were expecting the review to result in some financial charge, but not on this scale. "The review of business always carries the risk of unexpected findings, yet the magnitude of the $6.2 billion charge is far more staggering than the $3 billion that the market anticipated," research firm Audit Analytics wrote in a note to subscribers.

At its annual meeting last November, chief financial officer Jamie Miller told shareholders that GE was likely to take a charge of more than $3 billion.

Changes in insurance claim reserves typically are disclosed in advance as changes in accounting estimates related to long-term care reserves. Companies are only required to disclose adjustments that are material. In its note, Audit Analytics wrote it looked at 30 insurance companies and found 60 changes in accounting estimates filed with the SEC for adjustment to the long-term care loss reserves filed since 2004.

The last time GE disclosed any changes in reserves even partly attributable to the long-term care reinsurance portfolio, according to Audit Analytics, was in its 2004 annual report, the same year it spun off the Genworth Financial business—another insurance company. GE wrote that liabilities, reserves, and annuity benefits were $4.5 billion higher than in 2003 and "attributable to growth in annuities, long-term care insurance, structured settlements,

---

[1]Francine McKenna, "GE says shock multibillion-dollar insurance charge is a 'special case,' *MarketWatch,* January 30, 2018, https://www.marketwatch.com/story/ge-says-shock-multibillion-dollar-insurance-charge-is-a-special-case-2018-01-26.

the effects of the weaker U.S. dollar, increases in loss reserves for policies written in prior years and 2004 U.S. hurricane-related losses."

On the call when the charge was first announced, Chief Risk Officer Ryan Zanin told analysts that a large percentage of the policyholders in their book of business were sold the policies at a very early age and are only now reaching the prime claim paying period—ages 80 and up. Therefore, approximately 40% of inception-to-date claims have occurred in the last two years.

A GE spokeswoman told MarketWatch: "GE has tested the adequacy of its policy reserves for the runoff insurance business every year through premium deficiency testing." In all prior years, Zanin said on the call with analysts, "these tests resulted in a positive margin, which, under GAAP, requires that original assumptions above the book remain locked." JP Morgan analyst Stephen Tusa asked GE Chief Financial Officer Jamie Miller if the company was happy with its auditor. "If these guys reviewed this stuff every year for the last several years and this is kind of a result of that, doesn't that kind of raise questions?" he asked. Flannery said that he was not planning an auditor change.

KPMG, the GE auditor for more than 100 years, is also the external auditor for Genworth Financial. A spokesman for KPMG emailed MarketWatch to say this.

"We are confident that our audits and reviews were appropriately performed in accordance with applicable professional standards, and we stand behind our work. Our client confidentiality obligations prohibit us from commenting further."

Questions

1. Assume you are asked as part of an audit of GE's insurance business to assess fraud risks, what would you include in your report and why?

2. At GE's annual meeting in November 2017, CFO Jamie Miller told shareholders that GE was likely to take a charge of more than $3 billion. Just fourteen months later GE announced a charge of $6.2 billion. Do you believe this indicates a failure on the part of KPMG to adequately evaluate the estimates of insurance claim reserves and risk assessment, or is it reflective of a change in economic circumstances that could not have been anticipated?

3. According to the Financial Executives Research Foundation, "enhancing the effectiveness of corporate disclosures is of paramount importance to companies, investors, creditors, regulators and the capital markets at large. This has compelled many companies to take a fresh look at how effectively they 'tell their story.'"[2] Some worry that increased disclosures through different channels can be confusing and lead to "disclosure overload." What role should materiality play in determining what kinds of information should be disclosed and how frequently? What are the dangers from an audit perspective of having clients increasingly add to its disclosures, especially when estimates are involved? Did GE do the "right thing" when it warned of a $3 billion charge only to wind up taking a $6.2 billion charge?

Case 5-5 Tax Inversion (a GVV case)

Jamie Keller was pleased with his new job position as director of international consolidation for Gamma Enterprises. Gamma Enterprises was a consolidation of high-tech gaming companies, with subsidiaries of Alpha, Beta, Gamma, Delta, and Epsilon. This past year Gamma had completed a tax inversion with Epsilon, which is headquartered in Ireland, becoming the parent company. Gamma was the oldest company of the group and the only subsidiary with material inventory.

[2]Financial Executives Research Foundation, Disclosure effectiveness: Companies embraced the call to action, http://www.financialexecutives.org/ferf/download/2015%20Final/2015-022.pdf.

Jamie was preparing for a meeting with Jason Day, the CFO of the group, as well as the senior manager on the audit of Gamma. The discussion was planning for the year-end and issues with the tax inversion and consolidation with Epsilon as the parent company.

Jamie and Jason were in the conference room when Thomas Stein, the senior auditor, arrived. Jamie was surprised as Thomas was an accounting classmate from State University.

"Thomas, what a surprise! I did not know that we would be working together on the annual financial statements. Long time, no see," Jamie said.

"Yes, it's good to see you. We did many a team project together in school. Congratulations on your new position. Jason told me what a great job you were doing."

Jason cleared his throat and said, "I see we all know each other. Let's get started as I think there are a lot of year-end issues with this tax inversion. First, the company will keep the corporate physical headquarters here in Philadelphia, but many of the governance meetings will be at Epsilon headquarters in Dublin, Ireland. Jamie, I need you to prepare a study for the board to consider at the next meeting as to whether all the subsidiaries should change to IFRS for the consolidation or not. Thomas, can you briefly explain the issues with such a change?"

"Under IFRS most assets will be revalued to fair market values. That will increase the values on the balance sheet. The biggest drawback will be the taxes the company will owe with changing from LIFO to weighted average for Gamma's inventory," Thomas began.

"Hold on, a minute," Jason jumped in. "This tax inversion is to be a tax savings or tax-neutral situation, particularly this year when the stockholders are expecting profits. The U.S. government has allowed LIFO inventory for tax and financial reporting purposes so that is what Gamma is going to do."

Jamie asked, "Are you suggesting that Gamma continue using U.S. GAAP while the other subsidiaries change to the IFRS basis? If I remember correctly from school, a company must pick one financial reporting format and follow the principles in those standards. Besides, LIFO is not acceptable under IFRS."

"I don't see why it is a big deal to use IFRS for all but Gamma's inventory, Jason said. Thomas, what do you think?"

"I'm sure something can be worked out," Thomas replied.

The discussion changed to other issues. After the meeting, Jamie and Thomas went to lunch to catch up on old times. At lunch, Jamie commented, "Thomas, do you really mean to let Jason and Gamma Enterprises pick and choose which accounting standards to follow, using a mixed-bag approach?"

"No, you were right, Jamie. However, I could see that the issue was upsetting Jason. It may take time to convince him."

"I was just surprised that you seemed open to it at all. Aren't the auditors suppose to be the watchdogs of business?"

"Jamie, I am up for partner this next year. I need to keep Gamma as a happy client. The pressure to keep revenues coming into the accounting firm is a big weight on my shoulders."

"Well, just don't forget your values."

Questions

Assume you are Thomas's position and know that you have to let Jason know the correct way to convert to IFRS accounting.

- What will be the objections or pushback from Jason?

- What would you say next? What data and other information do you need to make your point and counteract the reasons and rationalizations you will likely have to address?

Consider whether Jamie and Thomas could work together to convince Jason (and the board) to change accounting methods. Identify the stakeholders in this case and their interests in addressing the following questions.

- What are the main arguments you are trying to counter? That is, what are the reasons and rationalizations you need to address?
- What is at stake for the key parties, including those who disagree with you?
- What levers can you use to influence those who disagree with you?
- What is your most powerful and persuasive response to the reasons and rationalizations you need to address? To whom should the argument be made? When and in what context?

Case 5-6 Rooster, Hen, Footer, and Burger

Barry Yellen, CPA, is a sole practitioner. The largest audit client in his office is Rooster Sportswear. Rooster is a privately owned company in Chicken Heights, Idaho, with a 12-person board of directors.

Barry is in the process of auditing Rooster's financial statements for the year ended December 31, 2019. He just discovered a related-party transaction that has him worried. For one thing, the relationship has existed for the past two years, but Barry did not discover it. What's just as troubling is that the client hid it from him.

Rooster bought out Hen Sportswear two years ago but still operates it as a separate entity, and since then has systematically failed to disclose to the private investors related-party transactions involving the CEO of Rooster, Frank Footer. It seems that Footer is borrowing money from Hen and is deeply in debt to the CEO of that company, who is his brother-in-law. Also, Hen has hired relatives of Footer, most of whom are unqualified for their jobs, and pays them an above-market salary. This has been hidden from Barry as well.

Barry was informed by an anonymous tipster that Rooster operates a secret off-balance-sheet cash account to pay for cash bonuses to senior officers, travel and entertainment expenses, an apartment rental for Footer, and cash and noncash gifts to local government officials to "grease the wheels" when permits need to be expedited in favor of Rooster. Barry doesn't know what to make of it, because he is too focused right now on the related-party transactions with Hen Sportswear.

Barry is in the process of questioning Hans Burger, CPA, who is the CFO of Rooster, about these transactions. Burger explains that he had raised these issues with Footer but was instructed in no uncertain terms to leave them alone. He did just that. Burger told Barry he needed this job and wouldn't jeopardize it out of a sense of "ethics."

Barry is in his office back at the firm and reflecting on how best to handle this matter.

Questions

1. Who are the stakeholders in this case and what are Barry's obligations to them?
2. What are related-party transactions? Why are related-party transactions a particularly sensitive area? What do you think Barry should do with respect to audit obligations for these transactions?
3. Has fraud been committed in this case? Explain. If so, what are Barry's obligations in this regard?

Case 5-7 Diamond Foods: Accounting for Nuts[1]

Diamond Foods, based in Stockton, California, is a premium snack food and culinary nut company with diversified operations. The company had a reputation of making bold and expensive acquisitions. Due to competition within the snack food industry, Diamond developed an aggressive company culture that placed high emphasis upon performance. The company's slogan was "Bigger is better." However, without strong ethical oversight, questionable behavior started to persist at Diamond Foods in 2009. Serious allegations of fraud against top management led to a restructuring of leadership. Here is the story we dub: "Accounting for Nuts."

On November 14, 2012, Diamond Foods Inc. disclosed restated financial statements tied to an accounting scandal that reduced its earnings during the first three quarters of 2012 as it took significant charges related to improper accounting for payments to walnut growers. The restatements cut Diamond's earnings by 57% for FY2011, to $29.7 million, and by 46% for FY2010, to $23.2 million. By December 7, 2012, Diamond's share price had declined 54% for the year.

Diamond Foods, long-time maker of Emerald nuts and subsequent purchaser of Pop Secret popcorn (2008) and Kettle potato chips (2010), became the focus of an SEC investigation after The Wall Street Journal raised questions about the timing and accounting of Diamond's payments to walnut growers. The case focuses on the matching of costs and revenues. At the heart of the investigation was the question of whether Diamond senior management adjusted the accounting for the grower payments on purpose to increase profits for a given period.

The case arose in September 2011, when Douglas Barnhill, an accountant who is also a farmer of 75 acres of California walnut groves, got a mysterious check for nearly $46,000 from Diamond. Barnhill contacted Eric Heidman, Diamond's director of field operations, on whether the check was a final payment for his 2010 crop or prepayment for the 2011 harvest. (Diamond growers are paid in installments, with the final payment for the prior fall's crops coming late the following year.) Though it was September 2011, Barnhill was still waiting for full payment for the walnuts that he had sent Diamond in 2010. Heidman told Barnhill that the payment was for the 2010 crop, part of FY2011, but that it would be "budgeted into the next year." The problem is, under accounting rules, you cannot legitimately record in a future fiscal year an amount for a prior year's crop. That amount should have been estimated during 2010 and recorded as an expense against revenue from the sale of walnuts.

An investigation by the audit committee in February 2012 found payments of $20 million to walnut growers in August 2010 and $60 million in September 2011 that were not recorded in the correct periods. The disclosure of financial restatements in November 2012 and audit committee investigation led to the resignation of former CEO Michael Mendes, who agreed to pay a $2.74 million cash clawback and return 6,665 shares to the company. Mendes' cash clawback was deducted from his retirement payout of $5.4 million. Former CFO Steven Neil was fired on November 19, 2012, and did not receive any severance. The SEC brought a lawsuit against Diamond Foods, Mendes, and Neil. It settled with the company and Mendes on January 9, 2014. In a separate action, Neil settled charges that he had directed the effort to fraudulently underreport money paid to walnut growers by delaying the recording of payments into later fiscal periods.

As a result of the audit committee investigation and the subsequent analysis and procedures performed, the company identified material weaknesses in three areas: control environment, walnut grower accounting, and accounts payable timing recognition. The company announced efforts to remediate these areas of material weakness, including enhanced oversight and controls, leadership changes, a revised walnut cost estimation policy, and improved financial and operation reporting throughout the organization.

---

[1]Stanford University, United States District Court Northern District of California San Francisco Division: Case No. 11-cv-05386, *In Re: Diamond Foods, Inc. Securities Litigation Consolidated Complaint Class Action,* Available at: http://securities.stanford.edu/filings-documents/1048/DMND00_01/2012730_r01c_11CV05386.pdf.

A number of questionable transactions took place, including unusual timing of payments to growers, a leap in profit margins, and volatile inventories and cash flows. Moreover, the company seemed to push hard on every lever to meet increasingly ambitious earnings targets and allowed top executives to pull in big bonuses, according to interviews with former Diamond employees and board members, rivals, suppliers, and consultants, in addition to reviews of public and nonpublic Diamond records.

Nick Feakins, a forensic accountant, noted the relentless climb in Diamond's profit margins, including an increase in net income as a percent of sales from 1.5% in FY2006 to more than 5% in FY2011. According to Feakins, "no competitors were improving like that; even with rising Asian demand." Reuters did a review of 11 companies listed as comparable organizations in Diamond's regulatory filings and found that only one, B&G Foods, which made multiple acquisitions, added earnings during the period.

Auditors often look at the relationship between earnings and cash flow as part of their risk assessment. At Diamond, net income growth is generally reflected in operating cash flow increases. However, the cash generation was sluggish in FY2010, when earnings were strong. Also, in September 2010, Mendes had promised EPS growth of 15% to 20% per year for the next five years. In FY2009, FY2010, and FY2011, $2.6 million of Mendes' $4.1 million in annual bonus was paid because Diamond beat its EPS goal, according to regulatory filings.

Diamond falsely disclosed its strong overall financial performance in conference calls with financial analysts. In its call for the third quarter FY 2011, Mendes said: "Earnings per share had increased 73% to 52 cents, exceeding the top end of the company's guidance range. Strong operating cash flow for the period helped fund a significant increase in new product and advertising investment as EBITDA [Earnings before interest, taxes, depreciations, and amortization] of $31 million was more than double the same period in the prior year." Based on these false reports, the analysts were optimistic about future earnings and share value. They informed the investment banking groups in their firms to recommend a "buy" to their clients.

As for the role of Deloitte in the fraud, the SEC charged that Neil misled them by giving false and incomplete information to justify the unusual accounting treatment for the payments. The SEC's order against Mendes found that he should have known that Diamond's reported walnut cost was incorrect because of information he received at the time, and he omitted facts in certain representations to Deloitte about the special walnut payments. One problem was Neil did not document accounting policies or design the process for which walnut grower payments and the walnut cost estimates were determined. This was exacerbated by the fact that management did not communicate the intent of the payments effectively.

Questions

1. Use the Fraud Triangle to analyze the business and audit risks that existed at Diamond Foods during the period of its accounting fraud.

2. How would you characterize Diamond's accounting? Did they commit an error in recording walnut grower payments? Was it an illegal act? A fraudulent act? For each one, explain the reporting requirements for Deloitte assuming they were aware of the transactions.

3. What are auditors' obligations with respect to accounting estimates and judgments made by management? Explain any concerns that should have existed about these areas of the audit. Assume that Deloitte was aware of these issues. Would any of them rise to the level of a critical audit matter? Explain.

4. Do you think non-GAAP information, such as that provided to financial analysts, should be audited? Consider the value of such information to the users of financial reports in answering this question.

Case 5-8 Critical Audit Matters or Potentially Damaging Disclosure?

Ronnie Maloney, an audit partner for Forrester and Loomis, a registered public accounting firm in Boston, just received a meeting request from Jack McDuff, the chairman of the audit committee of Digital Solutions, one of his clients. The audit committee wants to discuss the draft communication the firm prepared to meet its obligations under PCAOB AS 1301. Digital Solutions, a Fortune 1000 client, has expressed concerns over the skepticism raised by the firm over accounting policies. Moreover, McDuff was worried about the impact of critical audit matters included in the draft of the December 31, 2020 audit report. He claimed that publicly disclosing the critical audit matter would muddy the waters for investors as the financial statements for the year-ended December 31, 2020, were found to fairly represent the financial condition of the company in all material respects.

Maloney is the lead engagement partner on the Digital Solutions audit. He arranges a meeting with Haley Stone, another audit partner on the engagement team, to discuss McDuff's request. They review the audit team's findings about accounting policies. It seems there was concern about a related party transaction between the CEO of Digital and a vendor whereby Digital paid about 20% above market price for components received from the vendor. As a result, Digital's net earnings for the year declined rather than increased, and earnings per share were $0.10 less than it would have been had the transaction been at arms' length.

As to the critical audit matters, Maloney and Stone discussed an estimate Digital made of imputed interest on a non-interest-bearing note from the same vendor for a piece of machinery that was recorded on December 30, 2020. The company used a 2% rate on the $400,000 five-year note and calculated the present value as $362,292. The entry recorded was:

Debit—Machinery 362,292

Debit—Discount 37,708

Credit—Note Payable 400,000

Based on an analysis of the rate Digital would incur if it borrowed funds from another source, Maloney and Stone determined that 6% should have been used. That would have led to the following entry:

Debit—Machinery 298,904

Debit—Discount 101,096

Credit—Note Payable 400,000

The future interest expense would be $63,388 less given the 2% rate, which had a material effect on future earnings. Furthermore, the difference was close to the amount of the "premium" Digital Solutions paid to the vendor for the components.

Questions

1. Given the facts of the case, what communications do you believe Forrester & Loomis should have made with the audit committee with regard to the transactions with the vendor to comply with PCAOB AS 1301?

2. How should Forrester & Loomis have determined whether to communicate the critical audit matter with the audit committee under PCAOB AS 1301?

3. Are the differences discussed in the case a matter of judgment or are there other factors at work? What concerns do you have about the audit risk and ICFR?

4. Do you believe financial statement fraud exists in this case? Explain why or why not.

Case 5-9 Weatherford International

Cast of Characters[1]

Weatherford International PLC is a multinational Irish public limited company based in Switzerland, with U.S. offices in Houston, Texas. Weatherford's shares are registered with the SEC and are listed on the NYSE. Weatherford files periodic reports, including Forms 10-K and 10-Q, with the Commission pursuant to Exchange Act Section 13(a) and related rules thereunder.

James M. Hudgins, CPA, served as Weatherford's Director of Tax from January 1999 until mid-2000, when he became Vice President of Tax, and as an Officer from February 2009 until his resignation on March 31, 2012.

Darryl S. Kitay, CPA, served as Weatherford's Tax Manager and Senior Manager from April 2004 until 2011, then as Weatherford's Tax Director through January 2013. Kitay reported to Hudgins from April 2004 until March 2012. Weatherford relieved Kitay of all supervisory responsibilities associated with Weatherford's income tax accounting in May 2012, after the filing of the Second Restatement of financial statements. Weatherford terminated Kitay's employment in July 2013.

Ernst & Young LLP was Weatherford's external auditor from 2001 to March 2013. On March 7, 2013, Weatherford's audit committee decided not to re-appoint EY.

SEC Order Against EY

On October 18, 2016, the SEC announced that EY agreed to pay more than $11.8 million to settle charges related to failed audits of Weatherford based on the auditors' failure to detect deceptive income tax accounting to inflate earnings. The EY penalty is in addition to the $140 million penalty already agreed to. The combined $152 million will be returned to investors who were harmed by the accounting fraud. The Commission also charged the EY partner who coordinated the audits, Craig Fronckiewicz, and a former tax partner who was part of the audit engagement team, Sarah Adams. Both agreed to suspensions to settle charges that they disregarded significant red flags during the audits and reviews.

The SEC's order stated that, despite placing the Weatherford audits in a high-risk category, EY's audit team repeatedly failed to detect the company's fraud until it was more than four years ongoing. The audit team was aware of post-closing adjustments that Weatherford was making to significantly lower its year-end provision for income taxes each year, but it relied on Weatherford's unsubstantiated explanations instead of performing the required audit procedures to scrutinize the company's accounting. The SEC's order also found that EY did not take effective measures to minimize known recurring problems its audit teams experienced when auditing tax accounting.[2]

Facts of the Case

Between 2007 and 2012, Weatherford, a large multinational provider of oil and natural gas equipment and services, issued false financial statements that inflated its earnings by over $900 million in violation of U.S. GAAP. Weatherford issued materially false and misleading statements about its net income, EPS, effective tax rate ("ETR"), and other key financial information. Weatherford did not have sufficient internal accounting controls to identify and properly account for its accounting of income taxes throughout the relevant period.

---

[1]SEC, *In the Matter of Weatherford International PLC, F/K/A Weatherford International Ltd., James Hudgins, CPA, and Darryl Kitay, CPA,* Accounting and Auditing Enforcement Release No. 3806, September 27, 2016, https://www.sec.gov/litigation/admin/2016/33-10221.pdf.

[2]SEC, *In the Matter of Ernst & Young LLP, Craig R. Fronckiewicz, CPA, and Sarah E. Adams, CPA,* Accounting and Auditing Enforcement Release No. 3814, October 18, 2016, https://www.sec.gov/litigation/admin/2016/34-79109.pdf.

As a result, Weatherford was forced to restate its financial statements on three separate occasions over eighteen months. The first restatement was made public on March 1, 2011, when Weatherford announced that it would restate its financial results for 2007-2010 and that a material weakness existed in its ICFR for the accounting of income taxes. That restatement, filed on March 8, 2011, reduced previously reported net income by approximately $500 million (the "First Restatement"). $461 million of the First Restatement resulted from a four-year income tax accounting fraud orchestrated by Hudgins and Kitay. Hudgins and Kitay made numerous post-closing adjustments or "plugs" to fill gaps to meet ETRs that Weatherford previously disclosed to financial analysts and the public. This deceptive intercompany tax accounting improperly inflated Weatherford's earnings and materially understated its ETR and tax expense.

The fraud created the misperception that the tax structure Weatherford designed to reduce its tax expense and ETR was far more successful than it actually was. From 2007 to 2010, Weatherford regularly promoted its favorable ETR to analysts and investors as one of its key competitive advantages, which it attributed to a superior international tax avoidance structure that Hudgins constructed at the urging of senior management.

After announcing the First Restatement, Weatherford's stock price declined nearly 11% in one trading day ($2.38 per share), closing at $21.14 per share on March 2, 2011. The decline eliminated over $1.7 billion from Weatherford's market capitalization.

Weatherford announced additional restatements in February 2012 and July 2012 (the "Second Restatement" and "Third Restatement," respectively). After the First Restatement, Weatherford attempted to remediate its material weakness in internal control over income tax accounting. Throughout its remediation efforts in 2011, Weatherford filed its Forms 10-Q on a timely basis and falsely reassured investors that it was performing additional reconciliations and post-closing procedures to ensure that its financial statements were fairly presented in conformity with GAAP. However, Weatherford, through Hudgins and Kitay, failed to review, assess, and quantify known income tax accounting issues that had a high risk of causing additional material misstatement as early as July 2011. When Weatherford filed its Second Restatement on March 15, 2012, Weatherford reported a $256 million drop in net income from 2007-2011 as a result of additional errors in its income tax accounting, and its material weakness in internal control over income tax accounting remained. At least $84 million of that drop in net income resulted from an income tax accounting GAAP violation Hudgins and Kitay knew about, but failed to assess and quantify, before Weatherford filed its third quarter financial statements.

Four months after filing the Second Restatement, Weatherford announced that it was withdrawing reliance on all previous financial statements because it had discovered additional income tax errors that reduced prior period net income by $107 million. By the time Weatherford issued its Third Restatement on December 17, 2012, Weatherford had reduced net income from prior periods by an additional $186 million, largely driven by books, records, and internal accounting controls issues identified and corrected during Weatherford's remediation efforts in 2012.

Tax Strategy

A key component of Weatherford's tax strategy was to develop a superior international tax avoidance structure that reduced Weatherford's ETR and tax expense (and increased EPS and cash flow) while providing a competitive advantage over U.S.-based peer companies. In 2002, Weatherford changed its place of incorporation from the U.S. to Bermuda, a 0% tax jurisdiction, through a process known as inversion.

Weatherford further refined its international tax structure from 2003 through 2006 by implementing a series of hybrid instruments to facilitate the movement of revenue from higher tax rate jurisdictions (i.e., Canada and U.S.) to lower tax rate jurisdictions (i.e., Hungary and Luxembourg). Hybrid instruments are often used in international tax planning to achieve deductions in one, typically high tax rate, jurisdiction and shift income to another, typically low tax rate, jurisdiction. Hybrid instruments are structured to incorporate features of both debt and equity, such that the instrument typically qualifies as debt in one jurisdiction and equity in another. Payments on debt may be deducted in computing taxable income while the yields are accrued but not necessarily paid and, therefore, not calculated as taxable income. As a result, these international tax avoidance strategies reduced Weatherford's ETR from 36.3% in 2001 to 25.9% by the end of 2006.

Weatherford senior management and Hudgins understood that Weatherford's tax structure and resulting ETR added significant value and was material to analysts and investors alike. Wall Street analysts closely followed Weatherford's ETR and its effect on earnings. Each percentage point in Weatherford's ETR translated into $0.02 to $0.03 in EPS.

Weatherford's senior management knew its tax department was perpetually understaffed and overworked during the years leading up to the First Restatement. Hudgins led a tax staff that was roughly the same size as when he was hired, and Hudgins pressed his employees to work long hours to make Weatherford's tax structure extremely competitive. Weatherford and Hudgins quickly gained a reputation with the company's external auditor as a challenging and demanding client known for taking aggressive accounting positions, particularly in the area of income tax accounting.

Although Weatherford reduced its ETR by nearly 10% from 2001 to the end of 2006, its CFO remarked that Weatherford's ETR remained somewhat above that of other inverted peer companies in his response to an analyst's question during the year-end earnings call on January 30, 2007. Soon thereafter, Weatherford started reporting ETR results that created a false perception that its international tax structure was outperforming similarly-situated competitors by a significant margin. For example, in 2008 and 2009, fueled by its deceptive income tax accounting practices, Weatherford reported pre-restatement ETRs of 17.1% and 6.5%.

In connection with fiscal years 2007 through 2010, Hudgins and Kitay engaged in fraudulent practices relating to income tax accounting that violated GAAP and made Weatherford's financial statements materially false and misleading. During each of those years, Weatherford repeatedly and publicly disclosed ETR estimates and recorded tax expenses that Hudgins and Kitay knew, or were reckless in not knowing, were fabricated. Each year, Hudgins and Kitay made or authorized unsupported post-closing adjustments to accounting data that intentionally lowered Weatherford's actual ETR and tax expense. To do so, they reversed accounting data that had been correctly input into Weatherford's consolidated tax provision from the company's accounting system, and did not notify Weatherford's accounting department why they had made such adjustments.

Hudgins and Kitay performed no work to support the adjustments, which were merely a "plug" to arrive at the lower estimated ETR and tax expense amounts. Without disclosing how they arrived at their numbers, they provided these amounts for inclusion in Weatherford's consolidated financial statements, which senior management shared with analysts and investors repeatedly during earnings calls and public financial statements. This conduct went undetected for over four fiscal years. Kitay identified the existence of the adjustments to EY each year, but, when questioned about them, Kitay made misleading and inconsistent responses to the auditors and failed to disclose the true reason for the adjustments. Kitay sometimes asked Hudgins to review his responses before providing them to EY.

The errors were finally discovered in February 2011. By that time, a "phantom income tax receivable" had increased to such dramatically disproportionate heights, over $460 million, that it defied even the unsupported explanations of Hudgins and Kitay. Shortly thereafter, Weatherford released the First Restatement in March 2011.

Results for 2007

The following summarizes the accounting and tax maneuvers for 2007. We limit the discussion to 2007 for the sake of brevity.

Throughout the first three quarters of 2007, Weatherford recorded ETR and tax expense pursuant to FIN 18, *"Accounting for Income Taxes in Interim Periods."* FIN 18 prescribes an estimated annualized ETR approach for computing the tax provisions for the first three quarters of the year, which is based on a company's best estimate of current year ordinary income. GAAP, however, does not allow companies to use FIN 18 to calculate their year-end tax provisions.

To comply with GAAP, Weatherford was required to record ETR and tax expense at year end pursuant to FAS 109, *"Accounting for Income Taxes."* FAS 109 establishes standards on how companies should account for and report the effects of income taxes, including the calculation of the year-end consolidated tax provision. Tax department personnel reviewed that information, after which the tax provisions for legal entities were finalized and then combined on a region-by-region basis. The region-based tax provisions were then consolidated to arrive at a single tax provision from which current and deferred assets and liabilities, associated tax expense (or benefit), and ETR were calculated and recorded.

Shortly before Weatherford was scheduled to release its year-end financial results for 2007, however, Hudgins and Kitay discovered the year-end ETR and tax expense that had been calculated pursuant to FAS 109 far exceeded the ETR estimates and tax expense disseminated publicly to analysts and investors during the first three quarters of 2007 based on their ETR estimates. Faced with a deadline for reporting earnings, Hudgins and Kitay falsified the year-end consolidated tax provision by making an unsubstantiated manual $439.7 million post-closing "plug" adjustment to two different Weatherford Luxembourg entities. To do so, they intentionally reversed accounting data that had been correctly input to Weatherford's consolidated tax provision via the company's accounting system.[3]

The resulting plug adjustment, which Hudgins and Kitay then improperly applied a 35% tax rate to, allowed Weatherford to reduce its tax expense by $153.9 million for the year and to lower its ETR in line with previous ETR estimates publicly disclosed during quarterly calls with analysts.

Hudgins and Kitay took no steps to determine the necessity and accuracy of the plug adjustment, either before or after it was made. They performed no work at any time to determine whether plugging the gap was appropriate under GAAP and made no attempt to substantiate the difference between the their publicly disclosed ETR estimates and tax expenses with the FAS 109 actual results that they were witnessing. Both Hudgins and Kitay knew, or were reckless in not knowing, that they should have reviewed and substantiated the actual tax numbers after the close process, but they never did. Hudgins and Kitay made no attempt to alert Weatherford's accounting department, internal auditor, or senior management of the significant issues related to its FAS 109 actual ETR results. Nor did they notify EY of any discrepancy.

During 2007 and throughout the relevant period, Hudgins signed representation letters relied upon by Weatherford senior management and EY indicating, without exception, that the ICFR for the accounting of income taxes were effective and that the income tax accounting was completed in accordance with GAAP. These statements were false.

Phantom Income Tax Receivable

The inappropriate plug adjustments and the resulting improper tax benefits recorded from 2007 through 2010 created a $461 million debit balance to Weatherford's current income tax payable, which Respondents reclassified as an income tax receivable for reporting purposes. This improper accounting should have raised red flags long before the First Restatement.

Hudgins and Kitay made misleading statements about the true reasons for the growing tax debit balance, claiming falsely that they had made either sizeable prepayments or overpayments to foreign tax jurisdictions that they would be working to recover. For example, during the fourth quarter of 2009, Weatherford reclassified the large debit balance within the Current Income Tax Payable account to a Prepaid Other account. In response to EY inquiries about the large "Prepaid Other" debit balance, Kitay responded, "We do not believe it would be appropriate to classify these balances as receivables until such time as a claim for refund has been filed." By 2010, Hudgins was aware of the phantom receivable and told others at Weatherford that he was working to recover all overpaid amounts, although he knew there were no such overpaid amounts.

In performing its audit of Weatherford's financial statements, EY and Weatherford identified a number of additional income tax accounting errors that increased Weatherford's tax expense by tens of millions of dollars, including: (1) failure to timely accrue foreign taxes; (2) uncertain tax position accruals that were not reflected in Weatherford's consolidated tax provisions; (3) entries to prematurely reverse liabilities related to uncertain tax positions (some of which were improperly classified as current taxes payable); and (4) understatements of income tax expense related to deferred tax liability.

---

[3]Effective for interim and annual periods ending after September 15, 2009, FASB codified authoritative accounting literature in the Accounting Standards Codification. As such, FIN 18 and FAS 109 were superseded by ASC Topic 740. The substantive provisions of the codified guidance are consistent with the superseded standards.

Material Weakness in ICFR

On or about February 15, 2011, after consideration of the errors and issues discovered and after consultation with EY, Weatherford's internal audit group concluded that there was a material weakness in internal control surrounding accounting for income taxes due to inadequate staffing and technical expertise, ineffective review and approval practices, inadequate processes to effectively reconcile income tax accounts, and inadequate controls over the preparation of Weatherford's quarterly tax provision.

After the identification of the material weakness, EY expanded the audit procedures for all income tax accounts, including a reconciliation of Weatherford's current taxes payable (and receivable) accounts. On or about February 20, 2011, a review of Weatherford's income tax receivable balance uncovered the phantom $461 million receivable which, in turn, led to the First Restatement. At no time prior to this process did Hudgins or Kitay inform anyone of the true reason they made the post-closing adjustments.

On March 1, 2011, Weatherford filed a Form 8-K with the Commission in which it made public for the first time that it would be restating its financial results for 2007-2010 and that a material weakness existed in its ICFR for the accounting of income taxes. Weatherford's stock price dropped nearly 11% to $21.14 on the news.

Restated Financial Statements

On March 8, 2011, Weatherford filed its First Restatement in which it restated its previously reported financial results for the years ended December 31, 2007, 2008, 2009, and the first three quarters of 2010. According to Weatherford, the First Restatement was necessary to correct "errors in [the Company's] accounting for income taxes." The following table depicts the impact the Restatement had on Weatherford's reported net income for the periods covered by the First Restatement.

Year Ended	Reported Net Income (in millions)	Restated Net Income (in millions)	% Change
2007	$1,070.6	$ 940.6	13.8%
2008	$1,393.2	$1,246.5	11.3%
2009	$ 253.8	$ 170.1	42.6%
Q1 - Q3 2010	$ 78.3	$ (21.6)	462.0%

Violations

SEC Securities Act provisions prohibit any person/corporation from:

- Obtaining money or property in the offer or sale of securities by means of any untrue statement of a material fact or any omission to state a material fact necessary in order to make the statements made, in light of the circumstances under which they were made, not misleading;

- Engaging in any transaction, practice, or course of business which operates or would operate as a fraud or deceit upon the purchaser in the offer or sale of securities;

- Failing to make and keep books, records and accounts which, in reasonable detail, accurately and fairly reflect their transactions and dispositions of their assets;

- Devising and maintaining a system of internal accounting controls that doesn't sufficiently provide reasonable assurances that transactions are recorded as necessary to permit preparation of financial statements in accordance with GAAP.

Weatherford agreed to report to the SEC during a two-year term its compliance with Commission regulations and GAAP regarding its accounting for income taxes, financial reporting, and the status of any remediation, implementation, auditing, and testing of its internal accounting controls and compliance measures. Hudgins and Katay were denied the privilege of appearing and practicing before the Commission as an accountant for five years after which they could apply for reinstatement. Financial penalties included: $140 million, as to Weatherford; for Hudgins, disgorgement of $169,728, prejudgment interest of $39,339, and a civil money penalty in the amount of $125,000, for a total of $334,067 to the SEC; and for Kitay, a civil money penalty in the amount of $30,000 to the SEC.

Questions

1. Explain how pressures and incentives drove the actions taken by Hudgins and Kitay to commit financial statement fraud.

2. Describe the problems in the audit of Weatherford International by Ernst & Young. Are any of these issues reflective of a violation of the rules of conduct in the AICPA Code? Explain.

3. Describe the deficiencies in the internal accounting systems, ICFR, and corporate governance at Weatherford. Were there any violations of the rules of conduct in the AICPA Code by Hudgins or Kitay? Explain.

4. Explain how Weatherford and Hudgins used aggressive accounting positions in the area of income tax accounting.

Case 5-10 Groupon

Groupon is a deal-of-the-day recommendation service for consumers. Launched in 2008, Groupon—a fusion of the words *group* and *coupon*—combines social media with collective buying clout to offer daily deals on products, services, and cultural events in local markets. Promotions are activated only after a certain number of people in a given city sign up.

Groupon pioneered the use of digital coupons in a way that created an explosive new market for local business. Paper coupon use had been declining for years. But when Groupon made it possible for online individuals to obtain deep discounts on products in local stores using e-mailed coupons, huge numbers of people started buying. Revenues were reported as $14.5 million in 2009, $312.9 million in 2010, and $1.6 billion in 2011. At the same time, the company had a net loss from operations of $1.0 million, $420.3 million, and $233.4 million, respectively, in those same years. The cause of the huge losses was acquisition-related costs and marketing costs.

On November 5, 2011, Groupon took its company public with a buy-in price of $20 per share. Groupon shares rose from that IPO price of $20 by 40% in early trading on NASDAQ, and at the 4 p.m. market close, it was $26.11, up 31%. The closing price valued Groupon at $16.6 billion, making it more valuable than companies such as Adobe Systems and nearly the size of Yahoo. However, after disclosures of fraud and increased competition from the likes of AmazonLocal and LivingSocial, its value had dropped to about $6 billion.

Less than five months after its IPO on March 30, 2012, Groupon announced that it had revised its financial results, an unexpected restatement that deepened losses and raised questions about its accounting practices. As part of the revision, Groupon disclosed a "material weakness" in its internal controls saying that it needed to increase the refund reserve accrual to reflect a shift in the Company's fourth quarter 2011 deal mix and higher price point offers, which have higher refund rate, such as laser eye surgery. Groupon failed to set aside enough money to cover customer refunds. The news that day sent shares of Groupon tumbling 6%, to $17.29.

The following information was disclosed in Groupon's December 31, 2011 Form 10K Report.[1]

> We concluded there is a material weakness in the design and operating effectiveness of our internal control over financial reporting.
>
> We did not maintain financial close process and procedures that were adequately designed, documented and executed to support the accurate and timely reporting of our financial results. As a result, we made a number of manual post-close adjustments necessary in order to prepare the financial statements included in this Form 10-K.
>
> We did not have adequate policies and procedures in place to ensure the timely, effective review of estimates, assumptions and related reconciliations and analyses, including those related to customer refund reserves. As noted previously, our original estimate disclosed on February 8 of the reserve for customer refunds proved to be inadequate after we performed additional analysis.

The financial problems escalated after Groupon released its third-quarter 2012 earnings report, marking its first full-year cycle of earnings reports since its IPO. While the net operating results showed improvement year-to-year, the company still showed a net loss for the quarter. Moreover, while its revenue had been increasing in fiscal 2012, its operating profit had declined over 60%. This meant that its operating expenses were growing faster than its revenues, a sign that trouble might be lurking in the background. The company's stock price on NASDAQ dropped to $4.14 a share on November 30, 2012, a decline of more than 80% in one year. The company did not meet financial analysts' expectations for the third quarter of 2012.

There had been other oddities with Groupon's accounting that reflected a culture of indifference toward GAAP and its obligations to the investing public.

- It reported a 1,367% increase in revenue for the three months ending March 31, 2011 versus the same period in 2010.
- It admitted to recognizing as revenue commissions received on sales of coupons/gift certificates, but also recognized the total value of the coupons and gift certificates at the date of sale.

As Groupon prepared its financial statements for 2011, its independent auditor, Ernst & Young (EY), determined that the company did not accurately account for the possibility of higher refunds. By the firm's assessment, that constituted a "material weakness." Groupon said in its annual report, "We did not maintain effective controls to provide reasonable assurance that accounts were complete and accurate." This meant that other transactions could be at risk because poor controls in one area tend to cause problems elsewhere. More important, the internal control problems raised questions about the management of the company and its corporate governance.

In a related issue, on April 3, 2012, a shareholder lawsuit was brought against Groupon accusing the company of misleading investors about its financial prospects in its IPO and concealing weak internal controls. According to the complaint, the company overstated revenue, issued materially false and misleading financial results, and concealed the fact that its business was not growing as fast and was not nearly as resistant to competition as it had suggested. These claims identified a gap in the sections of SOX that deal with companies' internal controls. There is no requirement to disclose a control weakness in a company's IPO prospectus. The complaint does not name Groupon's accounting firm, Ernst & Young, which noted in the 10-K filing that Groupon has a material weakness in its internal controls related to financial reporting.

---

[1]Groupon, Inc. Form 10-K, For the Fiscal Year Ended December 31, 2011, https://www.sec.gov/Archives/edgar/data/1490281/000144530512000922/groupon10-k.htm.

Groupon's 10-K filing revised the figures executives had presented during the company's February 2012 earnings call. The revision shaved $14.3 million off fourth-quarter revenue (the new total was $492 million). The company's stock fell on the news, dropping to $15.28 per share by the end of trading Monday. That price was down from the $26.11 per share close on the day of Groupon's initial public offering last November.

Groupon reported the weakness in its internal controls through a Section 302 provision in SOX that requires public companies' top executives to evaluate each quarter whether their disclosure controls and procedures are effective. The company seems to have concluded that the internal control shortcoming was serious enough to treat as an overall deficiency in disclosure controls rather than pointing it out in its report on internal controls that is required under Section 404. EY expressed no opinion on the company's internal controls in its audit report, which makes us wonder whether it was willing to stand up to Groupon's management on the shortcomings in its internal controls and governance. In fact, the firm signed clean audit opinions for four years.

Questions

1. Does it matter that Groupon reported its weakness in internal controls as a disclosure control under SOX Section 302 rather than pointing it out in its report on internal controls under Section 404? Explain.

2. Describe the risks of material misstatements in the financial statements that should have raised red flags for EY.

3. According to a 2012 survey of 192 U.S. executives conducted by Deloitte & Touche LLP and Forbes Insights, social media was identified as the fourth-largest risk, on par with financial risk.[2] This ranking derives from social media's capacity to accelerate to other risks, such as financial risk associated with disclosures in violation of SEC rules, for example. Other risks inherent to social media include information leaks, reputational damage to brand, noncompliance with regulatory requirements, and third-party and governance risks.

   a. Why is it important for a firm such as EY, in a case such as Groupon, to fully understand the nature of risk when a company conducts its business online?

   b. What role can internal auditors play in dealing with such risks?

   c. How should external auditors adapt their risk assessment procedures for social media/networking clients?

---

[2]Deloitte & Forbes Insight, Aftershock: Adjusting to the New World of Risk Management, Available at: http://deloitte.wsj.com/cfo/files/2012/10/Aftershock_Adjusting-to-the-new-world-of-risk-management.pdf

Chapter 6

Legal, Regulatory, and Professional Obligations of Auditors

Learning Objectives

After studying Chapter 6, you should be able to:

LO 6-1 Describe common-law rulings and auditors' legal liability to clients and third parties.

LO 6-2 Explain the basis for auditors' statutory legal liability.

LO 6-3 Explain the provisions of the PSLRA.

LO 6-4 Discuss auditors' legal liabilities under SOX.

LO 6-5 Explain the provisions of the FCPA.

Ethics Reflection

Auditors owe a duty of care to the client and third parties who foreseeably rely on the their work. Auditors can be sued for negligence, a civil offense, or fraud, a criminal act. SEC auditing enforcement actions brought against auditors tend to focus on two themes: (1) protecting the integrity of the auditors' role as independent gatekeepers; and (2) sanctions against individuals and entities for failing to detect financial misrepresentation due to allegedly deficient audits. The SEC has increasingly chosen to file enforcement actions as administrative proceedings rather than filing in U.S. District Court to expedite actions against offending auditors and audit firms. Auditors are also subject to private litigation brought by shareholders and/or third parties in the form of class action lawsuits.

On April 20, 2015, PwC agreed to pay $65 million to settle claims over its failed audits of MF Global. According to the original complaint filed in U.S. District Court Southern District of New York, MF Global charged PwC with professional malpractice, breach of contract, and unjust enrichment in connection with its advice concerning, and approval of, the company's off-balance-sheet accounting for its investments.

The decision notes that:

> "But for PwC's erroneous accounting advice, MF Global Holdings could not have—and would not have—invested heavily in European sovereign debt to generate immediate revenues and would not have suffered the massive damages that befell the company in 2011. Had PwC met its duty to provide accounting advice and auditing services consistent with the professional standards of ordinary skill, prudence, and diligence, it would have advised MF Global Holdings that the transactions had to be recorded on the company's consolidated financial statements as secured financings and not as sales. In that circumstance, the company would never have amassed the enormous Euro exposure it did, nor would it have suffered massive damages as a direct and proximate result of PwC's negligence and malpractice."

MF Global collapsed in October 2011 after former New Jersey Governor and Senator Jon Corzine took over as chairman and CEO and pushed the firm to invest about $6.3 billion in risky sovereign debt from troubled countries in the Eurozone. MF Global had employed questionable transactions known as repo-to-maturity, using the sovereign debt bonds as collateral for the loans it took out, while earning money from the spread between the rate on the bonds and the rate it paid to the counterparty on the financing.[1]

MF Global shareholders had sued PwC for its audits of MF Global in 2010 and 2011. The shareholders had contended that PwC's audits gave MF Global a clean bill of health even though the accounting firm knew or should have known that the firm's financial statements were erroneous and its internal controls weren't effective. PwC settled the lawsuit without admitting wrongdoing.

On March 23, 2017, PwC finally settled a potential $3 billion lawsuit by the administrator of the bankrupt MF Global. The administrator argued accounting errors, including allowing MF Global to keep the bonds off its balance sheet. The premature settlement means that important questions about the extent to which an auditor can be held liable for its advice on complex accounting questions went untested. Thus, the risk that auditors' liability would be extended to include complex judgments was not decided so that auditors' role in providing reasonable assurances about financial statements remains intact.

In an analysis of the fraud, Dr. Barry Jay Epstein suggests that the root cause of the demise of MF Global was the auditors' failure to maintain a healthy skepticism when responding to client assertions regarding the financial statements. He criticizes the auditors for not acting on the axiom "trust but verify." He claims the auditors failed "to take steps to counteract the normal human judgmental biases—such as those of confirmation, anchoring and availability," all signs of a lack of professional skepticism.[2]

As you read this chapter, think about the following questions: (1) What is the link between professional ethics and auditors' legal liability? (2) What legal actions can be taken against auditors? (3) What are auditor obligations and defenses that can help them to avoid liability? (4) What are auditor liabilities for failing to comply with Sections 302 and 404 of SOX?

"Accountants must be prepared to compensate all foreseeable victims whose economic losses are proximately caused by the accountants' negligent statements."

Source: U.S. Supreme Court Justice Benjamin Cardozo

In the above statement from the case, *Ultramares Corporation v Touche 174 N.E. 441 (1932),* Justice Benjamin Cardozza created the first common-law legal liability standard for auditors, known as the privity/near privity rule. This standard would ultimately be accompanied by others that addressed third-party liability as more and more lawsuits were filed against auditors for negligence/gross negligence and fraud.

In 1924, the auditors of Touche Niven provided an unqualified audit certificate to Fred Stern and Company, having failed to discover that management had falsified entries to overstate accounts receivable. The auditors knew the accounts, when certified, would be used to raise money. Ultramares Corporation lent Stern and Company money. Stern declared bankruptcy in 1925. Ultramares sued Touche Niven for the amount of the Stern debt, declaring that a careful audit would have shown Stern to be insolvent. The fraud claim against Touche was dismissed by the court of first instance for the plaintiff's failure to present evidence to the court that it had deliberately been misled by Touche or indeed that the defendant had knowingly covered up the irregularity in Fred Stern's audited accounts. Although the audit was initially found to have been negligent, the negligence claim was also dismissed when a verdict of $186,000 was returned by the jury. The judge set the negligence finding aside based on the doctrine of privity (i.e. auditors' have a contractual relationship with the client only), which protects auditors from third party lawsuits. An intermediate appellate court reinstated the negligent verdict. The case went to the New York Court of Appeals where judge Cardozza held that the claim in negligence failed on the ground that the auditors owed the plaintiff no duty of care, there being no sufficiently proximate relationship. He said no "to a liability in an indeterminate amount for an indeterminate time to an indeterminate class."

Legal Liability of Auditors: An Overview

LO 6-1

Explain common-law rulings and auditors' legal liability to clients and third parties.

Zoe-Vonna Palmrose, a former professor at the University of Southern California and now at the University of Washington, identifies the four general stages in an audit-related dispute: (1) the occurrence of events that result in losses for users of the financial statements; (2) the investigation by plaintiff attorneys before filing, to link the user losses with allegations of material omissions or misstatements of financial statements; (3) the legal process, which commences with the filing of the lawsuit; and (4) the final resolution of the dispute.[3] The first stage comes about as a result of some loss-generating event, including client bankruptcy, fraudulent financial reporting, and the misappropriation of assets.

Auditors can be sued by clients, investors, creditors, and the government for failure to perform services adequately and in accordance with the profession's ethics standards. Auditors can be held liable under two classes of law: (1) common law and (2) statutory law. Common-law liability evolves from legal opinions issued by judges in deciding a case. These opinions become legal principles that set a precedent and guide judges in deciding similar cases in the future. Statutory law reflects legislation passed at the state or federal level that establishes certain courses of conduct that must be adhered to by covered parties.[4]

Exhibit 6.1 summarizes the types of liability and auditors' actions that result in liability.

EXHIBIT 6.1   Summary of Types of Liability and Auditors' Actions Resulting in Liability

Types of Liability	Auditors' Actions Resulting in Liability
Common law—clients	Breach of contract (privity relationship)
	Negligence
	Gross negligence/constructive fraud
	Fraud
Common law—third parties	Negligence
	Gross negligence/constructive fraud
	Fraud
Federal statutory law—civil liability	Negligence
	Gross negligence/constructive fraud
	Fraud
Federal statutory law—criminal liability	Willful violation of federal statutes

Source: William F. Messier Jr., Steven M. Glover, and Douglas F. Prawitt, *Auditing and Assurance Services: A Systematic Approach* (New York: McGraw-Hill Irwin, 2012), p. 664.

There are four basic theories of liabilities which, depending on the type of lawsuit, can render a defendant liable for injuries he causes.[5]

1. *Intent* (also called willfulness) means the person acted with the intent to cause harm.

2. *Recklessness* means the person knew (or should have known) that his or her actions were likely to cause harm.

3. *Negligence* means that the person acted in violation of a duty to someone else, with the breach of that duty causing harm to someone else.

4. *Strict liability* is reserved for certain specific situations where someone can be held liable for harms they cause no matter what their mental state was.

Common-Law Liability

Common-law liability requires the auditor to perform professional services with due care. Evidence of having exercised due care exists if the auditor can demonstrate having performed services with the same degree of skill and judgment possessed by others in the profession. Typically, an auditor would cite adherence to generally accepted auditing standards as evidence of having exercised due care in conducting the audit. Due care includes exercising the degree of professional skepticism expected in the audit of financial statements.

Tort actions (for wrongdoings) cover other civil complaints (e.g., fraud, deceit, and injury) arising from auditors' failure to exercise the appropriate level of professional care, sometimes referred to as substantiated performance. Clients or users of financial statements can bring tort actions against auditors.[6]

Lawsuits for damages under common law usually result when someone suffers a financial loss after relying on financial statements later found to be materially misstated. Plaintiffs in legal actions involving auditors, such as clients or third-party users of financial statements, generally assert all possible causes of action, including breach of contract, tort, deceit, fraud, and anything else that may be relevant to the claim. These cases are often referred to as "audit failures" in the financial press.

Liability to Clients—Privity Relationship

An accountant has a contractual obligation to the client that creates a *privity relationship*. Breach of contract is a claim that accounting and auditing services were not performed in a way consistent with the terms of a contract. Although auditors may have contractual relationships with third parties, cases involving breach of contract are brought most frequently against auditors by their clients.[7] Privity does not necessarily mean only clients. Third-party beneficiaries that are named in the contract also have a contractual relationship/privity. When privity exists, plaintiffs must demonstrate all of the following:[8]

1. They suffered an economic loss.

2. Auditors did not perform in accordance with the terms of the contract, thereby breaching that contract.

3. Auditors failed to exercise the appropriate level of professional care related to tort actions.

4. The breach of contract or failure to exercise the appropriate level of care caused the loss.

In addition to breach of contract, auditors may be liable to clients for tort liability that ranges from simple, ordinary negligence to the more serious case of fraud. It's worth noting the similarity between the claim that the auditor failed to exercise due care or the standard of care that other accountants would have done in similar situations and the universality perspective of Rights Theory. In other words: What would other accountants have done in similar situations (for similar reasons)?

Legal liability exists along a continuum of ordinary negligence to outright fraud—the intentional act to deceive another party. In between, an auditor might be held liable for gross negligence or constructive fraud that represents an extreme or reckless departure from professional standards of care.

Professional Negligence

Professional negligence is the liability theory most often referred to as an "accounting malpractice" claim. The elements of a professional negligence action against an accountant are similar to those present in any other type of negligence lawsuit. They are:[9]

- *Duty* – the accountant must have owed the plaintiff a duty to use reasonable care in delivering accounting services.

- *Breach of Duty* – the plaintiff must show that the accountant failed to use that degree of skill and learning normally possessed and used by public accountants in good standing in a similar practice and under like circumstances.

- *Damage* – the plaintiff must show that he or she suffered damage as a direct result of the accountant's breach of duty. In the words of one court, "no hurt, no tort."

- *Causation* – a causal nexus between the asserted breach and damages, such as a business driven into bankruptcy because it went into debt in reliance on overstated financial statements.

Defending Audit-Malpractice Cases

Contributory negligence of the client can be regarded as a defense to the liability of the accountant for malpractice. However, it has to be proved that the negligence of the client has proximately contributed to the accountant's failure to perform. Some courts have ruled that accountants are not immune from the consequences of their own negligence because their clients have conducted the business negligently. In *National Surety Corp. v. Lybrand,* the plaintiff sued its auditors for failing to detect embezzlement by a company employee. The auditors asserted they were not liable—even if they were negligent—because the client's claim was barred by its contributory negligence; failing to supervise the embezzler or by failing to follow its established internal controls. To avoid this harsh result, the court held that accountants should not be able to escape liability altogether by virtue of their client's negligence, and thus the client's negligence "is a defense only when it has contributed to the accountant's failure to perform his contract and to report the truth."[10]

In *Shapiro v. Glekel,* the accounting firm failed to detect and report inaccuracies in certain financial statements of the client during the course of an audit. The court observed that knowledge of the financial condition of the corporation by the president and board chairman will not constitute contributory negligence precluding the accountant's liability. Accountants cannot be allowed to avoid liability resulting from their own negligence except upon a showing of substantial negligence or fault by the client. The court did observe that if the doctrine of contributory negligence is repudiated, an accounting firm is entitled to assert the defense of *comparative negligence* in malpractice action instituted against the firm by a client.[11] But in some jurisdictions, auditors must contend with the *audit-interference rule.* The audit-interference rule may restrict the type of client conduct that counts for purposes of apportioning fault. In jurisdictions adopting this rule, an auditor may only assert a comparative-fault defense where it can establish that the client's negligence "interfered with" the auditor's performance of its duties.

Recklessness

Recklessness involves conduct that is short of actual intent to cause harm, but greater than simple negligence. Unlike negligence—which occurs when a person unknowingly takes a risk that they should have been aware of—recklessness means to knowingly take a risk.

Recklessness is a state of mind that is determined both subjectively and objectively. There are two types of reckless behavior. The first looks at what the actor knew or is believed to have been thinking when the act occurred (subjective test). The second considers what a reasonable person would have thought in the defendant's position (objective test). In both situations, the issue depends on conscious awareness, or whether the person knew (or should have known) his actions may cause harm to another.[12]

Liability to Third Parties

Near-Privity Relationship

While the *Ultramares* decision established a strict privity standard, a number of subsequent court decisions in other states moved away from this standard over time. Following years of broadening the auditor's liability to third parties to include those that were "foreseen"and "reasonably foreseeable" (which we will discuss shortly), in a 1985 decision, the court seemed to move the pendulum back in favor of limiting the liability of accountants to third parties based on the privity standard. The New York Court of Appeals expanded the privity standard in the case of *Credit Alliance v. Arthur Andersen & Co.*[13] to include a *near-privity relationship* between third parties and the accountant. In the case, Credit Alliance was the principal lender to the client and demonstrated that Andersen had known Credit Alliance was relying on the client's financial statements prior to extending credit. The court also ruled that there had been direct communication between the lender and the auditor regarding the client.

The *Credit Alliance* case establishes the following tests that must be satisfied for holding auditors liable for negligence to third parties: (1) knowledge by the accountant that the financial statements are to be used for a particular purpose; (2) the intention of the third party to rely on those statements; and (3) some action by the accountant linking him or her to the third party that provides evidence of the accountant's understanding of intended reliance. The 1992 New York Court of Appeals decision in *Security Pacific Business Credit, Inc. v. Peat Marwick Main & Co.*[14] sharpens the last criterion in its determination that the third party must be known to the auditor, who directly conveys the audited report to the third party or acts to induce reliance on the report.

Actually Foreseen Third Parties

The "middle ground" approach followed by the vast majority of states (and federal courts located within those states) expands the class of third parties that can sue successfully an auditor for negligence beyond near-privity to a person or limited group of persons whose reliance is (*actually*) *foreseen,* even if the specific person or group is unknown to the auditor.[15]

The courts have deviated from the *Ultramares* principle through a variety of decisions. For example, a federal district court in Rhode Island decided a case in 1968, *Rusch Factors, Inc. v. Levin,*[16] that held an accountant liable for negligence to a third party that was not in privity of contract. In that case, Rusch Factors had requested financial statements prior to granting a loan. Levin audited the statements, which showed the company to be solvent when it was actually insolvent. After the company went into receivership, Rusch Factors sued, and the court ruled that the *Ultramares* doctrine was inappropriate. In its decision, the court relied heavily on the *Restatement (Second) of the Law of Torts.*

Restatement (Second) of the Law of Torts

The Restatement (Second) of the Law of Torts approach, sometimes known as Restatement 552,[17] expands accountants' legal liability exposure for negligence beyond those with near privity to a small group of persons and classes who are or *should be* foreseen by the auditor as relying on the financial information. This is known as the *foreseen third-party* concept because even though there is no privity relationship, the accountant knew that that party or those parties would rely on the financial statements for a specified transaction.

Section 552 states: "The liability . . . is limited to loss (a) suffered by the person or one of the persons for whose benefit and guidance he or she intends to supply the information, or knows that the recipient [client] intends to supply it; and (b) through reliance upon it in a transaction which he or she intends the information to influence, or knows that the recipient so intends." For example, assume that a client asks an accountant to prepare financial statements and the accountant knows that those statements will be used to request a loan from one or more financial institutions. The accountant may not know the specific bank to be approached, but he does know the purpose for which the statements will be used. Thus, the third parties as a class of potential users can be foreseen.

A majority of states now use the modified privity requirement imposed by Section 552 of the *Restatement (Second) of the Law of Torts.* The *Restatement* modifies the traditional rule of privity by allowing nonclients to sue accountants for negligent misrepresentation, provided that they belong to a "limited group" and provided that the accountant had actual knowledge that his or her professional opinion would be supplied to that group. In some state court decisions, a less restrictive interpretation of Section 552 has been made. For example, a 1986 decision by the Texas Court of Appeals in *Blue Bell, Inc. v. Peat, Marwick, Mitchell & Co.* (now KPMG) held that if an accountant preparing audited statements knows or should know that such statements will be relied upon, the accountant may be held liable for negligent misrepresentation.[18]

Reasonably Foreseeable Third Parties

A third judicial approach to third-party liability expands the legal liability of accountants well beyond *Ultramares.* The *reasonably foreseeable third-party* approach results from a 1983 decision by the New Jersey Supreme Court in *Rosenblum, Inc. v. Adler.*[19] In that case, the Rosenblum family agreed to sell its retail catalog showroom business to Giant Stores, a corporation operating discount department stores, in exchange for Giant common stock. The Rosenblums relied on Giant's 1971 and 1972 financial statements, which had been audited by Touche. When the statements were found to be fraudulent and the stock was deemed worthless, the investors sued Touche. The lower courts did not allow the Rosenblums' claims against Touche on the grounds that the plaintiffs did not meet either the *Ultramares* privity test or the *Restatement* standard. The case was taken to the New Jersey Supreme Court, and it overturned the lower courts' decision, ruling that auditors can be held liable for ordinary negligence to all *reasonably foreseeable third parties* who are recipients of the financial statements for routine business purposes. In finding for Rosenblum on certain motions, the Court held, "Independent auditors have a duty of care to all persons whom the auditor should reasonably foresee as recipients of the statements from the company for proper business purposes, provided that the recipients rely on those financial statements. It is well recognized that audited financial statements are made for the use of third parties who have no direct relationship with the auditor. Auditors have responsibility not only to the client who pays the fee but also to investors, creditors, and others who rely on the audited financial statements."

Another important case that followed this approach was *Citizens State Bank v. Timm, Schmidt, & Company.*[20] In this case, the bank sued the public accounting firm after relying on financial statements for one of its debtors that had been audited by Timm. The Wisconsin court used a number of reasons for extending auditors' liability beyond privity. The following quote from the case demonstrates the court's rather liberal leanings with respect to auditor legal liability to third parties: "If relying third parties, such as creditors, are not allowed to recover, the cost of credit to the general public will increase because creditors will either have to absorb the cost of bad loans made in reliance on faulty information or hire independent accountants to verify the information received."

Since 1987, no state high court has adopted this foreseeability approach to accountants' legal liability, while a large number have approved or adopted one of the narrower standards.[21] For example, in its 1992 ruling in *Bily v. Arthur Young,* the California Supreme Court expressly rejected the foreseeability approach in favor of the *Rusch Factors* or *Restatement* standard. The court gave a number of reasons for rejecting the *Rosenblum* foreseeability approach, including that the foreseeability rule exposes auditors to potential liability in excess of their proportionate share and the sophisticated plaintiffs have other ways to protect themselves from the risk of inaccurate financial statements (e.g., they can negotiate improved terms or hire their own auditor).[22]

However, in its 2003 ruling in *Murphy v. BDO Seidman, LLP,* the California Court of Appeals ruled that "grapevine plaintiffs," who alleged indirect reliance based on what others (e.g., stockholders and stockbrokers) told them about the financial statements, had legal claims for ordinary negligence against the auditors so long as the auditor would have reasonably foreseen that stockholders or stockbrokers would tell other people of the content of the financial statements and that the other people would rely upon the misrepresentations in purchasing the corporate stock. The court ruled that nothing in the *Bily* decision precludes indirect reliance.[23]

The *Murphy* ruling seems to stretch auditors' legal liability to third parties beyond reasonable bounds. Imagine, for example, that you are watching Jim Cramer's television show "Mad Money" on CNBC, and Cramer recommends a stock that you then purchase online. Shortly thereafter, news breaks of an accounting fraud. You sue the auditors based on your belief that the auditors should have known the public would buy the stock after Cramer recommended it. It makes little sense to conclude that a plaintiff may be successful in a lawsuit against the auditors based on a claim of ordinary negligence in this situation, given that auditors cannot control every use of audit information.

The conflicting common-law rulings can be confusing in trying to apply legal precedent to current court cases. To assist students, we have developed a summary in Exhibit 6.2 of the primary legal issues and guiding principles addressed in important court cases in deciding the auditor's liability to third parties.

EXHIBIT 6.2   Auditor Legal Liability to Third Parties

Legal Approach	Case	Legal Principle	Legal Liability to Third Parties
Ultramares	*Ultramares v. Touche*	Privity	Possibly gross negligence that constitutes (constructive) fraud
Near-privity relationship	*Credit Alliance*	Three-pronged approach: knowledge of accountant that the statements will be used for a particular purpose; intention of third party to rely on those statements; some action by third party that provides evidence of the accountant's understanding of intended reliance	Ordinary negligence
Restatement (Second) of the Law of Torts	*Rusch Factors*	Foreseen third-party users	Ordinary negligence beyond near-privity
Foreseeable third party	*Rosenblum*	Reasonably foreseeable third-party users	Ordinary negligence with reliance on the statements

The legal liability of accountants is not limited to audited statements. In the 1967 case *1136 Tenants Corp. v. Max Rothenberg & Co.,*[24] an accounting firm was sued for negligent failure to discover embezzlement by the managing agent who had hired the firm to "write up" the books, which did not include any audit procedures. The firm was held liable for failure to inquire or communicate about missing invoices despite a disclaimer on the financial statements informing users that "No independent verification were undertaken thereon." The firm moved to dismiss the case, but the court denied the motion and held that even if a CPA "acted as a robot, merely doing copy work," there was an issue as to whether there were suspicious circumstances relating to missing invoices that imposed a duty on the firm to warn the client. When the case went to trial, the court found there to be an engagement to audit and entered a judgment for more than $237,000 despite the firm's oral evidence that it was employed for $600 annually to write up the books.

The *1136* case affected auditing standards in two notable areas. First, the engagement letter was developed to clarify the responsibilities of accountants and auditors in performing professional services. The engagement letter formalizes the relationship between the auditor and the client. It serves as a contract detailing the responsibilities of the accountant or auditor and expectations for management.

A second result was that the Accounting and Review Services Committee of the AICPA, a senior technical committee, was formed to formulate standards to be followed by accountants who perform two levels of service—a compilation and a review. A *review* provides limited assurance that the financial statements are free of material misstatements (a lower standard than the reasonable assurance requirement in the audit), while a *compilation* provides no assurance because the only services provided are of a bookkeeping nature.

SSARS 21

Many small businesses do not require an audit or review of financial statements and turn to compilations instead. SSARS 21 provides CPAs the opportunity to prepare financial statements without the burden of submitting a compilation report, or so-called 'plain paper financial statements.' The standard is designed to be a better fit for accountants using electronic or cloud-based services with clients, or firms that may work with clients remotely. In SSARS 21, the preparation of financial statements is separated from the reporting on these statements. This means a compilation report is based solely on whether the CPA was engaged by the client to prepare one. SSARS 21 became effective for engagements on financial statements for periods ending on or after December 15, 2015.

Compilation Services

Here is a brief overview of these new standards as they pertain to services with non-compilation reports.[25] It remains to be seen how auditors might be required to justify their conformity to these standards in a court of law.

- An engagement letter is still required for preparing financial statements, signed by the accountant and the client's management.

- If there is to be no compilation engagement, then each page of the financial statement must include language stating no assurance is being provided. Examples of such language include, "No assurance is provided on these financial statements," or "These financial statements have not been subjected to an audit or review or compilation engagement, and no assurance is provided on them."

- If an accountant cannot include a statement on each page of the financial statements as described above, then a disclaimer must be issued clarifying that no assurance is being provided. An example of a disclaimer would read, "The accompanying financial statements of XYZ Company as of and for the year ended December 31, 20XX, were not subjected to an audit, review, or compilation engagement by me and, accordingly, I do not express an opinion, a conclusion, nor provide any assurance on them." A signature line including the city, state, and date would follow the disclaimer.

- This is a non-attest service, so independence does not need to be determined by the accountant if they are engaged to prepare only financial statements.

- If an accountant prepares financial statements that omit substantially all disclosures required by the applicable reporting framework, the accountant should disclose such omission in the financial statements.

- If an accountant prepares financial statements that are an applicable reporting framework other than U.S. GAAP, the accountant should disclose such omission in the financial statements.

For purposes of comparison, SSARS 21 requires the following standards when an accountant is engaged by the client to perform a compilation on financial statements.

- The original submission of financial statement provision by CPAs is no longer required; they no longer need to determine if they "prepared and presented" the financial statements to the client.

- The engagement letter should state that the CPA will perform a compilation of financial statements and be signed by both the accountant and the client's management.

- Compilation engagements require a report, just as before, but there is a language change to make the report more streamlined compared to review and audit reports. An example of a compilation report prepared in accordance with GAAP:

"Management is responsible for the accompanying financial statements of XYZ Company, which comprise the balance sheets as of December 31, 20X2 and 20X1, and the related statements of income, changes in stockholders' equity and cash flows for the years then ended, and the related notes to the financial statements in accordance with accounting principles generally accepted in the United States of America. I (We) have performed compilation engagements in accordance with the Statements on Standards for Accounting and Review Services promulgated by the Accounting and Review Services Committee of the AICPA. I (We) did not audit or review the financial statements nor was (were) I (we) required to perform any procedures to verify the accuracy or completeness of the information provided by management. Accordingly, I (we) do not express an opinion, a conclusion, nor provide any form of assurance on these financial statements."

Legal Considerations

Vincent J. Love and Thomas R. Manisero explore the legal liability of CPAs who purport to perform SSARS 21 services.[26] The authors suggest that legal liability could turn on whether those CPAs actually performed procedures beyond what the standard contemplates—in which case they will be beyond the legal protection that the standard attempts to create. This is precisely what occurred in *1136 Tenants' Corp.* In that case, the accountant's testimony that certain services performed went beyond the scope of "write-up" work and the time records revealing that the accountants examined bank statements were sufficient to create an issue of fact as to the scope of services actually performed, with the accountants ultimately being held to the standard of having been engaged to perform an audit.

Love and Manisero caution that CPAs must take extra care not to create the appearance that a higher level of service was actually performed. In the past, similar arguments have been made by litigants trying to establish that a CPA did more than was required for a compilation. By SSARS 21's own terms, CPAs who undertake to do more in terms of verification or analysis could find themselves being measured against the higher standards applicable to compilation or review engagements. This is particularly a concern in jurisdictions where privity rules allow negligence suits to be brought against CPAs by third parties, as those non-clients would not be subject to the argument that their signatures on the engagement letters prevents them from arguing that a higher level of service was actually intended. It is entirely foreseeable that an opportunistic creditor or bankruptcy trustee would advance such an argument to establish a CPA's liability.[27]

Auditor Liability to Third Parties

Plaintiff Claims for Action

Common-law liability for fraud is available to third parties in any jurisdiction. The plaintiff (third party) must prove (1) a false representation by the accountant, (2) knowledge or belief by the accountant that the representation was false, (3) that the accountant intended to induce the third party to rely on false representation, (4) that the third party relied on the false representation, and (5) that the third party suffered damages.[28]

Courts have held that *scienter* or fraudulent intent may be established by proof that the accountant acted with knowledge of the false representation. However, liability for fraud is not limited to cases where the auditor was knowingly deceitful. Some courts have interpreted gross negligence or constructive fraud as an instance of fraud. An important case in this area is *State Street Trust Co. v. Ernst.*[29] In this case, the auditors issued an unqualified opinion on their client's financial statements, knowing that State Street Trust Company was making a loan based on those financial statements. A month later, the auditors sent a letter to the client indicating that receivables had been overstated. The auditors, however, did not communicate this information to State Street, and the client subsequently went bankrupt. The New York court ruled that the auditor's actions appeared to be grossly negligent and that "reckless disregard of consequences may take the place of deliberate intention." In such cases, while fraudulent intent may not be present, the court "constructs" fraud due to the grossness of the negligence.[30]

In *Phar-Mor v. Coopers & Lybrand,* (now PricewaterhouseCoopers) the auditors were found guilty of fraud under both common and statutory law, even though the plaintiffs acknowledged that the auditors had no intent to deceive. Instead, the plaintiff successfully argued reckless disregard for the truth which gives rise to an inference of fraud. An important part of this ruling is that plaintiffs who are barred from suing for ordinary negligence because they lack a privity relationship or are not foreseen users can choose to sue the auditor for fraud because to find an auditor guilty of fraud, the plaintiffs need only prove gross negligence.[31]

In more recent cases, the court ruled in *Houbigant, Inc. v. Deloitte & Touche LLP*[32] and *Reisman v. KPMG Peat Marwick LLP*[33] that for an auditor to be found guilty of fraud, the plaintiffs must prove only that the auditor was aware that its misrepresentations might reasonably be relied upon by the plaintiff, not that the auditor intended to induce the detrimental reliance. The court referred to recent audit failures in its *Houbigant* decision: "It should be sufficient that the complaint contains some rational basis for inferring that the alleged misrepresentation was knowingly made. Indeed, to require anything beyond that would be particularly undesirable at this time, when it has been widely acknowledged that our society is experiencing a proliferation of frauds perpetrated by officers of large corporations . . . unchecked by the 'impartial' auditors they hired."[34]

Auditor Defenses

The auditor's defense against third-party lawsuits for negligence that claim the auditor did not detect a misstatement or fraud requires proof that (1) the auditor did not have a duty to the third party, (2) the third party was negligent, (3) the auditor's work was performed in accordance with professional standards, (4) the third party did not suffer a loss, (5) any loss to the third party was caused by other events, or (6) the claim is invalid because the statute of limitations has expired.[35] Here are examples of the various defenses that an auditor can use:

1. Auditors can defend a common-law action by presenting arguments and evidence to rebut third-party plaintiffs' claims and evidence. Once a plaintiff has demonstrated an economic loss and materially misstated financial statements, defenses available to auditors against third parties include the following:[36] (1) the third party lacked standing to sue in a particular jurisdiction, as would be the case when bringing a lawsuit for ordinary negligence; and (2) the appropriate relationship between the auditor and third party did not exist (i.e., a privity relationship).

2. The third party's loss was due to events other than the financial statements and auditors' examination, as might be the case if poor business practices or stock market declines caused the loss.

3. Auditors' work was performed in accordance with accepted auditing standards (e.g., AICPA or PCAOB standards), which is generally interpreted to mean that auditors were not negligent (ordinary negligence).

Grant Thornton LLP v. Prospect High Income Fund, et al.

A Texas Supreme Court decision in 2010 in the case of *Grant Thornton LLP v. Prospect High Income Fund, et al.* has strengthened defenses available to auditors brought by third parties for negligent misrepresentation and fraud. The Court overruled what had been a broader standard for establishing liability in negligent misrepresentations when financial failings of their clients exist. The ruling also sets new limitations on "holder" claims, wherein investors contend that they were put at a disadvantage because they held securities based on an auditor's report that they otherwise would have sold.[37] Given the potential importance of the case, we present a summary of the ruling in Exhibit 6.3.

In *Prospect,* the Texas Supreme Court expressly rejected the standard set forth in *Blue Bell* in favor of the stricter standard set forth in the 1999 decision of *McCamish, Martin, Brown & Loeffler v. F. E. Appling Interests* (a lawyer case). In doing so, it stated: "*McCamish* has served as a guidepost for our courts of appeals in analyzing the tort of negligent misrepresentation, in contrast to earlier decisions applying a broader standard."[38] The only case the Supreme Court cited as applying the rejected broader standard was *Blue Bell.*

The significance of adopting *McCamish* for auditors and others is that it applies a strict standard for determining who can assert a negligent misrepresentation claim — a plaintiff must be "a known person" who relied upon the auditor's representations for "a known purpose." The importance of this limitation is apparent from the court's first holding — the Cayman Fund's claims were all dismissed because it was merely a potential public investor with no prior connections to either Grant Thornton or the issuer of the bonds. "[P]redicating scope of liability on [the auditor's] general knowledge that investors may purchase bonds would 'eviscerate the Restatement rule in favor of a *de facto* foreseeability approach — an approach [we] have refused to embrace.'"

Courts in Texas and other states have allowed negligent misrepresentation claims against auditors and others by persons who should not have been considered to be within the "limited group" that the authors of the Restatement of Torts intended to be able to sue. Adopting the *McCamish* standard of a "known person for a known purpose" to identify proper plaintiffs should reduce litigation against auditors, particularly by potential public investors. Requiring even a known person to have a direct communication with a defendant to assert a claim that a misrepresentation caused the plaintiff to hold onto an investment should eliminate additional claims against accountants and others in litigation. Equally important for both fraud and negligent misrepresentation defense is the finding that a plaintiff who knows the financial condition of a company cannot assert reliance upon an auditor's opinion as the basis of its damages.[39]

EXHIBIT 6.3 *Grant Thornton LLP v. Prospect High Income Fund, et al.*

Background

Epic Resorts, a timeshare operator, issued $130 million in corporate bonds in 1998 and sold them in the open market. Epic was required to make semiannual interest payments of $8.45 million to bondholders. To secure the interest payments, it was also required to maintain $8.45 million in an escrow account at U.S. Trust, which served as both the indenture trustee and escrow agent, for the benefit of the bondholders. Epic was required to provide annual audited financial statements, as well as a negative assurance statement from its auditors confirming that Epic was in compliance with the financial conditions of the indenture and related agreements.

Grant Thornton was engaged as Epic's auditor in March 2000 and subsequently audited Epic's financial statements for both 1999 and 2000. In the course of its 1999 audit, Grant discovered that Epic did not have the minimum required amount in the U.S. Trust account. Despite this deficiency, in April 2000, Grant issued an unqualified opinion on Epic's 1999 financial statements and confirmed in its negative assurance letter that Epic was in compliance with the escrow requirement. Grant's opinion and negative assurance were based, in part, upon representations from Epic that it was allowed to use more than one account to meet its escrow responsibilities, and the combined balances of escrow funds that it held never totaled less than the required minimum. U.S. Trust never objected to the lack of sufficient funds in the account that it maintained. In April 2001, Grant issued an unqualified opinion on Epic's 2000 financial statements despite a continuing shortfall of funds in the U.S. Trust account, but it did not issue a negative assurance letter to the trustee.

The plaintiffs in this case were hedge funds that over several years purchased Epic bonds. Prospect had made three purchases before Grant was hired to perform its first audit. Thereafter, Highland Capital Management Corporation and its portfolio manager, Davis Deadman, began managing Prospect's investments and, as a result, became familiar with Epic's bonds. Deadman, on behalf of the Cayman Fund, a second fund, purchased more Epic bonds in December 2000, two days before Epic made its semiannual interest payment. At about the same time, Epic's primary lender, Prudential, told Epic that it would not renew its credit arrangement. This credit was critical to Epic's survival and its ability to meet its obligations to bondholders. Deadman learned of Prudential's decision sometime in the first quarter of 2001 but continued to buy Epic bonds throughout the spring of 2001.

In June 2001, Epic defaulted on its interest payment to bondholders, claiming that Prudential's failure to renew the credit arrangement forced the timeshare operator to use that money to fund operations. Four days after this default, the hedge funds purchased more bonds and forced Epic into bankruptcy. The hedge funds then sued Grant Thornton, alleging that the audit reports misrepresented the status of the escrow account.

Procedural History

The plaintiff hedge funds sued Grant for negligent misrepresentation, direct negligence, fraud, conspiracy to commit fraud, aiding and abetting fraud, and third-party beneficiary breach of contract. They sought damages equal to the par value of the bonds, plus five years' interest. The trial court, two months before trial in August 2004, granted summary judgment to Grant Thornton on all counts. In October 2006, the Dallas Court of Appeals affirmed the judgment on certain claims, but reversed the judgment on the negligent misrepresentation, fraud, conspiracy, and aiding and abetting claims, finding genuine issues as to material facts.

Grant Thornton filed its petition for review with the Texas Supreme Court in January 2007. The petition argued that the Court of Appeals erred in not holding the following: (1) there was no evidence of a causal connection between Grant's alleged misrepresentation and the funds' alleged injury; (2) there was no evidence of actual and justifiable reliance; and (3) liability for fraudulent misrepresentations runs only to those whom the auditor knows and intends to influence, all of which was not present. The hedge funds responded that Grant's misrepresentations caused them to fail to take action to protect themselves earlier and to refrain from selling their bonds ("holder" claims). The petition was granted in August 2008. In a victory for the auditing profession, in July 2010, the Texas Supreme Court ruled the law does not impose on auditors an obligation to provide an accurate accounting to anyone who reads and relies upon an audit report.

The good news for accountants and other defendants is that this ruling sets forth a strong defense to the otherwise difficult-to-defend claim that "if I had known, I would have sold or taken other action to protect myself." Up until now, defendants have had little ability to defend holder claims because there is rarely any proof other than the plaintiff's testimony of what he did not do or would have done. *Prospect* significantly closes that door.

Statutory Liability

LO 6-2

Explain the basis for auditors' statutory legal liability.

Auditors may have legal liability under the Securities Act of 1933 and the Securities Exchange Act of 1934. These statutory liabilities may lead to convictions for crimes, provided their conduct was "willful."

The term "willful" and its application in criminal securities law cases often is influenced by the context of the situation. Section 32(a) of the Securities Exchange Act of 1934 provides that any person who "willfully" violates any provision of the Act can be charged with a crime, while Section 15(b)(4) authorizes the SEC to seek civil administrative penalties against any person who "willfully" violates certain provisions of the securities laws.

Securities Act of 1933

The Securities Act of 1933 regulates the disclosure of information in a registration statement for a new public offering of securities (i.e., IPO). Companies must file registration statements (S-1, S-2, and S-3 forms) and prospectuses that contain financial statements that have been audited by an independent CPA. Accountants who assist in the preparation of the registration statement are civilly liable if the registration statement (1) contains untrue statements of material facts, (2) omits material facts required by statute or regulation, or (3) omits information that if not given makes the facts stated misleading.[40]

Section 11 of the Securities Act of 1933 imposes a liability on issuer companies and others, including auditors, for losses suffered by third parties when false or misleading information is included in a registration statement. Any purchaser of securities may sue: The purchaser generally must prove that (1) the specific security was offered through the registration statements, (2) damages were incurred, and (3) there was a material misstatement or omission in the financial statements included in the registration statement. The plaintiff need not prove reliance on the financial statements unless the purchase took place after one year of the offering.

If items (2) and (3) are proven, it is a *prima facie* case (sufficient to win against the CPA unless rebutted) and shifts the burden of proof to the accountant, who may escape liability by proving the following: (1) after reasonable investigation, the CPA concludes that there is a reasonable basis to believe that the financial statements were true and there was no material misstatement (the materiality defense); (2) a "reasonable investigation" was conducted (the due diligence defense); (3) the plaintiff knew that the financial statements were incorrect when the investment was made (the knowledge of falsehood defense); or (4) the loss was due to factors other than the material misstatement or omission (the lack of causation defense).

Materiality Defense

An accountant might argue that the false or misleading information is not material and thus should not have had an impact on the purchaser's decision-making process. The SEC and the courts have attempted to define materiality in this context. The term *material* describes the kind of information that an average prudent investor would want to have so that he can make an intelligent, informed decision whether or not to buy the security. A material fact is one that, if correctly stated or disclosed, would have deterred or tended to deter the average prudent investor from purchasing the securities in question. The term does not cover minor inaccuracies or errors in matters of no interest to investors. Facts that tend to deter a person from purchasing a security are those that have an important bearing upon the nature or condition of the issuing corporation or its business.[41]

Due Diligence Defense

To establish a due diligence defense under Section 11, the defendant must prove that a reasonable investigation of the financial statements of the issuer and controlling persons was conducted. As a result, there was no reason to believe any of the information in the registration statement or prospectus was false or misleading. To determine whether a reasonable investigation has been made, the law provides that the standard of *reasonableness* is that required of a prudent person in the management of his own property. The burden of proof is on the defendant, and the test is as of the time the registration became effective. The due diligence defense, in effect, requires proof that a party was not guilty of fraud or negligence.[42]

Section 11 Liability Under Securities Act of 1933

A major opinion of the U.S. Supreme Court on March 24, 2015, in *Omnicare, Inc. v. Laborers District Council Construction Industry Pension Fund* changes the legal landscape with respect to when an issuer of financial statements may be held liable under Section 11 of the Securities Act of 1933 for statements of opinion made in a registration statement. The Court vacated and remanded the Sixth Circuit's 2013 decision holding that a Section 11 plaintiff need only allege that an opinion in a registration statement was "objectively false," notwithstanding the company's understanding when the statement was made. The Supreme Court ruled a statement of opinion in a registration statement may not support Section 11 liability merely because it is "ultimately found incorrect." Addressing Section 11's alleged misstatements of facts, the Supreme Court held that "liability under Section 11's false-statement provision would follow . . . not only if the speaker did not hold the belief she professed but also if the supporting facts she supplied were untrue." The Court held that with respect to potential misstatement liability under Section 11, "a sincere statement of pure opinion is not an 'untrue statement of material fact,' regardless whether an investor can ultimately prove the belief wrong."

The Court further held that an issuer may be liable under Section 11 for omitting material facts about the inquiry into or knowledge concerning a statement of opinion if those facts "conflict" with what a reasonable investor would "understand an opinion statement to convey" with respect to "how the speaker has formed the opinion" or "the speaker's basis for holding that view." The Court clarified that an issuer need not disclose every fact "cutting the other way" against an opinion because "[r]easonable investors understand that opinions sometimes rest on a weighing of competing facts."

The essence of the *Omnicare* opinion can be summarized as follows:

- An investor cannot state a claim by alleging only that an opinion was wrong; the complaint must also call into question the issuer's basis for offering the opinion;

- Statements of opinion are actionable under Section 11 of the Securities Act of 1933 as false or misleading only if the issuer of the opinion held a subjective belief inconsistent with the opinion;

- A Section 11 plaintiff must identify particular and material facts about an inquiry the issuer did or did not conduct or the knowledge it did or did not have whose omission makes the opinion statement questioned misleading to a reasonable person reading the statement fairly and in context.

In summary, the Court emphasized that Section 11 "does not allow investors to second-guess inherently subjective and uncertain assessments." Even if wrong, a genuinely held statement of pure opinion, therefore, cannot be an untrue statement of material fact." It is worth noting that the essence of this statement is motivation. In rendering an opinion, so long as the issuer believes the statement to be true, allegations of legal liability under Section 11 will not survive.

Section 11 Liability Standard for Auditors

In analyzing the *Omnicare* ruling with respect to auditors' opinions, Griggs, Mixter, and Rissier, writing for Bloomberg BNA, point to three statements in the audit report that can be examined using the *Omni* framework.[43]

- The auditor's "opinion" that "the financial statements . . . present fairly, in all material respects, the [consolidated] financial position of [the company at the identified balance sheet dates], and the [consolidated] results of [its] operations and [its] consolidated cash flows for [each of the three years in the period] ended in conformity with [U.S. generally accepted accounting principles ['GAAP']]";
- The auditor's statement that audits were conducted "in accordance with [the standards of the [PCAOB]]";
- The auditor's belief that the audits "provide a reasonable basis for [the] opinion."

According to the authors, under *Omnicare,* an auditor can be held liable under Section 11 for its audit opinion in only three circumstances: (1) if the auditor does not actually hold the opinion; (2) the opinion contains an embedded statement of fact that is misleading; or (3) if the opinion omits a fact that makes the opinion misleading to the ordinary investor. A material omission claim would require the plaintiff "to identify actual and material steps taken or not taken by [the defendant auditor] in its audit or knowledge it did or did not have in the formation of the opinion" rather than simply "claiming that any reasonable audit would have uncovered a material fact whose omission renders the opinion misleading to a reasonable person reading the statement fairly and in context."

The authors conclude their analysis by stating that Omnicare labels auditors' statements as opinions, which seems appropriate. Labeling or forming a statement as an opinion expresses uncertainty. Although a plaintiff could later prove that opinion erroneous, the words in the audit report "[We] believe" themselves admit to this possibility, thus precluding liability for an untrue statement of fact. Statements of fact express certainty; statements of opinion do not.

It remains to be seen what long-term effect the Section 11 liability standard will have on auditors under the Securities Act of 1934, especially Section 10 and Rule 10b-5, that pertain to annual and quarterly report filings in Forms 10-K and 10-Q.

Section 11 and Auditors' "Opinion" Statements

In their review of SEC Section 11 regulations with respect to registration statements, Douglas and Rowe point out that independent auditors and CPA firms have long been the target of plaintiffs' attorneys seeking to impose liability under federal securities laws. However, changes in these standards mean auditors may have a new shield to deflect frivolous claims. Recently, courts in a growing number of jurisdictions have required that plaintiffs asserting a Section 11 claim under the Securities Act of 1933 must plead both objective and subjective falsity to properly allege a misstated "opinion" statement with respect to financial-statement line items.[44]

Section 11 of the Securities Act provides a cause of action to investors who can prove that a registration statement "contained an untrue statement of a material fact or omitted to state a material fact required to be stated therein or necessary to make the statements therein not misleading."[45] Those potentially liable under Section 11 include every person who signed the registration statement, every director or partner of the issuer at the time of the filing, every underwriter, and, as relevant here, every accountant who consented to being named as having prepared or certified any part of the registration statement. Independent auditors who consent to being named as having prepared financial statements that are later included in a registration statement are frequent targets under Section 11.

Only recently have courts considered whether financial-statement line items constitute an opinion for purposes of Section 11 pleading, and, thus, whether an accountant's representation regarding its "opinion" can lead to Section 11 liability. At least two courts have now held that certain financial-statement line items are "opinions" such that a plaintiff must allege that the financial-statement account was objectively and subjectively false.

In *Fait v. Regions Financial Corp.*, the Second Circuit addressed whether goodwill and the loan-loss reserve were balance sheet "opinions." As to goodwill, the court recognized that "[e]stimates of goodwill depend on management's determination of the 'fair value' of the assets acquired and liabilities assumed, which are not matters of objective fact." Likewise, the Second Circuit found that a loan-loss reserve is similarly subject to the opinion of the accountant and registrant. That is, "loan loss reserves reflect management's opinion or judgment about what, if any, portion of amounts due on the loans ultimately might not be collectible." Because both determinations were "inherently subjective," the Second Circuit held that matters of opinion are actionable only if the statements "misstate the opinions or belief held, or, in the case of statements of reasons, the actual motivation for the speaker's actions, *and* they are false or misleading with respect to the underlying subject matter they address."[46]

A similar issue existed in *MHC Mutual Conversion Fund, L.P. v. United W. Bancorp, Inc.* There, the plaintiffs alleged that United Western Bancorp's registration statement materially misstated the value of certain collateralized mortgage obligations and mortgage-backed securities. Specifically, the plaintiffs alleged that United Western Bancorp failed to recognize timely as much as $69 million in other-than-temporary impairment (OTTI), which improperly inflated the value of the underlying securities. The court ruled that the OTTI account balance constituted an opinion. In so doing, the court reasoned, all impairment analysis requires the issuer to determine an asset's fair value, which itself takes into account such subjective indicia as "market forces, market trends, and buyers' whims," and it also observed that the issuer must subjectively assess its "expectation" as to whether it will recover the security's amortized cost.[47]

Ultimately, a significant number of financial-statement accounts and decisions require some degree of subjective input. If *Fait* and *MHC Mutual* are to serve as any guide, plaintiffs pursuing a Section 11 claim against the registrant's auditors must now plead that any material misstatement to such an account is both subjectively and objectively false.

Securities Exchange Act of 1934

The Securities Exchange Act of 1934 regulates the ongoing reporting by companies whose securities are listed and traded on stock exchanges. The Act requires ongoing filing of quarterly (10-Q) and annual (10-K) reports and the periodic filing of an 8-K form whenever a significant event takes place affecting the entity, such as a change in auditors. Entities having total assets of $10 million or more and 500 or more stockholders are required to register under the Securities Exchange Act. The form and content of 10-K and 10-Q filings are governed by the SEC through Regulation S-X (which covers annual and interim financial statements) and Regulation S-K (which covers other supplementary disclosures).[48]

In addition to these two regulations, auditors must be familiar with Financial Reporting Releases (FRRs), which express new rules and policies about disclosure, and Staff Accounting Bulletins (SABs), which provide unofficial, but important, interpretations of Regulations S-X and S-K. Taken together, these four pronouncements provide the authoritative literature for information that must be filed with the SEC.[49]

Section 18 of the Act imposes liability on any person who makes a material false or misleading statement in documents filed with the SEC. The auditor's liability can be limited if the auditor can show that he "acted in good faith and had no knowledge that such statement was false or misleading." However, a number of cases have limited the auditor's good-faith defense when the auditor's action has been judged to be grossly negligent.[50]

The liability of auditors under the act often centers on Section 10 and Rule 10b-5. These provisions make it unlawful for a CPA to (1) employ any device, scheme, or artifice to defraud; (2) make an untrue statement of material fact or omit a material fact necessary in order to make the statement made, in the light of the circumstances under which they were made, not misleading; or (3) engage in any act, practice, or course of business to commit fraud or deceit in connection with the purchase or sale of the security.[51]

Once a plaintiff has established the ability to sue under Rule 10b-5, the following elements must be proved: (1) a material, factual misrepresentation or omission; (2) reliance by the plaintiff on the financial statements; (3) damages suffered as a result of reliance on the financial statements; and (4) the intent to deceive, manipulate, or defraud.[52]

Reliance by Plaintiff

The first element can include materially misleading information or the omission of material information. Reliance cannot be established if the damages or loss suffered by the plaintiff would have occurred regardless of whether the audited financial statements were misstated. A good example of the failure to establish direct causation between the audited financial statements, reliance thereon, and damages to the plaintiff is the court ruling in *Maxwell v. KPMG LLP.* In this case, the court ruled that even if the other elements necessary to sue under Rule 10b-5 could be established, Maxwell's alleged reliance on the audited financial statements of an acquiring entity was irrelevant, as the business model of that entity was bound to fail because of the dot.com collapse, and thus Maxwell's harm was not caused by KPMG's audit.[53]

This ruling stands as an example of non-accounting events that are the proximate cause of a failed business being given more weight than audited statements. The necessary conditions for the demise of the audit client (Whittman-Hart) were, first, its decision to buy US Web, and, second, the precipitate decline of the dot.com business. The decision to buy US Web was not influenced by KPMG's approving Whittman-Hart's accounting decisions, and neither were the dot.com troubles. US Web's agreement to be bought may have been influenced by KPMG's advice to Whittman-Hart, but that is irrelevant because US Web was doomed by the coming collapse of its market and thus was not harmed by the advice.

Intent to Deceive or Defraud

Under Rule 10b-5, auditor liability is linked to the intent to deceive, manipulate, or defraud. It is not enough to assert the failure to exercise the appropriate level of care to cause liability. The *Louisiana School Employees'* case that appears in Exhibit 6.4 illustrates the stringent requirements for plaintiffs to successfully bring securities fraud cases against auditors. What follows is a brief discussion of key facts in the case.

Courts impose very difficult and, some would argue, unreasonably high barriers to imposing federal securities liability upon accountants and auditors. In *Louisiana School Employees' Retirement System v. Ernst & Young,*[54] the Sixth Circuit Court of Appeals affirmed the dismissal of a securities fraud complaint against EY finding that the recklessness necessary to establish auditor liability under the federal securities laws is

EXHIBIT 6.4 *Louisiana School Employees' Retirement System v. Ernst & Young*

Pleading Scienter Against an Outside Auditor

The Sixth Circuit Court of Appeals addressed the liability of an outside auditor named as a primary violator in a securities fraud action in *Louisiana School Employees' Retirement System v. Ernst & Young, LLP.*[56] There, the Circuit Court held that a plaintiff "may survive a motion to dismiss only by pleading with particularity facts that give rise to a strong inference that the defendant acted with knowledge or conscious disregard of the fraud being committed . . ." as to a defendant. However, "[t]he standard of recklessness is more stringent when the defendant is an outside auditor."

The case is based on the acquisition by Accredo Health, Inc., of a division of Gentiva Health Services, Inc. The deal closed in June 2002. EY issued an unqualified audit opinion on Accredo's 2002 fiscal year financial results. Prior to closing, EY participated in due diligence. According to the complaint, the audit firm learned that nearly $58.5 million of the receivables in one division were uncollectible. EY also recognized that the allowance for doubtful accounts was understated, resulting in revenue being materially overstated.

In May 2003, Accredo issued a press release stating that it was writing off the $58.5 million of accounts receivable acquired from Gentiva. In its Form 10-Q for the third quarter of 2003, the company noted that if the collection rates had been evaluated based on data as of January 1, 2003, the charge would have been recorded as of that date. Plaintiffs claim this statement was made to avoid a restatement. The company terminated EY and filed a malpractice suit against the firm, alleging violations of the antifraud provisions of the federal securities laws. The district court dismissed the complaint, finding that scienter had not been adequately pleaded as required by the Private Securities Litigation Reform Act (PSLRA) and the Supreme Court's decision in *Tellabs, Inc. v. Makor Issuers & Rights, Ltd.,* 551 U.S. 308 (2007).[57]

The Sixth Circuit affirmed the dismissal. The Court began by noting that the PSLRA requires a securities law plaintiff to state with particularity both the facts constituting the alleged violation of Section 10(b) and those establishing scienter. As *Tellabs* holds, the "strong inference" standard of the PSLRA was intended to "raise the bar" for pleading scienter. While reckless conduct will suffice, when the case is against an outside auditor, more is required. In that instance, "the complaint must identify specific, highly suspicious facts and circumstances available to the auditor at the time of the audit and allege that these facts were ignored, either deliberatively or recklessly." Those well-pleaded facts must give rise to a strong inference of scienter. In addition, a comparative analysis must be done regarding possible competing inferences.

The plaintiffs failed to adequately plead scienter. Pleading accounting irregularities or a failure to comply with GAAP is, by itself, insufficient. Central to plaintiffs' allegations is a claim that EY failed to adhere to proper professional standards. This keyed to a claim that its testing of the receivables was deficient because the firm used "old and stale" data. Even if true, this type of allegation does not constitute securities fraud, the Court noted.

Plaintiffs' claim was not bolstered by its assertion that the audit firm missed "red flags." To create a strong inference of scienter from such a claim, the factual allegations must demonstrate an "egregious refusal to see the obvious, or to investigate the doubtful." Typically, courts look for multiple, obvious red flags before drawing an inference of scienter. In this regard, the plaintiffs pointed only to a series of facts which support conflicting inferences or that are not supported by facts demonstrating that the audit firm was aware of it.

Likewise, the magnitude of the error does not support a finding of scienter, as plaintiffs claim. In this regard the court held, "[w]e decline to follow the cases that hold that the magnitude of the financial fraud contributes to an inference of scienter on the part of the defendant . . . Allowing such an inference would eviscerate the principle that accounting errors alone cannot support a finding of scienter." The Court opinion states "such a claim is little more that hindsight, speculation and conjecture."

Finally, the allegations regarding motive do not save the complaint. Plaintiffs accuse EY of committing fraud because of a promise of future professional fees. It is beyond dispute that the firm earned substantial fees from the company. There is no allegation, however, that the fees from Accredo were more significant than those from other clients. There are no facts in the complaint demonstrating that EY's motive to retain Accredo as a client was any different than its general desire to retain business. Overall, plaintiffs' claims are little more that the classic fraud by hindsight case.

conduct "akin to conscious disregard [that] is highly unreasonable [and] an extreme departure from standards of ordinary care" such that "any reasonable man would have known it." The Sixth Circuit imposed an even higher burden on plaintiffs attempting to plead securities fraud against an auditor, stating that "[t]he standard for recklessness is more stringent when the defendant is an outside auditor . . . and [proof of] recklessness [for an auditor defendant] requires a mental state so culpable that it approximates an actual intent to aid in the fraud being perpetrated by the audited company." In evaluating an auditor's application of accounting principles, the Sixth Circuit also held that, to establish scienter on the part of an auditor, a complaint must plead much more than misapplication of accounting principles. Specifically, the Sixth Circuit held that a plaintiff must prove that (1) the accounting practices were so deficient that the audit amounted to "no audit at all;" (2) an egregious refusal to see the obvious or investigate the doubtful; or (3) the accounting judgments made amounted to decisions that no reasonable accountant would have made under the same circumstances.[55]

Private Securities Litigation Reform Act (PSLRA)

LO 6-3

Explain the provisions of the PSLRA.

The Private Securities Litigation Reform Act (PSLRA) of 1995 amends the Securities Exchange Act of 1934 by adding Section 10A, "Audit Requirements," which specified that each independent auditor of an issuer under the Act must include "Procedures designed to provide reasonable assurance of detecting illegal acts that would have a direct and material effect on the determination of financial statements amounts." The Act also includes in federal law the auditor's responsibility to detect fraud and requires auditors to promptly notify the audit committee and board of directors of illegal acts. Recall that we had discussed the reporting requirements of illegal acts in Chapter 5.

Proportionate Liability

The attempts to reform auditor liability in the United States focused on the argument that the tort system was out of control, partly as a consequence of the 1933 Securities Act, which placed auditors under a joint-and-several liability regime and made them, not the plaintiffs, carry the burden of proof. The accounting profession had fought over time to effectuate this change because of what the profession perceived to be frivolous lawsuits that included the auditors as defendants primarily because the plaintiffs counted on out-of-court settlement by the auditors who had "deep pockets;" auditors also carry large amounts of professional liability insurance for such matters. The senior partners in the large firms argued that SEC Rule 10-b permits class action claims against companies and auditors where share prices have fallen. Because there is no provision in U.S. law for recovery of costs by successful defendants, auditors felt compelled to settle even meritless legal claims in order to avoid high costs of litigation. Prior to enactment of the PSLRA, the average claim in 1991 was $85 million; the average settlement was $2.6 million, with legal costs of $3.5 million. The audit firms claimed that legal costs represented nine percent of their revenues in 1991.[58]

The PSLRA changes the legal liability standard of auditors from joint-and-several liability to proportionate liability. The Act adopts proportionate liability for all unknowing securities violations under the Exchange Act. (It adopts the same rule for non-officer directors under Section 11 of the Securities Act.) This provision is particularly important for underwriters, venture capital firms, outside directors, accounting firms, and others pulled into securities cases as deep-pocketed defendants. Plaintiffs will no longer have the hammer of joint-and-several liability to coerce peripheral defendants into settlements because the risk to those defendants of defending the action is unacceptable and they fear being charged with the entire responsibility for the fraud rather than only their share of it. Only those whom the trier of fact finds to have committed "knowing" securities fraud—that is, had actual knowledge that (1) a statement was false and/or that an omission led to a misleading statement and (2) investors were reasonably likely to rely on the misrepresentation or omission—will suffer joint-and-several liability.

One of the most influential (and confusing) cases involving application of the PSLRA was *Tellabs, Inc. v Makor Issues & Rights.* Several plaintiffs brought a class action securities fraud lawsuit against Tellabs, a manufacturer of equipment for fiber optic cable networks. The plaintiffs alleged that Tellabs had misrepresented the strength of its products and earnings in order to conceal the declining value of the company's stock. The District Court dismissed the complaints. The court held that the plaintiff's allegations were too vague to establish a "strong inference" of scienter on the part of Tellabs.[59]

On appeal, the U.S. Court of Appeals for the Seventh Circuit reversed one of the lower court's dismissals. The Court of Appeals ruled that a plaintiff need only allege "acts from which, if true, a reasonable person could infer that the defendant acted with the required intent." The Court of Appeals decided to consider only the plausibility of the inference of a guilty mental state and not any competing inferences of an innocent mental state. This decision was due in part to the Court's concern that weighing competing inferences was more properly the task of a jury. The Appeals Court ruling conflicted with those of other Courts of Appeals, which required plaintiffs to show that the inference of scienter supported by the alleged facts was more plausible than any competing inference of innocent intent.

The case went to the U.S. Supreme Court, where Justice Ruth Bader Ginsburg wrote the opinion for the Court, which held that the Seventh Circuit's more relaxed standard was not strong enough to comport with Congress' intent in PSLRA to limit securities fraud litigation. "The strength of an inference cannot be decided in a vacuum. The inquiry is inherently comparative [. . .]," the Court ruled. A court must consider each plausible inference of intent, both fraudulent and nonfraudulent, and then decide whether a reasonable person would consider the guilty inference "at least as strong as any opposing inference."[60]

Establishing Scienter

Application of the PSLRA seems to rely as much on scienter after the passage of the Act as it did before. The key is for plaintiffs to establish a degree of recklessness sufficient to establish knowledge of the falsehood. Additionally, courts have sided with auditors, in some instances, when they successfully assert the fraud was hidden from them by management or when internal controls are overridden by management. A good example is the ruling in Doral Financial Corporation against PwC, which is summarized in Exhibit 6.5.

EXHIBIT 6.5   PricewaterhouseCoopers Escapes Liability in Doral Litigation[61]

In a 2010 decision with potential implications for securities fraud claims against accounting firms, the U.S. Court of Appeals for the Second Circuit upheld a lower court's dismissal of securities fraud claims by shareholders of Doral Financial Corporation (Doral) against Doral's auditor, PwC. The litigation arose after Doral, a financial services company that engages in mortgage and commercial banking, restated its financial statements for the years 2000 through 2004. The restatements showed that Doral had overstated its pre-tax income by $920 million and understated its debt by $3.3 billion.

The plaintiffs alleged that Doral engaged in at least two substantial frauds involving the securitization of mortgages. First, the plaintiffs claimed that Doral engaged in "side deals and oral agreements" that essentially turned the "sales" of the securities into secured borrowings, resulting in the overstatement of earnings and an

(*Continued*)

understatement of debt. Second, the plaintiffs claimed that Doral improperly valued the interest-only strips (IO Strips) that it retained as part of the securitizations by using "manufactured" assumptions to conceal losses in its IO Strip portfolio. With respect to PwC, the plaintiffs claimed that the firm's audit reports and its report on Doral's internal controls were materially false and allowed Doral to conceal and perpetuate its frauds. On this basis, the plaintiffs claimed that PwC, like Doral, violated Section 10(b) of the Securities and Exchange Act of 1934 and Rule 10b-5 thereunder.

Judge Jed Rakoff of the U.S. District Court for the Southern District of New York had dismissed the claims against PwC in 2009, holding that the plaintiffs failed to allege the requisite scienter under the PSLRA. In a summary order issued on September 3, 2009, the Second Circuit agreed. Citing the U.S. Supreme Court's 2007 decision in *Tellabs, Inc. v. Makor Issues & Rights, Ltd.,* the Second Circuit noted that, under the PSLRA, a plaintiff must "state with particularity facts giving rise to a strong inference" of scienter, or an intent to "deceive, manipulate or defraud." The inference of scienter must be such that a reasonable person would deem it "cogent and at least as compelling as any opposing inference one could draw" from the same alleged facts. The Second Circuit opinion states that this burden could be met by alleging facts showing that the defendant had "both motive and opportunity to commit the fraud," or constituting "strong circumstantial evidence of conscious misbehavior or recklessness." However, in determining whether the alleged facts were sufficient to raise a "strong inference" of scienter, the Court was required to "take into account plausible opposing inferences," even if neither party had raised them.

The Seventh Circuit acknowledged that the plaintiffs raised "numerous allegations of carelessness" by PwC, but concluded that the allegations failed to create a strong inference of recklessness. The plaintiffs alleged, for instance, that PwC recklessly failed to uncover the side agreements that altered the terms of the mortgage sales. However, the plaintiffs also alleged that the side agreements were a "tightly-held secret," known only to a few individuals within Doral's management. The court therefore held that it was more plausible that PwC failed to discover the side deals because Doral's management hid them from PwC.

The Seventh Circuit also held that PwC's failure to identify problems with Doral's system of internal controls was insufficient to establish recklessness. It noted that the plaintiffs had alleged that Doral overrode several of its internal controls, which further undermined any inference of recklessness by PwC.

The Court ruled that "the PSLRA requires . . . more than mere plausibility." Because the "competing inference" that Doral deceived PwC was stronger than the inference that PwC was reckless, it was proper to dismiss the claims. Indeed, it is not uncommon for securities fraud claims to allege that the individuals within a company who perpetuated an alleged fraud took steps to conceal their actions and ignored or circumvented the company's system of internal controls. Following the Court's rationale, allegations of this nature would give rise to a strong "competing inference" that the auditor, like the plaintiffs themselves, was a victim of the fraud, and therefore should not be held liable for it.

It should be noted that the competing inference prevailed even though, as the District Circuit had stated, the plaintiffs alleged that PwC personnel were "regularly present" at Doral and had "unlimited access" to information regarding its operations and that PwC violated GAAP and GAAS in conducting its audits. The District Court held that these allegations were insufficient to establish scienter unless accompanied by some evidence of "corresponding fraudulent intent." The same was true of the plaintiff's allegations that PwC had a financial incentive to ignore the fraud because it collected over $6 million in fees from Doral and provided non-audit services to Doral during the relevant period.

In effect, these court decisions require allegations of facts rising to the level of deliberate or willful ignorance of misconduct (if not conscious knowledge or active participation) in order to hold an auditor liable under Section 10(b) and Rule 10b-5. Indeed, the District Court framed the issue in these terms when it discussed and dismissed allegations based on information allegedly provided by a former Doral internal auditor that PwC personnel attended meetings of the Doral Audit Committee at which questions about the company's internal controls were raised: "At most, [the former internal auditor's] information may raise an inference the PwC was negligent in not following up on such discussions, but it certainly does not show the conscious turning away from the true facts required for recklessness."

We believe not much has changed, in reality, with respect to auditors' legal liability and what we are experiencing is different interpretations by different courts in somewhat different circumstances. The intent standard still should provide the legal basis, at least for fraud determination.

SOX and Auditor Legal Liabilities

LO 6-4

Discuss auditors' legal liabilities under SOX.

Major developments in auditor liability have occurred as a result of the Sarbanes-Oxley Act. SOX was passed to increase the transparency of financial reporting by enhancing corporate disclosure and governance practices and to foster an ethical climate.[62] SOX increases auditor liability to third parties by specifying or expanding the scope of third parties to whom an auditor owes a duty of care. SOX also increases auditor liability to third parties because it requires accounting firms to review and assess management's report on internal controls and issue its own report.

Section 404. *Internal Control over Financial Reporting*

Traditionally, because auditors had no duty to disclose control weaknesses or their effects on substantive audit testing in the audit report, courts deemed control irregularities immaterial for deciding auditors' liability under Section 11 of the Securities Exchange Act of 1933. The case of *Monroe v. Hughes* (1991) illustrates the current law.[63] In that case, the auditor found internal control irregularities, conferred with management and expanded the scope of its financial audit by performing more elaborate substantive testing. The auditor issued an unqualified audit report, but did not disclose the control irregularities in the audit report. In the following year, the auditor found significant deterioration in internal controls and was unable to issue an unqualified financial statement opinion for that year. The client collapsed and investors sued the auditor under Section 11, claiming that the auditor should have disclosed in its audit opinion the internal control irregularities it discovered. The *Monroe* court (and others facing similar questions) rejected the investors' argument, citing Section 11's due diligence defense, negligence standard, and observing that good faith compliance with GAAS discharges an auditor's professional obligation to act with reasonable care. No legal or accounting authority required auditors to disclose control irregularities.[64]

Under PCAOB AS 2201, the auditor must form an opinion on the ICFR and either prepare a separate report on such matters or include the assessment in the auditor's report. Since the assessment of ICFR is required under Section 404 of SOX, the auditor may be held legally liable for deficiencies in the audit of ICFR much like the deficiencies in applying GAAS and material misstatements in the financial statements.

Important Definitions

A *deficiency* in internal control over financial reporting exists when the design or operation of a control does not allow management or employees, in the normal course of performing their assigned functions, to prevent or detect misstatements on a timely basis.

A *material weakness* is a deficiency, or a combination of deficiencies, in internal control over financial reporting, such that there is a *reasonable possibility* that a material misstatement of the company's annual or interim financial statements will not be prevented or detected on a timely basis.

A *significant deficiency* is a deficiency, or a combination of deficiencies, in internal control over financial reporting that is less severe than a material weakness, yet important enough to merit attention by those responsible for oversight of the company's financial reporting.

Section 11 and 10(b) Liability and Attesting to Management's Assessment of ICFR

The auditors' assessment of management's assertions about ICFR and related audit of internal controls are intended, in part, to create an early warning system to alert financial statement users to material weaknesses in ICFR that may impair an issuer's ability to prepare reliable financial statements in current- and future-accounting periods.[65]

Cunningham et al. believe that PCAOB AS 2 (superseded by AS 2201) is likely to change the legal landscape for auditors. If auditors conclude that internal controls are effective when they are not, the situation is much like that occurring when they inappropriately conclude that financial statements are fair and conform to GAAP. The authors explore auditors' potential legal liability under Section 11 of the Securities Act. The authors suggest that, given the standards established in AS 2201, it seems reasonable to assume that a court might find auditor culpable for failing to disclose a material weakness in internal controls. Thus, auditors would have incentives when providing ICFR opinions to disclose discovered weaknesses and to err on the side of characterizing control deficiencies as material when they could alternatively be described instead as significant deficiencies not requiring disclosure. The problem, as the authors see it, is even though this incentive appears to be consistent with AS 2201's early warning system objectives, it may create false positive signals, which ultimately may render the adverse opinion less meaningful or result in lower pricing by the market of public offerings. Additionally, a definition of a material weakness in this way sets a low threshold that even some well-managed companies are likely to get caught up by the negative ICFR.[66]

Under Section 3 of the Securities Exchange Act of 1934, a violation of the Act or any rule of the PCAOB shall be treated for all purposes in the same manner as a violation of the Exchange Act of 1934. Looking at Section 10(b) of the Act, Cunningham et al. suggest that to the extent auditor behavior is influenced by applicable legal liability risks, Section 10(b)'s incentives could bias auditors' decisions to resolve uncertain cases as significant deficiencies rather than material weaknesses. This is because most courts apply a bright-line rule that an auditor must make a false or misleading statement to the public to be liable under section 10(b).[67]

Section 302. *Corporate Responsibility for Financial Reports*

Section 302 requires the certification of periodic reports filed with the SEC by the CEO and CFO of public companies. The certification states that "based on the officer's knowledge, the report does not contain any untrue statement of a material fact or omit to state a material fact necessary in order to make the statements, in light of the circumstances under which such statements were made, not misleading."

The certifications aim to prevent fraudulent financial disclosures by emphasizing the CEO's and CFO's personal accountability for integrity in financial reporting. As a result, CEOs and CFOs are exposed to personal civil and criminal liability if they sign false certificates for SEC registrants, which includes falsely certifying corporate financial reports and reports on internal controls.

The early cases set the tone for SEC's expectations with respect to Section 302 certifications. The first reported case was *Higginbotham v. Baxter Int'l.* in 2005. The plaintiffs argued that the 302 certifications concerning the adequacy of the company's internal controls were false, and accordingly, the court could infer that Section 10(b)'s scienter requirement was met as to the individuals signing those certifications. The *Higginbotham* court rejected this argument because plaintiffs provided "no specific allegations as to what the deficiencies in the controls were, nor [did they provide] any specific allegations as to [the certifying executives'] awareness of those deficiencies."[68] The ruling does not mean that a false statement with regard to internal controls is not an actionable offense. Instead, the conclusion to be drawn is that claims of scienter require more than just an assertion; specific proof of such knowledge must exist.

The next such case was *In re Lattice Semiconductor Corp.* In *Lattice Semiconductor,* plaintiffs alleged a series of accounting errors that resulted in materially misstated financial statements. In this case, plaintiffs argued that false 302 certifications raised a strong inference that the CEO and CFO were, at a minimum, deliberately reckless, thereby satisfying Section 10(b)'s scienter requirement. Defendants responded by arguing that if "these certifications raised a strong inference of *scienter,* every corporate officer who signed a certification for a Form 10-Q or 10-K filing that was later found to be incorrect would be subject to a securities fraud action."[69]

The *Lattice Semiconductor* court sided with plaintiffs, holding that the 302 certifications in that case did, in fact, give rise to an inference of scienter "because they provide evidence either that defendants knew about the improper journal entries and unreported sales credits that led to the over-reporting of revenues (because of the internal controls they said existed) or, alternatively, knew that the controls they attested to were inadequate."

Soon after *Lattice Semiconductor,* the court in *In re WatchGuard Secs. Litig.* considered allegedly false 302 certifications in the context of a private Section 10(b) action. In *WatchGuard,* plaintiffs alleged that the defendant company had made material misstatements about interest expenses and revenue recognition in its financial statements. Plaintiffs also contended that WatchGuard's quarterly 302 certifications were themselves actionable misstatements on which they could base a Section 10(b) and Rule 10b-5 claim. Plaintiffs also argued that the certifications demonstrated scienter under the "deliberate recklessness" standard because the certifying individual defendants either knew about WatchGuard's revenue recognition problems or were "deliberately reckless in not obtaining the information or conducting the investigations described in their certifications prior to publishing the false financial statements."[70]

The *WatchGuard* court rejected plaintiffs' arguments, holding that the individual defendants' 302 certifications were, by themselves, inadequate to support a strong inference of scienter. In so holding, the court stressed that the failure of plaintiffs to plead scienter adequately is what doomed their 302 argument. "In a case like this one, however, where the court finds no strong inference that any defendant was at least deliberately reckless in issuing corporate earnings statements, the court has no basis for a strong inference that the Sarbanes-Oxley certifications were culpably false."[71]

It is safe to say the courts are still finding their way with respect to legal liability issues and alleged violations of SOX under Section 302. However, based upon the reported private securities cases thus far, it appears that that Section 302 certifications that turn out to be inaccurate do not give rise to independent private claims under the securities laws, nor do they appear to alter the fundamental standards that are applied in Section 10(b) actions. Rather, they are viewed by courts in the overall context of a case and bear on civil liability only when other pleaded facts create a strong inference of scienter against the 302 certifier.[72]

As discussed in Chapter 3, most major corporations have implemented internal compliance systems that make it very difficult to show that the CEO or CFO knowingly signed a false certification. One reason is multiple layers of subcertification are put in place, requiring lower-level officials to attest to the accuracy of financial reports all the way up the chain of command to the CEO and CFO. The subcertifications provide cover for CEOs and CFOs from false certification charges. To prove SOX charges, prosecutors have to show that top officials signed off on financial reports they knew to be false. The subcertifications make it much tougher to prove since CEOs and CFOs can claim they relied on the attestations of their underlings.

Perspective on Accomplishments of SOX

SOX is sometimes faulted for not preventing the financial crisis and the Great Recession. But defenders argue that it wasn't designed to do more than ensure that accounting rules were followed. "If you've got employees who are stealing stuff out the back door of the warehouse, [SOX] would tell you whether you have inventory controls in place, not whether the door is locked," according to Gary Kabureck, vice president and chief accounting officer at Xerox Corp.

One consolation, says Lynn Turner, former chief accountant for the SEC, is that SOX no doubt mitigated the force of the financial crisis, which could have been worse. "We didn't see the huge rash of fraudulent reporting like we saw in the 1996–2002 time period," he says. "So that would tell you, 'Yes, the legislation did accomplish its goal.'"

Foreign Corrupt Practices Act (FCPA)

LO 6-5

Explain the provisions of the FCPA.

In addition to the PSLRA and SOX, other laws have influenced audit procedures, legal liability, requirements for internal controls over financial reporting, and ethics requirements under the due care principle. The law with the greatest effect in the United States is the Foreign Corrupt Practices Act (FCPA).

The FCPA establishes standards for the acceptability of payments made by U.S. multinational entities or their agent to foreign government officials. The act was motivated when, during the period of 1960 to 1977, the SEC cited 527 companies for bribes and other dubious payments that were made to win foreign contracts. Lockheed Corporation was one of the companies caught in this scandal. It was determined that Lockheed had made about $55 million in illegal payments to foreign governments and officials. One such payment, $1.7 million to Japanese premier Kukuei Tanaka, led to his resignation in disgrace in 1974.

The FCPA makes it a crime to offer or provide payments to officials of foreign governments, political candidates, or political parties for the purpose of obtaining or retaining business. It applies to all U.S. corporations, whether they are publicly or privately held, and to foreign companies filing with the SEC. The U.S. Department of Justice (DOJ) is responsible for all criminal enforcement and for civil enforcement of the antibribery provisions with respect to domestic entities and foreign companies and nationals. The SEC is responsible for civil enforcement of the antibribery provisions with respect to registrants.

Under the FCPA, a corporation that violates the law can be fined up to $1 million, while its officers who directly participated in violations of the act or had "reason to know" of such violations can be fined up to $10,000, imprisoned for up to five years, or both. The act also prohibits corporations from indemnifying fines imposed on directors, officers, employees, or agents. FCPA does not prohibit "grease payments" (i.e., *permissible facilitating payments*) to foreign government employees whose duties are primarily ministerial or clerical because such payments are sometimes required to persuade recipients to perform their normal duties.[73]

As a result of the criticisms of the antibribery provisions of the 1977 FCPA, Congress amended the act as part of the Omnibus Trade and Competitiveness Act of 1988 to clarify when a payment is prohibited, as follows:[74]

1. A payment is defined as illegal if it is intended to influence a foreign official to act in a way that is incompatible with the official's legal duty.

2. The "reason to know" standard is replaced by a "knowing" standard, so that criminal liability for illegal payments to third parties applies to individuals who "knowingly" engage in or tolerate illegal payments under the act.

3. The definition of "grease" payments is expanded to include payments to any foreign official that facilitates or expedites securing the performance of a routine governmental action.

4. Examples of acceptable payments include (1) obtaining permits, licenses, and the official documents to qualify a person to do business in a foreign country; (2) processing governmental papers, such as visas or work orders; (3) providing police protection, mail pickup, and delivery, or scheduling inspections associated with contract performance or inspections related to the transit of goods across country; (4) providing telephone service, power, and water, unloading and loading cargo, or protecting perishable product or commodities from deterioration; and (5) performing actions of a similar nature.

Two affirmative defenses for those accused of violating the act are that the payment is lawful "under the written laws" of the foreign country, and that the payment can be made for "reasonable and bona fide expenditures." These include lodging expenses incurred by or for a foreign official to promote products or services or to execute the performance of a contract.

Individuals can be prosecuted under the 1988 amendment even if the company for which they work is *not* guilty. Penalties for violations were raised to $2 million for entities and $100,000 for individuals. The maximum term of imprisonment is kept at five years. A $10,000 civil penalty also was enacted.

The health-care industry has been under increased SEC and DOJ scrutiny for a number of years now for potential FCPA violations. What has been described as an "industry sweep" has focused primarily on medical device and pharmaceutical companies. Exhibit 6.6 summarizes one of the most comprehensive FCPA actions taken by the SEC and DOJ against Pfizer on August 7, 2012.

EXHIBIT 6.6 The SEC Case Against Pfizer

The allegations by the SEC against Pfizer Inc. illustrate the vast global nature of foreign bribery. On August 7, 2012, the SEC charged Pfizer Inc. with violating the FCPA when its subsidiaries bribed doctors and other health-care professionals employed by foreign governments in order to win business.[75]

The SEC alleged that employees and agents of Pfizer's subsidiaries in Bulgaria, China, Croatia, Czech Republic, Italy, Kazakhstan, Russia, and Serbia made improper payments to foreign officials to obtain regulatory and formulary approvals, sales, and increased prescriptions for the company's pharmaceutical products. They tried to conceal the bribery by improperly recording the transactions in accounting records as legitimate expenses for promotional activities, marketing, training, travel and entertainment, clinical trials, freight, conferences, and advertising.

The SEC separately charged another pharmaceutical company that Pfizer acquired a few years ago—Wyeth LLC—with its own FCPA violations. Pfizer and Wyeth agreed to separate settlements in which they will pay more than $45 million combined to settle their respective charges. In a parallel action, the DOJ announced that Pfizer H.C.P. Corporation, an indirectly wholly-owned subsidiary of Pfizer, agreed to pay a $15 million penalty to resolve the investigation of its potential FCPA violations.

"Pfizer subsidiaries in several countries had bribery so entwined in their sales culture that they offered points and bonus programs to improperly reward foreign officials who proved to be their best customers," said Kara Brockmeyer, chief of the SEC Enforcement Division's FCPA Unit. "These charges illustrate the pitfalls that exist for companies that fail to appropriately monitor potential risks in their global operations."

(Continued)

According to the SEC's complaint against Pfizer filed in U.S. District Court for the District of Columbia, the misconduct dated back as far as 2001. Employees of Pfizer's subsidiaries authorized and made cash payments and provided other incentives to bribe government doctors to use Pfizer products. In China, for example, Pfizer employees invited "high-prescribing doctors" in the Chinese government to club-like meetings that included extensive recreational and entertainment activities to reward doctors' past product sales or prescriptions. Pfizer China also created various "point programs," under which government doctors could accumulate points based on the number of Pfizer prescriptions they wrote. The points were redeemed for various gifts ranging from medical books to cell phones, tea sets, and reading glasses.

The SEC further alleged that Wyeth subsidiaries engaged in FCPA violations primarily before but also after the company's acquisition by Pfizer in late 2009. Starting at least in 2005, subsidiaries marketing Wyeth nutritional products in China, Indonesia, and Pakistan bribed government doctors to recommend their products to patients by making cash payments or, in some cases, providing BlackBerrys and cell phones or travel incentives. They often used fictitious invoices to conceal the true nature of the payments. In Saudi Arabia, Wyeth's subsidiary made an improper cash payment to a customs official to secure the release of a shipment of promotional items used for marketing purposes. The promotional items were held in port because Wyeth Saudi Arabia had failed to secure a required Saudi Arabian Standards Organization Certificate of Conformity. (This could have been deemed a facilitating payment under FCPA.)

Following Pfizer's acquisition of Wyeth, Pfizer undertook a risk-based FCPA due diligence review of Wyeth's global operations and voluntarily reported the findings to the SEC staff. Pfizer diligently and promptly integrated Wyeth's legacy operations into its compliance program and cooperated fully with SEC investigators.

Pfizer consented to the entry of a final judgment ordering it to pay disgorgement of $16,032,676 in net profits, as well as prejudgment interest of $10,307,268, for a total of $26,339,944. Wyeth also is required to report to the SEC on the status of its remediation and implementation of compliance measures over a two-year period, and is permanently enjoined from further violations of Sections 13(b)(2)(A) and 13(b)(2)(B) of the Securities Exchange Act of 1934.

In a speech on compliance in the pharmaceutical industry on March 3, 2015, Andrew Ceresney, SEC's Director of the Division of Enforcement, pointed out that the best way for a company to avoid FCPA violations is to have a robust FCPA compliance program that includes compliance personnel, extensive policies and procedures, training, vendor reviews, due diligence on third-party agents, expense controls, escalation of red flags, and internal audits to review compliance.[76] An effective compliance program also includes performing risk assessments and monitoring internal controls over financial reporting.

In discussing the importance of internal controls and its relevance to FCPA reporting, Ceresny noted that the number of enforcement actions the SEC brought in the financial reporting area increased by over 40% in fiscal year 2014 compared to 2013, and the number of new financial reporting investigations opened increased by about 30% in the same period. "Many of these cases are focused on issuers and their executives and financial personnel. But we also are looking closely at gatekeepers, who play a critical role in ensuring accurate and reliable financial reporting. In every financial reporting investigation, we look at the work of the auditors to determine whether their audits were performed in accordance with professional standards."[77]

The FCPA violations at Pfizer clearly illustrate the importance of an effective system of internal controls, strong corporate governance, and a tone at the top that filters throughout the organization and strengthens compliance with regulations and ethical behavior. FCPA compliance is important for accountants and auditors who are charged with disclosing illegal acts and evaluating internal controls.

Internal Accounting Control Requirements

The FCPA requires all SEC registrants to maintain internal accounting controls to ensure that all transactions are authorized by management and recorded properly. The Act requires public company issuers to maintain adequate books and records that, in reasonable detail, accurately and fairly reflect an issuer's transactions and disposition of assets. In addition, public companies must maintain internal controls to ensure transparency in the financial condition of the company, the relevant risk to the company, and the transactions conducted by the company.

In Chapter 3 we examined the whistleblower case of Tony Menendez against Halliburton. Now, we look at a FCPA enforcement action against Halliburton for internal control failures in its business relationships in Angola. On July 27, 2017, the SEC charged Halliburton Company with violating the books and records and internal accounting controls provisions of the FCPA while selecting and making payments to a local company in Angola in the course of winning lucrative oilfield services contracts.

According to the SEC's order,[78] officials at Angola's state oil company Sonangol advised Halliburton management in 2008 that it was required to partner with more local Angolan-owned businesses to satisfy local content regulations for foreign firms operating in Angola. Halliburton assigned then vice president Jeannot Lorenz with leading these efforts. When a new round of oil company projects came up for bid, Lorenz began a lengthy effort to retain a local Angolan company owned by a former Halliburton employee who was a friend and neighbor of the Sonangol official who would ultimately approve the award of the contracts. It took three attempts, but Halliburton ultimately outsourced more than $13 million worth of business to the local Angolan company.

There were multiple issues in the enforcement action around internal controls, their effectiveness (or lack thereof), and management override of internal controls. The SEC's order found that Halliburton entered into contracts with the local Angolan company that were intended to meet local content requirements rather than the stated scope of work. Lorenz violated Halliburton's internal accounting controls by starting with the local Angolan company and then backing into a list of contract services rather than first determining the services and then selecting an appropriate supplier. Lorenz also failed to conduct competitive bidding or substantiate the need for a single source of supply, and he avoided an internal accounting control that required contracts of more than $10,000 in countries like Angola with high corruption risks to be reviewed and approved by a special committee within Halliburton. The company eventually paid $3.705 million to the local Angolan firm, and Sonangol approved the award of seven lucrative subcontracts to Halliburton.

Without admitting or denying the findings, Halliburton and Lorenz consented to the order requiring them to cease and desist from committing or causing any violations or any future violations of the books and records and internal accounting controls provisions of the FCPA. Halliburton agreed to pay $14 million in disgorgement plus $1.2 million in prejudgment interest and a $14 million penalty. Halliburton must retain an independent compliance consultant for 18 months to review and evaluate its anti-corruption policies and procedures, particularly in regard to local content obligations for business operations in Africa.

FCPA violations are troubling because they result from bribery of foreign government officials or agents of the government. If bribery occurs in a company, we can only wonder what other ethical transgressions exist. Halliburton is a case in point. It is rare when a company violates a law, oftentimes very blatantly, and toes the line in other areas of operations. The violations always reflect a failure of the corporate governance system and unethical tone at the top. As for the auditors, we have to wonder how they can miss FCPA violations given the heightened ethical requirements when operating in the global arena where different cultures establish different standards of ethical conduct.

Voluntary Disclosure of Violations of FCPA

On November 29, 2017, the U.S. DOJ issued a revised policy to encourage companies to voluntarily disclose violations of the FCPA. The revised policy follows an 18-month pilot program during which time the FCPA enforcement unit received 30 voluntary disclosures compared to 18 during the previous 18-month period. What follows is a summary of the revised policy.[79]

The revised policy states, in part:

> When a company has voluntarily self-disclosed misconduct in an FCPA matter, fully cooperated, and timely and appropriately remediated, all in accordance with the standards set forth below, there will be a presumption that the company will receive a declination absent aggravating circumstances involving the seriousness of the offense or the nature of the offender.
>
> The policy lays out some examples of aggravating circumstances that may warrant criminal resolution, but notes this is a non-exhaustive list: (1) involvement by executive management of the company in misconduct; (2) a significant profit to the company from the misconduct; (3) pervasiveness of the misconduct within the company; and (4) criminal recidivism.

In several places, the policy discusses the importance of having an effective compliance program in place. For example, for a company to receive full credit for timely and appropriate remediation in FCPA matters, it must have in place an "effective compliance and ethics program." Similarly, if criminal resolution is warranted, a company that has an effective compliance program, and has otherwise fully cooperated, self-reported and remediated, will not likely require the appointment of a monitor.

The policy provides the following, non-exhaustive list of what may be considered in evaluating effective compliance programs:

- The company's culture of compliance, including awareness among employees that any criminal conduct, including the conduct underlying the investigation, will not be tolerated;
- The resources the company has dedicated to compliance;
- The quality and experience of the personnel involved in compliance, so that they can understand and identify the transactions and activities that pose a potential risk;
- The authority and independence of the compliance function and the availability of compliance expertise to the board;
- The effectiveness of the company's risk assessment and the manner in which the company's compliance program has been tailored based on that risk assessment;
- The compensation and promotion of the personnel involved in compliance, in view of their role, responsibilities, performance, and other appropriate factors;
- The auditing of the compliance program to assure its effectiveness; and
- The reporting structure of any compliance personnel employed or contracted by the company.

It is worth noting the similarities between an effective compliance program and many of the issues we have addressed in these first six chapters. First and foremost, an effective compliance and ethics program and culture of compliance provide the foundation for an ethical compliance program, much like a code of ethics, ethics policies, and tone at the top establish strong ethics in an organization. Properly trained compliance personnel relate to trained auditors and audit planning. An independent compliance function is similar to the independent audit. Risk assessment of the compliance program equates to risk assessment in an audit. Compliance expertise available to the board is similar to having someone with financial expertise on the audit committee. Finally, the auditing of the compliance program can be said to equate to the way internal audit functions to ensure internal controls are operating as intended.

Although the prospect of a declination is encouraging for companies that would consider self-reporting, the issues of cooperation, what constitutes an effective compliance program, and whether aggravating circumstances are involved are subjective determinations. Ultimately, the government will still hold the power in deciding what credit should be given in any particular case.

Concluding Thoughts

Auditors are liable to clients and third parties for failing to conduct an audit in accordance with prescribed standards including PCAOB standards, AICPA rules of conduct, state board rules and regulations, SEC Securities Exchange Acts, violations of Sections 302 and 404 of SOX, and failing to keep proper records and internal controls when FCPA matters arise. The history of litigation against auditors indicates that the most important standards to protect auditors from legal liability are exercising due care in the performance of professional services, including professional skepticism; properly assessing whether material misstatements exist in ICFR; and conducting an audit in accordance with GAAS to determine whether material misstatements exist in the financial statements due to the failure to follow GAAP.

Auditors are required to report illegal acts including fraud under the PSLRA, as we discussed in Chapter 5. The PSLRA relies on scienter to determine whether auditors will be held legally liable for failing to identify illegal acts and fraud. Important questions to consider are: Did the auditor know about an illegal act or fraud or should the auditor have known about it? Was there an overt act by the auditors to induce reliance by third parties on materially misstated financial statements? Were the auditors reckless to the extent that constructive fraud exists? Did the auditors meet the requirements under SOX Section 404?

The importance of properly assessing ICFR under Section 404 cannot be overstated. Audit firms and auditors must do everything in their power to ensure that deficiencies are identified and determined to be either significant or material. Legal actions against auditors for their failure to properly assess internal controls and management's assessment of ICFR are likely to increase in the future now that a sufficient number of years have gone by and experiences have been gained with respect to the application of Section 404 to auditor legal liability.

Discussion Questions

1. As discussed in the opening reflection, MF Global filed a complaint charging PwC with professional malpractice, breach of contract, and unjust enrichment in connection with its advice concerning, and approval of, the company's off-balance-sheet accounting for its investments. On March 23, 2017, PwC finally settled a potential $3 billion lawsuit by the administrator of the bankrupt MF Global. The administrator argued accounting errors, including allowing MF Global to keep the bonds off its balance sheet. The premature settlement left open the question of whether auditors should be held legally liable for their advice on complex accounting questions that require complex judgments? What do you believe?

2. Distinguish between common-law liability and statutory liability for auditors. What is the basis for the difference in liability?

3. Is there a conceptual difference between an error and negligence from a reasonable care perspective? Give examples of each in your response.

4. Distinguish between the legal concepts of actually foreseen third-party users and reasonably foreseeable third-party users. How does each concept establish a basis for an auditor's legal liability to third parties?

5. Describe the possible entities that may sue an auditor and the possible reason for a lawsuit.

6. Explain the legal basis for a cause of action against an auditor. What are the defenses available to the auditor to rebut such charges? How does adherence to the ethical standards of the accounting profession relate to these defenses?

7. Assume a third party such as a successor audit firm quickly discovers a fraud that the predecessor external auditor has overlooked for years. How might a determination be made whether scienter existed?

8. What must a plaintiff assert in a Section 11 claim under the Securities Act of 1933 to properly allege an "opinion" statement is materially misleading? When might certain financial statement items constitute "opinions"?

9. What are the legal requirements for a third party to sue an auditor under Section 10 and Rule 10b-5 of the Securities Exchange Act of 1934? How do these requirements relate to the *Louisiana School Employees* decision?

10. What do you believe would be required for an auditor to successfully assert the fraud of a client's managers as a defense against the company's charges of breach of contract, failure to exercise due care, and failure to uncover fraud?

11. Valley View Manufacturing Inc. sought a $500,000 loan from First National Bank. First National insisted that audited financial statements be submitted before it would extend credit. Valley View agreed to do so, and an audit was performed by an independent CPA who submitted his report to Valley View. First National, upon reviewing the audited statements, decided to extend the credit desired. Certain ratios used by First National in reaching its decision were extremely positive, indicating a strong cash flow. It was subsequently learned that the CPA, despite the exercise of reasonable care, had failed to discover a sophisticated embezzlement scheme by Valley View's chief accountant. Under these circumstances, what liability might the CPA have?

12. Nixon & Co., CPAs, issued an unmodified opinion on the 2015 financial statements of Madison Corp. These financial statements were included in Madison's annual report and Form 10-K filed with the SEC. Nixon did not detect material misstatements in the financial statements as a result of negligence in the performance of the audit. Based upon the financial statements, Harry Corp. purchased stock in Madison. Shortly thereafter, Madison became insolvent, causing the price of the stock to decline drastically. Harry has commenced legal action against Nixon for damages based upon Section 10(b) and Rule 10b-5 of the Securities Exchange Act of 1934. What would be Nixon's best defense to such an action? Explain.

13. Explain your answers to the following questions about the PSLRA:

    a. Do you believe the standard for liability under the PSLRA better protects auditors from legal liability than the standards which existed before the Act was adopted by Congress?

    b. Do you believe the PSLRA standard better protects the public interest?

14. How has the Sarbanes-Oxley Act affected the legal liability of accountants and auditors?

15. Some auditors claim that increased exposure under Section 404 of SOX creates a litigation environment that is unfairly risky for auditors. Do you think that the inability of auditors to detect a financial statement misstatement due to gross deficiencies in internal controls over financial reporting should expose auditors to litigation? Why or why not?

16. Should Section 302 of SOX be broadened to establish legal liability for others in the certification process in addition to CEOs and CFOs? Explain.

17. Given the recent changes in audit committee responsibilities under SOX and PCAOB standards, when might audit committee members be held at least partially responsible for a financial reporting failure?

18. Carly Simmons is approached by a small sole proprietor to assist him in getting the record keeping for the enterprise organized to firm up receivables, payables, payroll, and other taxes necessary to run the business. It seems the owner intends to apply for a $50,000 loan at the bank. During the month following their initial discussion and agreement on services, Carly established a suitable internal control system, assisted the bookkeeper with setting up a "Quick Books" type of record

keeping, prepared adjusting and closing entries for the month, and discussed the computerized financial statements with the owner. Answer the following:

    a. Should Carly have gotten an engagement letter? If so, what should it have included?

    b. What type of compilation service has Carly performed? Does she have to prepare a compilation report?

    c. What legal liability issues would be of concern to you if you were Carly?

19. Answer the following with respect to deficiencies in ICFR.

    a. How should a SEC registrant evaluate whether a deficiency in ICFR is a material weakness?

    b. Why should SEC registrant's document why a significant deficiency in ICFR is not a material weakness?

20. Assume a U.S. company operates overseas and is approached by foreign governments officials with a request to provide family members with student internships with the company. The company does business in that country with foreign customers and is negotiating for a contract with one such customer to provide services. Under what circumstances might such a request violate the FCPA?

21. What is the importance of having an effective compliance and ethics program with respect to the FCPA? What is the role of confidential reporting and internal investigations in the compliance program?

22. Consider the practice of making "facilitating payments" to foreign officials and others as part of doing business abroad in the context of the following statement: International companies are confronted with a variety of decisions that create ethical dilemmas for the decision makers. "Right-wrong" and "just-unjust" derive their meaning and true value from the attitudes of a given culture. Some ethical standards are culture-specific, and we should not be surprised to find that an act that is considered quite ethical in one culture may be looked upon with disregard in another. How do cultural factors influence the acceptability of making facilitating payments in a country? Use rights theory and justice reasoning to analyze the ethics of allowing facilitating payments such as under the FCPA.

23. What are the costs and benefits of voluntarily disclosing violations of the FCPA assuming an internal compliance official threatens to blow the whistle on the company under the Dodd-Frank Financial Reform Act?

24. Has the accounting profession created a situation in which auditors' ethical behavior is impaired by their professional obligations? How does the profession's view of such obligations relate to how courts tend to view the legal liability of auditors?

25. How does auditors' meeting public interest obligations relate to avoiding legal liability?

Endnotes

1. JS 44/C/SDNY, REV. 2/2014, Available at: http://go.bloomberg.com/assets/content/uploads/sites/2/2014/03/3-28-14-8.pdf.

2. Epstein & Nach LLC, Auditor Liability and Professional Skepticism: A Look at Lehman Brothers and MF Global A White Paper By Dr. Barry Jay Epstein, CPA, CFF June, 2015, http://www.epsteinnach.com/wp-content/uploads/2015/06/Auditor_Liability_Professional_Skepticism_White_Paper_Final.pdf.

3. Zoe-Vonna Palmrose, *Empirical Research in Auditor Litigation: Considerations and Data, Studies in Accounting Research No. 33* (Sarasota, FL: American Accounting Association,1999).

4. William F. Messier Jr., Steven M. Glover, and Douglas F. Prawitt, *Auditing and Assurance Services: A Systematic Approach* (New York: McGraw-Hill Irwin, 2012).

5. Find Law, Recklessness, http://injury.findlaw.com/accident-injury-law/recklessness.html.

6. Timothy J. Louwers, Robert J. Ramsay, David H. Sinason, Jerry R. Strawser, and Jay C. Thibodeau, *Auditing and Assurance Services* (New York: McGraw-Hill Irwin, 2013).

7. Timothy J. Louwers, Robert J. Ramsay, David H. Sinason, Jerry R. Strawser, and Jay C. Thibodeau, *Auditing and Assurance Services* (New York: McGraw-Hill Irwin, 2013).

8. Louwers et al., pp. 637–638.

9. *In Re Gouiran Holdings, Inc.,* 165 B.R. 104 (E.D.N.Y. 1994), *U.S. District Court for the Eastern District of New York,* February 10, 1994, https://law.justia.com/cases/federal/district-courts/BR/165/104/1942863/.

10. Steven P. Garmisa, Supreme Court Debates Defense in Claims Against Service Providers, January 19, 2004, http://www.hoeyfarina.com/supreme-court-debates-defense-claims-against-service-providers.

11. *Shapiro v. Glekel,* US District Court for the Southern District of New York, *380 F. Supp. 1053 (S.D.N.Y. 1974),* https://law.justia.com/cases/federal/district-courts/FSupp/380/1053/1457899/.

12. Find Law, Recklessness.

13. *Credit Alliance v. Arthur Andersen & Co.,* 483 N.E. 2d 100 (N.Y. 1985).

14. *Security Pacific Business Credit v. Peat Marwick Main & Co.,* 165 A.D.2d 622 (N.Y. App. Div. 1991), Available at: https://casetext.com/case/security-pacific-v-peat-marwick.

15. Messier et al., pp. 692–693.

16. *Rusch Factors, Inc. v. Levin,* 284. F.Supp. 85, 91.

17. *Restatement (Second) of the Law of Torts,* Section 552A–E (1997), www.tomwbell.com/NetLaw/Ch05/R2ndTorts.html.

18. *Blue Bell, Inc. v. Peat, Marwick, Mitchell & Co.,* 715 S.W. 2d 408 (Dallas 1986).

19. *Rosenblum, Inc. v. Adler,* 93 N.J. 324 (1983).

20. *Citizens State Bank v. Timm, Schmidt & Co.* (1983), Available at: https://law.justia.com/cases/wisconsin/supreme-court/1983/81-801-9.html

21. Dan M. Goldwasser and Thomas Arnold, *Accountants' Liability* (New York: Practising Law Institute, 2009).

22. *Bily v. Arthur Young,* 834 P. 2d 745 (Cal. 1992).

23. Richard Mann and Barry Roberts, *Essentials of Business Law and the Legal Environment,* (Boston, MA: Cengage Learning, 2015).

24. *1136 Tenants Corp. v. Max Rothenberg & Co.,* 27 App. Div. 2d 830, 277 NYS 2d 996 (1967).

25. AICPA Accounting and Review Services Committee, *Statement on Standards for Accounting and Review Services 21,* October 21, 2014, https://www.journalofaccountancy.com/content/dam/jofa/archive/issues/2014/12/ssars-21-final.pdf.

26. Vincent J. Love and Thomas R. Manisero, "'Plain Paper' Financial Statements Made Not So Plain: An Overview of SSARS 21," The CPA Journal, May 2017, https://www.cpajournal.com/2017/05/26/plain-paper-financial-statements-made-not-plain-overview-ssars-21/.

27. Love and Manisero.

28. Messier et al., p. 705.

29. *State Street Trust Co. v. Ernst,* Court of Appeals, N.Y. (1938), 278 N.Y. 104. 15 N.E.2d 416.

30. Messier et al., p. 705.

31. *Phar-Mor v. Coopers & Lybrand,* Available at: www.cases.justia.com/us-court-of-appeals/F3/22/1228/579478/.

32. Supreme Court, New York County, *Water St. Leasehold LLC v Deloitte & Touche, Llp,* Available at: http://law.justia.com/cases/new-york/other-courts/2004/2004-51260.html.

33. *Howard Reisman & others vs. KPMG Peat Marwick LLP,* 57 Mass. App. Ct. 100, April 10, 2002 - January 15, 2003, November 24, 2003, Available at: http://masscases.com/cases/app/57/57massappct100.html.

34. *Houbigant, Inc. v. Deloitte & Touche LLP.*

35. Louwers et al., pp. 641–642.

36. Louwers et al., pp. 642–643.

37. *Grant Thornton LLP v. Prospect High Income Fund, et al.,* July 2, 2010, Available at: http://www.txcourts.gov/media/819887/OpinionsFY2010.pdf.

38. Supreme Court of Texas, *McCamish, Martin, Brown & Loeffler v. F.E. Appling Interests,* No. 97-0970, April 29, 1999, http://caselaw.findlaw.com/tx-supreme-court/1164179.html.

39. Wilson Elser Moskowitz Edelman & Decker LLP, Texas Supreme Court Clarifies Law Regarding Auditors' Liability to Third Parties, September 2010, https://www.wilsonelser.com/news_and_insights/insights/992-texas_supreme_court_clarifies_law_regarding.

40. Securities Exchange Act of 1934, Title 15 of the U.S. Code.

41. O. Lee Reed, Marisa Anne Pagnattaro, Daniel R. Cahoy, Peter J. Shedd, and Jere W. Morehead, *The Legal and Regulatory Environment of Business* (New York: McGraw-Hill Irwin, 2013).

42. Reed et al.

43. Linda Griggs, Christian Mixter, and Warren Rissier, A Matter of Opinion: Parsing the Independent Auditor's Report in the Context of Omnicare, Bloomberg BNA, https://www.morganlewis.com/-/media/files/publication/outside-publication/article/bna-a-matter-of-opinion-29jan16.ashx?la=en&hash=1E12AEC2D41F132D001B324F8A4ECDDA58F3CCF1.

44. Dana S. Douglas and Michael Rowe, Section 11 and Auditors' "Opinion" Statements, American Bar Association Section on Litigation: Professional Services Liability, http://apps.americanbar.org/litigation/committees/professional/articles/spring2013-0513-section-11-auditors-opinion-statements.html.

45. Cornell Law School Legal Information Institute, *15 U.S. Code § 77k - Civil liabilities on account of false registration statement,* https://www.law.cornell.edu/uscode/text/15/77k.

46. Leagle, *Fait v. Regions Financial Corp.,* 655 F.3d 105 (2011), https://www.leagle.com/decision/infco20110823108.

47. *MHC Mutual Conversion Fund v. United Western Bancorp, Inc.,* United States Court of Appeals, Tenth Circuit, No. 13-1016, http://caselaw.findlaw.com/us-10th-circuit/1674400.html.

48. Securities Exchange Act of 1934, Title 15 of the U.S. Code.

49. Louwers et al., p. 648.

50. Messier et al., p. 709.

51. Messier et al., p. 709.

52. Securities Exchange Act of 1934.

53. Jean Braucher (Editor), John Kidwell (Editor), William C Whitford (Editor), *Revisiting the Contracts Scholarship of Stewart Macaulay: On the Empirical and the Lyrical (International Studies in the Theory of Private Law),* Oxford: UK, Hart Publishing, 2013.

54. United States Court of Appeals Sixth Circuit *Louisiana School Employees Retirement System v. Ernst & Young, LLP,* No. 08-6194, December 22, 2010, http://caselaw.findlaw.com/us-6th-circuit/1538932.html.

55. SFMS Securities Law Bulletin, Fall 2010, https://www.sfmslaw.com/News-Events/Quarterly-Securities-Law-Bulletin/securities-bulletin-2010-11.pdf.

56. *Louisiana School Employees Retirement System v. Ernst & Young, LLP.*

57. United States Supreme Court, *Tellabs, Inc., et al. v. Makor Issues & Rights, Ltd., et al.,* No. 06-484, Decided June 21, 2007, https://supreme.justia.com/cases/federal/us/551/308/.

58. HR 3763: Sarbanes-Oxley Act in full, Available at: www.sec.gov/about/laws/soa2002.pdf.

59. U.S. Court of Appeals for the Seventh Circuit, Tellabs Inc. v. Makor Issues & Rights, Docket No. 06-484, Available at: http://www.oyez.org/cases/2000-2009/2006/2006_06_484.

60. U.S. Supreme Court, Tellabs Inc. v. Makor Issues & Rights, Ltd. et al., Available at: http://www.oyez.org/cases/2000-2009/2006/2006_06_484.

61. American Bar Association, "Second Circuit Affirms Dismissal of Securities Fraud Claims Against PricewaterhouseCoopers in Doral Litigation," Available at: https://apps.americanbar.org/litigation/committees/professional/casenotes/0110_doral.html.

62. Lawrence A. Cunningham, Stephen Kwaku, and Arnold Wright, "The Sarbanes-Oxley Act: Legal Implications and Research Opportunities," *Research in Accounting Regulation,* Vol. 19, 2006.

63. *Monroe v. Hughes,* 860 F. Supp. 733 (1991), Available at: http://law.justia.com/cases/federal/district-courts/FSupp/860/733/2159100/.

64. Cunningham et al.

65. PCAOB, AS 2201: An Audit of Internal Control Over Financial Reporting That Is Integrated with An Audit of Financial Statements, PCAOB Release No. 2007-005A, Fiscal years ending on or after Nov. 15, 2007, https://pcaobus.org/Standards/Auditing/Pages/AS2201.aspx.

66. Lawrence A. Cunningham, Stephen Kwaku Asare, and Arnold Wright, "The Sarbanes-Oxley Act: Legal Implications and Research Opportunities," GW Law Scholarly Commons 2006, http://lawdigitalcommons.bc.edu/cgi/viewcontent.cgi?article=1191&context=lsfp.

67. Cunningham et al.

68. *Higginbotham v. Baxter Int'l.,* 2005 WL 1272271 (N.D. Ill. May 25, 2005).

69. *In re Lattice Semiconductor Corp. Secs. Litig.,* 2006 U.S. Dist. LEXIS 262 (Jan. 3, 2006 Dist. Ore.).

70. *In re WatchGuard Secs. Litig.,* 2006 U.S. Dist. LEXIS 272717 (W.D.Wash., April 21, 2006).

71. *In re WatchGuard Secs. Litig.*

72. Timothy P. Harkness, Celiza P. Bragança and John Bessonnette, *Minding Your 302s: Assessing Potential Civil, Administrative, and Criminal Liability for False Financial Statement Certifications.* Available at: www.pli.edu/emktg/compliance_coun/Minding_302s_CC_34.pdf.

73. *United States v. Richard Scrushy,* Available at: www.justice.gov/archive/dag/cftf/chargingdocs/scrushyindictment.pdf.

74. Richard D. Ramsey and A. F. Alkhafaji, "The 1977 Foreign Corrupt Practices Act and the 1988 Omnibus Trade Bill," *Management Decision* 29, no. 6., pp. 22–39.

75. U.S. Securities and Exchange Commission, "SEC Charges Pfizer with FCPA Violations," Available at: http://www.sec.gov/News/PressRelease/Detail/PressRelease/1365171483696.

76. Andrew Ceresny, "FCPA, Disclosure, and Internal Controls Issues Arising in the Pharmaceutical Industry," Remarks at CBI's Pharmaceutical Compliance Congress, Washington, D.C., March 3, 2015, Available at: http://www.sec.gov/news/speech/2015-spch030315ajc.html.

77. Ceresny.

78. SEC, *In the Matter of Halliburton Company and Jeannot Lorenz,* Accounting and Auditing Enforcement Release No. 3884, July 27, 2017, https://www.sec.gov/litigation/admin/2017/34-81222.pdf.

79. Legal Alert: DOJ Announces Changes to FCPA Corporate Enforcement Policy, November 29, 2017, https://us.eversheds-sutherland.com/NewsCommentary/Legal-Alerts/206662/Legal-Alert-DOJ-Announces-Changes-to-FCPA-Corporate-Enforcement-Policy.

Chapter 6 Cases

Case 6-1 Advanced Battery Technologies: Reverse Merger

Auditors are not always found guilty of negligence, gross negligence, and fraud when lawsuits are filed against them. And they do not always settle lawsuits to avoid costly, protracted litigation. A good example is legal action taken against three accounting firms in *In re Advanced Battery Technologies, Incorporated and Ruble Sanderson v. Bagell, Josephs, Levine & Co., LLC, Friedman LLP, and EFP Rothenberg, LLP.* For purposes of this case, Advanced Battery is referred to as *ABAT* and the three accounting firms simply as "the auditors."

On March 25, 2015, the Second Circuit and Eleventh Circuit Courts of Appeal affirmed dismissals of securities fraud claims filed against the auditors that audited Chinese reverse-merger companies because the plaintiffs did not adequately plead scienter under the heightened pleading standard imposed by the Private Securities Litigation Reform Act of 1995.[1] Under the PSLRA, plaintiffs must "state with particularity facts giving rise to a strong inference that the defendant acted with the required state of mind" with respect to each act or omission of the defendant that is alleged to violate the securities laws.

The Second Circuit's opinion in *ABAT* stated that to allege scienter on a recklessness theory against an independent audit firm under Section 10(b) of the Securities Exchange Act of 1934 and Rule 10b-5, a plaintiff must allege facts showing that the audit firm's auditing practices were so deficient as to amount to "no audit at all" or that the audit firm disregarded signs of fraud that were "so obvious" that the audit firm must have been aware of them.

The *ABAT* ruling is significant because it is the first federal appellate case to expressly reject scienter arguments based on the alleged discrepancy between a company's filings with the U.S. SEC and with China's State Administration of Industry and Commerce (SAIC), a regulatory agency to which Chinese companies must submit financial statements as part of an annual examination. The decision reflects a growing trend of courts rejecting securities fraud claims filed against independent audit firms in the context of Chinese reverse-merger companies.

In *ABAT,* the plaintiffs alleged that the auditors falsely represented that they performed their audits in accordance with professional standards and that ABAT's financial statements were fairly presented. An amended complaint upon appeal of the lower court decision against ABAT alleged that the audit firms were reckless and committed an "extreme departure from the reasonable standards of care" by failing to identify several purported "red flags," including (1) conflicts between ABAT's financial statements filed with China's SAIC and with the SEC and (2) the unreasonably high profits that ABAT reported in its SEC filings, in contrast to the significant losses that it reported in its SAIC filings. The district court denied leave to amend, and the Second Circuit affirmed.[2]

The Second Circuit agreed with the district court that the proposed amended complaint, like the previous complaint, failed to adequately plead the audit firms' scienter under the theory of recklessness and that amendment would be futile. The appellate court explained that the plaintiff was required to allege conduct "that is highly unreasonable, representing an extreme departure from the standards of ordinary care," such that the conduct "must, in

---

[1]A reverse merger occurs when a privately-held Chinese company goes public in the U.S. by merging with U.S. publicly-traded "shell companies." The reverse merger trend was initially fueled by the difficulties of going public in China. Reverse mergers are often described as an inexpensive "back-door" way of taking a company public, but they have a sketchy history in the U.S. One reason is the publicly held shell company has virtually no assets or business of its own. Many shell companies are the remnants of failed companies, though some are created from scratch for the single purpose of merging with an existing private company.

[2]In re *Advanced Battery Technologies, Incorporated and Ruble Sanderson v. Bagell, Josephs, Levine & Co., LLC, Friedman LLP, and EFP Rothenberg, LLP,* 14-1410-cv, March 25, 2015, Available at: http://caselaw.findlaw.com/us-2nd-circuit/1695335.html.

fact, approximate an actual intent to aid in the fraud being perpetrated by the audited company as, for example, when a defendant conducts an audit so deficient as to amount to no audit at all, or disregards signs of fraud so obvious that the defendant must have been aware of them."

Much of the Second Circuit's analysis focused on the plaintiff's argument that the audit firms acted recklessly by failing to inquire about or review ABAT's financial filings with China's SAIC. In rejecting these arguments, the court noted that none of the "standards on which [the lead plaintiff] relies—the Generally Accepted Auditing Standards, Statements on Auditing Standards, or GAAP [generally accepted accounting principles]—specifically requires an auditor to inquire about or review a company's foreign regulatory filings."

The court declined to adopt the general rule, urged by the plaintiff, that allegations of an audit firm's failure to inquire about or review such foreign filings are adequate to plead recklessness under the PSLRA. Although the court noted that "such a legal duty could arise under certain circumstances" (which it did not explain), it concluded that those circumstances were not pleaded here. In addition, the Second Circuit held that ABAT's report of high profit margins in its SEC filings triggered, at most, a duty to perform a more rigorous audit of those filings, not of the company's SAIC-China filings. The court declined to infer recklessness from the allegations that one of the audit firms had access to, and "presumably relied" on, the financial data underlying ABAT's SAIC filings but failed to see that the data contradicted the company's SEC filings. Instead, the court found another inference more compelling—that ABAT maintained different sets of data for its Chinese and U.S. regulators and provided the audit firm with false data.

The *ABAT* opinion is significant because it illustrates the high burden plaintiffs face in pleading recklessness in Section 10(b) cases against independent audit firms. Notably, since under the PSLRA the plaintiffs filing suit must plead with particularity facts alleging that the audit firm's work was so deficient as to amount to no audit at all, the historical legal standards for auditor liability seem to have turned in favor of the auditors. Also, the Second Circuit's determination that allegations that an audit firm failed to review AIC filings is not sufficient to meet this high burden for pleading scienter is significant, as such allegations are frequently pleaded in matters involving audits of the financial statements of Chinese companies listed on U.S. securities exchanges.

Questions

1. Do you believe the legal standards of allegations with "particularity sufficient facts" and of "no audit at all" cited in *ABAT* under Section 10(b) of the Securities Exchange Act of 1934 are too strict, too lenient, or just about right with respect to auditors' legal liability in cases similar to *ABAT*? Explain.

2. In *ABAT*, the plaintiffs alleged that the auditors falsely represented that they performed their audits in accordance with professional standards and that ABAT's financial statements were fairly presented. The amended complaint alleged that the audit firms were reckless and committed an "extreme departure from the reasonable standards of care" by failing to identify several purported "red flags." Do you believe the failure to identify red flags should be sufficient in a court of law to successfully allege gross negligence? Include in your discussion the purpose of auditors looking to detect red flags as part of their audits in accordance with GAAS.

3. Do you believe that auditors should be held legally liable when their filings to the SEC are [overly] optimistic while filings with Chinese regulatory agencies are [unduly] pessimistic? Explain, using ethical reasoning to craft your answer.

Case 6-2   Joker & Wild LLC

Joker & Wild LLC has just been sued by its audit client, Canasta, Inc., claiming the audit failed to be conducted in accordance with generally accepted auditing standards, lacked the requisite care expected in an audit, and failed to point out that internal controls were not working as intended. The facts of the case are that the auditors failed to find the accounting manager's misappropriation of assets when he stole inventory and then improperly, knowingly, wrote down inventory for market declines.

Current market values of inventory were not provided to the auditors despite numerous requests for this information. The auditors relied on management's representations about these values, which understated inventory by 10%. The plaintiff client brought the suit against the CPA firm claiming negligence, asserting the firm's failure to find the vice president's misappropriations of inventory and false valuations damaged the company by prematurely recognizing losses and then causing large reversals in the subsequent fiscal year when the inventory was sold for 15% above the original cost. The defendant CPA firm sought to blame the client, claiming Canasta did not cooperate on the audit and the vice president overrode internal controls.

Questions

1. Are the auditors guilty of malpractice? Explain.

2. What defenses are available to Joker & Wild in this case? Explain what they must prove to successfully assert these defenses.

3. Assume you are not aware of state laws on auditor legal liability. What legal concepts might a court of law use to resolve the lawsuit?

4. Do you believe the auditors should be held legally liable? Why or why not?

Case 6-3 QSGI, Inc.

Overview of the Case[1]

QSGI, Inc., is in the business of purchasing, refurbishing, selling, and servicing used computer equipment, parts, and mainframes. During its 2008 fiscal year (FY) and continuing up to its filing for Chapter 11 bankruptcy on July 2, 2009 (the "relevant period"), Mark Sherman was the CEO and chairman of the board of directors. The SEC alleged that Sherman was aware of deficiencies in and the circumvention of internal controls for inventory and the resulting falsification of the Company's books and records. The SEC alleged that Sherman withheld this information from the Company's external auditors in connection with their audit of the financial statements for the FY 2008 and review of the financial statements for the quarter ended March 31, 2009, and made affirmative material misrepresentations and statements that were materially misleading as a result of his omission of information in management representation letters to the auditors about the design, maintenance, and operation of internal controls. It was further alleged that Sherman signed a Form 10-K and Form 10-K/A for the 2008 fiscal year, each containing a management's report on ICFR as required by Section 404 of SOX and Exchange Act rule 13a-15(c), which falsely represented that he, in his capacity as CEO, had participated in assessing the effectiveness of the ICFR. Sherman also signed certifications required under Section 302 of SOX and Rule 13a-14 of the Exchange Act included in filings with the SEC falsely representing that he had evaluated ICFR and, based on this evaluation, disclosed all significant deficiencies to the auditors. The certifications were attached to the 2008 Forms 10-K and 10-K/A, and to the first quarter 2009 Form 10-Q filed with the Commission, which Sherman also signed.

Facts of the Case

Leading up to its bankruptcy in 2009, QSGI experienced recurring inventory control problems. Throughout the relevant period, Company personnel: (1) shipped certain inventory out to customers without making the

---

[1]*In the Matter of March Sherman, Respondent,* SEC Administrative Proceeding File No. 3-15992 Release No. 74765, April 20, 2015, https://www.sec.gov/litigation/admin/2015/34-74765.pdf

appropriate entries and (2) removed items from physical inventory without reducing inventory on the Company's books. Company personnel removed component parts from the physical inventory for such parts without recording the parts removed and occasionally stripped component parts from operating systems without recording the parts removed. As a result, the Company's books and records incorrectly reflected certain components in inventory and operating systems as intact systems. These component parts were then sold by the Company or used for the Company's maintenance services. These internal control problems resulted in the falsification of QSGI's books and records relating to its inventory.

QSGI's efforts to introduce new controls during FY 2008 largely failed. The Company failed to design procedures taking into consideration the control environment, including the qualifications and experience level of persons employed to handle accounting. Controls were mostly ignored during FY 2008 and well into FY 2009. For example, sales and warehouse personnel often failed to document their removal of items from inventory or, to the extent they did prepare paperwork, accounting personnel often failed to process the paperwork and to adjust inventory in the company's financial reporting system. The Company's attempts to monitor compliance on an ongoing basis were also inadequate. Company personnel regularly circumvented controls.

During the relevant period, Sherman knew of ongoing deficiencies in and the circumvention of internal controls relating to inventory. As an example, in the final days of FY 2008, QSGI senior management, including Sherman, openly communicated amongst themselves about the failed implementation, including training in, and circumvention of, controls introduced into operations earlier in the year. Management agreed that corrective action was needed which, given the timing, could not be undertaken until 2009. Based on further communications, management, including Sherman, was aware that the problems continued through the Company filing for bankruptcy in July 2009.

Sherman's False Representations in Management's Report on ICFR and Critical Accounting Policies

At no time during the relevant period did Sherman disclose, or direct anyone to disclose, to QSGI's external auditors the foregoing inventory issues and the resulting falsification of QSGI's books and records. To the contrary, in the management representation letters to the auditors, Sherman made affirmative misrepresentations and made statements that were misleading as a result of his omitting material facts which were necessary in order to make the statements made not misleading. He represented to the auditors that either there were no significant deficiencies or that he had disclosed to the auditors all such deficiencies. At the conclusion of FY 2008, he provided yet another representation letter in connection with the auditor's audit of the FY 2008 financial statements in which he acknowledged his responsibility for establishing and maintaining ICFR. Omitted from the letter was any reference to the existence, or his disclosure to the auditors, of significant deficiencies. In the management representation letter relating to the auditors' review of the first quarter 2009 financial statements, Sherman affirmatively misrepresented that he had disclosed to the auditors all significant deficiencies.

QSGI's Form 10-K for FY 2008 included a Company management's report on ICFR, as required by Section 404 of SOX and Exchange Rule 13a-15(c). A management's report on ICFR was also included in a Form 10-K/A for FY 2008. These management reports falsely represented that QSGI's management, with the participation of CEO Sherman, had evaluated ICFR using the criteria set forth by COSO Internal Control – Integrated Framework (see chapter 3). In fact, Sherman did not participate as CEO, did not participate in the referenced evaluation, and was unfamiliar with the referenced framework.

The discussion on critical accounting policies in QSGI's Form 10-K for FY 2008 falsely stated that "[m]anagement continually monitors its inventory valuation. . ., closely monitors and analyzes inventory for potential obsolescence and slow-moving items on an item-by-item basis. Sherman knew, or was reckless in not knowing, that these statements were materially false and misleading because he knew that the Company did not closely monitor inventory in the manner described because the Company lacked the necessary resources. Sherman signed the 2008 Form 10-K and 10-K/A. He was the sole signing officer for the 10-K/A.

Sherman's False SOX Certifications

Pursuant to SOX Section 302 and Exchange Act Rule 13a-14, Sherman signed certifications attached to the financial statements that said, based on his and the other certifying officer's (CFO) "most recent evaluation of [ICFR]," they had disclosed to QSGI's external auditors all significant deficiencies, "in the design or operation of [ICFR] which are reasonably likely to adversely affect [QSGI's] ability to record, process, summarize and report financial information." Omitted from the certification attached to the Form 10-K, but included in the certification attached to the Form 10-Q, were Sherman's certifications to the effect that the other certifying officer and he: (1) had been responsible for establishing and maintaining ICFR and designing, or supervising others in the design of, ICFR and (2) had designed, or caused to be designed, such ICFR. These certifications were false because Sherman had not participated in or evaluated ICFR and did not make referenced disclosures to the external auditors.

Findings

The SEC found that Sherman violated various Sections of the Exchange Act dealing with proper financial statements and certifications under SOX. Sherman was ordered to cease and desist from committing or causing any future violations of the Act, prohibited for five years from acting as an officer or director of any issuer of stock, and pay a civil money penalty of $7,500.

Questions

1. Assume that a third party(ies) is considering whether to sue the external auditors of QSGI. What could they allege in their lawsuit and why?

2. Assuming a third party(ies) files the lawsuit, what defenses could the external auditors use to rebut the charges?

3. Did SOX fail to protect investors and other users of QSGI's financial statements? Explain.

Case 6-4 *Anjoorian et al.*: Third-Party Liability

In the 2007 case of *Paul V. Anjoorian v. Arnold Kilberg & Co., Arnold Kilberg, and Pascarella & Trench,* the Rhode Island Superior Court ruled that a shareholder can sue a company's outside accounting firm for alleged negligence in the preparation of the company's financial statements even though the accountant argued it had no duty of care to third parties like the shareholder with whom it never engaged in a direct financial transaction. Judge Michael A. Silverstein disagreed, saying an accountant owes a duty to any individual or group of people who are meant to benefit from or be influenced by the information the accountant provides. Silverstein relied on the *Restatement (Second) of the Law of Torts:* "The Restatement approach strikes the appropriate balance between compensating victims of malpractice and limiting the scope of potential liability for those who certify financial statements. While it remains to be proved that [the firm] actually did foresee that [its] financial statements would be used by the shareholders [in the manner alleged], the absence of a particular financial transaction does not preclude the finding of a duty in this case."[1]

The facts of the case are described in Exhibit 1.

[1] Paul V. Anjoorian v. Arnold Kilberg & Co., Arnold Kilberg, and Pascarella & Trench by and through its general partners, Stephen E. Pascarella and John J. Trench, Available at: http://law.justia.com/cases/rhode-island/superior-court/2006/97-1013.html.

EXHIBIT 1   *Anjoorian et al.:* Third-Party Liability

Facts of the Case

The defendants Pascarella and Trench, general partners of the accounting firm Pascarella & Trench (P&T), asked the court for summary judgment in their favor with respect to plaintiff Anjoorian's claim that P&T committed malpractice in the preparation of financial statements and that the plaintiff (Anjoorian) suffered pecuniary harm as a result.

Anjoorian formerly owned 50% of the issued shares of Fairway Capital Corporation (FCC), a Rhode Island corporation. The other 50% of the shares were held by the three children of Arnold Kilberg. Kilberg himself owned no stock in the corporation, but he served as the day-to-day manager of the company. FCC was in the business of making and servicing equity loans to small businesses under the regulation of the U.S. Small Business Administration (SBA), and was capitalized by loans from the SBA and a $1.26 million investment by Anjoorian.

Beginning in 1990, P&T provided accounting services to FCC. The firm audited FCC's annual financial statements following the close of each calendar year between 1990 and 1994. In its representation letter (similar to the current Section 302 requirement under SOX), P&T stated that FCC was "responsible for the fair presentation in the financial statements of financial position." P&T's responsibility was to perform an audit in accordance with GAAS and to "express an opinion on the financial statements" based on the firm's audit. The first page of each financial statement contained the auditor's opinion that "the financial statements referred to above present fairly, in all material respects, the financial position of FCC in conformity with generally accepted accounting principles." Each report is addressed to "The Board of Directors and Shareholders." The 1990–1994 statements indicate that "it is management's opinion that all accounts presented on the balance sheet are collectible." In addition, the 1991–1994 statements indicate that "all loans are fully collateralized" according to the board of directors.

On March 2, 1994, Anjoorian filed a complaint and motion for a temporary restraining order seeking the dissolution of FCC on various grounds. P&T was not a party to that suit. As a result of that action, the three Kilberg children exercised their right to purchase the plaintiff's shares of the corporation. The court appointed an appraiser to determine the value of Anjoorian's shares, which the other shareholders would have to pay. The bulk of FCC's assets comprised its right to receive payment for the loans that it had made. The appraiser determined that the value of the corporation was $2,395,000, plus a payroll adjustment of $102,000, and minus a "loss reserve" adjustment to account for the fact that 10 of FCC's 30 outstanding loans were delinquent. The loss reserve adjustment reduced the total appraised value of the corporation by $878,234. Consequently, Anjoorian's 50% interest in the corporation was reduced accordingly by $439,117. He ultimately received a judgment for $809,382.85 against the other shareholders in exchange for the buyout of his shares.

In 1997, Anjoorian brought the lawsuit against Kilberg, Kilberg's company, and P&T. He claimed that P&T was negligent in preparing the annual financial statements for FCC because it did not include an accurate loan loss reserve in the statements. Anjoorian argued that he relied on the financial statements prepared by the defendants, and that if the statements had included a loan loss reserve, he would have sought dissolution of the corporation much earlier than 1994, when his shares would have been more valuable. Anjoorian submitted an appraisal suggesting that the appropriate loan loss reserve figure would have been much less—and, therefore, his share value much higher—in the years 1990 and 1991. He alleged that he lost over $300,000 in share value between 1990 and March 2, 1994. Nine years later, the defendants moved for summary judgment on the grounds that P&T owed no duty to Anjoorian as a shareholder.

Accountants' Liabilities to Third Parties

Silverstein observed that while the question of accountant liability to third parties was unsettled in Rhode Island, the Rhode Island Supreme Court had identified three competing interpretations. The first interpretation was the "foreseeability test," under which an auditor has a duty to all foreseeable recipients of information he provides. "This rule gives little weight to the concern for limiting the potential liability for accountants and is not widely adopted," Silverstein noted.

The second interpretation, the judge continued, was the "privity test," requiring a contractual relationship to exist between an accountant or auditor and another party.

Finally, the *Restatement* test, found in §522 of the *Restatement (Second) of Torts,* states an accountant who does not exercise reasonable care "is only liable to intended persons or classes of persons, and only for intended transactions or substantially similar transactions," said Silverstein. "[This approach] applies not only [to] specific persons and transactions contemplated by the accountant, but also specific classes of persons and transactions." Silverstein settled on the *Restatement* rule.[2]

Applying the rule, Silverstein denied summary judgment for the accounting firm, concluding there was a genuine issue of material fact on whether the accounting firm could be liable. "This court would have no difficulty finding a duty in this case, in the absence of a specific financial transaction, if it can be shown that [the defendant] intended the shareholders to rely on the financial statements for the purpose of evaluating the financial health of the company, and therefore, their investment in the company," wrote Silverstein.[3]

Case Analysis

The court found that the addressing of the reports to the shareholders, while not conclusive, is a strong indication that P&T intended the shareholders to rely upon them. Therefore, the court concluded that genuine issues of fact exist as to whether P&T intended for Anjoorian to rely on these financial statements. Perhaps the court would have reached a different conclusion for a widely held public corporation with a potentially unlimited number of shareholders whose identities change regularly. Here, however, FCC was a close corporation with only four shareholders, giving greater significance to the fact that the financial statements were addressed "to the shareholders."

The defendants also argued that, in order to find a duty to third parties, an accountant must have contemplated a specific transaction for which the financial statement would be used and that no such transaction was contemplated here.[4] The court found this argument unconvincing, stating that the case is unusual in that the alleged malpractice did not arise from a specific financial transaction. The typical case involves a person whose reliance on a defective financial statement induces the person to advance credit or invest new equity into the corporation.[5] When the investment is lost, or the loan unpaid, the person sues the accountant. In this case, however, Anjoorian had already invested his capital in the corporation when P&T was hired, and he alleged that he used the financial statements as a tool to evaluate the value of that investment. The alleged malpractice did not result in his advancing new value to the corporation and then losing his investment, but instead resulted in Anjoorian failing to withdraw his capital from the corporation while its value was higher.

The court opined that it would have no difficulty finding a duty in this case, in the absence of a specific financial transaction, if it could be shown that P&T intended the shareholders to rely on the financial statements for the purpose of evaluating the financial health of the company and, therefore, their investment in the company. In this case, the "particular transaction" contemplated by the *Restatement* relates to the purpose for which the financial statements would be used—the shareholders' decision whether to withdraw capital or not. While it remains to be proved that P&T actually did foresee that its financial statements would be used by the shareholders in this manner, the absence of a particular financial transaction does not preclude the finding of a duty in this case. Because the value of the shareholders' investment was limited to the amounts reflected in the company balance sheets, any loss from malpractice was an insurable risk for which accounting professionals can plan.[6]

[2]Eric T. Berkman, "Shareholder can sue accounting firm," January 26, 2007. Available at: http://newenglandinhouse.com/2007/01/26/shareholder-can-sue-accounting-firm/.

[3]Berkman.

[4]Jenny Steele, *Tort Law: Text, Cases, and Materials,* 2 nd edition (2010) (Oxford, UK: Oxford University Press).

[5]*Rusch Factors, Inc. v. Levin, 284 F. Supp. 85 (D.R.I. 1968)*. U.S. District Court for the District of Rhode Island - 284 F. Supp. 85 (D.R.I. April 17, 1968), Available at: http://law.justia.com/cases/federal/district-courts/FSupp/284/85/1815507/.

[6]*Rusch Factors, Inc. v. Levin, 284 F. Supp. 85 (D.R.I. 1968).*

The defendants argued that the plaintiff's theory of damages was speculative and against public policy. Anjoorian based his damage claims on the assertion that he relied on four annual audited financial statements to evaluate the status of his $1.26 million investment in FCC. Because the statements failed to include a loan loss reserve figure, he argued that the statements overstated the value of the corporation at the end of each year from 1990 to 1993. When Anjoorian sought dissolution in 1994, the value he obtained for his shares was significantly less than his expectation. He contended that if he had accurate financial information, he would have liquidated his investment earlier when his shares were more valuable. At issue was the existence and amount of the loan loss reserve. An appraiser of the value of the corporation in the dissolution action determined that the inclusion of a loan loss reserve in the financial statements was proper, and that created a genuine issue as to whether a breach of the duty of care occurred. The defendant had questioned the computation of the loan loss reserve but the court disagreed. (A detailed analysis of the amount of loan loss reserve has been omitted.)

Questions

1. Analyze the potential for legal liability of P&T under each of the four basic theories of liabilities discussed in Chapter 6.

2. Were the auditors guilty of professional negligence? Explain.

3. Judge Silverstein relied on the *Restatement (Second) of the Law of Torts* for his ruling. Assume he had relied on the "near-privity relationship" ruling in *Credit Alliance,* and evaluate the legal liability of the auditors using that standard.

4. The defendants argued in the case that, in order to find a duty to third parties, an accountant must have contemplated a specific transaction for which the financial statement would be used and that no such transaction was contemplated here. Do you agree with this statements from the perspective of auditors' third party liability? Why or why not?

Case 6-5 *Vertical Pharmaceuticals Inc. et al. v. Deloitte & Touche LLP*[1]

On December 13, 2012, Vertical Pharmaceuticals Inc. and an affiliated company sued Deloitte & Touche LLP in New Jersey state court for alleged accountant malpractice, claiming the firm's false accusations of fraudulent conduct scrapped a public company's plans to acquire Vertical for more than $50 million.

Vertical is a privately owned company that sells niche prescription drugs geared toward women's health and pain management. Trigen Laboratories (TLI) sells and markets generic drugs. Deloitte was auditing the 2011 financial statements of Vertical and TLI, which are owned by the same three partners, when it abruptly suspended that review because of supposedly troubling items that two whistleblowers brought to the firm's attention, according to the complaint, which was filed November 21 in Morris County Superior Court.

Deloitte insisted that Vertical hire independent counsel and conduct an internal investigation with a forensic audit, the complaint said. Vertical agreed to those steps, but Deloitte eventually notified Vertical that it was resigning rather than finishing its work, according to the complaint.

"As a forensic audit later discovered—no money was being pilfered from the company. No partner was stealing money from another. No improper conduct was taking place," the complaint said.

---

[1]The case is *Vertical Pharmaceuticals Inc. et al v. Deloitte & Touche LLP,* case number L-2852-12, filed on December 13, 2012, in the Superior Court of New Jersey, Morris County.

The revelation that Deloitte resigned from the 2011 audit and the allegations of potential criminal conduct and financial improprieties that the auditor passed on to the audit committee left the acquisition for dead, the complaint said. The public company found another pharmaceutical company to acquire.

The deal would have helped rapidly grow Vertical's business and established a revenue stream for the company of more than $500 million, the complaint contended. "Deloitte knew the deal would be final once the 2011 audit was completed. Without Deloitte's interference in concocting a series of false, negligent statements regarding Vertical's financials, the 2011 audit would have been issued and the deal completed."

Vertical has asked for $200 million or more in damages on multiple counts, including accounting malpractice and breach of fiduciary duty. Deloitte also demanded and received $120,000 for all of its invoiced services before resigning, according to the complaint, which seeks back those funds as well.

Deloitte's allegedly slanted statements involved accusations that Vertical was pilfering company funds through two LLCs, inappropriately paying company employees through car allowances, committing fraud by having an owner's father as tax auditor, and paying an owner's wife off the books, according to the complaint.

The firm also falsely claimed Vertical's books were in terrible shape and that its management was unreliable, the complaint said. "A subsequent forensic audit initially to assuage Deloitte was ultimately completed . . . which found: None of these items had merit nor did they consider any resolution items justified to engender Deloitte's resignation; that Deloitte was well aware of the nature prior to its supposed whistleblower disclosures of the items; and that many of these items were in the process of being resolved based on advice provided by Deloitte as early as May 2011," the complaint said.

Questions

1. Do you believe Deloitte & Touche breached its fiduciary duty to Vertical Pharmaceuticals in this case? Explain.

2. Do you believe Deloitte was guilty of malpractice as alleged by Vertical? Why or why not?

3. When should an auditor withdraw from an engagement? Do you believe Deloitte was justified in resigning from the Vertical Pharmaceuticals engagement. Do you believe Deloitte acted ethically in this regard?

Case 6-6 *Kay & Lee, LLP*

Kay & Lee LLP was retained as the auditor for Holligan Industries to audit the financial statements required by prospective banks as a prerequisite to extending a loan to the client. The auditor knows whichever bank lends money to the client is likely to rely on the audited statements.

After the audit report is issued, the bank that ultimately made the loan discovers that the client's inventory and accounts receivable were overstated. The client subsequently went bankrupt and defaulted on the loan. The bank alleged that the auditor failed to communicate about the inadequacy of the client's internal recordkeeping and inventory control. Moreover, the bank claims that the auditors were grossly negligent in not discovering the overvaluation of inventory and accounts receivable.

The auditors asserted that there was no way for them to know that the client included in the inventory account $1 million of merchandise in transit to a customer on December 31, 2015. The shipping terms were unclear so the auditors accepted management's representations in that regard (FOB Destination). As for the receivables, the auditors claimed the client falsified confirmations by sending them to a post office address, retrieving them, and then confirming the stated balances.

Questions

1. What would the bank have to prove to successfully bring a lawsuit against Kay & Lee?

2. What defenses might the auditors use to rebut any charges made about their (deficient) audit?

3. Critically evaluate the auditors' statements about the inventory and receivables with respect to generally accepted auditing standards and the firm's ethical responsibilities.

Case 6-7 TransWays' FCPA Dilemma (a GVV case)

TransWays, Inc. is a global U.S. company and provider of offshore oil drilling services and equipment based in Houston, Texas. The company just received a multi-million-dollar contract to explore for oil off the African coast. Ben Jones is the controller for TransWays. He recently met with Lonnie Wilson, the chief accounting officer, to discuss certain payments that will be made to freight forwarding agents in various African countries. The meeting did not go well. Jones expressed his concern about the payments that, he believed, qualified as bribes under the FCPA. Wilson took a different view, classifying the payments as facilitating payments, not bribes. The two accountants couldn't resolve their differences so a meeting was set for the following day, at which time the two of them would discuss the matter. Each agreed to research the provisions of the FCPA to determine whether the payments violate the law.

The payments being discussed relate to business operations in several African countries. The transactions are for the import of goods and materials and deep-water oil rigs into African waters. The amounts in total are significant. The transactions involve payments by freight forwarding agents in these countries to customs officials to circumvent each country's customs regulations, which are unduly burdensome and will delay operations and extend the assignment beyond the agreed-upon completion date. In that case, TransWays will have to pay a penalty.

Wilson claims that the payments qualify as facilitating payments because they are designed to induce the customs officials to let TransWays begin its operations as soon as possible. The payments simply help the company to obtain the necessary permits, licenses, and the official documents to qualify the company to do business in these countries.

Jones, on the other hand, isn't so sure about the payments. He is concerned that the payments are a bribe to get things done.

Assume you are in Ben Jones' position and preparing for the meeting. You fully expect Lonnie Wilson to push hard for classifying the payments as facilitating.

Questions

1. Using the GVV framework, answer the following questions:
   - What are the main arguments you expect to hear from Wilson?
   - What are the reasons and rationalizations you need to address?
   - What is at stake for the key parties including TransWays?
   - What levers can you use to influence Wilson?
   - What are your most effective responses to the reasons and rationalizations?

2. Assume Wilson wins the argument and you are told that the payments should be treated as facilitating payments. What would you do next and why?

Case 6-8 Disclosing Material Weaknesses in ICFR or Protecting the Firm from Litigation? (A GVV case)

Billy Muldoon, CPA and CFO, just finished reading a preliminary draft of his company's annual audit report from PwC. He was pleased that they had given the company a clean audit opinion, but dismayed to learn that they had concluded and were planning to disclose that the company had a material weakness in their internal controls over financial reporting. Billy was concerned that such a disclosure might result in a large drop in the market price of the company's stock. Included with the draft of the report was the following note of explanation from the partner in charge of the engagement as to how PwC had reached this conclusion:

Dear Billy,

As you know, we perform an integrated audit which combines our testing of the adequacy of internal controls with our performance of our normal audit procedures. This process starts during our audit planning process with the review of managements' assertions surrounding the adequacy of internal controls, including those surrounding financial reporting. Unfortunately, as we conducted our work we discovered a series of deficiencies, which individually are immaterial. Taken together, we believe these significant deficiencies represent a more than remote likelihood that a material misstatement could occur and not be prevented or detected. Therefore, in accordance with Section 404 of SOX and PCAOB AS 2201, the deficiencies need to be disclosed as material in the audit report. We are also concerned that other internal control weaknesses could provide indirect evidence of managerial ability because the design and implementation of internal controls is a primary management responsibility.

Once you have had a chance to review, please feel free to reach out to me to discuss.

Identified Weaknesses:

- We found inadequate segregation of duties over access to your sales information system controls.
- We found several instances of transactions on the general ledger which were not also recorded in the appropriate subsidiary ledger: these transactions were not material individually or in aggregate.
- We found that timely reconciliations of certain intercompany transaction accounts were not being performed: the individual transactions were material on an individual basis and only impacted balance sheet accounts.
- We found insufficient procedures to qualitatively assess whether the fair value of a reporting unit is less than its carrying value in order to assess goodwill impairment.

Billy immediately shot off an email to the partner requesting a meeting stating he vehemently disagreed with his analysis. He further stated that he thought PwC was intentionally misclassifying these items as material weaknesses over fear of potential legal liability.

Questions

1. What are the main arguments that the partner from PwC will need to counter when he meets with Billy? That is, what are the reasons and rationalizations he should expect to hear from Billy as to why a material weakness in the ICFR does not exist?

2. What is at stake for both Billy and PwC should the partner be unable to convince Billy to accept the material weakness disclosure? Consider the requirements of certification under SOX 302 in your response in addition to those of SOX 404. Address the potential liability to both PwC and Billy's company for failure to follow AS 2201.

3. What levers does the partner have? Where can he go to for support?

4. Assume Billy suggests the opinion on ICFR be changed from material to significant? Should the PwC partner go along? What is at stake for PwC, Billy, and the company of characterizing the deficiency as significant if it is, in fact, material?

Case 6-9 Miller Energy Resources, Inc.

On August 15, 2017, the SEC completed an Administrative Hearing process initiated by a PCAOB investigation of KPMG, LLP and one of their audit partners John Riordan, CPA[1] for conducting a materially deficient audit of Miller Energy Resources Inc. KPMG became the successor auditor of Miller for fiscal 2011. Miller was charged with accounting fraud in 2015.

Among other things, the SEC found that KPMG and Riordan:

- failed to properly assess the risks associated with accepting Miller Energy as a client and to properly staff the audit;

- failed to adequately address the audit team's lack of industry experience resulting in a lack of planning, supervision, due care, and professional skepticism;

- failed to obtain sufficient competent evidence to assess the impact of the opening balance of the Alaska Assets on Miller Energy's current year financial statements;

- failed to adequately assess whether Miller Energy's valuation of the Alaska Assets conformed with GAAP (Miller inaccurately revalued an asset costing $4.5 million at $480 million);

- did not obtain sufficient competent evidence regarding the assumptions on which Miller Energy's valuation of the Alaska Assets was based; and

- failed to take reasonable steps to assess Miller Energy's recorded value of $110 million for certain fixed assets included in the Alaska acquisition.

In a class action lawsuit against one-half dozen former executives of Miller, the plaintiffs charged that Miller overlooked the overvaluation of certain oil and gas interests that the company had purchased in Alaska the previous year. According to the lawsuit, David M. Hall, who served as chief operating officer, understated the cost to run the oil field. Also, it charged that the former CFO, Paul W., Boyd, and Hall, provided expense projections that were, in many cases, significantly lower than expenses recorded by the previous owners of the field. For example, the lawsuit claims internal documents maintained by Hall indicated that the cost to drill a new well was roughly $13 million, however he told the engineering firm preparing reports used to determine the value of the company that the costs to drill at the field was only $4.6 million per well. Additional understatements were made.

As a result of the above, in addition to agreeing to pay $6.2 million in penalties to settle SEC charges that it failed to properly audit Miller Energy, KPMG agreed to complete a firm wide review and evaluation "of the sufficiency and adequacy of their quality controls, including their policies and procedures for audits and interim reviews" of specific items identified by the SEC. KPMG also had to hire and bear the cost of having an independent consultant evaluate the adequacy of KPMG's internal policies and procedures to ensure compliance with all relevant commission regulations and PCAOB standards. In addition, KPMG must certify they have implemented the recommendations of the consultant and then certify the adequacy of their controls at the end of 2018 and 2019, as well.

Questions

1. Analyze the facts of the case with respect to the AICPA Code and explain any perceived deviation from ethical standards.

2. Assume Miller Energy is considering bringing a lawsuit against KPMG for malpractice. What would it have to demonstrate to be successful? What defenses are available to KPMG to counteract the malpractice claim?

---

[1]*In the matter of KPMG LLP and John Riordan, CPA* , SEC Accounting and Auditing Enforcement Release No. 3888, August 15, 2017, https://www.sec.gov/litigation/admin/2017/34-81396.pdf.

3. Assume investors in Miller Energy met to discuss whether to bring a class action lawsuit against KPMG. On what basis might they bring the lawsuit?

4. Assume Miller Energy negotiated a $10 million loan with a financial institution during 2015. Subsequent to the SEC's finding of accounting fraud in 2015, the financial institution brought a lawsuit against KPMG for negligence. What judicial approaches might be used to decide the case?

Case 6-10 *In re Puda Coal Securities*

On May 23, 2016, the U.S. Court of Appeals for the Second Circuit affirmed the dismissal of federal securities claims, under Section 10(b) and Section 11 of the Securities Acts, against Moore Stephens, an accounting firm that performed audits of Puda Coal's 2009 and 2010 consolidated financial statements and of Puda's ICFR as of December 2009 and 2010. For each of these years, Moore Stephens issued Independent Auditors' Reports, in which it opined that Puda's consolidated financial statements conformed to GAAP and that Puda maintained effective ICFR. The court held a summary order that plaintiff-shareholders in the lawsuit failed to establish scienter under Section 10(b) and failed to establish subjective falsity under Section 11.[1] Significantly, the court held that auditors' reports are "statements of opinion subject to the . . . standard" established by the Supreme Court for Section 11 claims in *Omnicare, Inc. v. Laborers District Council.*

Case Summary

The case is *In re Puda Coal Securities Litigation.* Puda Coal was a China-based coal supplier that went public in the United States through a reverse merger in 2005 and began trading on the NYSE in 2009. In 2011, investors learned that the company's chairman, Ming Zhao, and his brother, Yao Zhao, had secretly transferred Puda Coal's only revenue-generating asset, a coal mining subsidiary named Shanxi Puda Coal Group Co. Ltd., to themselves and then pledged a 49% interest in Shanxi to a Chinese private equity group. In a securities class action, the plaintiffs alleged that Moore Stephens had violated Sections 10(b) and 11 of the Securities Act of 1933 when it gave Puda Coal clean opinions. The charge was that Moore Stephens had misrepresented material facts, concealed adverse material facts, and "fraudulently certified" Puda Coal's financial statements, the plaintiffs said in their complaint. In addition, plaintiffs argued Moore Stephens violated Section 11 when it claimed to have conducted its audits in accordance with PCAOB standards. The audits had not complied with those standards, the plaintiffs said.

Plaintiffs brought claims in the Southern District of New York alleging that Moore Stephens should have uncovered fraud at Puda Coal involving the transfer of its main operating subsidiary to a company executive thereby leaving Puda Coal a shell company. The District Court ruled there was no material fact on Section 10(b) scienter and that there was no evidence of and no triable issue on Section 11 subjective falsity.

On appeal, the Second Circuit affirmed the lower court's ruling on both claims. First, the court affirmed summary judgment on plaintiff's Section 10(b) claim because there was no triable fact as to whether Moore Stephens' audit was reckless or auditors acted with intent to deceive, manipulate, or defraud. There was "no factual basis for alleging that the . . . audits were 'extreme departure[s]' from PCAOB standards 'amounting to no audit at all.'" Further, summary judgment was granted because plaintiff's alleged "red flags" were "not obvious signs of fraud," holding that plaintiffs alleged, at most, "fraud by hindsight," which is not sufficient to meet the heightened scienter standard for auditors.

---

[1] Second Circuit Court of Appeals, *In re Puda Coal Securities, Inc. Litigation,* Summary Order, May 20, 2016, https://www.courtlistener.com/pdf/2016/05/20/in_re_puda_coal_securities_inc._litigation.pdf.

Finally, and most importantly, on Section 11 the court held that Moore Stephens' "[a]udit reports, labeled 'opinions' and involving considerable subjective judgment, are statements of opinion subject to the *Omnicare* standard for Section 11 claims." Applying *Omnicare,* the Second Circuit concluded that there was "no evidence that Moore Stephens did not believe its 'clean audit opinions'" or that "Moore Stephens omitted material facts about the basis for its audit reports." Accordingly, the court affirmed summary judgment for Moore Stephens on Plaintiff's Section 11 claim. Finding no evidence that Moore Stephens disbelieved its own audit opinions, the court had little trouble ruling against the plaintiffs.

Meaning of the Opinion

The Second Circuit's decision is important to accounting firms facing Section 11 claims because it clarifies that auditors' reports, which are crafted as opinions and not certifications of the company's financial statements, are opinions. Thus, to plead a successful case, plaintiffs must comply with the standards set forth in *Omnicare* by showing either subjective falsity — that the auditor did not believe its report when issued — or that the auditor omitted material facts from its report.

The Puda Coal decision builds on *Omnicare* to provide attorneys representing auditors a clear tool with which to defend against Section 10 or 11 claims predicated on alleged false statements contained in audit reports. Conclusory allegations that an audit opinion turned out to be wrong are not sufficient. Absent sufficient factual allegations that reasonably call into question that an auditor knew the statements were false, disbelieved their own opinions, or omitted material facts, such claims are unlikely to survive scrutiny.[2]

U.S. District Court Judge Katherine Forrest Opinion

In an opinion and order, U.S. District Court Judge Katherine Forrest wrote the following:

Section 10 and 11 claims regarding opinion statements require that the statement was both objectively false at the time that it was made and also subjectively false — that is, that defendants did not honestly believe that statements when they made them. Section 11 of the Securities Act requires subjective falsity because an auditor's opinion, just like those rendered by all or substantially all accounting firms, is explicitly labeled as just that — an opinion that the audit complied with these broadly stated standards.[3]

Because the plaintiffs presented no plausible evidence that Moore Stephens had known about the Zhao brothers' shenanigans when it issued its opinions, Judge Forrest dismissed the Sections 10 and 11 claims.

Questions

1. What exactly is the difference between an auditor's opinion and a statement of fact?

2. In her opinion, Judge Forrest wrote that: "Section 10 and 11 claims regarding opinion statements require the statement was both objectively false at the time that it was made and also subjectively false — that is, that defendants did not honestly believe the statements when they made them." Do you believe subjective falsity is a proper standard of care? What if the auditors did honestly believe the statements when they made them but failed to uncover the evidence needed to objectively determine that a material misstatement existed in the financial statements or ICFR. Should they be able to escape legal liability under Section 10(b) or Section 11?

3. Do you believe the rulings in *Omnicare* and *Puda Coal* swing the pendulum too far in the direction of the auditors with respect to when they can be held legally liable for violations of Section 10b and Section 11? Explain.

---

[2]James Thomas, Arthur Luk, and Said Saba, The Second Circuit Clarifies Liability Standard for Audit Opinions, American Bar Association, June 30, 2016, https://www.americanbar.org/groups/litigation/committees/professional-liability/practice/2016/063016-the-second-circuit-clarifies-liability-standard-for-audit-opinions.html.

[3]*In re Puda Coal Securities, Inc. Litigation,* Summary Order.

Chapter

7

Earnings Management

Learning Objectives

After studying Chapter 7, you should be able to:

LO 7-1 Describe the motivation for earnings management.
LO 7-2 Describe the scope and purpose of reporting non-GAAP financial measures.
LO 7-3 Explain the role of materiality in earnings management.
LO 7-4 Describe earnings management techniques in SEC enforcement actions.
LO 7-5 Explain the workings of financial shenanigans.
LO 7-6 Explain the causes and effects of financial restatements.

Ethics Reflection

Companies seem to look for an any advantage when they report GAAP earnings results. One approach that has caught on with virtually all public companies is to report non-GAAP earnings in conference calls with investors, financial analysts, and in quarterly financial reports. Companies have great latitude in choosing what they report as non-GAAP metrics because FASB has not set any rules in this area. The SEC did issue Regulation G, which applies whenever a company subject to the periodic reporting requirements under the Securities Exchange Act of 1934, or a person acting on the company's behalf, discloses publicly any material information that includes a "non-GAAP financial measure," whether orally or in writing and whether or not furnished to the SEC. Non-GAAP measures often exclude non-recurring, infrequent, or unusual expenses. Under Regulation G, a disclosure of a non-GAAP measure must be accompanied by disclosure of the comparable GAAP measure and a reconciliation of the differences between the non-GAAP measure and the GAAP measure. Beyond that, the Commission does provide guidelines in the form of Compliance and Disclosure Interpretations (C&DI) that address a variety of issues that will be discussed in this chapter. External auditors are required to read other information included with financial reports, such as Management's Discussion & Analysis (MD&A), to ensure it is materially consistent with financial statement information. Non-GAAP measures are often addressed in the MD&A.

The first enforcement action brought by the SEC pursuant to Regulation G was against SafeNet, Inc. The SEC reached an agreement with the company; its former Chief Executive Officer Anthony Caputo; its former Chief Financial Officer Kenneth Mueller; and three former SafeNet accountants, Clinton Ronald Greenman, John Wilroy, and Gregory Pasko. The allegations were that:[1]

- From the third quarter of 2004 through the second quarter of 2005, SafeNet, through the actions of top executives, engaged in a scheme to meet or exceed quarterly earnings per share targets through the use of improper accounting adjustments.
- During the relevant period, Caputo and Mueller were aware that SafeNet would be unable to meet its earnings targets through normal business operations, and, in response, took actions to ensure that SafeNet would meet its earnings targets.
- At Mueller's direction, the three accountants made, or caused others to make, improper accounting adjustments to various expenses including the improper classification of ordinary operating expenses as non-recurring integration expenses (costs incurred to integrate acquired companies into current operations), and the improper reduction of accruals and reserves.
- SafeNet, Mueller, and Caputo represented to investors that SafeNet's non-GAAP earnings results excluded certain non-recurring expenses, when, in fact, SafeNet had misclassified and excluded a significant amount of recurring operating expenses from its non-GAAP measure of operating income in order to meet or exceed quarterly EPS targets.
- In the course of the earnings management scheme, Mueller, Caputo, Greenman, Wilroy, and Pasko prepared, reviewed, and/or signed SafeNet's materially false and misleading securities filings and press releases.

An interesting aspect of this case is that non-GAAP earnings was the trigger for earnings management of the GAAP amounts by improperly classifying recurring expenses as non-recurring and improperly reducing accruals and reserves. This raises four important questions for you to consider in reading this chapter: (1) Should the SEC (and FASB) set specific rules governing non-GAAP disclosures? (2) Should auditors test these numbers to ensure there are no materially misleading amounts? (3) Should auditors include in their assessment of internal controls over financial reporting consideration of whether adequate controls exist to ensure the non-GAAP reported amounts comply with SEC guidelines and/or any regulations that are set? (4) How do considerations of earnings management influence the manner in which non-GAAP metrics are disclosed?

Increasingly, I have become concerned that the motivation to meet Wall Street earnings expectations may be overriding common sense business practices. Too many corporate managers, auditors, and analysts are participants in a game of nods and winks. In the zeal to satisfy consensus earnings estimates and project a smooth earnings path, wishful thinking may be winning the day over faithful representation.

Source: Arthur Levitt

This quote by former SEC chair Arthur Levitt from "The Numbers Game" links the practice of "earnings management" to an excessive zeal to project smoother earnings from year to year that casts a pall over the quality of the underlying numbers. Levitt identifies the cause as a "culture of gamesmanship" in business rooted in the emphasis on achieving short-term results such as meeting or exceeding financial analysts' earnings expectations.[2]

Warren Buffett once said, "Earnings can be as pliable as putty when a charlatan heads the company reporting them." The quote emphasizes the importance of having an ethical person at the head of a company because a CEO who practices fraud can twist earnings to make them look better than they really are, thereby deceiving the users of the financial statements.

The accounting scandals at companies such as Enron, WorldCom, and Tyco involved the use of inside information by top management to sell shares owned at a relatively favorable current price compared to future prices. Presumably, the executives knew the earnings had been manipulated, and either the manipulation could no longer be sustained or the bubble was about to burst. While the executives sold their shares and typically enhanced their wealth, thousands of employees lost millions of dollars of accumulated wealth in stock ownership and 401-k plans. If the company failed, employees lost their jobs as well. Typically, managers acted without due regard for their fiduciary obligations to the shareholders and in violation of securities laws. It was the old story: Managers act out of self-interest and greed; greed begets more greed. It was a classic example of egoistic behavior motivated by a sense that they would never be caught.

Companies manage earnings when they ask, "How can we best report desired results?" rather than "How can we best report economic reality (the actual results)?" Levitt attributes the practice of earnings management to the pressure on Wall Street to "make the numbers." He identifies a pattern created by earnings management whereby "companies try to meet or beat Wall Street earnings projections in order to grow market capitalization and increase the value of stock options." He notes that on the one hand auditors are under pressure to retain clients by the firm and on the other they are under pressure by management "not to stand in the way."

An important quality of useful information is *representational faithfulness.* To represent the transactions and events faithfully in the financial statements, the effects of transactions and events should be reported on the basis of economic substance of the transactions instead of legal form of the transaction. For example, if a company sells an asset but is still responsible for maintaining it or has other risks of "ownership," then reporting this transaction as a sale instead of secured loan does not faithfully represent the transaction and thus would distort the effect of the transaction on reported amounts and may have the potential to mislead the users of the statements.

Characteristics of Earnings Management

LO 7-1

Describe the motivation for earnings management.

What drives a manager to record transactions in a way that achieves a desired level of financial results even if the accounting treatment is not supportable by the facts? Is to meet budget expectations, put the best face possible on the financial statements, hit overly-optimistic earnings guidance, or flat out fraud? During the era of Enron and WorldCom, earnings management occurred to enhance executives' performance reputation and the desire to influence the stock price, which would make stock options more valuable.

Motivation for Earnings Management

Earnings management occurs when companies artificially inflate (or deflate) their revenues, profits, or earnings per share (EPS) figures. Gaa and Dunmore point out that earnings may be managed in many different ways, but they all boil down to two basic possibilities. One is to alter the numbers already in the financial records by using discretionary accruals and other adjustments, and the other is to create or structure real transactions for the purpose of altering the reported numbers. There are also two kinds of motivations for altering the financial reports through disclosure decisions. Management may either intend to influence stakeholders' beliefs and behavior or to influence how contracts are performed.[3]

Another perspective on earnings management is to divide the techniques into two categories: operating earnings management and accounting earnings management. Operating earnings management deals with altering operating decisions to affect cash flows and net income for a period such as easing credit terms to increase sales. Accounting earnings management deals with using the flexibility in accounting standards to alter earnings numbers.[4]

Generally, the end result of earnings management is to distort the application of GAAP, thereby bringing into question the quality of earnings. The question to ask is whether the distortion is the result of appropriate decision making given that choices exist in the application of GAAP, or if it is motivated by a conscious effort to manipulate earnings for one's advantage, which is fraud.

While some authors distinguish between earnings manipulation and earnings management, we believe earnings manipulation is a form of earnings management. For example, Hopwood et al. believe that earnings management is management's routine use of nonfraudulent accounting and economic discretion, while earnings manipulation can refer either to the legitimate or aggressive use, or fraudulent abuse, of discretion. By their reckoning, earnings management is legitimate, while earnings manipulation can be legitimate, marginally ethical, unethical, or illegal, depending on its extent.[5] The problem with this distinction is characterizing practices as ethical relies on what is a person's intent. If one intends to manipulate earnings through smoothing or other techniques, it is unethical because it is designed to alter the earnings picture and deceive another party; if not, why engage in the practice? Recall that intent or motivation is the third factor in Rest's Model of Ethical Decision Making.

Income Smoothing

Arthur Levitt talks about another motivation to manage earnings: to smooth net income over time. The ideal pattern of earnings for a manager is a steady increase each year over a period of time. The results make it appear that the company is growing and doing better than it really is, and the manager should be given credit for the positive results. The market reacts by bidding up the price of the stock, and the manager is rewarded for the results by a performance bonus and stock options with a prospective value that increases over time because of income smoothing that triggers stock price increases. Levitt believes "these practices lead to erosion in the quality of earnings and, therefore, the quality of financial reporting." The notion that accounting information should represent what it purports to represent, or representational faithfulness,[6] would be distorted in these cases through adjustments up or down to net income by the use of devices such as accelerating the recognition of revenue by stuffing the distribution channels with product (i.e., channel stuffing), delaying the recognition of an expense, and creating reserve accounts such as estimated sales rebates (i.e., "cookie-jar reserves").

A classic case of the use of cookie-jar reserves to manipulate income was at HealthSouth. The SEC investigated the practice and deemed it to be fraudulent. According to the SEC, the company fraudulently reduced contractual adjustments to increase revenue by more than $2.2 billion.[7] The contractual allowances represented the amount of the health-care billing not expected to be reimbursed. During the second quarter of 1996, HealthSouth began what was to become a systematic practice of reducing contractual adjustments—that is, narrowing the gap between standard health-care charges and anticipated reimbursements—even though the applicable contractual adjustments had not actually changed and there was otherwise no support for the reductions. This practice continued without interruption in every reporting period through mid-2002.

The contractual allowance account was a perfect tool to manipulate earnings from year to year to present a smoothing or increasing trend in earnings. The company historically had accounted for the provision of health-care services by recording both its standard charge for the service and a contractual adjustment. The first entry essentially is a constant, unaffected by the amount actually to be paid by or on behalf of a patient. The second is a variable, representing the company's estimate of a discount from the standard charge which it does not expect to collect. The amount of the variable—*the contractual adjustment*—is based on the source of payment, since different payors may reimburse different amounts for the same service. The difference between the standard charge and the contractual adjustment, frequently a significant amount, represents the company's net operating revenue.

One industry that routinely uses allowances to smooth net income over time is banking. Rivard et al. studied income smoothing techniques by banks and found them to be more aggressive in using loan-loss reserves as a tool of income smoothing. The provision for loan losses is a noncash accounting expense for banks. In theory, this expense represents expected future losses, which will eventually occur on loans extended during the previous period. These expenses accumulate on the bank's balance sheet in the loan-loss reserve account. When a loan is charged off, this reserve account is debited. Because banks have considerable flexibility in determining the size of the annual provision for loan losses, and because this is a noncash expense, it is an excellent tool for income smoothing. During periods of lower-than-normal earnings, the bank may understate its expected future loan loss and thus increase earnings. When profits are abnormally high, the opposite occurs. Over an extended period of time, the loan-loss reserve balance is maintained at the desired level and average earnings are unaffected. However, the variability of the earnings stream over that period is less than it would otherwise be. As the authors point out, income smoothing reduces not only earnings, but also tax liabilities in high-income years, and increases them in low-income years.[8]

A fertile area for income smoothing and earnings management is through the use of discretionary accruals. *Discretionary accruals* are items that management has full control over and is able to delay or eliminate.

Nondiscretionary accruals are items that are estimated based on changes in the fundamental economic performance of the firm, and management has no control over them. Dividing commitments into optional and non-optional confirms that total commitments are applied to offering better information for financial statements.

Unlike nondiscretionary accruals, which arise from transactions that can be considered "normal" for a firm (i.e., recording an accrual for unbilled services that have been provided), a discretionary accrual is a non-mandatory expense that is recorded within the accounting system but has yet to be realized. An example of this would be an anticipated management bonus. Discretionary accruals are those that arise from managerial discretion and are generally interpreted as indicative of managed earnings. By recognizing accruals at a "convenient" time, companies can smooth earnings and better meet or exceed analysts' earnings projections.

Acceptability of Earnings Management

There are a variety of perspectives on earnings management. Schipper defines it as a "purposeful intervention in the external reporting process, with the intent of obtaining some private gain (as opposed to, say, merely facilitating the neutral operation of the process)," as might be the case when earnings are manipulated to get the stock price up in advance of cashing in stock options.[9]

Healy and Wahlen define it as "when managers use judgment in financial reporting and in structuring transactions to alter financial reports to either mislead some stakeholders about the underlying economic performance of the company, or to influence contractual outcomes that depend on reported accounting numbers."[10] They focus on management's intent to deceive the stakeholders by using accounting devices to influence reported earnings positively.

Dechow and Skinner note the difficulty of operationalizing earnings management based on the reported accounting numbers because they center on managerial intent, which is unobservable. Dechow and Skinner offer their own view that a distinction should be made between making choices in determining earnings that may comprise aggressive, but acceptable, accounting estimates and judgments, as compared to fraudulent accounting practices that are clearly intended to deceive others.[11]

Thomas E. McKee wrote a book on earnings management from the executive perspective. He defines *earnings management* as "reasonable and legal management decision making and reporting intended to achieve stable and predictable financial results." McKee believes earnings management reflects a conscious choice by management to smooth earnings over time and it does not include devices designed to "cook the books." He criticizes Schipper, Healy and Wahlen, and Dechow and Skinner for taking "unnecessarily negative view[s] of earnings management." McKee contends that a more positive definition is needed that portrays managers' motives in a positive light rather than the negative view adopted by others.[12]

How Managers and Accountants Perceive Earnings Management

An early first survey of about how managers view the ethics of earnings management was conducted in 1990 by Bruns and Merchant. They found that managers disagreed considerably on whether earnings management is ethically acceptable. They also found that, in general, the respondents thought manipulating earnings via operating decisions (e.g., purposefully delaying making needed repairs to a subsequent year) was more ethically acceptable than manipulation by accounting methods. The authors were disturbed by these findings. They were concerned that these practices could be misleading to users of the information and, over time, reduce the credibility of accounting numbers, thereby damaging the reputation of the accounting profession.[13]

Rosenzweig and Fischer followed up on the Bruns and Merchant survey in 1995 by asking accounting professionals about factors causing earnings management. Two of these factors involve accounting manipulation, and two involve operating decisions designed to influence reported earnings. The accounting factors include actions that influence earnings by changing accounting methods. Examples include recording an expense in the wrong year or changing an inventory valuation in order to influence earnings. Examples of operating decision manipulations are deferring necessary expenditures to a subsequent year or offering unusually attractive terms to customers at year-end to include next year's sales into the current year.[14]

Elias conducted a study in 2004 of corporate ethical values and earnings management ethics. He defined corporate ethical values as a composite of the individual values of managers and both the formal and informal policies on the ethics of the organization. The tone at the top signals whether ethics policies are taken seriously by management and is, therefore, very important to create an ethical corporate environment. The study clearly shows that accountants in organizations with high ethical values perceived earnings management actions as more unethical. CPAs in industry occupations (i.e., controllers and CFOs) were significantly less likely than those in public accounting to perceive high ethical values in their organizations.[15] This may be attributable to the greater pressure internally to meet financial analysts' earnings projections and provide bonuses and stock options for top management.

In a 2006 survey, Akers, Giacomino, and Bellovary surveyed accounting students and practitioners about their views of earnings management. With respect to accounting practitioners, the results show that accounting manipulation is much less acceptable ethically than operating decision manipulation. This finding parallels the attitude that Bruns and Merchant found among managers.[16] Generally, the practitioners had few ethical qualms about operating decision manipulation, with scores indicating an average rating between (fully) ethical and questionable. The practitioners, however, generally felt that operating decisions that influenced expenses were somewhat more suspect than those that influenced revenues.

The five most serious infractions were (1) bury "scrap costs" in other expenses—no (operating) income effect; (2) request deferred billing from the supplier; (3) raise the return forecast (on purchases) from 22 to 35%, with actuals of 22%; (4) accelerate delivery to customers by 42 days; and (5) defer supply expenses by delaying recording the invoice. It is interesting to note that the most serious infraction did not even affect net income.[17] Instead, the action to bury scrap costs in other expenses shifts an operating expense into a nonoperating category, thereby increasing operating income, an amount on the income statement often considered to be a more important gauge of earnings than "bottom-line" net income. Other actions are clearly designed to manage earnings by either accelerating the recording of earnings or delaying the recording of operating expenses.

As to the 10 practices rated as minor infractions, the ethical significance of each is as follows: (1) reduce reserve for obsolescence to meet budget target, (2) increase reserve for obsolescence and reduce income, (3) accelerate delivery to the customer by 28 days, (4) defer expenses to meet the annual budget, (5) raise the return forecast from 22 to 35%, (6) request deferred billing from the supplier, (7) accelerate delivery to the customer by 16 days, (8) reduce reserve for obsolescence to continue work, (9) defer expenses to meet the quarterly budget, and (10) prepay expenses to reduce income by $60,000.[18]

Ethics of Earnings Management

Stanga and Kelton examined investors' ethicality judgments of earnings management in a 2008 study. The authors found no significant difference in ethicality judgments between accounting methods and operating methods of earnings management. Regardless of the method, participants perceive earnings management as unethical. They also found that ethicality judgments are positively associated with investment decisions.[19]

Johnson et al. conducted a study that focused on the consequences of earnings management behavior in response to the question: Do the ends of positive organizational consequences justify the means of earnings management? The authors investigated manager evaluations of, and reactions to, a scenario in which a hypothetical employee makes a choice whether or not to engage in earnings management behavior, with consequences that are either favorable or unfavorable to the organization. The results indicated that managers may be motivated to discount the ethical impact of earnings management behavior when the consequence has a favorable impact on the organization—implying that the ends justify the means. This finding, in turn, suggests that incrementalism, or the ethical "slippery slope" of overlooking seemingly minor ethical breaches, can undermine efforts to establish a strong ethical tone throughout the organization.[20]

The authors of this book believe that the acceptability of earnings management techniques should be judged using the ethics framework established earlier in the book. Virtue ethics examines the reasons for actions taken by the decision maker as well as the action itself. McKee's definition is self-serving from a management perspective and does not reflect virtues such as honesty (full disclosure/transparency) and reliability (representational faithfulness). The definition also ignores the rights of shareholders and other stakeholders to receive accurate and understandable financial information year-to-year. McKee's explanation that earnings management is good because it creates a more stable and predictable earnings stream by smoothing net income cannot overcome the fact that a smooth net income by choice does not reflect what investors and creditors need or want to know because it masks true performance. Hopwood et al. provide cover for their view of the ethics of earnings management by stating that "the ethics issue might possibly be mitigated by clearly disclosing aggressive accounting assumptions in the financial statement disclosures."[21] We disagree with this characterization because disclosure should not be used to mask the ills of improper accounting that tests the limits of what does and does not present fairly financial position, results of operations, and cash flows. A disclosure may be nothing more than a rationalization for an unethical action with respect to earnings management, thereby closing the Fraud Triangle.

One might be able to rationalize the ethics of earnings management from an act-utilitarian perspective. Under this view, a decision about how to account for and report a financial transaction could be made by weighing the benefits to management and the company of using a particular technique (to smooth net income) versus the costs of providing potentially misleading information to the shareholders. Under a rule-utilitarian perspective, however, financial statements should never be manipulated to put a rosier face on the financials or for personal gain regardless of any utilitarian benefits.

Needles points out that the difference between an ethical and an unethical accounting choice is often merely the degree to which the choice is carried out. Needles believes the problem with many accounting judgments is that there is no clear limit beyond which a choice is obviously unethical. Thus, a perfectly routine accounting decision, such as expense estimation, may be illegal if the estimated amount is extreme, but it is perfectly ethical if it is reasonable. He provides an interesting example of how a manager might use the concept of an earnings continuum to decide whether to record the expense amount at the conservative end or aggressive end.[22]

Needles' example is based on a rather modest difference in estimate from $6,000 to $30,000 (1.0% to 5.0% of net sales). Exhibit 7.1 shows a difference of $0.24 per share ($1.70–$1.94) or approximately 12–14% of EPS (assuming 100,000 shares outstanding). We recognize that judgment is an essential part of deciding when a difference is and is not material. Needles' continuum illustrates a possible basis for such judgments and how an auditor might go about deciding whether or not to accept management's position on the issue.

Earnings Quality

Dichev et al. released the results of a survey in 2016 that examined the views of 375 CFOs on the prevalence and identification of earnings misrepresentation. The authors were interested in identifying the characteristics of high-quality earnings. The authors asked the CFOs to rank order specific characteristics of earnings quality. The leading answers were consistent reporting choices through time and the absence of long-term estimates, both features of sustainable earnings. They reported one participants view that:

EXHIBIT 7.1   Where Do You Draw the Line? The Earnings Management Continuum of Ethical Financial Reporting

Questionable Conservative	Conservative	Neutral	Aggressive	Fraudulent

2a: The Earnings Management Continuum of Ethical Financial Reporting.

$1.70	$1.76	$1.82	$1.88	$1.94

Violates GAAP ←   Within GAAP   Violates GAAP →

2b: Overly Aggressive Earnings on the Continuum

Highly Conservative	Overly Conservative	Neutral	Overly Aggressive	Fraudulent
$1.70	$1.76	$1.82	$1.88	$1.94

Violates GAAP ←   Within GAAP   Violates GAAP →

Source: Copyright © 2011. Reprinted with permission of the author, Belverd E. Needles, Jr.

"You are not trying to essentially grab earnings from the future and drag them in to make it look better, nor are you trying to push earnings out into the future, but you somehow reflect the underlying economics of the long-run value of this bundle of net assets that is the firm." One key element is transparency and predictability. "Can investors anticipate what is going to happen?"[23]

One CFO pointed out that, over the long term, if earnings and cash flows are not highly linked, and if he were to consistently report a big gap between these two measures, then the market would start to wonder what is going on unless the company were in a huge growth phase. He added that if the gap between earnings and cash flows is persistently high, a significant discount in the company's stock price would be expected because, ultimately, if the cash is not being generated, then the earnings are either artificial or not a good indicator of value creation. Another CFO added that if earnings are not backed by actual cash flows, except for the very short term, then they are not good earnings.

The MD&A is the primary vehicle for management to inform investors about the quality of a company's earnings. Company's make many estimates and judgments in applying GAAP to the financial statements that readers should be made aware of for the sake of complete and transparent disclosures in the statements. The MD&A can be used to discuss nonrecurring and unusual transactions that bear on the level of operating earnings as might uncertainties and contingencies.

Deloitte looks at the quality of earnings from the audit committee perspective. The firm recommends that the committee follow a framework to assess the quality of earnings that includes:[24]

- Read the financial statements, annual report, and interim filings
- Be familiar with current press coverage regarding the financial performance and practices of the company
- Read the most recent analysts' reports on the company
- Consider earnings components in relation to the earnings continuum
- Consider the overall indicators of earnings quality
- Understand the sources of earnings and consider the characteristics affecting the quality of the various earnings components.

The assessment of earnings quality is more difficult today than ever before because companies increasingly discuss earnings information with financial analysts, conference calls with investors, and on their websites. Auditors cannot possibly examine this information although they should act if they believe it contradicts earnings filings with the SEC. Companies now use other forms of earnings guidance, such as non-GAAP metrics, that bear on the quality of earnings. These numbers need to be carefully scrutinized to ensure they are not false or misleading or inconsistent with published information.

Earnings Guidance

LO 7-2

Describe the scope and purpose of reporting non-GAAP financial measures.

Forward-looking Statements

Earnings guidance reflects the comments management gives about what it expects its company will do in the future. These comments are also known as "forward-looking statements" because they focus on sales revenues or earnings expectations in light of industry and macroeconomic trends. These comments are given for the sake of transparency and to guide investors and financial analysts in their evaluation of the company's earnings potential. The guidance may be described as a management discussion and analysis, operating and financial review, or something else.

There are a number of provisions in the federal securities laws that can create liability for forward-looking statements. In the context of a public offering, Section 11 and Section 12 of the Securities Act of 1933 impose liability on issuers, their officers and directors, and underwriters for misstatements of material fact or omissions of material facts necessary to make included statements not misleading. Rule 10b-5 under the Securities Exchange Act of 1934 applies to statements made in the context of securities offerings as well as in periodic reports and day-to-day communications with analysts and investors.

The Private Securities Litigation Reform Act of 1995 (PSLRA) enacted safe harbor provisions in both the Securities Act and the Exchange Act for forward-looking statements that are (1) identified as such and (2) accompanied by "meaningful cautionary statements identifying important factors that could cause actual results to differ materially from those in the forward-looking statement." These safe harbors also provide protection where a plaintiff fails to prove that a statement was made with actual knowledge that the statement was false or misleading if made by a natural person, or was made by or with the approval of an executive officer if made by a company. The PSLRA safe harbor provisions do not apply in the context of an IPO or to enforcement proceedings brought by the SEC.

Earnings Expectations

During the 1990s and early 2000s, meeting or beating analysts' earnings expectations emerged as an important earnings benchmark. Bartov et al. found that the stock market has been found to award firms that meet or beat analysts' forecasts and punish firms that miss earnings targets.[25] Meeting or beating earnings through earnings and expectations management has drawn concerns over the integrity of managers. For instance, an analysis of Nortel Networks Corporation by Fogarty et al. (separate from Case 7-1 later in this chapter) reveals that earnings expectations management is tied to many other missteps of managers that collectively contributed to the downfall of the giant telecommunications firm.[26] Consistent with Fuller and Jensen, this suggests that earnings expectations management sets in motion a variety of organizational behaviors that often end up damaging the firm.[27] Erhard et al. suggest that meeting or beating earnings by manipulating earnings and analysts' earnings expectations is indicative of low integrity in relations with the capital markets, resulting in calls for boards of directors to take accountability for integrity of the entire corporate system.[28] Graham et al. also advocate changes in the culture of boards of directors by focusing on long-term strategic goals and shielding managers from the short-term pressure from the capital markets.[29] Taken collectively, the arguments suggest that, while managing earnings expectations may help the firm avoid missing earnings targets and market penalties, it can be detrimental to the long-term value of the firm and the capital markets, as pointed out by Liu et al.[30]

Covenants in a long-term lending contract, such as required debt-to-equity ratio or minimum working capital requirements, exist to protect the lender from the potentially adverse actions of managers. Earnings management can serve as motivation to steer managers away from violating the terms of a debt contract, because such a violation would be highly costly to the manager and could affect her ability to operate the firm freely. Earnings management gives a manager the flexibility to choose those accounting policies that avoid a close proximity to covenant violation.

Earnings guidance appears in the earnings per share numbers. EPS is a barometer of a company's financial viability, or the ability to generate sufficient income to meet operating payments and debt commitments. A caveat in using non-GAAP earnings and EPS is that companies may purposefully predict low numbers to make it easier to meet or beat the estimates, thereby raising concerns about the quality of earnings.[31]

The range of methods used to manipulate earnings to achieve earnings guidance was evident when on April 19, 2016, the SEC announced a pair of financial fraud cases against companies that left investors without accurate depictions of company finances. In one case, technology manufacturer Logitech International had fraudulently inflated its fiscal year 2011 financial results to meet earnings guidance through manipulation of its warranty accrual accounting and failure to amortize intangibles from an earlier acquisition. The SEC found the company deliberately minimized the write-down of millions of dollars of excess component parts for a product for which Logitech had excess inventory in 2011. In the other case, battery manufacturer Ener1 materially overstated revenues and assets for year-end 2010 and overstated assets in the first quarter of 2011. The financial misstatements stemmed from management's failure to impair investments and receivables related to an electric car manufacturer that was one of its largest customers.[32]

Green Mountain Coffee Roasters

The Green Mountain case—*Employees' Retirement System, et al. v. Green Mountain Coffee Roasters, et al.*[33]—is unusual in that the fraud occurred not only through materially misleading financial statements but through conference calls that provided false earnings guidance to shareholders and analysts. Exhibit 7.2 provides an overview about the company and its inventory fraud. What follows is a discussion of the content of the conference calls.

Essentially, Green Mountain knowingly misled investors through conference calls claiming to have ramped up production to meet increasing demand for its single-cup coffee brewing system while keeping inventory levels in check. Allegations in a shareholder lawsuit included that, on numerous occasions before an inventory count or audit by PwC, "bags and bags of coffee would be loaded onto trucks" that would either leave temporarily or just sit behind the facility filled with product. When employees escorted auditors through the facility, they were not permitted "beyond a point blocked off by black plastic."

Green Mountain defendants continuously reassured investors that its business was booming. For example, Green Mountain held a conference call with investors on February 2, 2011, to discuss first quarter 2011 results. Green Mountain stated that "we remain focused on increasing production to fulfill unmet demand and achieving and maintaining optimum inventory levels." During its second quarter conference call on May 3, 2011, Green Mountain stated "we are not building any excess inventories at all at retail." On July 27, 2011, in another conference call to discuss third quarter results, defendant Frances Rathke—CFO, secretary, and treasurer of Green Mountain—stated that during the third quarter, "we got back into a place where we knew we had appropriate inventory levels." Lawrence Blanford, president, CEO, and director of the company, emphasized a need to increase production in 2012 to meet anticipated high consumer demand. When investors expressed concern about overproducing, Blanford reiterated that "we're at appropriate inventory levels."

The conference calls providing earnings guidance and other communications to the public about how well Green Mountain was doing seemed to raise red flags for some who follow such announcements. In fact, the initial class action lawsuit that was filed in October 2011 came after a high-profile presentation by hedge fund manager David Einhorn who, in a stock bet against Green Mountain, accused the company of misleading auditors and inflating its results. Einhorn raised questions about the company's future prospects and its accounting procedures. Wall Street took notice as the stock price started to decline.

Sam Antar, a financial analyst, examined the numbers and used analytical procedures to identify warning signs that were missed. If there is inventory growth that is higher than revenue growth over extended periods of time combined with declining inventory turnover trends, this can be considered a red flag that ending inventory is inflated, thereby overstating earnings. Table 7.1 shows the analysis.

TABLE 7.1	Green Mountain Coffee Roasters					
Fiscal Year 2012 vs. 2011 ($ in 000s)						
Quarter Ended	Reported Revenues: Fiscal Year 2012	Reported Revenues: Fiscal Year 2011	Change	Inventory at End of Current Quarter in 2012	Inventory at End of Previous Year Comparable Quarter in 2011	Increase in Inventory
6/23/2012	$869,194	$717,210	21%	$667,005	$417,496	60%
3/24/2012	$885,052	$647,658	37%	$602,121	$300,760	100%
12/24/2011	$1,158,216	$574,148	102%	$606,679	$269,132	125%
Fiscal Year 2011 vs. 2010 ($ in 000s)						
Quarter Ended	Reported Revenues: Fiscal Year 2011	Reported Revenues: Fiscal Year 2010	Change	Inventory at End of Current Quarter in 2011	Inventory at End of Previous Year Comparable Quarter in 2010	Increase in Inventory
9/24/2011	$711,883	$373,087	91%	$672,248	$262,478	156%
6/25/2011	$717,210	$316,583	127%	$417,496	$186,262	124%
3/26/2011	$647,658	$321,953	101%	$300,760	$109,929	174%
12/25/2010	$575,027	$345,152	67%	$269,132	$117,009	130%

Note: Revenues for the quarter ended 12/25/10 were later revised by Green Mountain Coffee from $575.027 million to $574.148 million after this blog reported discrepancies in its numbers.

According to Antar's analysis, Green Mountain inventory levels had been increasing much faster than revenue during a seven-quarter period in 2010–2012. Thus, the inventory turnover rate was declining, and it was taking Green Mountain longer to sell its products than in the past.

Antar provided the numbers, straight from Green Mountain's SEC filings. In September 2010, the SEC started a probe of Green Mountain's revenue accounting practices.[34]

Taking the analysis further, Antar showed that the inventory turnover was 102.04 days (to sell inventory) in the quarter ended in June 2012 versus only 72.12 days in the quarter ended in June 2011. Green Mountain claimed in SEC filings it was increasing inventory to meet holiday demand. The same explanation was given in a conference call by CFO Fran Rathke. Of course, that was just a smokescreen to hide the fraud.

The Green Mountain case is instructive because it illustrates that a company does not need to financially structure transactions and engage in a sophisticated accounting fraud, as did Enron, to pull the wool over the eyes of shareholders and auditors. A simple phone call can set the scheme in motion, as happened at Green Mountain. This raises an interesting question: Should auditors monitor conference calls with investors, analysts, and even the financial press to determine whether something is said that could be false, fraudulent, or deceptive?

EXHIBIT 7.2   Green Mountain False Earnings Guidance

Green Mountain manufactures the Keurig single-cup brewing system and many varieties of the associated "K-Cup" portion packs to brew single servings of coffee and other related products. The company operates on a razor/razor blade model—selling brewing machines but making its real money on the K-Cups. Between February 2, 2011, and November 9, 2011 (the "class period"), plaintiffs purchased or otherwise acquired Green Mountain common stock. A class-action lawsuit was brought against the company alleging fraud based on materially misleading statements made to deceive [with *scienter*] shareholders about the inventory levels and earnings of the company. The original district court decision went against the plaintiff-shareholders but it was appealed and the decision was remanded for further trial. In the end, the shareholders prevailed against Green Mountain.

During the class period, defendants represented to investors, including plaintiffs, that it was straining to meet consumer demand for its Keurig and K-Cup products and that the company was ramping up production without accumulating excess inventory. Accordingly, Green Mountain's stock price soared to record highs during the class period, from $32.96 per share on February 2, 2011, to a high of $111.62 per share on September 19, 2011.

News of a possible inventory fraud leaked out by third parties who make a living analyzing the financials of companies they feel may be playing fast and loose with the accounting rules. The plaintiff-shareholders brought a lawsuit claiming Green Mountain had represented to them that demand for its coffee makers (Keurig) was so high that it was increasing production without accumulating excess inventory. However, a number of confidential witnesses alleged that within the company excess inventory was piling "up to the rafters" and was being stored out of sight of the auditors from PricewaterhouseCoopers. There were allegations that the company claimed to ship 500,000 coffee brewers to customers, such as QVC, the home shopping channel, but the facts showed that the alleged shipments were never made. Indeed, most of the brewers never even left the dock and were instead taped off with a note saying "not to inventory." After the auditors left, the entire order was "put back in stock."

Green Mountain was accumulating a significant overstock of expiring and unsold product. The complaint includes observations from numerous confidential witnesses ("CWs")—Green Mountain employees from different tiers of the company—detailing the company's increasing inventory buildup.

Using Social Media to Report Earnings Guidance and Financial Results

Companies are required to make public information that is considered "material" to shareholders. Typically, companies will do that by filing that information with the SEC, but businesses are also allowed to bypass the SEC by posting information on their websites or by issuing a press release.

In a ruling that portends changes to how companies communicate with investors, the SEC said on April 2, 2013, that postings on sites such as Facebook and Twitter are just as good as news releases and company Web sites as long as the companies have told investors which outlets they intend to use. The ruling permits companies to use social media channels to announce financial and other key information and post earnings information to the investing public in compliance with Regulation Fair Disclosure (Regulation FD).

The move was sparked by an investigation into a Facebook posting from Netflix Inc. Chief Executive Reed Hastings, who boasted on the social media site that the streaming-video company had exceeded 1 billion hours in a month for the first time, sending the firm's shares higher. The SEC opened the investigation in December 2012, to determine if the post had violated rules that bar companies from selectively disclosing information. The SEC did not initiate an enforcement action or allege wrongdoing by Hastings or Netflix, recognizing that there has been market uncertainty about the application of Regulation FD to social media.

"An increasing number of public companies are using social media to communicate with their shareholders and the investing public," the SEC said. "We appreciate the value and prevalence of social media channels in contemporary market communications, and the commission supports companies seeking new ways to communicate."[35]

Given the SEC's openness to using social media for company communications about financial matters, we can only observe: Students, it is a brave new world out there, and one you all should thrive in.

Non-GAAP Financial Metrics

A 2017 study by Audit Analytics that focuses on non-GAAP usage indicates that 95% of the Standard & Poor's (S&P) 500 disclosed a non-GAAP measurement.[36] Most companies disclose non-GAAP financial metrics, yet little is known about the objectives of disclosing these numbers, how they are determined, management's intent in disclosing non-GAAP amounts, regulation of these disclosures, and the auditors' responsibilities.

A study by Calcbench examined 816 corporate filers that had already filed earnings releases with the SEC for fiscal 2015 that disclosed both GAAP and non-GAAP net income metrics. The study measured the difference between GAAP and non-GAAP net income and reviewed reconciliations. The most common reconciling items were restructuring costs (45.4%), acquisition-related costs (30.5%), stock compensation (20.0%), debt (2.4%), and legal costs (1.6%). From a sample of the 816 firms, it was determined that these companies made 4,632 adjustments to GAAP net income that inflated non-GAAP net income by $164.1 billion. Examples include Facebook, which reported GAAP net income of $3.688 billion in 2015 and non-GAAP net income of $6.518 billion, an increase of 76.7%. In its earnings release the company said:[37]

> We believe that excluding [stock compensation] expense provides investors and management with greater visibility to the underlying performance of our business operations, facilitates comparison of our results with other periods, and may also facilitate comparison with the results of other companies in our industry. . .

HP Inc. reported GAAP net income of $4.554 billion in 2015 and non-GAAP net income of $6.592 billion, an increase of 44.7%.

GAAP net income	$4,554
Amortization of intangibles	+931
Restructuring charges	+1,017
Acquisition-related charges	+90
Separation costs	+1,259
Pension plan settlement charges	+168
Impairment of data center assets	+136
Separation costs in interest & other	+167
Adjustment for taxes	−(927)
Valuation allowances	−(803)
Non-GAAP net income	**$6,592**

Merck & Co. reported GAAP net income of $4.442 billion and non-GAAP net income of $10.195 billion, a difference of $5.753 billion (129.5%). The upward adjustments were largely due to acquisition costs, plus restructuring costs, litigation settlements, and foreign exchange losses due to Venezuela operations.

GAAP net income	$4,442
Acquisition & divestiture costs	+1,110
Vioxx-related litigation	+680
Foreign exchange loss on Venezuela	+876
Gain on divestiture of certain assets	−(397)
Other	−(34)
Income tax benefit	−(1,880)
Non-GAAP net income	**$10,195**

Former SEC Chair Mary Jo White, speaking at a corporate governance meeting in June 2016, expressed her concern that "[i]n too many cases, the non-GAAP information, which is designed to supplement the GAAP information, has become the key message to investors, crowding out and effectively supplanting the GAAP presentation."[38] Beyond that, the diverse items that have been used by companies to adjust GAAP net income to non-GAAP adjusted net income raises questions about the consistency and comparability of non-GAAP amounts. Some companies present EPS on a non-GAAP basis adding another wrinkle to the understandability issue. For example, First Energy provided the following information for fiscal year 2016.

Basic Earnings (Loss) per share (GAAP)	$(14.49)
Excluding Special items:	
Mark-to-market adjustments:	
Pension/OPEB actuarial assumptions	0.21

(*Continued*)

Other	0.01
Merger accounting–commodity contracts	0.05
Regulatory charges	0.13
Asset impairment/Plant exit costs	16.67
Debt redemption costs	0.02
Trust securities impairment	0.03
Total Special Items	$17.12
Basic EPS—Operating (Non-GAAP)	**$2.63**

What is a Non-GAAP Financial Measure?

SEC Regulation G and Item 10(e) of Regulation S-K define a "non-GAAP financial measure" as a numerical measure of historical or future financial performance, financial position, or cash flows, that:

- Excludes amounts that are included in the most directly comparable measure calculated and presented in accordance with GAAP; or
- Includes amounts that are excluded from the most directly comparable measure so calculated and presented.

The SEC regulations further provide that the definition of a non-GAAP financial measure is intended to capture all measures that have the effect of depicting either:[39]

- A measure of performance that is different from that presented in the financial statements, such as income or loss before taxes, or net income or loss as calculated in accordance with GAAP; or
- A measure of liquidity that is different from cash flow or cash flow from operations computed in accordance with GAAP.

Regulation G applies to all public disclosures and is not limited to the registrant's written public filings. If a non-GAAP financial measure is made public orally, telephonically, by webcast, by broadcast, or by similar means, then the reconciliation requirements under Regulation G would exist if:[40]

- The required information (i.e., presentation and reconciliation) is provided on the registrant's website at the time the non-GAAP financial measure is made public; and
- The location of the website is made public in the same presentation in which the non-GAAP financial measure is made public.

Based on regulatory requirements, if a company takes a defined GAAP measure (such as GAAP net income) and thereafter "adjusts" for (i.e., excludes or includes) one or more expense or revenue items that are components of that GAAP measure (i.e., excluding a restructuring expense identified as "nonrecurring"), then the resulting measure (i.e., "adjusted net income") is a non-GAAP financial measure. One common non-GAAP measure is EBITDA (earnings before interest, taxes, depreciation, and amortization). Other variations include EBIT, EBITA, EBITD, EBITDAR (earnings before interests, taxes, depreciation, amortization, and restructuring costs), adjusted EBITDA, and so on. A joke making the rounds is perhaps the best measure is EBBS (earnings before the bad stuff).

Federal Securities Laws

The SEC did not regulate non-GAAP measures until Congress passed SOX in 2002.[41] The Act directed the SEC to implement and enforce rules requiring that, when non-GAAP financial measures are disclosed, they must be presented in a manner that (1) does not contain an untrue statement of a material fact or omit a material fact necessary to make the "pro forma financial information," in light of the circumstances under which it is presented, not misleading and (2) reconciles the "pro forma financial information" presented with the financial position and the results of operations of the company under U.S. GAAP.

The SEC adopted final rules that implemented the following requirements:[42]

- Regulation G, which applies to a company's public disclosures or releases of material information that include non-GAAP financial measures;
- Item 10(e) of Regulation S-K, which applies to the use of non-GAAP financial measures in filings with the Commission; and
- Item 2.02 of Form 8-K, which requires public companies to furnish to the SEC earnings releases or announcements that disclose material nonpublic information included in annual or quarterly fiscal periods.

Requirements under Item 10(e) of Regulation S-K

Item 10(e) applies to non-GAAP financial measures that are included in SEC filings. To comply with these requirements, the registrant must include the following:

- A presentation, with equal or greater prominence, of the most directly comparable financial measure or measures calculated and presented in accordance with GAAP;
- A non-GAAP measure should be presented in proximity to the GAAP measure with an appropriate balance of discussion;
- A quantitative reconciliation of the differences between the non-GAAP financial measure and the most directly comparable GAAP financial measure;
- The reconciliation should be presented with each adjustment clearly labeled and separately quantified;
- A statement disclosing why the registrant's management believes that presentation of the non-GAAP financial measure provides useful information to investors regarding the registrant's financial condition and results of operations; and
- To the extent material, a statement disclosing the additional purposes, if any, for which the registrant's management uses the non-GAAP financial measure.[43]

Item 10(e) of Regulation S-K specifically prohibits:

- Non-GAAP financial measures of liquidity that exclude charges or liabilities requiring cash settlement other than EBIT and EBITDA;
- Adjustments to non-GAAP financial measures of performance that eliminate or smooth items identified as "nonrecurring, infrequent or unusual," when the nature of the charge or gain is such that it is reasonably likely to recur within two years or there was a similar charge or gain within the prior two years;
- The presentation of non-GAAP financial measures on the face of the registrant's financial statements prepared in accordance with GAAP or in the accompanying notes;

- The presentation of non-GAAP financial measures on the face of any pro forma financial information required to be disclosed under Regulation S-X; and
- The use of titles or descriptions of non-GAAP financial measures that are the same as, or confusingly similar to, titles or descriptions used for GAAP financial measures.

When evaluating a company's use and presentation of non-GAAP financial measures, management and the audit committee should consider the following:

- What is management's intention in disclosing non-GAAP amounts? The audit committee's responsibility is to ensure management is not attempting to manage earnings.
- How does the non-GAAP measure provide investors with useful information?
- Where should the non-GAAP amounts be disclosed (i.e., in earnings releases, conference calls with financial analysts, filings with the SEC)?
- Are there appropriate controls over the calculation of non-GAAP measures? Are these amounts presented consistently from period to period?
- Is this information designed to supplement GAAP amounts, not substitute for it?
- Have these amounts been discussed with the external auditors?

Controls over non-GAAP Measures

Given the need to comply with SEC disclosure rules and the potential consequences of material errors and omissions or misleading non-GAAP presentations, companies should develop and implement controls over the creation and reporting of non-GAAP measures. Controls should address whether non-GAAP measures are sufficiently transparent, including their reconciliation to GAAP, whether their calculation may be biased and whether they are presented on a consistent basis from period to period. For example, in defining a non-GAAP profit metric, it is important for companies to treat gains and losses of a similar nature in the same manner by consistently including or excluding both.[44] Choosing to add back losses but not deduct gains is what the SEC refers to as "cherry-picking" adjustments within a non-GAAP financial measure that could mislead users.

Compliance and Disclosure Interpretations

On May 17, 2016, the SEC updated its interpretive guidance on non-GAAP metrics that provides examples of potentially misleading non-GAAP measures that could violate Regulation G, including:[45]

- Presenting a performance measure that excludes normal, recurring, cash operating expenses;
- Presenting non-GAAP measures inconsistently between periods without disclosing the change and reasons for the change;
- Presenting non-GAAP measures that exclude non-recurring charges but do not exclude non-recurring gains; and
- Using individually-tailored accounting principles to calculate non-GAAP earnings, for example, by presenting non-GAAP revenue that accelerates revenue recognition as though the revenue were earned sooner than for GAAP purposes.

The updated guidance also provides example disclosures that would cause a non-GAAP measure to be more prominent than the most directly comparable GAAP measure, such as:

- Omitting comparable GAAP measures from headlines of earnings releases;
- Presenting a non-GAAP measure that precedes the most directly comparable GAAP measure;

- Presenting a non-GAAP measure using a style of presentation (e.g., bold, larger font) that emphasizes non-GAAP over the comparable GAAP measures;

- Describing non-GAAP measures (e.g., record performance, exceptional) without equally prominent description of the comparable GAAP measure;

- Providing tabular disclosure of non-GAAP information without including the GAAP information in the same table or an equally prominent tabular disclosure; and

- Including unbalanced discussion and analysis of non-GAAP versus GAAP presentations.

Why Do Companies Use Non-GAAP Financial Measures?

Often, non-GAAP operating measures are used by research analysts, rating agencies, and other financial professionals in evaluating or comparing the performance of comparable companies. For instance, EBITDA is commonly found in debt covenants, widely used by analysts in valuing businesses, and making financial projections. Non-GAAP financial measures also enable management to convey a picture how they see the company's financial condition or results of operations in a manner that GAAP results alone may not be able to convey. The danger here is that management will use the occasion of disclosing non-GAAP numbers as a means of presenting its views on earnings rather than GAAP.[46] One example is if a company were to include deferred revenues as an adjustment from GAAP to non-GAAP operating income.

Marc Siegel, a member of the FASB Board, believes that the combination of non-GAAP data outside the financial statements with information inside the audited financial statements is more impactful than either dataset on its own. Siegel suggests that the combination of the two sets of information would be a "powerful analytical tool in understanding the underlying business because they complement each other."[47]

External Auditor Responsibilities

Professional standards require auditors only to read other information in a document containing the financial statements and accompanying audit report. There are no requirements for auditors to test non-GAAP disclosures, which are presented outside the financial statements, in earnings releases, or in the MD&A section of periodic filings. Consequently, the external auditor's opinion on the company's financial statements and, when required, the effectiveness of the company's internal controls do not cover non-GAAP measures. This raises an important question: Is there an expectation gap because users might expect that external auditors have reviewed earnings releases, or are attesting to the company's internal controls over non-GAAP measures, when they generally do not.[48]

The external auditor has no responsibility for determining whether non-GAAP financial information is properly stated. However, under PCAOB standards (AS 2710), the auditor should read the other information included in certain documents (such as annual or quarterly reports) and consider whether the information, or its manner of presentation, is materially consistent with the information appearing in the financial statements. If material inconsistencies exist, the auditor should consider whether the other information needs to be revised and communicate the matter to the client. If the other information is not revised to eliminate the material inconsistency, the auditor should communicate the material inconsistency to the audit committee and consider other actions, such as revising the audit report to include an explanatory paragraph, withholding the use of the report, and withdrawing from the engagement.[49]

Liability for Wrongful Use of Non-GAAP Financial Measures

Registrants are subject to the anti-fraud provisions of the federal securities law, in addition to the general disclosure requirement under Regulation G which provides that a registrant shall not make public a non-GAAP financial measure that, taken together with the information accompanying that measure, contains an untrue statement of material fact or omits to state a material fact necessary in order to make the presentation of the non-GAAP financial measure, in light of the circumstances under which it is presented, not misleading.[50]

Companies should ensure that the non-GAAP financial measures they use are neither misleading nor prohibited by the rules. Appropriate controls on the use of non-GAAP financial measures should be considered and established by management. Audit committees should carefully oversee and monitor the use of non-GAAP financial measures and disclosures. The audit committee should ask management to explain the usefulness of non-GAAP financial measures in the company's public disclosures. The audit committee should discuss the company's use of non-GAAP financial measures with the external auditors.

Is Non-GAAP Reporting Ethical?

Do companies purposefully choose non-GAAP measures that disclose the most positive results or do they select a method that best informs investors, analysts, and other users about their "true" performance? In other words, the non-GAAP method chosen should be designed to provide information to investors that are more meaningful than GAAP in portraying not only how the company is doing but provide insight into how it might do in the future. Since adjustments to GAAP can include transitory amounts, non-recurring items, and one-time events, the result should provide better guidance on the company's performance than would occur using GAAP only. The non-GAAP measures should better reflect economic reality than GAAP amounts alone.

It's possible that some managers turn to non-GAAP reporting because they are unable to produce GAAP earnings that meet or beat earnings targets or expectations—even after engaging in earnings management. It may be difficult for an auditor to make this determination without understanding management's motivation in disclosing non-GAAP amounts and in selecting one type of non-GAAP measure versus another. External auditors need to assess motivation, look for pressures on management to disclose earnings numbers that make the company look like it's doing better than it really is, and be aware of other factors that might incentivize management to find alternative ways to present operating performance that also portray them in the most positive light.

Earnings Management and Materiality Judgments

> ### LO 7-3
> Explain the role of materiality in earnings management.

The principle of materiality underscores the concept that some financial transactions are so insignificant that they are not worth measuring and reporting with exact precision. Materiality is an amount that makes a difference to the users of financial statements and linked to the audit concept of reasonable assurance. For instance, if a company has overstated its revenues by $1 million when its total revenues are $100 million, then this $1 million amount (1%) is considered immaterial. However, if the total revenues are $10 million, it would be material (10%). Materiality can be viewed from the perspective of the earnings continuum.

Materiality is a matter of professional judgment and should be assessed based on surrounding circumstances, including the size and nature of the misstatement. Accountants and auditors should consider both quantitative and qualitative factors. In the case of the latter, the potential effect of a misstatement on the company's compliance with loan covenants should be considered material regardless of the amount.

The possibility of fraud and illegal acts is another example. Now we can add the effect of misstatements of non-GAAP earnings when contrasted with investor expectations and analysts' forecasted earnings.

Gemstar–TV Guide International, Inc.

The danger of relying on only a quantitative analysis to make materiality judgments can be seen in the audit by KPMG of Gemstar–TV Guide International, Inc. *Accounting and Auditing Enforcement Release (AAER) 2125,* issued by the SEC, concludes that $364 million of revenue was reported improperly and that certain disclosure policies were inconsistent with Gemstar's accounting for revenue, did not comply with GAAP disclosure requirements, or both. *AAER 2125* found that the KPMG auditors concurred in Gemstar's accounting for overstated revenue from licensing and advertising transactions in March 2000, December 2000, December 2001, and March 2002. Also, KPMG did not object to Gemstar's disclosure and issued audit reports stating that KPMG had conducted its audits in conformity with generally accepted accounting standards (GAAS) and that the financial statements fairly presented its results in conformity with GAAP. In reaching these conclusions, the KPMG auditors unreasonably relied on representations by Gemstar management, unreasonably determined that the revenues were immaterial to Gemstar's financial statements, or both. The KPMG auditors' materiality determinations were unreasonable in that they considered only quantitative materiality factors (i.e., that the amount of revenue was not a large percentage of Gemstar's consolidated financial results) and failed to also consider qualitative materiality (i.e., that the revenue related to business lines were closely watched by securities analysts and had a material effect on the valuation of Gemstar stock).

The SEC complaint reads like a "what's what" in earnings management; it provides insight into the techniques that some companies use to manage earnings. The complaint alleges that Gemstar materially overstated its revenues by nearly $250 million through the following means:[51]

- Recording revenue under expired, disputed, or nonexistent agreements, and improperly reporting this as licensing and advertising revenue.

- Recording revenue from a long-term agreement on an accelerated basis in violation of GAAP and Gemstar's own policies, which required recording and reporting such revenue ratably over the terms of the agreement (consistent with the matching theory).

- Inflating advertising revenue by improperly recording and reporting revenue amounts from multiple-element transactions.

- Engaging in "round-trip" transactions, whereby Gemstar paid money to a third party to advertise its services and capitalized that cost while the third party used the funds received from Gemstar to buy advertising that Gemstar recorded 100% as revenue in the period of the transaction.

- Failing to disclose that it had structured certain settlements for the purpose of creating cookie-jar reserves of advertising revenue to smooth net income.

- Improperly recording advertising revenue from nonmonetary and barter transactions even though Gemstar could not establish the advertising's fair value properly.

Accrual accounting is not an exact science. A variety of assumptions and accounting estimates are used in arriving at the final earnings figures. These assumptions and estimates require sound judgment to protect against unacceptable forms of earnings management. Earnings management aims to report the numbers in such a way as to achieve a predetermined earnings target. The risks of managing earnings are more serious today than ever before because of the various ways in which earnings and earnings per share information is communicated with users, including shareholders, financial analysts, and the investment community.

While earnings management is not necessarily the result of an intentional fraud, but the culmination of a series of aggressive interpretations of the accounting rules and aggressive operating activities, it still should be considered unethical if the primary motive for managing earnings is to deceive users of the true results of operations, portray managerial performance in the best light, and present views of earnings and liquidity not conforming with GAAP. In many cases, earnings management is carried out by otherwise honest people who are motivated to tell the company's side of the story rather than strictly adhere to GAAP. The end result is misstatement of the financial results that oftentimes builds pressure to do the same in subsequent periods. One aggressive interpretation leads to another until the quality of the financial information is in doubt.

McGregor explains earnings manipulation as follows:

> The typical case of earnings manipulation begins with a track record of success. The company or division has posted significant sales and earnings growth over recent years. [Its] stock price trades at a high price earnings multiple as the market rewards its stellar growth. Unfortunately, it is becoming more difficult for the company to maintain the sales and earnings growth that analysts have grown to expect. Sales are behind target this quarter, so management runs special incentives for its sales force to accelerate sales and uses overtime to ship out its products. It works and the firm meets expectations.
>
> The next quarter, the analyst expectations are higher. However, sales still have not picked up to the level required, so the firm provides additional incentives to its sales force, uses overtime to boost shipments but now has additional expenses to contend with (incentives and overtime), so it does not fully accrue all its consulting expenses. The following quarter rolls around and sales still haven't recovered, but the analysts keep raising the bar. This time the operating tactics are not enough, so management pressures the CFO to make the numbers. The CFO is aggressive in the interpretation of installment sales and expense accruals, and the company again meets expectations. The expectations keep rising, as does the firm's stock price. As the fourth quarter comes around, sales still are not at expectations. The CFO creates sales and under-accrues expenses all to meet expectations. The company has gone from aggressive operating practices to financial fraud.[52]

Earnings management techniques have come to be known as "financial shenanigans." Financial shenanigans are actions or omissions of information or financial structuring of transactions intended to hide or distort the real financial performance or financial condition of an entity. They range from minor deceptions to more serious misapplications of accounting principles. We discuss these techniques in the following sections.

SEC Enforcement in Financial Reporting and Disclosure

LO 7-4

Describe earnings management techniques in SEC enforcement actions.

The SEC reported enforcement proceedings in its 2017 Year-End Update that is encouraging because the number of enforcement cases decreased by almost 19% over 2016, dropping from 548 standalone actions to 446. The following illustrates some of the enforcement actions.[53]

Overstating Assets (Related-Party Transactions)

The CEO of Integrated Freight Corporation, David Fuselier, who was also chair of the board, CFO and principal accounting officer, arranged for the company to sell non-performing subsidiaries with liabilities greater than assets to a new shell company called Deep South that was formed and controlled by the CEO's friend. The motivation was to improve the financial condition of the company. Fuselier concealed the true nature of the transactions from the companies' auditors and from July 2012 to April 2015, reviewed, approved, and signed SEC filings containing false and misleading information about the related-party nature of the sales and the issuers' financial condition. As a result, Integrated Freight filed with the SEC false and misleading reports. The liabilities purportedly transferred to Deep South remained liabilities of Integrated Freight because the purported indemnifications given by Deep South were worthless. Under FASB Accounting Standards Codification (ASC) Topic 850-10-50-6, Related Party Disclosures, if the reporting entity and one or more other entities are under common ownership or management control that could result in operating results or financial position of the reporting entity significantly different from those that would have been obtained if the entities were autonomous, the nature of the control relationship should be disclosed even *though there are no transactions between the entities.*[54]

Understating Liabilities (Contingencies)

General Motors failed to properly identify and accrue for vehicle recall contingencies after it was determined on February 7, 2014, that it would recall 619,122 vehicles to repair defective ignition switches that, under certain circumstances, might move out of the run/on position. If this occurred, the driver would lose the assistance of power steering and power brakes. Moreover, if a collision occurred while the switch was in the accessory/off position, the vehicle's airbags may fail to deploy. This recall, the first of three related to the defective switch, followed years of internal reviews. As early as April 2012, a GM engineer had reported that a probable root cause of the airbag non-deployment problem was the defective switch out of the on to the off position. Even though this was reported to the product senior manager and a GM attorney, the company failed to record a contingent liability for product recalls. Under GM's system of internal accounting controls, GM's processes were focused on recall accruals and only provided the warranty group with information about vehicle issues at the point a recall was considered probable and the costs of the recall were estimable, and did not provide information about potential vehicle issues to the warranty group prior to this point.[55]

Improper Revenue Recognition (Multiple-Element Arrangements)

Ixia sells network testing, visibility, and security products. It typically sells a bundle of its products—hardware, software, post-contract support, and services–to customers in a single transaction, with none of those component products having been separately negotiated or priced. These kinds of combination sales (known in accounting as "multi-element arrangements") are subject to GAAP that require Ixia to defer recognizing Ixia's software revenue from a given sale if certain criteria are not met.[56]

Under GAAP, revenue from a multi-element arrangement involving software must be allocated to each element (e.g., the separate products sold in the combination sale) based on the fair value of each element (e.g., the dollar value of that element as established through evidence of a consistent price paid by customers for the same or similar element), as measured by vendor-specific objective evidence of fair value ("VSOE"). Thus, if VSOE does not exist for an undelivered software element, then any software revenue from the multi-element arrangement must be deferred until either the point in time when all elements have been delivered to the customer, or when VSOE does exist for each individual element, whichever is earlier. Consistent with this, Ixia's internal revenue recognition policy provided that: "If we have not been able to establish VSOE for our professional services the entire order or group is recognized as revenue over the service term or when the service is completed, depending on the arrangement."

In 2012, Ixia was headed by Victor Alston, the CEO. Alston pushed for Ixia's revenue and other financial metrics to meet or exceed consensus market expectations. Discontent with the problems created by the deferral of Ixia's software revenue, Alston issued a directive to artificially split professional services onto a separate purchase order (POs) whenever they were included in any sale. Splitting POs gave the false appearance that customers were buying Ixia's professional services in a stand-alone sale, and not as part of a multi-element arrangement with the company's software products. It also allowed Ixia to prematurely recognize software revenue in contravention of its stated revenue recognition policy and GAAP. Until his resignation in 2014, Thomas Miller was the CFO. Ixia's director of accounting was William Liang, and, until 2014 when he was fired from the company, Liang was responsible for Ixia's revenue recognition accounting. Each of them took affirmative steps to mislead Ixia's auditors while allowing the most important revenue recognition policy at the company, as well as GAAP, to be violated. Following a 2014 internal investigation by its audit committee, Ixia restated its first and second quarter 2013 financial statements and, among other things, reversed in those periods nearly all revenue prematurely recognized because of Split POs. The audit committee further concluded that the company had not maintained effective ICFR in the first and second quarters of 2013.

Management's Discussion and Analysis (MD&A)

Item 303 of Regulation S-K requires issuers' quarterly filings to discuss material changes in the liquidity and financial resources which, in turn, requires that management discuss and analyze the registrant's financial condition, changes in financial condition, and results of operations, with a specific focus on "material events and uncertainties known to management that would cause reported financial information not to be necessarily indicative of future operating results or of future financial condition."

In the case of UTi Worldwide Inc. (UTi), its disclosures regarding serious risks to the company's liquidity and capital resources in its Form 10-Q for the quarter ending October 31, 2013, were inadequate under the standards appearing in Item 303. Beginning in October 2013, UTi internally identified a critical proprietary operating system as a possible contributing factor to UTi's lower than historical cash flow volumes. The company began to experience a liquidity crisis, including a backlog of receivables and an inability to meet its debt covenants. Despite these significant issues, UTi's Form 10-Q, which was signed and certified by both then-CEO Eric W. Kirchner and then-CFO Richard G. Rodick, did not include adequate information in the MD&A section to allow investors and others to meaningfully assess UTi's financial condition and results of operations, particularly as to UTi's future prospects.[57]

Revenue Recognition

Given the prominence of revenue recognition techniques in earnings management cases, we discuss some of the criteria for determining proper revenue and provide an example of how challenging it can be.

Generally, revenue is recognized only when a specific event has occurred and the amount of revenue is measurable. The specific event addresses when revenue is realized or realizable. These decisions can be challenging because uncertainties may exist about collectibility, side agreements may be made, contingencies added, and/or multiple elements may exist in a revenue transaction that need to be separately valued as discussed in the Ixia case above.

The bedrock revenue recognition principles are explained in SEC Staff Accounting Bulletin 101 (SAB 101), "Revenue Recognition in Financial Statements." The basic guidelines provide that revenue generally is realized or realizable and earned when all of the following criteria are met:[58]

1. Persuasive evidence of an arrangement exists.
2. Delivery has occurred or services have been rendered,

3. The seller's price to the buyer is fixed or determinable.

4. Collectibility is reasonably assured.

Here are some common revenue recognition devices that have been used to manage earnings.

Multiple Deliverables

Vendors often provide multiple products or services to their customers as part of a single arrangement or a series of related arrangements. These deliverables may be provided at different points in time or over different time periods. As a simple example, a vendor may enter into an arrangement with a customer to deliver and install a tangible product along with providing one year of maintenance services. In this arrangement, there are three deliverables: (1) the product, (2) installation, and (3) maintenance services. Issues often arise regarding how and whether to separate these deliverables and how to allocate the overall arrangement consideration. Subtopic 605-25, *Revenue Recognition–Multiple-Element Arrangements,* of the Financial Accounting Standards Board's Accounting Standards Codification (ASC) provides the guidance that should be followed in accounting for this and many other revenue arrangements with multiple deliverables.[59]

Channel Stuffing

Channel stuffing is a deceptive business practice used by a company to inflate its sales and earnings figures by deliberately sending retailers along its distribution channel more products than they are able to sell to the public. The goal is to beef up receivables and accelerate revenue into a period earlier than would normally be expected given the company's revenue cycle. One problem is concessions may need to be made to get customers to buy before they are ready to do so and/or receive the product. Another is that customers may return excess product at a later date, which may not be so bad for the vendor given it still recognizes a higher level of revenue when it wants; however, these kinds of transactions have a way of blowing up in your face when customers say "no" in the future. Moreover, the snowball effect makes it harder each year to maintain the charade. Sunbeam stuffed the channels with product because it sought to accelerate the recording of revenue to earlier periods. The company made deals with customers, such as Walmart, to take product sooner than they really wanted to. Sunbeam provided discounts and a liberal return policy to incentivize customers.

The legality of channel stuffing comes into question because these transactions may not meet the "economic substance" test. The *economic substance* of transactions and events must be recorded in the financial statements rather than just their *legal form* in order to present fairly financial position, results of operations, and cash flows. One issue of concern is: What if a company cannot estimate future sales returns or, at net, if the channel stuffing transactions substantially reduce future revenues?

Channel stuffing can be questioned from an operational earnings management perspective. It makes little sense to borrow from the future to make the current period look better only to add more pressure to future years to do the same. The house of cards may ultimately collapse, as it did at Sunbeam.

Round-Tripping

Global Crossing and Qwest were two telecommunications companies that engaged in "round-trip" transactions in the early 2000s. What happened is the companies were round-tripping revenues by recording a series of last-minute deals with other carriers, in which the contracts were for nearly identical amounts, for routes that had yet to be specified or, in some cases, on routes that had not yet been built. In a 2001 transaction between Global Crossing and Qwest, Global Crossing signed a $100 million contract only to "round-trip" the cash by purchasing a similar amount of undefined capacity from Qwest. Global Crossing would book the incoming contract as a large chunk of revenue and then book the outgoing contract as a capital expense. To an objective observer, these capacity swaps appear to be a transaction solely for the purpose of boosting revenues. Hence, it fails the economic substance test.

Bill and Hold

In a traditional bill-and-hold scheme, such as the one engaged in by Halliburton that was discussed in Chapter 3, a legitimate sales order is received, processed, and ready for shipment. The customer, however, is not ready to take and/or use the product. The seller holds the goods in its facility or ships them to a different location, such as a third-party warehouse, for storage until the customer is ready to accept shipment. The seller then recognizes revenue immediately upon shipment to the warehouse. Since the risk of ownership has not passed to the buyer, the recording of revenue is not justified.

In a new twist on bill-and-hold transactions, in August 2014, the SEC brought charges against Newport Beach, California, telecommunications equipment maker AirTouch Communications Inc., former president and CEO Hideyuki Kanakubo, and former CFO Jerome Kaiser, for orchestrating a fraudulent revenue recognition scheme that violated GAAP by recognizing revenue on inventory that was shipped to a Florida warehouse, but never sold. They are also accused of defrauding an investor from whom they secured a $2 million loan for the company based on misstatements and omissions associated with the shipments.[60]

When AirTouch reported net revenues of a little more than $1.03 million in its report for the third quarter of 2012, it included approximately $1.24 million in inventory that had been shipped to the company in Florida that agreed to warehouse AirTouch's products in anticipation of future sales. The Florida company had not purchased the inventory, and AirTouch had not sold the inventory to any of its customers.

MagnaChip Semiconductor, Ltd.

The MagnaChip Semiconductor fraud illustrates how much can go wrong when management seeks to manage earnings through revenue recognition transactions, internal controls are overriden, and the auditors are kept out of the loop.

MagnaChip Semiconductor, Ltd. designs and manufactures analog and mixed-signal semiconductor products for consumer, computing, communication, industrial, automotive, and Internet applications. The company offers display solutions for a range of flat panel display sizes used in LCD televisions, LCD monitors, notebooks, tablet PCs, public information displays, and other applications.

MagnaChip Semiconductor Corporation is a Delaware corporation headquartered in Luxembourg with the majority of its operations in South Korea. It maintains a U.S. sales subsidiary in Cupertino, California. MagnaChip's stock is listed on the New York Stock Exchange. MagnaChip Korea engaged in a variety of transactions to accelerate the recording of revenue into earlier periods through channel stuffing arrangements, recording revenue on sales of incomplete or unshipped products, and delaying recording obsolete inventory to manipulate its reported gross margin. The underlying motivation for the fraud was to hit earnings targets and was carried out through aggressive action directed by or in response to pressure from the former CFO, Margaret Sakai.[61]

MagnaChip stated in its public filings that it recognized revenue on a "sell-in" basis under GAAP (i.e., when it sold and shipped the product to a distributor, not when the distributor sold and shipped the product to an end customer). This revenue recognition treatment for sales to distributors is consistent with GAAP only when the aforementioned revenue recognition requirements are met.

The revenue recognition criteria in MagnaChip's quarterly and annual filings during the relevant period was signed off by Sakai. The filings stated that it utilized these criteria to recognize revenue "upon shipment, upon delivery of the product at the customer's location or upon customer acceptance . . . when the risks and rewards of ownership have passed to the customer" and that, outside of warranty obligations and contractual terms, its sales contracts "do not include any other post-shipment obligations that could have an impact on revenue recognition." Those statements were later determined to have been materially false and misleading because MagnaChip recognized substantial revenue even when the disclosed criteria were not met.

Contrary to the disclosures in its public filings, as well as to its written policies, from late 2011 through the third quarter of 2013, certain MagnaChip employees engaged in what they called a "pull-in" sales practice whereby they offered distributors undisclosed concessions via side agreements to incentivize them to order products earlier than wanted or needed so that MagnaChip would hit revenue targets. The concessions included payment term extensions, credit limit increases, unlimited return and stock rotation rights on unsold inventory, and price protection. As a result of the concessions, MagnaChip improperly recognized revenue on certain transactions that did not meet the requirements of GAAP.

Although the "pull-in" sales practice was known to numerous individuals throughout MagnaChip's Korean management structure, Sakai, as CFO of MagnaChip, approved payment term extensions and credit limit increases for certain of the improper pull-in sales, failed to correct the improper accounting treatment of other pull-in sales, and understood how they would impact MagnaChip's reported revenue. Sakai signed MagnaChip's financial statements disclosing the company's revenue recognition policy and GAAP requirements. She also represented to MagnaChip's auditors in management representation letters that MagnaChip had not entered into any side agreements, and certified MagnaChip's public filings. Sakai either knew or was reckless in not knowing that the concessions and side agreements precluded revenue recognition under GAAP and violated MagnaChip's disclosed revenue recognition policy. Further, Sakai either knew or was reckless in not knowing that the Company engaged in these practices solely to meet revenue targets.

MagnaChip also improperly recognized revenue on "sales" of non-existent or unfinished products in order to meet revenue targets. In 2011, some MagnaChip Korean sales employees met with some manufacturing employees to express concern about their ability to meet the sales targets set by senior management because manufacturing could not keep up. After that meeting, certain of MagnaChip's manufacturing employees in Korea began circumventing the Company's accounting controls and falsified books and records to create entries that made it appear that products that had not yet begun production or were still in production had been completed, shipped and billed to customers. MagnaChip then recognized revenue on the sales of those unfinished products. In so doing, MagnaChip violated GAAP because it recognized revenue on purported sales of products that had not yet completed manufacturing and therefore had not yet shipped or been delivered, and the risk of loss had not transferred to the purchaser.

The MagnaChip case illustrates how things can go so wrong, so quickly, when a top official (i.e., the CFO) directs a fraud and creates a pressure-laden culture to meet earnings targets. MagnaChip's misconduct was pervasive, from senior employees like Sakai down to manufacturing plant employees and employees in other departments. By late 2013, both Magna's outside auditors (Samil PricewaterhouseCoopers) and its audit committee suspected something was wrong. In March 2014, the audit committee disclosed its investigation to investors, and, in 2015, the company restated revenues for 2011, 2012, and most of 2013. The SEC began its investigation shortly thereafter and settled in June 2017 by imposing a $3 million fine against MagnaChip, deferred another $3 million in penalties, that it may impose in the future if the company has more trouble. Sakai must pay $135,000 in personal penalties, cannot appear before the SEC again as an accountant, and cannot serve as a director or officer of a U.S.-listed company ever again.[62]

New Revenue Recognition Standard

Given the myriad of problems in revenue recognition and lack of consistent standards, the Financial Accounting Standards Board (FASB) and the International Accounting Standards Board (IASB) jointly issued a new revenue recognition standard, *Revenue from Contracts with Customers,* to converge the revenue recognition rules of both bodies, thereby enhancing understandability on a global level. The FASB noted that public companies, certain nonprofits, and employee benefit plans were to implement the standard for fiscal years, and quarterly and interim financial statements within such years, beginning after December 15, 2017. Public companies were to adopt the standard for their 2018 first-quarter filings with the SEC. Private companies and other entities were scheduled to implement it for fiscal years beginning after December 15, 2018, as well as quarterly and interim financial statements for fiscal years beginning after December 15, 2019. The new standard provides a single, comprehensive accounting model for revenue recognition under U.S. GAAP and IFRS. The standard is complex so we limit the discussion to the very basics here.

Under the new standard, companies under contract to provide goods or services to a customer will be required to follow a five-step process to recognize revenue:[63]

1. *Determine whether you have a contract.* Do you have a deal with a customer?
2. *Identify the performance obligations.* What are the responsibilities of each party under the contract?
3. *Determine the transaction price.* What do you expect to be owed?
4. *Allocate the transaction price.* Assign a value to the separate performance obligations.
5. *Recognize revenue (or as) performance obligations are satisfied.* When has transfer of control occurred?

According to Prabhakar "PK" Kalavacherla, partner in the Audit Quality and Professional Practice group at KPMG LLP, companies that sell products and services in a bundle, or those engaged in major projects—in such industries as telecommunications, software, engineering, construction, and real estate—could see significant changes to the timing of revenue recognition. For telecommunications or cable companies, their current practice of recognizing revenue only to the extent of the cash received will be replaced by a requirement to estimate a stand-alone selling price for free or discounted goods or services (such as a wireless handset or free premium channel services for a limited time).[64] It remains to be seen whether a company can make reliable estimates of stand-alone selling prices that represent management's best estimate considering observable inputs. However, it could be more challenging if goods or services are not sold independently by the company or others.

The new standard requires extensive disclosures including disaggregation of total revenue, information about performance obligations, changes in contract asset and liability account balances between periods, and key judgments and estimates. Our concern is the devil is in the details and those can be quite complicated with revenue recognition. We'll reserve final comment until the standard goes fully into effect and any "tweaking" that is necessary is made.

Financial Shenanigans

LO 7-5
Explain the workings of financial shenanigans.

Financial Statement Effects

Financial shenanigans are a colorful way to describe earnings management techniques. Howard Schilit wrote a book that has become a classic in understanding the common types of financial shenanigans. We explain the basic financial shenanigan techniques below,[65] with the number of examples in each category limited to the three most common techniques. We also use Schilit's framework to discuss earnings manipulations at two companies charged by the SEC with accounting fraud—Xerox and Lucent.

The shenanigans can be broadly classified into two types: (a) schemes that overstate revenues and profits, which are designed to enhance reported results and earnings per share, and (b) schemes that understate revenues and profits that are typically done to smooth out net income over time periods and make it appear less volatile.

1. Recording Revenue Too Soon or of Questionable Quality

We have discussed this before and provided many examples where revenue is recorded before the earnings process has been completed or before an unconditional exchange has occurred. Examples of this shenanigan include:

- Recording revenue when future services remain to be provided.
- Recording revenue before shipment or before the customer's unconditional acceptance.
- Recording revenue even though the customer is not obligated to pay.

The Xerox case discussed later in this chapter illustrates how a company can move earnings into an earlier period by allocating more of the revenue in a multiyear contract to earlier years than justified given continuing servicing under the contract.

2. Recording Bogus Revenue

Typically, bogus revenue transactions lead to fictitious revenue. Examples include:

- Recording sales that lack economic substance.
- Recording as revenue supplier rebates that are tied to future required purchases.
- Releasing revenue that was held back improperly before a merger.

The ZZZZ Best case assignment in Chapter 5 illustrates how a master of deception like Barry Minkow can create nonexistent revenue by creating fictitious invoices for unperformed work.

3. Boosting Income with One-Time Gains

The gains (and losses) from the sale of operating and investment assets that should be recorded in another (e.g., miscellaneous) income account can be classified in other ways if the intent is to boost operating income. These include:

- Boosting profits by selling undervalued assets.
- Including investment income or gains as part of operating revenue.
- Including investment income or gains as a reduction in operating expenses.

IBM used the net proceeds from the sale of an operating unit ($300 million) to lower its operating costs, rather than accounting for it as a nonrecurring, one-time gain. We consider it fraud because it is a deliberate attempt to mislead users of the financial statements into thinking that operating income is larger than it really is. Financial analysts tend to put more emphasis on operating income than net income because of the miscellaneous, non-operating items recorded below the line of operating income to get net income.

4. Shifting Current Expenses to a Later or Earlier Period

A common approach to shifting expenses to a later period is by capitalizing a cost in the current period and expensing it over a period of time, rather than expensing the item completely in the current period. This was the technique used by WorldCom to inflate earnings by between $11 billion and $13 billion.

Additional examples include:

- Changing accounting policies and shifting current expenses to an earlier period.
- Failing to write down or write off impaired assets.
- Reducing asset reserves.

WorldCom capitalized its line costs that provided telecommunications capacity on other companies' systems rather than expense those costs as they were incurred. The effects on reported income were dramatic and illustrate how earnings management techniques can lead to reporting earnings when a loss has actually occurred. The following table illustrates just how that was done.

Form Filed with the Commission	Reported Line Cost Expenses	Reported Income (before Taxes and Minority Interests)	Actual Line Cost Expenses	Actual Income (before Taxes and Minority Interests)
10-Q, 3rd Q. 2000	$ 3.867 billion	$1.736 billion	$ 4.695 billion	$ 908 million
10-K, 2000	$15.462 billion	$7.568 billion	$16.697 billion	$6.333 billion
10-Q, 1st Q. 2001	$ 4.108 billion	$ 988 million	$ 4.879 billion	$ 217 million
10-Q, 2nd Q. 2001	$ 3.73 billion	$ 159 million	$ 4.29 billion	$ 401 million **loss**
10-Q, 3rd Q. 2001	$ 3.745 billion	$ 845 million	$ 4.488 billion	$ 102 million
10-K, 2001	$14.739 billion	$2.393 billion	$17.754 billion	$ 622 million **loss**
10-Q, 1st Q. 2002	$ 3.479 billion	$ 240 million	$ 4.297 billion	$ 578 million **loss**

5. Failing to Record or Improperly Reducing Liabilities

The liability account is often used to manipulate earnings because when liabilities that should be recorded are not, the expenses also are understated. When liabilities are reduced improperly, the same effect on expenses occurs. The result is to overstate earnings. Some examples include:

- Failing to record expenses and related liabilities when future obligations remain.
- Releasing questionable reserves (cookie-jar reserves) into income.
- Recording revenue when cash is received, even though future obligations remain.

The recording of discretionary accruals that was previously discussed is one application of the technique. The Lucent Technologies example discussed later in this chapter illustrates a variety of these techniques.

6. Shifting Current Revenue to a Later Period

Some companies act to delay the recording of revenue when the amount is relatively high in a given year. In a sense, this action sets up a "rainy day" reserve that can be used to restore earnings in low-earnings years. One way to accomplish this is to create a cookie-jar reserve with the excess revenues and release it back into the income stream at a later date, when it can do more good for the bottom line. Another method is through the use of deferred revenue. Examples include:

- Deliberately overstating the allowance for uncollectible accounts, thereby understating current revenue, and adjusting the allowance downward in future years to increase revenue.

- Deferring revenue recognition on a year-end service transaction that was completed by December 31 and then transferring it to earned revenue in subsequent years.

- Deliberately overstating the estimated sales returns account and adjusting it downward in future years.

The SEC went after W. R. Grace & Co. for manipulating earnings to meet Wall Street's expectations. The Commission alleged that senior Grace executives deferred reporting some 1991 and 1992 income from National Medical Care, then the main Grace health-care unit. Grace assigned $10 million to $20 million of this unexpected profit to "corporate reserves," which it then used to increase the reported earnings of both the health-care unit and the company between 1993 and 1995, the SEC said.[66]

The actual earnings of the unit and its parent company sometimes fell short of analysts' expectations during this period, the SEC alleged. Thus, Grace misled shareholders by reporting results buttressed by the reserves. The only problem was that Grace deferring reporting income by increasing or establishing reserves was not in conformity with GAAP. In fact, it smacks of using secret reserves to achieve a "cookie-jar reserve" effect.

7. Shifting Future Expenses to the Current Period as a Special Charge

A company might choose to accelerate discretionary expenses, such as repairs and maintenance, into the current period if the current year's revenue is relatively high in relation to expected future revenue or if future expenses are expected to be relatively high. The motivation to shift future expenses to the current period might be to smooth net income over time. This may not be illegal in this instance but certainly illustrates operating earnings management. The decision to delay needed repairs raises several ethical issues with respect to the company's operating decisions because it creates a risk that assets such as machinery and equipment may break down prematurely. The ethical issues and consequences are: (1) the quality of product may suffer, leading to extra quality control and rework costs; (2) production slows and fails to meet deadlines, thereby risking customer goodwill; and (3) the costs to repair the machines can be greater than they would have been had maintenance been completed on a timely basis. Imagine, for example, that you fail to change the oil in your car on a regular basis. The result may be serious, costly repairs to the engine later on.

Red Flags of Earnings Management

Auditors need to be attuned to the red flags that fraud may exist because of overly aggressive accounting and outright manipulation of earnings. The following are some of the signs that trouble may lie ahead:

- Growth in the market share that seems unbelievable.
- Frequent acquisitions of businesses.
- Management growth strategy and emphasis on earnings and/or EPS.
- Reliance on income sources other than core business.
- One-time sources of income.
- Growth in revenue that doesn't line up well with receivables or inventory.
- Unexpected increase in accounts receivable.
- Slowdown of inventory turnover.
- Reduction in reserves.
- Not reserving for possible future losses.
- Reduction in discretionary costs at year-end (i.e., advertising; R&D).

- Unusual increase in borrowings; short-term borrowing at year-end.

- Extension of trade payables longer than normal credit.

- Change in members of top management, especially the CFO.

- Change in auditors.

- Changes in accounting policies toward more liberal applications.

Sometimes, a forensic accountant is brought into a case to find suspected fraudulent activity or can be called in after the fraud has been detected to assess the magnitude of the fraudulent activity. These days we believe audit firms should have at least one forensic accountant on each audit to help identify the signs that something is amiss and prevent earnings management from getting started and stopping it in its track once under way.

Examples of Shenanigans

In this section, we describe the financial shenanigans that occurred at Xerox, Lucent, and Enron. We chose these companies because the techniques used to manage earnings vary from the relatively simple (recording revenue too soon) to the more exotic (using special-purpose entities to hide debt and inflate earnings).

The Case of Xerox

Motivation for Fraudulent Scheme of Top Management

On June 3, 2003, the SEC filed a civil fraud injunctive action in the U.S. District Court for the Southern District of New York charging six former senior executives of Xerox Corporation, including its former CEOs Paul Allaire and G. Richard Thoman and its former CFO Barry D. Romeril, with securities fraud and aiding and abetting Xerox's violations of the reporting, books and records, and internal control provisions of the federal securities laws. The complaint charged the former executives with engaging in a fraudulent scheme that lasted from 1997 to 2000 and misled investors about Xerox's earnings to "polish its reputation on Wall Street and to boost the company's stock price."[67]

The quality of the financial reports came into question as Xerox failed to disclose GAAP violations that led to acceleration in the recognition of approximately $3 billion in equipment revenues and an increase in pretax earnings by approximately $1.4 billion in Xerox's 1997–2000 financial results. The executives agreed to pay over $22 million in penalties, disgorgement, and interest without admitting or denying the SEC's allegations.

The tone at the top was one that viewed business success with meeting short-term earnings targets. Romeril directed or allowed lower-ranking defendants in Xerox's financial department to make accounting adjustments to results reported from operating divisions to accelerate revenues and increase earnings. These individuals used accounting methods to meet earnings goals and predictions of outside securities analysts. Allaire and Thoman then announced these results to the public through meetings with analysts and in communications to shareholders, celebrating that Xerox was enjoying substantially greater earnings growth than the true operating results warranted.

A description of two selected fraudulent accounting devices follows.

Fraudulent Lease Accounting

Xerox sold copiers and other office equipment to its customers for cash, but it more frequently entered into long-term lease agreements in which customers paid a single negotiated monthly fee in return for the equipment, service, supplies, and financing. Xerox referred to these arrangements as "bundled leases." We previously discussed the revenue recognition issues as "multiple deliverables."

The leases met the criteria under *SFAS 13* to be accounted for as "sales-type" leases, whereby the fair value of the equipment leased would be recognized as income in the period the lease is delivered, less any residual value the equipment was expected to retain once the lease expired. GAAP permits the financing revenue portion of the lease to be recognized only as it is earned over the life of the lease. *SFAS 13* also specifies that the portion of the lease payments that represents the fee for repair services and copier supplies be prorated over the term of the lease, matching it against the financing income.

Until the mid-1990s, Xerox followed satisfactory procedures for revenue recognition. However, the company encountered growing copier sales competition around the world and perceived a need to continue reporting record earnings. The management told KPMG that it was no longer able to reasonably assign a fair value to the equipment as it had in the past. The company abandoned the value determinations made at the lease inception for public financial reporting purposes but not for internal operating purposes and substituted a formula that management could manipulate at will. Xerox did not test the value determinations to assess the reliability of the original method or if the new method did a better job of accurately reflecting the fair value of copier equipment.[68]

Xerox's "topside" lease accounting devices consistently increased the amount of lease revenues that Xerox recognized at the inception of the lease and reduced the amount it recognized over the life of the lease. One method was called *return on equity (ROE),* which pulled forward a portion of finance income and recognized it immediately as equipment revenue. The second, called *margin normalization,* pulled forward a portion of service income and recognized it immediately as equipment revenue. These income acceleration methods did not comply with GAAP because there was no matching of revenue with the period during which (1) financing was provided, (2) copier supplies were provided, and (3) repairs were made to the leased equipment.

"Cushion" Reserves

From 1997 through 2000, Xerox violated GAAP through the use of approximately $496 million of reserves to close the gap between actual results and earnings targets. Xerox had created reserves through charges to income prior to 1997. These cookie-jar reserves were released into income to make the numbers look better than they really were. The result was a smoothing of net income over time. This practice violated *SFAS 5, Accounting for Contingencies,* which allows a company to establish reserves only for identifiable, probable, and estimable risks and precludes the use of reserves, including excess reserves, for general or unknown business risks because they do not meet the accrual requirements of *SFAS 5.*

Sanctions by the SEC on KPMG

The SEC issued a cease-and-desist order against KPMG on April 19, 2005, for its role in auditing the financial statements of Xerox from 1997 through 2000. *AAER 2234* details KPMG's consent to institute a variety of quality control measures, which included providing oversight of engagement partner changes of audit personnel and related independence issues.[69]

On February 22, 2006, the SEC announced that all four remaining KPMG staff members in the commission's action in connection with the $1.2 billion fraudulent earnings manipulation scheme by Xerox from 1997 through 2000 had agreed to settle the charges against them. Three KPMG partners agreed to permanent injunctions, payment of $400,000 in penalties, and suspensions from practice before the commission. Four partners were charged with filing materially false and misleading financial statements with the SEC and aiding and abetting Xerox's filing of false financial reports. The SEC charged that the partners knew or should have known about improper "topside adjustments" that resulted in $3 billion of the restated revenues and $1.2 billion of the restated earnings.[70]

The concurring review partner on the audit engagement team was cited because the adjustments enabled Xerox to change the allocations of revenues that it received from leasing photocopiers and other types of office equipment. The partner agreed to a censure from the SEC for failing to exercise due care and professional skepticism and adhere to GAAS.

On April 20, 2005, KPMG settled with the SEC over the financial fraud at Xerox, agreeing to pay $10 million in penalties, in addition to disgorging nearly $10 million in audit fees and paying another $2.7 million in interest.

The Case of Lucent Technologies

On May 20, 2004, the SEC charged Lucent Technologies, Inc., with securities fraud and violations of the reporting, books and records, and internal control provisions of the federal securities laws. The commission also charged current and former Lucent officers, executives, and employees with securities fraud and aiding and abetting Lucent's violations of federal securities laws. The SEC complaint alleged that Lucent fraudulently and improperly recognized approximately $1.148 billion of revenue and $470 million in pretax income during the fiscal year 2000.

The Lucent case is typical of the frauds that occurred in the late 1990s and early 2000s. The company's accounting techniques violated GAAP and were motivated by its drive to realize revenue, meet internal sales targets, and obtain sales bonuses. The internal controls were either violated or circumvented by top management. The board of directors and audit committee were either not involved or turned away from their obligations.

According to *AAER 2016,* Lucent officers improperly granted and/or failed to disclose various side agreements, credits, and other incentives (extracontractual commitments) made to induce Lucent's customers to purchase the company's products. The premature recognition of revenue occurred by "selling" $135 million in software to a customer that could choose from a software pool by September 29, 2001, and Lucent recognized $135 million in revenue in its fiscal year ending September 30, 2000. The parties reached an agreement to document separately additional elements of the software pool transaction that would give the customer more value in the form of side agreements. Top management postdated three letters documenting the side agreements with fictitious dates in October 2000. The effect of the postdated letters was to create the appearance that the side agreements were reached after September 30, 2000, and were not connected to the software pool agreement.[71] The accounting for these transactions enabled Lucent to manage earnings in a way that smoothed net income over time.

Lucent's story as a separate entity began in April 1996, when AT&T spun off the company. By 1999, operating income had reached $5.4 billion, tripling in two years. Net income had grown more than tenfold during that time period. These remarkable increases over a relatively short period of time should have raised a red flag for KPMG, but it did not. Exhibits 7.3 and 7.4 present the comparative amounts during the two-year period ended September 30, 1999.[72]

EXHIBIT 7.3 Lucent Technologies, Inc.: Comparative Sales and Income

| Item | Sales and Income Amounts (in billions) | | |
	September 1999	September 1998	September 1997
Sales	$48.3	$31.8	$27.6
Operating income	5.4	2.6	1.6
Net income	4.8	1.0	0.4

EXHIBIT 7.4   Lucent Technologies, Inc.: Percentage Change in Sales and Income

	Percentage Changes in Sales and Income Amounts	
	September 1998 to September 1999	**September 1997 to September 1998**
Sales	52%	15%
Operating income	104	63
Net income	380	150

Schilit points out that Lucent's stock price increased from a low of about $14 per share on January 1, 1997, to a high of about $78 by September 1999. The stock price began to decline after that, to a low of about $7 per share on January 1, 2002, as the fraud unfolded.

Exhibit 7.5 takes Lucent's earnings management techniques and classifies them into Schilit's financial shenanigan categories.

EXHIBIT 7.5   Lucent Technologies, Inc.: Financial Shenanigans

Technique	Description	Shenanigan Number
Recorded revenue too soon	Lucent restated year 2000 earnings, removing $679 million of improperly included revenue.	No. 1
Boosted income with one-time gains	During fiscal 1998, Lucent recorded $558 million of pension income—over 50% of earnings for the year.	No. 3
Failed to write down impaired assets	Lucent reduced the allowance for doubtful accounts and released the previous reserves despite an increase in receivables of 32%.	No. 4
Shifted current expenses to a later period	Lucent reduced the allowance for inventory obsolescence although the inventory balance increased.	No. 4
Reduced liabilities by changing accounting assumptions	Lucent modified its accounting approach and assumptions for pensions.	No. 5
Released reserves into income	Lucent released $100 million of a previously recorded restructuring reserve, boosting operating income.	No. 5
Created new reserves from 10 acquisitions	Lucent wrote off $2.4 billion (58% of the cumulative purchase price) as an in-process R&D. This new reserve could be released into earnings later.	No. 7

Accounting for Revenue in the Cloud

On February 21, 2017, Oracle settled a lawsuit from a high-ranking accountant who claimed she was fired for threatening to blow the whistle on its illegal accounting practices. Former senior finance manager Svetlana Blackburn sued Oracle in June 2016, claiming it fired her for refusing to create false financial reports that inflated the company's revenue.

In her original complaint, Blackburn said she was ordered to add millions of dollars in unsupported revenue to financial reports for Oracle's cloud services, despite lack of billings to support those numbers. The company sought to inflate its cloud revenue with accruals not supported by evidence that those numbers would actually ever roll in. After refusing to go along with the fraud and trying to report the improprieties to superiors, Blackburn was fired. The company said she was fired due to "ongoing performance issues," not because she threatened to expose the company's allegedly fraudulent accounting practices. The settlement out of court puts the lawsuit to bed but not the difficulties in accounting for cloud revenue.

Pat Walravens, an analyst at JMP Securities stated that accounting for cloud software "can get very complex and requires judgment calls and estimates which a third party might disagree with upon further review." Accountants and analysts say that classifying software sales as cloud or traditional remains something of an art. There is some subjectivity in "is it cloud, is it traditional software?" said Stave Biskie, an auditor and co-founder of compliance consultancy High Water Advisors. The most nebulous part of cloud accounting concerns situations where the customer buys a product that can be used partly in the cloud and partly on its own hardware. GAAP states that, in cases when use is mixed, companies should allocate the revenue between traditional, or licensed software, and cloud, or hosted software. Determining the fair value of the software license and hosting services may require the use of estimates, according to the rules. Management should consider all relevant information, such as information from the negotiation process with the vendor, in estimating the fair value of the license. That's the gray area. How can the cloud company determine how much a user uses its own hardware? Is it casual use or frequent use?[73]

Analysts report that various tricks can be used by a vendor trying to inflate its cloud figures, including:

- Lump on-premise and cloud figures together and then pretend it's all cloud;
- Give huge credit to customers moving their on-premise license value to the cloud and consider it as booked cloud sales;
- Give a cloud product for free and then extrapolate its sales value to other modules; and
- Sell a cloud subscription for a pilot population but book it as if it were for the whole company headcount.

Oracle claimed in 2015 that it made $1.5 billion from its cloud offerings. Dan Woods, chief technology officer and editor of CITO Research, claims that Oracle's cloud revenue numbers are bogus. Specifically, Woods claims that Oracle uses mechanisms such as "cloud credits" to move client revenue from traditional Oracle services to cloud computing without really achieving adoption. Frank Scavo, president of Computer Economics, said "As Oracle's traditional business in software licenses is under pressure, it needs to quickly ramp up cloud subscriptions to make up the difference. It's much easier to buy those customers than it is to grow them organically with cloud apps newly developed internally."[74] Exhibit 7.6 summarizes the FASB standards on cloud computing arrangements.

The standard provides some guidance on how to interpret the term "significant penalty." The ability to take delivery of the underlying software without significant cost and to use that software separately without a significant reduction in value would indicate there is not a significant penalty. Determining whether taking possession of the software will result in significant penalty will require judgment.

Arrangements that do not meet both of the criteria are considered service contracts, and separate accounting for a license will not be permitted. Arrangements that meet the criteria are considered multiple-element arrangements to purchase both a software license and a service of hosting the software. Existing guidance on internal-use software is applied to the purchased license.

Costs incurred by a customer in a CCA that includes a software license should be allocated between the license and hosting elements. The consideration should be allocated based on the relative fair value of each element. Determining the fair value of the software license and hosting service may require the use

EXHIBIT 7.6   Cloud Computing Revenue Recognition[75]

FASB issued Accounting Standards Update 2015-05, *Customer's Accounting for Fees Paid in a Cloud Computing Arrangement*, as part of its simplification initiative to reduce the diversity in practice and to reduce the costs and complexity of assessing fees paid in a cloud computing arrangement (CCA). While the new standard does not provide explicit guidance on how to account for fees paid in a CCA, it does provide guidance on which existing accounting model should be applied.

For purposes of applying the new guidance, a CCA includes software-as-a-service (SaaS) and SaaS-type services. "Hosting" refers to situations in which the end user does not take possession of the software; instead, the software resides on the vendor's or a third party's hardware, and the customer accesses the software remotely.

Under the new standard, fees paid by a customer in a CCA will be within the scope of the internal-use software guidance if both of the following criteria are met:

- The customer has the contractual right to take possession of the software at any time during the CCA period without significant penalty.
- It is feasible for the customer to run the software on its own hardware (or to contract with another party to host the software).

of estimates. Management should consider all relevant information, such as information from the negotiation process with the vendor, in estimating the fair value of the license. More observable inputs might be available to estimate the fair value of the hosting element.

The Story of Enron

The uniqueness of the decisions and manipulations at Enron and its link to the passage of SOX warrants a detailed discussion. The background details on the company and its shenanigans appears in **Exhibit 7.7**.

EXHIBIT 7.7   Enron Accounting Fraud

In the Beginning

Enron was created in 1985 through Omaha-based InterNorth Inc.'s takeover of Houston Natural Gas Corporation. InterNorth paid a huge premium for Houston Natural Gas, creating $5 million in debt. The company's debt payments of $50 million a month quickly led to the selloff of billions of dollars' worth of assets. Its debt load was so high that it forced the company into financing projects with borrowings that were kept off the balance sheet.

Former Enron CEO Jeff Skilling suggested that Enron's problems were due to a fluid market for natural gas; the industry needed long-term supply contracts. But prices were volatile, and contracts were available only for 30-day spot deals. Producers were unwilling to commit to the long term, always believing the price could go up.

Skilling's "Gas Bank" Idea

Enron needed to find a way to bridge the gap between what the producers and big gas users wanted. Skilling discussed ways to pool the investments in gas-supply contracts and then sell long-term deals to utilities through a Gas Bank. The Gas Bank called for Enron to write long-term contracts that enabled it to start accounting for those contracts differently. Traditionally, accounting would book revenue from a long-term contract when it came in. But Skilling wanted Enron to book all anticipated revenue immediately, as if it was writing up a marketable security. The technique lends itself to earnings management because of the subjectivity involved in estimating future market value.

(Continued)

Counting all expected profits immediately meant a huge earnings kick for a company that was getting deeply in debt. But it also put Enron on a treadmill: To keep growing, it would have to book bigger and bigger deals every quarter. The result was to shift focus from developing economically sound partnerships to doing deals at all costs.

The marketplace didn't seem to like the Enron deals. The initial Gas Bank plan hadn't persuaded gas producers to sell Enron their reserves. To entice the producers, the company needed to offer them money up-front for gas that would be delivered later. The problem was where to get the cash.

Fastow's Special-Purpose Entities

In 1991, to revitalize the Gas Bank, Enron's CFO, Andy Fastow, began creating a number of partnerships. The first series of deals was called Cactus. The Cactus ventures eventually took in money from banks and gave it to energy producers in return for a portion of their existing gas reserves. That gave the producers money up-front and Enron gas over time.

Fastow worked to structure ventures that met the conditions under GAAP to keep the partnership activities off Enron's books and on the separate books of the partnership. To do so, the equity financing of the partnership venture had to include a minimum of 3% outside ownership. Control was not established through traditional means, which was the ownership of a majority of voting equity and combining of the partnership entity into the sponsoring organization (Enron), as is done with parent and subsidiary entities in a consolidation. Instead, the independent third parties were required to have a controlling and substantial interest in the entity. Control was established by the third-party investors exercising management rights over the entity's operations. There were a lot of "Monday morning quarterbacks" in the accounting profession who questioned the economic logic of attributing even the possibility of control to those who owned only 3% of the capital.

Bethany McLean and Peter Elkind are two *Fortune* magazine reporters credited with prompting the inquiries and investigations that brought down the Enron house of cards. McLean had written a story posing the simple question: "How, exactly, does Enron make its money?" Well, in the go-go years of the 1990s, all too often no one asked these kinds of questions (or, perhaps, did not want to know the answers).

According to McLean and Elkind, a small group of investors were pulled together, known internally as the Friends of Enron. When Enron needed the 3% of outside ownership, it turned to the friends. However, these business associates and friends of Fastow and others were independent only in a technical sense. Though they made money on their investment, they didn't control the entities or the assets within them. "This, of course, was precisely the point," McLean and Elkind say.[79]

The 3% investments triggered a "special-purpose vehicle or special-purpose entity (SPE)." The advantage of the independent partnership relationship was that the SPE borrowed money from banks and other financial institutions that were willing to loan money to it with an obligation to repay the debt. The SPE enabled Enron to keep debt off its books while benefiting from the transfer and use of the cash borrowed by the SPE. The money borrowed by the SPE was often "transferred" to Enron in a sale of an operating asset no longer needed by Enron. The sale transaction typically led to a recorded gain because the cash proceeds exceeded the book value of the asset sold. The result was increased cash flow and liquidity and inflated earnings. The uniqueness of the transactions engaged in by Enron was that they initially didn't violate GAAP. Instead, Enron took advantage of the rules to engineer transactions that enabled it to achieve its goals for enhanced liquidity and profitability.

The Growth of Special-Purpose Entities

Eventually, Enron would grow addicted to these arrangements because they hid debt. Not only did the company turn to its "friends," but, increasingly, it had to borrow from banks and financial institutions that it did business with. These entities did not want to turn down a company like Enron, which was, at its peak, the seventh largest corporation in the United States. But Enron let the risk-shifting feature of the partnerships lapse, thus negating their conformity to GAAP. Over time, the financial institutions that were involved in providing the 3% for the SPEs became skeptical of the ability of the SPEs to repay the interest when due. These institutions asked Enron to relieve the risk of the SPEs' failure to repay the investments. Later, partnership deals were backed by promises of Enron stock. Thus, if something went wrong, Enron would be left holding the bag. Therefore, there was no true transfer of economic risk to the SPE, and, according to GAAP, the SPE should have been consolidated into Enron's financial statements.

The Culture at Enron

The tension in the workplace grew with employees working later and later—first until 6 p.m. and then 11 p.m. and sometimes even into the next morning. Part of the pressure resulted from Skilling's new employee-evaluation policy. Workers called it "rank and yank." Employees were evaluated in groups, with each person rated on a scale of 1 to 5. The goal was to remove the bottom 15% of each group every year.

Ultimately, the system was seen as a tool for managers to reward loyalists and punish dissenters. It was seen as a cutthroat system and encouraged a "yes" culture, in which employees were reluctant to question their bosses—a fear that many would later come to regret.

Let the Force Be With You

In late 1997, Enron entered a number of partnerships to improperly inflate earnings and hide debt. Enron created Chewco, named after the *Star Wars* character Chewbacca, to buy out its partner in another venture called JEDI, which was legally kept off the books. For JEDI to remain off the balance sheet, however, Chewco had to meet certain accounting requirements. But Enron skirted the already-weak rules required to keep Chewco off its books. JEDI helped overstate Enron's profits by $405 million and understate debt by $2.6 billion.

Because Enron needed to close the deal by year's end, Chewco was a rush job. Enron's executive committee presented the Chewco proposal to the board of directors on November 5. But CFO Fastow left out a few key details. He maintained that Chewco was not affiliated with Enron, but failed to mention that there was virtually no outside ownership in it. Nor did he reveal that one of his protégés, Michael Kopper, was managing the partnership. Indirectly (if not directly), Fastow would control the partnership through Kopper. Enron had a code of ethics that prohibited an officer from becoming involved with another entity that did business with Enron. Involvement by Fastow in these related-party entities was forbidden by the code. Nevertheless, the board of directors waived that requirement so Fastow could become involved with Chewco.

The board approved the deal even though Enron's law firm Vinson & Elkins prepared the requisite documents so quickly that very few people actually read it before approving it. Arthur Andersen, the firm that both audited Enron and did significant internal audit work for the company (pre-SOX), claimed that Enron withheld critical information. The firm billed the company only $80,000 for its review of the transaction, indicating a cursory review at best. Chewco, Fastow's involvement, the board approval, and a rapid approval process all were allowed because of a lack of internal controls. The *Star Wars* transactions were the beginning of the end for Enron. Chewco was inappropriately treated as a separate entity. Other SPE transactions eventually led to Enron's guaranteeing the debt of the SPE, using its stock as collateral. When Enron finally collapsed, its off-balance-sheet financing stood at an estimated $17 billion.

Enron Just Keeps on Going

The greatest pressures were in Fastow's finance group. In 1999, he constructed two partnerships called LJM Cayman and LJM2 that readily passed through the board, the lawyers, and the accountants. They were followed by four more, known as the Raptors. They did it once, it worked, and then they did it again. It didn't take long to blur the lines between what was legal and what was not. When asked by a student during an interview for a position with Enron what he did at the company, one Enron employee in the finance group answered by saying, "I remove numbers from our balance sheet and inflate earnings."

As Enron pushed into new directions—wind power, water, high-speed Internet, paper, metals, data storage, advertising, etc.—it became a different company almost every quarter. Entrepreneurship was encouraged; innovation was the mantra. The quarter-by-quarter scramble to post ever-better numbers became all-consuming. Enron traders were encouraged to use "prudence reserves"—to essentially put aside some revenue until another quarter

(Continued)

when it might be needed. Long-term energy contracts were evaluated using an adjustable curve to forecast energy prices. When a quarter looked tight, analysts were told to simply adjust the curve in Enron's favor.

Executive Compensation

Enron's goal of setting its executive pay in the 75th percentile of its peer group—including companies like Duke Energy, Dynegy, and PG&E, which it compared itself with to assess overall corporate performance—was easily exceeded. In 2000, Enron exceeded the peer group average base salary by 51%. In bonus payments, it outdistanced its peers by 383%. The stock options granted in 2000—valued at the time at $86.5 million—exceeded the number granted by peers by 484%. Top management became accustomed to the large pay-outs, and the desire for more became a part of the culture of greed at Enron.

While Enron was the first player into the new energy market, enabling it to score huge gains, competitors caught on over time, and profit margins shrank. Skilling began looking for new pastures, and, in 1996, he set his sights on electricity. Enron would do for power what it had done for natural gas. The push into electricity only added to the pressures mounting inside Enron. Earlier in 1996, Ken Lay, Enron's CEO before Skilling took over, had predicted that the company's profits would double by 2000. This was a statement that would come back to haunt Lay in his civil trial in 2006, which alleged that he hyped Enron's stock to keep funds flowing, even though he knew the company was coming apart at the seams.

Lay pushed on as if nothing was wrong. Enron instituted a stock-option plan that promised to double employee salaries after eight years. Fresh off a $2.1 billion takeover of Portland General Corporation, an electric utility, Lay said his goal was nothing less than to make Enron the "world's greatest energy company."

Growth at all costs was the mantra at Enron. It encouraged executives to buy into this philosophy by giving out stock options that would provide cash over time and added the sweetener that if profits and the stock price went up enough, the schedule for those options would be sharply accelerated. It provided the incentive to find ways of increasing profits and improving stock price. It looked the other way when questions about ethics came up. Clearly, Enron and its officers pursued their self-interests to the detriment of all other interests and created a culture of greed. The environment at Enron reminds us of the famous quote by Gordon Gekko in the 1987 movie *Wall Street:* "Greed is good. Greed captures the essence of the evolutionary spirit."

Congressional Investigation and Skilling's Departure

In 2000, Skilling was granted 867,880 options to buy shares, in addition to his salary and bonus that totaled $6.45 million. In that year, he exercised and sold over 1.1 million shares from options he received from prior years, and he pocketed $62.48 million. Skilling testified before Congress that he did not dump Enron shares as he told others to buy because he knew or suspected that the company was in financial trouble. Skilling's holdings of Enron shares increased because his number of options increased. Even under Enron's option plan, in which options vested fully in three years (an unusually quick rate), Skilling wound up holding many Enron shares that he couldn't legally sell.

Lay and Skilling used as their defense in the 2006 civil trial that Enron was a successful company brought down by a crisis of confidence in the market. The government contended that Enron appeared successful but actually hid its failures through dubious, even criminal, accounting tricks. In fact, Enron by most measures wasn't particularly profitable—a fact obscured by its share price until late in its history. But there was one area in which it succeeded like few others: executive compensation.

As the stock market began to decline in the late 1990s, Enron's stock followed the downward trend. The never-ending number of deals, even as business slowed, gave Wall Street pause. By April 2001, concerns mounted whether the company was disclosing financial information from its off-balance-sheet financing transactions adequately.

The pressure continued both internally and externally from a slowing economy, competition from other entities that were catching on to Enron's gimmicks, and stock market declines. Differences of opinion exist as to why he made the decision, but on August 14, 2001, Skilling, who just six months prior had been named the CEO of Enron, resigned. He gave as his public reason the ever-popular "I need to spend more time with my family."

The Final Days

In November 2001, Enron announced it had overstated earnings by $586 million since 1997. In December 2001, Enron made the largest bankruptcy filing ever at that time. By January 2002, the U.S. Department of Justice (DOJ) confirmed an investigation of Enron. The very next day, Andersen admitted to shredding documents related to its audit of Enron, an act of obstructing justice that would doom the firm following a DOJ lawsuit. It hardly mattered what the outcome of the lawsuit would be; Enron's clients started to abandon the firm in droves after the announcement of the lawsuit. Ultimately, the jury decided that the firm had obstructed justice, a decision that would be overturned later due to a technicality.

The Lay-Skilling Criminal Trial

Following the unanimous jury verdict on May 26, 2006, that found both Lay and Skilling guilty of fraud and conspiracy, Lay was quoted as saying, "Certainly we're surprised," and Skilling commented, "I think it's more appropriate to say we're shocked. This is not the outcome we expected."[80]

Skilling was convicted of 19 counts of fraud, conspiracy, and insider trading. Lay was convicted on 6 counts in the joint trial and four charges of bank fraud and making false statements to banks in a separate nonjury trial before U.S. District Judge Sam Lake related to Lay's personal finances. The sentencing for Lay and Skilling in the case, somewhat ironically, was set for September 11, 2006. Skilling faced a maximum of 185 years in prison. For Lay, the fraud and conspiracy convictions carried a combined maximum punishment of 45 years. The bank fraud case added 120 years, 30 years for each of the four counts. However, Ken Lay passed away just weeks after the verdict.

Skilling's Efforts to Overturn the Verdict

On October 23, 2006, Skilling was sentenced to 24 years and 4 months in prison, and fined $45 million. Skilling has fought to overturn that sentence almost from the beginning. On June 21, 2013, it was announced by the U.S. Department of Justice that Skilling will be freed 10 years early. This means he would spend a total of 14 years in jail and get release in 2020. Skilling is eligible for parole in 2017.

Below we discuss the accounting techniques used by Enron to cook the books. It's important to remember that Enron shares were worth $90.75 at their peak in August 2000 and dropped to $0.67 in January 2002. When everything was said and done, shareholders lost $64 billion. The Enron fraud caused more harm than any other and is remembered as the daddy of all frauds.

The Enron fraud was relatively simple. The company structured financial transactions in such a way to keep partnerships that were formed to borrow funds on behalf of Enron off Enron's books. These so-called "off-balance-sheet entities" (i.e., special-purpose entity/SPE) grew in size and number over the years. For many years, Enron was successful in setting them up and borrowing funds from financial institutions through the SPEs, after which Enron would concoct a transaction with these entities to take under-performing assets from Enron in return for the cash from the borrowing. Enron padded their cash account without carrying the debt and even recorded gains on some of the transactions.

Exhibit 7.8 depicts the typical transaction between Enron and the SPE.

Sherron Watkins' Role

One Enron executive tried to do the right thing—Sherron Watkins. Watkins was dubious, and she sent an anonymous letter to Ken Lay, the chair of the board of directors, warning him of an impending scandal. It said in part, "Has Enron become a risky place to work? For those of us who didn't get rich over the last few years, can we afford to stay?" She described in detail problems with Enron's partnerships, problems that the letter claimed would cause huge financial upheavals at the company in as little as a year. "I am

EXHIBIT 7.8 Enron Corporation's SPEs

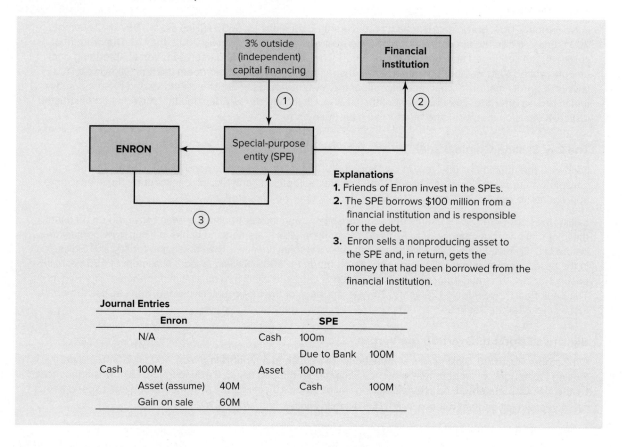

Explanations
1. Friends of Enron invest in the SPEs.
2. The SPE borrows $100 million from a financial institution and is responsible for the debt.
3. Enron sells a nonproducing asset to the SPE and, in return, gets the money that had been borrowed from the financial institution.

Journal Entries

Enron			SPE		
N/A			Cash	100m	
			Due to Bank		100M
Cash	100M		Asset	100m	
Asset (assume)	40M		Cash		100M
Gain on sale	60M				

incredibly nervous that we will implode in a wave of accounting scandals," Watkins wrote. "Skilling is resigning for 'personal reasons,' but I think he wasn't having fun, looked down the road, and knew this stuff was unfixable and would rather abandon ship now than resign in shame in two years."[76]

Lay took a copy of the letter to James V. Derrick Jr., Enron's general counsel, who agreed that it needed to be investigated. They decided to assign the task to Vinson & Elkins—which had helped prepare some of the legal documents for some of the partnerships. Enron wanted answers fast, seemingly regardless of due diligence, and the company instructed the outside lawyers not to spend time examining the accounting treatment recommended by Arthur Andersen—although that was at the heart of the letter's warnings.

Powers Committee Report

Vinson & Elkins began its investigation. Even while it investigated Andy Fastow's role as Enron CFO and managing partner of SPEs, the conflicts mounted. Michael Kopper, another Enron employee and managing partner of an SPE, sold his Chewco assets to Enron to deflect criticisms of Fastow's role. Kopper made a profit on the sale and then insisted that Enron cover the $2.6 million tax liability from the sale. The Powers Committee, formed by the audit committee to investigate the failure of Enron, concluded on this matter that "there is credible evidence that Fastow authorized Enron's payment to Chewco," adding that the payment—done against the explicit instructions of Enron's general counsel—was "one of the most serious issues we identified in connection with the Chewco buyout."[77]

Three days after beginning their investigation, the Vinson & Elkins lawyers investigating Watkins's warnings reported their findings to Lay and Derrick that there was no reason for concern. Everything in Fastow's operation seemed to be on the level. They promised a written report in a matter of weeks. By then, though, it would be too late.

Enron: A Review of Important Accounting Issues

The fraud at Enron was caused by a variety of factors, including these:

- Improperly failing to consolidate the results of an SPE (Chewco) with Enron. Consolidation was warranted because Chewco lacked the necessary independence from Enron's management because Andy Fastow had direct or indirect control over it.

- Failing to disclose adequately the related-party relationship between Enron and the SPEs, especially those that were independent of the company under GAAP.

- Overstating earnings from using mark-to-market accounting for investments in long-term gas contracts that relied on estimates of future market value to record unrealized gains.

The quality of financial reports was poor for the following reasons:

- Failure to disclose adequately the related-party transactions made it impossible for investors and creditors to know the full extent of these transactions, and loans were made to Enron based on vastly understated debt.

- The sale of assets to SPEs in return for the transfer of borrowed funds from the SPE, with the subsequent recording of a gain, masked Enron's true earnings and made it appear that the company was doing better than it really was.

- The use of reserves and failure to explain the basis for creation made it impossible to judge the acceptability of these transactions.

- The failure to disclose Fastow's dual role with the SPEs and as CFO of Enron made it impossible for investors and creditors to gain the information they had an ethical right to know in order to evaluate the legitimacy of off-balance-sheet transactions and their effect on the financial statements.

Enron managed earnings through the following techniques (Schilit's shenanigan numbers are indicated in parentheses):

- Used reserves to increase earnings when reported amounts were too low (#5).

- Used mark-to-market estimates to inflate earnings in violation of GAAP (#1).

- Selected which operating assets to "sell" to the SPEs, thereby affecting the amount of the gain on transfer and earnings effect (#3).

The lack of strong controls contributed to the fraud as evidenced by the following:

- Top management overrode or ignored internal controls in the approval process for Chewco, the LJM SPEs, and the Raptors.

- Oversight by the board of directors was either negligent, as was the case with the waiving of the ethics code for Fastow, or nonexistent.

- A culture was established to make the deals at any cost, thereby diluting the due diligence process that should have raised red flags on some of the transactions.

- A culture of fear was created within Enron with its "rank or yank" policy and cutthroat competition.

FASB Rules on SPEs

While it may seem that the GAAP rules on SPEs are naïve, there are legitimate reasons for establishing the concept that an entity could isolate a business operation or some corporate assets. The idea was to control risk in a project such as investing in a new oil refinery. By following the rules to set up an SPE, an oil company could keep the large amount of debt off the books while using the funds from the SPE to construct the refinery. The off-balance-sheet effect helps control risk if the project fails. The original motivation by FASB was to establish a mechanism to encourage companies to invest in needed assets while keeping the related debt off their books.

The "creativity" of Andy Fastow was in using a less-well-known technique under GAAP to satisfy Enron's unique needs. Enron became the leader of structured transactions designed to meet specific goals rather than to present accurately its financial position and the results of its operations. These are nothing more than elaborate attempts to manage earnings.

FASB Interpretation 46(R)

After much debate about how to fix the original SPE ownership percentage and consolidation rules, FASB issued on December 24, 2003, a revision of its proposed Interpretation: FASB Interpretation 46(R), Consolidation of Variable Interest Entities.[78] Basically, Interpretation 46(R) requires unconsolidated variable interest entities to be consolidated by their primary beneficiaries if the entities do not effectively disperse risk among parties involved. Variable-interest entities that effectively disperse risks would not be consolidated unless a single party holds an interest or combination of interests that recombines risks that were previously dispersed.

The new rules apply an economic reality test to the consolidation of a variable interest entity. No longer is there a percentage ownership test. Instead, it is the dispersion of risk that determines the consolidation status. By effectively dispersing risk, the primary beneficiary controls its own risk with respect to activities of the unconsolidated variable interest entity.

Enron's Role in the Creation and Passage of SOX

The Enron fraud was a direct cause, along with WorldCom's, of congressional passage of SOX and efforts to reform the accounting profession. The provisions of the act that were motivated by the Enron fraud include:

- Prohibiting the provision of internal audit services for audit clients. Andersen provided the major part of internal audit services for Enron. Overall, Andersen earned from Enron in its last full year as accountants $27 million from nonauditing services and $25 million from auditing services.

- Requiring that off-balance-sheet financing activities be disclosed in the notes to the financial statements. Enron's SPEs were never referred to as providing off-balance-sheet financing.

- Requiring that related-party transactions be disclosed in the notes. The activities with the SPEs qualify as related-party transactions. By some accounts, Enron had over 3,000 SPEs, yet the footnote disclosure in its last year before filing for bankruptcy was limited to one page.

Enron also suffered from the same lack of controls and inadequate corporate governance that infected so many other companies during the accounting scandals. For example, the board of directors did not act independently, and the audit committee members were not independent of management. The internal environment at Enron, especially the tone at the top, promoted a culture of making deals regardless of the risks.

The internal controls at Enron were either ignored or overridden by management (i.e., the board waived its ethics policy so that Andy Fastow could control Chewco indirectly while simultaneously serving as the

CFO for Enron). This created a conflict of interest that enabled Fastow to enrich himself through control of Chewco at the expense of Enron. The result was a serious breach of fiduciary responsibilities and the failure of management to meet its obligation as an agent for the shareholders.

Lessons to Be Learned from Enron

What is the moral of the Enron story? Certainly, we could say that weak internal controls equate with possible fraud. Also, we could point to the need for an ethical tone at the top to help prevent fraud. At Enron, once the company developed an appetite for establishing SPEs and keeping these transactions off the books, the company became more and more addicted to the cash provided through the SPEs. Even if it wanted to stop the transactions, Enron and its top management had set the company on a course that was difficult to change. Enron had started to slide down the ethical slippery slope, and there was no turning back.

The bottom-line factor that kept the Enron fraud going well past the point of no return was greed. Skilling saw Fastow getting rich, Lay saw Skilling getting rich, all the Enron employees thought they saw Lay getting rich, and then Lay hyped Enron stock to the employees for their 401-ks as a way for them, eventually, to get rich.

Enron ethics means that business ethics is a question of organizational "deep" culture rather than of cultural vestiges such as ethics codes, ethics officers, and the like. At Enron, everything was done with set purposes in mind—to make the deal at any cost; to line one's pockets with ill-gotten gains; and to deceive the stakeholders—including the company's own employees—into thinking Enron was doing better than it really was. The Enron affair illustrates just how quickly a company can go from good to bad when those at the top respect only nonethical values, such as power, wealth, and fame, rather than the ethical values of honesty, integrity, and responsibility.

Financial Statement Restatements

> **LO 7-6**
>
> Explain the causes and effects of financial statement restatements.

Characteristics of Restatements

Audit Analytics reports a detailed analysis and comparison of trends in financial restatements over a sixteen-year period. The report shows that 2016 saw an "all time low" in restatements, which might be attributed to tighter controls over financial reporting in accordance with the Sarbanes-Oxley Act of 2002.[81]

Reissuance Restatements have declined for the tenth year in a row since 2004, when the 8-K disclosure requirements came into effect. 2016 shows a record low of 130, a sharp decline from 2006's 941, the highest number in the sample period. While the number of Revision Restatements has remained fairly steady, the percentage compared to all restatements has been gradually increasing. So, while it's true that we are seeing less restatements in general, the vast majority of restatements have been Revision Restatements (78.3% in 2016).

In order to gauge the severity of restatements, Audit Analytics examines the impact of net income. According to the report, about 59.1% of the restatements disclosed by publicly traded companies had no impact on earnings. This is the second highest percentage in 9 years.

The report also looks at both the average number of days restated and the average number of issues found in restatements, both of which continue to be low. However, the average number of days needed to restate increased to 5.37 (Note: This number is likely to increase as there are still outstanding restatements disclosed in 2016 that will most likely raise the average).

Overall, the trend for restatements continues to be on the decline. Audit Analytics concludes that we are seeing fewer restatements, and those restatements that we do see, more often than not lack severity or material weakness. While the average amount of days to restate is slightly higher, the increase in Revision Restatements over Reissuance Restatements indicates more transparency and better-quality disclosures.

It is encouraging to see a decline in Reissuance Restatements. However, we are not convinced the good news will last forever as past history does indicate these things run in cycles. We are also concerned about non-GAAP disclosures that may need to be reissued down the line depending on how the standard-setting bodies decide to deal with these issues given almost every company now discloses such metrics.

Another cause for concern continues to be the number of "stealth restatements." The SEC requires companies to disclose within four business days a determination that past financial statements should no longer be relied on. This disclosure must appear in an 8-K report. The SEC defines a stealth restatement as one that is disclosed only in periodic reports and not in the 8-K or amended periodic report such as a 10-K/A or 10-Q/A.

A recent study of restatements shows that many companies are turning away from announcing restatements in Form 8-K and have avoided amending previously issued financial statements for the periods affected. Companies are instead revising the affected numbers for the previous periods and showing them in subsequent quarterly or annual reports (litttle "r" *restatements*).[82] This is troublesome because it gives the appearance that companies are going out of their way not to draw attention to the restatements rather than erring on the side of transparency.

Hertz Accounting Restatements

On July 16, 2015, Hertz Global Holdings, Inc., (Hertz) announced that it had filed its annual report on Form 10-K for the fiscal year ending December 31, 2014, which includes the restated results for 2012 and 2013 as well as selected unaudited restated financial information for 2011. In addition, the company had filed its quarterly report on Form 10-Q for the period ending March 31, 2015.

Financial Restatement

As discussed in the Form 10-K filed with the SEC, Hertz identified accounting misstatements for the years 2011 through 2013. The following information in Exhibit 7.9 summarizes the impact of misstatements identified.[83]

The Form 10-K contained audited restated financial information for 2012 and 2013, audited financial information for 2014, and unaudited restated selected financial information for 2011. The Form 10-K also contained quarterly information for the quarters in 2013, as restated, and 2014. The Form 10-Q contained quarterly information for the first quarter of 2015.

The company noted that the filing of its Form 10-K cures the filing deficiency notice from the New York Stock Exchange (NYSE) as reported on March 24, 2015, and brings Hertz back into compliance with the NYSE listing requirements.

EXHIBIT 7.9 Hertz Impact of Misstatements

(In millions)	Year Ended December 31, (Unaudited) Increase/ (Decrease)*		
	2011	**2012**	**2013**
As originally filed			
GAAP pretax income	$324	$451	$663
GAAP net income attributable to Hertz	$176	$243	$346
Misstatements previously disclosed and included in the originally filed 10-K/A**			
GAAP pretax income	$(19)	$ (9)	N/A
GAAP net income attributable to Hertz	$(12)	$ (4)	N/A
Additional misstatements identified			
GAAP pretax income	$(54)	$(81)	$(72)
GAAP net income attributable to Hertz	$(19)	$(58)	$(51)
Cumulative misstatements (Misstatements previously revised in 10-K/A plus additional errors identified)**			
GAAP pretax income	$(73)	$(90)	$(72)
GAAP net income attributable to Hertz	$(31)	$(62)	$(51)
Cumulative misstatements as a %			
GAAP pretax income	(23)%	(20)%	(11)%
GAAP net income attributable to Hertz	(18)%	(26)%	(15)%

*Increase/Decrease associated with misstatements and impact to GAAP pre-tax and GAAP net income.

**Amounts recorded as a revision in the 2013 Form 10-K/A.

***In addition, $114 and $87 in errors reducing GAAP pre-tax income and GAAP net income, respectively, related to periods prior to 2011 were recorded as a cumulative adjustment to opening retained earnings for 2011. Of these amounts, $7 and $5 GAAP pre-tax and GAAP net income, respectively, were recorded in the 2013 Form 10-K/A as a revision.

Restatements Due to Errors in Accounting and Reporting

An analysis of causes of restatement due to errors in accounting and reporting was made by Turner and Weirich. Results from their study with respect to the kinds of accounting errors that trigger restatements are particularly relevant to the discussion of earnings management. Exhibit 7.10 presents these results.[84]

Restatements due to errors also occur when a company switches from non-GAAP to GAAP. A good example of this occurred at Cubic Corporation, with its "development contracts." Cubic announced on August 1, 2012, that the audit committee of the company's board of directors, after consultation with EY, its independent auditor, determined that Cubic's financial statements for the fiscal years ending September 30, 2011, 2010, and 2009; the quarters ended March 31, 2012, and December 31, 2011; and each of the prior quarters of 2011 and 2010 could no longer be relied upon as complying with GAAP. Accordingly, Cubic informed the SEC that it would restate the financial statements.[85]

EXHIBIT 7.10 Accounting Errors that Trigger Financial Statement Restatements

Category	Cause of Restatements
Revenue recognition	Improper revenue recognition, including questionable items and misreported revenue
Expense recognition	Improper expense recognition, including period of recognition, incorrect amounts; includes improper lease accounting
Misclassification	Improper classification on income statement, balance sheet, or cash flow statement; includes non-operating revenue in the operating category; cash outflow from operating activities in investment activities
Equity	Improper accounting for EPS; stock-based compensation plans, options, warrants, and convertibles
Other comprehensive income (OCI)	Improper accounting for OCI transactions, including unrealized gains and losses on investments in debt and equity securities, derivatives, and pension-liability adjustments
Capital assets	Improper accounting for asset impairments; asset-placed-in-service dates and depreciation
Inventory	Improper accounting for valuation of inventory, including market adjustments and obsolescence
Reserves/allowances	Improper accounting for bad debt reserves on accounts receivable, reserves for inventory, and provision for loan losses
Liabilities/contingencies	Improper estimation of liability claims, loss contingencies, litigation matters, commitments, and certain accruals

Exhibit 7.11 provides additional information on how the Cubic restatements were identified and reported.

Errors in accounting and financial reporting that affect earnings are corrected through a prior period adjustment to retained earnings. The importance of such adjustments to users of the statements depend on materiality issues. In the context of potentially faulty financial statements, however, the process by which materiality is determined is complex and can be lengthy. Depending on the timing of the discovery of the error and its magnitude, this event can lead to negative effects with respect to share value.

The basic accounting standard for materiality judgments is in *Statement of Financial Accounting Concepts (SFAC) No. 8. SFAC No. 8* provides that: "The omission or misstatement of an item in a financial report is material if, in the light of surrounding circumstances, the magnitude of the item is such that it is probable that the judgment of a reasonable person relying upon the report would have been changed or influenced by the inclusion or correction of the item."[86]

It is important to note the trend that both FASB and the SEC want accountants and auditors to follow: the application of professional judgment in making materiality decisions. We agree with the SEC and reiterate that the application of professional judgment entails an ethical approach to decision making. The qualities of an ethical auditor of objectivity, integrity, due care, and professional skepticism are critical components of that judgment. The shift to more professional judgments should be accompanied by better training for auditors in the area of ethical decision making. We would like to see the SEC and PCAOB address this issue.

EXHIBIT 7.11 Cubic Corporation Restatement of Financial Statements (August 1, 2012)[87]

The Audit Committee's decision to restate these financial statements follows a recommendation by management that revenues in these previously issued financial statements should be adjusted due to errors in calculating revenues on certain long-term fixed-price development type contracts ("development contracts") and on certain long-term service contracts with non-U.S. Government customers ("service contracts").

Preliminary indications from the company's evaluation are that the changes described below will result in an increase in revenues and net income cumulatively over the period of the restatement and an increase in retained earnings as of March 31, 2012. Cubic Corporation is continuing to evaluate the total amount of the adjustments and the specific impact on each period covered by the restatement, which may result in an increase or decrease in previously reported amounts for individual periods.

Cubic has historically recognized sales and profits for development contracts using the cost-to-cost percentage-of-completion method of accounting, modified by a formulary adjustment. Under the cost-to-cost percentage-of-completion method of accounting, sales and profits are based on the ratio of costs incurred to estimated total costs at completion. Cubic has consistently applied a formulary adjustment to the percentage completion calculation for development contracts that had the effect of deferring a portion of the indicated revenue and profits on such contracts until later in the contract performance period.

Cubic believed that this methodology was an acceptable variation of the cost-to-cost percentage-of-completion method as described in Accounting Standards Codification ("ASC") 605-35. The company now believes that generally accepted accounting principles do not support the practice of using a formulary calculation to defer a portion of the indicated revenue and profits on such contracts. Instead, Cubic believes that sales and profits should have been recognized based on the ratio of costs incurred to estimated total costs at completion, without using a formulary adjustment. The company is in the process of evaluating the differences resulting from this change but has not yet completed this evaluation.

While evaluating its revenue recognition for development contracts, Cubic also evaluated its long-standing practice of using the cost-to-cost percentage-of-completion method to recognize revenues for many of its service contracts. Under the accounting literature the cost-to-cost percentage of completion method is acceptable for U.S. Government contracts but not for contracts with other governmental customers, whether domestic or foreign.

Concluding Thoughts

Earnings management is typically motivated by a desire to meet or exceed forecasted results, meet financial analysts' earnings estimates, inflate share price to make stock options more lucrative, and to enhance managerial performance. Earnings management can also occur through the use of non-GAAP measures that put the best face on the numbers even if they do not conform to GAAP.

We believe that when management manipulates earnings, the quality of such information suffers. It is hard enough for most readers of financial statements to understand the underlying accounting and financial reporting techniques used to develop the statements. When such methods are manipulated, or new ones developed to put a positive spin on company results, then there is a distortion effect that compromises the dependability of the statements. In the end it is the users of the statements that suffer.

At the end of the day, financial reporting needs to focus more on representational faithfulness, meaning that there should be a correspondence or agreement between the accounting measures or descriptions in financial reports and the economic events they purport to represent. Faithful representation does not mean accurate in all respects. Free from error means there are no errors or omissions in the description of the event, and the process used to produce the reported information has been selected and applied with no errors in the process. In other words, a representation of an estimate can be faithful if the amount is described clearly and accurately as being an estimate, the nature and limitations of the estimating process are explained, and no errors have been made in selecting and applying an appropriate process for developing the estimate.

While *revision restatements* are up and *reissuance restatements* are down, we have learned that it is not uncommon for companies to use language and characterize restatements in a way that may not be truthful. The public expects accountants and auditors to serve as a check on such behavior. The recent trend of not reporting restatements right away in Form 8-K is troubling because it serves managements' interests to delay until quarterly reports are prepared so as to minimize the impact in the minds of users; such information needs to be disclosed in a more timely manner.

As we have learned throughout this book, organizational ethics, effective ICFR, and strong corporate governance systems provide a foundation to ward off the temptation to manipulate reported results. In virtually all of the financial frauds discussed in this chapter, compromises were made in these systems in order to achieve desired results. Companies played fast and loose with the accounting rules and often were successful in deceiving the independent auditors.

What is lacking in virtually all cases of earnings management is ethical leadership. The tone at the top establishes the culture within an organization. An ethical culture is enhanced when top managers understand their responsibilities to shareholders, creditors, and the public at large. Ethical leadership entails a commitment to do what is right regardless of the consequences. It is not always an easy standard to achieve because of the inevitable pressures that build up in an organization to produce consistently better financial results. In the final chapter we will examine just how an organization can promote ethical leadership in the context of accounting decision making.

Discussion Questions

1. There is an old industry joke that if you ask an accountant what is four plus four, she will tell you it's whatever you want it to be. Explain what might be meant by this statement.

2. In Arthur Levitt's speech, referred to in the opening quote, he also said, "I fear that we are witnessing an erosion in the quality of earnings, and therefore, the quality of financial reporting. Managing may be giving way to manipulation; integrity may be losing out to illusion." Explain what you think Levitt meant by this statement. What role do financial analysts' earnings expectations play in the quality of earnings?

3. Relevance and faithful representation are the qualitative characteristics of useful information under *SFAC No. 8*.[88] How does ethical reasoning enter into making determinations about the relevance and faithful representation of financial information?

4. Evaluate the following statements from an ethical perspective:

   "Earnings management, in a narrow sense, is the behavior of management to play with the discretionary accrual component to determine high or low earnings."

   "Earnings are potentially managed because financial accounting standards still provide alternative methods."

5. Comment on the statement that materiality is in the eye of the beholder. How does this statement relate to the discussion in this chapter of how to gauge materiality in assessing financial statement restatements? Is materiality inconsistent with the notion of representational faithfulness?

6. Needles talks about the use of a continuum ranging from questionable or highly conservative to fraud to assess the amount to be recorded for an estimated expense. Do you believe that the choice of an overly conservative or overly aggressive amount would reflect earnings management? Explain.

7. Do you agree with Thomas McKee's conception of earnings management as applied to (a) operational earnings management and (b) accounting earnings management?

8. Comment on the statement that what a company's income statement reveals is interesting, but what it conceals is vital.

9. Why are non-GAAP financial measures used by many investors and analysts?

10. Explain the SEC rules and regulations applicable to the public disclosure of non-GAAP financial measures.

11. Maines and Wahlen[89] state in their research paper on the reliability of accounting information: "Accrual estimates require judgment and discretion, which some firms under certain incentive conditions will exploit to report non-neutral accruals estimates within GAAP. Accounting standards can enhance the information in accrual estimates by linking them to the underlying economic constructs they portray." How can accruals be used to manage non-GAAP operating earnings?

12. Krispy Kreme was involved in an accounting fraud where the company reported false quarterly and annual earnings and falsely claimed that, as a result of those earnings, it had achieved what had become a prime benchmark of its historical performance; that is, reporting quarterly earnings per share that exceeded its previously announced EPS guidance by 1¢. One method used to report higher earnings was to ship two or three times more doughnuts to franchisees than ordered in order to meet monthly quotas. Would you characterize what Krispy Kreme did as earnings management? Explain.

13. Safety-Kleen issued a major financial restatement in 2001. The next year, the company restated (reduced) previously reported net income by $534 million for the period 1997–1999. PwC withdrew its financial statement audit reports for those years. Do you believe that financial restatements and withdrawing an audit report are *prima facie* indicators that a failed audit has occurred? Explain.

14. Revenue recognition in the Xerox case called for determining the stand-alone selling price for each of the deliverables and using it to separate out the revenue amounts. Why do you think it is important to separate out the selling prices of each element of a bundled transaction? How do these considerations relate to what Xerox did to manage its earnings? Do you think the new revenue recognition standard will change the criteria in accounting for transactions like at Xerox?

15. Tinseltown Construction just received a $2.6 billion contract to construct a modern football stadium for the L.A. Rams and San Diego Chargers at the L.A. Sports and Entertainment District. The company estimates that it will cost $1.8 billion to construct the stadium. Explain how Tinseltown can make revenue recognition decisions each year that enable it to manage earnings over the three-year duration of the contract.

16. The SEC's new rules on posting financial information on social media sites such as Twitter means that companies can now tweet their earnings in 280 characters or less. What are the problems that may arise in using a social media platform to report key financial data, including the potential effects on shareholders and the company?

17. Do you agree with each of the following statements? Explain.

- EBITDA makes companies with asset-heavy balance sheets look healthier than they may actually be.

- EBITDA portrays a company's debt service ability— but only *some types of debt*.

- EBITDA isn't a determinant of cash flow *at all*.

18. What is the risk of management bias for each earnings judgment and estimate? What safeguards should be in place to mitigate the risk of management bias, if any? What is the external auditor's role in this process?

19. In the Enron case, the company eventually turned to "back-door" guaranteeing of the debt of Chewco, one of its SPEs, to satisfy equity investors. Assume that a $16 million loan agreement required that Enron stock should not fall below $40 per share. If the share price did decline below that trigger amount, either the loan would be called by the bank or the bank could choose to increase the guaranteed number of Enron shares based on the new price (assume $32). If the bank decides to increase the number of shares guaranteed, what would be (1) the original number of shares in the guarantee and (2) the new number of shares? Why would it be important from an accounting and ethical perspective for Enron to disclose information about the guarantee in its financial statements?

20. In the study of earnings quality by Dichev et al.,[90] CFOs stated that "current earnings are considered to be high quality if they serve as a good guide to the long-run profits of the firm." Discuss how and why current earnings may *not* be a good barometer of the long-term profits of the firm. How do non-GAAP measures of earnings address this issue?

21. Discuss the revenue recognition and internal control challenges when a company uses cloud computing.

22. Schlit describes a variety of financial shenanigans. What is the purpose of using those techniques? Would you call it gimmickry? Explain.

23. Distinguish between big R and little r restatements. What is required of management and the external auditors when such events occur? In well-governed companies, a sense of accountability and ethical leadership create a culture that places organizational ethics above all else. What role does organizational culture play in preventing financial shenanigans from being used to manage earnings?

24. Read the following statements made by Warren Buffet in a letter to shareholders included in the Berkshire Hathaway 2017 Annual Report. Should the external auditors have a role in responding to its information content? Can the statements be misleading to shareholders and the investing community?

I must first tell you about a new accounting rule—a generally accepted accounting principle (GAAP)—that in *future* quarterly and annual reports will severely distort Berkshire's net income figures and very often mislead commentators and investors.

The new rule says that the net change in *unrealized* investment gains and losses in stocks we hold must be included in all net income figures we report to you. That requirement will produce some truly wild and capricious swings in our GAAP bottom-line. Berkshire owns $170 billion of marketable stocks (not including our shares of Kraft Heinz), and the value of these holdings can easily swing by $10 billion or more within a quarterly reporting period. Including gyrations of that magnitude in reported net income will swamp the truly important numbers that describe our operating performance. For analytical purposes, Berkshire's "bottom-line" will be useless.

The new rule compounds the communication problems we have long had in dealing with the *realized* gains (or losses) that accounting rules compel us to include in our net income. In past quarterly and annual press releases, we have regularly warned you not to pay attention to these realized gains, because they—just like our unrealized gains—fluctuate randomly.

That's largely because we sell securities when that seems the intelligent thing to do, not because we are trying to influence earnings in any way. As a result, we sometimes have reported substantial realized gains for a period when our portfolio, overall, performed poorly (or the converse).

25. Review the numbers below. Assume you are an investor. What questions would you have about the numbers and presentation?

UNAUDITED ORGANIC REVENUE GROWTH RECONCILIATION
(in 000s, except percentages)

	Three Months Ended		Nine Months Ended	
	Revenue $	% Change	Revenue $	% Change
September 30, 2016–Revenues	$ 349,254		$ 995,343	
Organic revenue growth*	27,075	7.8%	83,556	8.4%
Impact of Non-GAAP acquisitions (dispositions), net	(3,153)	(0.9%)	36,489	3.7%
Foreign exchange impact, net	2,624	0.8%	(4,356)	(0.4%)
GAAP revenue growth	26,546	7.6%	115,689	11.6%
September 30, 2017–Revenues	$ 375,800		$ 1,111,032	

*"Organic revenue growth" and "organic revenue decline" refer to the positive or negative results, respectively, of subtracting both the foreign exchange and acquisition (disposition) components from total revenue growth. The acquisition (disposition) component is calculated by aggregating prior period revenue for any acquired businesses, less the prior period revenue of any businesses that were disposed of during the current period. The organic revenue growth (decline) component reflects the constant currency impact of (a) the change in revenue of the partner firms which the Company has held throughout each of the comparable periods presented, and (b) "non-GAAP acquisitions (dispositions), net". Non-GAAP acquisitions (dispositions), net consists of (i) for acquisitions during the current year, the revenue effect from such acquisition as if the acquisition had been owned during the equivalent period in the prior year and (ii) for acquisitions during the previous year, the revenue effect from such acquisitions as if they had been owned during that entire year (or same period as the current reportable period), taking into account their respective pre-acquisition revenues for the applicable periods, and (iii) for dispositions, the revenue effect from such disposition as if they had been disposed of during the equivalent period in the prior year.

Endnotes

1. SEC, *Securities and Exchange Commission v. SafeNet, Inc., et al.,* Accounting and Auditing Enforcement Release No. 3068. November 12, 2009, https://www.sec.gov/litigation/litreleases/2009/lr21290.htm.

2. Arthur Levitt, "The Numbers Game," Remarks made by the former SEC chairman before the NYU Center for Law and Business, September 28, 1998, Available at: https://www.sec.gov/news/speech/speecharchive/1998/spch220.txt.

3. Jim Gaa and Paul Dunmore, "The Ethics of Earnings Management," *Chartered Accountants Journal,* 2007, pp. 60–62.

4. Kenneth A. Merchant, *Rewarding Results: Motivating Profit Center Managers* (Boston: Harvard Business School Press, 1989).

5. William S. Hopwood, Jay J. Leiner, and George R. Young, *Forensic Accounting and Fraud Examination* (New York: McGraw-Hill Irwin, 2012).

6. Financial Accounting Standards Board, "Recognition and Measurement in Financial Statements of Business Enterprises," *Statement of Financial Accounting Concepts (SFAC) No. 5* (Stamford, CT: FASB, May 1986).

7. SEC, *HealthSouth Corporation Securities Litigation,* United States District Court Northern District of Alabama Southern Division. Available at: http://securities.stanford.edu/filings-documents/1008/HRC98/200482_r03c_031500.pdf

8. Richard J. Rivard, Eugene Bland, and Gary B. Hatfield Morris, "Income Smoothing Behavior of U.S. Banks under Revised International Capital Requirements," *International Advances in Economic Research* 9 (4), (November 2003) pp. 288–294.

9. K. Schipper, "Commentary on Earnings Management," *Accounting Horizons,* December 1989, pp. 91–102.

10. P. M. Healy and J. M. Wahlen, "A Review of Earnings Management Literature and Its Implications for Standard Setting," *Accounting Horizons* 13 (1999), pp. 365–383.

11. P. M. Dechow and P. J. Skinner, "Earnings Management: Reconciling the Views of Accounting Academics, Practitioners, and Regulation," *Accounting Horizons* 14 (2001), pp. 235–250.

12. Thomas E. McKee, *Earnings Management: An Executive Perspective* (Mason, OH: Thompson Corporation, 2005).

13. William J. Bruns Jr. and Kenneth A. Merchant, "The Dangerous Morality of Managing Earnings," *Management Accounting,* August 1990, pp. 62–69.

14. K. Rosenzweig and M. Fischer, "Is Managing Earnings Ethically Acceptable?" *Management Accounting,* March 1994, pp. 44–51.

15. R. Z. Elias, "The Impact of Corporate Ethical Values on Perceptions of Earnings Management," *Managerial Auditing Journal* 19 (2004), pp. 84–98.

16. Michael D. Akers, Don E. Giacomino, and Jodi L. Bellovary, "Earnings Management and Its Implications: Educating the Accounting Profession," *The CPA Journal,* August 2007, pp. 33–39.

17. Akers et al.

18. Akers et al.

19. Keith G. Stanga and Andrea S. Kelton, "Ethicality and Moral Intensity of Earnings Management: Does the Method Matter?," *Research on Professional Responsibility and Ethics in Accounting,* Vol. 13, 2008, *pp. 19-40.*

20. Eric N. Johnson, Gary Fleischman, Sean Valentine, and Kenton B. Walker, "Managers' Ethical Evaluations of Earnings Management and its Consequences," *Contemporary Accounting Research* Vol. 29, No. 3, July 2011.

21. Hopwood et al., p. 426.

22. Belverd E. Needles, "Teaching Judgment and Ethics in First-year Accounting: A Good Lecture," *Trends,* June 13, 2011, https://blog.cengage.com/wp-content/uploads/2014/07/SUMMER-2011.Trends.pdf

23. Ilia Dichev, John Graham, Campbell R. Harvey, and Shiva Rajgopal, "The Misrepresentation of Earnings, *Financial Analysts Journal,* Vol. 72, No. 1, 2016, pp. 22-35.

24. Deloitte, Quality of earnings: Focus on integrity and quality, 2009, https://www2.deloitte.com/content/dam/Deloitte/in/Documents/risk/Corporate%20Governance/Audit%20Committee/in-gc-guality-of-earning-how-can-boards-understand-noexp.pdf.

25. Eli Bartov, Dan Givoly, and Carla Hayn, "The Rewards to Meeting or Beating Earnings Expectations," *Journal of Accounting & Economics* 33 (2002), pp. 173–204.

26. Timothy Fogarty, Michel Magnan, Garen Markarian, and Serge Bohdjalian, "Inside Agency: The Rise and Fall of Nortel," February 1, 2008, Available at: http://papers.ssrn.com/sol3/papers.cfm?abstract_id=1092288.

27. Joseph Fuller and Michael C. Jensen, "Just Say No to Wall Street: Putting a Stop to the Earnings Game," *Journal of Applied Corporate Finance* 14 (4), (Winter 2002) pp. 41–46.

28. Werner Erhard and Michael C. Jensen, "Beyond Agency Theory: The Hidden and Heretofore Inaccessible Power of Integrity (PDF of Keynote Slides) (August 31, 2012)," Harvard Business School NOM Unit Working Paper No. 10-068; Barbados Group Working Paper No. 10-02, Available at SSRN: http://ssrn.com/abstract=1552009 or http://dx.doi.org/10.2139/ssrn.1552009.

29. John R. Graham, Harvey R. Campbell, and Shiva Rajgopal, "The Economic Implications of Corporate Financial Reporting," *Journal of Accounting & Economics* 40 (1), (December 2005) pp. 3–73.

30. Kim, Yangseon & Liu, Caixing & Rhee, S. (2018). The Effect of Firm Size on Earnings Management.

31. Dichev et al.

32. SEC, SEC Announces Financial Fraud Cases, April 19, 2016, https://www.sec.gov/news/pressrelease/2016-74.html.

33. *Employees' Retirement System, et al. v. Green Mountain Coffee Roasters, et al.,* United States Court of Appeals for the Second Circuit, July 24, 2015, Available at: http://caselaw.findlaw.com/us-2nd-circuit/1708736.html.

34. Green Mountain Coffee Roasters, Inc., *Annual Report on Form 10-K,* September 29, 2012, Available at: http://www.sec.gov/Archives/edgar/data/909954/000110465912080228/a12-21067_110k.htm.

35. Jessica Holzer and Greg Bensinger, "SEC Embraces Social Media," *The Wall Street Journal,* April 2, 2013, Available at: http://www.wsj.com/articles/SB10001424127887323611604578398862292997352.

36. Mercedes Erickson, Non-GAAP Reporting One Year After New SEC Guidance, December 21, 2017, http://www.auditanalytics.com/blog/non-gaap-reporting-one-year-after-new-sec-guidance/.

37. Calcbench & Radical Compliance, Measuring Non-GAAP Metrics: A Look at Adjusted Net Income, June 2016

38. Mary Jo White, Keynote Address, International Corporate Governance Network Annual Conference: Focusing the Lens of Disclosure to Set the Path Forward on Board Diversity, Non-GAAP, and Sustainability, June 2016, https://www.sec.gov/news/speech/chair-white-icgn-speech.html.

39. SEC Release No. 33-8145, Proposed Rule: Conditions for Use of Non-GAAP Financial Measures (Nov. 4, 2002), https://www.sec.gov/rules/proposed/33-8145.htm, and SEC Release No. 33-8176, Final Rule: Conditions for the Use of Non-GAAP Financial Measures (Jan. 22, 2004), https://www.sec.gov/rules/final/33-8176.htm.

40. Cornell Law School Legal Information Institute, 17 CFR 244.100—General Rules Regarding Disclosure of non-GAAP Financial Measures, https://www.law.cornell.edu/cfr/text/17/244.100.

41. SOX, Section 401, Disclosures in Periodic Reports, http://www.soxlaw.com/s401.htm.

42. SEC, Conditions for Use of Non-GAAP Financial Measures, 17 CFR PARTS 228, 229, 244 and 249, March 28, 2003, https://www.sec.gov/rules/final/33-8176.htm.

43. SEC, Regulation S-K, Item 10(e)(1)(i), https://www.sec.gov/divisions/corpfin/ecfrlinks.shtml.

44. Ernst & Young, Technical Line.

45. PwC, SEC Updates Interpretive Guidance on non-GAAP financial Measures, May 19, 2016. https://www.pwc.com/us/en/cfodirect/publications/in-brief/sec-non-gaap-financial-measures.html. These interpretations were updated in 2017: SEC, Non-GAAP Financial Measures, October 17, 2016, https://www.sec.gov/divisions/corpfin/guidance/nongaapinterp.htm.

46. Morrison and Foerster, Practice Pointers on Non-GAAP Financial Measures, https://media2.mofo.com/documents/160816-practice-pointers-on-non-gaap-financial-measures.pdf.

47. Marc Siegel, For the Investor: The Use of Non-GAAP Metrics, FASB, http://www.fasb.org/jsp/FASB/Page/SectionPage&cid=1176164442130.

48. BKD, Non-GAAP Financial Measures, https://www.bkd.com/docs/pdf/Non-GAAP-Financial-Measures.pdf. dit report.

49. PCAOB, AS 2710: Other Information in Documents Containing Audited Financial Statements, https://pcaobus.org/Standards/Auditing/Pages/AS2710.aspx.

50. SEC, Regulation G, Rule 102; 17 CFR 244.100(b), https://www.sec.gov/rules/final/33-8176.htm.

51. SEC, *In the Matter of KPMG [v. Gemstar], Accounting and Auditing Enforcement Release No. 2125,* Available at: https://www.sec.gov/divisions/enforce/friactions.shtml

52. Scott McGregor, "Earnings Management Manipulation," Available at: http://webpage.pace.edu/pviswanath/notes/corpfin/earningsmanip.html.

53. SEC Enforcement in Financial Reporting and Disclosure—2017 Year-End Update, Harvard Law School Forum on Corporate Governance and Financial Reporting, February 19, 2018, https://corpgov.law.harvard.edu/2018/02/19/sec-enforcement-in-financial-reporting-and-disclosure-2017-year-end-update/.

54. *SEC against David N. Fuselier and Roy W. Erwin, and Integrated Freight Corporation,* Case 1:17-cv-04240, June 6, 2017, https://www.sec.gov/litigation/complaints/2017/comp23855.pdf.

55. *In the Matter of General Motors Company,* Accounting and Auditing Enforcement Release No. 3850, January 18, 2017, https://www.sec.gov/litigation/admin/2017/34-79825.pdf.

56. *SEC v. Thomas Miller and William Liang,* Case 2:17-cv-00897, February 3, 2017, https://www.sec.gov/litigation/complaints/2017/comp23741.pdf.

57. *In the Matter of Eric W. Kirchner and Richard G. Rodick,* Accounting and Auditing Enforcement Release No. 3877, June 15, 2017, https://www.sec.gov/litigation/admin/2017/34-80947.pdf.

58. SEC, Staff Accounting Bulletin: No. 101—Revenue Recognition in Financial Statements, Available at: https://www.sec.gov/interps/account/sab101.htm.

59. Financial Accounting Standards Board, "Multiple-Deliverable Revenue Arrangements: a Consensus of the FASB Emerging Issues Task Force, Financial Accounting Standards Update No. 2009-13, October 2009, Available at: https://asc.fasb.org/imageRoot/62/6844362.pdf.

60. SEC, "California-Based Telecommunications Equipment Firm and Two Former Executives Charged in Revenue Recognition Scheme," August 22, 2014, Available at: http://www.sec.gov/News/PressRelease/Detail/PressRelease/1370542732440.

61. *In the Matter of MagnaChip Semiconductor Corporation and Margaret Hyeryoung Sakai, CPA,* Accounting and Auditing Enforcement Release 3869, May 1, 2017, https://www.sec.gov/litigation/admin/2017/33-10352.pdf.

62. Matthew Heller, MagnaChip Fined $3M Over Accounting Fraud, CFO.com, May 2, 2017, http://ww2.cfo.com/fraud/2017/05/magnachip-accounting-fraud/.

63. Kathryn Yeaton, "A New World of Revenue Recognition," *The CPA Journal,* July 2015, pp. 50–53.

64. Jason Bramwell, "FASB, IASB Unveil Final Standard on Revenue Recognition," May 28, 2014, Available at: http://www.accountingweb.com/aa/standards/fasb-iasb-unveil-final-standard-on-revenue-recognition.

65. Howard M. Schilit, *Financial Shenanigans: How to Detect Accounting Gimmicks and Fraud in Financial Reports,* 3rd ed. (New York: McGraw-Hill, 2010).

66. *W. R. Grace & Co.*

67. SEC, Litigation Release No. 18174, *Securities and Exchange Commission v. Paul A. Allaire, G. Richard Thoman, Barry D. Romeril, Philip D. Fishbach, Daniel S. Marchibroda, and Gregory B. Tayler,* June

5, 2003, *Accounting and Auditing Enforcement Release No. 1796,* Available at: https://www.sec.gov/litigation/litreleases/lr18174.htm

68. SEC, Litigation Release No. 17645, *Accounting and Auditing Enforcement Release No. 1542, Securities and Exchange Commission v. Xerox Corporation,* Civil Action No. 02-CV-2780 (DLC) (S.D.N.Y.), April 11, 2002.

69. SEC, *In the Matter of KPMG LLP, Accounting and Auditing Enforcement Release No. 2234,* April 19, 2005, Available at: www.sec.gov/litigation/admin/34-51574.pdf.

70. SEC, Litigation Release No. 19573, *Accounting and Auditing Enforcement Release No. 2379, SEC v. KPMG LLP et al.,* Civil Action No. 03-CV 0671 (DLC) (S.D.N.Y.), February 22, 2006.

71. SEC, Litigation Release No. 18715, *Accounting and Auditing Enforcement Release No. 2016, Securities and Exchange Commission v. Lucent Technologies, Inc., Nina Aversano, Jay Carter, A. Leslie Dorn, William Plunkett, John Bratten, Deborah Harris, Charles Elliott, Vanessa Petrini, Michelle Hayes-Bullock, and David Ackerman,* Civil Action No. 04-2315 (WHW) (D.N.J.), filed May 17, 2004, Available at: www.sec.gov/litigation/litreleases/lr18715.htm.

72. SEC, *Accounting and Auditing Enforcement Release No. 2380, In the Matter of Thomas J. Yoho, CPA, Respondent,* Administrative Proceeding File No. 3-12215, February 22, 2006.

73. Sarah McBride, Oracle whistleblower suit raises questions over cloud accounting, *Reuters,* June 6, 2016, https://www.reuters.com/article/us-oracle-lawsuit-accounting/oracle-whistleblower-suit-raises-questions-over-cloud-accounting-idUSKCN0YS0X1.

74. Steven J. Vaughn-Nichols, Is Oracle cooking its cloud books, *Computerworld,* June 13, 2016, https://www.computerworld.com/article/3082707/cloud-computing/is-oracle-cooking-its-cloud-books.html.

75. Financial Accounting Standards Board, Financial Accounting Series No. 2015-05, April 2015, *Customer's Accounting for Fees Paid in a Cloud Computing Arrangement,* http://www.fasb.org/jsp/FASB/Document_C/DocumentPage?cid=1176165941746&acceptedDisclaimer=true.

76. Mimi Swartz and Sherron Watkins, *Power Failure: The Inside Story of the Collapse of Enron* (New York: Doubleday, 2003), pp. 275–276.

77. Report of Investigation by the Special Investigative Committee of the Board of Directors of Enron Corp., William C. Powers, Jr., Chair, Available at: http://picker.uchicago.edu/Enron/PowersReport%282-2-02%29.pdf.

78. FASB, FASB Interpretation 46(R), Consolidation of Variable Interest Entities, December 24, 2003 (Norwalk, CT: FASB, 2003).

79. Bethany McLean and Peter Elkind, *The Smartest Guys in the Room: The Amazing Rise and Scandalous Fall of Enron* (New York: Penguin Books, 2003).

80. Michael Gracyzk, Enron Whistleblower: "I Warned Ken Lay," http://truth-out.org/archive/component/k2/item/61427:enron-whistleblower-i-warned-ken-lay.

81. Audit Analytics, 2016 Financial Restatements Review, June 12, 2017, http://www.auditanalytics.com/blog/2016-financial-restatements-review/.

82. Fatima Alali and Sophia I-Ling Wang, "Characteristics of Financial Restatements and Frauds: An Analysis of Corporate Reporting Quality from 2000-2014, *The CPA Journal,* November 2017, https://www.cpajournal.com/2017/11/20/characteristics-financial-restatements-frauds/.

83. PR Newswire, "Hertz Completes Financial Restatement; Provides 2015 Business Outlook," July 16, 2015, Available at: http://www.stockhouse.com/news/press-releases/2015/07/16/hertz-completes-financial-restatement-provides-2015-business-outlook.

84. Lynn E. Turner and Thomas R. Weirich, "A Closer Look at Financial Statement Restatements: Analyzing the Reasons Behind the Trend," *The CPA Journal,* December 2006, pp. 33–39.

85. Available at: https://www.businesswire.com/news/home/20140210006450/en/Cubic-Corporation-Restate-Financial-Statements

86. Cubic Corp., "Cubic Corporation to Restate Financial Statements," Company Press Release, August 1, 2012, Available at: https://www.cubic.com/news-events/news/cubic-corporation-restate-financial-statements

87. FASB, *Statement of Financial Accounting Concepts No. 8, Conceptual Framework for Financial Reporting* (NY: FASB, 2010).

88. FASB, *Statement of Financial Accounting Concepts No. 8, Conceptual Framework for Financial Reporting– Chapter 1,* The Objective of General Purpose Financial Reporting, *and Chapter 3,* Qualitative Characteristics of Useful Financial Information (a replacement of FASB Concepts Statements No. 1 and No. 2), September 2010, Available at http://www.fasb.org/cs/BlobServer?blobkey= id&blobwhere=1175822892635&blobheader=application%2Fpdf&blobcol=urldata&blob table=MungoBlobs.

89. Laureen A. Maines and James M. Wahlen, "The Nature of Accounting Information Reliability: Inferences from Archival and Experimental Research," November 3, 2003, Available at: http:// repository.binus.ac.id/content/m0034/m003421831.pdf.

90. Ilia D. Dichev, John R. Graham, Campbell R. Harvey, and Shivaram Rajgopal, The Misrepresentation of Earnings (August 10, 2015). Financial Analysts Journal, Forthcoming. Available at SSRN: http:// ssrn.com/abstract=2376408 or http://dx.doi.org/10.2139/ssrn.2376408.

Chapter 7 Cases

Case 7-1 Nortel Networks

Canada-based Nortel Networks was one of the largest telecommunications equipment companies in the world prior to its filing for bankruptcy protection on January 14, 2009, in the United States, Canada, and Europe. The company had been subjected to several financial reporting investigations by U.S. and Canadian securities agencies in 2004. The accounting irregularities centered on premature revenue recognition and hidden cash reserves used to manipulate financial statements. The goal was to present the company in a positive light so that investors would buy (hold) Nortel stock, thereby inflating the stock price. Although Nortel was an international company, the listing of its securities on U.S. stock exchanges subjected it to all SEC regulations, along with the requirement to register its financial statements with the SEC and prepare them in accordance with U.S. GAAP.

The company had gambled by investing heavily in Code Division Multiple Access (CDMA) wireless cellular technology during the 1990s in an attempt to gain access to the growing European and Asian markets. However, many wireless carriers in the aforementioned markets opted for rival Global System Mobile (GSM) wireless technology instead. Coupled with a worldwide economic slowdown in the technology sector, Nortel's losses mounted to $27.3 billion by 2001, resulting in the termination of two-thirds of its workforce.

The Nortel fraud primarily involved four members of Nortel's senior management as follows: CEO Frank Dunn, CFO Douglas Beatty, controller Michael Gollogly, and assistant controller Maryanne Pahapill. At the time of the audit, Dunn was a certified management accountant, while Beatty, Gollogly, and Pahapill were chartered accountants in Canada.

Accounting Irregularities

On March 12, 2007, the SEC alleged the following in a complaint against Nortel:[1]

- In late 2000, Beatty and Pahapill implemented changes to Nortel's revenue recognition policies that violated U.S. GAAP, specifically to pull forward revenue to meet publicly announced revenue targets. These actions improperly boosted Nortel's fourth quarter and fiscal 2000 revenue by over $1 billion, while at the same time allowing the company to meet, but not exceed, market expectations. However, because their efforts pulled in more revenue than needed to meet those targets, Dunn, Beatty, and Pahapill selectively reversed certain revenue entries during the 2000 year-end closing process.

- In November 2002, Dunn, Beatty, and Gollogly learned that Nortel was carrying over $300 million in excess reserves. The three did not release these excess reserves into income as required under U.S. GAAP. Instead, they concealed their existence and maintained them for later use. Further, Beatty, Dunn, and Gollogly directed the establishment of yet another $151 million in unnecessary reserves during the 2002 year-end closing process to avoid posting a profit and paying bonuses earlier than Dunn had predicted publicly. These reserve manipulations erased Nortel's *pro forma* profit for the fourth quarter of 2002 and caused it to report a loss instead.[2]

[1]U.S. District Court for the Southern District of New York, *U.S. Securities and Exchange Commission v. Frank A. Dunn, Douglas C. Beatty, Michael J. Gollogly, and Maryanne E. Pahapill,* Civil Action No. 07-CV-2058, https://www.sec.gov/litigation/litreleases/2007/lr20036.htm.

[2]Pro forma means literally as a matter of form. Companies sometimes report income to the public and financial analysts that may not be calculated in accordance with GAAP. For example, a company might report pro forma earnings that exclude depreciation expense, amortization expense, and nonrecurring expenses such as restructuring costs. In general, pro forma earnings are reported in an effort to put a more positive spin on a company's operations. Unfortunately, there are no accounting rules on just how pro forma should be calculated, so comparability is difficult at best, and investors may be misled as a result.

- In the first and second quarters of 2003, Dunn, Beatty, and Gollogly directed the release of at least $490 million of excess reserves specifically to boost earnings, fabricate profits, and pay bonuses. These efforts turned Nortel's first-quarter 2003 loss into a reported profit under U.S. GAAP, which allowed Dunn to claim that he had brought Nortel to profitability a quarter ahead of schedule. In the second quarter of 2003, their efforts largely erased Nortel's quarterly loss and generated a *pro forma* profit. In both quarters, Nortel posted sufficient earnings to pay tens of millions of dollars in so-called return to profitability bonuses, largely to a select group of senior managers.

- During the second half of 2003, Dunn and Beatty repeatedly misled investors as to why Nortel was conducting a purportedly "comprehensive review" of its assets and liabilities, which resulted in Nortel's restatement of approximately $948 million in liabilities in November 2003. Dunn and Beatty falsely represented to the public that the restatement was caused solely by internal control mistakes. In reality, Nortel's first restatement was necessitated by the intentional improper handling of reserves, which occurred throughout Nortel for several years, and the first restatement effort was sharply limited to avoid uncovering Dunn, Beatty, and Gollogly's earnings management activities.

The complaint charged Dunn, Beatty, Gollogly, and Pahapill with violating and/or aiding and abetting violations of the antifraud, reporting, and books and records requirements. In addition, they were charged with violating the Securities Exchange Act Section 13(b)(2)(B) that requires issuers to devise and maintain a system of internal accounting controls sufficient to provide reasonable assurances that, among other things, transactions are recorded as necessary to permit the preparation of financial statements in conformity with U.S. GAAP and to maintain accountability for the issuer's assets.

Dunn and Beatty were separately charged with violations of the officer certification provisions instituted by SOX under Section 302. The commission sought a permanent injunction, civil monetary penalties, officer and director bars, and disgorgement with prejudgment interest against all four defendants.

Specifics of Earnings Management Techniques

From the third quarter of 2000 through the first quarter of 2001, when Nortel reported its financial results for year-end 2000, Dunn, Beatty, and Pahapill altered Nortel's revenue recognition policies to accelerate revenues as needed to meet Nortel's quarterly and annual revenue guidance, and to hide the worsening condition of Nortel's business. Techniques used to accomplish this goal include:

1. *Reinstituting bill-and-hold transactions.* The company tried to find a solution for the hundreds of millions of dollars in inventory that was sitting in Nortel's warehouses and offsite storage locations. Revenues could not be recognized for this inventory because U.S. GAAP revenue recognition rules generally require goods to be delivered to the buyer before revenue can be recognized. This inventory grew, in part, because orders were slowing and, in June 2000, Nortel had banned bill-and-hold transactions from its sales and accounting practices. The company reinstituted bill-and-hold sales when it became clear that it fell short of earnings guidance. In all, Nortel accelerated into 2000 more than $1 billion in revenues through its improper use of bill-and-hold transactions.

2. *Restructuring business-asset write-downs.* Beginning in February 2001, Nortel suffered serious losses when it finally lowered its earnings guidance to account for the fact that its business was suffering from the same widespread economic downturn that affected the entire telecommunications industry. As Nortel's business plummeted throughout the remainder of 2001, the company reacted by implementing a restructuring that, among other things, reduced its workforce by two-thirds and resulted in a significant write-down of assets.

3. *Creating reserves.* In relation to writing down the assets, Nortel established reserves that were used to manage earnings. Assisted by defendants Beatty and Gollogly, Dunn manipulated the company's reserves to manage Nortel's publicly reported earnings, create the false appearance that his leadership and business acumen was responsible for Nortel's profitability, and pay bonuses to these three defendants and other Nortel executives.

4. *Releasing reserves into income.* From at least July 2002 through June 2003, Dunn, Beatty, and Gollogly released excess reserves to meet Dunn's unrealistic and overly aggressive earnings targets. When Nortel internally (and unexpectedly) determined that it would return to profitability in the fourth quarter of 2002, the reserves were

used to reduce earnings for the quarter, avoid reporting a profit earlier than Dunn had publicly predicted, and create a stockpile of reserves that could be (and were) released in the future as necessary to meet Dunn's prediction of profitability by the second quarter of 2003. When 2003 turned out to be rockier than expected, Dunn, Beatty, and Gollogly orchestrated the release of excess reserves to cause Nortel to report a profit in the first quarter of 2003, a quarter earlier than the public expected, and to pay defendants and others substantial bonuses that were awarded for achieving profitability on a *pro forma* basis. Because their actions drew the attention of Nortel's outside auditors, they made only a portion of the planned reserve releases. This allowed Nortel to report nearly break-even results (though not actual profit) and to show internally that the company had again reached profitability on a *pro forma* basis necessary to pay bonuses.

Role of Auditors and Audit Committee

In late October 2000, as a first step toward reintroducing bill-and-hold transactions into Nortel's sales and accounting practices, Nortel's then controller and assistant controller asked Deloitte to explain, among other things, (1) "[u]nder what circumstances can revenue be recognized on product (merchandise) that has not been shipped to the end customer?" and (2) whether merchandise accounting can be used to recognize revenues "when installation is imminent" or "when installation is considered to be a minor portion of the contract."[3]

On November 2, 2000, Deloitte presented Nortel with a set of charts that, among other things, explained the U.S. GAAP criteria for revenues to be recognized prior to delivery (including additional factors to consider for a bill-and-hold transaction) and also provided an example of a customer request for a bill-and-hold sale "that would support the assertion that Nortel should recognize revenue" prior to delivery.

Nortel's earnings management scheme began to unravel at the end of the second quarter of 2003. On the morning of July 24, 2003, the same day on which Nortel issued its second Quarter 2003 earnings release, Deloitte informed Nortel's audit committee that it had found a "reportable condition" with respect to weaknesses in Nortel's accounting for the establishment and disposition of reserves. Deloitte went on to explain that, in response to its concerns, Nortel's management had undertaken a project to gather support and determine proper resolution of certain provision balances. Management, in fact, had undertaken this project because the auditor required adequate audit evidence for the upcoming year-end 2003 audit. Nortel concealed its auditor's concerns from the public, instead disclosing the comprehensive review.

Shortly after Nortel's announced restatement, the audit committee commenced an independent investigation and hired outside counsel to help it "gain a full understanding of the events that caused significant excess liabilities to be maintained on the balance sheet that needed to be restated," as well as to recommend any necessary remedial measures. The investigation uncovered evidence that Dunn, Beatty, and Gollogly and certain other financial managers were responsible for Nortel's improper use of reserves in the second half of 2002 and first half of 2003.

In March 2004, Nortel suspended Beatty and Gollogly and announced that it would "likely" need to revise and restate previously filed financial results further. Dunn, Beatty, and Gollogly were terminated for cause in April 2004.

On January 11, 2005, Nortel issued a second restatement that restated approximately $3.4 billion in misstated revenues and at least another $746 million in liabilities. All of the financial statement effects of the defendants' two accounting fraud schemes were corrected as of this date, but there remained lingering effects from the defendants' internal control and other nonfraud violations.

Nortel also disclosed the findings to date of the audit committee's independent review, which concluded, among other things, that Dunn, Beatty, and Gollogly were responsible for Nortel's improper use of reserves in the second half of 2002 and first half of 2003. The second restatement, however, did not reveal that Nortel's top executives had also engaged in revenue recognition fraud in 2000.

In May 2006, in its Form 10-K for the period ending December 31, 2005, Nortel admitted for the first time that its restated revenues in part had resulted from management fraud, stating that "in an effort to meet internal and

---

[3]*U.S. SEC v. Nortel Networks Corporation and Nortel Networks Limited,* Civil Action No. 07-CV-8851, October 15, 2007, Available at: https://www.sec.gov/litigation/complaints/2007/comp20333.pdf.

external targets, the senior corporate finance management team . . . changed the accounting policies of the company several times during 2000," and that those changes were "driven by the need to close revenue and earnings gaps."

Throughout their scheme, the defendants lied to Nortel's independent auditor by making materially false and misleading statements and omissions in connection with the quarterly reviews and annual audits of the financial statements that were materially misstated. Among other things, each of the defendants submitted management representation letters to the auditors that concealed the fraud and made false statements, which included that the affected quarterly and annual financial statements were presented in conformity with U.S. GAAP and that they had no knowledge of any fraud that could have a material effect on the financial statements. Dunn, Beatty, and Gollogly also submitted a false management representation letter in connection with Nortel's first restatement, and Pahapill likewise made false management representations in connection with Nortel's second restatement.

The defendants' scheme resulted in Nortel issuing materially false and misleading quarterly and annual financial statements and related disclosures for at least the financial reporting periods ending December 31, 2000, through December 31, 2003, and in all subsequent filings made with the SEC that incorporated those financial statements and related disclosures by reference.

On October 15, 2007, Nortel, without admitting or denying the SEC's charges, agreed to settle the commission's action by consenting to be enjoined permanently from violating the antifraud, reporting, books and records, and internal control provisions of the federal securities laws and by paying a $35 million civil penalty, which the commission placed in a Fair Fund[4] for distribution to affected shareholders.[5] Nortel also agreed to report periodically to the commission's staff on its progress in implementing remedial measures and resolving an outstanding material weakness over its revenue recognition procedures.

On January 14, 2009, Nortel filed for protection from creditors in the United States, Canada, and the United Kingdom in order to restructure its debt and financial obligations. In June, the company announced that it no longer planned to continue operations and that it would sell off all of its business units. Nortel's CDMA wireless business and long-term evolutionary access technology (LTE) were sold to Ericsson, and Avaya purchased its Enterprise business unit.

The final indignity for Nortel came on June 25, 2009, when Nortel's stock price dropped to 18.5¢ a share, down from a high of $124.50 in 2000. Nortel's battered and bruised stock was finally delisted from the S&P/TSX composite index, a stock index for the Canadian equity market, ending a colossal collapse on an exchange on which the Canadian telecommunications giant's stock valuation once accounted for a third of its value.

Postscript

During testimony about the fraud at Nortel on June 13, 2012, the lead Deloitte auditor on the Nortel engagement, Don Hathway, suggested that CEO Frank Dunn "did not understand" the role of the external auditors from Deloitte & Touche as they probed issues related to the company's accounting in 2003. Hathway told the Toronto fraud trial of Dunn and two other former Nortel executives that, after almost a year of working daily with Nortel staff at the company's head office, he concluded that neither management nor the board's audit committee understood his role.[6]

Hathway was assigned to head the Nortel audit team in January 2003 and said he and Deloitte audit partner John Cawthorne quickly found themselves being pressured by Dunn to help Nortel find strategies to deal with its accounting issues. "He had lectured John Cawthorne and I on more than one occasion about the need to be creative and come up with solutions . . . It indicated to me that he did not understand our role as independent auditors."

---

[4]A Fair Fund is a fund established by the SEC to distribute "disgorgements" (returns of wrongful profits) and penalties (fines) to defrauded investors. Fair Funds hold money recovered from a specific SEC case. The commission chooses how to distribute the money to defrauded investors, and when completed, the fund terminates.

[5]Theresa Tedesco and Jamie Sturgeon, "Nortel: Cautionary Tale of a Former Canadian Titan," *Financial Post,* June 27, 2009.

[6]Janet McFarland, Nortel executives 'didn't understand' auditor was independent: testimony, *The Globe and Mail,* June 13, 2012, https://www.theglobeandmail.com/report-on-business/nortel-executives-didnt-understand-auditor-was-independent-testimony/article4256369/.

Hathway said the relationship with the Nortel board's audit committee, led by former bank executive John Cleghorn, also grew strained and needed to be "reset" by late 2003. "The audit committee seemed more interested in getting things done by a certain schedule than they did getting them done right," Hathway testified. "I was surprised by that, because my view of their function was to oversee the integrity of the financial reporting process."

He said he was criticized by Cleghorn for taking too long to review issues related to the press release announcing first-quarter financial results in 2003 and was "severely criticized" for expressing reservations about offering an assurance on the company's third-quarter financial statements that year.

Hathway testified he felt Nortel had a "macho" culture and that many of its senior executives had never worked anywhere else, so "hadn't seen how other companies do things. I think that type of culture was problematic," he said.

By November 2003, Hathway was removed as lead audit partner on the engagement after spending his brief tenure raising red flags about Nortel's use of accounting reserves in 2003. He instead became a senior technical adviser to the audit team. He said his supervisor told him he was being replaced because he "didn't communicate with the audit committee."

Hathway said he first discovered in the summer of 2003—just six months after being assigned to lead the Nortel audit—that senior executives at the company were unhappy with his work. At the time, Hathway was pressing the company to launch a comprehensive review of the accounting reserves it was carrying on its balance sheet—a review that later led to a controversial restatement of the company's books in the fall of 2003.

Hathway testified that he was shown the results of Deloitte client-survey interviews conducted in July 2003, with Mr. Beatty and Mr. Gollogly. In the interview summary, Gollogly reportedly complained that Deloitte's two new lead audit partners—Hathway and Cawthorne—were "night and day" compared with Deloitte partners previously assigned to Nortel and were "turning the audit on its head. Gollogly described Hathway and Cawthorne as 'inflexible,' the interview summary said, and not in 'solution mode.'"

The three former top executives of Nortel Networks Corp. were found not guilty of fraud on January 14, 2013. In the court ruling, Justice Frank Marrocco of the Ontario Superior Court found that the accounting manipulations that caused the company to restate its earnings for 2002 and 2003 did not cross the line into criminal behavior.

During the trial, lawyers for the accused said that the men believed that the accounting decisions they made were appropriate at the time, and that the accounting treatment was approved by Nortel's auditors from Deloitte & Touche. Judge Marrocco accepted these arguments, noting many times in his ruling that bookkeeping decisions were reviewed and approved by auditors and were disclosed adequately to investors in press releases or notes added to the financial statements.

Nonetheless, the judge also said that he believed that the accused were attempting to "manage" Nortel's financial results in both the fourth quarter of 2002 and in 2003, but he added he was not satisfied that the changes resulted in material misrepresentations. He said that, except for $80 million of reserves released in the first quarter of 2003, the rest of the use of reserves was within "the normal course of business." Judge Marrocco said the $80 million release, while clearly "unsupportable" and later reversed during a restatement of Nortel's books, was disclosed properly in Nortel's financial statements at the time and was not a material amount. He concluded that Beatty and Dunn "were prepared to go to considerable lengths" to use reserves to improve the bottom line in the second quarter of 2003, but he said the decision was reversed before the financial statements were completed because Gollogly challenged it.

In a surprising twist, Judge Marrocco also suggested the two devastating restatements of Nortel's books in 2003 and 2005 were probably unnecessary in hindsight, although he said he understood why they were done in the context of the time. He said the original statements were arguably correct within a threshold of what was material for a company of that size.

Questions

1. Describe each of the financial shenanigans used by Nortel and how they manipulated earnings.

2. What were the motivating factors that led to the fraud at Nortel? How should the auditors have considered these factors and the culture at Nortel in its risk assessment?

3. Assume you had to prepare an assessment of internal control over financial reporting at Nortel, what would your conclusion be and why?

4. Does it appear from the facts of the case that the Deloitte auditors met their ethical and professional responsibilities in the audit of Nortel's financial statements? Be specific.

Case 7-2 Solutions Network, Inc. (a GVV case)

"We can't recognize revenue immediately, Paul, since we agreed to buy similar software from DSS," Sarah Young stated.

"That's ridiculous," Paul Henley replied. "Get your head out of the sand, Sarah, before it's too late."

Sarah Young is the controller for Solutions Network, Inc., a publicly owned company headquartered in Sunnyvale, California. Solutions Network has an audit committee with three members of the board of directors that are independent of management. Sarah is meeting with Paul Henley, the CFO of the company on January 7, 2019, to discuss the accounting for a software systems transaction with Data Systems Solutions (DSS) prior to the company's audit for the year ended December 31, 2018. Both Young and Henley are CPAs.

Young has excluded the amount in contention from revenue and net income for 2018, but Henley wants the amount to be included in the 2018 results. Without it, Solutions Network would not meet earnings expectations. Henley tells Young that the order came from the top to record the revenue on December 28, 2018, the day the transaction with DSS was finalized. Young points out that Solutions Network ordered essentially the same software from DSS to be shipped and delivered early in 2019. Therefore, according to Young, Solutions Network should delay revenue recognition on this "swap" transaction until that time. Henley argues against Sarah's position, stating that title had passed from the company to DSS on December 31, 2018, when the software product was shipped FOB shipping point.

Background

Solutions Network, Inc., became a publicly owned company on March 15, 2014, following a successful initial public offering (IPO). Solutions Network built up a loyal clientele in the three years prior to the IPO by establishing close working relationships with technology leaders, including IBM, Apple, and Dell Computer. The company designs and engineers systems software to function seamlessly with minimal user interface. There are several companies that provide similar products and consulting services, and DSS is one. However, DSS operates in a larger market providing IT services management products that coordinate the entire business infrastructure into a single system.

Solutions Network grew very rapidly during the past five years, although sales slowed down a bit in 2018. The revenue and earnings streams during those years are as follows:

Year	Revenues (millions)	Net Income (millions)
2013	$148.0	$11.9
2014	175.8	13.2
2015	202.2	15.0
2016	229.8	16.1
2017	267.5	17.3

Young prepared the following estimates for 2018:

Year	Revenues (millions)	Net Income (millions)
2018 (projected)	$262.5	$16.8

The Transaction

On December 28, 2018, Solutions Network offered to sell its Internet infrastructure software to DSS for its internal use. In return, DSS agreed to ship similar software 30 days later to Solutions Network for that company's internal use. The companies had conducted several transactions with each other during the previous five years, and while DSS initially balked at the transaction because it provided no value added to the company, it did not want to upset one of the fastest-growing software companies in the industry. Moreover, Solutions Network might be able to help identify future customers for DSS's IT service management products.

The $15 million of revenue would increase net income by $1.0 million. For Solutions Network, the revenue from the transaction would be enough to enable the company to meet targeted goals, and the higher level of income would provide extra bonus money at year-end for Young, Henley, and Ed Fralen, the CEO.

Accounting Considerations

In her discussions with Henley, Young points out that the auditors will arrive on January 15, 2019; therefore, the company should be certain of the appropriateness of its accounting before that time. After all, says Young, "the auditors rely on us to record transactions properly as part of their audit expectations." At this point Henley reacts angrily and tells Young she can pack her bags and go if she doesn't support the company in its revenue recognition of the DSS transaction. Young is taken aback. Henley seems unusually agitated. Perhaps he was under a lot more pressure to "meet the numbers" than she anticipated. To defuse the matter, Young makes an excuse to end the meeting prematurely and asks if they could meet on Monday morning, after the weekend. Henley agrees.

Over the weekend, Sarah Young calls her best friend, Shannon McCollough, for advice. Shannon is a controller at another company and Sarah would often commensurate with Shannon over their mutual experiences. Shannon suggests that Sarah should explain to Paul Henley exactly what her ethical obligations are in the matter. Shannon thinks it might make a difference because Paul is a CPA as well.

After the discussion with Shannon, Sarah considers whether she is being too firm in her position. On the one hand, she knows that regardless of the passage of title to DSS on December 31, 2018, the transaction is linked to Solutions Network's agreement to take the DSS product 30 days later. While she doesn't anticipate any problems in that regard, Sarah is uncomfortable with the recording of revenue on December 31 because DSS did not complete its portion of the agreement by that date. She has her doubts whether the auditors would sanction the accounting treatment.

On the other hand, Sarah is also concerned about the fact that another transaction occurred during the previous year that she questioned but, in the end, went along with Paul's accounting for this transaction. On December 28, 2017, Solutions Network sold a major system for $20 million to Laramie Systems but executed a side agreement with Laramie on that date which gave Laramie the right to return the product for any reason within 30 days. Even though Solutions Network recorded the revenue in 2017 and Sarah felt uneasy about it, she did not object because Laramie did not return the product; her acceptance was motivated by the delay in the external audit until after the 30-day period had expired. Now, however, Sarah is concerned that a pattern may be developing.

Questions

1. What are the main arguments Sarah is trying to counter? That is, what are the reasons and rationalizations she needs to address in deciding how to handle the meeting with Paul Henley?

2. What is at stake for the key parties in this case? What are Sarah's ethical obligations to them?

3. Should Sarah's decision on revenue recognition in 2017 influence how she handles the DSS transaction? Explain.

4. Should Sarah follow Shannon's advice? What if she does and Paul Henley does not back off? What additional levers can she use to strengthen her position?

5. What is the most powerful and persuasive response to the reasons and rationalizations Sarah needs to address? To whom should the argument be made? When and in what context?

6. What should Sarah do next if all parties at Solutions Network support Paul Henley's position and flat out tell Sarah to be a team player?

Case 7-3 Allergan: Mind the GAP

Exhibit 1 presents the fourth quarter press release of Allergan. Allergan is a global pharmaceutical company and a leader in a new industry model–Growth Pharma. Allergan's product lines include Botox, Juvederm, Latisse, Namenda, and Restasis. Exhibit 2 presents the reconciliation from GAAP to non-GAAP income that was included with the release. Additional supporting information appears after the questions below.

Over the years, Allergan has had many disagreements with the SEC about the presentation of non-GAAP metrics in their financial reports and press releases. Allergan's responses to SEC staff comments has been to emphasize that its performance measures "are useful to both management and investors in assessing current performance and future operations." Moreover, Allergan contended in its response that "analysts for our industry group base their third-party consensus estimates on non-GAAP earnings per share metrics."

Review **Exhibit 1** below and answer the following questions.

1. Do you believe Allergan's financial information in its press release is useful? Why or why not?

2. Do you believe this kind of information should be subject to audit procedures? If so, what procedures should be used? If not, why not?

3. Do you believe the financial and non-financial information provided by Allergan in its press release is veiled attempt at earnings management? Explain.

Review **Exhibit 2** at the end of the case and answer the following questions.

4. Does the reconciliation shed light on the usefulness and understandability of the non-GAAP numbers? Explain.

5. Look at each item included in the reconciliation and briefly discuss whether you think each one should or should not be included in a reconciliation from GAAP to non-GAAP.

Allergan Reports Solid Finish to 2017 with 12% Increase in Fourth Quarter GAAP Net Revenues to $4.3 Billion:

- Q4 2017 GAAP Continuing Operations Income Per Share of $9.97; Q4 Non-GAAP Performance Net Income Per Share of $4.86

- Q4 2017 GAAP Operating Loss from Continuing Operations of $90.5 Million; Q4 Non-GAAP Adjusted Operating Income from Continuing Operations of $2.17 Billion

- Q4 2017 GAAP Revenue Growth Versus Prior Year Quarter Powered by BOTOX®, JUVÉDERM® Collection, ALLODERM®, CoolSculpting® and Launch Products

- Full-Year 2017 GAAP Net Revenues of $15.94 Billion

- Full-Year 2017 GAAP Continuing Operations Loss Per Share of $11.99; Full-Year Non-GAAP Performance Net Income Per Share of $16.35

- Company Continues to Advance R&D Pipeline Beyond Six "Star" Programs

- Provides Full-Year 2018 Guidance and First Quarter 2018 GAAP Net Revenue and Non- GAAP Performance Net Income Per Share Guidance

Dublin, Ireland—February 6, 2018—Allergan plc (NYSE: AGN) today reported its fourth quarter and full-year 2017 continuing operations performance.

Continuing on from the earnings release, the total fourth quarter net revenues were $4.33 billion, a 12.0% increase from the prior year quarter, driven by BOTOX® Cosmetic, BOTOX® Therapeutic, JUVÉDERM® Collection, ALLODERM®, CoolSculpting® and new products, including VRAYLAR™, NAMZARIC® and VIBERZI®. The increase was partially offset by lower revenues from products losing patent exclusivity, and the continuing decline in ACZONE® and NAMENDA XR®. For the full year 2017, Allergan reported total net revenues of $15.94 billion, a 9.4% increase versus the prior year, driven by continued strong growth across key therapeutic areas and key products, and the addition of Regenerative Medicine products and CoolSculpting®.

"2017 was a pivotal year for Allergan and we delivered solid results. We powered strong revenue growth of our top products and in each of our regions. We acquired, integrated and grew two new businesses and continued to advance our R&D pipeline. Allergan also continued to execute our capital deployment plan by completing a $15 billion share repurchase program, instituting a dividend and paying down debt in 2017," said Brent Saunders, Chairman and CEO of Allergan. "I believe that Allergan has a strong future and I am especially proud of our Allergan colleagues who continue to be Bold for Life by delivering treatments that make a difference for patients around the world."

Fourth Quarter 2017 Performance

GAAP operating loss from continuing operations in the fourth quarter 2017 was $90.5 million, including the impact of amortization, in-process research and development (R&D) impairments and charges associated with the December 2017 restructuring program announced on January 3, 2018. Non-GAAP adjusted operating income from continuing operations in the fourth quarter of 2017 was $2.17 billion, an increase of 16.4% versus the prior year quarter. Cash flow from operations for the fourth quarter of 2017 increased to approximately $2.05 billion.

Full-Year 2017 Performance

GAAP operating loss from continuing operations for the full year 2017 was $5.92 billion, compared with $1.83 billion in 2016 primarily due to impairment charges recognized in the third quarter of 2017 of $3.2 billion related to RESTASIS® and $646.0 million related to ACZONE®. Non-GAAP adjusted operating income from continuing operations for the full year 2017 was $7.65 billion, an increase of 5.6% versus prior year. GAAP Cash flow from operations for the full year of 2017 increased to approximately $5.87 billion, compared to $1.45 billion in 2016, which was negatively impacted by cash taxes paid in connection with the gain recognized on the businesses sold to Teva Pharmaceuticals Industries, Ltd ("Teva").

Operating Expenses

Total GAAP Selling, General and Administrative (SG&A) Expense was $1.27 billion for the fourth quarter 2017, compared to $1.28 billion in the prior year quarter. Included within GAAP SG&A in the fourth quarter and full

EXHIBIT 1 Allergan Earnings Release

(unaudited; $ in millions, except per share amounts)	Q4 '17	Q4 '16	Q3 '17	Q4 '17 v Q4 '16	Q4 '17 v Q3 '17	Year Ended December 31, 2017	Year Ended December 31, 2016	2017 v 2016
Total net revenues**	$4,326.10	$3,864.30	$4,034.30	12.0%	7.2%	$15,940.70	$14,570.60	9.4%
Operating (Loss)	$ (90.50)	$ 900.00	$(4,022.30)	−89.9%	−97.8%	$ (5,921.20)	$ (1,825.50)	224.4%
Diluted EPS—Continuing Operations	$ 9.97	$ (0.31)	$ (12.05)	n.m.	−182.7%	$ (11.99)	$ (3.17)	278.2%
SG&A Expense	$1,266.80	$ 1,276.80	$ 1,169.70	−0.8%	8.3%	$ 5,016.70	$ 4,740.30	5.8%
R&D Expense	$ 408.20	$ 913.30	$ 442.60	−55.3%	−7.8%	$ 2,100.10	$ 2,575.70	−18.5%
Continuing Operations Tax Rate	n.m.	96.4%	29.3%	n.m.	n.m.	64.2%	67.0%	−2.8%
Non-GAAP Adjusted Operating Income	$2,174.30	$1,868.70	$ 1,968.20	16.4%	10.5%	$ 7,647.50	$ 7,245.30	5.6%
Non-GAAP Performance Net Income Per Share	$ 4.86	$ 3.90	$ 4.15	24.6%	17.1%	$ 16.35	$ 13.51	21.0%
Non-GAAP Adjusted EBITDA	$2,284.50	$1,975.70	$2,051.70	15.6%	11.3%	$ 8,097.60	$ 7,628.70	6.1%
Non-GAAP SG&A Expense	$1,132.80	$1,067.00	$1,099.60	6.2%	3.0%	$ 4,554.80	$ 4,081.70	11.6%
Non-GAAP R&D Expense	$ 405.70	$ 425.90	$ 405.30	−4.7%	0.1%	$ 1,598.80	$ 1,433.80	11.5%
Non-GAAP Continuing Operations Tax Rate	11.4%	10.4%	13.1%	1.0%	−1.7%	12.6%	8.9%	3.7%

** Excludes the reclassification of revenues of ($80.0) million in the twelve months ended December 31, 2016 related to the portion of Allergan product revenues sold by our former Anda Distribution Business into discontinued operations.

year 2017 were charges related to the December 2017 restructuring program of $80.0 million. Total non-GAAP SG&A expense increased to $1.13 billion for the fourth quarter 2017, compared to $1.07 billion in the prior year period, primarily due to costs associated with the addition of the Regenerative Medicine and CoolSculpting® businesses. GAAP R&D investment for the fourth quarter of 2017 was $408.2 million, compared to $913.3 million in the fourth quarter of 2016. Non-GAAP R&D investment for the fourth quarter 2017 was $405.7 million, a decrease of 4.7% over the prior year quarter, due to reprioritization of R&D programs and tight expense management.

Asset Sales & Impairments, Net and In-Process R&D Impairments

The Company recorded impairment charges of $238.5 million and $456.0 million in the three months ended December 31, 2017 and 2016, respectively. The Company excludes asset sales and impairments, net and in-process research and development impairments from its non-GAAP performance net income attributable to shareholders as well as Adjusted EBITDA and Adjusted Operating Income.

Amortization, Other Income (Expense) Net, Tax and Capitalization

Amortization expense from continuing operations for the fourth quarter 2017 was $1.92 billion, compared to $1.64 billion in the fourth quarter of 2016.

The Company's GAAP continuing operations tax rate benefit in the fourth quarter of 2017 was primarily attributable to discrete income tax benefits recognized as a result of the Tax Cuts and Jobs Act ("TCJA"). The Company's non-GAAP adjusted continuing operations tax rate was 11.4% in the fourth quarter 2017. As of December 31, 2017, Allergan had cash and marketable securities of $6.45 billion and outstanding indebtedness of $30.1 billion.

Provisional Estimates of the Impact of U.S. Tax Reform

Allergan recorded a net provisional benefit of approximately $2.8 billion related to the TCJA. This amount includes a $730 million provisional expense representing the U.S. tax payable on deemed repatriated earnings of non-U.S. subsidiaries offset by a $3.5 billion net reduction of U.S. deferred tax liabilities due to the lower enacted U.S. tax rate and the change in assertion regarding permanently reinvested earnings as a result of the transition to a territorial tax system. These provisional estimates are based on the Company's initial analysis and current interpretation of the legislation. Given the complexity of the TCJA, anticipated guidance from the U.S. Treasury, and the potential for additional guidance from the Securities and Exchange Commission or the Financial Accounting Standards Board, these estimates may be adjusted during 2018.

Discontinued Operations and Continuing Operations

As a result of the divestiture of the Company's generics business and the divestiture of the Company's Anda Distribution business in 2016, the financial results of those businesses have been reclassified to discontinued operations for all periods presented in our consolidated financial statements up through the date of the divestitures.

Included within (loss) from discontinued operations for the three months ended December 31, 2017, was a charge to settle certain Teva related matters, net of tax of $387.4 million.

Included in segment revenues in the twelve months ended December 31, 2016, are product sales that were sold by the Anda Distribution business once the Anda Distribution business had sold the product to a third-party customer. These sales are included in segment results and are excluded from total continuing operations revenues through a reduction to Corporate revenues. Cost of sales for these products in discontinued operations is equal to our average third-party cost of sales for third-party branded products distributed by Anda Distribution.

EXHIBIT 2   Allergan PLC Reconciliation Table

| | (Unaudited; in millions except per share amounts) | | | |
| | Three Months Ended December 31, | | Twelve Months Ended December 31, | |
	2017	2016	2017	2016
GAAP to Non-GAAP Performance net income calculation				
GAAP income/(loss) from continuing operations attributable to shareholders	$ 3,506.6	$ (41.9)	$(3,722.6)	$ (941.1)
Adjusted for:				
Amortization	$ 1,922.2	$ 1,638.50	$ 7,197.1	$ 6,470.4
Acquisition, divestiture and licensing charges[1]	$ 108.4	$ 800.40	$ 4,083.4	$ 1,593.6
Accretion and fair-value adjustments to contingent consideration	$ (81.6)	$ (143.50)	$ (133.2)	$ (64.2)
Impairment/asset sales and related costs	$ 238.5	$ 456.00	$ 5,380.0	$ 748.9
Non-recurring losses/(gains)	$ 16.2	$ (9.50)	$ 210.1	$ 8.9
Non-acquisition restructurings, including Global Supply Chain initiatives	$ 113.6		$ 208.4	
Legal settlements	$ 22.2	$ 17.30	$ 96.5	$ 117.3
Income taxes on items above and other discrete income tax adjustments	$ (4,137.8)	$(1,242.20)	$ (7,508.8)	$(2,432.2)
Non-GAAP performance net income attributable to shareholders	$ 1,708.3	$ 1,475.1	$ 5,810.9	$ 5,501.6
Diluted earnings per share				
Diluted income/(loss) per share from continuing operations attributable to shareholders—GAAP	$ 9.97	$ (0.12)	$ (11.15)	$ (2.45)
Non-GAAP performance net income per share attributable to shareholders	$ 4.86	$ 3.90	$ 16.35	$ 13.51
Basic weighted average ordinary shares outstanding	331.3	356.8	333.8	384.9
Effect of dilutive securities:				
Dilutive shares	20.3	21.8	21.6	22.3
Dilutive weighted average ordinary shares outstanding	351.6	378.6	355.4	407.2

(1) Includes stock-based compensation primarily due to the Zeltiq, Allergan and Forest acquisitions as well as the valuation accounting impact in interest expense net.

Case 7-4 The Potential Darkside of Using Non-GAAP Metrics (a GVV case)

The CFO, King Bernard, of Blackswan Petfood, a large publicly traded manufacturer of organic gourmet dog and cat food, is getting ready for the quarterly conference call with major investors and financial analysts in two days. The King has been reviewing a draft of the quarterly financial statements for the fourth quarter ending September 30, 2018, and working with his financial team on how best to present the numbers in the conference call. During the current quarter, the company had two material transactions which to him appear to unfairly distort the financial condition of the company in the GAAP numbers provided by Debbie Doberman, the Senior Manager in charge of financial reporting. The first relates to a loss of $2 million due to a massive tsunami which wiped out their manufacturing facilities in Chihuahua, Mexico. This amount was included in Additional Income/Expense Items. The second item relates to a loss of $1 million from the disposal of their Red Rooster product line of gourmet chicken feed that was discontinued.

The income statement currently reads as follows:

Blackswan Pet Food Income Statement September 30, 2018	(in 000's)
Sales	$ 458,543
Cost of Goods Sold	$(257,678)
Gross Profit	$ 200,865
Selling and Administrative	$(123,738)
Depreciation and Amortization	$ (25,324)
Non-Recurring Items	$ (25,000)
Other Operating Items	$ (13,435)
Operating Income	$ 13,368
Additional Income/Expense Items	$ (2,456)
Earnings before Interest and Tax	$ 10,912
Interest Expense	$ (3,478)
Earnings before Tax	$ 7,434
Income Tax	$ 1,918
Net Income before Discontinued Operations	$ 5,516
Discontinued Operations (net of tax)	$ (7,500)
Net Income (loss)	$ (1,984)
Earnings (loss) per share	(0.20)

Loyal Doge, the newest member of the CFO's financial team (and recent college graduate), suggests that they provide the analysts with a number of GAAP and Non-GAAP metrics. He double majored in accounting and marketing to obtain the required 150 credits to sit for the CPA exam. He said he learned in his strategic marketing class that a lot of companies are now using non-GAAP metrics to "better" explain their financial results and provide more useful information to users of the financial reports. He also noted that the recent change to GAAP which eliminated the concept of Extraordinary Items was just bad accounting and he believed that alone was reason enough to create some metrics of their own. King Bernard thought his idea made a lot of sense as he, too, was wondering why the costs related to the tsunami should be included in operating income.

The group discussed providing the analysts with the following measures.

- Earnings before Interest, Tax, Depreciation and Amortization (EBITDA),
- Earnings before Discontinued Operations,
- Earnings before Extraordinary Items,
- Recurring Earnings which would exclude both the discontinued operation and extraordinary item.

Whichever number(s) were to be presented would be net of tax, and an EPS number would be calculated as well. In addition, they discussed highlighting these new measures in the financials presented on their website. The group had a very animated discussion, and excitement continued to build as they realized that, through the use of these new metrics, they could paint a much better picture of the operating results of the company.

"Dilly, Dilly", Loyal Doge said expressively. He was excitedly talking about using multiple colors, large fonts, and the bolding of non-GAAP numbers in the quarterly financials when Debbie Doberman decided to speak up. Since it was 5 pm, the group decided to stop for the day and meet at 8 am the following morning at which time they would address Debbie's concerns.

Assume you are in Debbie's place. You are a CPA, MBA, CFE. You have purposefully been silent up until now to first gather all the facts, hear everyone's opinion, and then provide guidance on what is and is not acceptable with respect to non-GAAP disclosures. Consider the following in developing a game plan for what to say when you address the group tomorrow.

Questions

1. What are the main arguments that you will need to counter? That is, what are the reasons and rationalizations you will need to address?

2. What is at stake should you not convince King Bernard to follow the SEC guidelines on the use of non-GAAP metrics? Include both short and long-term potential consequences in your answer.

3. What levers do you have available? Include in your answer a discussion of the specific rules and guidelines for the use of non-GAAP metrics.

4. If you cannot convince the King to follow the guidelines for using non-GAAP metrics, what is your next step?

5. If the earnings call goes forward and the non-GAAP measures are prominently highlighted as Loyal Doge suggests, what are your options then?

Case 7-5 Dell Computer

Background

For years, Dell's seemingly magical power to squeeze efficiencies out of its supply chain and drive down costs made it a darling of the financial markets. Now we learn that the magic was at least partly the result of a huge financial illusion. On July 22, 2010, Dell agreed to pay a $100 million penalty to settle allegations by the SEC that the company had "manipulated its accounting over an extended period to project financial results that the company wished it had achieved."

According to the commission, Dell would have missed analysts' earnings expectations in every quarter between 2002 and 2006 were it not for its accounting shenanigans. This involved a deal with Intel, a big microchip maker, under which Dell agreed to use Intel's central processing unit chips exclusively in its computers in return for a series of undisclosed payments, locking out Advanced Micro Devices (AMD), a big rival. The SEC's complaint said that Dell had maintained cookie-jar reserves using Intel's money that it could dip into to cover any shortfalls in its operating results.

The SEC said that the company should have disclosed to investors that it was drawing on these reserves, but it did not. And it claimed that, at their peak, the exclusivity payments from Intel represented 76% of Dell's quarterly operating income, which is a shocking figure. The problem arose when Dell's quarterly earnings fell sharply in 2007 after it ended the arrangement with Intel. The SEC alleged that Dell attributed the drop to an aggressive product-pricing strategy and higher-than-expected component prices, when the real reason was that the payments from Intel had dried up.

The accounting fraud embarrassed the once-squeaky-clean Michael Dell, the firm's founder and CEO. He and Kevin Rollins, a former top official of the company, agreed to each pay a $4 million penalty without admitting or denying the SEC's allegations. Several senior financial executives at Dell also incurred penalties. "Accuracy and completeness are the touchstones of public company disclosure under the federal securities laws," said Robert Khuzami of the SEC's enforcement division when announcing the settlement deal. "Michael Dell and other senior Dell executives fell short of that standard repeatedly over many years."

In its statement on the SEC settlement the company played down Michael Dell's personal involvement, saying that his $4 million penalty was not connected to the accounting fraud charges being settled by the company, but was "limited to claims in which only negligence, and not fraudulent intent, is required to establish liability, as well as secondary liability claims for other non-fraud charges."[1]

Accounting Irregularities

The SEC charged Dell Computer with fraud for materially misstating its operating results from FY2002 to FY2005. In addition to Dell and Rollins, the SEC also charged former Dell chief accounting officer (CAO) Robert W. Davis for his role in the company's accounting fraud. The SEC's complaint against Davis alleged that he materially misrepresented Dell's financial results by using various cookie-jar reserves to cover shortfalls in operating results and engaged in other reserve manipulations from FY2002 to FY2005, including improper recording of large payments from Intel as operating expense-offsets. This fraudulent accounting made it appear that Dell was consistently meeting Wall Street earnings targets (i.e., net operating income) through the company's management and operations. The SEC's complaint further alleged that the reserve manipulations allowed Dell to misstate materially its operating expenses as a percentage of revenue—an important financial metric that Dell highlighted to investors.[2]

The company engaged in the questionable use of reserve accounts to smooth net income. Davis directed Dell assistant controller Randall D. Imhoff and his subordinates, when they identified reserved amounts that were no longer needed for bona fide liabilities, to check with him about what to do with the excess reserves instead of just releasing them to the income statement. In many cases, he ordered his team to transfer the amounts to an "other accrued liabilities" account. According to the SEC, "Davis viewed the 'Corporate Contingencies' as a way to offset future liabilities. He substantially participated in the 'earmarking' of the excess accruals for various purposes."

Beginning in the 1990s, Intel had a marketing campaign that paid its vendors certain marketing rebates to use their products according to a written contract. These were known as market developing funds (MDFs), which, according to accounting rules, Dell could treat as reductions in operating expenses because these payments offset expenses that

---

[1]Facts of the case are available at http://www.economist.com/blogs/newsbook/2010/07/dells_sec_settlement.

[2]Securities and Exchange Commission, *Securities and Exchange Commission v. Robert W. Davis*, Civil Action No. 1:10-cv-01464 (D.D.C.) and *Securities and Exchange Commission v. Randall D. Imhoff,* Civil Action No. 1:10-cv-01465 (D.D.C.), *Accounting and Auditing Enforcement Release No. 3177* | August 27, 2010. Available at: www.sec.gov/litigation/litreleases/2010/lr21634.htm.

Dell incurred in marketing Intel's products. However, the character of these payments changed in 2001, when Intel began to provide additional rebates to Dell and a few other companies that were outside the contractual agreements.

Intel made these large payments to Dell from 2001 to 2006 to refrain from using chips or processors manufactured by Intel's main rival, AMD. Rather than disclosing these material payments to investors, Dell decided that it would be better to incorporate these funds into their component costs without any recognition of their existence. The nondisclosure of these payments caused fraudulent misrepresentation, allowing Dell to report increased profitability over these years.

These payments grew significantly over the years making up a rather large part of Dell's operating income. When viewed as a percentage of operating income, these payments started at about 10% in FY2003 and increased to about 76% in the first quarter of FY2007.

When Dell began using AMD as a secondary supplier of chips in 2006, Intel cut the exclusivity payments off, which resulted in Dell having to report a decrease in profits. Rather than disclose the loss of the exclusivity payments as the reason for the decrease in profitability, Dell continued to mislead investors.

Dell's Internal Investigation

On August 16, 2007, Dell announced it had completed an internal investigation, which had revealed a variety of accounting errors and irregularities and that it would restate results for FY2003 through FY2006, and the first quarter of 2007. The restatement cited certain accounting errors and irregularities in those financial statements as the reasons the previously issued statements should no longer be relied upon.

Dell said that the investigation of accounting issues found that executives wrongfully manipulated accruals and account balances, often to meet Wall Street quarterly financial expectations in prior years. The company was forced to restate its earnings during that time period, which lowered its total earnings during that time by $50 million to $150 million.

As result of the SEC's investigation, Dell took another hit to its bottom line. With the restatement, Dell's first quarter 2011 earnings looked like this: net income of $341 million and earnings of 17¢ per share. That's instead of the initially reported $441 million and 22¢ per share.

PriceWaterhouseCoopers (PwC)

PwC had been Dell's independent auditor since 1986 and had signed off on every one of Dell's financial statements that were on file with the SEC. From 2003 to 2007, Dell paid PwC more than $50 million to perform auditing and other services. PwC issued clean (*unmodified*) audit opinions for the 2003 to 2006 financial statements, saying that they fairly represented the financial position of Dell.

It was alleged that PwC had consistently approved the now-restated financial statements as prepared in accordance with generally accepted accounting principles and did not conduct an audit in accordance with generally accepted auditing standards. The argument was that the opinions that the financial statements fairly represented financial position were materially false and misleading. The court ruled that the restatement does not by itself satisfy the *scienter* (knowledge of the falsehood) requirement to hold the auditors legally liable for deliberate misrepresentation of material facts or actions taken with severe recklessness as to the accuracy of its audits or reports.

The legal standard for auditor liability under Section 10(b) of the Securities Exchange Act of 1934 and Rule 10b-5 requires that the plaintiff must show (1) a misstatement or omission, (2) of a material fact, (3) made with scienter, (4) on which the plaintiff relied, and (5) that proximately caused the injury. The court pointed out in its opinion that "the mere publication of inaccurate accounting figures, or failure to follow GAAP, without more, does not establish scienter." To establish scienter adequately, the plaintiffs must state with particularity facts giving rise to a strong inference that the party knew that it was publishing materially false information, or that it was severely reckless in publishing such information. The court ruled that the plaintiffs did not prove fraudulent intent.[3]

---

[3]*In re Dell Inc., Securities Litigation, U.S. District Court for the Western District of Texas Austin Division,* Case No. A-06-CA-726-55, October 6, 2008, Available at: http://securities.stanford.edu/filings-documents/1036/DELL_01/2008107_r01o_0600726.pdf.

In a suit by shareholders against the firm, PwC was accused of a variety of charges, including not being truly independent and ignoring red flags. These charges were dismissed on a basis of lack of evidence to support the accusations.

Questions

1. In his analysis of the Dell fraud for Forbes, Edward Hess comments: "Too often, the market's maniacal focus on creating ever-increasing quarterly earnings drives bad corporate behavior, as it apparently did at Dell. That behavior produces non-authentic earnings that obscure what is really happening in business. Short-termism can result in a range of corporate and financial games that may enrich management at the expense of market integrity and efficient investor capital allocation."[4] Comment on Hess's statement from two perspectives: earnings management and financial analysts earnings projections.

2. Explain the difference between financial statement fraud and disclosure fraud. How did Dell use each one to produce materially misstated financial results?

3. Do you agree with the court opinion that PwC did not act with fraudulent intent, therefore, not holding it legally liable? How can fraudulent intent be established in a case like Dell?

[4]Edward D. Hess, Stark Lessons From the Dell Fraud Case, Forbes, October 13, 2010, https://www.forbes.com/2010/10/13/michael-dell-fraud-leadership-governance-sec.html#4d9b8c046d6a.

Case 7-6 TierOne Bank

It took a long time, but the Securities and Exchange Commission finally acted and held auditors responsible for the fraud that occurred in banks during the financial recession in 2014. Surprisingly to some, the TierOne bank case explained below was the nation's first case brought by federal securities regulators against auditors of a company that went down in the multibillion-dollar financial crisis and real estate meltdown. Federal banking authorities had brought a handful of cases against auditors, but the SEC hadn't brought one until TierOne.

TierOne Corporation, a holding company for TierOne Bank, had $3 billion in assets when it collapsed in 2010. The facts of the case are drawn from the initial decision reached by the SEC, *In the Matter of John J. Aesoph, CPA, and Darren M. Bennett, CPA,* unless otherwise noted.[1] Aesoph and Bennett were the KPMG auditors of TierOne.

TierOne was a regional bank headquartered in Lincoln, Nebraska, that originated and purchased loans, and loan participation interests, with its primary market area in Nebraska, Iowa, and Kansas. From 2002 to 2005, TierOne opened or acquired nine loan production offices (LPO) in Arizona, Colorado, Florida, Minnesota, Nevada, and North Carolina, the main purpose of which was to originate construction and land-development loans. Over time, TierOne increased its portfolio in these high-risk loans. By September 2008, TierOne closed the LPOs in the wake of real estate market deterioration. By year-end 2008, TierOne had a total net loan portfolio of approximately $2.8 billion, with a quarter of its loans concentrated in the LPO states. In October 2008, TierOne's regulator, the Office of Thrift Supervision (OTS), issued a report following its June 2008 examination of the bank, in which it downgraded TierOne's bank rating, criticized management and loan practices, and found that the bank had collateral-dependent loans either without appraisals or with unsupported or stale appraisals. The bank was closed by OTS in 2010. TierOne Corp. filed for bankruptcy three weeks later.

[1]SEC, *In the Matter of John J. Aesoph, CPA, and Darren M. Bennett, CPA,* Initial Decision Release No. Administrative Proceeding File No. 3-151658, Available at: https://www.sec.gov/alj/aljdec/2014/id624cff.pdf.

Tier One Management

The SEC alleged in the indictment that TierOne's executives hid loan losses as OTS repeatedly requested information. On December 10, 2014, Gilbert Lundstrom, the former chief executive officer of TierOne, was indicted for hiding the condition of the bank from regulators, investors, and auditors. Allegedly, Lundstrom conspired with others to hide the bank's problems as losses mounted on its loan portfolio. "Lundstrom is essentially charged with having two sets of books, with the books shown to regulators concealing tens of millions of dollars in delinquent loans," said Christy L. Romero, special inspector general for the U.S. Troubled Asset Relief Program, established during the financial meltdown.[2]

The trigger for the fraudulent activities by TierOne management was that TierOne's core capital ratio had fallen below the 8.5% minimum threshold mandated by the OTS. Lundstrom and others caused the bank to issue false statements that it met or exceeded the ratio.

Lundstrom knew that the bank needed to increase its reserves to cover loan losses and didn't report this, according to the indictment. Lundstrom, in 2012, settled a lawsuit brought by the SEC claiming he understated TierOne's loan losses and losses on real estate repossessed by the bank so that the bank would appear to meet its mandated regulatory capital requirements. Lundstrom, who didn't admit the allegations when settling, agreed to pay $500,921 in penalties.

Another former TierOne executive, Don Langford, the bank's chief credit officer, pleaded guilty for his role in what prosecutors called a scheme to defraud shareholders and regulators. Langford played a major role in developing an internal estimate of losses embedded in TierOne's loan portfolio, but did not disclose that estimate to auditors or regulators. Langford's initial analysis indicated the bank needed an additional $65 million in loan loss reserves; a refined analysis, entitled the "Best/Worst Case Scenario," showed losses ranging from a "best case" of $36 million to a "worst case" of $114 million. Langford did not share any of this analysis with the bank's accounting staff or external auditors.

As the value of properties declined and defaults increased during 2008 and 2009, Lundstrom and others directed TierOne employees to forgo ordering new appraisals even when the old ones were stale or no longer accurate. In some cases, when appraisals were made and came in at lower values than recorded by TierOne, the new appraisals were rejected at the direction of Lundstrom and other bank executives. They also restructured loan terms to disguise the borrowers' inability to make timely interest and principal payments. As a result, Lundstrom and others were allegedly able to hide millions of dollars in losses from regulators and investors.

KPMG

KPMG LLP (KPMG) audited TierOne's 2008 financial statements. In March 2009, KPMG issued an unqualified audit opinion on TierOne's consolidated financial statements and effectiveness of its internal controls over financial reporting as of year-end 2008; certified that the audit was conducted in accordance with PCAOB standards that required KPMG to plan and perform the audit to obtain reasonable assurance whether the financial statements were free of material misstatement; and opined that the financial statements reflected in TierOne's year-end 2008 Form 10-K presented fairly, in all material respects, the financial position of TierOne and the results of its operations and cash flows, in conformity with U.S. Generally Accepted Accounting Principles (GAAP).

Subsequently, TierOne recorded $120 million in losses relating to its loan portfolio after obtaining updated appraisals. In April 2010, when KPMG learned that TierOne had failed to disclose the document created by Langford showing an internal analysis of varying estimates of additional loan loss reserves higher than what had been disclosed during the audit, the firm resigned and withdrew its audit opinion. Citing risk of material misstatement, KPMG had also warned the audit committee that TierOne's financials were not to be relied upon by investors. The two items

---

[2]SEC, *U.S. v. Lundstrom,* 14-cr-03136, U.S. District Court, District of Nebraska (Lincoln), Available at: http://www.justice.gov/criminal-vns/case/lundstromg.

cited in the report to the audit committee were: (1) TierOne's year-end 2008 financial statements contained "material misstatements related to certain out-of-period adjustments for loan loss reserves," and (2) TierOne's internal controls could not be relied on "due to a material weakness in internal control over financial reporting related to the material misstatements."

Aesoph and Bennett were charged with improper professional conduct in connection with the December 31, 2008, year-end audit of TierOne's financial statements. They failed to comply with Public Company Accounting Oversight Board (PCAOB) auditing standards because they failed to subject TierOne's loan loss estimates—one of the highest risk areas of a bank audit—to appropriate scrutiny. The SEC also said the pair "failed to obtain sufficient competent evidential matter to support their audit conclusions, and failed to exercise due professional care and appropriate professional skepticism."

According to the SEC's order instituting administrative proceedings against Aesoph and Bennett, they "rubber stamped" TierOne's accounting for loan losses. The auditors failed to comply with professional auditing standards in their substantive audit procedures over the bank's valuation of loan losses resulting from impaired loans. They relied principally on stale appraisals and management's uncorroborated representations of current value despite evidence that management's estimates were biased and inconsistent with independent market data rather than make an independent analysis of loan value and collectability.[3]

As for the internal controls, the SEC said that the controls over the allowance for loans and lease losses identified and tested by the auditing engagement team did not effectively test management's use of stale and inadequate appraisals to value the collateral underlying the bank's troubled loan portfolio. For example, the auditors identified TierOne's Asset Classification Committee as a key control. But there was no reference in the audit workpapers to whether or how the committee assessed the value of the collateral underlying individual loans evaluated for impairment, and the committee did not generate or review written documentation to support management's assumptions. Given the complete lack of documentation, Aesoph and Bennett had insufficient evidence from which to conclude that the bank's internal controls for valuation of collateral were effective. Robert Khuzami, director of the SEC's Division of Enforcement, said, "Aesoph and Bennett merely rubber-stamped TierOne's collateral value estimates and ignored the red flags surrounding the bank's troubled real estate loans."[4]

In 2016, Aesoph and Bennett appealed the original decision of the Administrative Law Judge that suspended them from practicing before the SEC for a term of one year and a term of six months, respectively. The SEC cross-appealed, asking for a three- and two-year term, respectively, after which time they could apply for reinstatement. In his appeal, Bennett took issue with statements made by the SEC that, he claimed, suggested that the auditors should be responsible for "auditing" each of TierOne's loan loss reserve estimates, whereas under PCAOB standards "[t]he auditor is responsible for evaluating the reasonableness of accounting estimates made by management in the context of the financial statements taken as a whole." The SEC, however, contended that in order to evaluate the reasonableness of the estimates in the context of the financial statements taken as whole, they were required to evaluate those estimates on a loan-by-loan basis. In the end the SEC cross-appeal won the day based on evidence provided that the two KPMG auditors violated PCAOB auditing standards in three specific areas with respect to the loan loss reserves: (1) their audit of the effectiveness of ICFR, (2) their substantive audit test work over the account, and (3) their post-audit procedures following the discovery of new appraisals in 2009.[5]

---

[3]"SEC Charges Two KPMG Auditors for Failed Audit of Nebraska Bank Hiding Loan Losses During Financial Crisis," Available at: http://www.sec.gov/News/PressRelease/Detail/PressRelease/1365171513624.

[4]SEC, "SEC Charges two KPMG Auditors for Failed Audit of Nebraska Bank Hiding Loan Losses During Financial Crisis," Available at: http://www.sec.gov/News/PressRelease/Detail/PressRelease/1365171513624.

[5]SEC, *In the Matter of John J. Aesoph and Darren M. Bennett,* Administrative Procedure File No. 3-15168, August 5, 2016, https://www.sec.gov/litigation/opinions/2016/34-78490.pdf.

Questions

1. Was TierOne's accounting for the loan loss reserve indicative of "managed earnings"? How would you make that determination?

2. What is the purpose of the auditor's assessment of ICFR? Describe the deficiencies in KPMG's audit work in that regard?

3. Would you conclude from the facts of this case that Tier One's fraud caused KPMG's auditing standards violations? Explain.

4. Which rules of conduct in the AICPA Code were violated by KPMG auditors? Be specific.

Case 7-7 Non-GAAP Metric Disclosure by General Electric: Value Added, Red Herring, or Red Flag?

According to an October 16, 2017, article by Richard Clough of Bloomberg News,[1] General Electric reported earnings per share of $.28, $.13, $.19 and $.15 for the quarter ending September 30, 2017, on an earnings call. Yes, you read that correctly, GE reported four different earnings per share figures for the same quarter. The numbers represent profit that includes or excludes certain items, such as pension costs and discontinued operations. For example, GE referred to one of these measures as 'industrial operating plus verticals earnings per share' rather than simply 'adjusted,' 'core,' or 'non-GAAP earnings per share' as is common place at most companies.[2] GE is not alone in the use of both GAAP and non-GAAP metrics they include in their financial reporting. However, according to Bloomberg, GE is only one of 21 S&P 500 companies to use more than one earnings per share figure.

Fast forward to the fourth quarter of 2017 and the fiscal year 2017, and we see a different picture in the MD&A. These results are presented in **Exhibit 1** below. Notice there are five measures of GAAP and five non-GAAP metrics. The numbers have declined from the third quarter in large part due to insurance adjustments. Beyond that, the descriptions do not seem to match up. To say this is confusing would be an understatement.

Back in July 2017, the SEC sent a comment letter to GE[3] in regard to their improper use of non-GAAP metrics and inconsistencies in their description and application of them. Per Tomi Kilgore's October 27, 2017 Market Watch article the SEC letter identified "16 items in its 10-K filing were listed as being potentially misleading to investors, with half the items mentioning the reporting of numbers that were inconsistent with Generally Accepted Accounting Principles (GAAP)."[4]

GE's response letter to the SEC seems to confuse matters even more. For example, the SEC asked: "We note your discussion regarding the $0.5 billion increase in industrial earnings. Explain to us how you determined industrial earnings and whether it is a non-GAAP measure. Tell us how the measure differs from industrial profit, the GAAP measure presented [in your report]." GE's response was: "With regard to how industrial earnings and industrial

[1]Richard Clough, GE's accounting for earnings is unfathomable, and investors and SEC are noticing, Bloomberg News, October 16, 2017, https://www.accountingtoday.com/articles/ge-earnings-and-non-gaap-measures-are-unfathomable-investors-and-sec-notice.

[2]Tomi Kilgore, GE's pledge to be more accountable comes after SEC comments, stock plunge, MarketWatch, October 31, 2017, https://www.accountingtoday.com/articles/ge-earnings-and-non-gaap-measures-are-unfathomable-investors-and-sec-notice.

[3]See https://www.sec.gov/Archives/edgar/data/40545/000004054517000047/filename1.htm.

[4]Tomi Kilgore, GE's pledge to be more accountable comes after SEC comments, stock plunge, MarketWatch, October 31, 2017, https://www.marketwatch.com/story/ges-pledge-to-be-more-accountable-comes-after-secs-urging-stock-plunge-2017-10-27

profits differ, industrial earnings is an after-tax measure that reflects an adjustment for earnings/losses attributable to noncontrolling interests, while industrial profit is a pre-tax measure."

This is the second time the SEC has called out GE for their use of non-GAAP metrics, as they sent them a series of letters on this topic during 2016 as well. However, GE is not being singled out as the only company who perhaps stretches the limit of their usage. In both 2016 and 2017, the SEC sent more comment letters regarding the use of non-GAAP measures than on any other topic (with 429 letters to 223 registrants in 2016 or 16.75% and 656 letters to 311 registrants in 2017 or 28.34% of all SEC comment letterssent).[5] The growing use of non-GAAP metrics is also of concern to the PCAOB, who are actively researching their use and questioning whether the current standards should require auditors to perform specific testing of non-GAAP metrics contained in public filings and even those used on earnings calls and other types of releases.[6]

Per Bloomberg, the use of non-GAAP metrics has increased from just 58% of publicly traded companies to virtually all of them in just 20 years. However, Bloomberg suggests that the use of this many metrics by GE has made their financials more confusing, resulting in investors shying away from GE and negatively impacting their market price per share. The Bloomberg article quotes an executive from Westwood Holdings who has been decreasing the size of a major stake in GE as saying, "GE somewhere along the line lost the benefit of the doubt that the non-GAAP adjusted EPS number was a good reflection of what they were earning." A look at GE's stock performance in relation to the overall market showing a steady decline supports this contention with their stock currently trading at close to its lowest level since the 2009 market crash. As of February 16, 2018, GE was trading at around $15 dollars per share, which was 50% of what it was trading at the same date in 2017, while the rest of the market was up over 18% during that same period.

It is also worth noting that, in late 2017, GE's CFO Jeff Bornstein left the company after 28 years working in various positions within GE. GE's CEO and incoming new CFO pledged to make life easier for investors, and reporters, not only by narrowing the focus of its businesses, but also by making its earnings reports simpler and more transparent. However, on January 24, 2018, Jamie Miller, the new CFO, announced that the SEC is now investigating GE's revenue recognition and controls for insurance contracts just days after the companies surprise announcement that they would be taking a $6.2 billion dollar loss from insurance claims and beefing up insurance contract reserves by $15 billion.[7] It would appear the troubles for GE are far from over and perhaps suggests that the use of non-GAAP metrics could be a red flag that there is trouble on the horizon. Matt Egan of CNN Money, on January 24, 2018, quotes Scott Davis, the head analyst at Melius Research, regarding GE as stating, "we can't be certain that prior management misled investors, but we certainly believe there were ethical lapses that deserve attention."[8]

Questions

1. Consider the costs/harms and benefits of disclosing non-GAAP financial numbers. What value, if any, do you see in the use of non-GAAP metrics?

2. What responsibilities do auditors currently have related to the use of non-GAAP measures by their attest clients? What responsibilities do you think they should have? Be specific.

3. Do you believe that GE is attempting to manage earnings by disclosing five different non-GAAP measures? Explain.

4. If you were a financial analyst looking at GE's metrics in Exhibit 1, what questions would you ask and why?

[5]Jessica McKeon and Olga Usvyatsky, A Look at Top SEC Comment Issues in 2017, Audit Analytics, December 4, 2017, http://www.auditanalytics.com/blog/a-look-at-top-sec-comment-letter-issues-in-2017/.

[6]PCAOB, Q&A: PCAOB Standard-Setting Initiatives, December 7, 2017, https://pcaobus.org/News/Speech/Pages/Harris-QA-PCAOB-standard-setting-initiatives-12-07-17.aspx.

[7]Tomi Kilgore.

[8]Matt Egan, GE is under investigation by the Securities and Exchange Commission, CNN Money, January 24, 2018, http://money.cnn.com/2018/01/24/investing/ge-sec-investigation-insurance-accounting/index.html.

EXHIBIT 1   General Electric Financial Metrics

(Dollars in millions; except per-share amounts) 31-12-2018	Fourth Quarter Results			Total Year Results		
	2017	**2016**	Year on Year	**2017**	**2016**	Year on Year
GAAP Metrics						
Continuing Operations EPS	$ (1.15)	$ 0.39	U	$ (0.68)	$ 1.00	U
Net Earnings EPS	$ (1.13)	$ 0.39	U	$ (0.72)	$ 0.89	U
Total Revenues	$ 31,402	$ 33,088	−5.0%	$1,22,092	$ 1,23,693	−1%
Industrial Margin	1.1%	12.0%	(1090) bps	5.7%	11.4%	(570) bps
GE CFOA	$ 6,990	$ 11,618	−40%	$ 11,040	$ 29,960	−63%
Non-GAAP Metrics						
Industrial Operating + Verticals EPS	$ (1.23)	$ 0.46	U	$ (0.45)	$ 1.49	U
Industrial Segment Organic Revenues	$ 28,712	$ 30,503	−6%	$1,09,430	$1,09,296	0%
Industrial Operating Profit/(Loss)c)	$ 3,526	$ 5,226	−33%	$ 13,868	$ 15,558	−11%
Industrial Operating Profis/(Loss) Marginb)	11.2%	16.8%	(560) bps	12.1%	14.0%	(190) bps
Adjusted Industrial CFOAa)	$ 7,757	$ 8,242	−6%	$ 9,698	$ 11,610	-16%

bps = book value per share
CFOA = cash flow from operating activities
a) Excluding deal taxes and GE Pension Plan funding, and with BHGE on a dividend basis
b) Excludes impact of acquisition and disposition activity in industrial segments
c) Excludes non-operating pension, gains/(losses) and restructuring & other

Case 7-8   Monsanto Company Roundup

Overview of the Case

Monsanto is an agricultural seed and chemical company that manufactures and sells glyphosate, an herbicide, under the trade name "Roundup." Roundup historically was one of Monsanto's most profitable products, and the company sells it to both retailers and distributors. After the patent expired in 2000, competition from generic products began to erode Monsanto's profit margins. By fiscal year 2009, generic competitors were undercutting Monsanto's prices in the U.S. and Canada by more than 70%. Monsanto was losing share in these markets as customers—concerned they could not profitably sell high-priced Roundup—shifted their purchases to generic brands. By the end of fiscal 2009, Monsanto had lost more than half of its share of the glyphosate market (dropping from 55% market share to less than 25%).

During fiscal years ended August 31 of 2009, 2010, and 2011, Monsanto improperly accounted for millions of dollars of rebates offered to Roundup distributors and retailers in the U.S. and Canada to incentivize them to purchase

Roundup. Monsanto also improperly accounted for rebate payments to Roundup customers in Canada, France, and Germany as selling, general, and administrative expenses ("SG&A") rather than rebates, which boosted Roundup gross profit in those countries. Monsanto did not have sufficient internal accounting controls to identify and properly account for rebate payments promised to customers.

As a result, Monsanto materially misstated its consolidated earnings and its revenues and earnings for its Roundup business lines in its periodic reports filed with the SEC for fiscal years 2009, 2010, and 2011. As a result of the improper accounting, Monsanto met consensus earnings-per-share analyst estimates for fiscal year 2009.

On November 14, 2011, Monsanto restated its 2009 and 2010 annual reports on Form 10-K and its 2011 quarterly reports on Form 10-Q (collectively "the Restatement").

As a result of the action of Monsanto and top managers, the company violated reporting provisions of Securities and Exchange Acts, the books and records provisions, and the internal accounting control provisions of Exchange Act Section 13(b)(2)(B).

Monsanto agreed to pay an $80 million penalty and retain an independent consultant to settle charges that it violated accounting rules and misstated company earnings as it pertained to its flagship product Roundup. Three accounting and sales executives also agreed to pay penalties to settle charges against them.

Cast of Characters

Sara M. Brunnquell was the External Reporting Lead at Monsanto from April 2009 through October 2015. In that capacity, she reported to the Controller of Monsanto. Brunnquell was a CPA during the time of the accounting fraud.

Jonathan W. Nienas was the U.S. Strategic Account Lead for the Roundup Division from September 1, 2009 until he retired in January 2014.

Anthony P. Hartke held the title of U.S. Business Analyst in the Roundup Division from July 2008 to August 2010. He was a CPA during the time of the accounting fraud.

Accounting Standards

The accounting standards governing Monsanto's rebate programs is set forth in FASB Emerging Issues Task Force ("EITF") Issue No. 01-9, "Accounting for Consideration Given by a Vendor to a Customer (Including a Reseller of the Vendor's Products)," codified as ASC 605-50.[1] Specifically, Issue 6 of EITF 01-9 (ASC 605-50-25-7) requires a vendor like Monsanto to recognize a rebate obligation as a reduction of revenue based on a systematic or rational allocation of the cost of honoring the rebate offer to each underlying transaction that results in progress by the customer towards earning the rebate. Issue 4 of EITF 01-9 (ASC 605-50-25-3) requires a vendor to recognize the cost of certain sales incentives at the later of either the date at which the related revenue is recognized or the date at which the sales incentive is offered.

Issue 1 of EITF 01-9 (ASC 605-50-45-1) addresses the circumstances in which a vendor may record payments to customers as a cost or expense [e.g., under the selling, general and administrative (SG&A) accounting classification] rather than as a reduction of revenue. EITF 01-9 (ASC 605-50-45-1) requires a vendor like Monsanto to recognize payments to customers to perform services on its behalf (and which provide an identifiable benefit to the vendor) as a reduction of revenue for the amount of the payments that exceeds the estimated fair value of the services rendered. If the services provided by customers do not provide a benefit to the vendor, it should recognize the total amount as a reduction of revenue.

---

[1]EITF 01-9 was the applicable accounting guidance during Monsanto's fiscal year 2009 and was codified into the Accounting Standards Codification ("ASC") within ASC 605-50 for fiscal years 2010 and 2011. See: http://www.fasb.org/jsp/FASB/ Document_C/DocumentPage?cid=1218220142394&acceptedDisclaimer=true.

Summary of the Facts

The SEC investigation found that Monsanto had insufficient internal accounting controls to properly account for millions of dollars in rebates offered to retailers and distributers of Roundup after generic competition had undercut Monsanto's prices and resulted in a significant loss of market share for the company. Monsanto booked substantial amounts of revenue resulting from sales incentivized by the rebate programs, but failed to recognize all of the related program costs at the same time. Therefore, Monsanto materially misstated its consolidated earnings in corporate filings during a three-year period.

According to the SEC's order instituting a settled administrative proceeding against Monsanto and three executives:[2]

- Monsanto's sales force began telling U.S. retailers in 2009 that if they "maximized" their Roundup purchases in the fourth quarter they could participate in a new rebate program in 2010.

- Hartke developed and Brunnquell approved talking points for Monsanto's sales force to use when encouraging retailers to take advantage of the new rebate program and purchase significant amounts of Roundup in the fourth quarter of the company's 2009 fiscal year. Approximately one-third of its U.S. sales of Roundup for the year occurred during that quarter.

- Brunnquell and Hartke knew, or should have known, that the sales force used this new rebate program to incentivize sales in 2009, and Generally Accepted Accounting Principles (GAAP) required the company to record in 2009 a portion of Monsanto's costs related to the rebate program. But Monsanto improperly delayed recording these costs until 2010.

- Monsanto also offered rebates to distributors who met agreed-upon volume targets. However, late in the fiscal year, Monsanto reversed approximately $57.3 million of rebate costs that had been accrued under these agreements because certain distributors did not achieve their volume targets (at the urging of Monsanto).

- Monsanto then created a new rebate program to allow distributors to "earn back" the rebates they failed to attain in 2009 by meeting new targets in 2010.

- Under this new program, Monsanto paid $44.5 million in rebates to its two largest distributors as part of side agreements arranged by Nienas, in which they were promised late in fiscal year 2009 that they would be paid the maximum rebate amounts regardless of target performance.

- Because the side agreements were reached in 2009, Monsanto was required under GAAP to record these rebates in 2009. But the company improperly deferred recording the rebate costs until 2010.

- Monsanto repeated the program the following year and improperly accounted for $48 million in rebate costs in 2011 that should have been recorded in 2010.

- Monsanto also improperly accounted for more than $56 million in rebates in 2010 and 2011 in Canada, France, and Germany. They were booked as SG&A expenses rather than rebates, which boosted gross profits from Roundup in those countries.

Scott W. Friestad, Associate Director in the SEC's Division of Enforcement, said, "Monsanto devised rebate programs that elevated form over substance, which led to the booking of substantial amounts of revenue without the recognition of associated costs. Public companies need to have robust systems in place to ensure that all of their transactions are recognized in the correct reporting period."

Monsanto consented to the SEC's order without admitting or denying the findings that it violated Sections 17(a)(2) and 17(a)(3) of the Securities Act of 1933; the reporting provisions of Section 13(a) of the Securities Exchange Act of 1934 and underlying rules 12b-20, 13a-1, 13a-11, and 13a-13; the books-and-records provisions of Exchange Act Section 13(b)(2)(A); and the internal accounting control provisions of Exchange Act Section 13(b)(2)(B).

---

[2]Monsanto Paying $80 Million Penalty for Accounting Violations, February 9, 2016, https://www.sec.gov/news/pressrelease/2016-25.html.

Brunnquell, Hartke, and Nienas also consented to the order without admitting or denying the findings that they violated Rule 13b2-1 and caused Monsanto's violations of various provisions. Nienas also was found to have violated Exchange Act Section 13(b)(5). Brunnquell, Nienas, and Hartke must pay penalties of $55,000, $50,000, and $30,000, respectively, and Brunnquell and Hartke agreed to be suspended from appearing and practicing before the SEC as an accountant, which includes not participating in the financial reporting or audits of public companies. The SEC's order permits Brunnquell to apply for reinstatement after two years, and Hartke is permitted to apply for reinstatement after one year.

The SEC's investigation found no personal misconduct by Monsanto CEO Hugh Grant and former CFO Carl Casale, who reimbursed the company $3,165,852 and $728,843, respectively, for cash bonuses and certain stock awards they received during the period when the company committed accounting violations. Therefore, it wasn't necessary for the SEC to pursue a clawback action under Section 304 of the Sarbanes-Oxley Act.

Ethics & Compliance Requirements

In determining to accept Monsanto's Offer, the Commission considered remedial acts undertaken/to be undertaken by Monsanto.[3]

- Retain a qualified independent ethics and compliance consultant to conduct an ethics and compliance program assessment of Monsanto's Crop Protection business. The Consultant shall also have expertise in, or retain someone with expertise in, internal accounting controls and public company financial reporting as well as vendor rebate and market funding programs.

- Analyze whether the components of Monsanto's ethics and compliance program for its Crop Protection business have been implemented successfully and are having the desired effects. The Consultant will determine whether the culture is supportive of ethical and compliant conduct, including strong, explicit, and visible support and commitment by the Board and senior management.

- In discharging this undertaking, the Consultant shall evaluate and assess the effectiveness of the internal accounting controls and financial reporting policies and procedures with respect to Monsanto's rebate and market funding programs for its Crop Protection business, including but not limited to:

  - Assess whether Monsanto's internal accounting controls with respect to Monsanto's rebate and market funding programs for its Crop Protection business are sufficient to provide reasonable assurances that the company is maintaining fair and accurate books, records, and accounts, with particular emphasis on whether they are designed to address the integrity of its revenue accounting and ensure consistent accuracy and integrity given the global nature of Monsanto's business; and

  - Determine whether Monsanto has specific accounting and financial reporting controls and procedures sufficient to ensure that all rebate and/or market funding programs for its Crop Protection business comply with applicable accounting rules and policies.

  - Provide a report to Commission staff and Monsanto's General Counsel and Chief Ethics and Compliance Officer regarding the Consultant's findings and recommendations.

Whistleblower

On August 30, 2016, the SEC announced the award of more than $22 million to an anonymous whistleblower whose detailed tip and extensive assistance helped the agency stop the well-hidden fraud at Monsanto, where the whistleblower worked. At the time, the $22 million-plus award was the second-largest total the SEC had awarded to a whistleblower under the Dodd-Frank Financial Reform Act.[4]

---

[3]SEC, *In the Matter of Monsanto Company, Sara M. Brunnquell, Anthony P. Hartke, and Jonathan W. Nienas,* Accounting and Auditing Enforcement Release No. 3741, February 9, 2016, https://www.sec.gov/litigation/admin/2016/33-10037.pdf.

[4]SEC Press Release, $22 Million Whistleblower Award for Company Insider Who Helped Uncover Fraud, August 30, 2016, https://www.sec.gov/news/pressrelease/2016-172.html.

The whistleblower's attorney, Stuart Meissner, shed light on the role of the external auditors Deloitte, in speaking on behalf of the whistleblower, in an interview with "Corporate Crime Reporter."[5] Meissner raised concerns about the role of outside auditors.

> We hope the agency will probe Monsanto's outside auditor Deloitte for the role we believe it played in enabling the company to overstate earnings and issue misleading financial statements—not only once, but twice. There was an initial misstatement by Monsanto and a subsequent restatement—the restatement is actually the bigger issue of the two in my view," Meissner said. When auditors are allowed to audit their own mistakes, it is difficult for them to be independent and objective. And when independence is impaired, the professional skepticism needed to recognize and flush out improprieties by management is not present. Professional skepticism of the auditor is the last line of defense for a management team that may have a clear bias in reporting positive results. To this day, Monsanto investors still do not have accurate financial statements for the periods involved in the case. I do not believe that investors have been able to reasonably access the performance of the company, including whether or not Monsanto hit the mid-teen percentage growth targets management committed to in 2010. If a true independent auditor not associated with the financials had been appointed to audit the restated financials, I believe there would be a higher likelihood that investors would know the true performance of the company and be in a better position to make fully informed decisions.

Questions

1. What is the underlying accounting and financial reporting concept at issue as described in EITF Issue No. 01-9 with respect to the way Monsanto accounted for customer rebates? Explain in your own words how Monsanto's accounting led to materially misstated financial statements.

2. Given that Monsanto was under great pressure from competitors that sold generic brands similar to Roundup, would you characterize the Monsanto situation as a business failure, an accounting failure, and/or an audit failure? Explain.

3. Of what value are the ethics and compliance requirements agreed to by Monsanto? Do you believe all companies that experience financial fraud should be required to institute such changes? Can such requirements change the culture of a global company such as Monsanto?

4. Do you believe restated financial statements should be audited by a different firm than the one that prepared the original financials? Why or why not? Consider costs and benefits in your analysis.

Case 7-9 The North Face, Inc.

The North Face, Inc. (North Face) is an American outdoor product company specializing in outerwear, fleece, coats, shirts, footwear, and equipment such as backpacks, tents, and sleeping bags. North Face sells clothing and equipment lines catered toward wilderness chic, climbers, mountaineers, skiers, snowboarders, hikers, and endurance athletes. The company sponsors professional athletes from the worlds of running, climbing, skiing, and snowboarding.

North Face is located in Alameda, California, along with an affiliated company, JanSport. These two companies manufacture about half of all small backpacks sold in the United States. Both companies are owned by VF Corporation, an American apparel corporation.

---

[5]Corporate Crime Reporter, Monsanto Whistleblower Wants SEC to Go after Deloitte, September 15, 2016, https://www.corporatecrimereporter.com/news/200/monsanto-whistleblower-wants-sec-to-go-after-deloitte/.

The North Face brand was established in 1968 in San Francisco. Following years of success built on sales to a high-end customer base, in the 1990s North Face was forced to compete with mass-market brands sold by the major discount retailers. It was at that point the company engaged in accounting shenanigans that led to it being acquired by VF Corporation.

Barter Transactions[1]

Consumer demand for North Face products was steadily growing by the mid-1980s, and the higher levels of demand for production were causing the manufacturing facilities to be overburdened. Pressure existed to maintain the level of production that was required. As North Face continued to grow in sales throughout the 1980s and into the 1990s, the management team set aggressive sales goals. In the mid-1990s, the team established the goal of reaching $1 billion in annual sales by the year 2003. The pressure prompted Christopher Crawford, the company's chief financial officer (CFO), and Todd Katz, the vice president of sales, to negotiate a large transaction with a barter company and then proceed to improperly account for it in the financial statements.[2]

North Face entered into two major barter transactions in 1997 and 1998. The barter company North Face dealt with typically bought excess inventory in exchange for trade credits. The trade credits could be redeemed by North Face only through the barter company, and most often the trade credits were used to purchase advertising, printing, or travel services.

North Face began negotiating a potential barter transaction in early December 1997. The basic terms were that the barter company would purchase $7.8 million of excess inventory North Face had on hand. In exchange for that inventory, North Face would receive $7.8 million of trade credits that were redeemable only through the barter company.

Before North Face finalized the barter transaction, Crawford asked Deloitte & Touche, North Face's external auditors, for advice on how to account for a barter sale. The auditors provided Crawford with the accounting literature describing GAAP relating to non-monetary exchanges. That literature generally precludes companies from recognizing revenue on barter transactions when the only consideration received by the seller is trade credits.

What Crawford did next highlights one of the many ways a company can structure a transaction to manage earnings and achieve the financial results desired rather than report what should be recorded as revenue under GAAP.

Crawford structured the transaction to recognize profit on the trade credits. First, he required the barter company to pay a portion of the purchase price in cash. Crawford agreed that North Face would guarantee that the barter company would receive at least a 60% recovery of the total purchase price when it resold the product. In exchange for the guarantee, the barter company agreed to pay approximately 50% of the total purchase price in cash and the rest in trade credits. This guarantee took the form of an oral side agreement that was not disclosed to the auditors.

Second, Crawford split the transaction into two parts on two days before the year-end December 31, 1997. One part of the transaction was to be recorded in the fourth quarter of 1997, the other to be recorded in the first quarter of 1998. Crawford structured the two parts of the barter sale so that all of the cash consideration and a portion of the trade credits would be received in the fourth quarter of 1997. The barter credit portion of the fourth quarter transaction was structured to allow profit recognition for the barter credits despite the objections of the auditors. The consideration for the 1998 first quarter transaction consisted solely of trade credits.

[1]The information in this case was taken from: Securities and Exchange Commission, A Civil Complaint filed in the United States District Court Northern District of California against Christopher F. Crawford and Todd F. Katz, February 20, 2003, www.sec.gov/litigation/complaints/comp17978.htm.

[2]"North Face Accounting Fraud," October 14, 2013, http://bethmichel.blogspot.com/2013/10/0-false-18-pt-18-pt-0-0-false-false.html.

On December 29, 1997, North Face recorded a $5.15 million sale to the barter company. The barter company paid $3.51 million in cash and issued $1.64 million in trade credits. North Face recognized its full normal profit margin on the sale. Just 10 days later on January 8, 1998, North Face recorded another sale to the barter company, this time for $2.65 million in trade credits, with no cash consideration. North Face received only trade credits from the barter company for this final portion of the $7.8 million total transaction. Again, North Face recognized its full normal profit margin on the sale.

Materiality Issues

Crawford was a CPA and knew all about the materiality criteria that auditors use to judge whether they will accept a client's accounting for a disputed transaction. He committed the fraud because he saw internal control weaknesses and believed no one would notice. Crawford realized that if he made sure the portion of the barter transaction recorded during the fourth quarter of fiscal 1997 was below a certain amount, the auditors would not look at it. He also believed that Deloitte & Touche would not challenge the profit recognized on the $3.51 million portion of the barter transaction because of the cash payment.

Crawford also realized that Deloitte would maintain that no profit should be recorded on the $1.64 million balance of the December 29, 1997, transaction with the barter company for which North Face would be paid exclusively in trade credits. However, Crawford was aware of the materiality thresholds that Deloitte had established for North Face's key financial statement items during the fiscal 1997 audit. He knew that the profit margin of approximately $800,000 on the $1.64 million portion of the December 1997 transaction fell slightly below Deloitte's materiality threshold for North Face's collective gross profit. As a result, he believed that Deloitte would propose an adjustment to reverse the $1.64 million transaction but ultimately "pass" on that proposed adjustment since it had an immaterial impact on North Face's financial statements. As Crawford expected, Deloitte proposed a year-end adjusting entry to reverse the $1.64 million transaction but then passed on that adjustment during the wrap-up phase of the audit.

In early January 1998, North Face recorded the remaining $2.65 million portion of the $7.8 million barter transaction. Crawford instructed North Face's accountants to record the full amount of profit margin on this portion of the sale despite being aware that accounting treatment was not consistent with the authoritative literature. Crawford did not inform the Deloitte auditors of the $2.65 million portion of the barter transaction until after the 1997 audit was completed.

The barter company ultimately sold only a nominal amount of the $7.8 million of excess inventory that it purchased from North Face. As a result, in early 1999, North Face reacquired that inventory from the barter company.

Audit Considerations

The auditors did not learn of the January 8, 1998, transaction until March 1998. Thus, when the auditors made the materiality judgment for the fourth quarter transaction, they were unaware that a second transaction had taken place and unaware that Crawford had recognized full margin on the second barter transaction.

In mid-1998 through 1999, the North Face sales force was actively trying to resell the product purchased by the barter company because the barter company was unable to sell any significant portion of the inventory. North Face finally decided, in January and February 1999, to repurchase the remaining inventory from the barter company. Crawford negotiated the repurchase price of $690,000 for the remaining inventory.

Crawford did not disclose the repurchase to the 1998 audit engagement team, even though the audit was not complete at the time of the repurchase.

During the first week of March 1999, the auditors asked for additional information about the barter transaction to complete the 1998 audit. In response to this request, Crawford continued to mislead the auditors by failing to disclose that the product had been repurchased, that there was a guarantee, that the 1997 and 1998 transactions were linked, and that the company sales force had negotiated almost all of the orders received by the barter company.

Crawford did not disclose any of this information until he learned that the auditors were about to fax a confirmation letter to the barter company that specifically asked if any of the product had been returned or repurchased. Crawford then called the chair of North Face's audit committee to explain that he had withheld information from the auditors. A meeting was scheduled for later that day for Crawford to make "full disclosure" to the auditors about the barter transactions.

Even at the "full disclosure" meeting with the auditors, Crawford was not completely truthful. He did finally disclose the repurchase and the link between the 1997 and 1998 transactions. He did not, however, disclose that there was a guarantee, nor did he disclose that the company's employees had negotiated most of the orders for the product.

Deloitte & Touche

Richard Fiedelman was the Deloitte advisory partner assigned to the North Face audit engagement. Pete Vanstraten was the audit engagement partner for the 1997 North Face audit. Vanstraten was also the individual who proposed the adjusting entry near the end of the 1997 audit to reverse the $1.64 million barter transaction that North Face had recorded in the final few days of fiscal 1997. Vanstraten proposed the adjustment because he was aware that the GAAP rules generally preclude companies from recognizing revenue on barter transactions when the only consideration received by the seller is trade credits. Vanstraten was also the individual who "passed" on that adjustment after determining that it did not have a material impact on North Face's 1997 financial statements. Fiedelman reviewed and approved those decisions by Vanstraten.

Shortly after the completion of the 1997 North Face audit, Vanstraten transferred from the office that serviced North Face. In May 1998, Will Borden was appointed the new audit engagement partner for North Face. In the two months before Borden was appointed the North Face audit engagement partner, Richard Fiedelman functioned in that role.

Fiedelman supervised the review of North Face's financial statements for the first quarter of fiscal 1998, which ended on March 31, 1998. While completing that review, Fiedelman became aware of the $2.65 million portion of the $7.8 million barter transaction that Crawford had instructed his subordinates to record in early January 1998. Fiedelman did not challenge North Face's decision to record its normal profit margin on the January 1998 "sale" to the barter company. As a result, North Face's gross profit for the first quarter of 1998 was overstated by more than $1.3 million, an amount that was material to the company's first-quarter financial statements. In fact, without the profit margin on the $2.65 million transaction, North Face would have reported a net loss for the first quarter of fiscal 1998 rather than the modest net income it actually reported that period.

In the fall of 1998, Borden began planning the 1998 North Face audit. An important element of that planning process was reviewing the 1997 audit workpapers. While reviewing those workpapers, Borden discovered the audit adjustment that Vanstraten had proposed during the prior year audit to reverse the $1.64 million barter transaction. When Borden brought this matter to Fiedelman's attention, Fiedelman maintained that the proposed audit adjustment should not have been included in the prior year workpapers since the 1997 audit team had *not* concluded that North Face could *not* record the $1.64 million transaction with the barter company. Fiedelman insisted that, despite the proposed audit adjustment in the 1997 audit workpapers, Vanstraten had concluded that it was permissible for North Face to record the transaction and recognize the $800,000 of profit margin on the transaction in December 1997.

Borden accepted Fiedelman's assertion that North Face was entitled to recognize profit on a sales transaction in which the only consideration received by the company was trade credits. Borden also relied on this assertion during the 1998 audit. As a result, Borden and the other members of the 1998 audit team did not propose an adjusting entry to require North Face to reverse the $2.65 million sale recorded by the company in January 1998.

After convincing Borden that the prior year workpapers misrepresented the decision that Vanstraten had made regarding the $1.64 million barter transaction, Fiedelman began the process of documenting this revised conclusion in the 1997 working papers that related to the already issued financial statements for 1997. The SEC had concluded in its investigation that Deloitte personnel prepared a new summary memorandum and proposed adjustments schedule reflecting the revised conclusion about profit recognition and replaced the original 1997 working papers with these newly created working papers.

SEC Actions against Crawford

In the SEC action against Crawford and Katz, the SEC charged that Crawford tried to conceal the true nature of the improperly reported transactions from North Face's accountants and auditors. He made, directly or indirectly, material misrepresentations and omissions to the auditors in an attempt to hide his misconduct. Katz also made, directly or indirectly, material misrepresentations and omissions to the accountants and auditors in an attempt to hide his misconduct.[3]

The commission charged that Crawford committed a fraud because his actions violated Section 10(b) of the Exchange Act of 1934, in that he knew or was reckless in not knowing that (1) it was a violation of GAAP to record full margin on the trade credit portion of the sale and (2) that the auditors would consider the amount of the non-GAAP fourth quarter profit recognition immaterial and would not insist on any adjusting entry for correction.

A second charge was that Crawford aided and abetted violations of Section 13(a) of the Exchange Act that requires every issuer of a registered security to file reports with the SEC that accurately reflect the issuer's financial performance and provide other information to the public.

A third charge dealt with record-keeping and alleged violations of Section 13(b) in that the Exchange Act requires each issuer of registered securities to make and keep books, records, and accounts that, in reasonable detail, accurately and fairly reflect the business of the issuer and to devise and maintain a system of internal controls sufficient to provide reasonable assurances that, among other things, transactions are recorded as necessary to permit preparation of financial statements and to maintain the accountability of accounts.

The SEC asked the U.S. District Court of the Northern District of California to enter a judgment:

- Permanently enjoining Crawford and the vice president of sales, Katz, from violating Sections 10(b) and 13(b)(5) of the Exchange Act;
- Ordering Crawford to provide a complete accounting for and to disgorge the unjust enrichment he realized, plus prejudgment interest thereon;
- Ordering Crawford and Katz to pay civil monetary penalties pursuant to Section 21(d)(3) of the Exchange Act; and
- Prohibiting Crawford and Katz from acting as an officer or director of a public company pursuant to Section 21(d)(2) of the Exchange Act.

Crawford agreed to the terms in a settlement with the SEC that included his suspension from appearing or practicing before the commission as an accountant for at least five years, after which time he could apply to the commission for reinstatement.

Questions

1. Use the fraud triangle to analyze the red flags that existed in the case and the role and responsibilities of the auditors at Deloitte & Touche. Assume the Deloitte auditors had confronted Crawford about the impropriety of accounting for barter transactions. What reasons and rationalizations do you think would have been provided by Crawford?

2. Why do auditors have a responsibility to assess the key decisions made by management? Which decisions in this case should the auditors have scrutinized more carefully?

3. Should materiality considerations have entered into the auditors' decisions whether to accept North Face's accounting? Does it matter that earnings management was the motivation for the accounting?

4. Comment on the quality of the audit performed by Deloitte.

---

[3]SEC, *In the matter of Christopher F. Crawford, Accounting and Auditing Enforcement Release No. 1751 (AAER No. 1751),* April 4, 2003, Available at: www.sec.gov/litigation/admin/34-47633.htm.

Case 7-10 Beazer Homes

Beazer Homes is a home-building company headquartered in Atlanta, Georgia. Its stock is listed on the New York Stock Exchange. Beazer is required to file Form 10-Q and Form 10-K, as well as an 8-K form when certain changes occur, such as restating financial statements.

As a homebuilder, Beazer often builds "model homes" for prospective homebuyers to tour while the remainder of a neighborhood and its future homes are under construction. As one of the last homes to be sold, model homes often may not be sold to a homebuyer for years, and thus may not provide a homebuilder with revenue and income on their sale until years after construction.

What follows is a description of the SEC's agreement in *SEC v. Michael T. Rand* to resolve charges that Beazer engaged in fraudulent accounting that led to material noncompliance with federal securities laws by improperly inflating Beazer's income by reducing or eliminating previously established artificial reserves and improperly recognizing sales revenue and income in sale-leaseback transactions involving its model homes.[1]

Sale-Leaseback Scheme

Under its sales-leaseback program, Beazer sold its model homes to investors, typically at a discounted price, thereby permitting it to recognize revenue and income from the sales. Under the "leaseback" portion of the transaction, Beazer leased back from the investor/buyer the same model homes, which Beazer could then use to show prospective home buyers.

In December 2005, the chief accounting officer, Michael T. Rand, CPA, entered into a secret side-agreement with one or more GMAC Model Home Finance personnel under which: (a) Beazer would "sell" the model homes and recognize revenue and income from such sales, (b) the homes would be leased back to Beazer for its use, but (c) Beazer would secretly receive a share of any profits from any subsequent sale of the model homes to a third party at the end of the leases. Under GAAP, a seller is not permitted to recognize revenue and income from a sale in a sale-leaseback transaction if the seller retains a continuing interest in the property after it has been sold. Beazer's continuing and secret interest in a share of any profits from the ultimate sale of the models was such a continuing interest.

What follows is a table showing model homes sold and improper pretax income recognized from the sale-leaseback transactions in violation of GAAP.

Overstated Pretax Income from Sale-Leaseback Transactions		
Quarter Ended	**# Homes Sold**	**Overstated Pretax Income**
December 31, 2005	90	$8.0 million
March 31, 2006	79	$4.2 million
June 30, 2006	37	$1.6 million
September 30, 2006	140	$8.3 million

Cookie-Jar Reserves

Prior to 2006, Rand and other Beazer employees engaged in an accounting scheme involving "cookie-jar accounting." Specifically, Rand improperly decreased Beazer's income by artificially establishing, increasing, and/or maintaining future anticipated expenses or "reserves." He executed this strategy by manipulating, among other accounts, Beazer's land development and house reserve accounts.

[1]*SEC v. Michael T. Rand,* U.S. District Court for the Northern District of Atlanta, Georgia, July 1, 2009, Available at: https://www.sec.gov/litigation/complaints/2009/comp21114.pdf.

In fiscal year 2006, when Beazer was in jeopardy of not meeting analysts' expectations, Rand eliminated certain unnecessary excess reserves that had been built up, thereby improperly boosting Beazer's pretax income by over $27.5 million. Beazer's arbitrary elimination of reserves to boost income resulted in financial statements that were not compiled in accordance with GAAP.

Land Inventory Accounting

As part of its home building and sale operations, Beazer purchased parcels of land upon which it constructed houses to form subdivisions. Beazer recorded the acquired land, along with costs for the common development of the parcel, such as sewer systems and streets, as an asset on Beazer's balance sheet in the land inventory accounts. As subdivisions were built, Beazer allocated the costs accumulated in the land inventory accounts to individual home lots, which were then offered for sale. When the home sale was recorded in Beazer's books, all associated homebuilding costs, including allocated costs recorded in the land inventory accounts, were expensed as a cost of the sale with a corresponding reduction or credit in the land inventory account.

Because Beazer sold houses within a subdivision as the development of that subdivision progressed, the land inventory expense recorded for any particular house sale was necessarily an estimate. The setting of inventory credits was done by each division based on estimates of costs to acquire, develop, and complete subdivisions plus an added amount for contingencies. Once established, divisions needed approval from Rand, who reviewed the reserves on a monthly basis, to make adjustments.

As additional houses in a subdivision were sold, the land inventory account continued to be decreased (credited) by amounts representing the land acquisition and development costs allocated to each individual house. If costs had been allocated properly, then, shortly after the final house in a development had been sold, the balance in the land inventory account should have been at or near zero.

What follows is a table showing the overstatement in land inventory costs between 2001 and 2005.

Overstatement of Land Inventory Costs			
	Quarter 1	**Quarter 2**	**Quarter 3**	**Quarter 4**
2001	$1,455,000	$ 584,000	$1,322,000	$2,571,000
2002	$1,827,000	$2,761,000	$1,270,000	$2,586,000
2003	$2,440,000	$1,422,000	$1,086,000	N/A
2004	$3,996,000	$4,253,000	$5,963,000	$2,227,000
2005	$3,388,000	$4,443,000	$5,122,000	$4,469,000

In order to reduce its first quarter 2002 earnings, which had exceeded analysts' EPS expectations, Rand fraudulently increased the land inventory expense recorded for homes sold during the quarter.

On January 8, 2002, after the end of the first quarter, Rand emailed a target earnings amount to the relevant financial personnel in numerous Beazer divisions with instructions not to exceed the target by a certain amount. The distributed target for each division was less than each division's previously expected quarterly results. Rand advised the divisions to review their land inventory accounts in order to increase expenses and reduce earnings. In one particular email, Rand instructed the Florida division to provide "more than adequate land allocations in communities closing out this year" as a means to reduce its earnings.

On January 10, 2002, Rand, via emails, directed certain divisions to, "[s]et aside all the reserves you reasonably can . . . the quarter is too high." This was followed by a series of emails in which Rand specified the amounts by which certain divisions should increase their reserves, along with targets for their EBIT (earnings before interest and taxes). The divisions substantially carried out his directions, and Rand was able to reduce Beazer's quarterly EPS from $2.60 to $2.47 a share, which exceeded analysts' consensus of $2.00 per share. In total, Beazer recorded approximately $1.827 million in excess land inventory costs for that quarter, or approximately 8% of its reported net income.

By increasing land inventory expenses, Rand caused Beazer to understate its net income by a total of $56 million ($33 million after tax effect; approximately 5% of reported net income) between 2000 and 2005. Beginning in the first quarter of 2006, Rand began to reverse the reserves existing in the land inventory accounts, which increased then-current period earnings. The credit balances in land inventory accounts were debited (i.e., zeroed out), and a cost of sales expense credited (i.e., reduced). These reversals improperly reduced expenses and increased Beazer's earnings. During all four quarters of 2006, Rand caused Beazer to release these land inventory reserves, boosting then-current period earnings by approximately $100,000 in the first quarter of 2006, approximately $301,000 in the second quarter of 2006, approximately $14,278,000 in the third quarter of 2006, and approximately $10,816,000 in the fourth quarter of 2006.

Manipulation of "House Cost-to-Complete" Reserves

Under its accounting policies, Beazer recorded revenue and profit on the sale of a house after the close of the sale of that house to a homebuyer. In the journal entries to record the sale, Beazer typically reserved a portion of its profit earned on the house. This reserve, called a "house cost-to-complete" reserve, was established to cover any unknown expenses that Beazer might incur on the sold house after the close, such as minor repairs or final cosmetic touch-ups. Although the amount of this reserve varied by region, it was typically $1,000 to $4,000 per house.

Beazer's policy was to reverse any unused portion of the house cost-to-complete reserve within four to nine months after the close, taking any unused portion into income at that time. As specified below, in various quarters between 2000 and 2005, Rand over-reserved house cost-to-complete expenses. Rand then took steps to maintain these reserves beyond the typical four to nine months and until increased earnings were required in future periods.

The following table shows the over-expensing of the cost-to-complete expense from 2000 to 2005.

Over-Expensing of the Cost-to-Complete Expense				
Year	Quarter 1	Quarter 2	Quarter 3	Quarter 4
2000	N/A	$610,000	$ 5,000	$2,288,000
2001	$1,138,000	$543,000	N/A	N/A
2002	$2,184,000	$813,000	N/A	N/A
2003	$1,380,000	N/A	N/A	N/A
2004	$1,057,000	N/A	$1,137,000	$2,051,000
2005	N/A	$805,000	$1,427,000	N/A

Beginning in 2006, Beazer began reversing some of the excess cost-to-complete reserves that it had previously recorded. As a result of Rand's directives, Beazer reduced its cost of sales expense by approximately $1.5 million by reducing the cost-to-complete reserve to zero on a number of houses. The following shows the amount of reversal of excess cost-to-complete reserves as earnings of the period that were previously recorded fraudulently.

Reversal of Excess Cost-to-Complete Reserves		
Year	**Quarter Ended**	**Amount of Reversal**
2006	March 31	$ 183,000
2006	September 30	$2,130,000
2006	December 31	$ 209,000
2007	March 31	$1,549,000

Additionally, at Rand's instruction, certain Beazer divisions, in order to report more income, failed to establish a house cost-to-complete reserve on house sales closing during the quarter. Beazer's Las Vegas division failed to record any cost-to-complete reserve for approximately 85 houses sold during December 2005. This resulted in an improper recognition, in violation of GAAP, of more than $200,000 of income for the period. All totaled, the additional income due to cost-to-complete reserve accounting added approximately $0.03 to Beazer's EPS.

Press Release

During the first quarter of fiscal year 2006, December 31, 2005, Beazer's stock price reached an all-time high of $82.03. The price was artificially inflated as a result of Beazer's false and misleading financial statements. On January 19, 2006, Beazer issued a press release titled "Beazer Homes Reports First Quarter 2006 EPS of $2.00, up 27%; Company expects Diluted EPS to Meet or Exceed $10.50 for Fiscal Year 2006." The company announced first quarter results as follows:

- Net income of $89.9 million, or $2.00 per diluted share (up 29% and 27.4%, respectively)
- Home closings: 3,829 (up 7.1%)
- Total revenues: $1.11 billion (up 21.3%)
- Operating income margin: 12.6% (up 40 basis points)
- New orders: 3,872 homes (up 9.2%), sales value $1.13 billion (up 11.3%)
- Backlog at 12/31/05: 9,276 homes (up 10.1%), sales value $2.78 billion (up 18.3%).

A statement released attributed Beazer's positive financial results to the success of Beazer's Profitable Growth Strategy: "These results illustrate the effectiveness of our Profitable Growth Strategy aimed at achieving greater profitability by optimizing efficiencies, *selectively increasing market penetration,* and leveraging our national brand."

Deloitte & Touche

Beazer's auditor, Deloitte & Touche, specifically advised Rand via email that Beazer's appreciation rights in the homes represented a continuing interest that, pursuant to GAAP, precluded Beazer from recognizing revenue when the homes were sold to GMAC. In an attempt to circumvent GAAP, and to deceive Deloitte, Rand caused the final, written versions of the sale-leaseback agreements to omit any reference to Beazer's continuing profit participation. Rand then directed, by email, his subordinates to record revenue at the time the model homes were initially sold to the GMAC investor pools. Rand provided Deloitte with copies of the sale-leaseback agreements that intentionally omitted the provisions relating to the continuing profit participation by Beazer. Rand also failed to disclose the side agreements to Deloitte.

Additionally, on January 18, 2006, Rand provided to Deloitte a memo that specifically stated Beazer would not "participate in the appreciation" of the leased assets (model homes). Based on Rand's concealment and misrepresentations, Deloitte agreed that immediate revenue recognition was proper.

As reported by *CFO Magazine* and summarized in the following paragraphs,[2] a class-action lawsuit filed against Deloitte was settled on May 7, 2009. The agreement said that the audit firm should have considered the homebuilder's "make the numbers" culture to be a red flag as the housing market tanked. Deloitte agreed to pay investors of Beazer Homes nearly $1 million to settle the claim.

The investors had accused Beazer of managing earnings, recognizing revenue earlier than allowed under generally accepted accounting principles, improperly accounting for sale-leaseback transactions, creating "cookie-jar" reserves, and not recording land and goodwill impairment charges at the proper time.

The investors accused Deloitte of turning "a blind eye" to the myriad of "red flags" that should have alerted the firm to potential GAAP violations. These warning signs included the "excessive pressure" employees were under to meet their higher-ups' sales goals, tight competition in Beazer's market, and weak internal controls. Accusing the auditor of "severe recklessness," the shareholders alleged, for example, that Deloitte should have noticed that Beazer was likely overdue in recording impairments on its land assets, as the real estate market began to decline, among the other alleged accounting violations.

"Deloitte either knowingly ignored or recklessly disregarded Beazer's wide-ranging material control deficiencies and material weaknesses during the class period," according to the shareholders' complaint. "For example, Deloitte was specifically aware that financial periods were regularly held open or re-opened because it had access to Beazer's detailed financial and accounting information via, among other means, access to Beazer's JD Edwards software."

In the Beazer settlement, Deloitte denied all liability and settled to avoid the expense and uncertainty of continued litigation, according to a spokeswoman.

Restatements of Financial Statements

Due to Beazer's material noncompliance with the financial reporting requirements of the federal securities laws, Beazer was required to issue accounting restatements. On May 12, 2008, Beazer filed accounting restatements for the fiscal year 2006. In various reports filed that day, Beazer restated its financial statements for fiscal 2006 and each of the first three quarters of fiscal 2006. Beazer admitted to the improper accounting with the following statement:

> During the course of the investigation, the Audit Committee discovered accounting and financial reporting errors and/or irregularities that required restatement resulting primarily from: (1) inappropriate accumulation of reserves and/or accrued liabilities associated with land development and house costs ("Inventory Reserves"), and (2) inaccurate revenue recognition with respect to certain model home sale-leaseback transactions.

In the filings, Beazer further acknowledged material weaknesses in its internal control over financial reporting "specifically related to the application of GAAP in accounting for certain estimates involving significant management judgments."

As set forth in those filings, Beazer acknowledged that its material weaknesses had several impacts on the Company's financial reporting, including "[i]nappropriate reserves and other accrued liabilities [being] recorded relating to land development costs, house construction costs and warranty accruals" and "[t]he accounting for certain model home sale and leaseback agreements [being] not in compliance with GAAP. . . [as the] Company's arrangement for certain sale and leaseback transactions."

Those filings went on to state that Beazer had "terminated our former Chief Accounting Officer who we believe may have caused, or allowed to cause, the internal control breakdown;" and that Beazer "believe[d] his termination has addressed concerns about the internal control deficiencies that we believe he caused or permitted to occur."

---

[2]Sarah Johnson, *CFO*, "Deloitte to Pay $1M in Beazer Suit," Available at: http://ww2.cfo.com/accounting-tax/2009/05/deloitte-to-pay-1m-in-beazer-suit/.

In July 2009, a federal bill of information was filed in U.S. District Court charging Beazer with, among other things, participation in the conspiracy and securities fraud with Rand. Beazer accepted responsibility for those charges and, in a deferred prosecution agreement, agreed to pay restitution of $50 million. Rand was indicted by a federal grand jury in August 2010.

On July 18, 2014, a federal jury convicted Rand of conspiracy and obstruction of justice charges stemming from the federal investigation into the seven-year accounting fraud and related conspiracy at Beazer. On April 30, 2015, U.S. District Judge Robert J. Conrad Jr. sentenced Rand to 120 months in prison and to three years of supervised release on conspiracy and obstruction of justice charges in connection with the investigation.[3]

A statement released by the U.S. Attorney's Office quotes John A. Strong, the special agent in charge for the Charlotte Division of the FBI:

> The U.S. Attorney's Office is committed to safeguarding the integrity of our financial markets from corporate executives like Rand, who put profits ahead of duty. Rand's actions breached his obligation to the investors and the public and jeopardized the stability of the housing industry. Today's verdict should send a clear message that corporate fraud, in this case cooking the books, will not be tolerated and you engage in such frauds at the risk of your freedom.[4]

Questions

1. Did Deloitte do an adequate job of evaluating the internal control environment at Beazer? Be specific.

2. Describe each of the financial shenanigans used by Beazer and how they manipulated earnings.

3. What do you believe should be done about companies like Beazer that engage in financial statement fraud for a period of time and issue false and misleading press releases during that time? Is it in the public interest to require external auditors to test this kind of information for accuracy and reliability? Explain by addressing the costs and benefits of such a requirement.

4. Assume you were hired to analyze the information in this case and write a two- to three-page report on your findings. Discuss each element of the fraud and why Beazer, Rand, and/or Deloitte violated ethical and professional standards.

---

[3]U.S. Attorney's Office Western District of North Carolina, "Federal Judge Hands Down 10-Year Sentence to Former Chief Accounting Officer for Beazer Homes USA, Inc.," . Available at: https://www.fbi.gov/charlotte/press-releases/2015/federal-judge-hands-down-10-year-sentence-to-former-chief-accounting-officer-for-beazer-homes-usa-inc.

[4]U.S. Attorney's Office Western District of North Carolina, "Charlotte Jury Finds Former Chief Accounting Officer for Beazer Homes USA Inc. Guilty of Accounting Fraud and Obstruction of Justice in Second Trial," July 18, 2014, Available at: https://www.fbi.gov/charlotte/press-releases/2014/charlotte-jury-finds-former-chief-accounting-officer-for-beazer-homes-usa-inc.-guilty-of-accounting-fraud-and-obstruction-of-justice-in-second-trial.

Chapter

8

Ethical Leadership and Decision-Making in Accounting

Learning Objectives

After studying Chapter 8, you should be able to:

LO 8-1	Explain the characteristics of ethical leaders.
LO 8-2	Distinguish between types of leadership.
LO 8-3	Describe what ethical leadership looks like in the accounting profession.
LO 8-4	Explain the relationship between personal responsibility, professional role, and whistleblowing.
LO 8-5	Describe the components of responsible leadership.
LO 8-6	Describe the characteristics of those with Ethical Leadership Competence.

Ethics Reflection

Ethical Leadership in Accounting

Dellaportas and Davenport point out that accountants protect the public interest when they consider not only the collective well-being of the people and institutions served, but also the economic interests of third parties by facilitating an efficient and effective economic decision-making process through the provision of relevant and reliable economic data.[1] The accounting profession's social contract centers on attesting to the fair presentation of corporate financial reports. Former SEC chairman Arthur Levitt said it best: "Accountants serve one of the most valuable functions in a capitalist society. Their stock in trade is neither numbers, nor pencils, nor columns, nor spreadsheets, but truth. Accountants are the people who protect the truth."[2]

Prior to the Sarbanes-Oxley Act, the SEC looked to the private sector for leadership in setting standards and improving financial reporting. Recall that former U.S. Supreme Court Chief Justice Warren Burger described accountants as public watchdogs certifying that public reports collectively depict a corporation's financial status. The failure of auditors' leadership at companies like Enron and WorldCom contributed to their demise. Time and time again the auditors stood idly by and did nothing about financial fraud.

The social contracts can be undermined by an inherent internal conflict — professionals not only provide necessary audit services for clients but are paid by those very same clients for whom the services are performed. This conflict tests the commitment to leadership by acting in the best interests of the public, not those of the client or self-interest.

Strong leadership in any field, and certainly in accounting, requires a commitment to ethical leadership as the foundation of an ethical organization. Ethical leaders create a culture of respect, trust, and accountability and always strive to do the right thing. Ethical leaders model ethical values such as honesty and integrity and communicate those values throughout the organization. Ethical leaders lead by example and earn the right to expect others to do so as well.

Leaders who lead ethically are role models, communicating the importance of ethical standards and holding their employees accountable to those standards. Leadership is the most important lever in an ethical system designed to support ethical conduct. Leadership in accounting means to insist that accountants and auditors carry out their professional services in accordance with ethical standards of behavior consistent with the public interest.

True leaders set an ethical tone at the top. There are times when the opposite occurs. The following discussion is taken from a PBS interview with Joseph Berardino, former worldwide CEO of Andersen, on May 1, 2002. Berardino was asked about the controversial decision to remove Carl Bass from oversight of the Enron audit. Bass was an Andersen partner at the Professional Standards Group — sometimes referred to as "The Keeper of the Holy Grail," an internal team of accounting experts that reviewed and passed judgment on tricky accounting issues facing local offices. Bass documented a conflict over how Enron should account for the sale of options owned by one of the partnerships managed by Andrew S. Fastow.

In the PBS interview, Berardino was asked about memos sent by Bass from 1999–2001 that said there was no substance to the partnerships that Enron was setting up off-books, Berardino claimed ignorance of the memos. When the PBS reporter probed further, perhaps out of disbelief, Berardino responded testily:

> Well, it didn't come to me. I've not read those memos. I've heard about them. There were disagreements. At the end of the day, what has happened is, if you look at the restatements that we agreed to on Enron, there were two restatements of some $500 million of earnings over a five-year period. In one instance, representing about 80% of that restatement. Frankly, we didn't have all the facts. Whether it was withheld from us purposefully or not, we didn't have all the facts. In the second instance—roughly 20% of the restatement—we did have the facts, and we made a bad judgment call. . . . At the end of October, when we reviewed the transaction, we realized our people had the information they needed to make a judgment call and they made the wrong call.

This is an astounding statement by the chairman of the once largest CPA firm in the world. Perhaps it is an extreme example of bad leadership; perhaps a one-time lapse in ethical judgment. We doubt it. Instead, it reflects ethical blindness toward what is the real mission of conducting an audit and who it serves. This statement is indicative of a culture that the most important goal was to keep the client happy at all costs. It was a failure of ethical leadership. Andersen violated the social contract with shareholders, investors, and the public at large.

As you read this chapter, think about the following: (1) What does it mean to be an ethical leader? (2) How does ethical leadership influence the judgments and decisions made by accounting professionals? (3) What can the accounting profession do to regain its position of ethical leadership and serving the public interest?

A leader is one who knows the way, goes the way, and shows the way.

John C. Maxwell

This quote by John Maxwell, an internationally recognized leadership expert, illustrates the followership nature of good leadership. Ethical leaders inspire others to be their best, make rightful decisions, create a pathway for others to make ethical decisions, and create a culture for leadership that emanates throughout the organization.

What Is Ethical Leadership?

One characteristic of ethical leadership is to influence others. Yukl emphasized the importance of influence when identifying a leader: "Leadership is the process of influencing others to understand and agree about what needs to be done and how to do it, and the process of facilitating individual and collective efforts to accomplish shared objectives."[3] Dhar and Mishra point out that leadership has been defined in terms of individual traits, leader behavior, interaction patterns, role relationships, followers' perceptions, influence over followers, influence on task goals, and influence on organizational culture.

The ethical leader understands that positive relationships built on respect, openness, and trust are critical to creating an ethical organization environment. The underlying principles of ethical leadership are: integrity, honesty, fairness, justice, responsibility, accountability, and empathy. Covey addresses a principle-centered leadership approach to one's personal life and organization development. He emphasizes that principle-centered leadership occurs when one's internal values form the basis of external actions. Principle-based leaders influence the ethical actions of those in the organization by transforming their own behavior first. Covey encourages principle-centered leaders to build greater, more trusting and communicative relationships with others in the workplace.[4]

Ethical leaders strive to honor and respect others in the organization and seek to empower others to achieve success by focusing on right action. An ethical organization is a community of people working together in an environment of mutual respect, where they grow personally, feel fulfilled, contribute to a common good, and share in the internal rewards, such as the achievement of a level of excellence common to a practice as well as the rewards of a job well done. By emphasizing community and internal rewards, ethical leaders commit to following a virtue-oriented approach to decision making based on a foundation of values-based leadership.

Leaders lead by example. They set an ethical tone at the top. They lead with an attitude of "Do what I say as well as what I do." Ciulla argues that what is distinctive of leadership is the concept of vision: "Visions are not simple goals, but rather ways of seeing the future that implicitly or explicitly entail some notion of the good."[5]

The Ethics and Compliance Initiative (ECI) points out that research has consistently shown that:[6]

- Ethical leadership is a critical factor driving down ethics and compliance risk;
- Leaders have a 'rosier' view of the state of workplace integrity and often have more positive beliefs than employees further down the chain of command; and
- The quality of the relationship between supervisors and employees goes a long way in determining whether employees report workplace integrity issues to management.

According to research conducted by Brown et al., most employees look outside themselves to significant others for ethical guidance. Therefore, in the workplace, leaders should be a central source of such guidance. The ethical dimension of leadership represents a small component that falls within the core of inspiring, stimulating, and visionary leader behaviors that make up transformational and charismatic leadership. The authors developed a measure of ethical leadership known as the "ethical leadership scale," which includes several behavioral characteristics of ethical leaders:[7]

- Talk about the importance of workplace integrity and doing the right thing
- Set a good example
- Do not blame others when things go wrong
- Support employees' efforts to do the right thing
- Hold themselves and others accountable for violating the organization's code of conduct
- Give positive feedback for acting with integrity
- Keep their promises and commitments.

Organizations suffer when leadership does not set an ethical tone at the top. The employees may be ethical, but acting ethically requires an ethical leader who supports such behavior, not a leader blinded by ambition or greed as occurred in so many of the financial failures of the early 2000s.

Lawton and Paez developed a framework for ethical leadership built on three interlocking questions: First, who are leaders and what are their characteristics? Second, how do ethical leaders do what they do? Third, why do leaders do as they do and what are the outcomes of ethical leadership?[8] The authors suggest that the three factors will not necessarily form discrete areas of ethics. For example, auditors need to be virtuous and exhibit the characteristics of honesty, integrity, objectivity, and professional skepticism. These traits are also essential in auditors' relations with clients because they enable professional judgment and ethical decision making in client relationships. They also facilitate the kind of probing audits and targeted inquiries of management that should be conducted selflessly and in the public interest, not that of the client or even self-interest.

Lawton and Paez state that virtues cannot be separated from the context within which they are practiced. This is certainly true of accounting professionals and the accounting profession. They also opine that different virtues will be appropriate to the different roles that leaders play. We agree that context is important. As leaders within their firms, partners must exhibit moral imagination through ethical perception of what it means to be ethical, professional, and successful. In dealing with conflicts in relationships with clients, auditors should demonstrate courage and moral judgment. Here, ethical reasoning and ethical decision-making skills become critically important.

Ethical problem solving is part of the role of being an accounting professional. Ethical leadership entails building an environment where those in the organization feel comfortable in talking to others to share perspectives of the importance of finding an ethical solution to problems. Internal accountants and auditors may possess ethical values, but it will mean nothing unless a supportive organization exists to help develop the courage to put those values into action. Voicing one's values when conflicts exist creates challenges that can be exacerbated by an indifferent leader and culture that operates by rationalizing unethical actions. Pressures imposed by top management to go along with financial wrongdoing under the guise of "It is expected practice around here" or "You need to be a team player" challenges a protagonist who must counter those reasons and give voice to one's values. As Patrick Kelly observes, "Ethical leaders must consistently make correct moral decisions, even under challenging circumstances."[9]

Copeland examined a model that examines ethical leadership and its impact on leader effectiveness for leaders within the accounting industry. The study examined leaders in a large regional CPA firm. She collected data on leadership attributes. Copeland found that there was a significant relationship between ethical leadership behaviors and leaders who were evaluated by their subordinates as more effective. Her analysis shows that ethical and transformational leadership make incremental independent contributions in explaining leader effectiveness. Ethical leadership was a significant predictor of leader effectiveness over and above transformational leadership, the number of years a subject has worked for a leader, the number of years the subject has worked for the organization, and the subordinates gender. Copeland concluded that a need exists for individuals to be ethical and to emerge as ethical leaders in the account-ing profession.[10]

Moral Person and Moral Manager

It has been claimed that part of the role of leadership includes creating the "moral organization," promot-ing development in others, and institutionalizing values within the organization's culture.[11] Trevino et al. discuss building ethical leadership through two pillars of character: moral person and moral manager. The executive as a moral person is characterized in terms of individual traits such as honesty and integrity. As a moral manager, the executive (i.e., CEO) creates a strong ethics message that gets employees' attention and influences their thoughts and behaviors. Both are necessary for moral leadership. To be perceived as an ethical leader, it is not enough to just be an ethical person. An executive ethical leader must also attend to cultivating the ethics and values and infuse the organization with principles that will guide the actions of all employees.[12]

The "moral person" pillar forms the basis of a reputation for ethical leadership and challenges the leader to convey that substance to others in the organization. The perception that a leader is an ethical person means that people think of the leader as having certain traits, engaging in certain behaviors, and making decisions based on ethical principles. A moral person exhibits the virtues of leadership and encourages followers to do the same.

Underlying ethical values found in ethical leaders include altruism, honesty, empathy, empowerment, fairness, and justice.[13] Mahsud et al. argued that these behaviors result in confidence and faith in leaders as they are observed to be fair and have high integrity.[14] Brown et al. stated that these behaviors result in subordinates being more likely to trust the leader and believe the leader is acting in their best interests; as a result, subordinates are more willing to follow the leader's direction.[15] O'Toole argued that, when lead-ers demonstrate that their focus is fair and ethical, and with the welfare of their followers as the primary goal, subordinates embrace these leaders. The result is that these leaders are highly effective at getting subordinates to follow their lead. Consequently, the leader is able to achieve superior results.[16]

Building trust is a critical component of moral managers and is demonstrated through consistency, cred-ibility, and predictability in relationships. Openness, respect, and fair treatment of others in relationships creates an environment where actions and decisions can be questioned in the interests of ethical decision making.

Moral leaders strive not only to do the right thing but do so for the right reason and communicate to others that the right thing is going to happen at all times. The right reason is not to maximize profits or increase share price but, instead, to build an ethical culture that creates the kind of environment that sup-ports both short-term and long-term ethical decision making.

A moral manager serves as a role model for ethical conduct in a way that is visible to employees. Moral managers communicate regularly and persuasively with employees about ethical standards, principles, and values. They use reward systems to hold employees accountable to ethical standards. They understand that doing the right thing is more than having a code of conduct but also requires carrying through ethical intent with ethical action. Moral managers are at a postconventional reasoning level in Kohlberg's model and have translated ethical judgments into ethical decision making consistent with Rest's model.

A distinguishing characteristic of many of the accounting frauds discussed in this book is that short-term factors were allowed to compromise long-term ethical decision making in the interest of creating the illusion that earnings were strong and sustainable. CFOs and CEOs acted based on non-ethical values, such as enhancing share prices and creating personal wealth. Those on the front line "held their nose" and carried out unethical orders that led to managed earnings. "Leaders" such as Jeff Skilling at Enron,

Bernie Ebbers at WorldCom, and Dennis Kozlowski at Tyco created hands-off environments that sent the message "all is well" while the companies were collapsing around them.

Building a reputation for ethical leadership means to enable ethics and values to shine through the fog of beating the competition and meeting financial projections. During the accounting scandals, the mantra was to meet or beat analysts' earnings expectations. All kinds of financial shenanigans were used to accomplish the goal, as explained in Chapter 7. Some companies even turned to non-GAAP measures of earnings, such as EBITDA, to project the image of exceeding expectations.

Values-Driven Leadership

The starting point of a values-driven organization is the individual leader. A leader needs to connect with organizational values. Leaders must ask what they stand for and why. Leaders must consider why others would want to follow them. The goal is to get in touch with what motivates one's actions and how best to motivate those in the organization who look to the leader for direction. Values-based leadership is best summed up by Kouzes and Posner in *The Leadership Challenge:* "Clearly articulating and, more importantly, demonstrating one's values, forms the basis of a leader's credibility—and credibility in leadership is character-based."[17]

The GVV approach to decision making distinguishes between organizational values and individual values. Organizational values link to the mission of an organization and guide relationships with stakeholders. They set the tone for those in the organization and serve as standards of ethical behavior. While organizational values should be highly visible within the organization, individual values are internal to the very being of an individual. When organizational values and actions differ from what one truly believes in, then a way should be found to voice one's values with the intent of changing hearts and minds.

Ethical organizations encourage employees to voice their values. Ethical leaders know that if employees feel comfortable speaking up about matters of concern in a supportive environment, then problems will not fester and the likelihood of whistleblowing activity is lessened.

According to Mary Gentile, often we hear, "When I'm CEO I can take action on this kind of decision, but as a middle manager, I have neither the power nor the influence to do so." On the other hand, when managers put themselves in the place of the CEO, they say: "Well, if I were lower in the organization, I might be able to take this kind of personal risk and stand up against this behavior. But I have the jobs and lives of thousands of employees and investors depending on me. I can't afford the luxury of having values." Sounds like Chuck Prince in July 2007, not long before he was deposed as the head of Citigroup, when he said, "As long as the music is playing, you've got to get up and dance."[18]

It's not that ethical theory and high-level strategic dilemmas are not important; they are. But they don't help future managers and leaders figure out what to do next when a boss wants to alter the financial report, or their sales team applies pressure to misrepresent the capabilities of their product, or they witness discrimination against a peer. These are the experiences that will shape their ability to take on the big, strategic, thorny ethical dilemmas in due time. The near-term skills needed to deal with these kinds of challenges involve knowing what to say, to whom, and how to say it when a manager knows what's right in a particular situation but doesn't feel confident about how to act on his or her convictions. Ethical leaders embrace these factors as central to ethical decision making.

Consider the following situation: Amy is an auditor at Black and White, LLP, a mid-sized accounting firm in New York City. Amy has identified what may be a major fraud at a client entity. It seems the client engaged in a "sell-through" product agreement whereby an apparent sale to another party included a side agreement that obligated that party to resell the merchandise prior to paying for the "acquisition." Thus, a contingency existed that should have delayed the recording of the sales revenue but did not. Amy has already spoken to Pat, the audit manager, who instructed her to leave the transaction alone. It seems the amount involved was not material, according to Pat. Moreover, it seems the client has exerted a great deal of pressure on the firm to go along with its accounting because the revenue involved is sufficient to change a loss for the year into a profit.

Amy is disappointed in Pat and what may be the firm's position on the matter. She knows the firm has a core set of values that do not square with the intended accounting. One such accounting value is how materiality is applied. Changing a loss to a profit is material in and of itself. It seems as though Amy may be facing an instance of organizational dissidence in that the way in which she expected the organization to act is not the way that it did act. She wants to find a way to give voice to her values but is not sure how to go about it. What are the key issues for Amy to consider? What road should she take?

Values-based leadership cuts both ways. Amy may be disappointed in the firm's leadership, but if she envisions herself as a leader (or potential leader), then she wants to demonstrate leadership instincts in deciding how to handle the matter. Perhaps she can influence the actions of the firm if she is successful in voicing her values using the GVV framework.

- What are the shared values that should drive my actions?
- With whom do I need to speak to enable voicing my values?
- What do I need to say to most effectively give importance to my values?
- What are the likely objections or push-back I should expect? And, then,
- What should I say next?

As we have discussed many times before, Amy should evaluate the reasons and rationalization she needs to address. One may be that the leader(s) in the firm she decides to approach may "play the loyalty card" or insist that they "keep the client happy." This is where the dissidence becomes a factor in Amy's decision.

Once Amy decides on a course of action, she needs to ask herself: What if I don't act and voice my values? How will I feel about myself? Would I be proud for others to know about it, including family members? What will happen if I do nothing and get blamed for inaction down the road? How will I feel if I do nothing and the organization implodes?

Authentic Leaders

> ### LO 8-2
> Distinguish between types of leadership.

Authentic leaders are focused on building long-term shareholder value, not in just beating quarterly estimates. Authentic leaders are individuals "who are deeply aware of how they think and behave and are perceived by others as being aware of their own and others' values/moral perspectives, knowledge, and strengths; aware of the context in which they operate; and confident, optimistic, resilient, courageous, and of high moral character. Authentic leaders acknowledge the ethical responsibilities of their roles, can recognize and evaluate ethical issues, and take moral actions that are thoroughly grounded in their beliefs and values."[19]

Authentic leaders hold altruistic values and are concerned with achieving a common good for the group or organization for which they are responsible. Authentic leadership produces a number of positive ethical effects in followers that significantly influence the creation of an ethical organization environment and help to promote values-based decision-making. Followers are likely to emulate the example of authentic leaders who set a high ethical standard. They are empowered to make ethical choices on their own without the input of the leader. They become moral agents of the organization.

Transformational Leadership

The need for good leaders to be ethical in their leadership is embedded within definitions of transformational leaders. Transformational leadership is defined as a leadership approach that causes change in individuals and social systems. In its ideal form, it creates valuable and positive change in the followers with the end goal of developing followers into leaders. Enacted in its authentic form, transformational leadership enhances the motivation, morale, and performance of followers through a variety of mechanisms. These include connecting the follower's sense of identity and self to the mission and the collective identity of the organization; being a role model for followers that inspires them; challenging followers to take greater ownership for their work; and understanding the strengths and weaknesses of followers, so the leader can align followers with tasks that optimize their performance.[20]

Transformational leadership is more effective than transactional leadership, where the appeal is to more selfish concerns. An appeal to social values thus encourages people to collaborate rather than working as individuals. Transformational leadership is an ongoing process rather than the discrete exchanges of the transactional approach.

A transformational leader is one who is able to influence major change in the attitudes of subordinates and inspire and empower them to support and commit to the organizational mission.[21] Transformational leaders raise the bar by appealing to higher ideals and values of followers. In doing so, they may model the values themselves and use appealing methods to attract people to the values and to the leader.

Followership and Leadership

The flip side of leadership is followership. First introduced by Hollander and Webb, the term *followership* is characterized as an independent relationship in which the leader's perceived legitimacy can affect the degree to which followers allow themselves to be influenced.[22] This early work emphasizes the reciprocal relationship in which followers play an active role not only by receiving but also exerting influence.

Servant leadership advocates a perspective that leaders have a responsibility to serve their followers by helping them achieve and improve by modeling leaders' ethical values, attitudes, and behaviors that influence organizational outcomes through the fulfillment of followers' needs. The basic premise of servant leadership is leaders should put the needs of followers before their own needs. Servant leaders use collaboration and persuasion to influence followers rather than coercion and control. They understand their stewardship role and are accountable for their actions. Servant leadership helps to create an ethical, trusting organizational climate.

Trust is a key component in developing successful relationships between leaders and followers. A trusting relationship is built on shared values, respect, open communication, and accountability. Trevino et al.'s pillars of ethical leadership are the relevant behaviors that leaders can employ to demonstrate integrity to followers and build trust. The pillars are antecedents to trust and include role-modeling through visible action, the use of rewards and discipline, and communicating about ethics and values.[23]

Followership, servant leaders, and authenticity all share one common characteristic: *leader ethicality.* De Cremer and Tenbrunsel define leader ethicality as the intention to demonstrate normatively appropriate conduct and to create an environment within which others will be encouraged to act ethically and discouraged from acting unethically. Demonstrating normatively appropriate conduct is in part determined by follower perceptions; thus, leader intent is important. Moreover, this definition takes into consideration the importance of moral perspectives and underscores the notion that ethical behavior is to some extent defined by how it is construed within the context of social prescriptions.[24] In accounting, the social contract with the public is the context within which leaders model ethical behavior to nourish the perception that the accounting profession is an ethical profession with norms and values.

The social perception of a leader's legitimacy may play an important role in determining how the leader's morally relevant actions are interpreted and the influence leaders have on followers. The social context created by followers' normative expectations is a significant determinant of leader legitimacy, and violations of such expectations can cast doubt on the leader's position, authority, status, and influence. Imagine, for example, if a controller was pressured by the CFO, who paid no regard to the ethical standards of the profession but allowed personal goals to influence professional values. The followers would be less likely to embrace the actions of such a leader.

De Cremer and Tenbrunsel posit that, due to the socially construed nature of leader legitimacy, leaders are vulnerable to follower judgments. Leaders may gain legitimacy from followers when they allow themselves to receive follower influence and behave in accordance with followers' normative expectations.[25] It stands to reason that, if leadership is important to performance, followership must have something to do with it too. Organizational dissidence is best controlled when both parties strive for high ethics in their behavior and decision making.

Social Learning Theory

Social learning theory has been used to understand how leaders influence followers more generally. Social learning theory holds that individuals look to role models in the work context and model or imitate their behavior. Modeling is acknowledged to be one of the most powerful means for transmitting values, attitudes, and behaviors. Employees learn what to do, as well as what not to do, by observing their leaders' behavior and its consequences. Leaders become role models by virtue of their assigned role, their status and success in the organization, and their power to affect the behavior and outcomes of followers.[26] Through social learning, people may adopt ethical behaviors, as evidenced by the impact of ethical leadership[27] or antisocial behaviors.[28]

Leaders who engage in unethical behaviors create a context supporting what Kemper calls "parallel deviance," meaning that employees observe and are likely to imitate the inappropriate conduct.[29] If leaders are observed "cooking the books," or enriching themselves at the expense of others, as did Skilling, Ebbers, and Kozlowski, followers learn that such behavior is expected. If leaders are rewarded for unethical conduct, the lesson for followers becomes particularly strong, and we might expect them to emulate such behavior, especially if no consequences exist for wrongful actions.

The social learning approach suggests a mostly instrumental understanding of what drives unethical behavior in organizations. It argues that, because of leaders' authority role and the power to reward and punish, employees will pay attention to and mimic leaders' behavior, and they will do what is rewarded and avoid doing what is punished in the organization. The rewards and punishments need not be direct but also can be learned by observing how others in the organization are rewarded and disciplined.

A good example of antisocial behavior in what might be called a game of corporate survivor was at Enron where a policy nicknamed "rank and yank" had employees give one another annual ratings, with the bottom 15% being fired. Every year, all employees were rated from 1 (best) to 5 (worst). The more money you made for the company, the better your rating. Skilling was fond of saying that money was the only thing that motivated people. Skilling mandated that between 10 and 15% of the employees had to be rated as 5s. And to get a rating of 5 meant that you were fired.

Unethical cultures that foster antisocial behavior are not limited to large corporations. An often overlooked aspect of cultural deviance in the accounting profession is the negative influence of leadership in accounting firms as described in the Introduction to this chapter. Joseph Berardino established a culture at Andersen that can best be characterized as "see no evil, hear no evil, and speak no evil." One could hardly claim that he was an authentic leader who encouraged followers to follow the ethical path in auditing Enron. In fact, his inability or unwillingness to perceive the ethical issues in the Enron audit and their moral intensity opened the door to antisocial behaviors by audit personnel.

Moral Intensity

We first discussed Thomas Jones' moral intensity model in Chapter 3. Jones conceptualized his model such that moral intensity might influence each of the components of Rest's model. It starts with moral awareness. Moral awareness and moral leadership go hand in hand. A moral leader is more likely to have his or her radar up and notice when ethical issues exist than one who is not attuned to the ethical dimension of decisions. The more intense the ethical issues, the more likely the decision maker will be aware of the ethical implications of her or his intended actions.

Jones argued that ethical decisions are primarily contingent upon the characteristics of the issue at stake so that judgments of ethicality would involve a systematic evaluation of the moral intensity of the characteristics of the issue. Factors need to be evaluated for moral intensity, including the magnitude of the consequences of the moral act, the degree of social consensus that the moral act is unethical, the feelings of proximity of the moral agent to the moral act, the likelihood that the moral act would take effect, the temporal immediacy of the effect of the moral act, and the concentration of the effect. Jones' model predicts that the perceived overall intensity of a moral issue would influence the decision maker's moral judgment and moral intent, as well as subsequent moral action.[30] All of these factors can be influenced by an ethical leader, one who is attuned to moral intensity.

The moral intensity of issues in an organization play a role in whether whistleblowing will occur. The predictor of whistleblowing and that of empathy corresponds directly to the two moral intensity dimensions of seriousness of issue and proximity. The degree of social consensus that the moral act is unethical is greatly influenced by the culture of the organization and whether ethical leadership exists. Thus, an ethical leader is more attuned to the magnitude of consequences and can use that in the pre-action decision stage to mitigate any bystander effect.

Taylor and Curtis studied whistleblowing among public accounting seniors and found that moral intensity is one of three significant factors affecting the intention to report wrongdoing, where intention to report is measured as the likelihood of reporting and perseverance in reporting. The other two factors were professional identity and locus of commitment (organization versus colleague). The authors found that, while high levels of professional identity increase the likelihood that an auditor will initially report an observed violation, the auditor's commitment to the organization drives perseverance in reporting. Auditors were more likely to report and to persevere when moral intensity is high.[31] More will be said about this study later on.

A greater degree of harm or benefit results in an increase in moral intensity because more stakeholders are at risk and the potential negative effects of unethical actions are more serious. We could equate moral intensity with materiality issues in accounting, where differences of opinion over proper accounting become more significant/intense as the amount involved increases and/or qualitative characteristics increase moral intensity—such as when an item in question masks a change in earnings or other trends. Moral intensity is high, as well, when non-GAAP measures are used to mask negative trends in GAAP earnings.

Ethical Leadership in the Accounting Profession

At an organizational level, ethical leaders build trust through actions and relationships with others. They set the tone that the value system is more important than producing numbers. In an interview with *Fraud Magazine,* Sherron Watkins characterizes the leadership of Ken Lay at Enron as follows:

> Ken Lay was setting the wrong tone. He was in effect letting his managers know that once you get to the executive suite, the company's assets are there for you to move around to yourself or your family. In some perverse way, Andy Fastow . . . could justify his behavior, saying to himself, "Well, my creative off-balance-sheet deals are helping Enron meet its financial statement goals. Why can't I just take a million here and there for myself as a 'structuring fee,' just like Lay has been taking a little Enron money and transferring it to his sister for all these years?"[32]

Watkins followed up by saying the CEO "must have pristine ethics if there is to be any hope of ethical behavior from the employees." She also suggested that CEOs must have a zero tolerance policy for ethically challenged employees, otherwise the internal control system will eventually be worthless.[33]

Ethical Leadership and Audit Firms

Personal ethical skills are primarily managed by the organizational structure of audit firms, and rules and processes have been developed with the sole aim of limiting the audit risk and guaranteeing audit quality. Ethical competencies are managed indirectly and promoted by the idea of responsible leadership and incentives to promote exemplary behaviors. Personal and professional ethics have roles to play in cultivating responsible leadership by management of audit firms. The promotion of responsible leadership is seen within audit firms as a way to improve audit quality.[34]

Responsible leadership in audit firms is essential to create an ethical environment within the firm. It is a critical component of setting the proper tone and encouraging members of the organization to ask probing questions when management's representations are unclear or unsubstantiated. Responsible leadership is an integral part of ethical leadership, although the latter also entails the ability to reason through ethical dilemmas and resolve conflicts in a morally appropriate way.

The ethical environment within an accounting firm is created through espoused values and management practices. The culture of the firm results from leadership style and may be the most important deterrent to unethical behavior.[35] Authentic (partner) leaders gain the confidence of audit staff and managers and create a foundation for ethical decision making.

Research by Ponemon found that leaders of accounting firms set the tone of their organizations, promoting those whose personal attributes more closely reflected the leaders' perceptions and moral reasoning development. He hypothesized there is a correlation between the organizational culture created by leaders of the accounting firms and the subordinates' personal characteristics and decision-making styles.[36]

Prior research has indicated that audit seniors' perceptions of their firm leaders and firm culture impact auditor behavior. Personal characteristics have an impact on individual behaviors. Shaub et al. found mixed evidence of "the ability of an accounting firm to either change an auditor's ethical orientation to match its own, or to provide an environment that closely matches an auditor's norms."[37]

The dissidence that is created when individual values do not fit into the expectations of the firm might lead the individual to alter behavior to conform to firm norms, the firing of the individual from the firm, or his voluntary departure. Ponemon confirmed the existence of a selection-socialization mechanism operating to control ethical reasoning in public accounting firms. The selection-socialization bias causes a firm to hire and promote individuals who fit into the prevailing firm culture and causes individuals unable to fit into that culture to leave.[38]

Douglas et al. studied the influence of ethical orientation and ethical judgment in situations of high and low moral intensity and found that ethical orientation is related to ethical judgments in high (but not low) moral intensity situations, which appears to support Jones' issue-contingent argument. They also found that perceived organizational culture is indirectly related to ethical judgments, as ethical culture affects individual values (i.e., idealism) and idealism affects judgments.[39]

Morris studied the influence of authentic leadership and ethical firm culture on auditor behavior. She used the definition of authentic leadership provided by Avolio and Gardner as follows:[40]

> A pattern of leader behavior that draws upon and promotes both positive psychological capacities and a positive ethical climate, to foster four constructs: greater self-awareness, an internalized moral perspective, balanced processing of information, and relational transparency on the part of leaders working with followers, fostering positive self-development.

Morris gathered data from 120 practicing senior auditors representing the Big Four firms, other international firms, large regional firms, and local firms. Participants were asked to indicate the frequency of selected dysfunctional behavior among audit seniors. Morris hypothesized that perceptions of authentic leadership are negatively related to the frequency of dysfunctional audit behaviors. The behaviors identified include under-reporting of time worked on an engagement, premature sign-off on audit procedures, and other dysfunctional behaviors.[41]

The results indicate that a typical audit senior at these firms more frequently under-reports time than prematurely signing off on audit work. The results also indicate there was a significant negative correlation between all measures of authentic leadership and dysfunctional audit behaviors with few exceptions. With respect to ethical culture, there was a negative relationship between the audit seniors' perceptions of their firms as ethical, and instances of dysfunctional audit behavior. The findings support the mediation of perceptions of authenticity in leaders on the auditors' perception of ethical firm culture and on auditors' instances of dysfunctional behavior. The results seem to indicate that the four constructs of authentic leadership, whether taken individually or in combination, have influence over the employee's perception of the ethical content of a firm's organizational culture.[42]

The takeaway from the Morris study is that authentic leaders can help to promote an ethical culture and reduce the instances of dysfunctional auditor behavior. Authentic leaders seek to eliminate ethical dissonance. As we discussed in Chapter 3, ethical (authentic) leaders commit to a high person-organization fit where organizational ethics are high and the culture promotes high individual ethics (High-High). Any other combination may jeopardize ethical decision making and sacrifice the public trust in the audit profession—at least in that instance.

Consider what might have happened at Andersen if Joseph Berardino were an authentic leader who placed ethical values ahead of non-ethical values. The culture within the firm would have been quite different. The message sent would have been that the red flags raised by Carl Bass about accounting for the off-balance-sheet partnerships had to be dealt with, not swept under the rug. Perhaps Berardino's biggest fault was in not balancing processing of information; instead, the negative aspects of what was happening at Enron were shoved in the background and hidden from view.

Gender Influence on Decision Making of Public Accounting Professionals

In a study published in *Behavioral Research in Accounting,* Bobek et al. describe the results of an investigation of how professional role (auditor or tax professional), decision context (an audit or tax issues), and gender influence public accounting professionals' ethical decision making. Participants were asked to respond to hypothetical sets of facts about contentious client conflicts for which they were asked to recommend whether to concede to the client's wishes and to indicate their own behavioral intentions. The decision context (an audit or tax environment) was manipulated to explore individual attributes in contexts with different types of professional responsibility.[43]

The results of the study may have implications for leadership in CPA firms because the factors that influence how males and females see their role as accounting professionals differ. Males were less likely to recommend conceding, and less likely themselves to concede, in an audit condition versus a tax condition. This is not surprising given the role of a tax accountant as an advisor with an advocacy relationship, whereas an accounting professional's audit role is that of an independent judge of the fairness of the financial statements.

Looking at the responses of females, there was no significant difference based on either condition or professional role. However, it was found that females appeared to use a different decision-making process than males. Females may be more likely to use an intuitionist approach. This implies a more deliberative approach may not be used, nor one that relies more heavily on systematic ethical reasoning to resolve conflicts. If so, the implications for resolving ethical dilemmas in dealing with clients may be significant. Another surprising result was that perceptions of moral intensity were seen as a factor that might mediate context in decision making in males but not females. Thus, the results show that professional role, context, and moral intensity potentially affect male decision making in a significant way but not female decision making.

The results of the study are one snapshot in time and limited by the choice of subjects studied. It will be interesting to see if the results are duplicated in other environments. Nevertheless, they do point out that leaders of audit firms need to pay attention to gender differences in designing decision systems to ensure audit quality.

Ethical Leadership and the Internal Audit Function

Chambers identifies seven attributes of internal audit leadership as a standard for ethical behavior including honesty, courageousness, accountability, empathy, trustworthiness, respect, and proactiveness. These are important qualities for internal auditors who are on the front lines of dealing with financial fraud.[44]

Studies of ethical leadership have relied on manipulating variables such as integrity and ethical standards (i.e., high versus low), treatment of employees (i.e., fair versus not fair), and holding of employees accountable for ethical conduct (i.e., held accountable versus not held accountable).[45] The internal audit function has been conceptualized as a multi-dimensional construct with a position within the corporate governance structure of a company based on to whom the internal audit function reports (i.e., audit committee versus chief financial officer), the primary role of the internal audit function within the company (i.e., assurance versus consulting), and the work product produced (i.e., history of finding versus missing deficiencies).[46]

Internal auditors can sometimes be bullied by CFOs, or at least an attempt to do so occurs, which makes it more difficult for them to carry out their ethical obligations. This occurred at WorldCom, where Cynthia Cooper was consistently pressured by Scott Sullivan to not act on the improper accounting. An internal auditor with a weak character might go along, but Cooper demonstrated strong ethical leadership skills in working with her team to uncover the scope of the fraud. She wouldn't take no for an answer and went to the audit committee first, then to the outside auditors, and persisted in her efforts to correct the wrongdoing.

When deciding whether to record a questionable journal entry (i.e., any entry for which a reasonable business case can be made for either recording it or not recording it), auditors may take their cue from executive management's behavior, especially if such behavior is the social norm and has been rewarded in the past.[47] In addition, a high-quality internal audit function can reinforce the tone at the top and provide guidance for decision makers by monitoring internal control and management's actions. For instance, accountants may hesitate to record a questionable entry if they know that internal audit is likely to detect inappropriate financial reporting practices. Prawitt et al. discovered from their study of earnings management that a quality internal audit function is associated with moderation in the level of earnings management using abnormal accruals and the propensity to meet or beat analysts' earnings forecasts as proxies.[48]

Arel et al. studied the impact of ethical leadership, the internal audit function, and moral intensity on a decision to record a questionable entry. The authors found that the joint influence of ethical leadership and internal audit quality on accountants' willingness to book a questionable accrual entry is fully mediated by participants' perception of the moral intensity of the issue. Specifically, a strong internal audit function and weak ethical leadership combined to alter accountants' perception of the moral intensity of the issue. As a result, accounting professionals who perceive greater moral intensity associated with the controller's request to record a questionable entry are less willing to book the questionable entry.[49]

The Arel study also found that a strong internal audit function may cause accountants to question the appropriateness and ethicalness of an undocumented journal entry when combined with weak ethical leadership. Conversely, a weak internal audit function removes the most important internal control to help prevent and detect financial statement fraud. A case in point is at HealthSouth. Maron Webster, a former internal auditor at HealthSouth, testified that CEO Richard Scrushy had fired him in 1989 after he questioned accounting at a company operation in Miami. Webster said he raised concerns about improperly booked receivables and was told by Scrushy that "we're under certain pressures to make certain numbers. We have an obligation to stockholders and shareholders."[50]

Former chief internal auditor Teresa Rubio Sanders, who was hired by Scrushy in 1990 and quit in late 1999, testified that her office wasn't allowed to see the general ledger, where previous testimony showed a $2.7 billion earnings overstatement occurred from 1996 through 2002. Under questioning from defense lawyer Jim Parkman, Sanders testified she never complained to HealthSouth directors about the lack of access to corporate records. She also said she rarely met with directors or the audit committee.[51] Her lack of concern for the welfare of the company or its shareholders speaks volumes about the importance of ethical leadership to the internal audit function. Internal auditors, like Sanders, who bury their head in the sand while fraud occurs not only fail in their ethical leadership role but make it more difficult for the external auditors to uncover what is still hidden under the surface.

Ethical Leadership and Tax Practice

Studies have shown a disconnect exists between the perceptions of organizational ethics between higher and lower levels of an organization. Employees at higher levels perceive organizational ethics at a higher level.[52] In accounting, Bobek et al. found a disconnect exists between tax partners and nonpartner tax practitioners with respect to perceptions of organizational ethics when they described a self-identified ethical dilemma. On average, they found tax partners rated the ethical environments of their firms as stronger than nonpartner tax practitioners, especially with respect to firm leadership. While tax partners were more likely to describe an actual ethical dilemma than nontax practitioners, the group who described a dilemma rated the ethical environment as weaker, and this discrepancy was more pronounced for nontax practitioners.[53] This raises a question whether the ethical expectations of tax professionals are being met by their firms.

In a later study, Bobek et al. probed the reasons for the difference in perceptions of tax partners and non-partner tax practitioners. They found that, when nonpartners believe they have a meaningful role in shaping and maintaining the ethical environment of their firms and/or have strong organizational fit with the firm, they are more likely to perceive the ethical environment as strong and perceive it similarly to firm leaders. They also found that, among firm leaders (i.e., tax partners), the sense of having a stronger public interest responsibility and a higher frequency of receiving mentoring are both associated with stronger perceptions of the ethical environment.[54]

Earlier in this chapter and in Chapter 3, we discussed the relationship between organizational fit and ethical culture. It is not surprising that a strong (ethical) fit positively influences perceptions of an ethical culture. Beyond that, an important issue is what steps a firm can take to provide a meaningful role to nonpartners in shaping the ethical environment of their firm. Studies indicate that the weakest part of the ethical environment appears to be outcomes (e.g., rewards and sanctions) and "explicitly rewarding (and punishing) ethical (unethical) behavior is a tangible way to encourage nonleaders to participate in maintaining a strong ethical environment for the firm."[55]

The Role of CFOs

CFOs are in a position of ethical leadership when it comes to preventing fraud. Rather than promoting the CEOs point of view on earnings, or going along with it to deal with pressures to conform to the company's narrative, CFOs need to stand strong and refuse to be a part of the fraud. Unfortunately, in the scandals of the early 2000s, all too often CFOs either masterminded the fraud or pressured the controllers to go along.

The CFOs at HealthSouth uniformly allowed themselves to be influenced by Scrushy, even bullied into recording improper entries to make things look better than they really were. The motivating factors to go along with the fraud are stunning in the case of Aaron Beam, the first CFO at HealthSouth. In an interview with CFO.com, Beam said "When we started the company my net worth wasn't even $100,000." As the years went by, he built a large home. As soon as he could, he sold some stock and paid cash for a Mercedes. On trips to New York City, Beam noticed that most investment bankers wore expensive Hermes ties.[56] "I bought $30,000 worth of them," he said. Beam's ill-advised purchases set the stage for his willingness to go along with the fraud. Beam had gotten used to the trappings of success. If we look at Beam's actions in light of the Seven Signs of Ethical Collapse, Beam allowed himself to be pressured by Scrushy to make the numbers, he feared reprisals if he had not gone along, he was loyal to Scrushy as a co-founder of the company, overlooked conflicts of interest, and took advantage of a weak board of directors. Over time, Beam hated to go to work. He didn't want to be the whistleblower, instead adhering to the bystander effect.

Here's how Beam characterized what happened at the company:

> It's a process. When you're the CFO of a publicly traded company, you're under a lot of pressure to deliver good numbers. I think over time, just the culture of Wall Street, you learn to "put lipstick on the pig." You're careful not to say anything negative. Over time, there's a possibility you learn how to be deceptive, because you want to protect the price of the stock. We were starting to not quite make our numbers for Wall Street. . .[57]

Exhibit 8.1 further details the glaring lapses in ethical leadership and toxic corporate culture at HealthSouth.

EXHIBIT 8.1   *Ethical Leadership and Corporate Culture at HealthSouth*

The following is largely drawn from a story in the University of Chicago Booth School of Business News following a presentation at the College by HealthSouth's former CFOs, Aaron Beam and Weston Smith.[58] The HealthSouth story took place in the 1990s and early 2000s and is about a corporate network of rehabilitation hospitals that skyrocketed up Wall Street and then plunged off a cliff. It's a story about sketchy ethics, tyrannical leadership, and crossing the line so often that boundaries disappeared.

Founded in 1984 by Beam and Richard Scrushy, the company's former chairman and CEO, HealthSouth went public two years later, after Scrushy impressed a group of Wall Street investors with a presentation on the company's potential. By 1995, the company had health centers in all 50 states, plus 40,000 employees, 10 to 12 jets, and a spot on the Fortune 500 list. Beam spent his millions on cars, condos, and a collection of French neckties that equaled an entry-level salary. It sounds a lot like what Dennis Kozlowski did at Tyco.

All the while, Beam said he was allowing Scrushy to bully him and other HealthSouth executives into manipulating financial reports to reflect the numbers Scrushy promised investors. During a meeting in 1996, Beam told Scrushy they would have to finally report a bad quarter. Scrushy said no, and they devised a way to hide the earnings shortfall.

"I should have had the courage to stand up and say, 'No, we can't cross this line,'" Beam said. Scrushy promised to deny everything if Beam reported the fraud and accused Beam of not being a team player. In 1997, Beam retired from HealthSouth, selling his company stock and walking away from a half-million-dollar annual salary. He thought the deception was behind him—until March 2003, when he heard on national television that a massive fraud had been uncovered at HealthSouth.

The $2.8 billion HealthSouth fraud involved recording fake revenues on the company's books from 1996 through 2012 and correspondingly adjusting the balance sheets and paper trails. Methods included overestimating insurance reimbursements, manipulating fixed-asset accounts, improperly booking capital expenses, and overbooking reserve accounts.[59]

According to the testimony of former CFOs Beam, Smith, Michael D. Martin, William T. Owens, and Malcolm McVay, each one realized the error of his ways, but most felt helpless to blow the whistle or even leave the company. Scrushy "managed greatly by fear and intimidation," according to Owens, who served as HealthSouth's third CFO from 2000 to 2001. Second CFO Martin testified that he tried to quit at least three times during his 1997 to 2000 tenure. "[Scrushy] said, 'Martin, you can't quit. You'll be the fall guy.'"

Apart from the organizational culture, what made the fraud possible on a structural level was Scrushy's elevation of so many decisions to the executive level, which limited checks and balances along the way. The accounting systems in the field did not interface with the corporate enterprise resource planning software, making it necessary for results to be consolidated by hand at the corporate level. That made it easy to fudge numbers, since the internal-audit staff was directed to review only the field numbers, not the consolidated numbers. In fact, Ernst & Young auditors noted in 2001 that "management is dominated by one or a few individuals without effective oversight by the board of directors or audit committee." EY also observed that the internal-audit function was understaffed, undertrained, and lacking in independence.

HealthSouth maintained impeccable corporate policies—on paper. A confidential whistleblowers' hotline had been set up in 1997. The company's nonretaliation policy gave the compliance director direct access to the board of directors.

Many employees of HealthSouth, particularly those who worked at medical centers in other parts of the country, thought they worked for an ethical company. A former regional manager who oversaw finances for facilities in several states says that the message from headquarters never conflicted with her personal values. "They were always stressing honesty in what we did, and that was how we ran it in the field," she says. "We had no reason to think they did any different."

HealthSouth is a case study in how a seemingly ethical company, at least one that had the trappings of an ethical consciousness, bowed to the unethical intentions and behaviors of its CEO and ignored the very systems that were put into place to build an ethical culture. It is a case study in how unethical leaders can corrupt the ethical culture and drag others, willingly or unwillingly, into a financial fraud that destroys a company and ruins lives along the way.

What happened at HealthSouth was not an uncommon occurrence, although the direct involvement of the CEO in pressuring other executives to execute the fraud was unusual. In most other cases (i.e., Enron and WorldCom), it was the CFOs who masterminded the fraud and carried it out. They exerted the pressure, perhaps so that the CEOs had "plausible deniability."

Personal Responsibility, Professional Role, and Whistleblowing

LO 8-4

Explain the relationship between personal responsibility, professional role, and whistleblowing.

Failed audits sometimes occur because unethical accountants agree to falsify the numbers to protect equally unethical clients. But that's only part of the story. The deeper, more pernicious problem with corporate auditing is its vulnerability to unconscious bias. Bazerman et al. looked at unconscious bias in auditing and concluded that the subjective nature of accounting and "tight relationships between accounting firms and their clients, even the most honest and meticulous of auditors can unintentionally distort the numbers in ways that mask a company's true financial status, thereby misleading investors, regulators, and sometimes management. Indeed, even seemingly egregious accounting scandals, such as Andersen's audits of Enron, may have at their core a series of unconsciously biased judgments rather than a program of criminality."[60]

Bazerman et al. suggest that bias thrives wherever there is a possibility of interpreting information in different ways, because people tend to reach self-serving conclusions whenever ambiguity surrounds a piece of evidence. Accountants need to interpret the ambiguous information in several situations. For example, what is the value of an investment, when should an expense be recorded, when should revenue be recognized? As Joseph Berardino said in his congressional testimony on the Enron collapse, "Many people think accounting is a science, where one number, namely earnings per share, is *the* number, and it's such a precise number that it couldn't be two pennies higher or two pennies lower. I come from a school that says it really is much more of an art."[61]

An audit ultimately endorses or rejects the client's accounting – in other words, it assesses the judgments of an auditor in the firm has already made. Research shows that self-serving biases become even stronger when people are endorsing others' biased judgments – provided those judgments align with their own biases – than when they are making original judgments themselves.[62] It implies that an auditor is likely to accept more aggressive accounting from his client than what he might suggest independently.

Culture and Whistleblowing in Accounting

Accountants and auditors are less likely to report financial wrongdoing if they perceive that past attempts by others in the organization to blow the whistle internally lead to retaliation against the reporter. According to Mesmer-Magnus and Viswesvaran, organizational employees have three options to address an unsatisfactory situation faced within an organization: (1) exit the organization, (2) voice discontent (i.e., blow the whistle), or (3) remain silent.[63] Employees with greater organizational commitment may prefer voicing discontent to exiting. Near and Miceli suggest that internal reporters will demonstrate high levels of firm loyalty in their initial decision to report.[64] However, absent ethical leadership and support for the reporter, it's less likely voicing discontent will occur.

Sims and Keenan studied organizational and interpersonal values as predictors of external whistleblowing. They found employees were more likely to engage in external whistleblowing if they had the support of their supervisor or they perceived that company policies suggested that such behavior was acceptable. The study also reported that external whistleblowing channels would be used only if would-be whistleblowers believed internal whistleblowing would be ineffective. The desire to use internal channels to report wrongdoing puts the ball in the court of companies to develop ethical systems to facilitate such reporting.[65] Ethical dissonance can be avoided by cultivating high organizational ethics and high individual ethics.

The locus of organizational commitment represents the strength of employees' identification with and involvement in a particular organization, a strong belief in organizational goals and values, and a willingness to exert considerable effort on behalf of the organization.[66] In public accounting, organizational commitment is heavily emphasized through identification with the ethical systems, quality controls, and firm leadership.

Commitment to the organization contrasts with colleague commitment, with the latter dependent on a sense of responsibility and readiness to support colleagues within the organization. Auditors may choose to act on behalf of their colleagues, mindless of the welfare of the firm as a whole. Thus, unlike professional identity, which exists independent of organizational affiliation, organizational colleague commitment and firm commitment are linked together in many cases with one sustaining the other, and, in other circumstances, such as when a colleague performs an unethical act, they create conflicting allegiances.[67]

In their study of whistleblowing, Taylor and Curtis examined the complex relationships in accounting firms that influence an individual's decision to report an ethical violation. They conceive of the environment of the firm as a series of concentric circles with the accounting profession as the outermost layer. An auditor can think of his professional identity as his affinity for and identification with the audit profession. Auditors can be committed to the firm and the profession, neither one, or one or the other. Individuals also vary in their commitment to colleagues within the organization. At the center of these potentially conflicting layers of commitment is the ethical violation itself and the individual's personal reaction to it. Even if an auditor is committed to the profession and the firm, he may choose not to report an unethical or illegal event because it is deemed as not being a critical event. On the other hand, the auditor may show evidence of low commitment to the profession and the firm, but the event is so egregious that he feels he must act. Individuals must weigh all of these influences and weigh their significance in arriving at their reporting intention.[68]

Taylor and Curtis theorize that, when assessing whether to report, an individual will weigh the harm to the organization from not reporting against the harm to the colleague from reporting, and those with greater colleague commitment would demonstrate lower reporting intentions. They expected individuals with greater organizational commitment to exhibit greater reporting intentions. However, the locus of commitment and likelihood of reporting were not significantly related, although locus of commitment and perseverance of reporting are significantly related. Thus, it would appear that the longer an individual persists in attempting to resolve an issue, the more likely one's commitment to a colleague versus the organization becomes an influencing factor in determining whether to report.[69] Examining persistence as a virtue, we can see that it is likely to reflect one's commitment to ethical standards (i.e., due care and professional skepticism), and it reflects a strong sense of professional identity.

Personal responsibility for reporting is also an important consideration. Senior auditors take their cue from managers and others higher-up in the chain of command in the firm. Ethical leadership by those in this group means greater support should exist for audit seniors' position than otherwise. A correlation exists between the likelihood of audit seniors reporting audit staff for premature sign-off behavior based on whether the audit step was a necessary (unnecessary) step and whether the staff member had a good (poor) performance history. Senior auditors were more likely to report a manager's ethical violation when they perceived personal costs of disclosure were low or when personal responsibility for reporting was perceived to be high.[70]

Brennan and Kelly studied some of the factors that influence propensity or willingness to blow the whistle among trainee auditors. The factors studied include audit firm organizational structures, personal characteristics of whistleblowers, and situational variables. The authors found that formal structures for whistleblowing and internal (versus external) reporting channels increase the likelihood of the subjects' reporting of an ethical violation by an audit partner. Their findings indicate that audit firms should examine their structures for reporting suspected or actual wrongdoing and, where necessary, improve such structures by encouraging staff to voice their concerns internally. A key issue is whether the firms have in place a system of quality controls to report internally. This is important because the respondents showed a reluctance to report externally. Brennan and Kelly's results have potentially significant implications for whether auditors use external reporting mechanisms, such as those of Dodd-Frank, if internal reporting has not resolved the differences between the auditor and firm management.[71]

Miceli et al.[72] studied the whistleblower intentions of internal auditing directors and found those directors less likely to report incidents of wrongdoing "when they did not feel compelled morally or by role prescription to do so." The authors note that these feelings of moral compunction and role prescriptions form the basis of the moral intensity of the situation.

Graham suggests that the positive contextual motivations toward reporting the unethical acts of others are a combination of the perceived seriousness of an unethical behavior and the perceived responsibility to act on this behavior. These two individual constructs are highly correlated with the seriousness of an issue generating increased feelings of responsibility to respond.[73] The more serious the matter (i.e., high moral intensity), the higher likelihood it will be reported. In such instances, the professional identity of the person reporting takes precedence over organizational and colleague commitment.

Whistleblowing can be perceived as an effective response to an organization's failure to establish accountability mechanisms internally. For auditors, the act of whistleblowing is internally required when differences exist on accounting issues with management because of their compliance obligations. External auditors have a similar obligation and additional reporting requirements to the SEC under Section 10(A) of the Securities Exchange Act of 1934, as discussed in Chapter 3.

A monkey wrench of sorts has been added to whistleblowing legislation through two major court decisions that were discussed in Chapter 3. The U.S. Supreme Court decision in *Digital Realty Trust, Inc. v. Somers*[74] clarifies that Dodd-Frank protections are only available to whistleblowers who report the matter to the SEC whether or not they follow the internal compliance reporting mechanism. This may hasten whistleblowing reports and be harmful to employers' interests. District Court Judge Cynthia Bashant's decision in *Erhart v. BofI Holdings*[75] clarifies that employer confidentiality agreements do not supersede federal whistleblower rights and signals that retaliatory lawsuits against whistleblowers are unlikely to succeed. Here, an employee can use confidential employer information as part of the whistleblowing claim reported under Sarbanes-Oxley, Dodd-Frank, and other federal laws.

To summarize, auditors are more likely to report wrongdoing if: (1) superiors and top management do not place obstacles in their way; (2) the reporter has a high commitment to the organization and/or colleagues; (3) the issue has high moral intensity; (4) ethical dissonance is not present; (5) the reporter perceives the organization provides reliable outlets (i.e., hotline) to report wrongdoing and retaliation will not occur; and (6) new whistleblowing legislation opens the door wider to whistleblowers who report to the SEC and under federal laws.

Accountants' and auditors' propensity to blow the whistle is closely linked to regulatory support for whistleblowers. As we have learned in this book, while SOX provides a process to blow the whistle if retaliated against, the Commission turns over investigation to the Department of Labor, which does not have a good track record of supporting whistleblowers. Moreover, those who report to the SEC after failing to change improper financial reporting may be ostracized and retaliated against, as was Tony Menendez in the Halliburton fraud.

From an ethical perspective, the recent *Digital Realty* decision casts a shadow over the willingness of a would-be-whistleblower to inform the SEC for fear of being fired because of that act. The *Erhart* decision may do the same because using confidential employer information is not likely to go over well with management. These rulings make it more difficult for whistleblowers to act morally and model ethical leadership. After all, if an internal accountant knows of a wrongful act but chooses to resolve the matter internally rather than report it to the SEC, an ethical action to be sure, it may be too late to report it to the SEC subsequent to being fired for the internal report.

Notwithstanding Dodd-Frank requirements, external auditors have to wrestle with their conscience when differences with management on financial reporting matters exist. They have to choose between confidentiality requirements and their public interest obligation, all the while evaluating the moral intensity of the issue.

A Case Study in Ethical Leadership

A good example of where an auditor acted based on her sense of right and wrong and identity as a professional is the case of Diem-Thi Le. She was faced with an ethical dilemma where her values and beliefs contradicted the values and beliefs of her employer, the Defense Contract Audit Agency (DCAA). Le was a senior auditor and had performed an accounting system audit at the corporate office of a contractor when she found that the accounting system was inadequate because the contractor was misallocating and mischarging costs to the government. Le's supervisor (regional audit manager) concurred with her audit findings; however, subsequently, the supervisor told Le that their branch manager disagreed with her.

The regional audit manager told Le that, because the branch manager was the one who signed the audit report, her opinion took precedence over Le's. Essentially, the person performing the audit had no say in the final audit report opinion. Moreover, the regional manager instructed Le's supervisor to put Le's working papers in the "superseded work paper folder." Her supervisor then deleted the audit findings from Le's working papers and, without performing any additional audit work, represented those changed working papers as Le's original working papers to support the change in the audit opinion from an inadequate accounting system to an adequate system. Shortly afterward, the audit report was issued, and the contractor accounting system was deemed adequate. Consequently, the contractor did not have to propose or implement any corrective actions to eliminate its accounting system deficiencies, which resulted in misallocating and mischarging costs to the government contracts.

Le did try to find an answer internally as to why her working papers were set aside and her audit opinion changed. Was it an anomaly or systemic problem? To satisfy her curiosity and give her branch manager the benefit of the doubt, she went to the office common drive that contained other audits and reviewed some system audits. She discovered a pattern of branch managers changing auditors' opinions, but Le did not know why these branch managers were doing it. She found out the reason after consulting with other supervisory auditors of other offices. By making the contractor systems and related internal controls adequate, less audit risk would be perceived and, consequently, fewer audit hours would be incurred on other audits. Because one of the DCAA's performance metrics was productivity rate, which measures the hours incurred versus the dollar examined, having fewer audit hours incurred for the same amount of dollars examined would increase the productivity rate. The productivity rate was one of the factors on which a branch manager's annual performance review was based.

On September 10, 2008, Le testified before the U.S. Senate Committee on Homeland Security and Governmental Affairs, which was investigating the DCAA audit, that an audit opinion she had developed on the audit of a contractor receiving funds from the U.S. government had been changed by a branch manager without her knowledge or approval. Ultimately, Le was responsible for a ruling by the U.S. Office of the Special Counsel that the DCAA violated the Whistleblower Protection Act when it retaliated against Le for blowing the whistle on fraudulent practices.

In reflecting on the incident in an interview with the *Orange County Register,* Le admitted to struggling with her conscience for weeks, trying through sleepless nights to get the courage to report the bad audits. She said, "I got to live with myself when I look in the mirror at the end of the day." She told the interviewer that management viewed her as the enemy, and even sympathetic coworkers were afraid of being associated with her: "When [I] walked into the break room, everybody walked out."[76]

A summary of Le's actions as a whistleblower and subsequent testimony before the U.S. Senate Committee on Homeland Security and Governmental Affairs appears in Exhibit 8.2.

EXHIBIT 8.2   *Diem-Thi Le and Whistleblowing at the DCAA*[77]

Diem-Thi Le testified before the U.S. Senate Committee on Homeland Security and Governmental Affairs on September 10, 2008. She told the committee that, because of the emphasis on the increase of the productivity rate, DCAA auditors, including herself, were pressured by management to perform audits within certain numbers of budgeted hours. Given the change in audit opinions by management without performing additional audit work or without discussing it with the auditors whose opinions were altered, she concluded that it was a lack of due professional care, at best, and negligent and fraudulent, at worst. She confided with other colleagues about her findings and was told she had no choice but to call the Department of Defense Inspector General (DoD IG) Hotline. She did so in November 2005.

Le said she never imagined that she would call the hotline and make an allegation against her management. She became disillusioned when she found out the complaint was sent back to her own agency for investigation. The independent process of review and determination of action by DoD IG personnel had been compromised. She followed up on her complaint several times, and, in February 2006, she was told that it might take a long time for someone to work on her case due to limited staff. She then decided to contact the local office of the Defense Criminal Investigative Services (DCIS) and met with a special agent on March 4, 2006. She also found out that her complaint had been referred to DCAA headquarters and that the referral included specific personal identifying information about her, such as her name and cell phone number, as well as details of the accounting system audit that triggered the hotline complaint. She concluded that her identity as a whistleblower had not been adequately protected; therefore, she suffered reprisal from DCAA management.

She made the following points about her experiences in her testimony:

- In September 2005, my management overruled my audit findings. In October 2005, I was transferred to another team. In the November 2005 Staff Conference, the regional audit manager stated that if we auditors did not like management's audit opinion, we should find another job.
- In early July 2006, I was transferred to another team. In late July 2006, my management was interviewed by the DCIS special agent. In October 2006, I found out that I was the only auditor with an "Outstanding" performance rating who did not get a performance award.
- In early April 2007, the Office of Special Counsel (OSC) investigator contacted DCAA Western Region management to inform them of my OSC complaint. Shortly after that happened, my supervisor told me that I should seek mental health counseling because of the stress I was under. She gave me an Employee Assistance Form and asked that I sign it.
- In August 2007, I was given my annual performance evaluation for the period of July 2006 through June 2007. I was downgraded from an "Outstanding" rating to a "Fully Successful" rating (two notches down). Also, my promotion points came down from 78 (out of a maximum of 120) to 58 points. Please note that prior to this job performance evaluation, I had been an outstanding auditor for several years.

(Continued)

- On August 31, 2007, I was given a memorandum signed by my supervisor and prepared by the DCAA headquarters' legal counsel. The memo instructed me that I was not allowed to provide any documents generated by a government computer, including e-mails and job performance evaluations, to any investigative units, including the OSC.
- On September 10, 2007, my supervisor advised me to read the 18 USC 641, Theft of Government Property. My supervisor stated that the unauthorized distribution of agency documents is theft, and it does not matter if the purpose is to respond to a hotline or OSC complaint.
- In August 2008, I was given my job performance evaluation for the period of July 2007 through June 2008. I remained at "Fully Successful," which is one notch above the rating that one would be put on a Performance Improvement Plan (PIP). My promotion points came down to 53.

Le concluded her testimony by stating that it was her opinion that DCAA management had become so metric driven that the quality of its audits and independence had suffered. Audits were not dictated by audit risks, but rather by the established budgeted hours and due dates. The pressure to close out audits and to meet the productivity rate was so intense that it often prevented auditors from following their instincts in questioning the contractor costs, reporting internal control deficiencies, and evaluating any suspected irregular conduct. In the end, contractors were "getting away with murder" because they knew that DCAA was so metric driven. She also pointed out that DCAA management had reduced the number of audit staff and created layers of personnel who did nothing but monitor metrics. She had hoped the culture would change and enable auditors to perform high-quality audits in accordance with generally accepted government auditing standards in order to protect the government's interest and taxpayers' money.

It is not easy to put everything on the line by questioning decisions and actions of your colleagues and the organization you work for. Diem-Thi Le's experience stands as an example of when doing the right thing can lead to right results, at least in the end, and that acting on one's conscience and a sense of professional identity can lead to positive results.

Responsible Leadership

LO 8-5

Describe the components of responsible leadership.

Researchers have addressed the audit report as a determinant of audit quality and linked it to responsible leadership. The promotion of responsible leadership, of which ethics is a key element, is taken to account by audit firms as a way to improve audit quality. Researchers have increasingly placed greater value on the humanist qualities of auditors,[78] much in line with the Six Pillars of Character discussed in Chapter 1.

According to Pless and Maak, becoming a responsible leader requires not only cognitive abilities but a combination of cognitive, emotional, relational, and moral qualities. Responsible leaders show interpersonal qualities in interacting with the different stakeholders and generating fair solutions. They need to be cooperative and empathetic in order to build and rely on social structures and resources both internal and external to the organization, which allow them to facilitate responsible actions.[79]

Ethical intelligence is an integral component of responsible leadership. Ethical intelligence depends on three ethical qualities: moral awareness (or ethical sensitivity), reflection skills (abilities to judge from a critical distance), and moral imagination (ability to develop new structures of thinking). Much of the literature addressing the ethical intelligence of leaders focuses predominately on the individual as a conscious decision maker and on the measure of his ethical sensitivity. In Rest's model, moral awareness plays a crucial role in different steps of the decision-making process.[80]

Lord and DeZoort point out that social influence pressures may counteract the effect of organizational commitments to promoting auditors' ethical intentions.[81] Krohmer and Noel suggest that the influence of the ethical climate and human resources practices within the audit firm on ethical behavior needs to be investigated. They proposed to better understand the development of future responsible leaders in audit firms by examining the ethical skills of the Big Four. Their results reveal an apparent discordance between discourse related to ethical management and human resource practices. Furthermore, ethics-related human resource practices are generally restricted to the identification of shortcomings in ethical competencies which are defined as being limited to the ability to effectively apply legal and organizational rules. Personal ethical skills are mainly managed by the organizational structure of the Big Four, and rules and processes have been developed with the sole aim of limiting the audit risk and guaranteeing audit quality. Moreover, ethical competencies are managed indirectly and promoted by the idea of responsible leadership and several incentives to exemplary behaviors.[82]

The results of the study of ethical skills of the Big Four show strong similarities in ethical skills management among those firms. They have similar organizations, almost identical values, and similar required competencies or in-firm day-to-day management. Ethical skills are defined by auditors as the capacity to rigorously apply rules and procedures. It is first of all a matter of keeping a professional distance from the client, which restricts auditors from holding shares with the firm's clients, accepting gifts, or having personal or business relationships with clients that violate independence and mask the need for objective decision making. The Big Four have quality control systems to monitor compliance with the rules. Professional confidentiality is also a predominant aspect of auditors' ethical skills. Auditors must not divulge confidential client information unless exceptions apply. Auditors must not use such information for personal gain.[83]

The study shows ethics are primarily personal skills. Character traits, such as integrity, perseverance, humility, and the ability to be objective, were mentioned by the auditors as being necessary to conduct a quality audit. As some auditors mentioned, it is always possible to lie or pretend. What distinguishes auditors, therefore, are their values. One senior auditor talked of the following case: "For example, you find an error and it's a pain, because it's going to waste your time. It's your sense of ethics that makes you sort out the error anyway. And on every level you are confronted with this type of problem. For me, ethics means having a professional conscience. You have to act like a professional. You are there to represent your company. So your behavior could tarnish your employer's image. It's not only your reputation at stake, but the profession you represent." Krohmer and Noel concluded from their study that the perceived image auditors have of their employer and the respect they have for him/her come into play as a factor capable of reinforcing auditors' ethical behavior.[84]

Ethical Leadership Competence

LO 8-6
Describe the characteristics of those with Ethical Leadership Competence.

Ethical Leadership Competence refers to the ability to handle all kinds of moral problems that may arise in an organization. It means to develop the problem-solving and decision-making skills to make difficult decisions. Leaders might try to deal with a moral problem in an automatic way, essentially using their authority for the basis of decision making. However, this System 1 approach is fraught with danger because the interests of all stakeholders may not be adequately considered, subtle moral issues may go unnoticed, and expediency is emphasized instead of thought and deliberation. As we have pointed out throughout the text, what is needed is to develop the competency to reason through ethical conflicts in a systematic way. There is no shortcut to making ethical decisions. It requires judgment and reflection on what the right thing to do is.

Thornton identifies five levels of ethical competence: personal, interpersonal, organizational, professional, and societal.[85] On a personal level, accounting professionals should internalize the values of the profession, including objectivity, integrity, diligence, and duty to society. Auditors are part of a larger social environment within the organization that may lead to pressures to conform with organizational expectations. The influence of organizational systems and ethics can create ethical dissonance. Auditors have a professional role to play in their organizations. Auditors work in teams so how they deal with others (i.e., showing respect, fair-mindedness) is a critical component of ethical competence. As members of an accounting firm, auditors should follow the ethics codes and expectations of their organizations, but they should never compromise their professional identity.

Kelly and Earley developed three measures called *The Ethical Leadership Scales,* which provide a measure of personal ethical competence, ethical leadership, and ethical organization. We have found the scales useful in teaching ethical leadership because they enable students to self-evaluate their leadership skills. Beginning with the understanding that effective ethical leadership depends on personal ethical competence, the *Ethical Competence Scale* provides a measuring stick of whether one's values consistently direct behavior. Questions to ask yourself include: Are you reliable and dependable? Are you willing to admit mistakes? Are you true to your word? Are you worthy of confidence? Do you keep promises and commitments?[86]

The *Ethical Leadership Scale* fits nicely with GVV methodology. It engages participants in reflecting on specific leadership qualities that can support voicing one's beliefs when conflicts exist in an organization and when interacting with others in organizational relationships. In discussing the usefulness of the Scales, Kelly and Earley point out that techniques of role-playing, simulation, and scenario writing can be used to enhance the experience.

The perception that followers have of managers in an organization, whether they are viewed as ethical leaders, depends on whether they are seen as moral persons and moral managers. Being a moral person is not enough to encourage ethical behavior of followers because of the distance between both parties. Moral managers gain legitimacy only if employees believe they are principled and caring, and say what they will do and do what they say.

Consistency in words and actions underlies ethical leadership. Followers must be comfortable that, if they follow the ethical path, they will be rewarded for doing so. In most of the companies that we have discussed in this book, the opposite was the case. Still, there are ethical organizations out there and leaders truly committed to doing the right thing.

When people face a moral problem, they sometimes have great difficulties in not confusing moral goals, values, feelings, and emotions with the problem-solving and decision-making processes and the methods adopted for the solution of the problem. By now you know these skills can be learned but require practice, commitment, reflection, and a continuous cycle of re-examining whether you need to adjust your thinking to match the ethical demands of a situation. We suggest that a worthwhile goal is to strive to eliminate any cognitive dissonance so that your behaviors match your values and beliefs.

We end this section with a quote from Shakespeare's Hamlet: "To thine own self be true, and it must follow, as the night the day, thou canst not then be false to any man [or woman]."

Concluding Thoughts

We began this book by discussing Aristotle and the ancient Greek ethics of virtue. It is fitting that we end it by discussing the Socratic Method. The philosophical position of ethics as a choice, which focuses on the way choices are made and the skills involved, starts from the Socratic dialogue. The goal is not so much to impart knowledge, as teachers, about what is the "truth." Instead, it is to help you discover the truth for yourselves through a collaborative process of asking questions. In this way we have tried to develop critical thinking skills in our discussions and assignments. The bottom line is that as students you are more likely to value knowledge if you discover it for yourselves than if we, as teachers, just tell you what it is. As Benjamin Franklin famously said, "Tell me and I forget, teach me and I may remember, involve me and I learn."

Armed with a strong desire to do the right thing, students should look for responsible leaders within their firms and the accounting profession for guidance. Ethical leadership does not occur in a vacuum. Instead, ethical leadership occurs within the broader structure of firm ethics. Ethical leaders seek to encourage followers to follow their path and they will be rewarded for their efforts.

Ethical behavior relies on personal commitment, courage and perseverance that is guided by strong ethical values. Ethical leadership is enhanced when we direct our moral compass due north. Having accounting professionals with a strong moral compass is essential to maintaining the public trust.

Now that we have reached the end of the course, it's up to each of you to internalize the leadership characteristics of an ethical person and apply them in your daily work. Our emphasis on virtue and the GVV methodology has been to engage you directly in discussions that can provide a pathway to the truth and stoke the fire of integrity that burns in the souls of good people. It is now up to you to summon up the courage to do the right thing; act the right way; and influence others to do so as well, which is the true test of leadership.

Discussion Questions

1. Choose someone from the business or accounting world who you think is an authentic leader and explain why you believe that to be true.

2. Distinguish between authentic leadership, transformational leadership, and servant leadership. Are all necessary to change individuals and social systems within an organization?

3. Identify three reasons why there may be ethical leadership failures and explain why failed leadership occurs.

4. Values-driven leadership as envisioned in the Giving Voice to Values technique poses the following question: Once I know what is right, how do I get it done and get it done effectively? Discuss how an authentic leader would go about addressing this question.

5. Describe the role of professional judgment in ethical leadership as it pertains to accountants and auditors and the link to their moral role in society.

6. It might be said that an effective, ethical leader is one who adheres to 'situational' ethics. Explain what this means. Do you agree?

7. How might an accounting firm influence whether non-tax practitioners view a contentious issue with a client as having been handled ethically?

8. How does an auditor's commitment to the firm, view of oneself as a professional, and loyalty to colleagues influence whether he will blow the whistle on financial wrongdoing?

9. Evaluate the moral intensity of the issues faced by Diem-Thi Le in her whistleblowing experience at DCAA.

10. How does organizational dissonance influence ethical leadership and decision making?

11. Why do you think studies show that no single factor has a bigger impact on the ethicality of a firm's culture than the personal examples set by firm leaders?

12. Audit firms are expected to establish and maintain a system of quality control. PCAOB inspections often cite the lack of quality controls as a deficiency of audit firms. What role does leadership play in developing the kind of quality control system that supports ethical decision making in audits?

13. Explain how the circumstances under each of the following might reflect failed leadership by auditors and the audit firm:

    • Under-reporting of time on an engagement

    • Premature sign-off on audit procedures

    • Accepting weak client explanations for accounting

14. Bruns and Merchant found that managers did not agree on the types of earnings management activities that are acceptable.[87] Refer to the definitions of earnings management in Chapter 7. Explain how leadership traits influence how managers might perceive the acceptability of earnings management.

15. Auditors are supposed to "sniff out" fraud. How can being an effective leader help in this regard?

16. Moral legitimacy refers to the generalized perception or assumption of observers that the actions of an entity are desirable, proper, or appropriate within some socially constructed system of norms, values, and beliefs. Explain how moral legitimacy might be applied to assess the actions of audit firms.

17. The court rulings in Digital Reality and Earhart establish standards of behavior for accountants and auditors. Which elements of ethical leadership might influence that behavior?

18. In talking about transformational leadership, Jennifer Wilson, Co-founder & Partner of ConvergenceCoaching, stresses the importance of getting people to believe in what they do, excited about what they do, and understanding the broader ideals of their work. What does this mean to you and your expectations in working for an employer?

19. Assume you are asked in an interview: Give me one word that describes you best? Then, explain why it is important in effective leadership.

20. It has been said that "Businesses don't fail – Leaders do." Explain what this means.

Endnotes

1. Steven Dellaportas and Lauren Davenport, "Reflections on the public interest in accounting," *Critical Perspectives in Accounting,* Vol. 19, pp. 1080–1098.

2. Arthur Levitt, Remarks by Chairman Arthur Levitt, SEC and Financial Reporting Institute, June 6, 1996, https://www.sec.gov/news/speech/speecharchive/1996/spch106.txt.

3. Gary Yukl, *Leadership in Organizations,* 8th edition, Pearson Education: London, England, 2012)

4. Stephen Covey, *Principle-Centered Leadership* (New York: NY, Simon and Schuster, 1991).

5. Joanne Ciulla, "The State of Leadership Ethics and the Work that Lies Before Us," *Business Ethics: A European Review,* Vol. 14, No. 4 (2005), pp. 323–335.

6. ECI, Executive Summary: Ethical Leadership Around the World, https://higherlogicdownload. s3.amazonaws.com/THEECOA/11f760b1-56e0-43c6-85da-03df2ce2b5ac/UploadedImages/ research/EthicalLeadership-ExecutiveSummary.pdf.

7. Michael Brown, Linda Klebe Trevino, and David A. Harrison, "Ethical Leadership: A Social Learning Perspective for Construct Development and Testing," *Organizational Behavior and Human Decision Processes*, Vol. 97, Issue 2 (July 2005), pp. 117–134.

8. Alan Lawton and Iliana Paez, "Developing a Framework for Ethical Leadership," *Journal of Business Ethics,* Vol. 130 (2015), pp. 639–649.

9. Patrick Kelly, "Developing Ethical Leader for the Accounting Profession," *The CPA Journal,* March 2017, https://www.cpajournal.com/2017/03/20/developing-ethical-leaders-accounting-profession/.

10. Mary Kay Copeland, "The Importance of Ethics and Ethical leadership in the Accounting Profession," *Research in Professional Responsibility and Ethics in Accounting,* Vol. 19, 2015, pp. 61-98.

11. See, for example, Chester I. Bernard, *The Functions of the Executive* (Cambridge, MA: Harvard University Press, 1971); and James MacGregor Burns, *Leadership* (New York, NY: Harper & Row, 1978).

12. Linda Klebe Trevino, Laura Pincus Hartman, and Michael Brown, "Moral Person and Moral Manager: How Executives Develop a Reputation for Ethical Leadership," *California Management Review,* Vol. 42, Issue 4 (Summer 2000), pp. 128–142.

13. Michael E. Brown and Linda K. Trevino, "Ethical leadership: A review and future directions," *The Leadership Quarterly,* Vol. 17, Issue 6, December 2006, pp. 595-616.

14. Rubina Mahsud, Gary Yukl, and Greg Prussia, "Leader empathy, ethical leadership, and relations-oriented behaviors as antecedents of leader-member exchange quality," *Journal of Managerial Psychology,* Vol. 25, Issue 6, 2010, pp. 561-577.

15. Michael E. Brown, Linda K. Trevino, and David A. Harrison, "Ethical leadership: A social learning perspective for construct development and testing, *Organizational Behavior and Human Decision Processes,* Vol. 97, Issue 2, July 2005, pp. 117-134.

16. James O'Toole, Leading Change: The Argument for Values-Based Leadership. NY: Random House, 1996.

17. James M. Kouzes and Barry P. Posner, *The Leadership Challenge,* 4th ed. (San Francisco: Jossey-Bass, 2008).

18. Mary Gentile, Giving Voice to Values in Leadership: How to Speak Your Mind When You Know What's Right, http://www.babson.edu/executive-education/thought-leadership/leadership-management/Pages/ giving-voice-to-values.aspx.

19. Bruce J. Avolio and William L. Gardner, "Authentic Leadership Development: Getting to the Root of Positive Forms of Leadership," *The Leadership Quarterly,* Vol. 16 (2005), pp. 315–338.

20. James MacGregor Burns, *Leadership* (New York, NY: Harper & Row, 1978).

21. Gary Yukl, *Leadership in Organizations*, 8th edition,Pearson Education: London, England, 2012).

22. Edwin P. Hollander and Wilse B. Webb, "Leadership, Followership, and Friendship," *The Journal of Abnormal and Social Psychology,* Vol. 50, No. 2 (1955), pp. 163–167.

23. Trevino et al.

24. David De Cremer and Ann E. Tenbrunsel, *Behavioral Business Ethics* (New York, NY: Taylor & Francis Group LLC, 2012).

25. De Cremer and Tenbrunsel, pp. 84–88.

26. Trevino et al.

27. Michael Brown, Linda Klebe Trevino, and David A. Harrison, "Ethical Leadership: A Social Learning Perspective for Construct Development and Testing," *Organizational Behavior and Human Decision Processes,* Vol. 97, Issue 2 (July 2005), pp. 117–134.

28. Sandra L. Robinson and Anne M. O'Leary-Kelly, "Monkey See, Monkey Do: The Influence of Work Groups on the Antisocial Behavior of Employees,". *The Academy of Management Journal,* Vol. 41, No. 6 (December 1998), pp. 658–672.

29. Theodore D. Kemper, "Representative Roles and the Legitimization of Deviance," *Social Problems,* Vol. 13 (1966), pp. 288–298.

30. Thomas M. Jones, "Ethical Decision Making by Individuals in Organizations: An Issue-Contingent Model," *Academy of Management Review,* Vol. 16 (1991), pp. 366–395.

31. Eileen Z. Taylor and Mary B. Curtis, "An Examination of the Layers of Workplace Influences in Ethical Judgments: Whistleblowing Likelihood and Perseverance in Public Accounting," *Journal of Business Ethics,* Vol. 93 (2010), pp. 21–37.

32. Dick Carozza, "Interview with Sherron Watkins: Constant Warning," *Fraud Magazine,* January/ February 2007, Available at: http://www.fraud-magazine.com/article.aspx?id=583.

33. Carozza.

34. Cathy Krohmen and Christine Noel, "Responsible Leadership for Audit Quality: How Do the Big Four Manage the Personal Ethics of their Employees?" Unpublished Manuscript by the University of Provence, France, Available at: http://sites.univ-provence.fr/ergolog/Bibliotheque/noel/responsible_leadership_for_corporate_responsability.pdf.

35. Patricia Casey Douglas, Ronald A. Davidson, and Bill N. Schwartz, "The Effect of Organizational Culture and Ethical Orientation on Accountants' Ethical Judgments," *Journal of Business Ethics,* Vol. 34 (2001), pp. 101–121.

36. Larry A. Ponemon, "Ethical Judgments in Accounting: A Cognitive-Developmental Perspective," *Critical Perspectives on Accounting,* Vol. 1 (1990), pp. 191–215.

37. Michael K. Shaub, Donald W. Finn, and Paul Munter, "The Effects of Auditors' Ethical Orientation on Commitment and Ethical Sensitivity," *Behavioral Research in Accounting,* Vol. 5 (1993), pp. 145–169.

38. Ponemon, pp. 199–201.

39. Douglas et al.

40. Avolio and Gardner, pp. 320–325.

41. Jan Taylor Morris, "The Impact of Authentic Leadership and Ethical Firm Culture on Auditor Behavior," *Journal of Behavioral Studies in Business,* Vol. 7 (September 2014), pp. 1–32.

42. Morris.

43. Donna D. Bobek, Amy M. Hageman, and Robon R. Radtke, "The Effects of Professional Role, Decision Context, and Gender on the Ethical Decision Making of Public Accounting Professionals," *Behavioral Research in Accounting,* Vol. 27, No. 1 (2015), pp. 55–78.

44. Richard Chambers, "Seven Attributes of the Ethical Internal Audit Leader," *Internal Auditor,* April 1, 2013, Available at: https://iaonline.theiia.org/seven-attributes-of-the-ethical-internal-audit-leader.

45. Brown et al. (2005).

46. Audrey A. Gramling, Mario J. Maletta, Arnold Schneider, and Bryan K. Church, "The Role of the Internal Audit Function in Corporate Governance: A Synthesis of the Extant Internal Auditing Literature and Directions for Future Research," *Journal of Accounting Literature,* Vol. 23 (2004), pp. 194–244.

47. David M. Mayer, Maribeth Kuenzi, Rebcca Greenbaum, Mary Bardes, and Rommel (Bombie) Salvador, "How Does Ethical Leadership Flow? Test of a Trickle-Down Model," *Organizational Behavior and Human Decision Processes,* Vol. 108 (2009), pp. 1–13.

48. Douglas F. Prawitt, Jason L. Smith, and David A. Wood, "Internal Audit Quality and Earnings Management, *The Accounting Review,* Vol. 84, No. 4 (2009), pp. 1255–1280.

49. Barbara Arel, Cathy A. Beaudoin, and Anna M. Cianci, "The Impact of Ethical Leadership and Internal Audit Function, and Moral Intensity on a Financial Reporting Decision," *Journal of Business Ethics,* Vol. 109, No. 3 (2012), pp. 351–366.

50. *The New York Times,* "Fifth Chief Financial Officer at HealthSouth to Admit Fraud," April 25, 2003, Available at: http://www.nytimes.com/2003/04/25/business/fifth-chief-financial-officer-at-healthsouth-to-admit-fraud.html.

51. *SEC v. HealthSouth Corporation and Richard Scrushy, Defendants,* United States District Court for the Southern Division of Alabama, 261 F. Supp. 2d 1298 (May 7, 2003), Available at: http://law.justia.com/cases/federal/district-courts/FSupp2/261/1298/2515723/.

52. See, for example, Linda Klebe Trevino, Gary R. Weaver, and Michael E. Brown, "It's Lovely at the Top: Hierarchical Levels, Identities, and Perceptions of Organizational Ethics," *Business Ethics Quarterly,* Vol. 18, No. 2 (2008), pp. 233–252; and Jill M. D'Aquila, "Financial Accountants' Perceptions of Management's Ethical Standards,"*Journal of Business Ethics,* Vol. 31, No. 3 (June 2001), pp. 233–244.

53. Donna D. Bobek, Amy M. Hageman, and Robin R. Radtke, "The Ethical Environment of Tax Professionals: Partner and Non-Partner Perceptions and Experiences," *Journal of Business Ethics,* Vol. 92 (2010), pp. 637–654.

54. Donna D. Bobek, Amy M. Hageman, and Robin R. Radtke, "The Influence of Roles and Organizational Fit on Accounting Professionals' Perceptions of Their Firms' Ethical Environment," *Journal of Business Ethics,* Vol. 126 (2015b), pp. 125–141.

55. Donna D. Bobek and Robin R. Radtke, "An Experiential Investigation of the Ethical Environment of Tax Professionals," *Journal of American Tax Association,* Vol. 29, No. 2 (2007), pp. 63–84.

56. David McCann, Two CFOs Tell a Tale of Fraud at HealthSouth, CFO.com, March 27, 2017, http://ww2.cfo.com/fraud/2017/03/two-cfos-tell-tale-fraud-healthsouth/.

57. David Jacobs, "Aaron Beam, Who Served Time in Jail after the HealthSouth Scandal, Opens Up about the Wrongdoing and His New Work,"*Business Report,* July 22, 2015, Available at: https://www.businessreport.com/business/aaron-beam-served-time-jail-healthsouth-scandal-opens-wrongdoing-new-work.

58. Kadesha Thomas, "From Wall Street to Prison: The HealthSouth Story," May 31, 2011, Available at: http://www.chicagobooth.edu/news/2011-05-31-healthsouth.aspx.

59. Alix Stuart, "Keeping Secrets: How Five CFOs Cooked the Books at HealthSouth," *CFO Magazine,* June 1, 2005, Available at: http://ww2.cfo.com/human-capital-careers/2005/06/keeping-secrets/.

60. Max H. Bazerman, George Lowenstein, and Don Moore, "Why Good Accountants Do Bad Audits," *Harvard Business Review,* November 2002, https://hbr.org/2002/11/why-good-accountants-do-bad-audits.

61. Bazerman et al.

62. Kristina Diekmann, Steven M. Samuels, Lee Ross, and Max H. Bazerman, "Self-Interest and Fairness in Problems in Resource Allocation," *Journal of Personality and Social Psychology,* Vol. 72, No. 5, May 1997, pp. 1061-1074.

63. Jessica R. Mesmer-Magnus and Chockalingam Viswesvaran, "Whistleblowing in Organizations: An Examination of Correlates of Whistleblowing Intentions, Actions, and Retaliation," *Journal of Business Ethics,* Vol. 62, No. 3 (2005), pp. 277–297.

64. Janet P. Near and Marcia P. Miceli, "Organizational Dissidence: The Case of Whistle-blowing," *Journal of Business Ethics,* Vol. 4, No. 1 (1985), pp. 1–16.

65. Randi L. Sims and John P. Keenan, "Predictors of External Whistleblowing: Organizational and Intrapersonal Variables," *Journal of Business Ethics,* Vol. 17 (1998), pp. 411–421.

66. Lyman W. Porter, Richard M. Steers, Richard T. Mowday, and Paul V. Boulian, "Organizational Commitment, Job Satisfaction, and Turnover among Psychiatric Technicians," *Journal of Applied Psychology,* Vol. 59, No. 5 (October 1974), pp. 603–609.

67. Linda Klebe Trevino and Bart Victor, "Peer Reporting of Unethical Behavior: A Social Context Perspective," *The Academy of Management Journal,* Vol. 35, No. 1 (March 1992), pp. 38–64.

68. Taylor and Curtis.

69. Taylor and Curtis.

70. Bobek et al. (2010).

71. N. Brennan and J. Kelley, "A Study of Whistleblowing among Trainee Auditors," *The British Accounting Review,* Vol. 39 (2007), pp. 61–87.

72. Marcia P. Miceli, Janet P. Near, and Charles R. Schwenk, "Who Blows the Whistle and Why?" *Industrial and Labor Relations Review,* Vol. 45, No. 1 (October 1991), pp. 113–130.

73. Jill W. Graham, "Principled Organizational Dissent: A Theoretical Essay," *Research in Organizational Behavior,* Vol. 8 (December 1985), pp. 1–52.

74. Supreme Court of the United States, *Digital Realty Trust, Inc. v. Somers,* February 21, 2018, https://www.supremecourt.gov/opinions/17pdf/16-1276_b0nd.pdf.

75. *Charles Matthew Erhart v. BOFI Holding, Inc., Case No. 15-cv-02287-BAS(NLS),* February 14, 2017, https://cases.justia.com/federal/district-courts/california/casdce/3:2015cv02287/486757/22/0.pdf?ts=1474967833.

76. Tony Saavedra, "This Whistleblower Saved You Money," *Orange County Register,* August 21, 2013, Available at: http://www.ocregister.com/articles/agency-325266-whistleblower-defense.html.

77. Statement of Diem-Thi Le, DCAA Auditor, before the Senate Committee on Homeland Security and Governmental Affairs, September 10, 2008, Available at: http://www.hsgac.senate.gov/download/091008le.

78. Cathy Krohmer and Christine Noel, Responsible Leadership for Audit Quality: How Do the Big Four Manage the Personal Ethics of Their Employees, https://allsh.univ-amu.fr/sites/allsh.univ-amu.fr/files/responsible_leadership_for_corporate_responsability.pdf.

79. Nicola M. Pless and Thomas Maak, "Responsible Leadership: Pathways to the Future," *Journal of Business Ethics,* Vol. 74, Issue 4, September 2007, https://link.springer.com/article/10.1007%2Fs10551-011-1114-4.

80. Cathy Krohmer and Christine Noel.

81. Alan T. Lord and F. Todd DeZoort, "The impact of commitment and moral reasoning on auditors' responses to social influence pressure, *Accounting, Organizations and Society,* Vol. 26 2001), pp. 215-235.

82. Cathy Krohmer and Christine Noel.

83. Cathy Krohmer and Christine Noel.

84. Cathy Krohmer and Christine Noel.

85. Thornton.

86. Patrick T. Kelly and Christine E. Earley, "Ethical Leaders in Accounting," in Anthony H. Catanach Jr. and Dorothy Feldmann (eds.), *Advances in Accounting Education: Teaching and Curriculum Innovations, Vol. 12* (Bingley, U.K.: Emerald, 2011), pp. 53-76.

87. William J. Bruns Jr. and Kenneth A. Merchant, "The Dangerous Morality of Managing Earnings," *Management Accounting,* Vol. 72, No. 2 (1990), Available at: https://www.researchgate.net/publication/265235024_The_Dangerous_Morality_of_Managing_Earnings.

Chapter 8 Cases

Case 8-1 Research Triangle Software Innovations (a GVV case)

Research Triangle Software Innovations is a software solutions company specializing in enterprise resource planning (ERP) business management software. Located in the Research Triangle Park, North Carolina, high-tech area, Research Triangle Software Innovations is a leader in ERP software.

Oak Manufacturing is located in Raleigh, North Carolina. Oak is a publicly owned company that produces oak barrels for flavoring and storage of wine products. As the largest company of its kind in the Southeast, Oak Manufacturing serves all 50 states and other parts of North America.

Tar & Heel, LLP, is a mid-sized professional services firm in Durham, North Carolina. It provides audit, assurance, and advisory services to clients, many of whom are in the Research Triangle area. The firm audits the financial statements of Oak Manufacturing and was just contacted by the client to assist in selecting and implementing an ERP system so the company can improve its collection, storage, management, and interpretation of data from a variety of business activities.

Steve Michaels is Tar & Heel's advisory manager in charge of the Oak Manufacturing engagement. He is reviewing the criteria used for software selection as follows:

- Alignment with client's needs
- Operations integration
- Software reliability
- Vendor support
- Scalability for growth
- Pricing

Everything seems in order for the criteria. However, Steve is concerned about the selection of the ERP software of Research Triangle Software Innovations, for one, because Research Triangle is also an audit client of the firm. Given that Research Triangle is the major client in the Durham office, Steve worries about perceptions if the firm selects its client's software product. Moreover, he knows his firm's partnership is pushing for sales of its own software and this might be an occasion to do so.

Steve calls Rosanne Field into his office to discuss her selection. This is Rosanne's first job as the lead advisory staff member on a software selection decision. She has great credentials having graduated with a bachelor's degree from the University of North Carolina, a masters from North Carolina State, and a computer science doctorate from Duke University. She has five years of experience in advisory services and has received glowing evaluations.

Rosanne explains that there were four ERP software products that made it to the "final four," including the firm's own product. The others were Research Triangle Software Innovations, Longhorn Software Systems in Austin, Texas, and Tex-Mex Software in El Paso, Texas.

Steve asks Rosanne to explain why Research Triangle Innovations was selected over the firm's own package. She goes through the ranking of the criteria. It seems the total score for Research Triangle's software was slightly below that of Longhorn Software but significantly above Tex-Mex. Rosanne told Steve she never considered the firm's own package. Her selection of Longhorn Software was overturned by Gary Booth, the senior on the job, ostensibly because Gary saw it as an opportunity to gain additional services for the firm by making the client – Research Triangle – happy and earning a feather in his cap by bringing in additional revenue.

Steve is unhappy with what he has learned so he calls for a meeting with Rosanne and Gary later in the week. Put yourself in Rosanne's position and consider the following in developing a game plan for what you will say at the meeting and then answer the questions that follow.

- What is at stake for the key parties, including the firm?
- What are the likely positions of Steve and Gary. What will you say to counteract those positions?
- Are there any levers you can use to get your point across? Explain.
- What is your most powerful and persuasive response to the reasons and rationalizations you need to address?

Questions

1. Describe the leadership style of Steve in this case.
2. Assume Steve decides to support Gary's explanation for choosing the firm's own package. What will you do next?
3. Have there been any violations of the AICPA Code of Professional Conduct in this case? Be specific.

Case 8-2 New Leadership at General Electric

On June 12, 2017, GE announced that 30-year GE veteran and current President and CEO of GE Healthcare John Flannery would be replacing Jeff Immelt as CEO of the company as of August 1, 2017.[1] Immelt had been the CEO for 16 years, taking over that role from the iconic Jack Welch. GE stated that the announcement was the culmination of a 6-year succession planning process for the company's top spot. Flannery started at GE in 1987 fresh out of Wharton Business School's MBA program and has worked in many positions, including successfully turning around the failing health care division of the company. The Company's CFO Jeff Bornstein was named Vice Chairman.[2] Bornstein was one of three other final candidates considered for the CEO position. Barclays' analyst, Scott Davis, observed that Jeff Immelt has been criticized for his inability to connect with investors, and now many are expecting "fairly dramatic changes" under Flannery.[3]

GE's Market Cap at $153.6 Billion, while greater than 93% of the rest of the companies in the S&P 500, has dropped $240 billion in the last 10 years. Analysts at Seeking Alpha issued a statement saying that: "General Electric has gotten absolutely crushed over the last two days, falling 15% from $20.50 down to $17.50. GE's peak of the current bull market for the S&P 500 came on July 20th of last year (2016), but since then it's down 47%. Even more shocking is that at $17.50, GE's share price is trading at the same level it was at 20 years ago in early 1997. Of course, there have been dividends paid, but it's not a good look for a company when share price is unchanged on a 20-year basis."[4]

On the GE July 21, 2017 second quarter earnings call with financial analysts and investors, Flannery stated that, while he does not officially start his new role as CEO until August 1, he was already underway conducting a "deep dive" into all the business areas within GE.[5] He stated, "In addition to the business reviews, I want to repeat the process I used in

[1]https://www.ge.com/reports/john-flannery-named-chairman-ceo-ge/.

[2]https://www.usatoday.com/story/money/business/2017/06/12/ge-ceo-immelt-stepping-down/102771682/.

[3]https://www.cnbc.com/2017/06/12/general-electrics-immelt-is-stepping-down-john-flannery-named-chairman-and-ceo.html.

[4]https://seekingalpha.com/article/4125006-general-electric-market-cap-240-billion-last-10-years.

[5]https://seekingalpha.com/article/4089530-general-electrics-ge-ceo-jeff-immelt-q2-2017-results-earnings-call-transcript?page=2.

healthcare to really get out and listen to what people are thinking, good and bad about the Company. I always start with customers and employees, but it's also important to get the view of our government partners and especially our investors." His plan was to take his first 90 days in his role to develop a new strategic plan for the company with the intent to report back to the investors in regard to that plan in November. The rest of this earnings call was handled by the current CEO Immelt and CFO Bornstein and was relatively optimistic as to earnings for the year and into the future.

On the October 20, 2017 third quarter earnings call with investors, Flannery led the call with Bornstein as CFO and Bornstein's successor Jamie Miller who would be taking over as CFO on November 1. Flannery kicked off the call by stating, "While the company has many areas of strength, it's also clear from our current results that we need to make some major changes with urgency and a depth of purpose. Our results are unacceptable, to say the least. He went on to say that his review of the company has been, and continues to be, exhaustive. The team and I have performed deep dives on all aspects of the Company," and left no stone unturned. "We are evaluating our business [structure], corporate [systems], our culture, how decisions are made, how we think about goals and accountability, how we incentivize people, how we prioritize investments in the segments; and at the overall Company level, including global research, digital and additive. We have also reviewed our operating processes, our team, capital allocation and how we communicate to investors. Everything is on the table, and there have been no sacred cows." One of those changes was that Jeff Bornstein would be leaving the company and not be the new vice chairman.

While stating he would give more details on the November call, he further stated that "We are driving sweeping change and moving with speed and purpose. I'm focusing on the culture of the Company. Our culture needs to be driven by mutual candor and intense execution, and the accountability that must come with that. We have announced changes in our team at the highest levels of the Company. In addition to changes in our culture and our team, I will also share more with you in November on our capital allocation methods, changes we are making to analytics and metrics, and process improvements. In particular, these changes will be focused on improving the cash generation of the Company. We have to manage the Company for cash and profitability in addition to growth."

On the November 17, 2017 call, Flannery led an Investor Update to provide a detailed analysis of his "deep dive" into the business and his plans for the company. He reiterated, "that the current operating results were unacceptable" and "the management team is completely devoted to doing what it takes to correct that." He went on to say, "going forward, we really just have to focus on how we can create the most value and portfolio of assets that we have for our owners and we're going to do that with a very dispassionate eye, very critical analytical dispassionate eye. The GE of the future is going to be a more focused industrial company, it will leverage a lot of really game changing capabilities in digital in Additive in industrial research, culture of the company much more open, much more transparent, much more connected. And at the end of the day, we really exist to deliver outcomes for the customers, performance for the owners and have an environment where our employees are motivated by, excited by, rewarded for delivering on those two things."[6]

Only time will tell whether Flannery is able to turn GE around and deliver on these promises.

Questions

1. Describe the characteristic traits of leadership at GE. How would you describe Flannery's leadership style?

2. Do you believe that leadership style and connection with employees can influence operating systems? Explain.

3. Scott Davis criticized Immelt's tenure as CEO and observed: "Jack Welch brought much needed energy and charisma to the CEO job and streamlined the bureaucracy." Can a leader's personal qualities be directly responsible for a higher level of earnings? Explain.

4. Review the GAAP and non-GAAP third-quarter 2017 earnings information released to the public. As an astute student of accounting, what questions would you have for John Flannery about these numbers if you were on a conference call and knew about the information described in this case?

---

[6]https://seekingalpha.com/article/4124617-general-electrics-ge-ceo-john-flannery-hosts-investor-update-conference-call-transcript.

GE 3Q 2017 EARNINGS

Continuing operations EPS (GAAP) of $0.22, (4%)
Industrial operating + Verticals EPS (non-GAAP) of $0.29, (9%)
EPS Impact of $(0.16) resulting from impairments of $(0.13); higher restructuring and lower gains of $(0.03)
3Q '17 GE CFOA of $0.5 billion; $1.7 billion industrial CFOA*
Industrial segment revenues +10%, (1%) organically*
Orders +11%; organic orders flat

	EARNINGS/EPS		REVENUES	MARGINS
	CONTINUING OPS/EPS[a]	**NET EARNINGS/EPS**[b]	**TOTAL REVENUES**	**INDUSTRIAL MARGIN**
GAAP	**$1.9B**	**$1.8B**	**$33.5B**	**7.6%**
	EPS: $0.22, (4%)	EPS: $0.21, (5%)	14%	(240) bps
	INDUSTRIAL OPERATING + VERTICALS/EPS		**INDUSTRIAL SEGMENT ORGANIC REVENUES**	**INDUSTRIAL OP MARGIN**[c]
non-GAAP	**$2.6B**		**$26.9B**	**11.8%**
	EPS: $0.29, (9%)		(1%)	(220) bps

We present both GAAP and non-GAAP measures to provide investors with additional information. The non-GAAP measures are focused on our ongoing operations and may exclude the effects of gains/losses on business dispositions, non-operating pension costs, and restructuring & other charges.

[a] Excluding deal taxes and GE Pension Plan funding
[b] Amounts attributable to GE common shareowners
[c] Excludes non-operating pension, gains and restructuring & other
* Non-GAAP measure

Case 8-3 KPMG Tax Shelter Scandal

In Chapter 4 we discussed the artificial tax shelter arrangements developed by KPMG LLP for wealthy clients that led to the settlement of a legal action with the Department of Treasury and the Internal Revenue Service. On August 29, 2005, KPMG admitted to criminal wrongdoing and agreed to pay $456 million in fines, restitution, and penalties as part of an agreement to defer prosecution of the firm. In addition, nine members of the firm were criminally indicted for their role in relation to the design, marketing, and implementation of fraudulent tax shelters.

In the largest criminal tax case ever filed, KPMG admitted it engaged in a fraud that generated at least $11 billion dollars in phony tax losses, which, according to court papers, cost the United States at least $2.5 billion dollars in evaded taxes. In addition to KPMG's former deputy chairman, the individuals indicted included two former heads of KPMG's tax practice and a former tax partner in the New York City office of a prominent national law firm.

The facts of the tax shelter arrangement are complicated, so we have condensed them for purposes of this case and present them in Exhibit 1.

Back in Chapter 4 we discussed the "realistic possibility of success" standard in taking tax positions under the Statements on Standards for Tax Services of the AICPA. This is a high standard to meet. Generally, there would need to be a 70–80% of prevailing if a tax position were challenged by the IRS. The "more likely than not" standard

EXHIBIT 1   Summary of Tax Shelter Transactions Developed by KPMG[1]

KPMG developed tax shelters to generate losses of $11.2 billion dollars for 601 wealthy clients that enabled them to avoid paying $2.5 billion in income taxes. KPMG mainly used four methods to help the wealthy clients avoid their tax liabilities or tax charges on capital gains. The shelters implemented were the Foreign Leveraged Investment Program (FLIP), Offshore Portfolio Investment Strategy (OPIS), Bond Linked Issue Premium Structure (BLIPS), and Short Option Strategy (SOS/SC 2). These shelters were designed to artificially create substantial phony capital losses through the use of an entity created in the Cayman Islands (a tax haven) for the purpose of the tax shelter transactions. The client purportedly entered into an investment transaction with the Cayman entity by purchasing purported warrants or entering into a purported swap. The Cayman entity then made a prearranged series of purported investments, including the purchase from either Bank A, which at the time was a KPMG audit client, Bank D, or both using money purportedly loaned by Bank A or Bank D, followed by redemptions of those stock purchases by the pertinent bank. The purported investments were devised to eliminate economic risk to the client beyond the cost to develop the tax shelters.

In the implementation of FLIP and OPIS, KPMG issued misleading opinion letters with assistance from its co-conspirators. The opinion letters were misleading because KPMG knew that the tax positions taken were more likely than not to prevail against the IRS, and the opinion letters and other documents used to implement FLIP and OPIS were false and fraudulent in a number of ways. For instance, the opinion letters began by falsely stating that the client requested KPMG's opinion regarding the U.S. federal income tax consequences of certain investment portfolio transactions, while the real fact is that the conspirators targeted wealthy clients based on the clients' large taxable gains and offered to generate phony tax losses to eliminate income tax on that gain as well as to provide a "more likely than not" opinion letter.

The "more likely than not" opinion letters provided an ambiguous and confusing view of the tax shelters to the users, but it brought an income of $50,000 to KPMG for each such opinion letter. In addition to that, the opinion letter continued by falsely stating that the investment strategy was based on the expectation that a leveraged position in the foreign bank securities would provide the investor with the opportunity for capital appreciation, when in fact the strategy was based on the expected tax benefits promised by certain conspirators in the tax frauds.

appears in Treasury Circular 230, which covers rules of conduct for those who practice before the IRS, including CPAs, attorneys, and enrolled agents. A tax preparer who fails to comply with Circular 230 will likely be subject to penalties and possibly other sanctions if she advises a client to take a position on a tax return or a document that does not meet the applicable tax reporting standard.

The three standards for tax positions in Treasury Circular 230, ranked from lowest to highest, are reasonable basis, substantial authority, and more likely than not. A description of each of these standards appears in Exhibit 2.

KPMG admitted that its personnel took specific, deliberate steps to conceal the existence of the shelters from the IRS by, among other things, failing to register the shelters with the IRS as required by law, fraudulently concealing the shelter losses and income on tax returns, and attempting to hide the shelters using sham attorney-client privilege claims.

The information and indictment alleged that top leadership at KPMG made the decision to approve and participate in shelters; issue KPMG opinion letters despite significant warnings from KPMG tax experts and others throughout the development of the shelters; and, at critical junctures, that the shelters were close to frivolous and would not withstand IRS scrutiny, that the representations required to be made by the wealthy individuals were not credible, and the consequences of going forward with the shelters—as well as failing to register them—could include criminal investigation, among other things.

[1]The facts are taken from the Report Prepared by the Minority Staff of the Permanent Subcommittee on Investigations of the Committee on Governmental Affairs of the United States Senate, titled "U.S. Tax Shelter Industry: The Role of Accountants, Lawyers and Financial Professionals—Four KPMG Case Studies: FLIP, OPIS, BLIPS, and SC2," November 18 and 20, 2003, Available at: http://www.gpo.gov/fdsys/pkg/CPRT-108SPRT90655/html/CPRT-108SPRT90655.htm.

EXHIBIT 2 Circular 230 Tax Positions and Compliance Standards[2]

Reasonable basis: Reasonable basis is the minimum standard for all tax advice and for preparation of all tax returns and other required tax documents to avoid a penalty under Section 6694 for the underpayment of taxes. If a return position is reasonably based on at least one relevant and persuasive tax authority cited, the return position will generally satisfy this standard.

Substantial authority: Substantial authority for the tax treatment of an item exists only if the weight of the tax authorities (Internal Revenue Code, Treasury regulations, court cases, etc.) supporting the treatment is substantial in relation to the weight of authorities supporting contrary treatment. All authorities relevant to the tax treatment of an item, including the authorities contrary to the treatment, are taken into account in determining whether substantial authority exists. This standard may be measured as a greater than 40% likelihood of being sustained on its merits.

More likely than not: More likely than not is "the standard that is met when there is a greater than 50% likelihood of the position being upheld." This is the standard for tax shelters under Section 6694 and reportable transactions.

As we noted in Chapter 4, an unusual aspect to the case is the culture that apparently existed in KPMG's tax practice during the time the shelters were sold, which was to aggressively market tax shelter arrangements targeting wealthy clients by approaching them with the deals rather than the clients coming to KPMG. Back in the late 1990s, the stock market was booming, and the firm sought to take advantage of the increasing number of wealthy clients by accelerating its tax-services business. The head of KPMG's tax department at the time, Jeffrey M. Stein, and its CFO, Richard Rosenthal, created an environment that treated those who didn't support the "growth at all costs" effort as not being team players.

Once it became clear that the firm faced imminent criminal indictment over its tax shelters, KPMG turned to its head of human resources, Timothy Flynn, to somehow persuade the government not to indict. He knew that criminal charges against the firm would probably kill it, as they did Arthur Andersen after the Enron scandal.

For years, KPMG had stoutly denied any impropriety, calling its tax advice legal. But Flynn took a gamble and met with Justice Department officials to acknowledge that KPMG had engaged in wrongdoing. He got no promises in return, and the admission could have sunk the firm. Instead, it provided flexibility to the prosecutors, who were aware that the collapse of one of only four remaining accounting giants could harm the financial markets. Two months later, the government gave KPMG a deferred-prosecution deal, holding off indicting if KPMG paid a $456 million penalty and met other conditions.

The agreement between KPMG and the IRS required permanent restrictions on KPMG's tax practice, including the termination of two practice areas, one of which provided tax advice to wealthy individuals, and permanent adherence to higher tax practice standards regarding the issuance of certain tax opinions and the preparation of tax returns. In addition, the agreement banned KPMG's involvement with any prepackaged tax products and restricted KPMG's acceptance of fees not based on hourly rates. The agreement also required KPMG to implement and maintain an effective compliance and ethics program; to install an independent, government-appointed monitor to oversee KPMG's compliance with the deferred prosecution agreement for a three-year period; and its full and truthful cooperation in the pending criminal investigation, including the voluntary provision of information and documents.

Questions

1. Describe the link between the tax culture at KPMG and leadership. Do you believe there is a direct correlation between dysfunctional tax decisions and culture?

[2] *Regulations Governing Practice before the Internal Revenue Service, Title 31 Code of Federal Regulations, Subtitle A, Part 10,* published June 12, 2014, Treasury Department Circular No. 230 (Rev. 6-2014), Available at: http://www.irs.gov/pub/irs-pdf/pcir230.pdf.

2. How can tax positions taken reflect leadership style?

3. Describe the relationship between the tax shelters developed by KPMG and management of the tax practice at the firm.

4. What's wrong with a CPA firm, such as KPMG, aggressively seeking to establish tax shelters for wealthy clients? Did KPMG's role in this regard reflect a failure of leadership or a failure of judgment? Explain.

Case 8-4 Krispy Kreme Doughnuts, Inc.[1]

On March 4, 2009, the SEC reached an agreement with Krispy Kreme Doughnuts, Inc., and issued a cease-and-desist order to settle charges that the company fraudulently inflated or otherwise misrepresented its earnings for the fourth quarter of its FY2003 and each quarter of FY2004. By its improper accounting, Krispy Kreme avoided lowering its earnings guidance and improperly reported earnings per share (EPS) for that time period; these amounts exceeded its previously announced EPS guidance by 1 cent.

The primary transactions described in this case are "round-trip" transactions. In each case, Krispy Kreme paid money to a franchisee with the understanding that the franchisee would pay the money back to Krispy Kreme in a prearranged manner that would allow the company to record additional pretax income in an amount roughly equal to the funds originally paid to the franchisee.

There were three round-trip transactions cited in the SEC consent agreement. The first occurred in June 2003, which was during the second quarter of FY2004. In connection with the reacquisition of a franchise in Texas, Krispy Kreme increased the price that it paid for the franchise by $800,000 (i.e., from $65,000,000 to $65,800,000) in return for the franchisee purchasing from Krispy Kreme certain doughnut-making equipment. On the day of the closing, Krispy Kreme debited the franchise's bank account for $744,000, which was the aggregate list price of the equipment. The additional revenue boosted Krispy Kreme's quarterly net income by approximately $365,000 after taxes.

The second transaction occurred at the end of October 2003, four days from the closing of Krispy Kreme's third quarter of FY2004, in connection with the reacquisition of a franchise in Michigan. Krispy Kreme agreed to increase the price that it paid for the franchise by $535,463, and it recorded the transaction on its books and records as if it had been reimbursed for two amounts that had been in dispute with the Michigan franchisee. This overstated Krispy Kreme's net income in the third quarter by approximately $310,000 after taxes.

The third transaction occurred in January 2004, in the fourth quarter of FY2004. It involved the reacquisition of the remaining interests in a franchise in California. Krispy Kreme owned a majority interest in the California franchise and, beginning in or about October 2003, initiated negotiations with the remaining interest holders for acquisition of their interests. During the negotiations, Krispy Kreme demanded payment of a "management fee" in consideration of Krispy Kreme's handling of the management duties since October 2003. Krispy Kreme proposed that the former franchise manager receive a distribution from his capital account, which he could then pay back to Krispy Kreme as a management fee. No adjustment would be made to the purchase price for his interest in the California franchise to reflect this distribution. As a result, the former franchise manager would receive the full value for his franchise interest, including his capital account, plus an additional amount, provided that he paid back that amount as the management fee. Krispy Kreme, acting through the California franchise, made a distribution to the former franchise manager in the amount of $597,415, which was immediately transferred back to Krispy Kreme as payment of the management fee. The company booked this fee, thereby overstating net income in the fourth quarter by approximately $361,000.

[1]Unless otherwise indicated, the facts of this case are taken from Securities and Exchange Commission, *Accounting and Auditing Enforcement Release No. 2941, In the Matter of Krispy Kreme Doughnuts, Inc.,* March 4, 2009, Available at: https://www.sec.gov/litigation/admin/2009/34-59499.pdf.

Additional accounting irregularities were unearthed in testimony by a former sales manager at a Krispy Kreme outlet in Ohio, who said a regional manager ordered that retail store customers be sent double orders on the last Friday and Saturday of FY2004, explaining "that Krispy Kreme wanted to boost the sales for the fiscal year in order to meet Wall Street projections." The manager explained that the doughnuts would be returned for credit the following week—once FY2005 was under way. Apparently, it was common practice for Krispy Kreme to accelerate shipments at year-end to inflate revenues by stuffing the channels with extra product, a practice known as "channel stuffing."

Some could argue that Krispy Kreme's auditors—PwC— should have noticed a pattern of large shipments at the end of the year with corresponding credits the following fiscal year during the course of their audit. Typical audit procedures would be to confirm with Krispy Kreme's customers their purchases. In addition, monthly variations analysis should have led someone to question the spike in doughnut shipments at the end of the fiscal year. However, PwC did not report such irregularities or modify its audit report.

In May 2005, Krispy Kreme disclosed disappointing earnings for the first quarter of FY2005 and lowered its future earnings guidance. Subsequently, as a result of the transactions already described, as well as the discovery of other accounting errors, on January 4, 2005, Krispy Kreme announced that it would restate its financial statements for 2003 and 2004. The restatement reduced net income for those years by $2,420,000 and $8,524,000, respectively.

In August 2005, a special committee of the company's board issued a report to the SEC following an internal investigation of the fraud at Krispy Kreme. The report states that every Krispy Kreme employee or franchisee who was interviewed "repeatedly and firmly" denied deliberately scheming to distort the company's earnings or being given orders to do so; yet, in carefully nuanced language, the Krispy Kreme investigators hinted at the possibility of a willful cooking of the books. "The number, nature, and timing of the accounting errors strongly suggest that they resulted from an intent to manage earnings," the report said. "Further, CEO Scott Livengood and COO John Tate failed to establish proper financial controls, and the company's earnings may have been manipulated to please Wall Street." The committee also criticized the company's board of directors, which it said was "overly deferential in its relationship with Livengood and failed to adequately oversee management decisions."

Krispy Kreme materially misstated its earnings in its financial statements filed with the SEC between the fourth quarter of FY2003 and the fourth quarter of FY2004. In each of these quarters, Krispy Kreme falsely reported that it had achieved earnings equal to its EPS guidance plus 1 cent in the fourth quarter of FY2003 through the third quarter of FY2004 or, in the case of the fourth quarter of FY2004, earnings that met its EPS guidance.

On March 4, 2009, the SEC reached agreement with three former top Krispy Kreme officials, including one-time chair, CEO, and president Scott Livengood. Livengood, former COO John Tate, and CFO Randy Casstevens all agreed to pay more than $783,000 for violating accounting laws and fraud in connection with their management of the company.

Livengood was found in violation of fraud, reporting provisions, and false certification regulations. Tate was found in violation of fraud, reporting provisions, record keeping, and internal controls rules. Casstevens was found in violation of fraud, reporting provisions, record keeping, internal controls, and false certification rules. Livengood's settlement required him to pay about $542,000, which included $467,000 of what the SEC considered as the "disgorgement of ill-gotten gains and prejudgment interest" and $75,000 in civil penalties. Tate's settlement required him to return $96,549 and pay $50,000 in civil penalties, while Casstevens had to return $68,964 and pay $25,000 in civil penalties. Krispy Kreme itself was not required to pay a civil penalty because of its cooperation with the SEC in the case.

SEC Charges against PricewaterhouseCoopers[2]

In a lawsuit brought on behalf of the Eastside Investors group against Krispy Kreme Doughnuts, Inc., members of management, and PricewaterhouseCoopers, a variety of the fraud charges leveled against the company were extended to the alleged deficient audit by PwC. These charges were settled and reflect the following findings.

[2]Material in this section was taken from United States District Court Middle District North Carolina, No. 1:04-CV-00416, *In re Eastside Investors v. Krispy Kreme Doughnuts, Inc., Randy S. Casstevens, Scott A. Livengood, Michael C. Phalen, John Tate, and PricewaterhouseCoopers, LLP*, 2005 , Available at: http://securities.stanford.edu/filings-documents/1030/KKD04-01/2005215_r01c_04416.pdf.

PwC provided independent audit services and rendered audit opinions on Krispy Kreme's FY2003 and FY2004 financial statements. The firm also provided significant consulting, tax, and due diligence services. Of the total fees received during this period, 66% (FY2003) and 61% (FY2004) were for nonaudit services. The lawsuit alleged that PwC was highly motivated not to allow any auditing disagreements with Krispy Kreme management to interfere with its nonaudit services.

PwC was charged with a variety of failures in conducting its audit of Krispy Kreme. These include: (1) failure to obtain relevant evidential matter whether it appears to corroborate or contradict the assertions in the financial statements; (2) failure to act on violations of GAAP rules with respect to accounting for franchise rights and the company's relationship with its franchisees; and (3) ignoring numerous red flags that indicated risks that should have been factored into the audit and in questioning of management. These include:

- Unusually rapid growth, especially compared to other companies in the industry;
- Excessive concern by management to maintain or increase earnings and share prices;
- Domination of management by a single person or small group without compensating controls such as effective oversight by the board of directors or audit committee;
- Unduly aggressive financial targets and expectations for operating personnel set by management; and
- Significant related-party transactions not in the ordinary course of business or with related entities not audited or audited by another firm.

The legal action against PwC referenced Rule 10b-5 of the Securities Exchange Act of 1934 in charging the firm with making untrue statements of material fact and failing to state material facts necessary to make Krispy Kreme's financial statements not misleading. The company wound up restating its statements for the FY2003 through FY2004 period.

Questions

1. How was mismanagement at Krispy Kreme reflective of leadership failure?

2. Describe the financial shenanigans used by Krispy Kreme. In this regard, is earnings management always a sign of failed leadership?

3. PwC had been Krispy Kreme's auditor since 1992. How can a firm's length of service influence audit decisions? What biases may creep up over time? Does it seem this occurred at PwC?

4. One of the reasons behind Krispy Kreme's financial shenanigans was its failure to meet earnings guidance. How might earnings guidance and the choice of non-GAAP measures reflect a particular style of leadership?

Case 8-5 Audit of Friars for Life

David Norris is the manager of the audit of Friars for Life (FFL), a new-age health food company headquartered in Providence, Rhode Island, that has been expanding by leaps and bounds. Norris is preparing for a meeting with Alan Morse, the partner in charge of the engagement. The meeting on January 4, 2019 concerns three controversial decisions by the auditors. They are described as follows:

- Why are we allowing the client to record $1 million of revenue in 2018 for a January 12, 2019 scheduled transaction whereby FFL agreed to sell $1 million of health food products to Ocean State Health in return for a stock issuance of that company?

- Why didn't we insist FFL writedown $100,000 in fixed assets as being impaired based on calculations as of December 31, 2018, the close of the fiscal year?
- Why was Lindsay Farrow removed from the position of audit senior on the engagement?

Norris was very concerned about these matters as he made the final decision in each case. Norris went back through his personal audit notes and workpaper explanations for each of these issues. The January 12, 2019 transaction was recorded in 2018 at the client's insistence. Norris was concerned the client might pull the engagement if he did not go along. The impairment issue was one of judgment. Norris reasoned that, since the impairment was temporary, he would accept the client's position not to writedown the fixed assets and wait to record any loss until 2019. The Lindsay Farrow matter was different. Norris had dated Lindsay for six months during the audit of FFL, but their relationship did not end amicably.

Questions

1. Describe the leadership style of David Norris? Include in your explanation the nature of the relationship he had with Lindsay Farrow.

2. Do you consider the decisions made by Norris dysfunctional audit behavior? Explain.

3. What should Alan Morse do once he learns about these issues?

Major Cases

The following cases can serve as detailed reviews of major issues discussed in the text. The cases vary in length to provide flexibility for instructors. The longer ones (Logitech International, Cendant Corporation, and Vivendi Universal) are ideal for final projects. Kiley Nolan's Ethical Dilemma can be used to review the Giving Voice to Values methodology. The Colonial Bank case is current and one of the most important cases affecting the accounting profession in the past few years. It was the biggest bank failure of 2009. Five major cases from the third and fourth editions have been removed from the text and are accessible in the Instructor's Resources: Adelphia Communications, Cumberland Lumber, Parmalat, Royal Ahold N.V., and Waste Management.

Major Case 1: Colonial Bank

- Auditor responsibility when client management commits fraud
- Auditors' inability to understand underlying cause of fraud: accounting for mortgage securitizations
- Reliance on work of outsourced internal audit and internal control issues
- Application of AICPA Code and auditing standards

Major Case 2: Logitech International

- Application of lower of cost or market valuations to inventory
- Corporate governance failures
- Application of AICPA Code and auditing standards
- Ethical dilemma for staff accountant: Application of Sarbanes-Oxley and Dodd-Frank

Major Case 3: Kiley Nolan's Ethical Dilemma (a GVV case)

- Inability to meet loan covenant amounts
- Application of FASB revenue recognition standard, *Revenue from Contracts with Customers*
- Ethical reasoning and cognitive development
- Whistleblowing

Major Case 4: Cendant Corporation

- Income smoothing
- Application of the Fraud Triangle
- Professional judgment/AICPA Code
- Trust in relationship between client and auditor

Major Case 5: Vivendi Universal

- Ethical leadership
- Role of internal controls and ethical corporate culture
- Financial disclosure fraud
- Earnings releases, EBITDA, and earnings management

Major Case 1

Colonial Bank

Case Overview

On January 2, 2018, U.S. District Court Judge Barbara Rothstein ruled that PricewaterhouseCoopers (PwC) negligently failed to uncover a $2.3 billion fraud scheme between PwC audit client Colonial Bank and Taylor, Bean & Whitaker. Colonial Bank is now in receivership under Federal Deposit Insurance Corporation (FDIC) rules. Taylor Bean is a bankrupt mortgage lender. PwC already paid an undisclosed amount in 2016 to settle related claims by Taylor Bean's trustee.[1] The decision in the case means it now moves into a damages phase, where the FDIC is seeking as much as $2.1 billion.

The collapse of Colonial Bank, which had $25 billion in assets and $20 billion in deposits, was the biggest bank failure of 2009. The FDIC estimates Colonial's failure will ultimately cost its insurance fund $5 billion, making it one of the most expensive bank failures in U.S. history. The lawsuit against PwC was the first of its kind filed against an accounting firm in the aftermath of the financial recession. In August 12, 2012, some former Colonial Bank directors and officers agreed to settle the securities class action lawsuit against them for the bank's collapse. The settlement did not include PwC.

While Judge Rothstein held PwC liable for negligence, it rejected similar claims by the bankruptcy trustee for Colonial BancGroup because the bank itself was responsible for the fraud. That professional negligence claim was barred by the *in pari delicto* doctrine and the audit interference rule. Latin for "in equal fault," *in pari delicto* means, if the fault of the fraud is more or less equal between two or more parties (i.e., Colonial Bank and PwC), neither party can claim breach of the contract by the other. The audit interference rule holds that an auditor may assert a comparative-fault defense where it can establish that the client's negligence "interfered with" the auditor's performance of its duties, as in the Colonial Bank case.

In her opinion, Judge Rothstein emphasized that PwC had relied on the chief architect of the fraud, Taylor Bean chair Lee Farkas, to verify key information about the collateral underlying a Colonial credit facility for Taylor Bean. PwC signed off on Colonial's audit without ever understanding the underlying accounting event, which was based on phantom mortgage securitizations. PwC allowed Colonial to account for certain types of mortgages from Taylor Bean as sales rather than as loans from Colonial to Taylor Bean that were secured by mortgages.

Judge Rothstein ruled PwC was guilty of professional negligence. It rapped the firm for failing to follow "illogical dates" and to check whether an entire class of loans—nearly 20% of its mortgage lending warehouse—existed. She also cited testimony from a PwC partner in an earlier, related case that that "our audit procedures were not designed to detect fraud."

PwC gave the bank's parent, Colonial BancGroup, a clean audit opinion for years before it was disclosed that substantial portions of Colonial's loans to Taylor Bean were secured against assets that did not exist. In the malpractice case, Judge Rothstein agreed with the FDIC that PwC failed to meet professional accounting standards in its audits of Colonial. "PwC did not design its audits to detect fraud and PwC's failure to do so constitutes a violation of the auditing standards," Rothstein ruled.[2]

[1.] Alison Frankel, At heart of FDIC's win v. PwC, an unsettled theory, *Reuters,* January 2, 2018, https://www.reuters.com/article/us-otc-fdic/at-heart-of-fdics-win-v-pwc-an-unsettled-theory-idUSKBN1ER1U1.

[2.] Matthew Heller, PwC Found Liable for $2B Colonial Bank Fraud, cfo.com, January 2, 2018, http://ww2.cfo.com/fraud/2018/01/pwc-found-liable-2b-colonial-bank-fraud/.

PwC Defense of Audit

PwC, in its defense, said it was duped by Farkas, who skimmed millions of dollars from Colonial to buy a private jet, vintage cars, and a vacation home. Rothstein had ruled that Colonial executives lied to PwC's auditors, circumvented internal controls by "recycling" mortgage data, and even created wire transfers to trick PwC into believing Taylor Bean's collateral mortgages had been paid off.

PwC put its own spin on the verdict by stating that the court's ruling recognized that in addition to those Colonial Bank employees who perpetrated the fraud, numerous other employees at Colonial BancGroup actively and substantially interfered with their audit. But Rothstein faulted PwC for failing to inspect or even request to inspect the underlying documents for some Taylor Bean mortgages. "PwC argues that even if it had attempted to inspect the underlying loan documents, it would not have uncovered the fraud because the fraudsters would simply have created fake documents. This, of course, is something that we will never know."[3]

A rather unusual aspect to the claim that PwC did not follow appropriate professional standards is the allegation that PwC did not understand the nature and scope of the transactions. After a PwC auditor who was supposed to make sense of the transactions gave up, saying they were "above his pay grade," PwC assigned a college-graduate intern to evaluate the nearly $600 million asset. Rothstein was distinctly harsh about PwC's failings. Basing Colonial's certification on Farkas' account of Taylor Bean's collateral was "quintessentially the same as asking the fox to report on the condition of the hen house." She added that expecting an intern to decipher a loan facility beyond the expertise of a senior auditor was a "truly astonishing" departure from PwC's mandate.[4]

Internal Audit and ICFR

Colonial Bank had outsourced internal audit to another accounting firm, Crowe Horwath. PwC was required to review Crowe's work product, and it did so. Crowe, however, never identified or performed any evaluation of internal controls specifically relating to the credit facility, and there was no documentation suggesting otherwise. Nonetheless, PwC concluded that internal controls for Colonial's Treasury operation (including the credit facility) were effective and could be relied upon by PwC to reduce its substantive audit procedures. PwC reached this conclusion in the absence of any evidence that Crowe (or anyone else) had tested any internal controls for the credit facility.[5]

Digging deeper, PwC knew that Colonial's Treasury and Securities Purchased Under Agreements to Resell (which included $51.5 billion in credit facility financing for Taylor Bean at December 31, 2007) was a "Significant Process" for which it would test controls. During the actual audit however, PwC excluded the credit facility entirely from the key controls that it tested despite the credit facility significant account balance and distinct class of transactions that called for transaction-specific controls.

PwC did not perform any walkthrough, skipping this crucial step because key controls were not identified by Crowe, and/or PwC did not properly assess the inherent risks regarding the existence and validity of credit facility assets. PwC instead decided that it would rely on Crowe to perform all walkthroughs.

The FDIC's claims against Crowe Horwath, who acted under a consulting contract as Colonial's internal audit department, were unusual. PwC's workpapers gave FDIC a glimpse into PwC's opinion of the quality of Crowe's work. Regardless of what PwC thought, the FDIC believed that PwC did not do enough to compensate for any failings or verify the assertions about internal controls Crowe made on behalf of Colonial management.[6]

[3]Matthew Heller.

[4]Allison Frankel.

[5]Francine McKenna, A Tale of Two Lawsuits—PricewaterhouseCoopers and Colonial Bank, forbes.com, November 10, 2012, https://www.forbes.com/sites/francinemckenna/2012/11/10/a-tale-of-two-lawsuits-pricewaterhousecoopers-and-colonial-bank/#435a.

[6]Francine McKenna.

The FDIC asserted gross negligence by Crowe. Allegedly, there was concealment and collusion to perpetrate a fraud within the bank and from outside sources. Crowe was held to the AICPA's standards for consulting work which, while stringent as the AICPA Code of Professional Conduct standards, do not carry the force of law that the Sarbanes-Oxley Act and the PCAOB auditing standards do. The FDIC also maintained that Crowe should have followed the professional standards promulgated by the Institute of Internal Auditors. Would an internal audit function staffed by Colonial employees instead of an outside consultant have been sued under the same circumstances?

The Colonial ruling marks the first time an auditor has been held liable for fraud in many years. Lawyers who defended auditors were outraged by the ruling, calling it "an aggressive interpretation," "extremely disturbing," and a "one-off decision that will be reversed upon appeal." They are particularly upset that the case ever went to trial. In most auditing failure cases, companies are barred from suing their auditors for failing to detect fraud if—as happened at Colonial—their employees actively participated in the malfeasance. But in this case, the bank went bankrupt, and the FDIC sued to recover money for taxpayers. Courts around the country are split on whether the government can do that, and Judge Rothstein opted to let the FDIC sue. Attorney Michael Dell argued that the Colonial decision would fundamentally change the nature of auditing: "Audit firms would effectively be insurers for the wrongdoing of their clients." If the ruling stands, some lawyers believe investors will find it easier to hold auditors accountable in future corporate fraud cases.[7]

Questions

1. Update the facts of this case for any relevant events that have taken place since the January 2018 ruling.

2. Which rules of conduct in the AICPA Code of Professional Conduct were violated by PwC? Explain.

3. Which PCAOB auditing standards were violated by PwC? Explain why those violations occurred and whether PwC should be held responsible.

4. Attorney Michael Dell argued that the Colonial Bank ruling would effectively hold audit firms liable for the wrongdoing of their clients. Is that the way you read the facts of the case and Judge Rothstein's ruling? Is there anything wrong with holding auditors responsible for the wrongdoing of their clients when client employees actively participate in the malfeasance? Explain.

5. Is it in the public interest to allow auditors to escape legal liability under the in pari delicto doctrine?

6. When should auditors disclose critical audit matters (CAMs)? Assume the Colonial Bank case occurred subsequent to the effective dates of the new auditing standard on disclosing CAMs. Which disclosures should PwC have included in the audit report of Colonial Bank?

Major Case 2

Logitech International

Logitech International S.A. (LOGI) is incorporated in Switzerland and has substantial operations in the United States. LOGI is primarily involved in manufacturing and selling peripherals for computers and electronic devices. Its shares are listed on both the Nasdaq Global Select Market, under the trading symbol LOGI, and the SIX Swiss Exchange, under the trading symbol LOGN. The company maintains an executive office and its Americas region headquarters in Newark, California. LOGI's common stock is registered with the Securities Exchange Commission (SEC) pursuant to the Exchange Act of 1933.

---

[7]Brooke Masters, PwC's Failure to Spot Colonial Fraud Spells Trouble for Auditors, January 5, 2018, https://www.ft.com/content/c2cc45d6-f1f6-11e7-b220-857e26d1aca4

In the fourth quarter of 2010, LOGI released the Revue, a TV set-top box designed to integrate cable/satellite TV with internet content. The Revue Google search bar was designed to find any desired content from any provider and project that content to the TV screen. The Revue was manufactured by contract manufacturers, not LOGI itself. In the arrangement with the contract manufacturers, the company authorized the manufacturers to purchase about $11 million of parts before production of the Revue began. LOGI was gearing up for high sales during the 2010 holiday season.[1]

Overview of the Case

During the 2010 holiday season, sales of Revue were much less than LOGI anticipated. In the fourth quarter of 2010, 165,000 Revues were sold, far less than the 350,000 units the company expected to sell. The Revue's high price, the blocking of content from Hulu, CBS, and ABC, and numerous software bugs doomed the Revue to be discontinued less than one year after its arrival. LOGI had millions of dollars invested in excess inventory of Revue component parts.

Despite knowing that the component parts in inventory would not be used in manufacturing other LOGI parts and that the market value of those components was minimal, the lower-of-cost-or-market (LCM) inventory write-down that the company did make fell far short of the actual decline in market value.

In 2016, the SEC alleged that some of LOGI's executives and accounting staff committed accounting fraud. LOGI paid a fine of $7.5 million to settle with the SEC over this improper inventory accounting and two other accounting issues. Individuals from the company including the former CFO paid fines of $25,000–$50,000.[2]

In a separate filing, the SEC brought a case against Erik K. Bardman, former Senior Vice President of Finance, and Jennifer F. Wolf, CPA, Chief Financial Officer (CFO) and Acting Controller of LOGI. The SEC filing details facts about Revue, that it was projected to be a significant percentage of LOGI's sales revenue, and that it represented a new strategic direction for the company—but the product failed to live up to expectations. Its sales were 70% lower than internal projections by the fourth quarter of the 2011 fiscal year (March 31, 2011). Compounding the poor sales performance of Revue, in March 2011, LOGI lowered its forecast of operating income to $140-150 million, causing an immediate 16% drop in the company's share price. Given the shortfall, senior management, including Bardman and Wolf, were under substantial pressure to meet the lowered guidance. Rather than ensure that Logitech accurately account for its problems, Bardman and Wolf engaged in a scheme to materially inflate the operating income that the company reported to its investors in a late April 2011 earnings release and in its annual report, or Form 10-K, filed with the SEC on May 27, 2011, for the fiscal year ended March 31, 2011.

By this time, LOGI had 163,000 units of Revue in storage in the United States that the company had not sold, and it had halted production of additional units in light of the poor sales performance. LOGI's current price for the product at that time—$299—was more than double the price of competing products and part of the reason Revue was not selling. Indeed, by at least May 19, 2011, Bardman knew that the company's Chief Executive Officer had been evaluating whether to "shut [Revue] down now."

Through their scheme, Bardman and Wolf concealed the extent of these problems by, among other forms of misconduct: (1) improperly calculating Revue's inventory valuation reserves by falsely assuming that

---

[1]Wendy Tietz, What could a Logitech staff accountant have done if he/she knew that the CFO and controller failed to write-down the discontinued Revue parts inventory?, *Accounting in the Headlines,* May 25, 2017, https://accountingintheheadlines.com/2017/05/25/what-could-a-logitech-staff-accountant-have-done-if-heshe-knew-that-the-cfo-and-controller-failed-to-write-down-the-discontinued-revue-parts-inventory/.

[2]*In the Matter of Logitech International, S.A., Michael Doktorczyk and Sherralyn Bolles, CPA,* Accounting and Enforcement Release No. 3765, April 19, 2016, https://www.sec.gov/litigation/admin/2016/34-77644.pdf.

Logitech would build excess component parts it was trying to sell into finished units of Revue; (2) misrepresenting to LOGI's independent auditor that the Company's excess component parts would be used in production and the company's future plans for Revue; and (3) misrepresenting to the independent auditor the proper amount of LOGI's write-down of finished goods inventory by failing to incorporate probable future pricing adjustments. As a result of this misconduct, LOGI overstated its fiscal 2011 operating income by $30.7 million (over 27%).

In addition, in a letter to LOGI's independent auditors dated May 27, 2011, Bardman and Wolf falsely represented that the company's accounting was compliant with GAAP. These representations, demanded by and relied upon by Logitech's independent auditors, were designed to ensure that the company's accounting was done in accordance with accepted standards and did not mislead the investing public. Bardman misled the company's independent auditors regarding the extent of Logitech's problems with Revue. He signed and certified the accuracy of Logitech's 2011 financial statements, thereby misleading investors as to these same misstatements and omissions. At the time, Bardman knew, was reckless in not knowing, or should have known that the financial statements he was certifying were materially false or misleading.

Bardman and Wolf violated rules related to the antifraud provisions of the Securities Act of 1933 and Section 10(b) and Rule 10b-5 of the Securities Exchange Act of 1934. They violated the internal controls and books and records provisions of Section 13(b)(5) of the Exchange Act and aided and abetted Logitech's violations of the antifraud, reporting, books and records, and internal controls provisions. The two also violated the lying to accountants' provision of the Act. Bardman violated the certification provision of the Exchange Act and the clawback provision of the Sarbanes-Oxley Act of 2002.

The SEC sought injunctive relief, including an officer and director bar, disgorgement of ill-gotten gains, prejudgment interest, civil penalties, and other appropriate and necessary equitable relief from Bardman and Wolf. In addition, the Commission sought an order requiring Bardman to forfeit any bonus, incentive-based compensation, or stock sales profits received during the relevant period. The case against Bardman and Wolf was unresolved at the time of writing.

The following is a summary of the accounting issues in this case.[3]

Accounting for Revue Product/Components

From the outset, Revue sales were significantly below LOGI's internal forecasts. By late November 2010, sales and finance personnel, including senior executives, were addressing whether the market price of $299 should be cut. LOGI's CFO at the time and its acting controller were aware that LOGI might have to evaluate taking a "lower of cost or market" (LCM) charge if the value of Revue inventory was impaired.

Under GAAP, the Company was required to value its inventory at the lower of the inventory's cost or market value. Specifically, if the market value of a company's inventory (generally calculated for finished goods as the estimated selling prices in the ordinary course of business, less reasonably predictable costs of completion, disposal, and transportation) is less than its cost, then the company must write-down the inventory value in its financial statements.

On or around December 7, 2010, because of high inventory levels and weak sales, LOGI directed the contract manufacturer to stop manufacturing Revue, including halting all work in progress. LOGI also instructed the manufacturer not to ship over 26,000 finished Revue units. Further, because the manufacturer, at LOGI's direction, had purchased parts for future manufacturing, LOGI was liable for approximately $11 million of excess components.

---

[3]*Securities and Exchange Commission v. Erik K. Bardman and Jennifer F. Wolf* Complaint Demand for Jury Trial April 18, 2016, https://www.sec.gov/litigation/complaints/2016/comp-pr2016-74.pdf.

At the end of the third quarter of fiscal year 2011 (December 31, 2010), Revue sales were only 40% of LOGI's forecasts for that product. As part of its financial closing process, LOGI performed an LCM analysis of the Revue finished goods inventory and concluded that no adjustment, or write-down, was required.

On or around January 5, 2011, LOGI's Senior Vice-President (SVP) of Operations informed several executives that he intended to "dispose of the components" awaiting assembly by the manufacturer in light of Revue's "current trajectory." Shortly thereafter, the SVP-Operations instructed the VP of Global Sourcing/Supplier Management (VP-Global Sourcing) to "sell all of the components we could."

Later in January 2011, LOGI management informed the Board of Directors about the poor sales of Revue and about management's future plans for the product, including a plan to lower the retail price of Revue to $249 in the first quarter of 2012 and to $199 in the third quarter. Management did not inform its independent auditor of this pricing plan strategy.

On January 27, 2011, LOGI issued its third quarter 2011 earnings release, reporting strong results, increasing its guidance for annual revenue for fiscal year-end March 31, 2011, and affirming its guidance for annual operating income in a range of $170-$180 million.

During LOGI's fourth quarter fiscal 2011, Revue sales continued to be far below projections. For all of quarter four, despite regular discounting and promotions, Revue sales were 30% of internal product forecasts. By quarter end, retailers were selling fewer than 1,000 Revue units per week.

At the end of the fourth quarter 2011, LOGI had over 163,000 units of Revue finished inventory in its U.S. distribution centers, with another 52,000 finished and work-in-progress units in Asia. Based on the sales rate for that quarter, LOGI had over a year's supply of Revue. At the quarter-end sales rate to retailers, LOGI had over three years of inventory.

In mid-March 2011, an accountant in LOGI's Regional Finance area asked LOGI's VP-Global Sourcing about financial risk for the Revue product and the number of units that could be built from on-hand components. The VP-Global Sourcing informed her that there was no plan to use the components and that Global Sourcing was attempting to sell whatever could be sold. He also noted: "If we need to scrap [work-in-progress] and components, we should assume a recoverable value of zero."

On or around March 23, 2011, a LOGI Finance employee sent Wolf a summary of potential excess and obsolete inventory for contract manufacturers in preparation for a meeting the next day to discuss required accounting adjustments for the year-end financials. The summary highlighted a total potential excess inventory of $19.4 million for Revue units and components that "should be reserved."

On March 31, 2011, LOGI announced that, for reasons unrelated to Revue, it would miss the guidance it had provided to the market two months earlier. LOGI lowered the previous guidance for operating income by $30 million (to a range of $140-$150 million). Internally, the CEO characterized the guidance miss as a "disaster" and informed his executive team, including Barden and Wolf, that management's credibility with the market was damaged.

For its fiscal year 2011 year-end financial close process, LOGI initially prepared an LCM analysis indicating that no LCM adjustment was required for Revue finished-goods inventory. The company's independent auditor arranged separate meetings with Barden and Wolf to discuss the importance of the assumptions in the LCM analysis. In the meetings, the independent auditor stressed the need to consider future pricing assumptions and strategies. Within days, LOGI revised the LCM analysis and, based on a planned price cut to $249 in the first quarter of 2012, recorded a $2.2 million adjustment. However, in the revised analysis, LOGI did not account for the planned third quarter of 2012 price cut to $199, nor did LOGI consider the excess component inventory.

After receiving the revised LCM with the $2.2 million adjustment, the independent auditor noted the roughly $11 million of excess component inventory and informed Barden and Wolf that LOGI was also required to evaluate and, if necessary, record an adjustment for the component inventory.

LOGI's Regional Finance accountant resisted adjusting for the component inventory. When the independent auditor persisted, Regional Finance again emailed the VP-Global Sourcing, notifying him there was "heated discussion" with the independent auditor about Revue and asking him to determine the number of Revue units that could be built from the component inventory.

The VP-Global Sourcing, who was responsible for managing the component inventory liability, informed Regional Finance and Wolf that production had been stopped for months and that he did not "see a chance that we are ever going to build [the components] into units." He wrote that a build-out of components was a "far-fetched scenario that has never been formulated."

On the next day (April 18, 2011), Wolf received a detailed list of the excess components. Less than an hour later, she sent a spreadsheet containing an LCM component analysis to the independent auditor, calculating an adjustment of $1.1 million, based on a hypothetical build-out of 79,000 additional finished units of Revue. Wolf ignored the fact (communicated to her two days earlier) that LOGI had been actively attempting to sell all of the components, with only limited success and below cost. Instead, she based the Company's accounting on the implausible scenario.

On or around April 18, 2011, after forwarding the component LCM analysis spreadsheet to the independent auditor, Wolf met with members of the independent audit team. At that meeting, Wolf discussed LOGI's plans to use the $11 million of excess components to build 79,000 finished Revue units. She also represented that LOGI could use excess components (beyond what was needed to make 79,000 Revue units) to manufacture even more Revue units. These representations were false.

During the week of April 18, 2011, Barden and Wolf met with senior members of the independent audit team, where they confirmed the assumptions used in the LCM analyses, and represented that LOGI was committed to the Revue product for the long-term and was going to build at least 79,000 additional units using excess components. These representations were false.

At the time the representations were made, Barden and Wolf knew or were reckless in not knowing that LOGI had no plan to produce additional units of Revue. They knew or were reckless in not knowing that the contract manufacturer had not shipped any Revue units since late November 2010 and had stopped production in early December 2010. In fact, they knew or were reckless in not knowing that LOGI had no timetable for re-starting production or even for completing the work-in-progress units and, for months, had been attempting to sell excess component inventory at substantial discounts.

On or around May 27, 2011, Barden and Wolf signed a management representation letter to the independent audit firm. The letter contained material misrepresentations concerning the valuation of inventory and the LCM analysis for Revue inventory. Specifically, with respect to the Revue LCM analysis, the letter represented that "we considered future pricing adjustments/discounts which are probable of occurring." This representation was false because the LCM analysis did not consider the planned price drop to $199 in the third quarter of 2012 or other discounting or promotions that would likely be required to sell the excess finished goods inventory. The company acknowledged the falsehood in its November 2014 restatement of financial statements.

On May 27, 2011, LOGI filed its Form 10-K with the SEC. Wolf signed the Form 10-K as the Company's CFO and Principal Accounting Officer. LOGI reported operating income of $142.7M, which was within the lowered range of $140M-$150M that LOGI had communicated to investors on March 31, 2011.

On November 14, 2014, LOGI restated its financial results for fiscal years 2011 and 2012 because of errors in the timing of the Revue-related inventory write-downs. At the time it initially filed its fiscal 2011 financial statements, LOGI overstated its operating income by $30.7 million (27%). If LOGI had properly accounted for Revue-related inventory in May 2011, it would have reported operating income of approximately $112 million, far below the lowered guidance of $140-$150 million.

Questions

1. Analyze the corporate governance systems at Logitech. Describe any weaknesses in these systems and how they affected the work of the external auditors.

2. Identify the red flags that indicate earnings management took place at LOGI. Discuss the accounting for inventory in the context of financial shenanigans.

3. Can you identify any violations of the AICPA Code of Professional Conduct by Jennifer Wolf? How about the external auditors in their audit of LOGI? Be specific.

4. There is no indication that LOGI staff accountants knew of the improper inventory accounting during 2010-2011. However, assume that one LOGI staff accountant, who is a CPA, did know about it. What steps should the staff accountant have taken once aware of the inventory issue? Be sure to explain each of the steps and why they would be taken.

5. Notwithstanding your answer to #4, assume the staff accountant decides to blow the whistle on the improper inventory accounting to the SEC. What protections are available to the staff accountant under the (a) Sarbanes-Oxley Act and (b) Dodd-Frank Financial Reform Act? Are there any conditions for these protections?

Major Case 3

Kiley Nolan's Ethical Dilemma (a GVV Case)

South City Electronics is involved in printed circuit board assembly (PCBA), dealing with the assembly of complex electronic system processes. The equipment is sold to a variety of customers throughout the United States and abroad. The electronics company, based in the city of South San Francisco, is publicly owned. Josh Goldberg is the chief executive officer of the company. David Levin is the chief financial officer.

It's March 30, 2019, and Kiley Nolan, controller for South City Electronics, has just gotten off the phone with her supervisor, South City's CFO David Levin, who reiterated the points he made in a face-to-face meeting with her earlier that day—that the company would be in default on a $10 million loan if its cash flow and earnings for the quarter ended March 31, 2019, did not meet set goals in the loan agreement.

At that date, the company's cash flow was $920,000 and the earnings were $460,000. This is $380,000 and $240,000, respectively, below prescribed levels. Gilmore knew her boss wanted her to agree to immediate revenue treatment for the transaction described below.

The Transaction

South City transferred title to equipment sold to Victor Systems on March 29, 2019, the date of delivery on a $1.6 million sale. The arrangement allowed for the transfer of title upon delivery to Victor's site, as had occurred. However, customer-specific acceptance provisions permit the customer to return the equipment unless the equipment satisfies certain performance tests. South City cannot demonstrate that, at the time of delivery, the equipment already met all the criteria and specifications in the customer-specific acceptance provisions. The arrangement also called for the vendor to perform the installation. South City also provides technical support for the installation and use of the equipment going forward.

Kiley is agonizing about what she should do. She believes it would be wrong to record the transaction as revenue in the first quarter of 2019 under GAAP and the recently adopted FASB revenue recognition standard,

Revenue from Contracts with Customers. However, she is under a great deal of pressure to do so. Levin, her boss, took the position that the conditions under which the customer intends to operate the equipment were replicated in pre-shipment testing. Kiley knew, however, that the performance of the equipment, once installed and operated at the customer's facility, may reasonably be different from that tested prior to shipment.

Meeting between Kiley and Levin

Kiley and Levin's face-to-face meeting earlier in the day featured an acrimonious dispute over whether to record the $1.6 million as revenue.

"Kiley, we have fallen below debt covenant requirements," Levin said. "The only option is to record the sale to Victor Systems. Besides, revenue recognition rules allow us to do so."

"The accounting rules are quite clear on this matter," Kiley said. "We can't recognize the revenue, given the terms of the sale, because the performance of tests at our end may result in a different outcome once it is installed by Victor Systems and it does independent testing."

"I understand your concerns, Kiley. But you're relying on a new accounting standard that just went into effect. I disagree with how you have defined the performance obligations and responsibilities we have and that of Victor Systems under the contract."

"You're using an aggressive accounting interpretation that may have passed muster before the new standard but doesn't anymore," Kiley responded.

"You're being hyper-technical," Levin responded. "We can't afford such a luxury given our precarious position."

"You and I both know," said Kiley, "that we can't just pick and choose how to apply accounting standards. As CPAs, we need to follow both the letter of the new standard and the spirit of it."

Levin became visibly upset. "Now wait a minute. This is an operating decision made by me, not an accounting decision. The accounting should reflect my operating decision. You'd better get on board."

Kiley hesitated to answer. She wasn't sure what to say next. She decided to buy some time to develop a game plan to counter Levin's position. Levin and Kiley decided to meet the next day to put this matter to bed.

Questions

1. Review the requirements of *Revenue from Contracts with Customers* as discussed in Chapter 7. Do you believe Kiley interpreted the new rules correctly? Be specific.

2. Explain the role of behavioral ethics and cognitive thinking in Kiley's decision to ask Levin for a one-day delay to rethink her position. What are the challenges facing her from these perspectives and the actions she might take?

3. Use ethical reasoning to evaluate the appropriateness of Levin's position.

4. Assume you are in Kiley Nolan's position. Answer the following questions as you prepare for the meeting with Levin tomorrow.

   - What are the main arguments you are trying to counter?

   - What is at stake for the key parties?

   - What levers can you use to influence Levin?

   - What is your most powerful and persuasive response to the reasons and rationalizations you need to address?

5. Assume the meeting concludes and Kiley has failed to change Levin's mind. In fact, he insists Kiley get on board. What should Kiley do next and why?

6. Regardless of your answer to #5, assume Levin takes it upon himself to record the $1.6 million revenue as of March 31, 2019. Should Kiley go to the SEC and blow the whistle on financial wrongdoing? Would it be appropriate to do so under the Sarbanes-Oxley Act and/or the Dodd-Frank Financial Reform Act? If so, under what conditions should she report her concerns? Explain.

Major Case 4

Cendant Corporation[1]

The Merger of HFS and CUC

HFS Incorporated (HFS) was principally a controller of franchise brand names in the hotel, real estate brokerage, and car rental businesses, including Avis, Ramada Inn, Days Inn, and Century 21. Comp-U-Card (CUC) was principally engaged in membership-based consumer services such as auto, dining, shopping, and travel "clubs." Both securities were traded on the NYSE. Cendant Corporation was created through the December 17, 1997, merger of HFS and CUC. Cendant provided certain membership-based and Internet-related consumer services and controlled franchise brand names in the hotel, residential real estate brokerage, car rental, and tax preparation businesses.

Overview of the Scheme

The Cendant fraud was the largest of its kind until the late 1990s and early 2000s. Beginning in at least 1985, certain members of CUC's senior management implemented a scheme designed to ensure that CUC always met the financial results anticipated by Wall Street analysts. The CUC senior managers used a variety of means to achieve their goals, including:

- Manipulating recognition of the company's membership sales revenue to accelerate the recording of revenue.

- Improperly using two liability accounts related to membership sales that resulted from commission payments.

- Consistently maintaining inadequate balances in the liability accounts, and, on occasion, reversing the accounts directly into operating income.

With respect to the last item, to hide the inadequate balances, senior management periodically kept certain membership sales transactions off the books. In what was the most significant category quantitatively, the CUC senior managers intentionally overstated merger and purchase reserves and subsequently reversed those reserves directly into operating expenses and revenues. CUC senior management improperly wrote off assets—including assets that were unimpaired—and improperly charged the write-offs against the company's merger reserves. By manipulating the timing of the write-offs and by improperly determining the nature of the charges incurred, the CUC senior managers used the write-offs to inflate operating income. As the scheme progressed over the course of several years, larger and larger year-end adjustments were required to show smooth net income over time. The scheme added more than $500 million to pretax operating income during the fiscal years ended January 31, 1996; January 31, 1997; and December 31, 1997.

---

[1]The information for this case comes from a variety of litigation releases on the SEC Web site, including www.sec.gov/litigation/admin/34-42935.htm (June 14, 2000); www.sec.gov/litigation/admin/34-42934.htm (June 14, 2000); www.sec.gov/litigation/admin/34-42933.htm (June 14, 2000); www.sec.gov/litigation/litreleases/lr16587.htm (June 14, 2000); and www.sec.gov/litigation/complaints/comp18102.htm (April 24, 2003).

SEC Filings against CUC and Its Officers

SEC complaints filed on June 14, 2000, alleged violations of the federal securities laws by four former accounting officials, including Cosmo Corigliano, CFO of CUC; Anne M. Pember, CUC controller; Casper Sabatino, vice president of accounting and financial reporting; and Kevin Kearney, director of financial reporting. The allegations against Corigliano included his role as one of the CUC senior officers who helped engineer the fraud, and he maintained a schedule that management used to track the progress of their fraud. Corigliano regularly directed CUC financial reporting managers to make unsupported alterations to the company's quarterly and annual financial results. The commission alleged that Corigliano profited from his own wrongdoing by selling CUC securities and a large number of Cendant securities at inflated prices while the fraud he helped engineer was under way and undisclosed.

The commission alleged that Pember was the CUC officer most responsible for implementing directives received from Corigliano in furtherance of the fraud, including implementing directives that inflated Cendant's annual income by more than $100 million, primarily through improper use of the company's reserves. According to the SEC, Pember profited from her own wrongdoing by selling CUC and Cendant stock at inflated prices while the fraud she helped implement was under way and undisclosed.

Sabatino and Kearney, without admitting or denying the commission's allegations, consented to the entry of final judgments settling the commission's action against them. The commission's complaint alleged that Sabatino was the CUC officer most responsible for directing lower-level CUC financial reporting managers to make alterations to the company's quarterly financial results.

In the first of the three separate administrative orders, the commission found that Steven Speaks, the former controller of CUC's largest division, made or instructed others to make journal entries that effectuated much of the January 1998 income inflation directed by Pember. In a second, separate administrative order, the commission found that Mary Sattler Polverari, a former CUC supervisor of financial reporting, at the direction of Sabatino and Kearney, regularly and knowingly made unsupported alterations to CUC's quarterly financial results.

In a third administrative order, the commission found that Paul Hiznay, a former accounting manager at CUC's largest division, aided and abetted violations of the periodic reporting provisions of the federal securities laws by making unsupported journal entries that Pember had directed. Hiznay consented to the issuance of the commission's order to cease and desist from future violations of the provisions.

In a fourth and separate administrative order, the commission found that Cendant violated the periodic reporting, corporate record-keeping, and internal controls provisions of the federal securities laws, in connection with the CUC fraud. Among other things, the company's books, records, and accounts had been falsely altered, and materially false periodic reports had been filed with the commission, as a result of the long-running fraud at CUC. Simultaneous with the institution of the administrative proceeding, and without admitting or denying the findings contained therein, Cendant consented to the issuance of the commission order, which ordered Cendant to cease and desist from future violations of the provisions.

On February 28, 2001, the SEC filed a civil enforcement action in the U.S. District Court for the District of New Jersey against Walter A. Forbes, the former chair of the board of directors at CUC, and E. Kirk Shelton, the former vice chair, alleging that they directed a massive financial fraud while selling millions of dollars' worth of the company's common stock. For the period 1995–1997 alone, pretax operating income reported to the public by CUC was inflated by an aggregate amount of over $500 million. Specific allegations included:

- Forbes, CUC's chair and CEO, directed the fraud from its beginnings in 1985. From at least 1991 on, Shelton, CUC's president and COO, joined Forbes in directing the scheme.

- Forbes and Shelton reviewed and managed schedules listing fraudulent adjustments to be made to CUC's quarterly and annual financial statements. CUC senior management used the adjustments to pump up income and earnings artificially, defrauding investors by creating the illusion of a company that had ever-increasing earnings and making millions for themselves along the way.

- Forbes and Shelton undertook a program of mergers and acquisitions on behalf of CUC in order to generate inflated merger and purchase reserves at CUC to be used in connection with the fraud. Forbes and Shelton sought out HFS as a merger partner because they believed that the reserves that would be created would be big enough to bury the fraud. To entice HFS management into the merger, Forbes and Shelton inflated CUC's earnings and earnings projections.

- Forbes and Shelton profited from their own wrongdoing by selling CUC and Cendant securities at inflated prices while the fraud they had directed was under way and undisclosed. The sales brought Forbes and Shelton millions of dollars in ill-gotten gains.

- After the Cendant merger, Forbes served as Cendant's board chair until his resignation in July 1998. At the time of the merger, Shelton became a Cendant director and vice chair. Shelton resigned from Cendant in April 1998.

Specific Accounting Techniques Used to Manage Earnings

Making Unsupported Postclosing Entries

In early 1997, at the direction of senior management, Hiznay approved a series of entries reversing the commissions payable liability account into revenue at CUC. The company paid commissions to certain institutions on sales of CUC membership products sold through those institutions. Accordingly, at the time that it recorded revenue from those sales, CUC created a liability to cover the payable obligation of its commissions. CUC senior management used false schedules and other devices to support their understating of the payable liability of the commissions and to avoid the impact that would have resulted if the liability had been properly calculated. Furthermore, in connection with the January 31, 1997 fiscal year-end, senior management used this liability account by directing postclosing entries that moved amounts from the liability directly into revenue.[2]

In February 1997, Hiznay received a schedule from the CUC controller setting forth the amounts, effective backdates, and accounts for a series of postclosing entries that reduced the commissions payable account by $9.12 million and offsetting that reduction by increases to CUC revenue accounts. Hiznay approved the unsupported entries and had his staff enter them. They all carried effective dates spread retroactively over prior months. The entries reversed the liability account directly into revenues, a treatment that, under the circumstances, was not in accordance with GAAP.

Keeping Rejects and Cancellations Off-Books: Establishing Reserves

During his time at CUC, Hiznay inherited, but then supervised, a longstanding practice of keeping membership sales cancellations and rejects off CUC's books during part of each fiscal year. Certain CUC membership products were processed through various financial institutions that billed their members' credit cards for new sales and charges related to the various membership products. When CUC recorded membership sales revenue from such a sale, it would allocate a percentage of the recorded revenue to cover estimated cancellations of the specific membership product being sold, as well as allocating a percentage to cover estimated rejects and chargebacks.[3] CUC used these percentage allocations to establish a membership cancellation reserve.

---

[2] *Post-closing journal entries* means entries that are made after a reporting period has ended, but before the financial statements for the period have been filed, and that have effective dates spread retroactively over prior weeks or months.

[3] Rejects resulted when the credit card to be charged was over its limit, closed, or reported as lost or stolen. Chargebacks resulted when a credit card holder disputed specific charges related to a particular membership program.

Over the years, CUC senior management had developed a policy of keeping rejects and cancellations off the general ledger during the last three months of each fiscal year. Instead, during that quarter, the rejects and cancellations appeared only on cash account bank reconciliations compiled by the company's accounting personnel. The senior managers then directed the booking of those rejects and cancellations against the membership cancellation reserve in the first three months of the next fiscal year. Because rejects and cancellations were not recorded against the membership cancellation reserve during the final three months of the fiscal year, the policy allowed CUC to hide the fact that the reserve was understated dramatically at each fiscal year-end. At its January 31, 1997 fiscal year-end, the balance in the CUC membership cancellation reserve was $29 million; CUC accounting personnel were holding $100 million in rejects and $22 million in cancellations off the books. Failing to book cancellations and rejects at each fiscal year-end also had the effect of overstating the company's cash position on its year-end balance sheet.

Accounting and Auditing Issues

Kenneth Wilchfort and Marc Rabinowitz were partners at Ernst & Young (EY), which was responsible for audit and accounting advisory services provided to CUC and Cendant. During the relevant periods, CUC and Cendant made materially false statements to the defendants and EY about the company's true financial results and its accounting policies. CUC and Cendant made these false statements to mislead the defendants and EY into believing that the company's financial statements conformed to GAAP. For example, as late as March 1998, senior Cendant management had discussed plans to use over $100 million of the Cendant reserve fraudulently to create fictitious 1998 income, which was also concealed from the defendants and EY. CUC and Cendant made materially false statements to the defendants and EY that were included in the management representation letters and signed by senior members of CUC's and Cendant's management. The statements concerned, among other things, the creation and utilization of merger-related reserves, the adequacy of the reserve established for membership cancellations, the collectability of rejected credit card billings, and income attributable to the month of January 1997.[4]

The written representations for the calendar year 1997 falsely stated that the company's financial statements were fairly presented in conformity with GAAP and that the company had made available to EY all relevant financial records and related data. Those written representations were materially false because the financial statements did not conform to GAAP, and, as discussed further, the company's management concealed material information from the defendants and EY.

In addition to providing the defendants and EY with false written representations, CUC and Cendant also adopted procedures to hide its income-inflation scheme from the defendants and EY. Some of the procedures that CUC and Cendant employed to conceal its fraudulent scheme included (1) backdating accounting entries; (2) making accounting entries in small amounts and/or in accounts or subsidiaries the company believed would receive less attention from EY; (3) in some instances, ensuring that fraudulent accounting entries did not affect schedules already provided to EY; (4) withholding financial information and schedules to ensure that EY would not detect the company's accounting fraud; (5) ensuring that the company's financial results did not show unusual trends that might draw attention to its fraud; and (6) using senior management to instruct middle- and lower-level personnel to make fraudulent entries. Notwithstanding CUC and Cendant's repeated deception, defendants improperly failed to detect the fraud. They were aware of numerous practices by CUC and Cendant indicating that the financial statements did not conform to GAAP, and, as a consequence, they had a duty to withhold their unqualified opinion and take appropriate additional steps.

---

[4]Available at: www.sec.gov/litigation/complaints/comp18102.htm.

Improper Establishment and Use of Merger Reserves

The company completed a series of significant mergers and acquisitions and accounted for the majority of them using the pooling-of-interests method of accounting.[5] In connection with this merger and acquisition activity, company management purportedly planned to restructure its operations. GAAP permits that certain anticipated costs may be recorded as liabilities (or reserves) prior to their incurrence under certain conditions. However, here CUC and Cendant routinely overstated the restructuring charges and the resultant reserves and would then use the reserves to offset normal operating costs—an improper earnings management scheme. The company's improper reversal of merger and acquisition–related restructuring reserves resulted in an overstatement of operating income by $217 million.

The EY auditors provided accounting advice and auditing services to CUC and Cendant in connection with the establishment and use of restructuring reserves. The auditors excessively relied on management representations concerning the appropriateness of the reserves and performed little substantive testing, despite evidence that the reserves were established and utilized improperly.

One example of auditor failures with reserve accounting is the Cendant reserve. Cendant recorded over $500 million in merger, integration, asset impairment, and restructuring charges for the CUC-side costs purportedly associated with the merger of HFS and CUC. The company recorded a significant portion of this amount for the purpose of manipulating its earnings for December 31, 1997, and subsequent periods, and, in fact, Cendant had plans, which it did not disclose to defendants and EY, to use a material amount of the reserve to inflate income artificially in subsequent periods.

In the course of providing accounting and auditing services, the auditors failed to recognize evidence that the company's establishment and use of the Cendant reserve did not conform to GAAP. For example, CUC and Cendant provided EY with contradictory drafts of schedules when EY requested support for the establishment of the Cendant reserve. The company prepared and revised these various schedules, at least in part as a result of questions raised and information provided by the defendants. The schedules were inconsistent with regard to the nature and amount of the individual components of the reserve (i.e., component categories were added, deleted, and changed as the process progressed). While the component categories changed over time, the total amount of the reserve never changed materially. Despite this evidence, the auditors did not obtain adequate analyses, documentation, or support for changes that they observed in the various revisions of the schedules submitted to support the establishment of the reserves. Instead, they relied excessively on frequently changing management representations.

The company planned to use much of the excess Cendant reserve to increase operating results in future periods improperly. During the year ended December 31, 1997, the company wrote off $104 million of assets that it characterized as impaired as a result of the merger. Despite the size and timing of the write-off, the defendants never obtained adequate evidence that the assets were impaired as a result of the merger and, therefore, properly included in the Cendant reserve. In fact, most of the assets were not impaired as a result of the merger.

Cash Balance from the Membership Cancellation Reserve

CUC and Cendant also inflated income by manipulating their membership cancellation reserve and reported cash balance. Customers usually paid for membership products by charging them on credit cards. The company recorded an increase in revenue and cash when it charged the members' credit card. Each month, issuers of members' credit cards rejected a significant amount of such charges. The issuers would deduct the amounts of the rejects from their payments to CUC and Cendant. CUC and Cendant

---

[5.]*Statement of Financial Accounting Standards (SFAS) 141, Business Combinations,* which eliminated the pooling methods for business combinations. The purchase method now must be used for all acquisitions.

falsely claimed to EY auditors that when it resubmitted the rejects to the banks for payment, it ultimately collected almost all of them within three months. CUC and Cendant further falsely claimed that, for the few rejects that were not collected after three months, it then recorded them as a reduction in cash and a decrease to the cancellation reserve. The cancellation reserve accounted for members who canceled during their membership period and were entitled to a refund of at least a portion of the membership fee, as well as members who joined and were billed, but never paid for their memberships.

At the end of each fiscal year, the company failed to record three months of rejects (i.e., it did not reduce its cash and decrease its cancellation reserve for these rejects). CUC and Cendant falsely claimed to the defendants and EY that it did not record rejects for the final three months of the year because it purportedly would collect most of the rejects within three months of initial rejection. According to CUC and Cendant, the three months of withheld rejects created a temporary difference at year-end between the cash balances reflected in the company's general ledger and its bank statements. The rejects were clearly specified on reconciliations of the company's numerous bank accounts, at least some of which were provided to EY and retained in its workpapers. CUC and Cendant falsely claimed to the defendants and EY that the difference between the general ledger balance and bank statement balance did not reflect an overstatement of cash and understatement in the cancellation reserve since it collected most rejects. In fact, the majority of rejects were not collected. By not recording rejects and cancellations against the membership cancellation reserve during the final three months of each fiscal year, CUC and Cendant dramatically understated the reserve at each fiscal year-end and overstated its cash position. CUC and Cendant thus avoided the expense charges needed to bring the cancellation reserve balance up to its proper amount and the entries necessary to record CUC and Cendant's actual cash balances.

The rejects, cancellation reserve balance, and overstatement of income amounts for the period 1996 to 1997 are as follows:

($ in millions)			
Date	Rejects	Cancellation Reserve Balance	Understated Reserve/Overstated Income
01/31/96	$ 72	$37	$35
01/31/97	$100	$29	$28
12/31/97	$137	$37	$37

The EY defendants did not adequately test the collectability of these rejects and the adequacy of the cancellation reserve and instead relied primarily on management representations concerning the company's successful collection history and inconsistent statements concerning the purported impossibility of substantively testing these representations.

Membership Cancellation Rates

The company also overstated its operating results by manipulating its cancellation reserve. The cancellation reserve accounted for members who canceled during their membership period. A large determinant of the liability associated with cancellations was CUC and Cendant's estimates of the cancellation rates. During the audits, CUC and Cendant intentionally provided EY with false estimates that were lower than the actual estimated cancellation rates. This resulted in a significant understatement of the cancellation reserve liability and an overstatement of income. To justify its understated cancellation reserve, CUC and Cendant provided to EY small, nonrepresentative samples of cancellations that understated the actual cancellation rates. The defendants allowed the company to choose the samples. EY did not test whether the samples provided were representative of the actual cancellations for the entire membership population.

Audit Opinion

EY issued audit reports containing unqualified (i.e., unmodified) audit opinions on, and conducted quarterly reviews of, the company's financial statements that, as already stated, did not conform to GAAP. The Securities Exchange Act requires every issuer of a registered security to file reports with the commission that accurately reflect the issuer's financial performance and provide other information to the public. For the foregoing reason, the firm aided and abetted violations of the securities laws.

Legal Issues

Sec Settlements

Between Hiznay's arrival at CUC in July 1995 and the discovery of the fraudulent scheme by Cendant management in April 1998, CUC and Cendant filed false and misleading annual reports with the commission that misrepresented their financial results, overstating operating income and earnings and failing to disclose that the financial results were falsely represented.

The commission's complaint alleged that Sabatino, by his actions in furtherance of the fraud, violated, or aided and abetted violations of, the anti-fraud, periodic reporting, corporate record-keeping, internal controls, and lying to auditors provisions of the federal securities laws. Sabatino consented to entry of a final judgment that enjoined him from future violations of those provisions and permanently barred him from acting as an officer or director of a public company.

Kearney consented to entry of a final judgment that enjoined him from future violations of those provisions, ordered him to pay disgorgement of $32,443 in ill-gotten gains (plus prejudgment interest of $8,234), and ordered him to pay a civil money penalty of $35,000. Kearney also agreed to the issuance of a commission administrative order that barred him from practicing before the commission as an accountant, with the right to reapply after five years.

Corigliano, Pember, and Sabatino each pleaded guilty to charges pursuant to plea agreements between those three individuals and the SEC. Pursuant to his agreement, Corigliano pleaded guilty to a charge of wire fraud, conspiracy to commit mail fraud, and causing false statements to be made in documents filed with the commission, including signing CUC's periodic reports filed with the commission and making materially false statements to CUC's auditors. Pember pleaded guilty to a charge of conspiracy to commit mail fraud and wire fraud. Sabatino, pursuant to his agreement, pleaded guilty to a charge of aiding and abetting wire fraud.

In another administrative order, the commission found that Hiznay aided and abetted violations of the periodic reporting provisions of the federal securities laws in connection with actions that he took at the direction of his superiors at CUC. Among other things, the commission alleged that Hiznay made unsupported journal entries that Pember had directed. Additional orders were entered against lower-level employees.

The commission found that Cendant violated the periodic reporting, corporate record-keeping, and internal controls provisions of the federal securities laws in connection with the CUC fraud in that the company's books, records, and accounts had been falsely altered, and materially false periodic reports had been filed with the SEC.

On December 29, 2009, the SEC announced a final judgment against Forbes, the former chair of Cendant, arising out of his conduct in the Cendant fraud.[6] The commission alleged that Forbes orchestrated an earnings management scheme at CUC to inflate the company's quarterly and annual financial results improperly during the period 1995 to 1997. CUC's operating income was inflated improperly by an aggregate amount exceeding $500 million.

---

[6] *Securities and Exchange Commission v. Walter A. Forbes et al.,* District Court N.J., filed February 28, 2001.

The final judgment against Forbes, to which he consented without admitting or denying the commission's allegations, enjoined him from violating relevant sections of the securities laws and barred him from serving as an officer or director of a public company.

Class Action Lawsuits

A class action suit by stockholders against Cendant and its auditors, led by the largest pension funds, alleged that stockholders paid more for Cendant stock than they would have had they known the truth about CUC's income. The lawsuit ended in a record $3.2 billion settlement. Details of the settlement follow.

By December 1999, a landmark $2.85 billion settlement with Cendant was announced that far surpassed the recoveries in any other securities law class action case in history. Until the settlements reached in the WorldCom case in 2005, this stood as the largest recovery in a securities class action case by far and clearly set the standard in the field. In addition to the cash payment by Cendant, which was backed by a letter of credit that the company secured to protect the class, the Cendant settlement included two other very important features. First, the settlement provided that if Cendant or the former HFS officers and directors were successful in obtaining a net recovery in their continuing litigation against EY, the class would receive half of any such net recovery. As it turned out, that litigation lasted another seven years— until the end of 2007—when Cendant and EY settled their claims against each other in exchange for a payment by EY to Cendant of nearly $300 million. Based on the provision in the Cendant settlement agreement and certain further litigation and a court order, in December 2008, the class received another $132 million. This brought the total recovered from the Cendant settlement to $2.982 billion.

Second, Cendant was required to institute significant corporate governance changes that were far-reaching and unprecedented in securities class action litigation. Indeed, these changes included many of the corporate governance structural changes that would later be included within the Sarbanes-Oxley Act of 2002 (SOX). They included the following:

- The board's audit, nominating, and compensation committees would be comprised entirely of independent directors (according to stringent definitions, endorsed by the institutional investment community, of what constituted an independent director).

- The majority of the board would be independent within two years following final approval of the settlement.

- Cendant would take the steps necessary to provide that, subject to amendment of the certificate of incorporation declassifying the board of directors by vote of the required supermajority of shareholders, all directors would be elected annually.

- No employee stock option could be "repriced" following its grant without an affirmative vote of shareholders, except when such repricings were necessary to take into account corporate transactions such as stock dividends, stock splits, recapitalization, a merger, or distributions.

The Settlement with EY

On December 17, 1999, it was announced that EY had agreed to settle the claims of the class for $335 million. This recovery was and remains today as the largest amount ever paid by an accounting firm in a securities class action case. The recovery from EY was significant because it held an outside auditing firm responsible in cases of corporate accounting fraud. The claims against EY were based on EY's "clean" (i.e., unmodified) audit and review opinions for three sets of annual financial statements, and seven quarterly financial statements, between 1995 and 1997.

The district court approved the settlements and plan of allocation in August 2000, paving the way for Cendant and EY to fund the settlements. Approximately one year later, in August 2001, the settlements and plan of allocation were affirmed on appeal by the U.S. Third Circuit Court of Appeals. And in March 2002, the U.S. Supreme Court determined that it would not hear any further appeals in the case.

Questions

1. Cendant manipulated the timing of write-offs and improperly determined charges in an attempt to smooth net income. Is income smoothing an ethical practice? Are there circumstances where it might be considered ethical and others where it would not? What motivated Cendant to engage in income smoothing practices in this case?

2. Analyze the actions taken by the company and its management from the perspective of the Fraud Triangle.

3. Describe the role of professional judgment in the audits by EY. Did the firm meet its ethical obligations under the AICPA Code? Did it adhere to all appropriate auditing standards?

4. Trust is a basic element in the relationship between auditor and client. Explain how and why trust broke down in the Cendant case, including shortcomings in corporate governance.

5. Do you believe auditors should be expected to discover fraud when a client goes to great lengths, as did Cendant, to withhold evidence from the auditors and mask the true financial effects of transactions? Explain.

Major Case 5

Vivendi Universal

"Some of my management decisions turned wrong, but fraud? Never, never, never." This statement was made by the former CEO of Vivendi Universal, Jean-Marie Messier, as he took the stand in November 20, 2009, for a civil class action lawsuit brought against him, Vivendi Universal, and the former CFO, Guillaume Hannezo. The class action suit accused the company of hiding Vivendi's true financial condition before a $46 billion three-way merger with Seagram Company and Canal Plus. The case was brought against Vivendi, Messier, and Hannezo after it was discovered that the firm was in a liquidity crisis and would have problems repaying its outstanding debt and operating expenses (contrary to the press releases by Messier, Hannezo, and other senior executives that the firm had "excellent" and "strong" liquidity); that it participated in earnings management to achieve earnings goals; and that it had failed to disclose debt obligations regarding two of the company's subsidiaries.[1] The jury decided not to hold either Messier or Hannezo legally liable because "scienter" (i.e., knowledge of the falsehood) could not be proven. In other words, the court decided it could not be shown that the two officers acted with the intent to deceive other parties.

The stock price of the firm dropped 89%, from $111 on October 31, 2000, to $13 on August 16, 2002, over the period of fraudulent reporting and press releases to the media.

As you read the case, consider whether Messier was accurate in his belief that fraud was not committed and whether this was an ethics failure.

Background

Vivendi is a French international media giant, rivaling Time Warner Inc., that spent $77 billion on acquisitions, including the world's largest music company, Universal Music Group (UMG). Messier took the firm to new heights through mergers and acquisitions that came with a large amount of debt.

In December 2000, Vivendi acquired Canal Plus and Seagram, which included Universal Studios and its related companies, and became known as Vivendi Universal. At the time, it was one of Europe's largest companies in terms of assets and revenues, with holdings in the United States that included Universal Studios Group, UMG, and USA Networks Inc. These acquisitions cost Vivendi cash, stock, and assumed

---

[1] *SEC v. Vivendi Universal, S.A., Jean-Marie Messier, and Guillaume Hannezo,* United States District Court Southern District of New York, December 23, 2003, Available at: https://www.sec.gov/litigation/complaints/comp18523.htm.

debt of over $60 billion and increased the debt associated with Vivendi's Media & Communications division from approximately $4.32 billion at the beginning of 2000 to over $30.25 billion in 2002.

In July 2002, Messier and Hannezo resigned from their positions as CEO and CFO, respectively, and new management disclosed that the company was experiencing a liquidity crisis that was a very different picture than the previous management had painted of the financial condition of Vivendi Universal. This was due to senior executives using four different methods to conceal Vivendi Universal's financial problems:

- Issuing false press releases stating that the liquidity of the company was "strong" and "excellent" after the release of the 2001 financial statements to the public.

- Using aggressive accounting principles and adjustments to increase EBITDA and meet ambitious earnings targets.

- Failing to disclose the existence of various commitments and contingencies.

- Failing to disclose part of its investment in a transaction to acquire shares of Telco, a Polish telecommunications holding company.

Earnings Releases/EBITDA

On March 5, 2002, Vivendi issued earnings releases for 2001, which were approved by Messier, Hannezo, and other senior executives, that their Media & Communications business had produced $7.25 billion in EBITDA and just over $2.88 billion in operating free cash flow. These earnings were materially misleading and falsely represented Vivendi's financial situation because, due to legal restrictions, Vivendi was unable unilaterally to access the earnings and cash flow of two of its most profitable subsidiaries, Cegetel and Maroc Telecom, which accounted for 30% of Vivendi's EBITDA and almost half of its cash flow. This contributed to Vivendi's cash flow actually being "zero or negative," making it difficult for Vivendi to meet its debt and cash obligations. Furthermore, Vivendi declared $1.44 per share dividend because of its excellent operations for the past year, but Vivendi borrowed against credit facilities to pay the dividend, which cost more than $1.87 billion after French corporate taxes on dividends. Throughout the following months before Messier's and Hannezo's resignations, senior executives continued to lie to the public about the strength of Vivendi as a company.

In December 2000, Vivendi and Messier predicted a 35% EBITDA growth for 2001 and 2002, and, in order to reach that target, Vivendi used earnings management and aggressive accounting practices to overstate its EBITDA. In June 2001, Vivendi made improper adjustments to increase EBITDA by almost $85 million, or 5% of the total EBITDA of $1.61 billion that Vivendi reported. Senior executives did this mainly by restructuring Cegetel's allowance for bad debts. Cegetel, a Vivendi subsidiary whose financial statements were consolidated with Vivendi's, took a lower provision for bad debts in the period and caused the bad debts expense to be $64.83 million less than it would have been under historical methodology, which in turn increased earnings by the same amount. Furthermore, after the third quarter of 2001, Vivendi adjusted earnings of UMG by at least $14.77 million or approximately 4% of UMG's total EBITDA of $360.15 million for that quarter. At that level, UMG would have been able to show EBITDA growth of approximately 6% versus the same period in 2000 and to outperform its rivals in the music business. It did this by prematurely recognizing revenue of $4.32 million and temporarily reducing the corporate overhead charges by $10.08 million.

Financial Commitments

Vivendi failed to disclose in its financial statements commitments regarding Cegetel and Maroc Telecom that would have shown Vivendi's potential inability to meet its cash needs and obligations. It was also worried that, if it disclosed this information, companies that publish independent credit opinions would have declined to maintain their credit rating of Vivendi. In August 2001, Vivendi entered into an undisclosed current account borrowing with Cegetel for $749.11 million and continued to grow to over $1.44 billion at certain periods of time. Vivendi maintained cash pooling agreements with most of its subsidiaries, but the current account with Cegetel operated much like a loan, with a due date of the balance at December 31, 2001 (which was later pushed back to July 31, 2002), and there was a clause in the agreement that provided Cegetel with the ability to demand immediate reimbursement at any time during the loan period. If this information would have been disclosed, it would have shown that Vivendi would have trouble repaying its obligations.

Regarding Maroc Telecom, in December 2000, Vivendi purchased 35% of the Moroccan government–owned telecommunications operator of fixed line and mobile telephone and Internet services for $3.39 billion. In February 2001, Vivendi and the Moroccan government entered into a side agreement that required Vivendi to purchase an additional 16% of Maroc Telecom's shares in February 2002 for approximately $1.58 billion. Vivendi did this in order to gain control of Maroc Telecom and consolidate its financial statements with Vivendi's own because Maroc carried little debt and generated substantial EBITDA. By not disclosing this information on the financial statements, Vivendi's financial information for 2001 was materially false and misleading.

Stakeholder Interests

The major stakeholders in the Vivendi case include (1) the investors, creditors, and shareholders of the company and its subsidiaries—by not providing reliable financial information, Vivendi misled these groups into lending credit and cash and investing in a company that was not as strong as it seemed; (2) the subsidiaries of Vivendi and their customers—by struggling with debt and liquidity, Vivendi borrowed cash from the numerous subsidiaries all over the globe, jeopardizing their operations; (3) the governments of these countries—because some of Vivendi's companies were government owned (such as the Moroccan company Maroc Telecom), and these governments have to regulate the fraud and crimes that Vivendi committed; and (4) Vivendi, Messier, Hannezo, and other senior management and employees—Messier was putting his future, the employees of Vivendi, and the company itself in jeopardy by making loose and risky decisions involving the sanctity of the firm.

SEC Actions Under Section 1103 of SOX

Section 1103 of SOX provides that:

> Whenever, during the course of a lawful investigation involving possible violations of the Federal securities laws by an issuer of publicly traded securities or any of its directors, officers, partners, controlling persons, agents, or employees, it shall appear to the Commission that it is likely that the issuer will make extraordinary payments (whether compensation or otherwise) to any of the foregoing persons, the Commission may petition a Federal district court for a temporary order requiring the issuer to escrow, subject to court supervision, those payments in an interest-bearing account for 45 days. In the Fair Funds provisions of SOX, Congress gave the SEC increased authority to distribute ill-gotten gains and civil money penalties to harmed investors. These distributions reflect the continued efforts and increased capacity of the commission to repay injured investors, regardless of their physical location and their currency of choice.

Based on these provisions, Messier was required to relinquish his claim to a severance package of about $29.4 million, which includes back pay and bonuses for the first half of 2002, and to pay a civil money penalty of $1 million and disgorgement of $1. Hannezo was required to disgorge $148,149 and to pay a penalty of $120,000.

On August 11, 2008, the SEC announced the distribution of more than $48 million to more than 12,000 investors who were victims of fraudulent financial reporting by Vivendi Universal. Investors receiving checks resided in the United States and 15 other countries. More than half bought their Vivendi stock on foreign exchanges and received their Fair Fund distribution in euros.

Failure of Ethical Leadership

In his analysis of the fraud at Vivendi, Soltani points to failures in ethical practice, corporate governance, and leadership as the root cause of the failure at Vivendi. He characterizes the actions of Messier as motivated by egoism, using one's authoritative position to influence others to ignore ethical practices, failure to set an ethical tone at the top, and failed corporate governance. What follows is an analysis of the points he makes in dissecting the fraud.[2]

- Use of company funds for personal benefit, including to enhance lifestyle choices.
- Failure to conceptualize core values and ethical standards in the company.
- Lack of internal control mechanisms to prevent and detect fraud.
- Ineffective control environment to prevent and detect fraud.
- Excessive risk taking.
- Opportunistic behavior.
- False earnings announcements.
- Aggressive earnings management.
- Use of loopholes in financial reporting standards to alter numbers as far as possible to achieve a desired goal.
- Lapses in accountability.
- Inability of external auditors to exercise their functions in an independent manner and detect material misstatements and fraudulent financial reporting.

It is clear that the culture at Vivendi enabled the fraud to occur and prevented the company from dealing with the crisis as it unfolded.

Questions

1. What is the role of internal controls in facilitating ethical behavior in an organization? Briefly describe the problems with internal controls at Vivendi with respect to its relationships with Cegetel and Maroc Telecom.

2. Why are disclosures in financial statements important? Why were they important in the relationship between Vivendi and Cegetel and Maroc Telecom? Is there such a thing as disclosure fraud? Explain.

3. Why do financial analysts look at measures such as EBITDA and operating free cash flow to evaluate financial results? How do these measures differ from GAAP earnings? Do you believe auditors should be held responsible for auditing such information?

4. Is using earnings management and aggressive accounting in EBITDA calculations just as serious as doing the same with the financial statements prepared under GAAP? Explain.

5. Analyze the appropriateness of the provisions in Section 1103 of SOX from an ethical reasoning perspective. Specifically, are the payments to harmed investors a good thing?

---

[2]Bahram Soltani, "The Anatomy of Corporate Fraud: A Comparative Analysis of High Profile American and European Corporate Scandals," *Journal of Business Ethics,* Vol. 120 (2014), pp. 251–274.

Name Index

Note: Page numbers followed by n indicate notes.

Subject Index

Note: Page numbers followed by n indicate notes.